McGraw-Hill Ryerson

Functions 11

Authors

Roland W. Meisel
B.Sc., B.Ed., M.Sc.
Port Colborne, Ontario

David Petro
B.Sc. (Hons.), B.Ed., M.Sc.
Windsor Essex Catholic District
School Board

Jacob Speijer
B.Eng., M.Sc.Ed., P.Eng.
District School Board of Niagara

Ken Stewart
B.Sc. (Hons.), B.Ed.
York Region District School
Board

Barb Vukets
B.Ed., M.Ed.
Waterloo Region District School
Board

Contributing Authors

Bryce Bates
Toronto District School Board

Kirsten Boucher
Durham District School Board

Mary Card
Toronto District School Board

Wayne Erdman
Toronto District School Board

Rob Gleeson
Bluewater District School Board

Consultants

Assessment Consultant

Antonietta Lenjosek
Ottawa Catholic School Board

Technology Consultants

Dan Ciarmoli
Hamilton-Wentworth District
School Board

Roland W. Meisel
Port Colborne, Ontario

**Mathematical Processes
Consultant**

Susan Siskind
Toronto, Ontario

Literacy Consultant

Carol Miron
Toronto District School Board

Pedagogical Consultants

Antonietta Lenjosek
Ottawa Catholic School Board

Larry Romano
Toronto Catholic District School
Board

Senior Program Consultant

Wayne Erdman
Toronto District School Board

Advisors

Kirsten Boucher
Durham District School Board

Patricia Byers
Georgian College

Chris Dearling
Burlington, Ontario

Dr. Steven J. Desjardins
University of Ottawa

Karen Frazer
Ottawa-Carleton District School
Board

Rob Gleeson
Bluewater District School Board

Jeff Irvine
Peel District School Board

Colleen Morgulis
Durham Catholic District School
Board

Andrzej Pienkowski
Toronto District School Board

Antonio Stancati
Toronto Catholic District School
Board

McGraw-Hill
Ryerson

Toronto   Montréal   Boston   Burr Ridge, IL   Dubuque, IA   Madison, WI   New York
San Francisco   St. Louis   Bangkok   Bogotá   Caracas   Kuala Lumpur   Lisbon   London
Madrid   Mexico City   Milan   New Delhi   Santiago   Seoul   Singapore   Sydney   Taipei

The McGraw·Hill Companies

COPIES OF THIS BOOK MAY BE OBTAINED BY CONTACTING:

McGraw-Hill Ryerson Ltd.

E-MAIL:

orders@mcgrawhill.ca

TOLL-FREE FAX:

1-800-463-5885

TOLL-FREE CALL:

1-800-565-5758

OR BY MAILING YOUR ORDER TO:

McGraw-Hill Ryerson Order Department 300 Water Street Whitby, ON L1N 9B6 Please quote the ISBN and title when placing your order.

Student Text ISBN:

978-0-07-000978-3

McGraw-Hill Ryerson

Functions 11

ISBN-13: 978-0-07-000978-3
ISBN-10: 0-07-000978-3

5 6 7 8 9 DOW 1 9 8 7 6 5 4 3

Care has been taken to trace ownership of copyright material contained in this text. The publishers will gladly accept any information that will enable them to rectify any reference or credit in subsequent printings.

The Geometer's Sketchpad® and *Fathom Dynamic Statistics*™ Software, Key Curriculum Press, 1150 65th Street, Emeryville, CA 94608, 1-800-995-MATH. Microsoft® Excel is a registered trademark of Microsoft Corporation in the United States and/or other countries.
TI-Nspire™ and CBR™ are trademarks of Texas Instruments Incorporated.

Statistics Canada information is used with the permission of Statistics Canada. Users are forbidden to copy the data and redisseminate them, in an original or modified form, for commercial purposes, without permission from Statistics Canada. Information on the availability of the wide range of data from Statistics Canada can be obtained from Statistics Canada's Regional Office, and its toll-free access number 1-800-263-1136.

PUBLISHER: Linda Allison
ASSOCIATE PUBLISHER: Kristi Clark
PROJECT MANAGERS: Maggie Cheverie, Janice Dyer
DEVELOPMENTAL EDITORS: Maggie Cheverie, Jacqueline Lacoursiere, Darren McDonald, Paul McNulty
MANAGER, EDITORIAL SERVICES: Crystal Shortt
SUPERVISING EDITOR: Janie Deneau
COPY EDITING: Julia Cochrane
PHOTO RESEARCH: Maria De Cambra, Monika Schurmann
EDITORIAL ASSISTANT: Erin Hartley
REVIEW COORDINATOR: Jennifer Keay
MANAGER, PRODUCTION SERVICES: Yolanda Pigden
PRODUCTION COORDINATOR: Paula Brown
COVER DESIGN: Michelle Losier
INTERIOR DESIGN: Valid Design and Layout
ART DIRECTION: Brian Lehen Graphic Design Ltd.
ELECTRONIC PAGE MAKE-UP: Brian Lehen Graphic Design Ltd.
TECHNICAL ART: Brian Lehen Graphic Design Ltd.
COVER IMAGE: ©Andrew Kornylak/Getty Images

Acknowledgements

Reviewers of *Functions 11*

The publishers, authors, and editors of *McGraw-Hill Ryerson Functions 11* wish to extend their sincere thanks to the students, teachers, consultants, and reviewers who contributed their time, energy, and expertise to the creation of this textbook. We are grateful for their thoughtful comments and suggestions. This feedback has been invaluable in ensuring that the text and related teacher's resource meet the needs of students and teachers.

John Giroux
Niagara Catholic District School Board

Russell Gordon
Peel District School Board

Beverly Hitchman
Upper Grand District School Board

Paul Hargot
Hamilton-Wentworth Catholic District School Board

Ursula Irwin
Simcoe County District School Board

Murray Johnston
Halton District School Board

David Keffer
Durham Catholic District School Board

Jane Lee
Toronto District School Board

Sheila Mascarin
Halton Catholic District School Board

Ria McNicholls-Ramrattan
Peel District School Board

Donald Mountain
Thames Valley District School Board

Marc Nimigon
York Region District School Board

Tina Poldervaart
Upper Canada District School Board

Monica Preiner
Halton District School Board

Silvia Rotolo
Toronto Catholic District School Board

Mary Schofield
Thames Valley District School Board

Peggy Slegers
Thames Valley District School Board

Robert Slemon
Toronto District School Board

Nancy Tsiobanos
Dufferin-Peel Catholic District School Board

Sharon Young
Halton District School Board

Dedication

The *Functions 11* resource is dedicated in honour of John Santarelli. John was an outstanding educator and mentor who had the unique ability to understand the needs of all students and teachers. He put his actions into words by conceptualizing and developing the best possible material. We are grateful to have had John's expertise with the initial development of this resource. John's spirit, laughter, and friendship will be truly missed.

Linda Allison
Mathematics Publisher

Contents

Preface   vi

Chapter 1   Functions   1

Prerequisite Skills   2

1.1   Functions, Domain, and Range   4

1.2   Functions and Function Notation   16

1.3   Maximum or Minimum of a Quadratic Function   25

Use Technology Use a TI-Nspire™ CAS Graphing Calculator to Find Maximum or Minimum and the Zeros of a Quadratic Function   33

1.4   Skills You Need: Working With Radicals   34

Use Technology Use a TI-Nspire™ CAS Graphing Calculator to Explore Operations With Radicals   41

1.5   Solve Quadratic Equations   43

1.6   Determine a Quadratic Equation Given its Roots   52

1.7   Solve Linear-Quadratic Systems   60

Chapter 1 Review   70

Chapter 1 Practice Test   72

Task: Laser Beams   74

Chapter 2   Transformations of Functions   75

Prerequisite Skills   76

2.1   Functions and Equivalent Algebraic Expressions   78

Use Technology Graph Functions Using a TI-Nspire™ CAS Graphing Calculator   86

2.2   Skills You Need: Operations With Rational Expressions   88

2.3   Horizontal and Vertical Translations of Functions   97

2.4   Reflections of Functions   105

2.5   Stretches of Functions   113

Use Technology Use *The Geometer's Sketchpad*® to Explore Transformations   123

2.6   Combinations of Transformations   125

2.7   Inverse of a Function   132

Chapter 2 Review   142

Chapter 2 Practice Test   144

Task: Functions in Design   146

Chapter 3   Exponential Functions   147

Prerequisite Skills   148

3.1   The Nature of Exponential Growth   150

Use Technology Use Lists and Trace Features on a TI-Nspire™ CAS Graphing Calculator   158

3.2   Exponential Decay: Connecting to Negative Exponents   160

3.3   Rational Exponents   170

3.4   Properties of Exponential Functions   178

3.5   Transformations of Exponential Functions   188

3.6   Making Connections: Tools and Strategies for Applying Exponential Models   199

Chapter 3 Review   210

Chapter 3 Practice Test   212

Chapters 1 to 3 Review   214

Task: Radioactive Isotopes   218

Chapter 4   Trigonometry   219

Prerequisite Skills   220

4.1   Special Angles   222

4.2   Co-terminal and Related Angles   232

Use Technology Use a Computer Algebra System to Find Exact Trigonometric Ratios and Angles   241

4.3   Reciprocal Trigonometric Ratios   243

4.4   Problems in Two Dimensions   249

Use Technology Use Geometry Software to Test for the Ambiguous Case   259

4.5   Problems in Three Dimensions   261

4.6   Trigonometric Identities   270

Chapter 4 Review   276

Chapter 4 Practice Test   278

Task: Pyramids and Angles of Elevation   280

Chapter 5 Trigonometric Functions 281

Prerequisite Skills   282
5.1 Modelling Periodic Behaviour   284
5.2 The Sine Function and the Cosine Function   294
Use Technology Dynamically Unwrap the Unit Circle   302
5.3 Investigate Transformations of Sine and Cosine Functions   304
5.4 Graphing and Modelling with $y = a\sin[k(x - d)] + c$ and $y = a\cos[k(x - d)] + c$ 313
5.5 Data Collecting and Modelling   322
5.6 Use Sinusoidal Functions to Model Periodic Phenomena Not Involving Angles   333
Use Technology Create a Scatter Plot and a Function Using a TI-Nspire™ CAS Graphing Calculator   343
Chapter 5 Review   344
Chapter 5 Practice Test   346
Chapters 4 and 5 Review   348
Task: Modelling a Rotating Object   350

Chapter 6 Discrete Functions 351

Prerequisite Skills   352
6.1 Sequences as Discrete Functions   354
Use Technology Use a TI-Nspire™ CAS Graphing Calculator to Write Terms in a Sequence   364
6.2 Recursive Procedures   365
6.3 Pascal's Triangle and Expanding Binomial Powers   373
6.4 Arithmetic Sequences   380
6.5 Geometric Sequences   388
6.6 Arithmetic Series   395
6.7 Geometric Series   402
Chapter 6 Review   410
Chapter 6 Practice Test   412
Task: Mathematics in Media Studies   414

Chapter 7 Financial Applications 415

Prerequisite Skills   416
7.1 Simple Interest   418
7.2 Compound Interest   426
7.3 Present Value   436
7.4 Annuities   444
7.5 Present Value of an Annuity   456
Chapter 7 Review   464
Chapter 7 Practice Test   466
Chapters 6 and 7 Review   468
Task: Loans and Annuities Due   470
Course Review   471

Prerequisite Skills Appendix   478
Technology Appendix   496
Answers   517
Glossary   587
Index   595
Credits   600

Preface

McGraw-Hill Ryerson Functions 11 is designed for students planning to qualify for college or university. The book introduces new mathematical principles, while providing a wide variety of applications linking the mathematical theory to real situations and careers.

Text Organisation

- Chapter 1 introduces the concept of a function and associated notation. Linear, quadratic, reciprocal, and radical functions, their domain and range, and other key properties are explored.

- In Chapter 2, you will learn how the equations of functions show related transformations.

- In Chapter 3 you extend your knowledge and understanding of exponents and apply the concepts to exponential functions.

- Chapter 4 extends your understanding of trigonometry by defining trigonometric ratios of any angle and solving oblique triangles. These concepts are then used in Chapter 5 to analyse trigonometric functions.

- In Chapter 6, concepts of arithmetic and geometric sequences and series are developed. In Chapter 7, these concepts are applied to financial situations involving simple and compound interest and annuities.

Mathematical Processes

Reasoning and Proving

Representing — Selecting Tools

Problem Solving

Connecting — Reflecting

Communicating

- This text integrates the seven mathematical processes: problem solving, reasoning and proving, reflecting, selecting tools and computational strategies, connecting, representing, and communicating. These processes are interconnected and are used throughout the course. Some examples and exercises are flagged with a math processes graphic to show you which processes are involved in solving the problem.

Chapter Features

- The **Chapter Opener** introduces what you will learn in the chapters. It includes a list of the specific curriculum expectations that the chapter covers.

- **Prerequisite Skills** reviews key skills from previous mathematical courses that are needed to be successful with the current chapter. Examples and further practice are given in the Prerequisite Skills Appendix on pages 478 to 495. The **Chapter Problem** is introduced at the end of the Prerequisite Skills. Questions related to this problem are identified in the exercises, and the **Chapter Problem Wrap-Up** is found at the end of the Chapter Review.

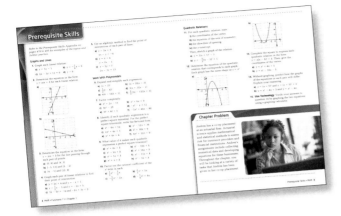

- Most numbered sections start with an **Investigate** which allows you to construct your own understanding of new concepts. Many of these investigations are best done using graphing calculators or dynamic geometry software, but in most instances the choice of tool is optional.

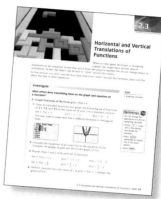

- Worked **Examples** provide model solutions that show how the new concepts are used. They often include more than one method, with and without technology. New mathematical terms are **highlighted** and defined in context. Refer to the **Glossary** on pages 587 to 594 for a full list of definitions of mathematical terms used in the text.

- The **Key Concepts** box summarizes the ideas in the lesson, and the **Communicate Your Understanding** questions allow you to reflect on the concepts of the section.

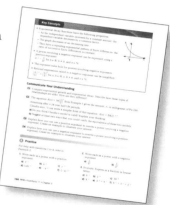

- Exercises are organized into sections **A: Practice**, **B: Connect and Apply**, and **C: Extend**. Any questions that require technology tools are identified as **Use Technology**. Most C exercises end with a few **Math Contest** questions to provide extra challenge.

- Each chapter ends with a section-by-section **Chapter Review. Cumulative Reviews** occur after chapters 3, 5, and 7.

- A **Practice Test** is also included at the end of each chapter.

- A **Task** is presented at the end of each chapter. These are more involved problems that require you to use several concepts from the preceding chapters. Some tasks may be assigned as individual or group projects.

- A **Course Review** follows the task at the end of Chapter 7. This comprehensive selection of questions will help you to determine if you are ready for the final examination.

Assessment

- Some questions are designated as an **Achievement Check**. These questions provide you with an opportunity to demonstrate your knowledge and understanding, and your ability to apply, think about, and communicate what you have learned.

- The **Chapter Problem Wrap-Up** occurs at the end of the Chapter Review. It consists of a summary problem, and may be assigned as a project.

Technology

- The text shows examples of the use of the TI-83Plus or TI-84Plus graphing calculator, *The Geometer's Sketchpad*®, *Fathom Dynamic Statistics™ Software,* and Microsoft® Excel spreadsheets.

- The TI-Nspire™ CAS calculator is introduced as an alternative tool.

Use Techology

- These optional features use technology to extend the concepts of the preceding sections. Techniques with the TI-Nspire™ CAS calculator or extensions with *The Geometer's Sketchpad*® provide you with interesting activities to challenge and engage you in new mathematical ideas.

Connections

This margin item includes:

- connections between topics in the course, or to topics learned previously

- interesting facts related to topics in the examples or exercises

- suggestions for how to use the Internet to help you solve problems or to research or collect information—direct links are provided on the *Functions 11* page on the McGraw-Hill Ryerson Web site.

Answers

- Answers to the **Prerequisite Skills**, numbered sections, **Chapter Review**, and **Practice Test** are provided on pages 517 to 586.

- Responses for the **Investigate**, **Communicate Your Understanding**, **Achievement Check** questions, and **Chapter Problem Wrap-up** are provided in *McGraw-Hill Ryerson Functions 11 Teacher's Resource*.

- Full solutions to all questions, including proof questions, are on the *McGraw-Hill Ryerson Functions 11 Solutions* CD-ROM.

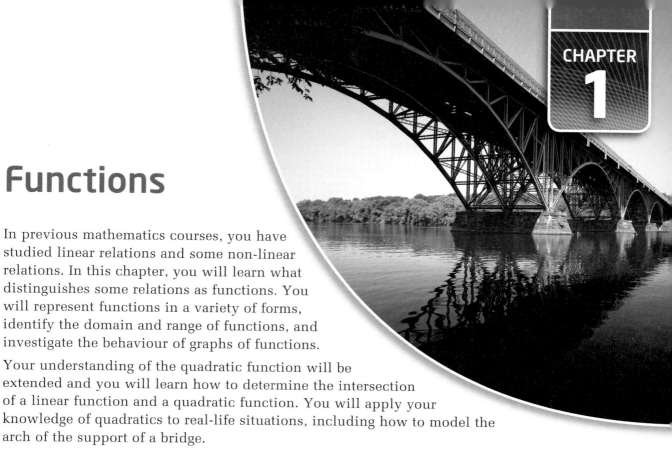

Functions

In previous mathematics courses, you have studied linear relations and some non-linear relations. In this chapter, you will learn what distinguishes some relations as functions. You will represent functions in a variety of forms, identify the domain and range of functions, and investigate the behaviour of graphs of functions.

Your understanding of the quadratic function will be extended and you will learn how to determine the intersection of a linear function and a quadratic function. You will apply your knowledge of quadratics to real-life situations, including how to model the arch of the support of a bridge.

By the end of this chapter, you will

- explain the meaning of the term *function* and distinguish a function from a relation that is not a function, through investigation of linear and quadratic relations using a variety of representations

- represent linear and quadratic functions using function notation, given their equations, tables of values, or graphs, and substitute into and evaluate functions

- explain the meanings of the terms *domain* and *range*, through investigation using numeric, graphical, and algebraic representations of the functions $f(x) = x$, $f(x) = x^2$, $f(x) = \sqrt{x}$, and $f(x) = \frac{1}{x}$; describe the domain and range of a function appropriately; and explain any restrictions on the domain and range in contexts arising from real-world applications

- determine the number of zeros of a quadratic function, using a variety of strategies

- determine the maximum or minimum value of a quadratic function whose equation is given in the form $f(x) = ax^2 + bx + c$, using an algebraic method

- solve problems involving quadratic functions arising from real-world applications and represented using function notation

- determine, through investigation, the transformational relationship among the family of quadratic functions that have the same zeros, and determine the algebraic representation of a quadratic function, given the real roots of the corresponding quadratic equation and a point on the function

- solve problems involving the intersection of a linear function and a quadratic function graphically and algebraically

- verify, through investigation with and without technology, that $\sqrt{ab} = \sqrt{a} \times \sqrt{b}$, $a \geq 0$ and $b \geq 0$, and use this relationship to simplify radicals and radical expressions obtained by adding, subtracting, and multiplying

Prerequisite Skills

Refer to the Prerequisite Skills Appendix on pages 478 to 495 for examples of the topics and further practice.

Graphs and Lines

1. Graph each linear relation.

   a) $y = 3x - 1$ **b)** $y = -\frac{1}{4}x + 5$

   c) $2x - 3y + 12 = 0$ **d)** $y = 6$

2. Determine the equation in the form $y = mx + b$ for each linear relation.

   a)

   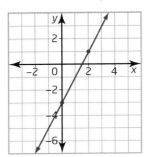

   b)

   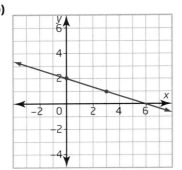

3. Determine the equation in the form $y = mx + b$ for the line passing through each pair of points.

   a) $(0, 8)$ and $(4, 3)$

   b) $(-3, 13)$ and $(2, -2)$

   c) $(4, -1)$ and $(12, 9)$

4. Graph each pair of linear relations to find their point of intersection.

   a) $y = 2x + 4$ and $y = -x + 1$

   b) $y = \frac{1}{2}x - 5$ and $y = -2x + 5$

   c) $3x - 5y = -4$ and $-2x + 3y = 2$

5. Use an algebraic method to find the point of intersection of each pair of lines.

   a) $y = 3x + 5$
   $2x - y = -6$

   b) $y = x + 4$
   $y = 2x - 1$

   c) $x - 2y = 7$
   $2x - 3y = 13$

Work With Polynomials

6. Expand and simplify each expression.

   a) $(x + 2)^2$ **b)** $(n + 3)(n - 3)$

   c) $\frac{1}{2}(t - 4)^2$ **d)** $3(x + 3)(x - 2)$

   e) $4(k - 1)(k + 1)$ **f)** $\frac{2}{3}(3x - 1)(2x + 3)$

7. Factor completely.

   a) $x^2 + 2x - 15$ **b)** $x^2 + 6x + 9$

   c) $9n^2 - 25$ **d)** $-x^2 - x + 12$

   e) $3t^2 + 6t + 3$ **f)** $-5x^2 + 40x - 80$

8. Identify if each quadratic expression is a perfect square trinomial. For the perfect square trinomials, write the factored form.

   a) $x^2 - 6x + 12$ **b)** $x^2 - 12x + 36$

   c) $2x^2 + 4x + 1$ **d)** $x^2 + 18x + 9$

   e) $x^2 + 4x + 4$ **f)** $4n^2 + 12n + 9$

9. What value of k makes each quadratic expression a perfect square trinomial?

   a) $x^2 + 8x + k$ **b)** $x^2 - 10x + k$

   c) $x^2 - 2x + k$ **d)** $x^2 + 14x + k$

   e) $x^2 + 5x + k$ **f)** $x^2 - 11x + k$

   g) $x^2 + x + k$ **h)** $x^2 - 3x + k$

10. Factor out the rational coefficient of the x^2-term in each.

   a) $\frac{1}{2}x^2 - \frac{3}{2}x$ **b)** $\frac{2}{3}x^2 + 5x$

   c) $-\frac{1}{5}x^2 - 2x$ **d)** $-\frac{3}{4}x^2 + 9x$

Quadratic Relations

11. For each quadratic relation, state

   i) the coordinates of the vertex

   ii) the equation of the axis of symmetry

   iii) the direction of opening

   iv) the y-intercept

Then, sketch a graph of the relation.

a) $y = 2(x + 1)^2 - 3$

b) $y = -\dfrac{5}{3}(x - 3)^2 + 1$

12. Determine the equation of the quadratic relation that corresponds to each graph. Each graph has the same shape as $y = x^2$.

a)

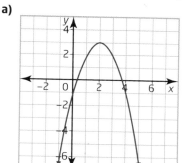

b)

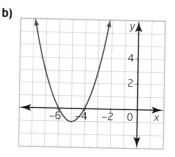

13. Complete the square to express each quadratic relation in the form $y = a(x - h)^2 + k$. Then, give the coordinates of the vertex.

a) $y = x^2 + 4x + 1$

b) $y = x^2 - 10x - 5$

14. Without graphing, predict how the graphs of the equations in each pair will differ. Explain your reasoning.

a) $y = (x + 5)^2$ and $y = (x + 5)^2 + 2$

b) $y = x^2 - 4x + 3$ and $y = x^2 - 4x$

15. Use Technology Verify your answers to question 14 by graphing the two equations using a graphing calculator.

Chapter Problem

Andrea has a co-op placement at an actuarial firm. Actuarial science applies mathematical and statistical methods to assess risk for insurance providers and financial institutions. Andrea's assignments include collecting numerical data and developing equations for these businesses. Throughout the chapter, you will be looking at a variety of tasks that Andrea has been given in her co-op placement.

1.1

Functions, Domain, and Range

When mathematicians and scientists recognize a relationship between items in the world around them, they try to model the relationship with an equation. The concept of developing an equation is used in other fields too. Economists predict the growth of sectors of the economy using equations. Pollsters try to predict the outcome of an election using equations. Does the value of one measured quantity guarantee a unique value for the second related quantity? This question defines the difference between a **relation** and a **function**.

relation

- an identified pattern between two variables that may be represented as ordered pairs, a table of values, a graph, or an equation

function

- a relation in which each value of the independent variable (the first coordinate) corresponds to exactly one value of the dependent variable (the second coordinate)

Investigate A

How can you tell if a relation is a function?

Data on summer jobs are collected from some students in a grade 11 class. Some analysis is done to look for patterns in the data.

A: Neil's Time Worked and Amount Earned, by Week

Time Worked (h)	Amount Earned ($)
20	190
18	171
26	247
22	209
30	285
24	228
10	95
14	126

B: Number of Weeks Worked and Amount Earned by 10 Different Students

Number of Weeks Worked	Total Amount Earned ($)
10	1850
8	675
6	520
9	480
8	1100
10	1400
8	975
6	1200
8	1580
9	1740

1. Graph the given sets of data.

2. Describe any trends in the two graphs.

3. From the graph of the data in table A, can you predict how much Neil would earn if he worked 28 h one week?

4. From the graph of the data in table B, can you predict the amount that a student who worked for 8 weeks would earn?

5. **Reflect** Which set of data is a function? Explain using the terms *independent variable* and *dependent variable*.

Tools

• grid paper

or

• graphing calculator

Investigate B

Tools

• grid paper

How can you make connections between equations, graphs, and functions?

Method 1: Use Pencil and Paper

The first Investigate illustrated that one value for the independent variable can be associated with more than one different value for the dependent variable. Any relation that has this property is not a function. In this Investigate, you will look at how this concept can be related to the equation for a relation.

1. Copy and complete the tables of values for the relations $y = x^2$ and $x = y^2$.

x	$y = x^2$	Coordinates
−3	9	(−3, 9)
−2	4	(-2,4)
−1	1	(-1,1)
0	0	(0,0)
1	1	(1,1)
2	4	(2,4)
3	9	(3,9)

$x = y^2$	y	Coordinates
9	−3	(9, −3)
	−2	
	−1	
	0	
	1	
	2	
	3	

2. Graph both relations on the same set of axes.

3. On the same set of axes, draw vertical lines with equations $x = -3$, $x = -2$, $x = -1$, $x = 1$, $x = 2$, and $x = 3$.

4. **Reflect** Compare how the lines drawn in step 3 intersect each of the relations. Which relation is a function? Explain why.

Technology Tip

Refer to the Technology Appendix, pages 496 to 516, if you need help with graphing equations.

Method 2: Use a Graphing Calculator

1. Graph **Y1** = x^2.
Use the standard window settings.

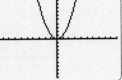

2. • Press (2nd) (DRAW) to access the **Draw** menu.

• Choose **4:Vertical**.

• Use the left and right cursor arrows to move the vertical line.

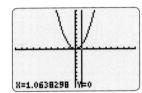

If you press (ENTER), the line will be secured at that spot. Press (2nd) (DRAW) and select **1:ClrDraw** to remove the vertical line.

3. Is $y = x^2$ a function? Explain why or why not.

4. Graph $x = y^2$ by first solving the equation for y to obtain $y = \pm\sqrt{x}$.

• Enter **Y1** = $(x)^{\wedge}0.5$ and **Y2** = $-(x)^{\wedge}0.5$.

5. Repeat step 2. Is $x = y^2$ a function? Explain why or why not.

Example 1

Use the Vertical Line Test

vertical line test

• a method of determining whether a relation is a function

• If every vertical line intersects the relation at only one point, then the relation is a function.

Use the **vertical line test** to determine whether each relation is a function. Justify your answer.

a)

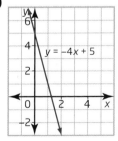

b)

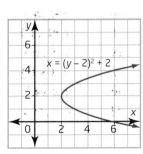

c)

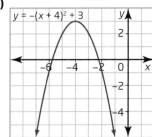

d)

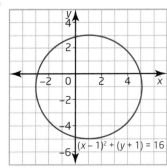

Solution

a) This relation is a function. No vertical line can be drawn that will pass through more than one point on the line.

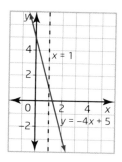

b) This relation is a not function. An infinite number of vertical lines can be drawn that will pass through more than one point on the curve. For example, the vertical line $x = 6$ passes through the points (6, 4) and (6, 0).

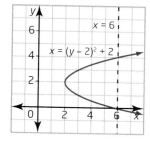

c) This relation is a function. No vertical line can be drawn that will pass through more than one point on the curve.

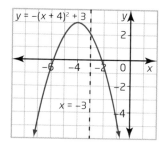

d) This relation is not a function. An infinite number of vertical lines can be drawn that will pass through more than one point on the circle.

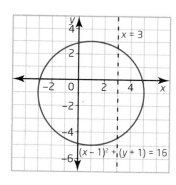

domain

- the set of first coordinates of the ordered pairs in a relation

range

- the set of second coordinates of the ordered pairs in a relation

For any relation, the set of values of the independent variable (often the *x*-values) is called the **domain** of the relation. The set of the corresponding values of the dependent variable (often the *y*-values) is called the **range** of the relation. For a function, for each given element of the domain there must be exactly one element in the range.

Example 2

Determine the Domain and Range From Data

Determine the domain and range of each relation. Use the domain and range to determine if the relation is a function.

a) $\{(-3, 4), (5, -6), (-2, 7), (5, 3), (6, -8)\}$

b) The table shows the number of children of each age at a sports camp.

Age	Number
4	8
5	12
6	5
7	22
8	14
9	9
10	11

Connections

Brace brackets { } are used to denote a set of related data points or values.

Solution

a) domain $\{-3, -2, 5, 6\}$, range $\{-8, -6, 3, 4, 7\}$

This relation is not a function. The *x*-value $x = 5$ has two corresponding *y*-values, $y = -6$ and $y = 3$. The domain has four elements but the range has five elements. So, one value in the domain must be associated with two values in the range.

b) domain $\{4, 5, 6, 7, 8, 9, 10\}$, range $\{5, 8, 9, 11, 12, 14, 22\}$

This is a function because for each value in the domain there is exactly one value in the range.

real number

- a number in the set of all integers, terminating decimals, repeating decimals, non-terminating decimals, and non-repeating decimals, represented by the symbol $\mathbb{R}$

When the equation of a relation is given, the domain and range can be determined by analysing the allowable values from the set of **real numbers**.

Example 3

Determine the Domain and Range From Equations

Determine the domain and the range for each relation. Sketch a graph of each.

a) $y = 2x - 5$ **b)** $y = (x - 1)^2 + 3$ **c)** $y = \dfrac{1}{x + 3}$

d) $y = \sqrt{x - 1} + 3$ **e)** $x^2 + y^2 = 36$

Solution

a) $y = 2x - 5$ is a linear relation. There are no restrictions on the values that can be chosen for x or y.

domain $\{x \in \mathbb{R}\}$ Read as "the domain is all real

range $\{y \in \mathbb{R}\}$ numbers."

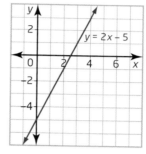

Connections

The notation $\{x \in \mathbb{R}\}$ is set notation. It is a concise way of expressing that x is any real number. The symbol $\in$ means "is an element of."

b) $y = (x - 1)^2 + 3$ is a quadratic relation.

There are no restrictions on the values that can be chosen for x, so the domain is all real numbers.

domain $\{x \in \mathbb{R}\}$

The parabola has a minimum at its vertex $(1, 3)$.

All values of y are greater than or equal to 3.

range $\{y \in \mathbb{R}, y \geq 3\}$

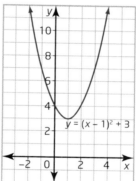

c) Division by zero is undefined. The expression in the denominator of $\dfrac{1}{x + 3}$ cannot be zero. So, $x + 3 \neq 0$, which means that $x \neq -3$. All other values can be used for x. The vertical line $x = -3$ is called an **asymptote**.

domain $\{x \in \mathbb{R}, x \neq -3\}$ Read as "the domain is all real numbers that are not equal to -3."

For the range, there can never be a situation where the result of the division is zero, as 1 divided by a non-zero value can never result in an answer of 0. This function has another asymptote, the x-axis. Any real number except -3 can be used for x and will result in all real numbers except 0 for the range. Use a table of values or a graphing calculator to check this on the graph.

range $\{y \in \mathbb{R}, y \neq 0\}$

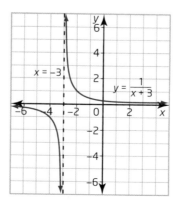

asymptote

- a line that a curve approaches more and more closely but never touches
- For example, for the graph of $y = \dfrac{1}{x}$, the x-axis and the y-axis are asymptotes.

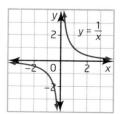

d) The expression under a radical sign must be greater than or equal to zero. So, in $\sqrt{x-1} + 3$, $x - 1 \geq 0$, or $x \geq 1$.

domain $\{x \in \mathbb{R}, x \geq 1\}$

The value of the radical is always 0 or greater and is added to 3 to give the value of y. So, the y-values are always greater than or equal to 3. This gives the range.

range $\{y \in \mathbb{R}, y \geq 3\}$

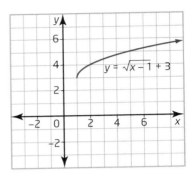

$y = \sqrt{x-1} + 3$

Connections

In grade 10, you learned that $x^2 + y^2 = r^2$ is the equation of a circle with centre the origin and radius r.

e) In $x^2 + y^2 = 36$, x^2 must be less than or equal to 36, as must y^2, since both x^2 and y^2 are always positive. So, the values for x and y are from -6 to 6.

domain $\{x \in \mathbb{R}, -6 \leq x \leq 6\}$

Read as "the domain is all real numbers that are greater than or equal to -6 and less than or equal to 6."

range $\{y \in \mathbb{R}, -6 \leq y \leq 6\}$

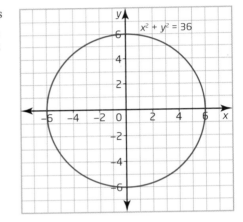

$x^2 + y^2 = 36$

Example 4

Determine the Domain and Range of an Area Function

Amy volunteers to help enclose a rectangular area for a dog run behind the humane society. The run is bordered on one side by the building wall. The society has 100 m of fencing available.

a) Express the area function in terms of the width.

b) Determine the domain and range for the area function.

Solution

Let x represent the width of the rectangular pen and $100 - 2x$ represent the length, both in metres. Let A represent the area, in square metres.

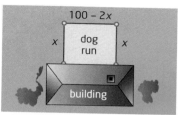

a) $A(x) = x(100 - 2x)$ Area = length × width
$\quad = -2x^2 + 100x$

b) For the domain, $x > 0$, since there must be a width to enclose an area. For the length to be greater than zero, $x < 50$.

domain $\{x \in \mathbb{R}, 0 < x < 50\}$

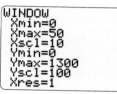

The area function is a quadratic opening downward. Graph the area function to find its maximum. The vertex is at $(25, 1250)$.

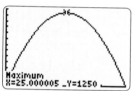

Connections

You could find the vertex algebraically by expressing the area function in vertex form, $y = a(x - h)^2 + k$.

The maximum value of the area function is 1250.

range $\{A \in \mathbb{R}, 0 < A < 1250\}$

An area must be greater than zero.

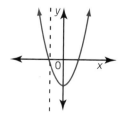

Key Concepts

- A relation is a function if for each value in the domain there is exactly one value in the range. This table of values models a function.

x	-2	-1	0	1	2
y	5	3	1	-1	-3

- The vertical line test can be used on the graph of a relation to determine if it is a function. If every vertical line passes through at most one point on the graph, then the relation is a function.

- The domain and the range of a function can be found by determining if there are restrictions based on the defining equation. Restrictions on the domain occur because division by zero is undefined and because expressions under a radical sign must be greater than or equal to zero. The range can have restrictions too. For example, a quadratic that opens upward will have a minimum value.

- Set notation is used to write the domain and range for a function. For example, for the function $y = x^2 + 2$:

  domain $\{x \in \mathbb{R}\}$ and range $\{y \in \mathbb{R}, y \geq 2\}$

Communicate Your Understanding

C1 Suzanne is unclear as to why the graphs of $y = x^2$ and $x = y^2$ are different, and why one is a function and the other is not. How would you help Suzanne?

C2 Is it possible to determine if a relation is a function if you are only given the domain and range in set notation? Explain your reasoning.

C3 Sagar missed the class on restrictions and has asked you for help. Lead him through the steps needed to find the domain and range of the function $y = \dfrac{-4}{2x + 1}$.

A Practise

For help with questions 1 and 2, refer to Example 1.

1. Which graphs represent functions? Justify your answer.

a)

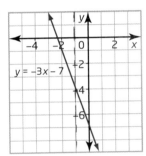

$y = -3x - 7$

a). Is a function

No vertical line can be drawn that will be pass through more than one point on the line.

b)

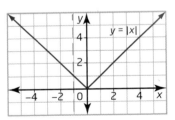

$y = |x|$

b) Is a function.

The same as a.

c)

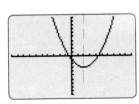

c) Is a function.

No vertical line can be drawn that will be pass through more than one point on the curve.

d)

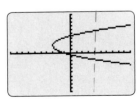

d) Is not a function. An infinite number of verticle line can be drawn that will pass through more than one point on the curve.

2. Is each relation a function? Explain. Sketch a graph of each.

a) $y = x - 5$ Is a function.

b) $x = y^2 - 3$ Is a function

c) $y = 2(x - 1)^2 - 2$ ✓

d) $x^2 + y^2 = 4$ ✓

For help with questions 3 and 4, refer to Example 2.

3. State the domain and the range of each relation. Is each relation a function? Justify your answer.

a) $\{(5, 5), (6, 6), (7, 7), (8, 8), (9, 9)\}$

b) $\{(3, -1), (4, -1), (5, -1), (6, -1)\}$

c) $\{(1, 6), (1, -14), (1, 11), (1, -8), (1, 0)\}$

d) $\{(1, 5), (4, 11), (3, 9), (5, 1), (11, 4)\}$

e) $\{(3, 2), (2, 1), (1, 0), (2, -1), (3, -2)\}$

4. The domain and range of some relations are given. Each relation consists of five points. Is each a function? Explain.

a) domain $\{1, 2, 3, 4, 5\}$, range $\{4\}$ ✗

b) domain $\{-3, -1, 1, 3, 5\}$, range $\{2, 4, 6, 8, 10\}$

c) domain $\{2, 3, 6\}$, range $\{-4, 6, 7, 11, 15\}$

d) domain $\{-2\}$, range $\{9, 10, 11, 12, 13\}$

Because each values in the domain there is exactly one values in the range.

B Connect and Apply

For help with questions 5 and 6, refer to Example 3.

5. State the domain and the range of each relation.

a)

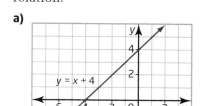

$y = x + 4$

d $\{x \in R\}$

R $\{y \in R\}$

b)

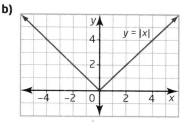

$y = |x|$

$\{x \in R\}$

$\{y \geq 0, y \in R\}$

c)

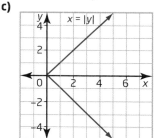

$x = |y|$

$\{x \geq 0, x \in R\}$

$\{y \in R\}$

d)

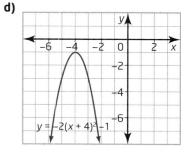

$y = -2(x + 4)^2 - 1$

$\{x \in R\}$

$\{y \leq -1, y \in R\}$

e)

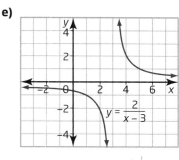

$y = \dfrac{2}{x - 3}$

$\{x \neq 3, x \in R\}$

$\{y \in R\}$

$x - 3 \neq 0$

$x \neq 3$.

6. Determine the domain and the range of each relation. Use a graph to help you if necessary.

a) $y = -x + 3$

b) $y = (x + 1)^2 - 4$

c) $y = -3x^2 + 1$

d) $x^2 + y^2 = 9$

e) $y = \dfrac{1}{x + 3}$

f) $y = \sqrt{2x + 1}$.

7. For each given domain and range, draw one relation that is a function and one that is not. Use the same set of axes for each part.

a) domain $\{x \in \mathbb{R}\}$, range $\{y \in \mathbb{R}\}$

b) domain $\{x \in \mathbb{R}, x \geq 4\}$, range $\{y \in \mathbb{R}\}$

c) domain $\{x \in \mathbb{R}\}$, range $\{y \in \mathbb{R}, y \leq -1\}$

d) domain $\{x \in \mathbb{R}, x \leq 2\}$, range $\{x \in \mathbb{R}, y \geq -2\}$

For help with questions 8 and 9, refer to Example 4.

8. Soula has 90 m of fencing to enclose an area in a petting zoo with two dividers to separate three types of young animals. The three pens are to have the same area.

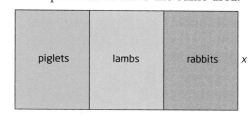

a) Express the area function for the three pens in terms of x.

b) Determine the domain and the range for the area function.

9. Is each relation a function? Justify your answer. If the relation is a function, state the independent variable and the dependent variable.

a) The amount of money taken in for the fundraiser is related to the number of raffle tickets a hockey team sells.

b) The age of students is related to their grade level.

c) The time it takes Jung Yoo to walk to school is related to the speed at which he walks.

10. A rectangular part of a parking lot is to be fenced off to allow some repairs to be done. The workers have fourteen 3-m sections of pre-assembled fencing to use. They want to create the greatest possible area in which to work.

Reasoning and Proving

Representing · Selecting Tools · Problem Solving · Connecting · Reflecting · Communicating

a) How can the fencing be used to create as large an enclosed area as possible?

b) Show why this produces the greatest area using the given fencing sections, but does not create the greatest area that can be enclosed with 42 m of fencing.

11. Determine the range of each relation for the domain {1, 2, 3, 4, 5}.

a) $y = 6x - 6$
b) $y = x^2 - 4$
c) $y = 3$
d) $y = 2(x - 1)^2 - 1$
e) $y = \dfrac{1}{x + 2}$
f) $x^2 + y^2 = 25$

12. Use Technology Use a graphing calculator or graphing software.

a) Copy and complete the table of values. Create a scatter plot of the resulting data using a graphing calculator.

$x = y^2 - 3$	y
6	-3
	-2
	-1
	0
	1
	2
	3

b) Enter the equations
$y = \sqrt{x + 3}$ and
$y = -\sqrt{x + 3}$ and display their graphs.

c) Explain the result of the display of the data and the equations.

d) Explain how this illustrates that the equation $x = y^2 - 3$ defines a relation that is not a function.

> **Technology Tip**
>
> Refer to the Technology Appendix, pages 496 to 516, if you need help with plotting data or graphing equations.

13. It is said that you cannot be in two places at once. Explain what this statement means in terms of relations and functions.

14. Describe the graph of a relation that has

a) one entry in the domain and one entry in the range

b) one entry in the domain and many entries in the range

c) many entries in the domain and one entry in the range

15. Sketch a relation with the following properties.

a) It is a function with domain all the real numbers and range all real numbers less than or equal to 5.

b) It is not a function and has domain and range from -3 to 3.

16. A car salesperson is paid according to two different relations based on sales for the week. In both relations, s represents sales and P represents the amount paid, both in dollars.

Reasoning and Proving

Representing · Selecting Tools · Problem Solving · Connecting · Reflecting · Communicating

For sales of less than $100 000,
$P = 0.002s + 400$.
For sales of $100 000 and over,
$P = 0.0025s + 400$.

a) State the domain and range for each relation.

b) Does each relation define a function? Justify your answer.

c) Graph the two relations on the same set of axes.

d) Connect what happens on the graph at $s = 100\ 000$ to its meaning for the salesperson.

C Extend

17. Is it possible for two different functions to have the same domain and range? Explain, giving examples.

18. State the domain and the range for the two relations shown. Is each a function?

a)

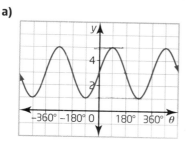

b)

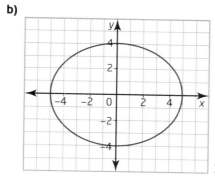

19. Math Contest What is the domain of the function $y = \dfrac{\sqrt{x - 3}}{\sqrt{5 - x}}$?

20. Math Contest Frank bought supplies for school. In the first store, he spent half his money plus $10. In the second store, he spent half of what he had left plus $10. In the third store, he spent 80% of what he had left. He came home with $5. How much did he start out with?

21. Math Contest Find the number of factors of 2520.

22. Math Contest For what values of x is $\sqrt{x + 2} > x$?

Career Connection

Khaldun completed a 4-year degree in mineral engineering at the University of Toronto. He works in northern Canada for an international diamond-mining company. In his job as a mining engineer, Khaldun uses his knowledge of mathematics, physics, geology, and environmental science to evaluate the feasibility of a new mine location. Whether the mine is excavated will be a function of the value of the diamond deposit, accessibility, and safety factors. Since mining a site costs millions of dollars, the analysis stage is crucial. Khaldun examines rock samples and the site itself before carefully estimating the value of the underground deposit. The diamonds will be mined only if the profits outweigh the many costs.

1.2

Functions and Function Notation

The first instances of notation may have occurred when early humans attempted to show the concept of numbers. A jawbone in the Deutsches Museum in Munich, Germany, which has been dated at approximately 30 000 B.C.E., shows this early attempt. It has 55 equally spaced notches carved into it, arranged in groups of 5. This is one of the earliest pieces of evidence that show human interest in designing a notation for others to understand and convey the concept of a number system.

In this section, you will extend the concept of a function and formalize several notations that are used to represent a function.

Tools

Optional
• grid paper
or
• graphing calculator

Connections

It is not by accident that we use the term *digit*. People started counting on their fingers, or digits. When there were too many items to count on 10 fingers, items such as stones or small pebbles were used. The Latin word for *pebble* is *calculus*, from which we get the word *calculate*.

Investigate

How can you use a function machine?

A function machine generates ordered pairs by performing mathematical operations on an input value. For each input value from the domain that enters a particular function machine, a unique output value in the range emerges. The output is determined by the rule of the defining function. If some values for x and their associated y-values are known, it is often possible to determine what function was used by the machine.

Suppose you are told that a linear function machine has two steps. The first step involves a multiplication or a division, and the second step involves an addition or a subtraction. You are told that when the input value is $x = 5$, the output value is $y = -9$. As well, when the input value is $x = 1$, the output value is $y = 3$.

Input
$x = 5$ → result of the first step is unknown → Output $y = -9$

Input
$x = 1$ → result of the first step is unknown → Output $y = 3$

1. From the information above, what are the coordinates of two points of the linear function?

2. Use the two points to determine the equation of the linear function in the form $y = mx + b$.

3. Use the defining function to find

    a) y if $x \in \{-3, -2, -1\}$

    b) x if $y \in \{-6, -15, -18\}$

4. Reflect Use the defining equation to describe the steps that are performed by the function machine in generating the data.

5. Reflect At the start of this Investigate, you were told that the first step was a multiplication or a division and that the second step was an addition or a subtraction.

    a) What type of value for m would suggest that the first step is a multiplication? a division?

    b) What type of value for b would suggest that the second step is an addition? a subtraction?

6. Make up your own linear function machine. Exchange two ordered pairs that your function machine generates with a partner. Determine the defining function for each other's function machine.

To write a function using function notation, the form $f(x) = \ldots$ is used to indicate a function, f, with independent variable x. The notation $f(3)$ means the value obtained when $x = 3$ is substituted. $f(3)$ is read as "f at 3" or "f of 3."

Connections

Letters other than f can be used in function notation. Often, scientists and mathematicians will use a letter related to the quantity being measured. For example, if the height is being measured as a function of time, express the function as $h(t)$.

Example 1

Find Values Using Function Notation

For each function, determine $f(-2)$, $f(5)$, and $f\left(\frac{1}{2}\right)$.

    a) $f(x) = 2x - 4$

    b) $f(x) = 3x^2 - x + 7$

    c) $f(x) = 11$

    d) $f(x) = \dfrac{2x}{x^2 - 3}$

Solution

a) $f(x) = 2x - 4$

    $f(-2) = 2(-2) - 4$ Substitute $x = -2$.

    $ = -8$

    $f(5) = 2(5) - 4$

    $ = 6$

    $f\left(\frac{1}{2}\right) = 2\left(\frac{1}{2}\right) - 4$

    $\phantom{f\left(\frac{1}{2}\right)} = 1 - 4$

    $\phantom{f\left(\frac{1}{2}\right)} = -3$

b) $f(x) = 3x^2 - x + 7$

$$f(-2) = 3(-2)^2 - (-2) + 7$$
$$= 12 + 2 + 7$$
$$= 21$$

$$f(5) = 3(5)^2 - 5 + 7$$
$$= 75 - 5 + 7$$
$$= 77$$

$$f\left(\frac{1}{2}\right) = 3\left(\frac{1}{2}\right)^2 - \frac{1}{2} + 7$$
$$= \frac{3}{4} - \frac{1}{2} + 7$$
$$= 7\frac{1}{4}$$

c) $f(x) = 11$ is a constant function.

$$f(-2) = 11 \qquad f(5) = 11 \qquad f\left(\frac{1}{2}\right) = 11$$

d) $f(x) = \dfrac{2x}{x^2 - 3}$

$$f(-2) = \frac{2(-2)}{(-2)^2 - 3} \qquad\qquad f(5) = \frac{2(5)}{5^2 - 3} \qquad\qquad f\left(\frac{1}{2}\right) = \frac{2\left(\frac{1}{2}\right)}{\left(\frac{1}{2}\right)^2 - 3}$$

$$= \frac{-4}{4 - 3} \qquad\qquad\qquad = \frac{10}{22} \qquad\qquad\qquad = \frac{1}{\frac{1}{4} - 3}$$

$$= -4 \qquad\qquad\qquad\quad = \frac{5}{11} \qquad\qquad\qquad\quad = \frac{1}{-\frac{11}{4}}$$

$$\qquad\qquad\qquad\qquad\qquad\qquad\qquad\qquad\qquad\qquad\qquad = -\frac{4}{11}$$

mapping diagram

- a graphical representation that relates the values in one set (the domain) to the values in a second set (the range) using directed arrows from domain to range

A **mapping diagram** is a representation that can be used when the relation is given as a set of ordered pairs. In a mapping diagram, the domain values in one oval are joined to the range values in the other oval using arrows. In a mapping diagram, a relation is a function if there is exactly one arrow leading from each value in the domain. This indicates that each element in the domain corresponds to exactly one element in the range.

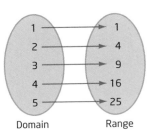

Domain   Range

Example 2

Interpret Mapping Diagrams

Use the mapping diagrams to

i) write the set of ordered pairs of the relation

ii) state if the relation is a function

a)

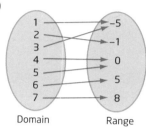

b)

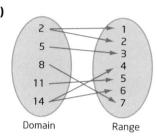

Solution

a) i) $\{(1, -5), (2, -1), (3, -5), (4, 0), (5, 0), (6, 5), (7, 8)\}$

ii) Since every value in the domain maps to exactly one value in the range, this relation is a function.

b) i) $\{(2, 1), (2, 2), (5, 3), (8, 7), (11, 5), (14, 4), (14, 6)\}$

ii) Since the values $x = 2$ and $x = 14$ both map to more than one value in the range, this relation is not a function.

While mapping diagrams are useful in situations where the relations are given in ordered pair form, they are impractical when a function is written in function notation. For this reason, a second form of mapping has been developed. This form is referred to as *mapping notation* and is illustrated in the next example.

Example 3

Represent Functions Using Mapping Notation

Write each function in mapping notation.

a) $f(x) = 3x^2 - 2x + 1$

b) $g(x) = 3x + 4$

c) $h(t) = -4.9t^2 - 4$

d) $P(x) = (500 - 2x)(300 + x)$

Solution

a) $f : x \rightarrow 3x^2 - 2x + 1$ 　　　Read "f is a function that maps x to $3x^2 - 2x + 1$."

b) $g : x \rightarrow 3x + 4$ 　　　Read "g is a function that maps x to $3x + 4$."

c) $h : t \rightarrow -4.9t^2 - 4$ 　　　Read "h is a function that maps t to $-4.9t^2 - 4$."

d) $P : x \rightarrow (500 - 2x)(300 + x)$ 　Read "P is a function that maps x to $(500 - 2x)(300 + x)$."

Example 4

Solve a Problem Using Function Notation

Connections

Great Slave Lake in the Northwest Territories is the deepest lake in North America. At its deepest, it is 614 m deep. Lake Ontario has an average depth of 96 m and is 235 m deep at its deepest.

The temperature of the water at the surface of a deep lake is 22 °C on a warm summer's day. As Renaldo scuba dives to the depths of the lake, he finds that the temperature decreases by 1.5 °C for every 8 m he descends.

a) Model the water temperature at any depth using function notation.

b) Use this function to determine the water temperature at a depth of 40 m.

c) At the bottom of the lake, the temperature is 5.5 °C. How deep is the lake?

Solution

a) Let d represent the depth, in metres, below the surface of the lake and T represent the temperature, in degrees Celsius, at this depth.

$$T(d) = 22 - 1.5\left(\frac{d}{8}\right)$$ 　　The temperature decreases by 1.5°C for each 8 m.

b) For a depth of 40 m, substitute $d = 40$.

$$T(40) = 22 - 1.5\left(\frac{40}{8}\right)$$
$$= 22 - 7.5$$
$$= 14.5$$

The temperature at a depth of 40 m is 14.5 °C.

c) Substitute $T(d) = 5.5$ and solve for d.

$$5.5 = 22 - 1.5\left(\frac{d}{8}\right)$$
$$1.5\left(\frac{d}{8}\right) = 22 - 5.5$$
$$1.5d = 8 \times 16.5$$
$$d = \frac{8 \times 16.5}{1.5}$$
$$d = 88$$

The depth of the lake is 88 m.

Key Concepts

- In function notation, the symbol $f(x)$ represents the dependent variable. It indicates that the function f is expressed in terms of the independent variable x. For example, $y = 3x^2 - 5$ is written as $f(x) = 3x^2 - 5$.

- Relations and functions given as ordered pairs can be represented using mapping diagrams. This involves using directed arrows from each value in an oval representing the domain to the corresponding value or values in an oval representing the range.

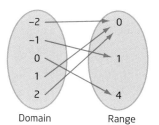

- In a mapping diagram, a relation is not a function when an element from the domain has two or more arrows leading to different elements of the range.

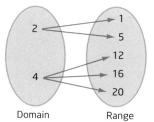

- Mapping notation can replace function notation. For example, $f(x) = 3x^2 - 5$ can be written as $f : x \rightarrow 3x^2 - 5$.

Communicate Your Understanding

C1 Samuel missed the explanation of function notation. Explain how to answer the following. Given $f(x) = x^2 + 5$, find $f(-2)$.

C2 Michelle has written the function defined by $y = 3t^2 + 5t - 5$ as $f(x) = 3t^2 + 5t - 5$. Is she correct? Explain why or why not.

C3 A quadratic function has the same shape as $y = x^2$, but it opens downward and has its vertex at $(0, 3)$. Is each of the following a representation of the same function?

A $y = -x^2 + 3$ **B** $f : x \rightarrow -x^2 + 3$ **C** 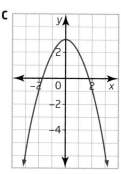   **D** $f(x) = 3 - x^2$

A Practise

For help with questions 1 to 4, refer to Example 1.

1. For each function, determine $f(4)$, $f(-5)$, and $f\left(-\frac{2}{3}\right)$.

   a) $f(x) = \frac{2}{5}x + 11$ ✓

   b) $f(x) = 3x^2 + 2x + 1$ ✓

   c) $f(x) = 2(x + 4)^2$ ✓

   d) $f(x) = -6$

   e) $f(x) = \frac{1}{x}$

   f) $f(x) = \sqrt{x + 5}$

2. Find the value of each function at $x = 0$. Sketch the graph of each function.

   a) $f(x) = 5x + 4$

   b) $k(x) = 4x$

   c) $p(x) = -4$

   d) $g(x) = 11x^2 + 3x - 1$

   e) $f(x) = (3x - 3)(2x + 2)$

   f) $h(x) = -\frac{2}{3}(5 - 4x)(x - 7)$

3. A linear function machine uses a function of the form $f(x) = ax$. Find the value of a for each given point on the function, and then write the defining equation of the function.

   a) $(3, -12)$ **b)** $(5, 15)$

   c) $\left(1, \frac{2}{3}\right)$ **d)** $(-3, 3)$

4. Give an example of a linear function and a constant function, both in function notation. Describe the similarities and the differences between the two functions.

Reasoning and Proving

Representing — Selecting Tools

Problem Solving

Connecting — Reflecting

Communicating

For help with questions 5 to 8, refer to Example 2.

5. Show each set of data in a mapping diagram.

   a) $\{(1, 4), (2, 1), (3, -2), (4, -5), (5, -8), (6, -11), (7, -14), (8, -17)\}$

   b) $\{(-3, 4), (-2, -1), (-1, -4), (0, -5), (1, -4), (2, -1)\}$

   c) $\{(-5, 6), (-4, 9), (-3, 1), (-5, -6), (1, -2), (3, 8), (8, 8)\}$

   d) $\{(9, 9), (7, 9), (5, 9), (3, 9)\}$

6. Determine if each relation in question 5 is a function. Justify your answer.

7. Write the ordered pairs associated with each mapping diagram.

   a)

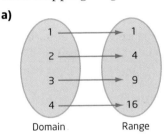

Domain   Range

   b)

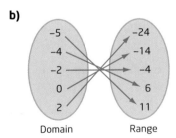

Domain   Range

   c)

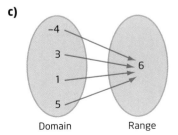

Domain   Range

8. Determine whether each relation in question 7 is a function. Justify your answer.

9. What advantages do mapping diagrams have over a list of ordered pairs?

For help with question 10, refer to Example 3.

10. Write each function in mapping notation.
   a) $f(x) = -x + 4$
   b) $g(x) = x^2 + 5x - 3$
   c) $s(x) = \sqrt{4x - 4}$
   d) $r(k) = -\dfrac{1}{2k - 1}$

B **Connect and Apply**

11. Describe two different ways to determine if a relation is a function.

12. Use Technology If the output of a quadratic function machine gives data that fit an equation of the form $f(x) = ax^2 + bx + c$, a graphing calculator can be used to determine the equation if at least three data points are given. Data are given from such a function machine as follows: $\{(1, 4), (2, 11), (3, 24)\}$.
   a) Enter the values of the domain in **L1** and the values of the range in **L2**.
   b) Plot the data.
   c) Run quadratic regression to determine the quadratic equation that fits these data. Record the equation that results from this regression.
   d) Use this function to determine the range values for the domain values $x = -3$, $x = 0$, and $x = 5$.

> **Technology Tip**
> Refer to the Technology Appendix, pages 496 to 516, if you need help with displaying data, quadratic regression, or finding values.

13. a) Complete a table of values for the relation $f(x) = \sqrt{x}$ and graph the data.

Reasoning and Proving
Representing — Selecting Tools
Problem Solving
Connecting — Reflecting
Communicating

   b) Is this relation a function? Explain.
   c) Could you have identified whether the relation was a function from the data in the table of values? Explain.

For help with questions 14 to 16, refer to Example 4.

14. Rivers located near an ocean experience a large wave called a tidal bore due to the tides. The speed, v, in kilometres per hour, of the tidal bore in a river is a function of the depth, d, in metres, of the river. The function is $v(d) = 11.27\sqrt{d}$.
   a) Determine the domain and the range of this function.
   b) Make a table of values and graph the function.

15. The value, V, in dollars, of an n-year-old car is given by $V(n) = \dfrac{23\,000}{n + 1} + 1000$.
   a) How much was this car worth when it was first purchased?
   b) Determine the value of the car after
      i) 10 years   **ii)** 12 years
   c) How long would it take the car to depreciate to a value of $2000?
   d) Is $V(n)$ a function? Justify your answer.

16. The amount, A, in dollars, that needs to be invested at an interest rate i to have $100 after 1 year is given by the relation $A(i) = \dfrac{100}{1 + i}$. Note that i must be expressed in decimal form.
   a) Determine the domain and the range for this relation.
   b) Graph the relation.
   c) How much money needs to be invested at 5% to give $100 after 1 year?
   d) What rate of interest is required if $90 is invested?

17. Create a linear function machine and two points that are generated by the machine. Trade points with a classmate to determine the function that generated the points.

18. Create a quadratic function machine of the form $f(x) = ax^2 + b$. Determine the coordinates of the y-intercept and of one other point that is generated by the machine. Trade points with a classmate to determine the function.

19. Chapter Problem While working at her co-op placement, Andrea is asked to work with a two-variable function to determine premiums for insurance policies. She is to calculate some values of the function and place them in the appropriate cell in a spreadsheet. The function is $f(n, r) = 500 + 2n - 10r$ for a driver with a rating of r (related to the driver's record, 1 being a poor driver up to 5 being an excellent driver) and an age of n (from 40 to 45 years of age). For example, a 42-year-old driver with a rating of 4 would have a policy premium of

$$f(42, 4) = 500 + 2(42) - 10(4)$$
$$= 500 + 84 - 40$$
$$= 544$$

This value has been placed in the spreadsheet for you.

Rating, r / Age, n	1	2	3	4	5
40					
41					
42				544	
43					
44					
45					

Help Andrea by copying and completing the spreadsheet.

✔ **Achievement Check**

20. On Earth, the time, t, in seconds, taken for an object to fall from a height, h, in metres, to the ground is given by the formula $t(h) = \sqrt{\dfrac{h}{4.9}}$. On the moon, the formula changes to $t(h) = \sqrt{\dfrac{h}{1.8}}$.

a) Express each relation using mapping notation.

b) Determine the domain and the range of each relation.

c) Is each relation a function? Explain.

d) Graph both relations on the same set of axes. Compare the graphs and describe any similarities or differences.

e) Determine the difference between the time it takes for an object to fall from a height of 25 m on Earth and the time it takes on the moon. Justify your answer.

C Extend

21. The initial velocity, v, in kilometres per hour, of a skidding car can be determined from the length, d, in metres, of the skid mark made by using the relation $v(d) = 12.6\sqrt{d} + 8$.

a) Determine the domain and the range of the relation.

b) Graph the relation.

c) Is the relation a function? Justify your answer.

22. Math Contest Given $f(x) = f(x + 1) + 3$ and $f(2) = 5$, what is the value of $f(8)$?

A 5   **B** 11   **C** 20   **D** -13

23. Math Contest Given $f(x) + 2g(x) = 12x^2 + 3x + 8$ and $2f(x) + 3g(x) = 18x^2 + 6x + 13$, find the value of $f(2) + g(3)$.

24. Math Contest $f(x)$ is a linear function. Given $f(f(3)) = 2$ and $f(f(2)) = 1$, what is the value of $f(0)$?

A 1   **B** 0   **C** -0.5 **D** -1

Maximum or Minimum of a Quadratic Function

Some bridge arches are defined by quadratic functions. Engineers use these quadratic functions to determine the maximum height or the minimum clearance under the support of the bridge at a variety of points. They can give this information to the bridge builders.

A quadratic function can be written in a number of forms. Each form has different advantages. In all forms, a determines the direction of opening and the shape.

- From the standard form, $f(x) = ax^2 + bx + c$, the y-intercept can be identified as c.

- From the factored form, $f(x) = a(x - r)(x - s)$, the x-intercepts can be identified as r and s.

- From the vertex form, $y = a(x - h)^2 + k$, the coordinates of the vertex can be identified as (h, k). If a is positive, the minimum value is k. If a is negative, the maximum value is k.

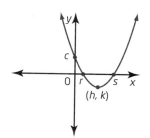

Tools

- graphing calculator

or

- grid paper

Investigate A

How can you connect different forms of the same quadratic function?

1. Graph each pair of functions.

a) $f(x) = (x + 2)^2 + 3$ and $f(x) = x^2 + 4x + 7$

b) $f(x) = (x + 3)^2 - 4$ and $f(x) = x^2 + 6x + 5$

c) $f(x) = 2(x - 3)^2 + 4$ and $f(x) = 2x^2 - 12x + 22$

d) $f(x) = 3(x - 1)^2 - 7$ and $f(x) = 3x^2 - 6x - 4$

2. Why are the graphs of the functions in each pair the same?

3. How can you rewrite the first equation in each pair in the form of the second equation?

4. How can you rewrite the second equation in each pair in the form of the first equation?

5. **Reflect** How can you use a graph to verify that two quadratic functions in different forms represent the same function? If you are using a graphing calculator, is it enough to observe that the graphs look the same on your screen? Explain.

To convert a quadratic function from standard form to vertex form, you can use the technique of completing the square.

Example 1

Find the Vertex by Completing the Square

Find the vertex of each function by completing the square. Is the vertex a minimum or a maximum? Explain.

a) $f(x) = x^2 + 5x + 7$

b) $f(x) = -\dfrac{2}{3}x^2 + 8x + 5$

Solution

a) $f(x) = x^2 + 5x + 7$

$$= x^2 + 5x + \left(\frac{5}{2}\right)^2 - \left(\frac{5}{2}\right)^2 + 7$$

Add half the coefficient of x, squared, to make the first three terms a perfect square trinomial. Subtract the same amount, $\left(\frac{5}{2}\right)^2$, so the value of the function does not change.

$$= \left(x + \frac{5}{2}\right)^2 - \frac{25}{4} + \frac{28}{4}$$

$$= \left(x + \frac{5}{2}\right)^2 + \frac{3}{4}$$

The vertex is at $\left(-\dfrac{5}{2}, \dfrac{3}{4}\right)$. This is a minimum because a is 1, a positive value, so the parabola opens upward.

b) $f(x) = -\dfrac{2}{3}x^2 + 8x + 5$

$$= -\frac{2}{3}(x^2 - 12x) + 5$$

Factor out the coefficient of x^2.

$$8 \div \left(-\frac{2}{3}\right) = 8 \times \left(-\frac{3}{2}\right)$$
$$= -12$$

$$= -\frac{2}{3}(x^2 - 12x + 36 - 36) + 5$$

Add and subtract $6^2 = 36$ to make a perfect square trinomial.

$$= -\frac{2}{3}[(x - 6)^2 - 36] + 5$$

$$= -\frac{2}{3}(x - 6)^2 + 24 + 5$$

$-\frac{2}{3} \times (-36) = 24$

$$= -\frac{2}{3}(x - 6)^2 + 29$$

The vertex is at $(6, 29)$. This is a maximum because the value of a is negative, indicating that the parabola opens downward.

Investigate B

Tools

- graphing calculator

or

- grid paper

How can you use partial factoring to find a minimum or a maximum?

1. Graph the function $f(x) = 2x^2 + 4x$.

2. How many x-intercepts does this function have?

3. Use the x-intercepts to find the vertex of the parabola.

4. Graph the functions $g(x) = 2x^2 + 4x + 2$ and $h(x) = 2x^2 + 4x + 5$ on the same set of axes as $f(x)$.

5. How many x-intercepts does $g(x)$ have? $h(x)$?

6. Describe how to find the vertex of the new parabolas, $g(x)$ and $h(x)$, based on the vertex of the original parabola, $f(x)$.

7. **Reflect** Using your answer from step 6, suggest a method that can be used to find the maximum or minimum of a parabola of the form $f(x) = 2x^2 + 4x + k$ for any value of k.

Example 2

Use Partial Factoring to Find the Vertex of a Quadratic Function

Find the vertex of the function $y = 4x^2 - 12x + 3$ by partial factoring. Is the vertex a minimum or a maximum value? Explain.

Solution

Work with the function $y = 4x^2 - 12x$ to find the x-coordinate of the vertex, since the x-coordinate of the vertex of $y = 4x^2 - 12x + 3$ will be the same.

$y = 4x(x - 3)$

For $y = 0$:

$0 = 4x(x - 3)$

$4x = 0$ or $x - 3 = 0$ Use the zero principle. If $AB = 0$, then either $A = 0$ or $B = 0$.

$x = 0$ or $x = 3$ These give the x-intercepts of the function $y = 4x^2 - 12x$.

The average of these two x-intercepts will give the x-coordinate of the vertex for $y = 4x^2 - 12x$ and $y = 4x^2 - 12x + 3$:

$\dfrac{0 + 3}{2} = \dfrac{3}{2}$

Connections

The vertex of a quadratic function is on the line of symmetry, which is halfway between the x-intercepts.

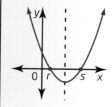

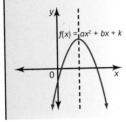
To find the y-coordinate of the vertex, substitute $x = \dfrac{3}{2}$ into $y = 4x^2 - 12x + 3.$

$$y = 4\left(\dfrac{3}{2}\right)^2 - 12\left(\dfrac{3}{2}\right) + 3$$

$$= 4\left(\dfrac{9}{4}\right) - 18 + 3$$

$$= 9 - 18 + 3$$

$$= -6$$

The vertex of the function $y = 4x^2 - 12x + 3$ is at $\left(\dfrac{3}{2}, -6\right)$. It is a minimum, because the value of a is positive.

Example 3

Solve a Problem Involving a Minimum or a Maximum

Rachel and Ken are knitting scarves to sell at the craft show. The wool for each scarf costs $6. They were planning to sell the scarves for $10 each, the same as last year when they sold 40 scarves. However, they know that if they raise the price, they will be able to make more profit, even if they end up selling fewer scarves. They have been told that for every 50¢ increase in the price, they can expect to sell four fewer scarves. What selling price will maximize their profit and what will the profit be?

Solution

Let x represent the number of 50¢ price changes.

Since each scarf cost $6 and was sold for $10, the profit was $4 per scarf. As they raise the price, their profit per scarf will be $(4 + 0.5x)$ for x changes to the price. They will sell $40 - 4x$ scarves when they make the price change.

Profit = profit per scarf × number sold

$$P(x) = (4 + 0.5x)(40 - 4x)$$

$$= -2x^2 + 4x + 160$$

Method 1: Complete the Square to Determine the Vertex

$$P(x) = -2(x^2 - 2x) + 160$$

$$= -2(x^2 - 2x + 1 - 1) + 160$$

$$= -2(x - 1)^2 + 2 + 160$$

$$= -2(x - 1)^2 + 162$$

The maximum value of this quadratic function is 162 when $x = 1$. This means that they will make a maximum profit of $162 if they increase the price once. The selling price is $10 + 0.5(1)$ or $10.50.

Method 2: Use Partial Factoring to Determine the Vertex

Find the x-coordinate of the vertex of the function $Q(x) = -2x^2 + 4x$, knowing that the vertex of $P(x) = -2x^2 + 4x + 160$ has the same x-coordinate.

$$Q(x) = -2x(x - 2)$$

Substitute $Q(x) = 0$ to find the x-intercepts.

$$0 = -2x(x - 2)$$
$$-2x = 0 \text{ or } x - 2 = 0$$
$$x = 0 \text{ or } \quad x = 2$$

The x-coordinate of the vertex is $x = 1$ (the average of 0 and 2).

$$P(1) = -2(1)^2 + 4(1) + 160$$
$$= 162$$

The vertex of this function is at (1, 162). This means that they will make a maximum profit of $162 if they increase the price once. The selling price is $10 + 0.5(1)$ or $10.50.

Example 4

Connect Projectiles to Quadratic Functions

Jamie throws a ball that will move through the air in a parabolic path due to gravity. The height, h, in metres, of the ball above the ground after t seconds can be modelled by the function $h(t) = -4.9t^2 + 40t + 1.5$.

a) Find the zeros of the function and interpret their meaning.

b) Determine the time needed for the ball to reach its maximum height.

c) What is the maximum height of the ball?

Connections

The zeros of a function are the values of the independent variable for which the function has value zero. They correspond to the x-intercepts of the graph of the function.

Solution

a) • Use the window settings shown.

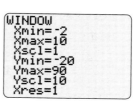

• Graph **Y1** $= -4.9x^2 + 40x + 1.5$.

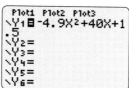

• Press (2nd) [CALC] to access the **CALCULATE** menu.

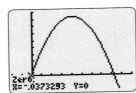

See the Use
Technology feature at
the end of this section
for a TI-Nspire™ CAS
graphing calculator
solution.

Technology Tip

• Select **2:zero** to find the x-intercepts of the function.

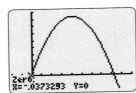 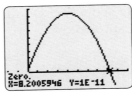

The zeros are approximately -0.037 and 8.2.

The solution $t = -0.037$ indicates when, in the past, the ball would have been thrown from ground level in order for it to follow the given path. The solution $t = 8.2$ indicates when the ball will return to the ground. The ball returns to the ground 8.2 s after Jamie threw it.

b) The maximum is midway between the two zeros. So, find the average of the two solutions from part a).

$$\frac{-0.037 + 8.2}{2} = 4.0815$$

The ball will take approximately 4.1 s to reach its maximum height.

c) The maximum height can be found by substituting $t = 4.1$ into the function.

$$h(t) = -4.9t^2 + 40t + 1.5$$
$$h(4.1) = -4.9(4.1)^2 + 40(4.1) + 1.5$$
$$\doteq 83.13$$

The ball will reach a maximum height of approximately 83.1 m.

This solution can be verified using the maximum function on the graphing calculator.

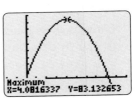

Key Concepts

• The minimum or maximum value of a quadratic function occurs at the vertex of the parabola.

• The vertex of a quadratic function can be found by

  – graphing
  – completing the square: for $f(x) = a(x - h)^2 + k$, the vertex is (h, k)
  – partial factoring: for $f(x) = ax\left(x + \dfrac{b}{a}\right) + k$, the x-coordinate of the vertex is $-\dfrac{b}{2a}$

• The sign of the coefficient a in the quadratic function
  $f(x) = ax^2 + bx + c$ or $f(x) = a(x - h)^2 + k$ determines
  whether the vertex is a minimum or a maximum.
  If $a > 0$, then the parabola opens upward and has a minimum.
  If $a < 0$, then the parabola opens downward and has a maximum.

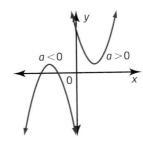

Communicate Your Understanding

C1 In one step of completing the square, you divide the coefficient of x by 2 and square the result. Why?

C2 How are the functions $f(x) = 4x(x - 3)$, $g(x) = 4x(x - 3) + 2$, and $h(x) = 4x(x - 3) - 1$ related? Explain using words and diagrams.

C3 Ryan does not understand the concept of partial factoring to determine the vertex. Use the function $y = 3x^2 - 9x - 17$ to outline the technique for him.

A Practise

For help with questions 1 and 2, refer to Example 1.

1. Complete the square for each function.

a) $y = x^2 + 4x$

b) $f(x) = x^2 + 7x + 11$

c) $g(x) = x^2 - 3x + 1$

d) $y = x^2 - 11x - 4$

e) $f(x) = x^2 + 13x + 2$

f) $y = x^2 - 9x - 9$

2. Determine the vertex of each quadratic function by completing the square. State if the vertex is a minimum or a maximum.

a) $f(x) = x^2 + 10x + 6$

b) $f(x) = 2x^2 + 12x + 16$

c) $f(x) = -3x^2 + 6x + 1$

d) $f(x) = -x^2 + 12x - 5$

e) $f(x) = -\dfrac{1}{2}x^2 - x + \dfrac{3}{2}$

f) $f(x) = \dfrac{2}{3}x^2 + \dfrac{16}{3}x + \dfrac{25}{3}$

For help with question 3, refer to Example 2.

3. Use partial factoring to determine the vertex of each function. State if the vertex is a minimum or a maximum.

a) $f(x) = 3x^2 - 6x + 11$

b) $f(x) = -2x^2 + 8x - 3$

c) $f(x) = \dfrac{1}{2}x^2 - 3x + 8$

d) $f(x) = -\dfrac{5}{3}x^2 + 5x - 10$

e) $f(x) = 0.3x^2 - 3x + 6$

f) $f(x) = -0.2x^2 - 2.8x - 5.4$

4. Use Technology Use a graphing calculator to verify your answers to questions 2 and 3.

B Connect and Apply

For help with questions 5 and 6, refer to Example 3.

5. An electronics store sells an average of 60 entertainment systems per month at an average of $800 more than the cost price. For every $20 increase in the selling price, the store sells one fewer system. What amount over the cost price will maximize revenue?

6. Last year, a banquet hall charged $30 per person, and 60 people attended the hockey banquet dinner. This year, the hall's manager has said that for every 10 extra people that attend the banquet, they will decrease the price by $1.50 per person. What size group would maximize the profit for the hall this year?

For help with question 7, refer to Example 4.

Reasoning and Proving

Representing ・ Selecting Tools

Problem Solving

Connecting ・ Reflecting

Communicating

7. A ball is kicked into the air and follows a path described by $h(t) = -4.9t^2 + 6t + 0.6$, where t is the time, in seconds, and h is the height, in metres, above the ground. Determine the maximum height of the ball, to the nearest tenth of a metre.

8. The cost, C, in dollars, of fuel per month for Sanjay to operate his truck is given by $C(v) = 0.0029v^2 - 0.48v + 142$, where v represents his average driving speed, in kilometres per hour. Find the most efficient speed at which Sanjay should drive his truck.

9. Arnold has 24 m of fencing to surround a garden, bounded on one side by the wall of his house. What are the dimensions of the largest rectangular garden that he can enclose?

10. The area shown is to be enclosed by 30 m of fencing. Find the dimensions that will maximize the enclosed area.

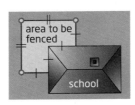

11. The sum of two numbers is 10. What is the maximum product of these numbers? 25.

12. A function models the effectiveness of a TV commercial. After n viewings, the effectiveness, e, is $e = -\frac{1}{90}n^2 + \frac{2}{3}n$.

Reasoning and Proving

Representing — Selecting Tools

Problem Solving

Connecting — Reflecting

Communicating

a) Determine the range for the effectiveness and the domain of the number of viewings. Explain your answers for the domain and range.

b) Use either completing the square or partial factoring to find the vertex. Is it a minimum or a maximum? Explain.

c) What conclusions can you make from this function?

d) Graph the function on a graphing calculator to verify your conclusions from part c).

13. All quadratic functions of the form $y = 2x^2 + bx$ have some similar properties.

a) Choose five different values of b and graph each function.

b) What are the similar properties?

c) Determine the vertex of each parabola.

d) Find the relationship between the vertices of these parabolas.

C **Extend**

14. A sheet of metal that is 30 cm wide and 6 m long is to be used to make a rectangular eavestrough by bending the sheet along the dotted lines.

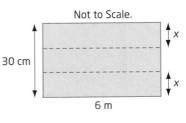

Not to Scale.

30 cm

6 m

What value of x maximizes the capacity of the eavestrough?

15. A ball is thrown vertically upward with an initial velocity of v metres per second and is affected by gravity, g. The height, h, in metres, of the ball after t seconds is given by $h(t) = -\frac{1}{2}gt^2 + vt$.

a) Show that the ball will reach its maximum height at $t = \frac{v}{g}$.

b) Show that the maximum height of the ball will be $\frac{v^2}{2g}$.

16. **Math Contest** Given that $x^2 = y^3 = z$, where x, y, and z are integers, how many different values of z are there for $z < 1001$?

A 0   **B** 3   **C** 4   **D** 10

17. **Math Contest** A function of two variables is defined as $f(x, y) = x^2 + y^2 + 4x - 6y + 7$. What is the minimum value of this function?

A 7   **B** -13 **C** -6 **D** 0

18. **Math Contest** A dog's 15-m-long leash is attached to a building. The leash is attached 10 m from one corner of the building. Assume that the sides of the building are long enough that the dog cannot go around any of the other corners. The greatest area that the dog can cover, in square metres, is

10 m

building

A 250π **B** $\frac{475\pi}{4}$ **C** 112.5π **D** 125π

Use a TI-Nspire™ CAS Graphing Calculator to Find the Maximum or Minimum and the Zeros of a Quadratic Function

Tools

• TI-Nspire™ CAS graphing calculator

Jamie throws a ball that will move through the air in a parabolic path due to gravity. The height, h, in metres, of the ball above the ground after t seconds can be modelled by the function $h(t) = -4.9t^2 + 40t + 1.5$.

a) Find the zeros of the function and interpret their meaning.

b) Determine the time needed for the ball to reach its maximum height.

c) What is the maximum height of the ball?

Solution

Connections

Example 4 on page 29 is used to model the steps needed to find the maximum or minimum and the zeros of a quadratic function using a TI-Nspire™ CAS graphing calculator.

a) Turn on the TI-Nspire™ CAS graphing calculator.

- Press ⌂ and select **6:New Document**.
- Select **2:Add Graphs & Geometry**.
- Type $-4.9x^2 + 40x + 1.5$ for function f1 and press ⏎.
- Press (menu). Select **4:Window**.
- Select **1:Window Settings**. Set **XMin** to -2, **XMax** to 10, **Ymin** to -40, and **YMax** to 100. Tab down to **OK** and press ⏎.
- Press (menu) and select **6:Points & Lines**.
- Select **2:Point On**. Move the cursor to the graph and press ⏎.
- Press (esc).
- Press (ctrl) and then ✋ to grab the point. Use the cursor keys (the arrows on the NavPad) to move the point along the graph toward the left zero. When you reach the zero, "zero" will appear in a box. Read the coordinates of the zero. It occurs at a time of approximately -0.037 s.

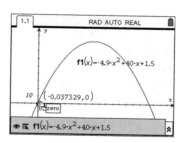

Similarly, you can find the right zero at a time of about 8.20 s.

b) To find the maximum height of the ball, move the point toward the maximum on the graph. When you reach the maximum, "maximum" will appear inside a box. Read the coordinates of the maximum. It occurs at a time of approximately 4.08 s.

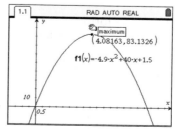

c) The maximum height of the ball is approximately 83.13 m.

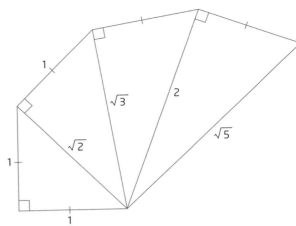

1.4

Skills You Need: Working With Radicals

The followers of the Greek mathematician Pythagoras discovered values that did not correspond to any of the rational numbers. As a result, a new type of number needed to be defined to represent these values. These values are called **irrational numbers**. One type of irrational number is of the form $\sqrt{n}$, where n is not a perfect square. Such numbers are sometimes referred to as radicals.

In this section, you will see how to use the operations of addition, subtraction, and multiplication with radicals.

irrational number

• a number that cannot be expressed in the form $\frac{a}{b}$, where a and b are integers and $b \neq 0$

Investigate

How do you multiply radicals?

1. Copy and complete the table. Where necessary, use a scientific calculator to help you evaluate each expression, rounding to two decimal places.

A	B
$\sqrt{4} \times \sqrt{4} = \blacksquare$	$\sqrt{4 \times 4} = \blacksquare$
$\sqrt{81} \times \sqrt{81} = \blacksquare$	$\sqrt{81 \times 81} = \blacksquare$
$\sqrt{225} \times \sqrt{225} = \blacksquare$	$\sqrt{225 \times 225} = \blacksquare$
$\sqrt{5} \times \sqrt{5} = \blacksquare$	$\sqrt{5 \times 5} = \blacksquare$
$\sqrt{31} \times \sqrt{31} = \blacksquare$	$\sqrt{31 \times 31} = \blacksquare$
$\sqrt{12} \times \sqrt{9} = \blacksquare$	$\sqrt{12 \times 9} = \blacksquare$
$\sqrt{23} \times \sqrt{121} = \blacksquare$	$\sqrt{23 \times 121} = \blacksquare$

2. What do you notice about the results in each row?

3. What conclusion can you make from your observations? Explain.

4. **Reflect a)** Make a general conclusion about an equivalent expression for $\sqrt{a} \times \sqrt{b}$.

   b) Do you think that this will be true for any values of a and b? Justify your answer.

The number or expression under the radical sign is called the **radicand**. If the radicand is greater than or equal to zero and is not a perfect square, then the radical is an irrational number. An approximate value can be found using a calculator. In many situations, it is better to work with the exact value, so the radical form is kept. Use the radical form when an approximate answer is not good enough and an exact answer is needed. Sometimes **entire radicals** can be simplified by removing perfect square factors. The resulting expression is called a **mixed radical**.

radicand

- a number or ex under a radical sign

entire radical

- a radical in the form $\sqrt{n}$, where $n > 0$, such as $\sqrt{45}$

mixed radical

- a radical in the form $a\sqrt{b}$, where $a \neq 1$ or -1 and $b > 0$, such as $3\sqrt{5}$

Example 1

Change Entire Radicals to Mixed Radicals

Express each radical as a mixed radical in simplest form.

a) $\sqrt{50}$

b) $\sqrt{27}$

c) $\sqrt{180}$

Solution

a) $\sqrt{50} = \sqrt{25 \times 2}$ Choose 25×2, not 5×10, as 25 is a perfect square factor.

$\qquad = (\sqrt{25})(\sqrt{2})$ Use $\sqrt{ab} = \sqrt{a} \times \sqrt{b}$.

$\qquad = 5\sqrt{2}$

b) $\sqrt{27} = \sqrt{9 \times 3}$

$\qquad = (\sqrt{9})(\sqrt{3})$ Use $\sqrt{ab} = \sqrt{a} \times \sqrt{b}$.

$\qquad = 3\sqrt{3}$

c) $\sqrt{180} = \sqrt{36 \times 5}$

$\qquad = (\sqrt{36})(\sqrt{5})$

$\qquad = 6\sqrt{5}$

or

$\sqrt{180} = \sqrt{9 \times 4 \times 5}$

$\qquad = (\sqrt{9})(\sqrt{4})(\sqrt{5})$

$\qquad = (3)(2)\sqrt{5}$

$\qquad = 6\sqrt{5}$

Adding and subtracting radicals works in the same way as adding and subtracting polynomials. You can only add like terms or, in this case, like radicals. For example, the terms in the expression $2\sqrt{3} + 5\sqrt{7}$ do not have the same radical, so they cannot be added, but the terms in the expression $3\sqrt{5} + 6\sqrt{5}$ have a common radical, so they can be added: $3\sqrt{5} + 6\sqrt{5} = 9\sqrt{5}$.

Example 2

Add or Subtract Radicals

Simplify.

a) $9\sqrt{7} - 3\sqrt{7}$

b) $4\sqrt{3} - 2\sqrt{27}$

c) $5\sqrt{8} + 3\sqrt{18}$

d) $\frac{1}{4}\sqrt{28} - \frac{3}{4}\sqrt{63} + \frac{2}{3}\sqrt{50}$

Solution

a) $9\sqrt{7} - 3\sqrt{7} = 6\sqrt{7}$

b) $4\sqrt{3} - 2\sqrt{27} = 4\sqrt{3} - 2\sqrt{9 \times 3}$ Simplify $\sqrt{27}$ first.

$$= 4\sqrt{3} - 2\sqrt{9} \times \sqrt{3}$$
$$= 4\sqrt{3} - 2 \times 3\sqrt{3}$$
$$= 4\sqrt{3} - 6\sqrt{3}$$
$$= -2\sqrt{3}$$

c) $5\sqrt{8} + 3\sqrt{18} = 5\sqrt{4 \times 2} + 3\sqrt{9 \times 2}$ First simplify both radicals.

$$= 5\sqrt{4}\sqrt{2} + 3\sqrt{9}\sqrt{2}$$
$$= 5 \times 2\sqrt{2} + 3 \times 3\sqrt{2}$$
$$= 10\sqrt{2} + 9\sqrt{2}$$
$$= 19\sqrt{2}$$

d) $\frac{1}{4}\sqrt{28} - \frac{3}{4}\sqrt{63} + \frac{2}{3}\sqrt{50} = \frac{1}{4}\sqrt{4 \times 7} - \frac{3}{4}\sqrt{9 \times 7} + \frac{2}{3}\sqrt{25 \times 2}$

$$= \frac{1}{4}\sqrt{4}\sqrt{7} - \frac{3}{4}\sqrt{9}\sqrt{7} + \frac{2}{3}\sqrt{25}\sqrt{2}$$
$$= \frac{1}{4} \times 2\sqrt{7} - \frac{3}{4} \times 3\sqrt{7} + \frac{2}{3} \times 5\sqrt{2}$$
$$= \frac{2}{4}\sqrt{7} - \frac{9}{4}\sqrt{7} + \frac{10}{3}\sqrt{2}$$
$$= -\frac{7}{4}\sqrt{7} + \frac{10}{3}\sqrt{2} \text{ or } -\frac{7\sqrt{7}}{4} + \frac{10\sqrt{2}}{3}$$

Example 3

Multiply Radicals

Simplify fully.

a) $(2\sqrt{3})(3\sqrt{6})$ **b)** $2\sqrt{3}(4 + 5\sqrt{3})$ **c)** $-7\sqrt{2}(6\sqrt{8} - 11)$

d) $(\sqrt{3} + 5)(2 - \sqrt{3})$ **e)** $(2\sqrt{2} + 3\sqrt{3})(2\sqrt{2} - 3\sqrt{3})$

Solution

a) $(2\sqrt{3})(3\sqrt{6}) = (2 \times 3)(\sqrt{3} \times \sqrt{6})$ Use the commutative property and the associative property.

$$= 6\sqrt{3 \times 6}$$ Multiply coefficients and then multiply radicands.

$$= 6\sqrt{18}$$

$$= 6\sqrt{9 \times 2}$$

$$= 6 \times 3\sqrt{2}$$

$$= 18\sqrt{2}$$

Connections

Recall that
$3(x + 2) = 3x + 6$ by the distributive property. The same property can be applied to multiply radicals.

b) $2\sqrt{3}(4 + 5\sqrt{3}) = 2\sqrt{3}(4) + (2\sqrt{3})(5\sqrt{3})$ Use the distributive property.

$$= 8\sqrt{3} + 10\sqrt{9}$$

$$= 8\sqrt{3} + 10(3)$$

$$= 8\sqrt{3} + 30$$

c) $-7\sqrt{2}(6\sqrt{8} - 11) = (-7\sqrt{2})(6\sqrt{8}) - (7\sqrt{2})(-11)$

$$= -42\sqrt{16} + 77\sqrt{2}$$

$$= (-42)(4) + 77\sqrt{2}$$

$$= -168 + 77\sqrt{2}$$

d) $(\sqrt{3} + 5)(2 - \sqrt{3}) = \sqrt{3}(2) + \sqrt{3}(-\sqrt{3}) + 5(2) + 5(-\sqrt{3})$

$$= 2\sqrt{3} - \sqrt{9} + 10 - 5\sqrt{3}$$

$$= 2\sqrt{3} - 3 + 10 - 5\sqrt{3}$$

$$= -3\sqrt{3} + 7$$

Connections

Recall the difference of squares:
$(a + b)(a - b) = a^2 - b^2$.
The factors in part e) have the same pattern. They are called conjugates.

e) $(2\sqrt{2} + 3\sqrt{3})(2\sqrt{2} - 3\sqrt{3}) = (2\sqrt{2})^2 - (3\sqrt{3})^2$

$$= 4(2) - 9(3)$$

$$= 8 - 27$$ Simplify and collect like terms.

$$= -19$$

Example 4

Solve a Problem Using Radicals

A square-based pyramid has a height of 9 cm. The volume of the pyramid is 1089 cm³. Find the exact side length of the square base, in simplified form.

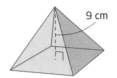

9 cm

Solution

Let x represent the side length of the base.

$$V = \frac{1}{3} \times \text{area of base} \times \text{height}$$

$$1089 = \frac{1}{3}x^2(9)$$

$$1089 = 3x^2$$

$$x^2 = \frac{1089}{3}$$

$$x^2 = 363$$

$$x = \sqrt{363} \qquad \text{Only the positive root is needed because } x \text{ is a length.}$$

$$x = \sqrt{121 \times 3}$$

$$x = 11\sqrt{3}$$

The exact side length of the square base of the pyramid is $11\sqrt{3}$ cm.

Connections

The answer $11\sqrt{3}$ cm is exact. An approximate answer can be found using a calculator. To the nearest hundredth, the side length is 19.05 cm.

Key Concepts

- $\sqrt{a} \times \sqrt{b} = \sqrt{ab}$ for $a \geq 0$ and $b \geq 0$.

- An entire radical can be simplified to a mixed radical in simplest form by removing the largest perfect square from under the radical to form a mixed radical.
  For example, $\sqrt{50} = \sqrt{25 \times 2}$
  $$= 5\sqrt{2}$$

- Like radicals can be combined through addition and subtraction. For example, $3\sqrt{7} + 2\sqrt{7} = 5\sqrt{7}$.

- Radicals can be multiplied using the distributive property.
  For example, $4\sqrt{2}(5\sqrt{3} - 3) = 20\sqrt{6} - 12\sqrt{2}$ and
  $(\sqrt{2} - 3)(\sqrt{2} + 1) = \sqrt{4} + \sqrt{2} - 3\sqrt{2} - 3$
  $$= 2 - 2\sqrt{2} - 3$$
  $$= -2\sqrt{2} - 1$$

Communicate Your Understanding

C1 Marc is asked to simplify the expression $\sqrt{3} - \sqrt{75}$. He says that since the radical expressions are unlike, the terms cannot be combined. Is he correct? Explain why or why not.

C2 Describe the steps needed to simplify the expression $\sqrt{3}(2\sqrt{3} - 4\sqrt{2})$.

C3 Ann wants to simplify the radical $\sqrt{108}$. She starts by prime factoring 108:
$108 = 2 \times 2 \times 3 \times 3 \times 3$
Rayanne looks for the greatest perfect square that will divide into 108 to produce a whole number. Rayanne finds that this value is 36.
Explain why both techniques will result in the same solution.

A Practise

For help with question 1, refer to the Investigate.

1. Simplify.

a) $3(4\sqrt{5})$

b) $\sqrt{3}(5\sqrt{2})$

c) $\sqrt{5}(-2\sqrt{7})$

d) $5\sqrt{3}(-4\sqrt{5})$

e) $2\sqrt{3}(3\sqrt{2})$

f) $-6\sqrt{2}(-\sqrt{11})$

For help with question 2, refer to Example 1.

2. Express each as a mixed radical in simplest form.

a) $\sqrt{12}$

b) $\sqrt{242}$

c) $\sqrt{147}$

d) $\sqrt{20}$

e) $\sqrt{252}$

f) $\sqrt{392}$

For help with questions 3 and 4, refer to Example 2.

3. Simplify.

a) $2\sqrt{3} - 5\sqrt{3} + 4\sqrt{3}$

b) $11\sqrt{5} - 4\sqrt{5} - 5\sqrt{5} - 6\sqrt{5}$

c) $\sqrt{7} - 2\sqrt{7} + \sqrt{7}$

d) $2\sqrt{2} - 8\sqrt{5} + 3\sqrt{2} + 4\sqrt{5}$

e) $\sqrt{6} - 4\sqrt{2} + 3\sqrt{6} - \sqrt{2}$

f) $2\sqrt{10} - \sqrt{10} - 4\sqrt{10} + \sqrt{5}$

4. Add or subtract as indicated.

a) $8\sqrt{2} - 4\sqrt{8} + \sqrt{32}$

b) $4\sqrt{18} + 3\sqrt{50} + \sqrt{200}$

c) $\sqrt{20} - 4\sqrt{12} - \sqrt{125} + 2\sqrt{3}$

d) $2\sqrt{28} + \sqrt{54} + \sqrt{150} + 5\sqrt{7}$

e) $5\sqrt{3} - \sqrt{72} + \sqrt{243} + \sqrt{8}$

f) $\sqrt{44} + \sqrt{88} + \sqrt{99} + \sqrt{198}$

For help with questions 5 to 7, refer to Example 3.

5. Expand and simplify.

a) $5\sqrt{6}(2\sqrt{3})$

b) $-2\sqrt{2}(4\sqrt{14})$

c) $8\sqrt{5}(\sqrt{10})$

d) $3\sqrt{15}(-2\sqrt{3})$

e) $11\sqrt{2}(5\sqrt{3})$

f) $-2\sqrt{6}(2\sqrt{6})$

6. Expand. Simplify where possible.

a) $3(8 - \sqrt{5})$

b) $\sqrt{3}(5\sqrt{2} + 4\sqrt{3})$

c) $\sqrt{3}(\sqrt{6} - \sqrt{3})$

d) $-2\sqrt{5}(4 + 2\sqrt{5})$

e) $8\sqrt{2}(2\sqrt{8} + 3\sqrt{12})$

f) $3\sqrt{3}(2\sqrt{7} - 5\sqrt{2})$

7. Expand. Simplify where possible.

a) $(\sqrt{2} + 5)(\sqrt{2} + 5)$

b) $(2\sqrt{2} + 4)(\sqrt{2} - 4)$

c) $(\sqrt{3} + 2\sqrt{2})(5 + 5\sqrt{2})$

d) $(3 + 2\sqrt{5})(\sqrt{5} - 5)$

e) $(1 + \sqrt{5})(1 - \sqrt{5})$

f) $(4 - 3\sqrt{7})(\sqrt{7} + 1)$

8. Simplify.

a) $\frac{1}{4}\sqrt{54} - \frac{1}{4}\sqrt{150}$

b) $2\sqrt{20} + \frac{3}{4}\sqrt{80} - \sqrt{125}$

c) $\frac{1}{2}\sqrt{8} + \frac{3}{5}\sqrt{50} - \frac{2}{3}\sqrt{18}$

d) $\frac{2}{5}\sqrt{125} - \frac{2}{3}\sqrt{243} - \frac{1}{3}\sqrt{45} + \frac{1}{2}\sqrt{48}$

B Connect and Apply

For help with questions 9 to 11, refer to Example 4.

9. Find a simplified expression for the area of each shape.

a)

b)

c)

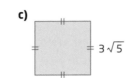

d)

10. Explain the steps you would need to take to fully simplify $\sqrt{2880}$.

11. A square has an area of 675 cm². Find the length of a side in simplified radical form.

12. On a square game board made up of small squares of side length 2 cm, the diagonal has a length of $20\sqrt{2}$ cm. How many small squares are on this board?

13. Find the area and the perimeter of the rectangle shown.
Express your answers in simplified radical form.

14. Why is $\sqrt{16 + 9}$ not equal to $\sqrt{16} + \sqrt{9}$? Justify your reasoning.

15. Is the expression $1 + \sqrt{3}$ a solution to the equation $x^2 - 2x - 2 = 0$? Explain.

C Extend

16. Simplify.

a) $\dfrac{10 + 15\sqrt{5}}{5}$

b) $\dfrac{21 - 7\sqrt{6}}{7}$

c) $\dfrac{\sqrt{14}}{\sqrt{2}}$

d) $\dfrac{12 - \sqrt{48}}{4}$

e) $\dfrac{-10 + \sqrt{50}}{5}$

17. A square root is simplified by finding factors that appear twice, and leaving all other factors under the radical sign. Simplifying a cube root requires the factor to appear three times under the cube root sign. Any factor that does not appear three times is left under the cube root. Simplify each cube root.

a) $\sqrt[3]{54}$ b) $\sqrt[3]{3000}$ c) $\sqrt[3]{1125}$

18. a) For what values of a is $\sqrt{a} < a$?

b) For what values of a is $\sqrt{a} > a$?

Explain your reasoning.

19. **Math Contest** If $\sqrt{4^2 + 4^2 + \cdots + 4^2} = 16$, how many 4^2's are under the radical?

A 4   **B** 8   **C** 12   **D** 16

20. **Math Contest** The roots of the equation $\sqrt{3x - 11} = x - 3$ are m and n. A possible value for $m - n$ is

A 9   **B** 0   **C** -1   **D** -5

21. **Math Contest** If $\sqrt{128} = \sqrt{2} + \sqrt{x}$, what is the value of x?

A 126   **B** 64   **C** 98   **D** 256

22. **Math Contest** Given that $f(a + b) = f(a)f(b)$ and $f(x)$ is always positive, what is the value of $f(0)$?

Use a TI-Nspire™ CAS Graphing Calculator to Explore Operations With Radicals

Tools

- TI-Nspire™ CAS graphing calculator

1. a) Turn on the TI-Nspire™ CAS graphing calculator.

- Press ⌂ and select **8:System Info**. Then, select **2:System Settings...**.

- Use the (tab) key to scroll down to **Auto or Approx** and ensure that it is set to **Auto**. Continue down to **OK**, and press ⊙ twice.

b) Press ⌂ and select **6:New Document**. Select **3:Add Lists & Spreadsheet**.

c) Use the cursor keys on the NavPad to move to cell **A1**. Press (ctrl) ⊙ to enter the square root symbol. Then, press **2** and (enter).

d) Move to cell **B1** and enter $\sqrt{3}$.

e) Move to the cell above cell **C1** and enter the formula =a*b. Press (enter). Note the result in cell **C1**, as shown.

f) Enter $\sqrt{5}$ in cell **A2** and $\sqrt{7}$ in cell **B2**. Note the result in cell **C2**.

g) Try a few more examples of your choice.

2. You can use the CAS to help you change entire radicals to mixed radicals.

a) Press ⌂ and select **1:Add Calculator**.

b) Press (menu) and select **3:Algebra**. Select **2:Factor**.

c) Type 50 and press (enter). Note the result.

d) Press (ctrl) ⊙ to access the square root.

e) Press (ctrl) (ans) to access the previous answer. Press (enter). Note the result.

f) Try this shortcut. Enter the square root symbol first. Then, enter the **factor()** command, followed by the 50. Press (enter).

g) Try a few more examples of your choice.

3. You can check your work on addition or subtraction of radicals.

a) Enter $9\sqrt{7} - 3\sqrt{7}$ and press ⏎. Note the result.

1.1	1.2	DEG AUTO REAL	
$9 \cdot \sqrt{7} - 3 \cdot \sqrt{7}$			$6 \cdot \sqrt{7}$
$4 \cdot \sqrt{3} - 2 \cdot \sqrt{3}$			$2 \cdot \sqrt{3}$
$5 \cdot \sqrt{8} + 3 \cdot \sqrt{18}$			$19 \cdot \sqrt{2}$

3/99

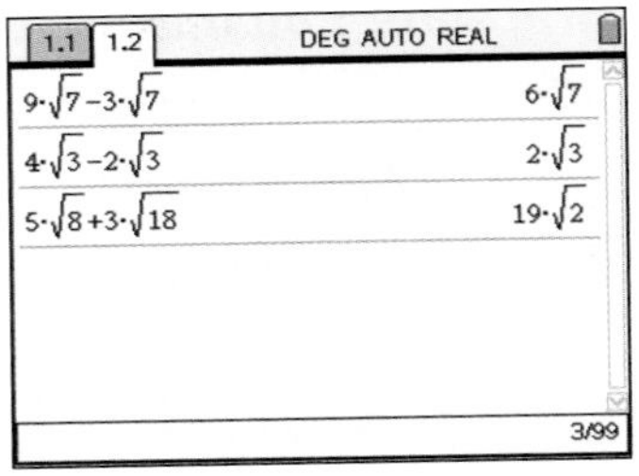

b) Try a few more, such as

$$4\sqrt{3} - 2\sqrt{3}$$
$$5\sqrt{8} + 3\sqrt{18}$$

Be sure you can explain where the last answer came from.

c) Try some examples of your choice.

4. Try some multiplication of radicals. Start with the examples shown. Then, try some of your own.

1.1	1.2	DEG AUTO REAL	
$2 \cdot \sqrt{3} \cdot 4 \cdot \sqrt{2}$			$8 \cdot \sqrt{6}$
$5 \cdot \sqrt{2} \cdot 3 \cdot \sqrt{7}$			$15 \cdot \sqrt{14}$
$3 \cdot \sqrt{2} \cdot 7 \cdot \sqrt{6}$			$42 \cdot \sqrt{3}$

3/99

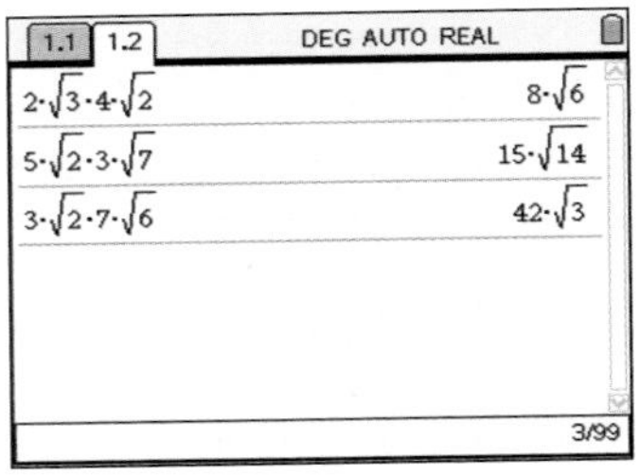

5. Try some mixed operations. Start with the examples shown. Then, try some of your own.

1.1	1.2	DEG AUTO REAL	
$2 \cdot \sqrt{3} \cdot (4 + 5 \cdot \sqrt{3})$			$8 \cdot \sqrt{3} + 30$
$-7 \cdot \sqrt{2} \cdot (6 \cdot \sqrt{8} - 11)$			$77 \cdot \sqrt{2} - 168$
$(\sqrt{3} + 5) \cdot (2 - \sqrt{3})$			$7 - 3 \cdot \sqrt{3}$
$(2 \cdot \sqrt{2} + 3 \cdot \sqrt{3}) \cdot (2 \cdot \sqrt{2} - 3 \cdot \sqrt{3})$			-19

4/99

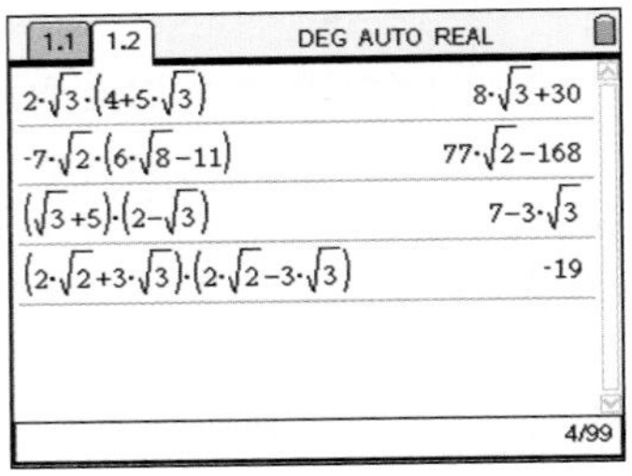

Solve Quadratic Equations ✓

Alexandre Despatie is a Canadian diver who has won two Olympic silver medals. One of the keys to a successful dive is for Alexandre to jump upward and outward to ensure that he is far enough away from the dive tower so that he will not hit it on the way down and so that he stays in the air long enough to complete the dive.

A mathematician analyses the dives of a team. The path of a dive can be modelled by the quadratic function $f(t) = -4.9t^2 + 3t + 10$. How can this function be used to determine how long a diver is in the air? What part of the equation needs to change for the diver to stay in the air longer? If this change is made, how much longer will the diver be in the air?

In this section, you will look at the concepts needed to answer questions such as these. One of the concepts is the solution of **quadratic equations**.

quadratic equation

• an equation of the form $ax^2 + bx + c = 0$, where a, b, and c are real numbers and $a \neq 0$

Investigate

How can you solve quadratic equations of the form $a(x - h)^2 + k = 0$?

1. Solve $x^2 = 4$. How many solutions are there?

2. Solve $(x + 1)^2 = 4$.

3. Solve $2(x + 1)^2 = 8$.

4. Solve $2(x + 1)^2 - 8 = 0$.

5. How are the equations in steps 1 to 4 related?

6. Reflect Describe a method for solving $a(x - h)^2 + k = 0$. Use your method to solve $2(x - 3)^2 - 32 = 0$.

Example 1

Select a Strategy to Solve a Quadratic Equation

a) Solve $2x^2 - 12x - 14 = 0$ by

    i) completing the square

    ii) using a graphing calculator

    iii) factoring

    iv) using the quadratic formula

b) Which strategy do you prefer? Justify your reasoning.

Solution

a)   **i)**

$$2x^2 - 12x - 14 = 0$$
$$x^2 - 6x - 7 = 0 \qquad \text{Divide both sides by 2.}$$
$$x^2 - 6x + 9 - 9 - 7 = 0$$
$$(x - 3)^2 - 16 = 0$$
$$(x - 3)^2 = 16$$
$$x - 3 = 4 \text{ or } x - 3 = -4 \qquad \text{Take the square root of both sides.}$$

The solutions are $x = 7$ and $x = -1$.

ii) • Use the window settings shown.

    • Graph **Y1** $= 2x^2 - 12x - 14$.

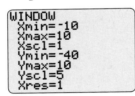 

    • Use the **Zero** operation to find the x-intercepts.

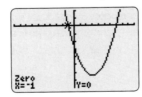 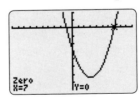

The solutions are $x = -1$ and $x = 7$.

iii) $2x^2 - 12x - 14 = 0$

$$x^2 - 6x - 7 = 0 \qquad \text{Divide both sides by 2.}$$
$$(x - 7)(x + 1) = 0 \qquad \text{Find the binomial factors of the trinomial}$$
$$\qquad\qquad\qquad\qquad\qquad\quad x^2 - 6x - 7.$$
$$x - 7 = 0 \text{ or } x + 1 = 0$$
$$x = 7 \text{ or } \qquad x = -1$$

iv) $2x^2 - 12x - 14 = 0$

$$x^2 - 6x - 7 = 0 \qquad \text{Divide both sides by 2.}$$

$a = 1, b = -6,$ and $c = -7.$

$$x = \frac{-b \pm \sqrt{b^2 - 4ac}}{2a} \qquad \begin{array}{l}\text{Substitute the values of } a, b, \text{ and } c \text{ into the}\\\text{quadratic formula and simplify.}\end{array}$$

$$= \frac{-(-6) \pm \sqrt{(-6)^2 - 4(1)(-7)}}{2(1)}$$

$$= \frac{6 \pm \sqrt{64}}{2}$$

$$= \frac{6 \pm 8}{2}$$

$$= \frac{14}{2} \text{ or } \frac{-2}{2}$$

$$= 7 \text{ or } -1$$

b) While all four methods produce the same solutions, factoring is probably the best strategy for this example. The quadratic expression is easy to factor, so this method is the fastest. If the quadratic expression could not be factored, either the graphing calculator method or using the quadratic formula would be preferred.

Connections

In this example, the roots are integers. However, many quadratic equations have irrational roots. If exact roots are asked for, then either completing the square or the quadratic formula is a better method to use. The graphing calculator method will only provide approximations.

Solving $2x^2 - 12x - 14 = 0$ is equivalent to finding the zeros, or x-intercepts, of the function $f(x) = 2x^2 - 12x - 14$. The two solutions in Example 1 represent the two x-intercepts of the function $f(x) = 2x^2 - 12x - 14$. However, not all quadratic functions have two x-intercepts. Some have one x-intercept, while others have no x-intercepts. The next example illustrates this.

Example 2

Connect the Number of Zeros to a Graph

For each quadratic equation given in the form $ax^2 + bx + c = 0$, graph the related function $f(x) = ax^2 + bx + c$ using a graphing calculator. State the number of solutions of the original equation. Justify each answer.

a) $-2x^2 + 8x - 5 = 0$

b) $8x^2 - 11x + 5 = 0$

c) $-4x^2 + 12x - 9 = 0$

Solution

a) The parabola opens downward and the vertex is located above the x-axis, so the function has two zeros.

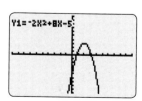

The equation $-2x^2 + 8x - 5 = 0$ has two solutions.

b) The parabola opens upward and the vertex is located above the x-axis, so the function has no zeros.

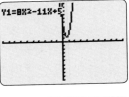

The equation $8x^2 - 11x + 5 = 0$ has no real solutions.

c) The parabola opens downward and the vertex is located on the x-axis. This function has one zero.

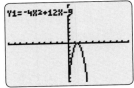

The equation $-4x^2 + 12x - 9 = 0$ has one solution.

The graph of a quadratic function gives you a visual understanding of the number of x-intercepts. Without a graphing calculator, it can be quite time-consuming to create this visualization. Is there a way that the number of zeros can be identified without drawing a graph? The next example revisits Example 2 using the quadratic formula to see if a pattern can be identified that will tell the number of zeros without graphing.

Example 3

Connect the Number of Zeros to the Quadratic Formula

Solve each quadratic equation in Example 2 using the quadratic formula. Give answers for the x-intercepts as exact values. Compare the results with the conclusion for the number of x-intercepts found in Example 2.

Solution

a) $-2x^2 + 8x - 5 = 0$

$a = -2$, $b = 8$, and $c = -5$.

$$x = \frac{-b \pm \sqrt{b^2 - 4ac}}{2a}$$

$$= \frac{-8 \pm \sqrt{8^2 - 4(-2)(-5)}}{2(-2)}$$

$$= \frac{-8 \pm \sqrt{24}}{-4}$$

$$x = \frac{-8 + 2\sqrt{6}}{-4} \text{ or } x = \frac{-8 - 2\sqrt{6}}{-4}$$

$$x = \frac{4 - \sqrt{6}}{2} \quad \text{ or } x = \frac{4 + \sqrt{6}}{2}$$

The answer of two solutions from Example 2 is verified by the quadratic formula. There are two solutions because the value under the radical sign is positive, so it can be evaluated to give two approximate roots.

Connections

Engineers use the zeros of a quadratic function to help mathematically model the support structure needed for a bridge that must span a given distance.

b) $8x^2 - 11x + 5 = 0$

$a = 8$, $b = -11$, and $c = 5$.

$$x = \frac{-b \pm \sqrt{b^2 - 4ac}}{2a}$$

$$= \frac{-(-11) \pm \sqrt{(-11)^2 - 4(8)(5)}}{2(8)}$$

$$= \frac{11 \pm \sqrt{-39}}{16}$$

Since the square root of a negative value is not a real number, there is no real solution to the quadratic equation.

c) $-4x^2 + 12x - 9 = 0$

$a = -4$, $b = 12$, and $c = -9$.

$$x = \frac{-b \pm \sqrt{b^2 - 4ac}}{2a}$$

$$= \frac{-12 \pm \sqrt{12^2 - 4(-4)(-9)}}{2(-4)}$$

$$= \frac{-12 \pm \sqrt{0}}{-8}$$

$$= \frac{-12}{-8}$$

$$= \frac{3}{2}$$

There is one solution because the value under the square root is zero. This means that there is exactly one root to the equation $-4x^2 + 12x - 9 = 0$.

Example 3 shows that the value under the radical sign in the quadratic formula determines the number of solutions for a quadratic equation and the number of zeros for the related quadratic function.

Example 4

Use the Discriminant to Determine the Number of Solutions

For each quadratic equation, use the **discriminant** to determine the number of solutions.

a) $-2x^2 + 3x + 8 = 0$ **b)** $3x^2 - 5x + 11 = 0$ **c)** $\frac{1}{4}x^2 - 3x + 9 = 0$

Solution

a) $-2x^2 + 3x + 8 = 0$

$a = -2$, $b = 3$, and $c = 8$.

$b^2 - 4ac = 3^2 - 4(-2)(8)$

$\quad\quad\quad\quad = 9 + 64$

$\quad\quad\quad\quad = 73$

discriminant

- the expression $b^2 - 4ac$, the value of which can be used to determine the number of solutions to a quadratic equation $ax^2 + bx + c = 0$
- When $b^2 - 4ac > 0$, there are two solutions.
- When $b^2 - 4ac = 0$, there is one solution.
- When $b^2 - 4ac < 0$, there are no solutions.

Since the discriminant is greater than zero, there are two solutions.

You can check this result using a graphing calculator.

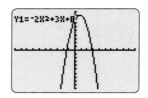

b) $3x^2 - 5x + 11 = 0$

$a = 3$, $b = -5$, and $c = 11$.

$$b^2 - 4ac = (-5)^2 - 4(3)(11)$$
$$= 25 - 132$$
$$= -107$$

Since the discriminant is less than zero, there are no solutions.

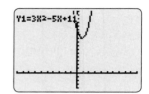

c) $\frac{1}{4}x^2 - 3x + 9 = 0$

$a = \frac{1}{4}$, $b = -3$, and $c = 9$.

$$b^2 - 4ac = (-3)^2 - 4\left(\frac{1}{4}\right)(9)$$
$$= 9 - 9$$
$$= 0$$

Since the discriminant is equal to zero, there is one solution.

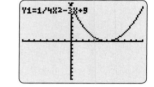

Key Concepts

- A quadratic equation can be solved by
  - completing the square
  - factoring
  - using the quadratic formula
  - graphing

- The number of solutions to a quadratic equation and the number of zeros of the related quadratic function can be determined using the discriminant.

If $b^2 - 4ac > 0$, there are two solutions (two distinct real roots).

If $b^2 - 4ac = 0$, there is one solution (two equal real roots).

If $b^2 - 4ac < 0$, there are no real solutions.

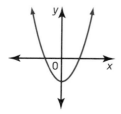

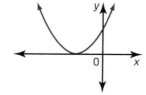

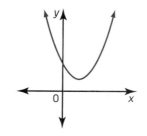

Communicate Your Understanding

C1 Minh has been asked to solve a quadratic equation of the form $ax^2 + bx + c = 0$, but he is unclear whether he should factor, complete the square, use the quadratic formula, or use a graphing calculator. What advice would you give him? Explain.

C2 While many techniques can be used to solve a quadratic equation of the form $ax^2 + bx = 0$, what is the easiest technique to use? Why?

C3 Deepi wants to determine how many x-intercepts a quadratic function has. How can she find the number of x-intercepts for the function without graphing? Justify your reasoning.

A Practise

For help with questions 1 to 3, refer to Example 1.

1. Solve each quadratic equation by factoring.

a) $x^2 + 2x - 3 = 0$

b) $x^2 + 3x - 10 = 0$

c) $4x^2 - 36 = 0$

d) $6x^2 - 14x + 8 = 0$

e) $15x^2 - 8x + 1 = 0$

f) $6x^2 + 19x + 10 = 0$

2. Check your answers to question 1 using a graphing calculator or by substituting each solution back into the original equation.

3. Solve each quadratic equation using the quadratic formula. Give exact answers.

a) $2x^2 - 17x + 27 = 0$

b) $-4x^2 + 3x + 8 = 0$

c) $-x^2 - x + 7 = 0$

d) $x^2 + 6x - 4 = 0$

e) $3x^2 + x - 11 = 0$

f) $-\frac{1}{2}x^2 + 4x - 1 = 0$

For help with question 4, refer to Example 2.

4. Use Technology Use a graphing calculator to graph a related function to determine the number of roots for each quadratic equation.

a) $3x^2 - 4x + 5 = 0$

b) $8x^2 - 20x + 12.5 = 0$

c) $-x^2 + 2x + 5 = 0$

d) $\frac{3}{4}x^2 - 5x + 2 = 0$

For help with question 5, refer to Example 3.

5. Determine the exact values of the x-intercepts of each quadratic function.

a) $f(x) = 6x^2 + 3x - 2$

b) $f(x) = -\frac{1}{3}x^2 + 4x - 8$

c) $f(x) = \frac{3}{4}x^2 - 2x - 7$

d) $f(x) = \frac{1}{4}x^2 - 2x + 4$

For help with question 6, refer to Example 4.

6. Use the discriminant to determine the number of roots for each quadratic equation.

a) $x^2 - 5x + 4 = 0$

b) $3x^2 + 4x + \frac{4}{3} = 0$

c) $2x^2 - 8x + 9 = 0$

d) $-2x^2 + 0.75x + 5 = 0$

B Connect and Apply

7. Which method would you use to solve each equation? Justify your choice. Then, solve. Do any of your answers suggest that you might have used another method? Explain.

a) $2x^2 - 5x - 12 = 0$ b) $x^2 - 25 = 0$

c) $2x^2 + 3x - 1 = 0$ d) $\frac{1}{2}x^2 + 4x = 0$

e) $3x^2 - 4x + 2 = 0$ f) $x^2 - 4x + 4 = 0$

g) $0.57x^2 - 3.7x - 2.5 = 0$

h) $9x^2 - 24x + 16 = 0$

8. Determine the value(s) of k for which the quadratic equation $x^2 + kx + 9 = 0$ will have

a) two equal real roots

b) two distinct real roots

9. a) Create a table of values for the function $f(x) = 2x^2 - 3x$ for the domain $\{-2, -1, 0, 1, 2, 3, 4\}$.

Reasoning and Proving

Representing — Selecting Tools

Problem Solving

Connecting — Reflecting

Communicating

b) Graph this quadratic function.

c) On the same set of axes, graph the line $y = 6$.

d) Use your graph to determine the approximate x-values where the line $y = 6$ intersects the quadratic function.

e) Determine the x-values for the points of intersection of $f(x) = 2x^2 - 3x$ and the horizontal line $y = 6$ algebraically.

10. Use Technology Check your answer to question 9 using a graphing calculator.

11. What value(s) of k, where k is an integer, will allow each quadratic equation to be solved by factoring?

a) $x^2 + kx + 12 = 0$

b) $x^2 + kx = 8$ c) $x^2 - 3x = k$

12. The height, h, in metres, above the ground of a football t seconds after it is thrown can be modelled by the function $h(t) = -4.9t^2 + 19.6t + 2$. Determine how long the football will be in the air, to the nearest tenth of a second.

13. A car travelling at v kilometres per hour will need a stopping distance, d, in metres, without skidding that can be modelled by the function $d = 0.0067v^2 + 0.15v$. Determine the speed at which a car can be travelling to be able to stop in each distance. Round answers to the nearest tenth.

a) 37 m   b) 75 m   c) 100 m

14. A by-law restricts the height of structures in an area close to an airport. To conform with this by-law, fuel storage tanks with different capacities are built by varying the radius of the cylindrical tanks. The surface area, A, in square metres, of a tank with radius r, in metres, can be approximately modelled by the quadratic function $A(r) = 6.28r^2 + 47.7r$. What is the radius of a tank with each surface area?

a) 1105 m²

b) 896.75 m²

15. The length of a rectangle is 2 m more than the width. If the area of the rectangle is 20 m², what are the dimensions of the rectangle, to the nearest tenth of a metre?

16. A building measuring 90 m by 60 m is to be built. A paved area of uniform width will surround the building. The paved area is to have an area of 9000 m². How wide is the paved area?

paved area

17. If the same length is cut off three pieces of wood measuring 21 cm, 42 cm, and 45 cm, the three pieces of wood can be assembled into a right triangle. What length needs to be cut off each piece?

18. In Vancouver, the height, h, in kilometres, that you would need to climb to see to the east coast of Canada can be modelled by the equation $h^2 + 12\ 740h = 20\ 000\ 000$. If the positive root of this equation is the solution, find the height, to the nearest kilometre.

19. Chapter Problem Andrea has been asked to determine when (if ever) the volume, V, in hundreds of shares, of a company's stock, which can be modelled by the function $V(x) = 250x - 5x^2$, after being listed on the stock exchange for x weeks, will reach

a) 275 000 shares in a week

b) 400 000 shares in a week

What answer should Andrea give?

20. Small changes to a quadratic equation can have large effects on the solutions. Illustrate this statement by solving each quadratic equation.

a) $x^2 + 50x + 624 = 0$

b) $x^2 + 50x + 625 = 0$

c) $x^2 + 50x + 626 = 0$

✔ **Achievement Check**

21. A diver followed a path defined by $h(t) = -4.9t^2 + 3t + 10$ in her dive, where t is the time, in seconds, and h represents her height above the water, in metres.

a) At what height did the diver start her dive?

b) For how long was the diver in the air?

c) The -4.9 in front of the t^2 term is constant because it relates to the acceleration due to gravity on Earth. If the diver always starts her dives from the same height, what other value in the quadratic expression will never change?

d) What is the only value in the quadratic expression that can change? Suggest a way in which this value can change.

e) If the value in part d) changed to 6, how much longer would the diver be in the air?

C Extend

22. Complete the square on the expression $ax^2 + bx + c = 0$ to show how the quadratic formula is obtained.

23. A cubic block of concrete shrinks as it dries. The volume of the dried block is 30.3 cm³ less than the original volume, while the length of each edge has decreased by 0.1 cm. Determine the edge length and volume of the concrete block before it dried.

24. In the diagram, the square has side lengths of 6 m. The square is divided into three right triangles and one isosceles triangle. The areas of the three right triangles are equal.

a) Find the value of x.

b) Find the area of the acute isosceles triangle.

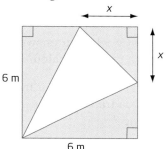

25. Math Contest If $f(x) = 2x^2 - 13x + c$ and $f(c) = -16$, then one possible value for c is

A -2 **B** 2 **C** -4 **D** 8

26. Math Contest The function $f(x) = 3x^2 + 9x - 3$ has x-intercepts p and q. The value of $p - pq + q$ is

A -2 **B** $3 + 5\sqrt{13}$

C 0 **D** -4

27. Math Contest The squares MNOP and IJKL overlap as shown. K is the centre of MNOP. What is the area of quadrilateral KROQ in terms of the area of MNOP?

Determine a Quadratic Equation Given Its Roots

Bridges like the one shown often have supports in the shape of parabolas. If the anchors at either side of the bridge are 42 m apart and the maximum height of the support is 26 m, what function models the parabolic curve of the support? Engineers need to determine this function to ensure that the bridge is built to proper specifications. How can the given data be used to model the equation of the parabola?

Tools

• grid paper

Investigate

How can you connect the zeros to a form of the quadratic function?

In the introduction, information was given about a parabolic support under a bridge. What equation will model the parabolic curve of the support if the vertex is on the y-axis and the points of attachment of the supports are on the x-axis?

Method 1: Use Pencil and Paper

1. Use the information given to identify three points: the two x-intercepts and the vertex. Sketch the function. Label the three known points.

2. The intercept form of a quadratic function is $y = a(x - r)(x - s)$, where r and s are the x-intercepts. Write the function in this form using the data from the original problem for the x-intercepts.

3. How can you use the third known point to find the value of a?

4. **a)** Write a function in factored form for the bridge support.

   b) Express the function from part a) in standard form.

5. **Reflect** Can you write the equation of a quadratic function given its zeros? If so, describe how. If not, explain why not.

Method 2: Use a Graphing Calculator

1. Use the information given to identify three points and draw a sketch. Enter the three data points into a graphing calculator using **L1** and **L2**.

2. Use quadratic regression to find the equation of the quadratic function in the form $y = ax^2 + bx + c$.

3. Enter the function for **Y1** and graph the equation to verify.

4. **a)** The intercept form of a quadratic function is $y = a(x - r)(x - s)$, where r and s are the x-intercepts. Write this form of the function, using the same value of a as found in step 2 and the data from the original problem. Enter this form of the function as **Y2** on the graphing calculator, choose a different thickness for the new line, and graph this line.

   b) What do you notice occurs on the display of the graphing calculator as the second parabola is graphed?

5. **Reflect** Can you determine the equation of a quadratic function given its zeros? If so, describe how. If not, explain why not.

Tools

• graphing ca...

Example 1

Find the Equation of a Family of Quadratic Functions

Find the equation, in factored form, for a family of quadratic functions with the given x-intercepts. Sketch each family, showing at least three members.

a) 4 and 2

b) 0 and -5

c) -3 and 3

d) 6 is the only x-intercept

Connections

Functions that have a common property are called a *family*. In grade 9, you worked with families of linear functions that have the same slope: they are parallel lines.

Solution

a) Since $x = 4$ and $x = 2$ are roots of the equation, $x - 4$ and $x - 2$ are factors of the function.

The equation for this family is $f(x) = a(x - 4)(x - 2)$.

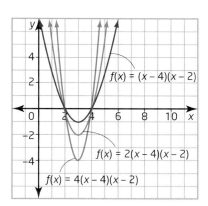

$f(x) = (x - 4)(x - 2)$

$f(x) = 2(x - 4)(x - 2)$

$f(x) = 4(x - 4)(x - 2)$

b) Since $x = 0$ and $x = -5$ are roots of the equation, x and $x + 5$ are factors of the function. The equation for this family is $f(x) = ax(x + 5)$.

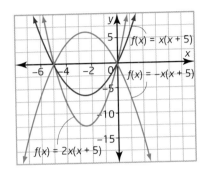

c) Since 3 and -3 are the x-intercepts, $x - 3$ and $x + 3$ are factors. The equation for this family is $f(x) = a(x - 3)(x + 3)$.

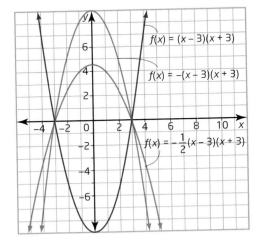

d) Since $x = 6$ is the only zero, $x - 6$ must be a repeated factor.

The equation for this family is $f(x) = a(x - 6)^2$.

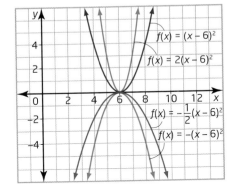

Example 2

Determine the Exact Equation of a Quadratic Function

Find the equation of the quadratic function with the given zeros and containing the given point. Express your answers in standard form.

a) 2 and -3, containing the point $(0, 3)$

b) double zero at $x = -2$, containing the point $(3, 10)$

c) $3 + \sqrt{5}$ and $3 - \sqrt{5}$, containing the point $(2, -12)$

Solution

a) Since 2 and -3 are zeros, then $x - 2$ and $x + 3$ are factors.

$f(x) = a(x - 2)(x + 3)$

Substitute the given point: $f(0) = 3$

$3 = a(0 - 2)(0 + 3)$

$3 = -6a$

$a = -\dfrac{1}{2}$

The function, in factored form, is $f(x) = -\dfrac{1}{2}(x - 2)(x + 3)$.

In standard form: $f(x) = -\dfrac{1}{2}(x^2 + x - 6)$

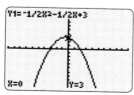

$$= -\dfrac{1}{2}x^2 - \dfrac{1}{2}x + 3$$

Check by graphing the function using a graphing calculator.

b) Since -2 is a double zero, the factor $x + 2$ is repeated.

$f(x) = a(x + 2)^2$

Substitute the point: $f(3) = 10$

$10 = a(3 + 2)^2$

$10 = 25a$

$a = 0.4$ Simplify and solve for a.

The function, in factored form, is
$f(x) = 0.4(x + 2)^2$.

In standard form:

$f(x) = 0.4(x^2 + 4x + 4)$

$\quad = 0.4x^2 + 1.6x + 1.6$

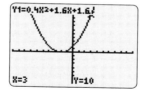

c) Since $3 + \sqrt{5}$ and $3 - \sqrt{5}$ are zeros, then

$\left(x - \left(3 + \sqrt{5}\right)\right)$ and $\left(x - \left(3 - \sqrt{5}\right)\right)$ are factors.

$f(x) = a\left(x - \left(3 + \sqrt{5}\right)\right)\left(x - \left(3 - \sqrt{5}\right)\right)$

$\quad = a\left(x - 3 - \sqrt{5}\right)\left(x - 3 + \sqrt{5}\right)$ This is in the form $(c - d)(c + d)$, where

$\quad = a\left[(x - 3)^2 - \left(\sqrt{5}\right)^2\right]$ $c = x - 3$ and $d = \sqrt{5}$.

$\quad = a(x^2 - 6x + 9 - 5)$

$\quad = a(x^2 - 6x + 4)$

Substitute the point: $f(2) = -12$

$-12 = a(2^2 - 6(2) + 4)$

$-12 = a(-4)$

$a = 3$

The function, in factored form, is
$f(x) = 3(x^2 - 6x + 4)$.

In standard form:
$f(x) = 3(x^2 - 6x + 4)$

$\quad = 3x^2 - 18x + 12$

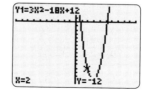

Example 3

Represent Given Information as a Quadratic Function

The parabolic opening to a tunnel is 32 m wide measured from side to side along the ground. At the points that are 4 m from each side, the tunnel entrance is 6 m high.

a) Sketch a diagram of the given information.

b) Determine the equation of the function that models the opening to the tunnel.

c) Find the maximum height of the tunnel, to the nearest tenth of a metre.

Solution

a) The point $(12, 6)$ comes from the information given. You are told that 4 m from each side, the height is 6 m. The point $(-12, 6)$ can also be used, giving the same answer.

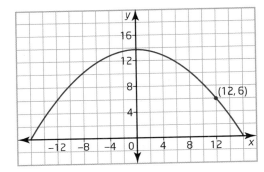

Connections

If you assume that one side of the tunnel is at the origin, you will get a different form of the equation. It will be a translation of the one found here. You will examine the effects of translations on the equation of a function in Chapter 2.

b) Use the x-intercepts -16 and 16. Write the general function,
$f(x) = a(x - 16)(x + 16)$.
To solve for a, substitute the point $(12, 6)$.
$$6 = a(12 - 16)(12 + 16)$$
$$6 = a(-4)(28)$$
$$6 = a(-112)$$
$$a = -\frac{6}{112}$$
$$= -\frac{3}{56}$$
The function that models the opening to the tunnel is
$$f(x) = -\frac{3}{56}(x - 16)(x + 16).$$

c) The maximum height of the tunnel will occur halfway between the two x-intercepts. This means a value of $x = 0$.
$$f(0) = -\frac{3}{56}(0 - 16)(0 + 16)$$
$$= -\frac{3}{56}(-16)(16)$$
$$\doteq 13.71$$
The maximum height of the tunnel is 13.7 m, to the nearest tenth of a metre.

Key Concepts

- The zeros can be used to find the equation of a family of quadratic functions with the same x-intercepts.

- To determine an individual quadratic function, you also need to be given one other point on the function.

Communicate Your Understanding

C1 Outline the steps needed to find the equation of a quadratic function given the x-intercepts and one other point on the function.

C2 You are given an equation for a family of quadratic functions with the same x-intercepts. Rita says, "The vertex is the only point that will not allow you to determine the exact equation, as it is at the centre of the function, and more than one function can be found." Ronnie claims, "The vertex is as good as any other point in finding the exact function." Who is correct? Explain.

C3 Mona has decided that if she is given a fraction such as $-\frac{1}{2}$ as one of the x-intercepts, she can use the binomial $(2x + 1)$ instead of $\left(x + \frac{1}{2}\right)$ and get the same quadratic function. Is she correct? Explain.

A Practise

For help with questions 1 and 2, refer to Example 1.

1. Determine the equation, in factored form, of a family of quadratic functions with each pair of roots. Sketch a graph to show four graphs in each family.

a) $x = 3$ and $x = -6$

b) $x = -1$ and $x = -1$

c) $x = -3$ and $x = -4$

2. Express each equation in question 1 in standard form.

For help with question 3 to 5, refer to Example 2.

3. Find the equation of a quadratic function that has the given x-intercepts and contains the given point. Express each function in factored form. Graph each function to check.

a) -3 and 5, point $(4, -3)$

b) -4 and 7, point $(-3, -12)$

c) 0 and $-\frac{2}{3}$, point $(-1, 5)$

4. Write each function in question 3 in standard form.

5. Find the equation of the quadratic function that has the given zeros and contains the given point. Express each function in standard form. Graph each function to check.

a) $1 \pm \sqrt{11}$, point $(4, -6)$

b) $-2 \pm \sqrt{7}$, point $(1, 2)$

c) $-5 \pm \sqrt{2}$, point $(-2, -14)$

6. Find the equation of the quadratic function that has the given zeros and contains the given point. Express each function in vertex form. Graph each function to check.

a) 3 and -1, point $(1, -2)$

b) 1 and -2, point $(0, 4)$

c) 3 and -5, point $(1, -4)$

B Connect and Apply

For help with question 7, refer to Example 3.

7. A soccer ball is kicked from the ground. After travelling a horizontal distance of 35 m, it just passes over a 1.5-m-tall fence before hitting the ground 37 m from where it was kicked.

Reasoning and Proving

Representing · Selecting Tools · Problem Solving · Connecting · Reflecting · Communicating

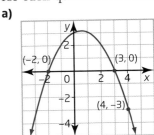

a) Considering the ground to be the x-axis and the vertex to be on the y-axis, determine the equation of a quadratic function that can be used to model the parabolic path of the ball.

b) Determine the maximum height of the ball.

c) How far has the ball travelled horizontally to reach the maximum height?

d) Develop a new equation for the quadratic function that represents the height of the ball, considering the ball to have been kicked from the origin.

e) Outline the similarities and differences between the functions found in parts a) and d).

f) **Use Technology** Use a graphing calculator to compare the solutions.

8. Determine the equation in standard form for each quadratic function shown.

a)

b)

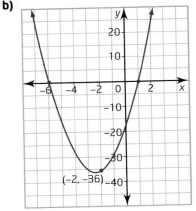

c)

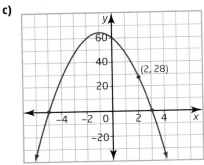

9. **Use Technology** For each part in question 8, use a graphing calculator to verify your solution by plotting the three points as well as entering the quadratic function. Explain how you can use this method to check that your solution is correct.

10. Explain how the technique studied in this section can be used to find the equation for the quadratic function if the only x-intercept is the origin and you are given one other point on the function.

11. Find the quadratic function that has only one x-intercept and passes through the given point.

a) x-intercept of 0, point $(5, -2)$

b) x-intercept of 5, point $(4, 3)$

c) x-intercept of -1, point $(2, 6)$

12. **Use Technology** Verify your solutions to question 11 using a graphing calculator.

13. If the function $f(x) = ax^2 + 5x + c$ has only one x-intercept, what is the mathematical relationship between a and c?

14. Chapter Problem The actuarial firm where Andrea has her co-op placement was sent a set of data that follows a quadratic function. The data supplied compared the number of years of driving experience with the number of collisions reported to an insurance company in the last month. Andrea was asked to recover the data lost when the paper jammed in the fax machine. Only three data points can be read. They are (5, 22), (8, 28), and (9, 22). The values of $f(x)$ for $x = 6$ and $x = 7$ are missing. Andrea decided to subtract the y-value of 22 from each point so that she would have two zeros: (5, 0), (8, 6), and (9, 0).

a) Use these three points to find a quadratic function that can be used to model the adjusted data.

b) Add a y-value of 22 to this function for a quadratic function that models the original data.

c) Use this function to find the missing values for $x = 6$ and $x = 7$.

15. An arch of a highway overpass is in the shape of a parabola. The arch spans a distance of 12 m from one side of the road to the other. The height of the arch is 8 m at a horizontal distance of 2 m from each side of the arch.

Reasoning and Proving

Representing · Selecting Tools

Problem Solving

Connecting · Reflecting

Communicating

a) Sketch the quadratic function if the vertex of the parabola is on the y-axis and the road is along the x-axis.

b) Use this information to determine the function that models the arch.

c) Find the maximum height of the arch to the nearest tenth of a metre.

16. Use the information from question 15, but instead of having the vertex on the y-axis, put one side of the archway at the origin of the grid. You will get a different equation because the zeros are now at 0 and 12, rather than at -6 and 6.

a) Find the equation of the quadratic function for this position.

b) Find the maximum height of the overpass and compare the result to the height calculated in question 15.

17. Explain how the two equations developed in questions 15 and 16 can model the same arch, even though the equations are different.

✓ **Achievement Check**

18. A quadratic function has zeros -2 and 6 and passes through the point (3, 15).

a) Find the equation of the quadratic function in factored form.

b) Write the function in standard form.

c) Complete the square to convert the standard form to vertex form, and state the vertex.

d) Use partial factoring to verify your answer to part c).

e) Find a second quadratic function with the same zeros as in part a), but passing through the point (3, -30). Express the function in standard form.

f) Graph both functions. Explain how the graphs can be used to verify that the equations in parts a) and e) are correct.

C Extend

19. Is it possible to determine the defining equation of a function given the following information? If so, justify your answer and provide an example.

a) the vertex and one x-intercept

b) the vertex and one other point on the parabola

c) any three points on the parabola

20. Math Contest Determine an equation for a quadratic function with zeros at $x = \dfrac{-1 \pm \sqrt{7}}{3}$.

21. Math Contest Show that the graph of $f(x) = ax^2 + c$ has no x-intercept if $ac > 0$.

Solve Linear-Quadratic Systems

Marina is a set designer. She plans movie sets using freehand sketches and her computer. In one scene, a banner will hang across a parabolic archway. To make it look interesting, she has decided to put the banner on an angle. She sets the banner along a line defined by the linear equation $y = 0.24x + 7.2$, with x representing the horizontal distance and y the vertical distance, in metres, from one foot of the archway. The archway is modelled by the quadratic equation $y = -0.48x^2 + 4.8x$. How can Marina use the equations to determine the points where the banner needs to be attached to the archway and the length of the banner? In this section, you will develop the tools needed to help Marina with these calculations.

Tools

- grid paper
Optional
- graphing calculator

Investigate A

How can a line and a parabola intersect?

Work with a partner.

1. Consider a line and a parabola. At how many points could they intersect? Draw sketches to illustrate your answer.

2. Create pairs of equations for each possibility that you identified in step 1. Use algebraic reasoning to show that your examples are correct.

3. In your algebraic reasoning in step 2, you will have solved a quadratic equation for each situation. Compute the value of the discriminant for each example.

4. **Reflect** Describe how you can predict the number of points of intersection of a linear function and a quadratic function using algebraic reasoning.

Investigate B

How can you connect the discriminant to the intersection of a linear and a quadratic function?

Tools

- grid paper

or

- graphing calculator

In this Investigate, you will create the equations of lines with slope -2 that intersect the quadratic function $y = x^2 + 4x + 4$.

1. Write a linear function, in slope y-intercept form, with slope -2 and an unknown y-intercept represented by k.

2. Eliminate y by substituting the expression for y from the linear equation into the quadratic equation. Simplify so you have a quadratic equation of the form $ax^2 + bx + c = 0$.

3. Substitute the values or expressions for a, b, and c into the discriminant $b^2 - 4ac$.

4. In Section 1.6, you learned that the discriminant determines the number of solutions for a quadratic equation. Take advantage of this fact to answer the following questions.

   a) What values of k will make the discriminant positive? How many points of intersection do the line and the quadratic have in this case?

   b) What values of k will make the discriminant zero? How many points of intersection do the line and the quadratic have in this case?

   c) What values of k will make the discriminant negative? How many points of intersection do the line and the quadratic have in this case?

5. **Reflect** With the solutions from step 4, write an equation for a linear equation, in slope y-intercept form $y = mx + b$, with slope -2, that

   a) intersects the quadratic function at two points

   b) intersects the quadratic function at one point

   c) does not intersect the quadratic function

6. Verify each solution in step 5 by graphing the quadratic function $y = x^2 + 4x + 4$ and each of your linear functions.

Example 1

Find the Points of Intersection of a Linear-Quadratic System of Equations

In the opening of this section, you were introduced to Marina. In a set design, she has a banner on an angle across an archway. She is working with the equations $y = 0.24x + 7.2$ and $y = -0.48x^2 + 4.8x$, where x represents the horizontal distance and y the vertical distance, both in metres, from one foot of the archway.

a) Determine the coordinates of the points where the two functions intersect.

b) Interpret the solutions in the context.

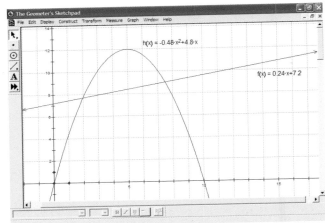

Solution

a) Method 1: Use Pencil and Paper

Eliminate y by equating the two functions.

$$-0.48x^2 + 4.8x = 0.24x + 7.2$$

$-0.48x^2 + 4.8x - 0.24x - 7.2 = 0$ Rearrange the terms so the right side is zero.

$-0.48x^2 + 4.56x - 7.2 = 0$ Simplify.

$2x^2 - 19x + 30 = 0$ Divide both sides by -0.24.

$2x^2 - 4x - 15x + 30 = 0$ Use grouping to factor.

$2x(x - 2) - 15(x - 2) = 0$

$(x - 2)(2x - 15) = 0$

Therefore, $x = 2$ or $x = 7.5$.

Substitute into either function to find the corresponding values for y. The linear function is easier to use here.

$y = 0.24x + 7.2$

For $x = 2$:

$y = 0.24(2) + 7.2$

$= 7.68$

For $x = 7.5$:

$y = 0.24(7.5) + 7.2$

$= 9$

The coordinates of the points where the two functions intersect are $(2, 7.68)$ and $(7.5, 9)$.

Method 2: Use a Graphing Calculator

- Enter the two functions:
  Y1 $= -0.48x^2 + 4.8x$ and **Y2** $= 0.24x + 7.2$.
- Use the window settings shown.
- Press (GRAPH).

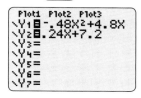 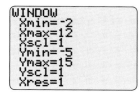 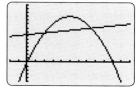

- Press (2nd) [CALC].
- Use the **Intersect** operation to find the coordinates of each point of intersection.

 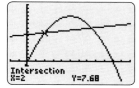 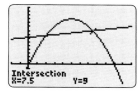

The coordinates of the points where the two functions intersect are (2, 7.68) and (7.5, 9).

Method 3: Use a TI-Nspire™ CAS Graphing Calculator

Turn on the TI-Nspire™ CAS graphing calculator.

- Press (⌂) and select **6:New Document**.
- Select **2:Add Graphs & Geometry**.
- Type $-0.48x^2 + 4.8x$ for function **f1**. Press (enter).
- Type $0.24x + 7.2$ for function **f2**. Press (enter).
- Press (menu). Select **4:Window**.
- Select **6:Zoom – Quadrant 1**.

The graphs will be displayed.

- Press (menu). Select **6:Points & Lines**.
- Select **3:Intersection Point(s)**. Move the cursor to the first graph and press (enter). Move the cursor to the second graph and press (enter). Press (esc).

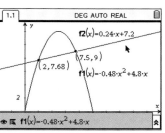

The coordinates of the points where the two functions intersect are displayed as (2, 7.68) and (7.5, 9).

b) These solutions tell Marina that one end of the banner should be attached 2 m horizontally from the left foot of the arch and 7.68 m upward. The other end of the banner should be attached 7.5 m horizontally and 9 m upward.

Example 2

Determine Whether a Linear Function Intersects a Quadratic Function

Determine algebraically whether the given linear and quadratic functions intersect. If they do intersect, determine the number of points of intersection.

a) $y = 3x + 5$ and $y = 3x^2 - 2x - 4$

b) $y = -x - 2$ and $y = -2x^2 + x - 3$

Solution

a) Equate the expressions and simplify.

$$3x^2 - 2x - 4 = 3x + 5$$

$3x^2 - 2x - 4 - 3x - 5 = 0$ Rearrange the terms so the right side is zero.

$3x^2 - 5x - 9 = 0$ Simplify.

$a = 3$, $b = -5$, and $c = -9$.

Use the discriminant:

$$b^2 - 4ac = (-5)^2 - 4(3)(-9)$$
$$= 25 + 108$$
$$= 133$$

Since the discriminant is greater than zero, there are two solutions. This means that the linear-quadratic system has two points of intersection.

b) Equate the expressions and simplify.

$$-2x^2 + x - 3 = -x - 2$$

$-2x^2 + x - 3 + x + 2 = 0$ Rearrange the terms so the right side is zero.

$-2x^2 + 2x - 1 = 0$ Simplify.

$a = -2$, $b = 2$, and $c = -1$.

Use the discriminant:

$$b^2 - 4ac = 2^2 - 4(-2)(-1)$$
$$= 4 - 8$$
$$= -4$$

Since the discriminant is less than zero, there are no solutions. This means that the linear-quadratic system has no points of intersection.

In this section, you have considered how a line can intersect a curve such as a quadratic function. One type of intersection results in a **secant** and the other results in a **tangent line** to the quadratic function.

secant

- a line that intersects a curve at two distinct points

tangent line

- a line that touches a curve at one point and has the slope of the curve at that point

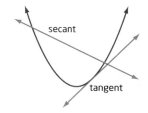

Example 3

Determine the *y*-intercept for a Tangent Line to a Quadratic Function

If a line with slope 4 has one point of intersection with the quadratic function $y = \frac{1}{2}x^2 + 2x - 8$, what is the *y*-intercept of the line? Write the equation of the line in slope *y*-intercept form.

Solution

The line can be modelled as $y = 4x + k$, where k represents the *y*-intercept.

Substitute for *y* in the quadratic function:

$$\frac{1}{2}x^2 + 2x - 8 = 4x + k$$

$$\frac{1}{2}x^2 - 2x - 8 - k = 0$$

$$\frac{1}{2}x^2 - 2x + (-8 - k) = 0$$

Then, $a = \frac{1}{2}$, $b = -2$, and $c = -8 - k$.

If the discriminant equals zero, there is only one root.

Substitute into $b^2 - 4ac = 0$.

$$(-2)^2 - 4\left(\frac{1}{2}\right)(-8 - k) = 0$$

$$4 - 2(-8 - k) = 0$$

$$4 + 16 + 2k = 0$$

$$2k = -20$$

$$k = -10$$

The *y*-intercept of the line that touches the quadratic at one point is -10. The equation of the line is $y = 4x - 10$.

This solution can be verified using a graphing calculator. Graph

Y1 $= \frac{1}{2}x^2 + 2x - 8$ and **Y2** $= 4x - 10$. Use the

Intersect operation to see that these two functions have only one point of intersection, at $(2, -2)$, so the line is a tangent.

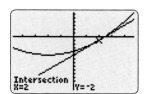

Connections

One of the main topics that you will study in calculus is determining the slope of a tangent to a curve at a point on the curve.

Technology Tip

Sometimes a "friendly window" is needed to cause the calculator to display exact values. Choose multiples of 94 for the domain. To show the exact point of intersection in Example 3, **Xmin** = −4.7 and **Xmax** = 4.7 were used. After this, the zoom feature **0:ZoomFit** can be used to choose an appropriate range.

Example 4

Solve a Problem Involving a Linear-Quadratic System

Dudley Do-Right is riding his horse, Horse, at his top speed of 10 m/s toward the bank, and is 100 m away when the bank robber begins to accelerate away from the bank going in the same direction as Dudley Do-Right. The robber's distance, d, in metres, away from the bank after t seconds can be modelled by the equation $d = 0.2t^2$.

a) Write a corresponding model for the position of Dudley Do-Right as a function of time.

b) Will Dudley Do-Right catch the bank robber? If he does, find the time and position where this happens. If not, explain why not.

Solution

a) Let the position of the bank be at the origin. Since Dudley Do-Right is 100 m away from the bank and the robber is moving in the same direction away from the bank, represent Dudley Do-Right's position as -100. He is moving at 10 m/s toward the bank, so his position, relative to the bank, is given by $d = 10t - 100$.

b) For Dudley Do-Right to catch the bank robber, the two equations need to be equal:

$$10t - 100 = 0.2t^2$$

Solve the equation:

$$0 = 0.2t^2 - 10t + 100$$
$$0 = t^2 - 50t + 500 \qquad \text{Multiply by 5.}$$

In the quadratic formula, $a = 1$, $b = -50$, and $c = 500$.

$$t = \frac{-b \pm \sqrt{b^2 - 4ac}}{2a}$$
$$= \frac{-(-50) \pm \sqrt{(-50)^2 - 4(1)(500)}}{2(1)}$$
$$= \frac{50 \pm \sqrt{2500 - 2000}}{2}$$
$$= \frac{50 \pm \sqrt{500}}{2}$$
$$= \frac{50 \pm 10\sqrt{5}}{2}$$
$$= 25 \pm 5\sqrt{5}$$

Then, $t \doteq 13.8$ s or $t \doteq 36.2$ s. The first time is when Dudley Do-Right catches the bank robber.

The second time means that if Dudley does not stop to catch the robber at 13.8 s, he will pass him. But since the robber is accelerating and Dudley is moving at a constant speed, the robber will catch up to Dudley at some point.

Dudley Do-Right will catch the bank robber after 13.8 s.

For the position, substitute $t = 13.8$ into either original function.

$$d(t) = 10t - 100$$
$$d(13.8) = 10(13.8) - 100$$
$$= 138 - 100$$
$$= 38$$

Dudley Do-Right will catch the robber 38 m past the bank.

Key Concepts

- A linear function and a quadratic function may
  - intersect at two points (the line is a secant)
  - intersect at one point (the line is a tangent line)
  - never intersect
- The discriminant can be used to determine which of the above situations occurs.
- The quadratic formula can be used to determine the x-values of actual points of intersection.

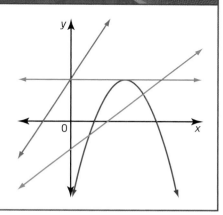

Communicate Your Understanding

C1 Larissa always uses the full quadratic formula to determine the number of zeros that a quadratic function has. What would you tell her that would help her understand that she only needs to evaluate the discriminant?

C2 After Randy has solved a quadratic equation to find the x-values for the points of intersection of a given linear-quadratic system, he substitutes the values for x into the linear function to find the values for y. Is this a good idea? Explain why or why not.

C3 What are the advantages and disadvantages in determining the points of intersection of a linear-quadratic system using each method?
- algebraic
- graphical

A Practise

For help with questions 1 and 2, refer to Example 1.

1. Determine the coordinates of the point(s) of intersection of each linear-quadratic system algebraically.

a) $y = x^2 - 7x + 15$ and $y = 2x - 5$

b) $y = 3x^2 - 16x + 37$ and $y = 8x + 1$

c) $y = \frac{1}{2}x^2 - 2x - 3$ and $y = -3x + 1$

d) $y = -2x^2 - 7x + 10$ and $y = -x + 2$

2. Verify the solutions to question 1 using a graphing calculator or by substituting into the original equations.

For help with questions 3 and 4, refer to Example 2.

3. Determine if each quadratic function will intersect once, twice, or not at all with the given linear function.

   a) $y = 2x^2 - 2x + 1$ and $y = 3x - 5$

   b) $y = -x^2 + 3x - 5$ and $y = -x - 1$ **once**

   c) $y = \frac{1}{2}x^2 + 4x - 2$ and $y = x + 3$

   d) $y = -\frac{2}{3}x^2 + x + 3$ and $y = x$ **twice**

4. Verify your responses to question 3 using a graphing calculator.

For help with questions 5 and 6, refer to Example 3.

5. Determine the value of the y-intercept of a line with the given slope that is a tangent line to the given curve.

   a) $y = -2x^2 + 5x + 4$ and a line with a slope of 1

   b) $y = -x^2 - 5x - 5$ and a line with a slope of -3 **-4**

   c) $y = 2x^2 + 4x - 1$ and a line with a slope of 2

   d) $y = 3x^2 - 4x + 1$ and a line with a slope of -2 **$-\frac{2}{3}$**

6. Verify your solutions to question 5 using a graphing calculator or by substituting into the original equations.

B Connect and Apply

7. The path of an underground stream is given by the function $y = 4x^2 + 17x - 32$. Two new houses need wells to be dug. On the area plan, these houses lie on a line defined by the equation $y = -15x + 100$. Determine the coordinates where the two new wells should be dug.

8. Part of the path of an asteroid is approximately parabolic and is modelled by the function $y = -6x^2 - 370x + 100\ 900$. For the period of time that it is in the same area, a space probe is moving along a straight path on the same plane as the asteroid according to the linear equation $y = 500x - 83\ 024$.

A space agency needs to determine if the asteroid will be an issue for the space probe. Will the two paths intersect? Show all your work.

Reasoning and Proving
Representing · Selecting Tools · Problem Solving · Connecting · Reflecting · Communicating

9. **Use Technology** Check your solutions to questions 7 and 8 using a graphing calculator.

10. Determine the value of k in $y = -x^2 + 4x + k$ that will result in the intersection of the line $y = 8x - 2$ with the quadratic at

    a) two points b) one point c) no point
       $k > -6$ $k = -6$ $k < -6$.

11. Determine the value of k in $y = kx^2 - 5x + 2$ that will result in the intersection of the line $y = -3x + 4$ with the quadratic at

    a) two points b) one point c) no point
       $k > -\frac{1}{2}$ $k = -\frac{1}{2}$ $k < -\frac{1}{2}$

12. A bridge has a parabolic support modelled by the equation

$$y = -\frac{1}{200}x^2 + \frac{6}{25}x - 5,$$

Reasoning and Proving
Representing · Selecting Tools · Problem Solving · Connecting · Reflecting · Communicating

where the x-axis represents the bridge surface. There are also parallel support beams below the bridge. Each support beam must have a slope of either 0.8 or -0.8. Using a slope of -0.8, find the y-intercept of the line associated with the longest support beam. Hint: The longest beam will be the one along the line that touches the parabolic support at just one point.

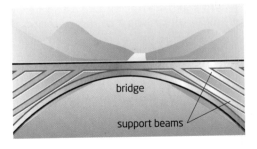

bridge

support beams

13. The line $x = 2$ intersects the quadratic function $y = x^2 - 9$ at one point, $(2, -5)$. Explain why the line $x = 2$ is not considered a tangent line to the quadratic function.

14. Chapter Problem Andrea's supervisor at the actuarial firm has asked her to determine the safety zone needed for a fireworks display. She needs to find out where the safety fence needs to be placed on a hill. The fireworks are to be launched from a platform at the base of the hill. Using the top of the launch platform as the origin and taking some measurements, in metres, Andrea comes up with the following equations.

Cross-section of the slope of one side of the hill: $y = 4x - 12$

Path of the fireworks: $y = -x^2 + 15x$

a) Illustrate this situation by graphing both equations on the same set of axes.

b) Calculate the coordinates of the point where the function that describes the path of the fireworks will intersect the equation for the hill.

c) What distance up the hill does the fence need to be located? **Hint:** Use the Pythagorean theorem.

15. A parachutist jumps from an airplane and immediately opens his parachute. His altitude, y, in metres, after t seconds is modelled by the equation $y = -4t + 300$. A second parachutist jumps 5 s later and freefalls for a few seconds. Her altitude, in metres, during this time, is modelled by the equation $y = -4.9(t - 5)^2 + 300$. When does she reach the same altitude as the first parachutist?

16. The UV index on a sunny day can be modelled by the function $f(x) = -0.15(x - 13)^2 + 7.6$, where x represents the time of day on a 24-h clock and $f(x)$ represents the UV index. Between what hours was the UV index greater than 7?

17. The support arches of the Humber River pedestrian bridge in Toronto can be modelled by the quadratic function $y = -0.0044x^2 + 21.3$ if the walkway is represented by the line $y = 0$.

A similar bridge, planned for North Bay, will have the same equation for the support arches. However, since the walkway is to be inclined slightly across a ravine, its equation is $y = 0.0263x + 1.82$.

a) Determine the points of intersection of the bridge support arches and the inclined walkway, to one decimal place.

b) **Use Technology** Use a graphing calculator to check your solution in part a).

c) Determine the length of the bridge.

d) How much shorter will this walkway be than the walkway that spans the Humber River in Toronto? Justify your answer.

C Extend

18. The technique of substitution has been used in this section to find the points where a line intersects a parbola. This technique can be used with other curves as well.

a) Determine the points at which the circle given by $(x - 5)^2 + (y - 5)^2 = 25$ is intersected by the line $y = -\frac{1}{3}x + \frac{5}{3}$.

b) Check your answer on a graphing calculator by graphing the line and the two functions
$$y = 5 + \sqrt{25 - (x - 5)^2} \text{ and}$$
$$y = 5 - \sqrt{25 - (x - 5)^2}.$$

19. Math Contest Find the point(s) of intersection of the line $y = 7x - 42$ and the circle $x^2 + y^2 - 4x + 6y = 12$.

20. Math Contest The two circles $x^2 + y^2 = 11$ and $(x - 3)^2 + y^2 = 2$ intersect at two points, P and Q. The length of PQ is

A 2   **B** $2\sqrt{2}$ **C** 13   **D** $\sqrt{13}$

Chapter 1 Review

1.1 Functions, Domain, and Range, pages 4 to 15

1. State the domain and range of each relation.

a)

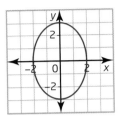

b)

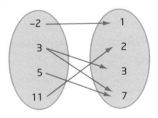

c) {(1, 4), (2, 6), (3, 10), (4, 18), (5, 29)}

d) $y = 2x^2 + 11$

2. Which relations in question 1 are functions? Justify your answers.

1.2 Functions and Function Notation, pages 16 to 24

3. A linear function machine produces the points $(2, 5)$ and $(-3, -15)$.

  a) Determine the equation of the function.

  b) Is it possible for a second function to exist that will generate these values? Explain.

4. a) Draw a mapping diagram for these data:
{(4, −2), (6, 1), (11, −7), (6, 7), (4, −7)}

  b) Is this relation a function? Explain.

1.3 Maximum or Minimum of a Quadratic Function, pages 25 to 33

5. A hall charges $30 per person for a sports banquet when 120 people attend. For every 10 extra people that attend, the hall will decrease the price by $1.50 per person. What number of people will maximize the revenue for the hall?

6. The power, P, in watts, produced by a solar panel is given by the function $P(I) = -5I^2 + 100I$, where I represents the current, in amperes.

  a) What value of the current will maximize the power?

  b) What is the maximum power?

1.4 Skills You Need: Working With Radicals, pages 34 to 42

7. Perform each radical operation and simplify where needed.

  a) $\sqrt{27} - 4\sqrt{3} + \sqrt{243} - 8\sqrt{81} + 2$

  b) $-3\sqrt{3}(\sqrt{3} + 5\sqrt{2})$

  c) $(\sqrt{3} + 5)(5 - \sqrt{3})$

  d) $5\sqrt{2}(11 + 2\sqrt{2}) - 4(8 + 3\sqrt{2})$

8. Find a simplified expression for the area of each shape.

a)

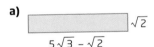

$\sqrt{2}$

$5\sqrt{3} - \sqrt{2}$

b)

$3\sqrt{3}$

1.5 Solving Quadratic Equations, pages 43 to 51

9. Solve each quadratic equation. Give exact answers.

  a) $3x^2 - 2x - 2 = 0$

  b) $6x^2 - 23x + 20 = 0$

10. Use the discriminant to determine the number of roots for each equation.

  a) $3x^2 + 4x - 5 = 0$

  b) $-2x^2 + 5x - 1 = 0$

  c) $9x^2 - 12x + 4 = 0$

11. Jessica reasoned that since $2 \times 2 = 4$ and $2 + 2 = 4$, $\sqrt{2} + \sqrt{2}$ must have the same value as $\sqrt{2} \times \sqrt{2}$. Is she correct? Justify your answer.

1.6 Determine a Quadratic Equation Given Its Roots, pages 52 to 59

12. Determine the equation in standard form for each quadratic function.

a) x-intercepts -2 and 5, containing the point (3, 5)

b) x-intercepts $-2 \pm \sqrt{5}$, containing the point $(-4, 5)$

13. A golf ball is hit, and it lands at a point on the same horizontal plane 53 m away. The path of the ball took it just over a 9-m-tall tree that was 8 m in front of the golfer.

a) Assume the ball is hit from the origin of a coordinate plane. Find a quadratic function that describes the path of the ball.

b) What is the maximum height of the ball?

c) Is it possible to move the origin in this situation and develop another quadratic function to describe the path? If so, find a second quadratic function.

14. Use Technology Use a graphing calculator to verify your solution to question 13.

1.7 Solve Linear-Quadratic Systems, pages 60 to 69

15. Determine the points of intersection of each pair of functions.

a) $y = 4x^2 - 15x + 20$ and $y = 5x - 4$

b) $y = -2x^2 + 9x + 9$ and $y = -3x - 5$

16. For what value of b will the line $y = -2x + b$ be tangent to the parabola $y = 3x^2 + 4x - 1$?

17. Do all linear-quadratic systems result in a solution? Justify your answer using a real-life example.

Chapter Problem   WRAP-UP

Part A

For her final duty at her co-op placement, Andrea is given two investments to analyse.
- Investment 1 asks investors to invest $5000, and the investment grows according to the equation $A(t) = 10t^2 - 48t + 5000$.
- Investment 2 asks investors to invest $10 000, and the investment grows according to the equation $A(t) = 10\ 000 + 497t$.

In both equations, t is time, in weeks, and A is the amount, in dollars.

a) After how long will both investments be worth the same amount?

b) Under what circumstances should Andrea recommend investment 1?

Part B

In this chapter, you explored some of the types of calculations that are associated with actuarial science. Conduct an Internet search to gather more information about the profession.

Chapter 1 Practice Test

1. Is each statement true or false?

    a) Every relation is a special type of function.

    b) Every function is a special type of relation.

    c) For $f(x) = \dfrac{3}{x - 2}$, x can be any real number except $x = 2$.

    d) $\sqrt{81}$ can be fully simplified to $3\sqrt{9}$.

    e) A quadratic function and a linear function always intersect at least once.

For questions 2 to 6, select the best answer.

2. A vertical line test can be used to determine

    A if a relation is a function

    B if a relation is constant

    C if a function is a relation

    D all of the above are true

3. The range of the function $f(x) = -x^2 + 7$ is

    A $\{y \in \mathbb{R}, y \geq 7\}$ B $\{y \in \mathbb{R}, y \leq 7\}$

    C $\{y \in \mathbb{R}, y > 0\}$ D $\{y \in \mathbb{R}\}$

4. Which function would produce an output of $y = 9$ for $x = 1$ and for $x = -1$?

    A $y = 2x + 7$ B $y = x^2 - 3x + 1$

    C $y = 2x^2 + 7$ D all of the above

5. The vertex of $y = -3x^2 + 6x - 2$ is

    A $(1, -2)$ B $(1, 1)$

    C $(-1, 1)$ D $(-1, -2)$

6. Given $f(x) = x^2 - 6x + 10$, if $f(a) = 1$, what is the value of a?

    A 5   B 3

    C 2   D 1

7. Sketch a relation that is

    a) a function with domain $\{x \in \mathbb{R}\}$ and range $\{y \in \mathbb{R}, y \leq 3\}$

    b) not a function with domain $\{x \in \mathbb{R}, -5 \leq x \leq 5\}$ and range $\{y \in \mathbb{R}, -5 \leq y \leq 5\}$

8. State the domain and the range of each function.

    a)

    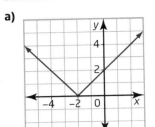

    b)

x	$f(x)$
0	−5
1	−8
2	−12
3	−21

9. The time needed for a pendulum to make one complete swing is called the period of the pendulum. The period, T, in seconds, for a pendulum of length ℓ, in metres, can be approximated using the function

    $T = 2\sqrt{\ell}$.

    a) State the domain and the range of T.

    b) Sketch a graph of the relation.

    c) Is the relation a function? Explain.

10. Write the ordered pairs that correspond to the mapping diagram. Is this a function?

    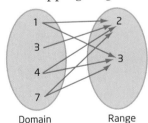

    Domain   Range

11. a) Find the vertex of the parabola defined by $f(x) = -\dfrac{1}{2}x^2 + 4x + 3$.

    b) Is the vertex a minimum or a maximum? Explain.

    c) How many x-intercepts does the function have? Explain.

12. Pat has 30 m of fencing to enclose three identical stalls behind the barn, as shown.

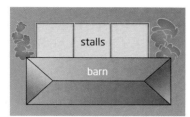

a) What dimensions will produce a maximum area for each stall?

b) What is that maximum area of each stall?

13. Simon knows that at $30 per ticket, 500 tickets to a show will be sold. He also knows that for every $1 increase in price, 10 fewer tickets will be sold.

a) Model the revenue as a quadratic function.

b) What ticket price will maximize revenue?

c) What is the maximum revenue?

14. Perform each radical multiplication and simplify where possible.

a) $3\sqrt{2}\left(2\sqrt{3} - 3\sqrt{2}\right)$

b) $\left(\sqrt{2} + x\right)\left(\sqrt{2} - x\right)$

15. For what value of x is

$\sqrt{x} + \sqrt{x} = \sqrt{x} \times \sqrt{x}$, where $x > 0$? Justify your answer.

16. Consider the quadratic function

$f(x) = -\dfrac{1}{2}x^2 + 4x + 10$.

a) Find the x-intercepts.

b) Use two methods to find the vertex.

c) Sketch a graph of the function.

17. A rectangle has a length that is 3 m more than twice the width. If the total area is 65 m², find the dimensions of the rectangle.

18. Find the equation, in standard form, of the quadratic function that has x-intercepts $-5 \pm \sqrt{3}$ and passes through the point $(-3, 8)$.

19. The graph of a quadratic function is given.

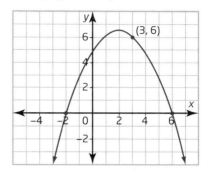

a) Find the equation of the function.

b) Find the maximum value of the function.

20. Find the point(s) of intersection of $y = -x^2 + 5x + 8$ and $y = 2x - 10$.

21. a) Compare the graphs of $f(x) = 3x^2 - 4$ and $g(x) = 3(x - 2)(x + 2)$.

b) What needs to be changed in the equation for $f(x)$ to make the two functions part of the same family of curves with the same x-intercepts? Explain.

c) Describe the family of curves, in factored form, that has the same x-intercepts as $h(x) = 5x^2 - 7$.

22. A baseball is travelling on a path given by the equation $y = -0.011x^2 + 1.15x + 1.22$. The profile of the bleachers in the outfield can be modelled with the equation $y = 0.6x - 72$. All distances are in metres. Does the ball reach the bleachers for a home run? Justify your answer.

Laser Beams

A concert stage has a parabolic roof. The front edge of the roof is defined by the equation $h(x) = -\frac{1}{8}x^2 + 8$, where x is the horizontal distance from the centre and h is the height, both in metres. A vertical lighting tower is built at $x = 9$. Coloured laser lights are installed at various intervals going up the tower. The beams of light are to shine on the front edge of the roof, with their paths defined by the following equations.

Blue: $6x + 8y - 73 = 0$

Green: $x + 2y - 17 = 0$

Orange: $x + y - 10 = 0$

Red: $2x + 8y - 67 = 0$

a) Sketch the graph of $h(x)$.

b) Determine the coordinates of any point(s) of intersection of each laser beam with the edge of the roof.

c) All but one of these laser beams share a common property. Describe the property.

d) Determine the height of each light source on the tower.

e) Determine an equation for the path of a fifth laser beam that is to be tangent to the edge of the roof at the vertex. Where should this light source be located on the tower?

f) Consider the one laser light that does not share the common property. Keeping the location of the light source fixed, determine a new equation for the path of the laser light so that it now shares the common property. Where does it intersect the edge of the roof?

Transformations of Functions

In this chapter, you will investigate properties associated with transformations of functions and learn about a variety of ways in which complex functions are related to simple functions. You will explore the connection between the graphical changes and the parameters in the equations. You will also develop a standard set of procedures for working with and analysing transformations that can be applied to new types of functions.

By the end of this chapter, you will

- relate the process of determining the inverse of a function to your understanding of reverse processes
- determine the numeric or graphical representation of the inverse of a linear or quadratic function, given the numeric, graphical, or algebraic representation of the function, and make connections, through investigation using a variety of tools, between the graph of a function and the graph of its inverse
- determine, through investigation, the relationship between the domain and range of a function and the domain and range of the inverse relation, and determine whether or not the inverse relation is a function
- determine, using function notation when appropriate, the algebraic representation of the inverse of a linear or quadratic function, given the algebraic representation of the function, and make connections, through investigation using a variety of tools, between the algebraic representations of a function and its inverse

- determine, through investigation using technology, the roles of the parameters a, k, d, and c in functions of the form $y = af[k(x - d)] + c$, and describe these roles in terms of transformations on the graphs of
  $f(x) = x$, $f(x) = x^2$, $f(x) = \sqrt{x}$, and $f(x) = \dfrac{1}{x}$
- sketch graphs of $y = af[k(x - d)] + c$ by applying one or more transformations to the graphs of
  $f(x) = x$, $f(x) = x^2$, $f(x) = \sqrt{x}$, and $f(x) = \dfrac{1}{x}$, and state the domain and range of the transformed functions
- simplify polynomial expressions by adding, subtracting, and multiplying
- simplify rational expressions by adding, subtracting, multiplying, and dividing, and state the restrictions on the variable values
- determine if two given algebraic expressions are equivalent

Prerequisite Skills

Refer to the Prerequisite Skills Appendix on pages 478 to 495 for examples of the topics and further practice.

Properties of Quadratic Functions

1. Compare the graph of each quadratic function to the graph of $y = x^2$. Identify the direction of opening and state whether the parabola has been vertically stretched or compressed. Justify your answer.

   a) $y = 3x^2$

   b) $y = -0.5x^2$

   c) $y = 0.1x^2 - 0.1x + 3$

   d) $y = \frac{3}{5}(x - 6)^2 + 5$

2. Determine the vertex of each parabola.

   a) $y = -(x - 5)^2 + 10$

   b) $y = \frac{3}{2}(x + 6)^2 + 20$

   c) $y = 2(x - 1)^2 - 5$

   d) $y = \frac{1}{4}(x + 3)^2 - 4$

Translations

3. Draw the graph of each relation after a vertical translation of 2 units up.

   a)

   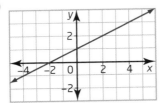

   b)

   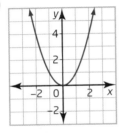

c)

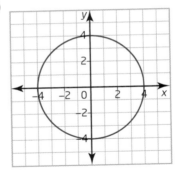

d)

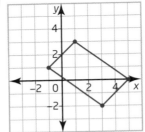

4. Draw each relation in question 3 after a horizontal translation of 4 units left.

Graph Functions

5. Graph each function.

   a) $y = \frac{1}{4}x + 5$

   b) $y = x^2 + 2x - 3$

   c) $y = (x - 2)(x + 3)$

   d) $y = -0.5(x - 2)^2 + 10$

Distributive Property

6. Expand and simplify.

   a) $3x(5x - 8)$

   b) $12x^2y(5x - 10y)$

   c) $-3x(4x^2 + 13x - 7)$

   d) $(3x + 4)(2x - 5)$

   e) $(4x - 5)(4x + 5)$

   f) $3x(4x - 5) - 4x(6 - 10x)$

Common Factors

7. Determine the greatest common factor of each set.

a) 16, 40

b) 15, 18, 30

c) 48, 72, 108

d) $4x^2y^3$, $8xy^2$, $16x^3y^2$

e) $3x^2 + 6x$, $5x^2 + 10x$

f) $x^2 + 5x + 4$, $x^2 - 3x - 28$

8. Factor fully.

a) $15x^2 + 10x$

b) $-35x^3 - 45x^2$

c) $18x^2y^3 - 36xy^3 + 6y^3$

d) $-5x^5 - 100x^4 - 30x^2$

e) $2x(4x - 10) + 5(4x - 10)$

f) $x(6 - 11x) - (6 - 11x)$

Factor Quadratic Expressions

9. Factor fully.

a) $x^2 + 5x + 6$ **b)** $x^2 - 4x - 12$

c) $x^2 + 6x - 27$ **d)** $x^2 - 14x + 49$

e) $x^2 - 64$ **f)** $3x^2 - 9x - 120$

g) $2x^2 + 20x + 50$ **h)** $4x^2 - 256$

10. Factor fully.

a) $2x^2 - 7x - 15$ **b)** $9x^2 + 24x + 16$

c) $12x^2 - 2x - 2$ **d)** $18x^2 - 54x - 20$

e) $4x^2 + 10x - 24$ **f)** $20x^2 + 47x + 24$

Work With Fractions

11. Determine the least common multiple (LCM) of each set.

a) 18, 30, 42

b) $4x^2y$, $2xy$, $6xy^2$

c) $x^2 + 3x - 40$, $x^2 - 11x + 30$

12. Add or subtract using the LCM of the denominator.

a) $\dfrac{3}{5} + \dfrac{8}{15}$ **b)** $\dfrac{8}{9} - \dfrac{1}{4}$

c) $\dfrac{x}{6} + \dfrac{y}{4}$ **d)** $\dfrac{2x}{3} - \dfrac{3y}{8}$

13. Simplify.

a) $\left(\dfrac{5}{6}\right)\left(-\dfrac{3}{20}\right)$ **b)** $\left(\dfrac{12}{7}\right)\left(\dfrac{28}{15}\right)$

c) $\dfrac{20}{9} \div \dfrac{15}{32}$ **d)** $-\dfrac{24}{25} \div \left(-\dfrac{12}{125}\right)$

Rearrange Formulas

14. Solve for the indicated variable in each expression.

a) $A = \pi r^2$, for r

b) $P = 2(\ell + w)$, for w

c) $x^2 + y^2 = 16$, for y

d) $y = x^2 - 20$, for x

e) $y = \sqrt{x^2 - 5}$, for x

f) $A = 2\pi r^2 + 2\pi rh$, for h

Chapter Problem

Matthew works at the local traffic safety bureau. Part of his job is the study of how traffic flows and how automobiles behave in various situations. In this chapter, you will see how transformations relate to this very important field of research.

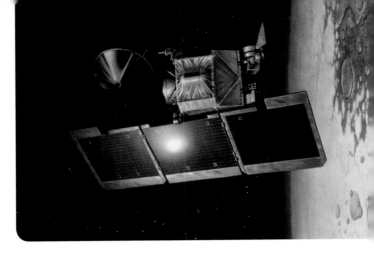

Functions and Equivalent Algebraic Expressions

On September 23, 1999, the Mars Climate Orbiter crashed on its first day of orbit. Two scientific groups used different measurement systems (Imperial and metric) for navigational calculations, resulting in a mix-up that is said to have caused the loss of the $125-million (U.S.) orbiter. Even though the National Aeronautics and Space Administration (NASA) requires a system of checks within their processes, this error was never detected.

This mix-up may have been caused by people not understanding complex equations. In general, to reduce the likelihood of errors in calculations, mathematicians and engineers simplify equations and expressions before applying them.

Example 1

Determine Whether Two Functions Are Equivalent

Determine whether the functions in each pair are equivalent by

i) testing three different values of x

ii) simplifying the expressions on the right sides

iii) graphing using graphing technology

a) $f(x) = 2(x - 1)^2 + (3x - 2)$ and $g(x) = 2x^2 - x$

b) $f(x) = \dfrac{x^2 - 2x - 8}{x^2 - x - 12}$ and $g(x) = \dfrac{x + 2}{x + 3}$

Solution

a) i) Choose three values of x that will make calculations relatively easy.

x	$f(x) = 2(x - 1)^2 + (3x - 2)$	$g(x) = 2x^2 - x$
−1	$f(-1) = 2(-1 - 1)^2 + (3(-1) - 2)$ $= 2(-2)^2 + (-5)$ $= 8 - 5$ $= 3$	$g(-1) = 2(-1)^2 - (-1)$ $= 2(1) + 1$ $= 3$
0	$f(0) = 2(0 - 1)^2 + (3(0) - 2)$ $= 2(-1)^2 + (-2)$ $= 0$	$g(0) = 2(0)^2 - 0$ $= 0$
1	$f(1) = 2(1 - 1)^2 + (3(1) - 2)$ $= 2(0)^2 + 1$ $= 1$	$g(1) = 2(1)^2 - 1$ $= 1$

Based on these three calculations, the functions appear to be equivalent. However, three examples do not prove that the functions are equivalent for every x-value.

ii) In this pair, $g(x)$ is already simplified, so concentrate on $f(x)$.

$$\begin{aligned}
f(x) &= 2(x - 1)^2 + (3x - 2) \\
&= 2(x^2 - 2x + 1) + 3x - 2 \\
&= 2x^2 - 4x + 2 + 3x - 2 \\
&= 2x^2 - x
\end{aligned}$$

Algebraically, these functions are equivalent.

iii) Use a graphing calculator to graph the two equations as **Y1** and **Y2**. Change the line display for **Y2** to a thick line.

- Cursor left to the slanted line beside **Y2**.
- Press (ENTER) to change the line style.

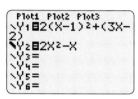

- From the **ZOOM** menu, select **6:ZStandard**.

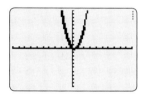

The graph of $y = 2(x - 1)^2 + (3x - 2)$ will be drawn first. Then, the graph of $y = 2x^2 - x$ will be drawn using a heavier line. You can pause the plot by pressing (ENTER). Pressing (ENTER) again will resume the plot.

This seems to yield the same graph. These functions appear to be equivalent.

Using a TI-Nspire™ CAS graphing calculator, you can graph the functions $f(x) = 2(x - 1)^2 + (3x - 2)$ and $g(x) = 2x^2 - x$ side by side for comparison.

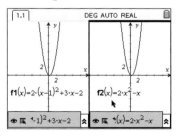

Technology Tip

Refer to the Use Technology feature on pages 86 and 87 to see how to graph multiple functions using a TI-Nspire™ CAS graphing calculator.

b) **i)**

x	$f(x) = \dfrac{x^2 - 2x - 8}{x^2 - x - 12}$	$g(x) = \dfrac{x + 2}{x + 3}$
−1	$f(-1) = \dfrac{(-1)^2 - 2(-1) - 8}{(-1)^2 - (-1) - 12}$ $= \dfrac{1 + 2 - 8}{1 + 1 - 12}$ $= \dfrac{-5}{-10}$ $= \dfrac{1}{2}$	$g(-1) = \dfrac{-1 + 2}{-1 + 3}$ $= \dfrac{1}{2}$
0	$f(0) = \dfrac{0^2 - 2(0) - 8}{0^2 - 0 - 12}$ $= \dfrac{-8}{-12}$ $= \dfrac{2}{3}$	$g(0) = \dfrac{0 + 2}{0 + 3}$ $= \dfrac{2}{3}$
1	$f(1) = \dfrac{1^2 - 2(1) - 8}{1^2 - 1 - 12}$ $= \dfrac{-9}{-12}$ $= \dfrac{3}{4}$	$g(1) = \dfrac{1 + 2}{1 + 3}$ $= \dfrac{3}{4}$

Based on these three calculations, the functions appear to be equivalent. However, three examples do not prove that these functions are equivalent for every x-value.

ii) In this pair, $g(x)$ is already simplified, so concentrate on $f(x)$. To simplify $f(x)$, factor the numerator and the denominator.

$$f(x) = \frac{x^2 - 2x - 8}{x^2 - x - 12}$$

$$= \frac{(x - 4)(x + 2)}{(x - 4)(x + 3)} \qquad \text{Factor the numerator and the denominator.}$$

$$= \frac{x + 2}{x + 3} \qquad \text{Divide by the common factor.}$$

Algebraically, it appears as though the two functions are equivalent. However, the effect of dividing by a common factor involving a variable needs to be examined.

iii) Use a graphing calculator to graph the two equations. In this case, there is a slight difference between the graphs. To see the graphs properly, press (ZOOM) and select **4:ZDecimal**.

Technology Tip

Using a "friendly window," such as **ZDecimal**, makes it easier to see any gaps in the graph of a function. This is because each pixel represents one tick mark.

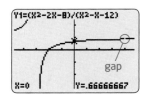

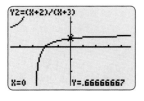

There appears to be a gap in the first graph.

This can be verified further by using the **TABLE** function on a graphing calculator.

Based on the evidence, this pair of functions is equivalent everywhere but at $x = 4$.

X	Y1	Y2
0	.66667	.66667
1	.75	.75
2	.8	.8
3	.83333	.83333
4	ERROR	.85714
5	.875	.875
6	.88889	.88889

Y1=ERROR

Connections

An open circle is used to indicate a gap or a hole in the graph of a function.

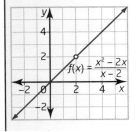

$f(x) = \dfrac{x^2 - 2x}{x - 2}$

Polynomial expressions that can be algebraically simplified to the same expression are equivalent. However, with **rational expressions**, this may not be the case.

More specifically, since division by zero is not defined, you must define restrictions on the variable. For example, the function $f(x) = \dfrac{x^2 - 2x - 8}{x^2 - x - 12}$ has a factored form of $f(x) = \dfrac{(x - 4)(x + 2)}{(x - 4)(x + 3)}$. Since the denominator is zero if

$$x - 4 = 0 \quad \text{or} \quad x + 3 = 0$$
$$x = 4 \qquad\qquad x = -3$$

the simplified function is written as $f(x) = \dfrac{x + 2}{x + 3}$, $x \neq -3$, $x \neq 4$.

rational expression
• the quotient of two polynomials, $\dfrac{p(x)}{q(x)}$, where $q(x) \neq 0$

Example 2

Determine Restrictions

Simplify each expression and determine any restrictions on the variable.

a) $\dfrac{x^2 + 10x + 21}{x + 3}$

b) $\dfrac{6x^2 - 7x - 5}{3x^2 + x - 10}$

Solution

a) $\dfrac{x^2 + 10x + 21}{x + 3} = \dfrac{(x + 3)(x + 7)}{x + 3}$ Factor the numerator and the denominator. Before reducing, determine restrictions. In this case, $x \neq -3$.

$\qquad = \dfrac{(x + 3)(x + 7)}{x + 3}$, $x \neq -3$ Divide by any common factors.

$\qquad = x + 7$, $x \neq -3$

So, $\dfrac{x^2 + 10x + 21}{x + 3} = x + 7$, $x \neq -3$.

b) $\dfrac{6x^2 - 7x - 5}{3x^2 + x - 10} = \dfrac{(2x + 1)(3x - 5)}{(3x - 5)(x + 2)}$ Factor the numerator and the denominator.

$\qquad = \dfrac{(2x + 1)(3x - 5)}{(3x - 5)(x + 2)}$, $x \neq -2$, $x \neq \dfrac{5}{3}$ Divide by any common factors.

$\qquad = \dfrac{2x + 1}{x + 2}$, $x \neq -2$, $x \neq \dfrac{5}{3}$

So, $\dfrac{6x^2 - 7x - 5}{3x^2 + x - 10} = \dfrac{2x + 1}{x + 2}$, $x \neq -2$, $x \neq \dfrac{5}{3}$.

Example 3

Simplify Calculations

A square of side length 7 cm is removed
from a square of side length x.

a) Express the area of the shaded region as
a function of x.

b) Write the area function in factored form.

c) Use both forms of the function to
calculate the area for x-values of
8 cm, 9 cm, 10 cm, 11 cm, and
12 cm. Which form is easier to use?

d) What is the domain of the area function?

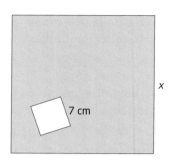

Solution

a) $A_{\text{shaded}} = A_{\text{large}} - A_{\text{small}}$
$$= x^2 - 7^2$$
$$= x^2 - 49$$

b) $A_{\text{shaded}} = x^2 - 49$
$$= (x - 7)(x + 7)$$

c)

x	$A = x^2 - 49$	$A = (x - 7)(x + 7)$
8	$A = 8^2 - 49$ $= 15$	$A = (8 - 7)(8 + 7)$ $= 15$
9	$A = 9^2 - 49$ $= 32$	$A = (9 - 7)(9 + 7)$ $= 32$
10	$A = 10^2 - 49$ $= 51$	$A = (10 - 7)(10 + 7)$ $= 51$
11	$A = 11^2 - 49$ $= 72$	$A = (11 - 7)(11 + 7)$ $= 72$
12	$A = 12^2 - 49$ $= 95$	$A = (12 - 7)(12 + 7)$ $= 95$

The areas are 15 cm², 32 cm², 51 cm², 72 cm², and 95 cm²,
respectively.

Both expressions have similar numbers of steps involved.
However, it is easier to use mental math with the factored form.

d) Since this function represents area, it must be restricted to x-values
that do not result in negative or zero areas.
So, the domain is $\{x \in \mathbb{R}, x > 7\}$.

- To determine if two expressions are equivalent, simplify both to see if they are algebraically the same.

- Checking several points may suggest that two expressions are equivalent, but it does not prove that they are.

- Rational expressions must be checked for restrictions by determining where the denominator is zero. These restrictions must be stated when the expression is simplified.

- Graphs can suggest whether two functions or expressions are equivalent.

Communicate Your Understanding

C1 The points $(-3, 5)$ and $(5, 5)$ both lie on the graphs of the functions $y = x^2 - 2x - 10$ and $y = -x^2 + 2x + 20$. Explain why checking only a few points is not sufficient to determine whether two expressions are equivalent.

C2 A student submits the following simplification.

$$\frac{x^2 + 6x + 3}{6x + 3} = \frac{x^2 + \cancel{6x + 3}}{\cancel{6x + 3}}$$

$$= x^2$$

Explain how you would show the student that this is incorrect.

C3 Explain why the expression $4x^3 + 4x^2 - 5x + 3$ does not have any restrictions.

Ⓐ Practise

For help with questions 1 to 6, refer to Examples 1 and 2.

1. **Use Technology** Use a graphing calculator to graph each pair of functions. Do they appear to be equivalent?

   a) $f(x) = 5(x^2 + 3x - 2) - (2x + 4)^2$,
   $g(x) = x^2 - x - 26$

   b) $f(x) = (8x - 3)^2 + (5 - 7x)(9x + 1)$,
   $g(x) = x^2 - 10x - 14$

   c) $f(x) = (x^2 + 3x - 5) - (x^2 + 2x - 5)$,
   $g(x) = 2(x - 1)^2 - (2x^2 - 5x - 1)$

   d) $f(x) = (x - 3)(x + 2)(x + 5)$,
   $g(x) = x^3 + 4x^2 - 11x - 30$

   e) $f(x) = (x^2 + 3x - 5)(x^2 - 5x + 4)$,
   $g(x) = x^4 - 2x^3 - 15x^2 + 37x - 20$

2. Refer to question 1. If the functions appear to be equivalent, show that they are algebraically. Otherwise, show that they are not equivalent by substituting a value for *x*.

3. State the restriction for each function.

   a)

   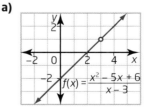

   b)

   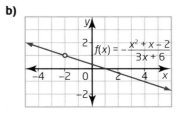

4. State the restrictions for each function.

a)

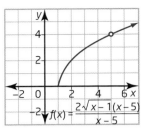

$$f(x) = \frac{2\sqrt{x-1}(x-5)}{x-5}$$

b)

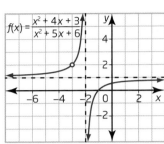

$$f(x) = \frac{x^2 + 4x + 3}{x^2 + 5x + 6}$$

5. Determine whether $g(x)$ is the simplified version of $f(x)$. If it is, then state the restrictions needed. If not, determine the correct simplified version.

a) $f(x) = \dfrac{x^2 + 11x + 30}{x + 6}$, $g(x) = x + 5$

b) $f(x) = \dfrac{x^2 - 16}{x^2 - 8x + 16}$, $g(x) = x + 4$

c) $f(x) = \dfrac{x^2 + 6x + 5}{x + 5}$, $g(x) = x^2$

d) $f(x) = \dfrac{x^2 + 10x + 16}{x^2 + 2x - 48}$, $g(x) = \dfrac{x + 2}{x - 6}$

e) $f(x) = \dfrac{12x^2 - 5x - 2}{3x^2 - 2x}$, $g(x) = \dfrac{4x + 1}{x}$

f) $f(x) = \dfrac{5x^2 - 23x - 10}{5x + 2}$, $g(x) = -23x - 2$

6. Simplify each expression and state all restrictions on x.

a) $\dfrac{x - 8}{x^2 - 13x + 40}$

b) $\dfrac{3(x - 7)^2(x - 10)}{x^2 - 17x + 70}$

c) $\dfrac{x^2 - 3x - 18}{x^2 + x - 42}$

d) $\dfrac{x^2 + 7x - 18}{x^2 + 3x - 10}$

e) $\dfrac{x + 8}{x^2 - 6x - 16}$

f) $\dfrac{25x^2 + 10x - 8}{10x^2 + 26x - 12}$

B Connect and Apply

7. Evaluate each expression for x-values of -2, -1, 0, 3, and 10. Describe any difficulties that occur.

a) $(x - 6)(x - 2) - (x - 11)(x + 2)$

b) $\dfrac{2x^3 + 12x^2 + 10x}{x^2 + 6x + 5}$

For help with question 8, refer to Example 3.

8. A circle of radius 3 cm is removed from a circle of radius r.

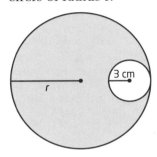

a) Express the area of the shaded region as a function of r.

b) State the domain and range of the area function.

9. A company that makes modular furniture has designed a scalable box to accommodate several different sizes of items. The dimensions are given by $L = 2x + 0.5$, $W = x - 0.5$, and $H = x + 0.5$, where x is in metres.

Reasoning and Proving

Representing · Selecting Tools · Problem Solving · Connecting · Reflecting · Communicating

a) Express the volume of the box as a function of x.

b) Express the surface area of the box as a function of x.

c) Determine the volume and surface area for x-values of 0.75 m, 1 m, and 1.5 m.

d) State the domain and range of the volume and surface area functions.

10. Chapter Problem At the traffic safety bureau, Matthew is conducting a study on the stoplights at a particular intersection. He determines that when there are 18 green lights per hour, then, on average, 12 cars can safely travel through the intersection on each green light. He also finds that if the number of green lights per hour increases by one, then one fewer car can travel through the intersection per light.

a) Determine a function to represent the total number of cars that will travel through the intersection for an increase of x green lights per hour.

b) Matthew models the situation with the function $f(x) = 216 - 6x - x^2$. Show that your function from part a) is the same.

c) How many green lights should there be per hour to maximize the number of cars through the intersection?

11. In the novel *The Curious Incident of the Dog in the Night-Time* by Mark Haddon, the young boy, who is the main character, loves mathematics and is mildly autistic. Throughout the book, he encounters several math problems. One of the problems asks him to prove that a triangle with sides given by $x^2 + 1$, $x^2 - 1$, and $2x$ will always be a right triangle for $x > 1$.

a) Use the Pythagorean theorem to verify that this statement is true for x-values of 2, 3, and 4.

b) Based on the three expressions for the sides, which one must represent the hypotenuse? Justify your answer.

c) Use the Pythagorean theorem with the expressions for the side lengths to prove that these will always be sides of a right triangle for $x > 1$.

12. The function $y = \dfrac{a^3}{a^2 + x^2}$ is sometimes called the witch of Agnesi after Maria Gaetana Agnesi (1718−1799). The equation generates a family of functions for different values of $a \in \mathbb{R}$.

a) **Use Technology** Use graphing technology to graph this function for a-values of 1, 2, 3, and 4.

b) Explain why this rational function does not have any restrictions.

c) Research the history of Maria Gaetana Agnesi and find out who else studied this curve before her.

Connections

Maria Gaetana Agnesi originally referred to this function as *versiera*, which means "to turn." Later, in translation, it was mistakenly confused with *avversiere*, which means "witch" or "wife of the devil," and thus its current name was born.

C Extend

13. What does the graph of
$$f(x) = \frac{(x + 6)(2x^2 - x - 6)}{x^2 + 4x - 12}$$
look like?

14. Algebraically determine the domain and range of the area function that represents the shaded region.

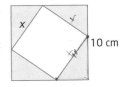

15. A student wrote the following proof. What mistake did the student make?

Let $a = b$.
Then, $a^2 = ab$.
$a^2 + a^2 = a^2 + ab$
$2a^2 = a^2 + ab$
$2a^2 - 2ab = a^2 + ab - 2ab$
$2a^2 - 2ab = a^2 - ab$
$2(a^2 - ab) = 1(a^2 - ab)$
Dividing both sides by $(a^2 - ab)$
gives $2 = 1$.

16. Math Contest Given the two linear functions $y = 6x - 12$ and $\dfrac{y}{x - 2} = 6$, what ordered pair lies on the graph of the first line but not on the graph of the second line?

Use Technology

Graph Functions Using a TI-Nspire™ CAS Graphing Calculator

1. Open a new document. Open a page using the **Graphs & Geometry** application.

2. In the entry line, you will see $f1(x)=$.

   • Type x^2 as a sample function.

   • Press $\boxed{enter}$.

   Note that the function is displayed with its equation as a label and the entry line has changed to $f2(x)=$.

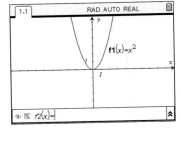

3. Look at the axes. This is the standard window.

   To view or change the window settings:

   • Press $\boxed{menu}$.

   • Select **4:Window**, and then select **1:Window Settings**.

   You can change the appearance of the window.

   • Press $\boxed{menu}$.

   • Select **2:View**.

   There are several options. For example, if you select **8:Show Axes End Values**, you can display the range of each axis.

4. Press the up arrow key once. The function $f1(x)$ will be displayed in the entry line. You can change the appearance of a line:

   • Press $\boxed{tab}$ until the **Attributes** tool, ▤, at the left of the entry line, is selected.

   • Press $\boxed{enter}$.

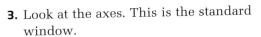

   You can use this tool to adjust the line weight, the line style, the label style, and the line continuity.

   • Use the up and down arrow keys to highlight an attribute.

   • Then, use the left and right arrow keys to move through the options for that attribute.

   Experiment with the attributes. When you are finished, press $\boxed{esc}$.

5. You can move a function label.

   • Press $\boxed{tab}$. The entry line will grey out, and the cursor will move to the graphing window.

   • Use the arrow keys to move the cursor over the function label. When you are in the correct place, the word "label" will appear, along with a hand symbol.

- Press (ctrl) (✥). The hand will close to "grab" the label.
- Use the arrow keys to move the label around the screen.
- When you are finished, press (esc).

You can also move the entire graph.

- Move the cursor to a blank space in the second quadrant.
- Press (ctrl) (✥). A hand will appear.
- Use the arrow keys to move the entire graph around the screen.
- When you are finished, press (esc).

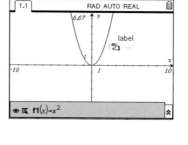

Technology **Tip**

If you are on the entry line and want to move to the graphing window, press (esc).

If you are in the graphing window and want to move to the entry line, press (tab).

6. You can display a table of values for the function.

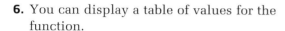

- Press (tab) to return to the entry line.
- Press the up arrow key to return to the function $f1(x)$.
- Press (menu) and select **2:View**.
- From the **View** menu, select **9:Add Function Table**.

You can scroll up and down to inspect different values.

To adjust the **Table Start** value and the **Table Step** value:

- Press (menu) and select **5:Function Table**.
- From the **Function Table** menu, select **3:Edit Function Table Settings**.

7. You can split the screen to display two functions at once.

- Open a new document. Open a page using the **Graphs & Geometry** application.
- Graph the function $f1(x) = x^2$.
- Press (ctrl) (⌂) to access the **Tools** menu.
- From the **Tools** menu, select **5:Page Layout**, and then select **2:Select Layout**.

You will see a menu of possible layouts.

For example, to display two graphs side by side:

- Select **2:Layout 2**. A blank window will appear.
- Press (ctrl) (tab) to switch windows.
- Press (menu) and select **2:Add Graphs & Geometry**.
- Graph the function $f2(x) = x^3$.

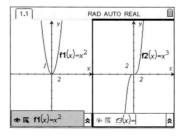

Technology **Tip**

You can hide the entry line.
- Press (ctrl) (G). The entry line is hidden.
- Press (ctrl) (G) again to view the entry line.

If you press a key or make a selection by mistake, you can undo the operation.
- Press (ctrl) (Z).

This will work several times to step back through a series of operations.

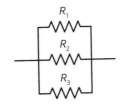

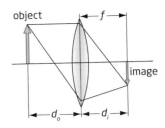

Skills You Need: Operations With Rational Expressions

$$\frac{1}{R_T} = \frac{1}{R_1} + \frac{1}{R_2} + \frac{1}{R_3}$$

$$\frac{1}{f} = \frac{1}{d_o} + \frac{1}{d_i}$$

The ability to manipulate rational expressions is an important skill for engineers, scientists, and mathematicians. Some examples of such situations are the calculation of the resistance in parallel circuits and the calculation of the focal length in curved lenses.

Example 1

Multiply and Divide Rational Expressions

Simplify each expression and state any restrictions on the variables.

a) $\dfrac{4x^2}{3x} \times \dfrac{12x^3}{2x}$

b) $\dfrac{10ab^2}{4a} \div \dfrac{15a^2}{12b^2}$

Solution

a) Method 1: Multiply and Then Simplify

$$\frac{4x^2}{3x} \times \frac{12x^3}{2x} = \frac{48x^5}{6x^2} \qquad \text{Multiply the numerators and multiply the denominators.}$$

$$= \frac{\overset{8}{48}x^{\overset{3}{5}}}{\underset{}{6}x^{2}}, x \neq 0 \quad \text{Divide by the common factors.}$$

$$= 8x^3$$

Thus, $\dfrac{4x^2}{3x} \times \dfrac{12x^3}{2x} = 8x^3, x \neq 0.$

Method 2: Simplify and Then Multiply

$$\frac{4x^2}{3x} \times \frac{12x^3}{2x} = \frac{\overset{2}{4}x^{\overset{1}{2}}}{\underset{}{3}x} \times \frac{\overset{4}{12}x^{\overset{2}{3}}}{\underset{}{2}x}, x \neq 0 \quad \text{Divide by the common factors.}$$

$$= 2x \times 4x^2$$

$$= 8x^3$$

Thus, $\dfrac{4x^2}{3x} \times \dfrac{12x^3}{2x} = 8x^3, x \neq 0.$

b) $\dfrac{10ab^2}{4a} \div \dfrac{15a^2}{12b^2} = \dfrac{10ab^2}{4a} \times \dfrac{12b^2}{15a^2}$ Multiply by the reciprocal.

$\qquad\qquad\quad = \dfrac{120ab^4}{60a^3}$ Multiply the numerators and multiply the denominators.

$\qquad\qquad\quad = \dfrac{\overset{2}{\cancel{120}}ab^4}{\underset{}{\cancel{60}}a^{3\ 2}}, a \neq 0$ Divide by the common factors.

$\qquad\qquad\quad = \dfrac{2b^4}{a^2}$

In the original expression, both a and b were in the denominator, so neither of them can be equal to zero.

So, $\dfrac{10ab^2}{4a} \div \dfrac{15a^2}{12b^2} = \dfrac{2b^4}{a^2}, a \neq 0, b \neq 0.$

Example 2

Multiply and Divide Rational Expressions Involving Polynomials

Simplify and state any restrictions.

a) $\dfrac{a^2 + 2a}{3a} \times \dfrac{20a^2}{5a^2 + 10a}$

b) $\dfrac{2x^2 - 8x}{x^2 - 3x - 10} \div \dfrac{4x^2}{x^2 - 9x + 20}$

Solution

a) $\qquad \dfrac{a^2 + 2a}{3a} \times \dfrac{20a^2}{5a^2 + 10a}$

$= \dfrac{a(a + 2)}{3a} \times \dfrac{20a^2}{5a(a + 2)}$ Factor binomials where possible.

$= \dfrac{\cancel{a}\cancel{(a + 2)}}{3\cancel{a}} \times \dfrac{\overset{4}{\cancel{20}}a^{\overset{1}{\cancel{2}}}}{\cancel{5}\cancel{a}\cancel{(a + 2)}}, a \neq -2, a \neq 0$ Divide by the common factors.

$= \dfrac{1}{3} \times 4a$ Multiply the numerators and multiply the denominators.

$= \dfrac{4a}{3}$

So, $\dfrac{a^2 + 2a}{3a} \times \dfrac{20a^2}{5a^2 + 10a} = \dfrac{4a}{3}, a \neq -2, a \neq 0.$

b) $\dfrac{2x^2 - 8x}{x^2 - 3x - 10} \div \dfrac{4x^2}{x^2 - 9x + 20}$

$= \dfrac{2x(x - 4)}{(x - 5)(x + 2)} \div \dfrac{4x^2}{(x - 4)(x - 5)}$

Factor binomials and trinomials where possible. Multiply by the reciprocal.

$= \dfrac{2x(x - 4)}{(x - 5)(x + 2)} \times \dfrac{(x - 4)(x - 5)}{4x^2}$

$= \dfrac{2x(x - 4)}{(x - 5)(x + 2)} \times \dfrac{(x - 4)(x - 5)}{4x^2 \; 1} , \; x \neq -2, x \neq 0, x \neq 5$

Divide by any common factors.

$= \dfrac{(x - 4)^2}{2x(x + 2)}$

When considering restrictions, you must include any instance where the denominator can be zero. From the original expression, this occurs when $x - 5 = 0$, $x + 2 = 0$, and $x - 4 = 0$. When the second rational expression is inverted, then its denominator can be zero when $x = 0$.

So, $\dfrac{2x^2 - 8x}{x^2 - 3x - 10} \div \dfrac{4x^2}{x^2 - 9x + 20} = \dfrac{(x - 4)^2}{2x(x + 2)}$,

$x \neq -2, x \neq 0, x \neq 4, x \neq 5$.

Example 3

Add and Subtract Rational Expressions With Monomial Denominators

Simplify and state the restrictions.

a) $\dfrac{1}{5x} + \dfrac{1}{2x}$

b) $\dfrac{ab^2 + 2}{2ab^2} - \dfrac{b + 2}{2b}$

Solution

a) Start by determining the least common multiple (LCM) of the denominators.

$5x = (5)(x)$

$2x = (2)(x)$

$(5)(2)(x) = 10x$

The LCM is the least common denominator (LCD) of the two rational expressions.

$\dfrac{1}{5x} + \dfrac{1}{2x} = \dfrac{1(2)}{5x(2)} + \dfrac{1(5)}{2x(5)}$

Multiply each rational expression by a fraction equal to 1 that makes each denominator $10x$.

$= \dfrac{2}{10x} + \dfrac{5}{10x}$

$= \dfrac{7}{10x}$

Add the numerators.

Thus, $\dfrac{1}{5x} + \dfrac{1}{2x} = \dfrac{7}{10x}$, $x \neq 0$.

b) Determine the LCM of the denominators.

$2ab^2 = (2)(a)(b)(b)$

$2b = (2)(b)$

$(2)(a)(b)(b) = 2ab^2$

The LCD is $2ab^2$.

$$\frac{ab^2 + 2}{2ab^2} - \frac{b + 2}{2b} = \frac{ab^2 + 2}{2ab^2} - \frac{(b + 2)(ab)}{2b(ab)}$$

Multiply each rational expression by a fraction equal to 1 that makes each denominator $2ab^2$.

$$= \frac{ab^2 + 2}{2ab^2} - \frac{ab^2 + 2ab}{2ab^2}$$

$$= \frac{2 - 2ab}{2ab^2}$$

Subtract the numerators.

$$= \frac{2(1 - ab)}{2ab^2}$$

Factor 2 from the numerator.

$$= \frac{1 - ab}{ab^2}$$

Divide by the common factor of 2.

Thus, $\dfrac{ab^2 + 2}{2ab^2} - \dfrac{b + 2}{2b} = \dfrac{1 - ab}{ab^2}$, $a \neq 0$, $b \neq 0$.

Example 4

Add and Subtract Rational Expressions With Polynomial Denominators

Simplify and state the restrictions.

a) $\dfrac{x + 5}{x - 3} + \dfrac{x - 7}{x + 2}$

b) $\dfrac{x + 9}{x^2 + 2x - 48} - \dfrac{x - 9}{x^2 - x - 30}$

Solution

a) There are no common factors in the denominators, so the LCD is just $(x - 3)(x + 2)$.

$$\frac{x + 5}{x - 3} + \frac{x - 7}{x + 2}$$

$$= \frac{(x + 5)(x + 2)}{(x - 3)(x + 2)} + \frac{(x - 7)(x - 3)}{(x + 2)(x - 3)}$$

Multiply each rational expression by a fraction equal to 1 that makes each denominator $(x - 3)(x + 2)$.

$$= \frac{x^2 + 7x + 10}{(x - 3)(x + 2)} + \frac{x^2 - 10x + 21}{(x - 3)(x + 2)}$$

$$= \frac{2x^2 - 3x + 31}{(x - 3)(x + 2)}$$

Add the numerators.

Thus, $\dfrac{x + 5}{x - 3} + \dfrac{x - 7}{x + 2} = \dfrac{2x^2 - 3x + 31}{(x - 3)(x + 2)}$, $x \neq -2$, $x \neq 3$.

b) Determine the LCM of the denominators.

$x^2 + 2x - 48 = (x + 8)(x - 6)$

$x^2 - x - 30 = (x - 6)(x + 5)$

$(x + 8)(x - 6)(x + 5)$

The LCD is $(x + 8)(x - 6)(x + 5)$.

$$\frac{x + 9}{x^2 + 2x - 48} - \frac{x - 9}{x^2 - x - 30}$$

$$= \frac{(x + 9)(x + 5)}{(x + 8)(x - 6)(x + 5)} - \frac{(x - 9)(x + 8)}{(x - 6)(x + 5)(x + 8)}$$

Multiply each rational expression by a fraction equal to 1 that makes each denominator $(x + 8)(x - 6)(x + 5)$.

$$= \frac{x^2 + 14x + 45}{(x + 8)(x - 6)(x + 5)} - \frac{x^2 - x - 72}{(x + 8)(x - 6)(x + 5)}$$

$$= \frac{15x + 117}{(x + 8)(x - 6)(x + 5)}$$

Add the numerators.

Thus, $\dfrac{x + 9}{x^2 + 2x - 48} - \dfrac{x - 9}{x^2 - x - 30} = \dfrac{15x + 117}{(x + 8)(x - 6)(x + 5)}$,

$x \neq -8, x \neq -5, x \neq 6$.

Example 5

Bicycle Relay

Raj and Mack are competing as a relay team in a 50-km cycling race. There are two legs in the race. Leg A is 30 km and leg B is 20 km.

a) Assuming that each cyclist travels at a different average speed, determine a simplified expression to represent the total time of the race.

b) If Raj can maintain an average speed of 35 km/h and Mack an average speed of 25 km/h, determine the minimum time it will take to complete the race.

Solution

a) For any distance-speed-time calculation, the expression for the time, t, is given by $t = \dfrac{d}{v}$, where d represents the distance and v represents the speed. To calculate the total time, add the times for the two legs. Let t_A and t_B represent the times and v_A and v_B represent the speeds of legs A and B, respectively.

$$t = t_A + t_B$$

$$= \frac{30}{v_A} + \frac{20}{v_B}$$

$$= \frac{30v_B}{v_A v_B} + \frac{20v_A}{v_A v_B} \qquad \text{Write with a common denominator.}$$

$$= \frac{30v_B + 20v_A}{v_A v_B} \qquad \text{Add the numerators.}$$

b) It makes sense that for the minimum time, the fastest person should ride the longest leg. So, Raj will ride leg A and Mack will ride leg B.

$$t = \frac{30(25) + 20(35)}{35(25)} \qquad \text{Substitute the value for each person's speed.}$$

$$\doteq 1.66$$

It will take the team approximately 1.66 h to complete the race.

Key Concepts

- When multiplying or dividing rational expressions, follow these steps:
  - Factor any polynomials, if possible.
  - When dividing by a rational expression, multiply by the reciprocal of the rational expression.
  - Divide by any common factors.
  - Determine any restrictions.
- When adding or subtracting rational expressions, follow these steps:
  - Factor the denominators.
  - Determine the least common multiple of the denominators.
  - Rewrite the expressions with a common denominator.
  - Add or subtract the numerators.
  - Simplify and state the restrictions.

Communicate Your Understanding

C1 Describe how you would simplify $\dfrac{(x + 3)(x - 6)}{(x + 4)(x + 5)} \div \dfrac{(x - 6)(x + 8)}{(x + 4)(x - 7)}$. What are the restrictions on the variable?

C2 Write two rational expressions whose product is $\dfrac{x + 5}{x - 2}$, $x \neq -4$, $x \neq 1$, $x \neq 2$.

C3 A student simplifies the expression $\dfrac{x + 3}{4} + \dfrac{x - 3}{6}$ and gets an answer of $\dfrac{2x}{12}$. What did the student probably do incorrectly to get this answer?

C4 Describe how you would simplify $\dfrac{5}{x + 3} - \dfrac{7x}{x - 1}$. What are the restrictions on the variable?

A Practise

For help with questions 1 and 2, refer to Example 1.

1. Simplify and state the restrictions on the variables.

   a) $\dfrac{14y}{11x} \times \dfrac{121y}{7x}$

   b) $\dfrac{20x^3}{7x} \times \dfrac{35x^5}{4x}$

   c) $\dfrac{15b^3}{4b} \times \dfrac{20b}{30b^2}$

   d) $\dfrac{30ab}{12a^2} \times \dfrac{18a}{45b^2}$

2. Simplify and state the restrictions on the variables.

   a) $\dfrac{5x}{9y} \div \dfrac{5x}{18y^2}$

   b) $\dfrac{55xy}{8y} \div \dfrac{1}{48x^2}$

   c) $\dfrac{26ab}{4a} \div \dfrac{39a^4b^3}{12b^4}$

   d) $\dfrac{32a^2b}{6c} \div \dfrac{16ab}{24c^3}$

For help with questions 3 to 6, refer to Example 2.

3. Simplify and state the restrictions on the variable.

   a) $\dfrac{25}{x + 10} \times \dfrac{x + 10}{5}$

   b) $\dfrac{x - 1}{x} \times \dfrac{2x}{x - 1}$

   c) $\dfrac{x + 5}{x - 3} \times \dfrac{x - 3}{x + 7}$

   d) $\dfrac{2x + 3}{x + 8} \times \dfrac{x + 8}{2x + 3}$

4. Simplify and state the restrictions on the variable.

   a) $\dfrac{3x^2}{12x^2 + 18x} \times \dfrac{4x + 6}{3x + 30}$

   b) $\dfrac{4x + 24}{x^2 + 8x} \times \dfrac{12x^2}{3x + 18}$

   c) $\dfrac{x^2 + 10x + 21}{x + 3} \times \dfrac{x + 2}{x^2 + 9x + 14}$

   d) $\dfrac{x^2 + 2x - 15}{x^2 - 9x + 18} \times \dfrac{x - 6}{x + 5}$

5. Simplify and state the restrictions on the variable.

   a) $\dfrac{x + 1}{x} \div \dfrac{x + 1}{2x}$

   b) $\dfrac{x}{x - 3} \div \dfrac{1}{x - 3}$

   c) $\dfrac{x + 12}{x + 10} \div \dfrac{x + 12}{x - 5}$

   d) $\dfrac{x - 7}{x + 3} \div \dfrac{x - 7}{x + 3}$

6. Simplify and state the restrictions on the variable.

   a) $\dfrac{x^2 + 15x}{4x + 24} \div \dfrac{3x}{3x + 18}$

   b) $\dfrac{6x}{8x - 72} \div \dfrac{9x}{2x - 18}$

   c) $\dfrac{x^2 + 15x + 26}{6x^2} \div \dfrac{x^2 - 3x - 10}{30x^3}$

   d) $\dfrac{x^2 + 11x + 24}{x^2 + 2x - 3} \div \dfrac{x - 8}{x - 1}$

For help with question 7, refer to Example 3.

7. Simplify and state any restrictions.

   a) $\dfrac{x + 1}{18} + \dfrac{x - 1}{45}$

   b) $\dfrac{x + 10}{12} - \dfrac{2x - 1}{15}$

   c) $\dfrac{2}{3x} - \dfrac{1}{4x}$

   d) $\dfrac{7}{6x} + \dfrac{3}{8x}$

   e) $\dfrac{3}{ab} + \dfrac{5}{4b}$

   f) $\dfrac{13}{10a^2b} + \dfrac{11}{4b^2}$

   g) $\dfrac{2 + a}{a^2b} + \dfrac{4 - a}{3ab^2}$

   h) $\dfrac{4 - ab}{9ab} + \dfrac{2ab}{6a^2b^2}$

For help with questions 8 and 9, refer to Example 4.

8. Simplify and state the restrictions.

   a) $\dfrac{1}{x - 6} - \dfrac{1}{x + 6}$

   b) $\dfrac{12}{x + 8} + \dfrac{3}{x - 9}$

   c) $\dfrac{x + 10}{x - 6} - \dfrac{x - 3}{x + 4}$

   d) $\dfrac{x + 5}{x + 1} + \dfrac{x + 2}{x - 2}$

9. Simplify and state the restrictions.

   a) $\dfrac{x}{x^2 - 9x + 8} + \dfrac{2}{x - 8}$

   b) $\dfrac{x + 3}{x + 5} + \dfrac{x + 2}{x^2 + 3x - 10}$

   c) $\dfrac{x}{x^2 + 3x + 2} - \dfrac{3x - 2}{x^2 + 8x + 7}$

   d) $\dfrac{x + 4}{x^2 - 121} - \dfrac{2x - 1}{x^2 + 8x - 33}$

B Connect and Apply

For help with question 10, refer to Example 5.

10. Alice is in a 20-km running race. She always runs the first half at an average speed of 2 km/h faster than the second half.

a) Let x represent her speed in the first half. Determine a simplified expression in terms of x for the total time needed for the race.

b) If Alice runs the first half at 10 km/h, how long will it take her to run the race?

11. Binomial expressions can differ by a factor of -1. Factor -1 from one of the denominators to identify the common denominator. Then, simplify each expression and state the restrictions.

a) $\dfrac{1}{x - 2} - \dfrac{1}{2 - x}$ **b)** $\dfrac{2x - 7}{x - 3} + \dfrac{x - 9}{3 - x}$

c) $\dfrac{a + 1}{5 - 2a} - \dfrac{a - 4}{2a - 5}$ **d)** $\dfrac{2b + 3}{4b - 1} + \dfrac{b + 6}{1 - 4b}$

12. An open-topped box is to be created from a 100-cm by 80-cm piece of cardboard by cutting out a square of side length x from each corner.

Reasoning and Proving

Representing   Selecting Tools

Problem Solving

Connecting   Reflecting

Communicating

a) Express the volume of the box as a function of x.

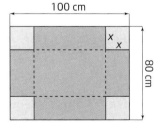

100 cm

x
x

80 cm

b) Express the surface area of the open-topped box as a function of x.

c) Write a simplified expression for the ratio of the volume of the box to its surface area.

d) Based on your answer in part c), what are the restrictions on x? What are the restrictions in the context?

13. Resistors are components found on most circuit boards and in most electronic devices. Since resistors do not come in every size, they have to be arranged in various ways to get the needed resistance. When three resistors are in parallel, then the total resistance, R_T, can be calculated using the equation $\dfrac{1}{R_T} = \dfrac{1}{R_1} + \dfrac{1}{R_2} + \dfrac{1}{R_3}$, where each of the resistances is in ohms (Ω).

a) Determine an expression for the total resistance, R_T.

b) Determine an expression for the total resistance if $R_1 = R_2 = R_3$.

c) Determine an expression for the total resistance if $R_1 = 2R_2 = 6R_3$.

14. Consider a cylinder of height h and radius r.

a) Determine the ratio of the volume of the cylinder to its surface area.

b) What restrictions are there on r and h?

r

h

15. Olivia can swim at an average rate of v metres per second in still water. She has two races coming up, one in a lake with no current and the other in a river with a current of 0.5 m/s. Each race is 800 m, but in the river race she swims the first half against the current and the second half with the current.

Reasoning and Proving

Representing   Selecting Tools

Problem Solving

Connecting   Reflecting

Communicating

a) Determine an expression for the time for Olivia to complete the lake swim.

b) Determine an expression for the time for Olivia to complete the river swim.

c) Olivia thinks that if she swims each race exactly the same and the current either slows her down or speeds her up by 0.5 m/s, both races will take the same amount of time. Is she correct? Explain.

16. Use Technology

a) Use graphing technology to graph
$$f(x) = \frac{1}{x + 2} + \frac{1}{x - 2}.$$

b) Rewrite the function using a common denominator. Then, graph the rewritten function.

c) Compare the graphs. Identify how the restrictions affect the graph.

✓ **Achievement Check**

17. a) Simplify the expressions for A and B, where $A = \dfrac{x + 4}{x^2 + 9x + 20}$

and $B = \dfrac{3x^2 - 9x}{x^2 + 3x - 18}$. State the restrictions.

b) Are the two expressions equivalent? Justify your answer.

c) Write another expression that appears to be equivalent to each expression in part a).

d) Determine $A + B$, AB, and $B \div A$.

C Extend

18. Archimedes of Syracuse (287−212 BCE) studied many things. One was the relationship between a cylinder and a sphere. In particular, he looked at the situation where the sphere just fits inside the cylinder so that they have the same radius and the height of the cylinder equals the diameter of the sphere.

a) Determine the ratio of the volume of the sphere to the volume of the cylinder in this situation.

b) Determine the ratio of the surface area of the sphere to the surface area of the cylinder in this situation.

c) What seems to be true about your answers from parts a) and b)?

Connections

Archimedes was so fond of the sphere and cylinder relationship that he had the image of a sphere inscribed in a cylinder engraved on his tombstone.

19. Simplify the expression and state any restrictions.
$$\frac{x + 8}{2x^2 + 9x + 10} - \frac{x^2 + 13x + 40}{2x^2 - x - 15}$$
$$\div \frac{x^2 + 10x + 16}{x^2 - 9}$$

20. a) Evaluate the expression

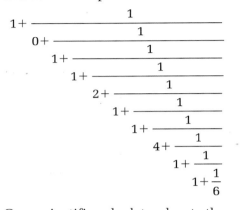
$$1 + \cfrac{1}{0 + \cfrac{1}{1 + \cfrac{1}{1 + \cfrac{1}{2 + \cfrac{1}{1 + \cfrac{1}{1 + \cfrac{1}{4 + \cfrac{1}{1 + \cfrac{1}{1 + \frac{1}{6}}}}}}}}}}$$

b) On a scientific calculator, locate the e^x button and enter e^1. Compare your answer for part a) to the constant e.

c) The pattern shown in part a) continues on forever. What are the next three steps in this pattern? How do they affect your comparison from part b)?

21. Math Contest When n is divided by 4, the remainder is 3. When $6n$ is divided by 4, the remainder is

A 1   **B** 2   **C** 3   **D** 0

22. Math Contest The sum of the roots of
$(x^2 + 4x + 3)(x^2 + 3x - 10)$
  $- (8x^2 - 8x - 16) = 0$ is

A −7   **B** −6   **C** 6   **D** 8

23. Math Contest Given
$$f(x) = \frac{36}{x - 2} + \frac{35}{x - 1},$$ what is the smallest integral value of x that gives an integral value of $f(x)$?

24. Math Contest Given
$$\frac{2x}{x - 3} = \frac{3y}{y - 4} = \frac{4z}{z - 5} = 5, \text{ then}$$
$x + y + z$ is

A 40   **B** −40   **C** 200   **D** −200

Horizontal and Vertical Translations of Functions

When a video game developer is designing a game, she might have several objects displayed on the computer screen that move from one place to another but do not change shape or orientation. In fact, the object can be said to "slide" around the screen.

In this section, you will consider how base functions "slide" around the Cartesian plane and the effect this has on their equations.

Investigate

What effect does translating have on the graph and equation of a function?

A: Graph Functions of the Form $g(x) = f(x) + c$

1. Clear any graphed functions and graph the following set of functions as **Y1**, **Y2**, and **Y3** on the same set of axes. Use a standard window.

   Set 1: $f(x) = x^2$ $g(x) = x^2 + 2$ $h(x) = x^2 - 2$

   You may want to make each line a different thickness to distinguish them.

   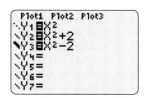 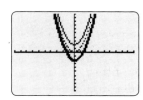

2. Compare the equations of $g(x)$ and $h(x)$ to the equation of $f(x)$. Compare the graphs of $g(x)$ and $h(x)$ to the graph of $f(x)$.

3. Repeat steps 1 and 2 with each set of functions.

   Set 2: $f(x) = \sqrt{x}$ $g(x) = \sqrt{x} + 2$ $h(x) = \sqrt{x} - 2$

   Set 3: $f(x) = \frac{1}{x}$ $g(x) = \frac{1}{x} + 2$ $h(x) = \frac{1}{x} - 2$

4. **Reflect** Describe how the value of c in $g(x) = f(x) + c$ changes the graph of $f(x)$.

Tools
- graphing calculator

Technology **Tip**

You can change the appearance of a line on a graphing calculator.

- Press (Y=). Cursor left to the slanted line beside the equation.

- Press (ENTER) repeatedly to choose one of the seven options.

- Press (GRAPH).

B: Graph Functions of the Form $g(x) = f(x - d)$

1. Clear any graphed functions and graph the following set of functions as **Y1**, **Y2**, and **Y3** on the same set of axes. Use a standard window.

   Set 1: $f(x) = x^2$ $g(x) = (x + 2)^2$ $h(x) = (x - 2)^2$

   You may want to make each line a different thickness to distinguish them.

2. Compare the equations of $g(x)$ and $h(x)$ to the equation of $f(x)$. Compare the graphs of $g(x)$ and $h(x)$ to the graph of $f(x)$.

3. Repeat steps 1 and 2 with each set of functions.

   Set 2: $f(x) = \sqrt{x}$ $g(x) = \sqrt{x + 2}$ $h(x) = \sqrt{x - 2}$

   Set 3: $f(x) = \dfrac{1}{x}$ $g(x) = \dfrac{1}{x + 2}$ $h(x) = \dfrac{1}{x - 2}$

4. **Reflect** Describe how the value of d in $g(x) = f(x - d)$ changes the graph of $f(x)$.

5. **Reflect** Compare the **transformations** on the functions in parts A and B. Describe any similarities and differences.

transformation

- a change made to a figure or a relation such that the figure or the graph of the relation is shifted or changed in shape
- Translations, stretches, and reflections are types of transformations.

translation

- a transformation that results in a shift of the original figure without changing its shape

Transformations that shift a function up, down, right, or left without affecting the shape are called **translations**.

The graph of the function $g(x) = f(x) + c$ is a vertical translation of the graph of $f(x)$ by c units. If c is positive, the graph moves up c units. If c is negative, the graph moves down c units.

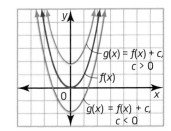

The graph of the function $g(x) = f(x - d)$ is a horizontal translation of the graph of $f(x)$ by d units. If d is positive, the graph moves to the right d units. If d is negative, the graph moves to the left d units.

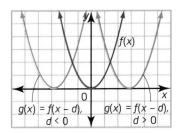

Example 1

Graph Translations by Using Points

Given the graph of a function $f(x)$, sketch the graph of $g(x)$ by determining **image points** for any original key points.

image point

- any point that has been transformed from a point on the original figure or graph

a) $g(x) = f(x) + 4$

b) $g(x) = f(x + 4)$

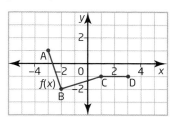

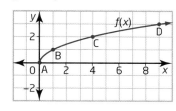

Solution

a) Since $y = f(x)$, the function $g(x) = f(x) + 4$ can be rewritten as $g(x) = y + 4$.

The corresponding transformation is a vertical translation of 4 units up. For each point, only the value of the y-coordinate changes, as shown in the table.

$f(x)$: $(x, f(x))$	$g(x)$: $(x, f(x) + 4)$
A(−3, 1)	A′(−3, 1 + 4) = (−3, 5)
B(−2, −2)	B′(−2, −2 + 4) = (−2, 2)
C(1, −1)	C′(1, −1 + 4) = (1, 3)
D(3, −1)	D′(3, −1 + 4) = (3, 3)

It is common notation to use a prime (′) next to each letter representing an image point.

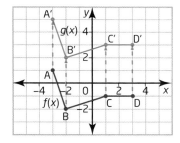

b) Write $g(x) = f(x + 4)$ as $g(x) = f(x − (−4))$. Since $d = −4$, each point is translated 4 units to the left. Subtract 4 from the x-coordinate of each point. The y-coordinate does not change.

Create a table using the key points.

$f(x)$: $(x, f(x))$	$g(x)$: $(x − 4, f(x))$
A(0, 0)	A′(0 − 4, 0) = (−4, 0)
B(1, 1)	B′(1 − 4, 1) = (−3, 1)
C(4, 2)	C′(4 − 4, 2) = (0, 2)
D(9, 3)	D′(9 − 4, 3) = (5, 3)

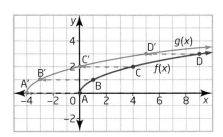

To ensure an accurate sketch of a transformed function, translate key points on the base function first and then draw a smooth curve through the new points.

Example 2

Describe Transformations

For each function $g(x)$, describe the transformation from a base function of $f(x) = x$, $f(x) = x^2$, $f(x) = \sqrt{x}$, or $f(x) = \frac{1}{x}$, first using function notation and then using words. Transform the graph of $f(x)$ to sketch the graph of $g(x)$ and then state the domain and range of each function.

a) $g(x) = (x + 5)^2 + 1$

b) $g(x) = \dfrac{1}{x + 3} - 7$

c) $g(x) = \sqrt{x - 2} + 4$

Solution

a) The base function is $f(x) = x^2$. By comparison,

$$g(x) = (x + 5)^2 + 1$$
$$= f(x + 5) + 1$$

This is a horizontal translation of 5 units to the left ($d = -5$) and a vertical translation of 1 unit up ($c = 1$). To help with the sketch, start with the vertex $(0, 0)$ from $f(x)$ and translate it to the point $(0 - 5, 0 + 1) = (-5, 1)$.

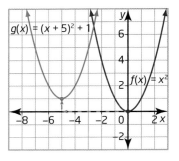

For $f(x)$, the domain is $\{x \in \mathbb{R}\}$ and the range is $\{y \in \mathbb{R}, y \geq 0\}$.

For $g(x)$, the domain is $\{x \in \mathbb{R}\}$ and the range is $\{y \in \mathbb{R}, y \geq 1\}$.

b) The base function is $f(x) = \frac{1}{x}$. By comparison,

$$g(x) = \dfrac{1}{x + 3} - 7$$
$$= f(x + 3) - 7$$

This is a horizontal translation of 3 units to the left ($d = -3$) and a vertical translation of 7 units down ($c = -7$). To help with the sketch, start with the point $(1, 1)$ from $f(x)$ and translate it to the point $(1 - 3, 1 - 7) = (-2, -6)$. Similarly, the point $(-1, -1)$ becomes $(-4, -8)$. The base function has asymptotes at $x = 0$ and $y = 0$, so the translated function will have asymptotes at $x = -3$ and $y = -7$.

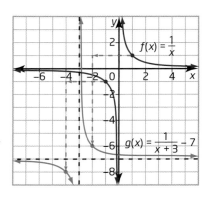

For $f(x)$, the domain is $\{x \in \mathbb{R}, x \neq 0\}$ and the range is $\{y \in \mathbb{R}, y \neq 0\}$.

For $g(x)$, the domain is $\{x \in \mathbb{R}, x \neq -3\}$ and the range is $\{y \in \mathbb{R}, y \neq -7\}$.

c) The base function is $f(x) = \sqrt{x}$. By comparison,

$$g(x) = \sqrt{x - 2} + 4$$
$$\qquad = f(x - 2) + 4$$

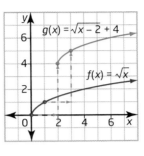

This is a horizontal translation of 2 units to the right ($d = 2$) and a vertical translation of 4 units up ($c = 4$). To help with the sketch, start with the point $(0, 0)$ from $f(x)$ and translate it to the point $(0 + 2, 0 + 4) = (2, 4)$. Similarly, the point $(1, 1)$ becomes $(3, 5)$.

For $f(x)$, the domain is $\{x \in \mathbb{R}, x \geq 0\}$ and the range is $\{y \in \mathbb{R}, y \geq 0\}$.

For $g(x)$, the domain is $\{x \in \mathbb{R}, x \geq 2\}$ and the range is $\{y \in \mathbb{R}, y \geq 4\}$.

Key Concepts

- Translations are transformations that cause functions to shift from one place to another without changing shape.

- The graph of $g(x) = f(x) + c$ is a vertical translation of the graph of $f(x)$ by c units. If $c > 0$, the graph moves up c units. If $c < 0$, the graph moves down c units.

- The graph of $g(x) = f(x - d)$ is a horizontal translation of the graph of $f(x)$ by d units. If $d > 0$, the graph moves to the right d units. If $d < 0$, the graph moves to the left d units.

- A sketch of the graph of any transformed function can be created by transforming the related base function.

- In general, the domain and range of a function of the form $g(x) = f(x - d) + c$ can be determined by adding the d-value and the c-value to restrictions on the domain and range, respectively, of the base function.

Communicate Your Understanding

C1 Given the graph of the function $f(x)$, describe how you would sketch the graph of $g(x) = f(x + 2) - 3$.

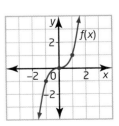

C2 Explain why the graph of $g(x) = f(x) + c$ translates the graph of $f(x)$ vertically and not horizontally.

C3 Explain why the graph of $g(x) = f(x - d)$ translates the graph of $f(x)$ to the right and not to the left for $d > 0$.

A Practise

For help with questions 1 to 5, refer to Example 1.

1. a) Copy and complete the table of values.

x	$f(x) = \sqrt{x}$	$r(x) = f(x) + 7$	$s(x) = f(x - 1)$
0			
1			
4			
9			

b) Use the points to graph all three functions on the same set of axes.

c) Explain how the points of the translated functions relate to the actual transformations.

2. Copy the graph of $f(x)$. Apply each transformation by determining the image points A′, B′, C′, D′, E′, and F′.

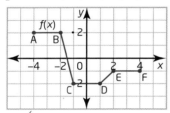

a) $b(x) = f(x) + 5$

b) $g(x) = f(x) - 7$

c) $h(x) = f(x - 8)$

d) $m(x) = f(x + 6)$

3. Copy the graph of $f(x)$ in question 2. Apply each transformation by determining the image points A′, B′, C′, D′, E′, and F′.

a) $n(x) = f(x - 3) + 6$

b) $r(x) = f(x - 2) - 10$

c) $s(x) = f(x + 5) + 4$

d) $t(x) = f(x + 12) - 3$

4. Copy the graph of $f(x)$. Apply each transformation by determining the image points A′, B′, C′, and D′.

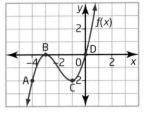

a) $b(x) = f(x) + 3$

b) $g(x) = f(x) - 6$

c) $h(x) = f(x - 4)$

d) $n(x) = f(x + 7)$

5. Copy the graph of $f(x)$ in question 4. Apply each transformation by determining the image points A′, B′, C′, and D′.

a) $m(x) = f(x - 2) + 10$

b) $r(x) = f(x - 5) - 9$

c) $s(x) = f(x + 8) + 9$

d) $t(x) = f(x + 1) - 11$

For help with questions 6 to 8, refer to Example 2.

6. For each function $g(x)$, identify the base function as one of $f(x) = x$, $f(x) = x^2$, $f(x) = \sqrt{x}$, and $f(x) = \frac{1}{x}$ and describe the transformation first in the form $y = f(x - d) + c$ and then in words. Transform the graph of $f(x)$ to sketch the graph of $g(x)$ and then state the domain and range of each function.

a) $g(x) = x - 9$

b) $g(x) = x + 12$

c) $g(x) = x^2 + 8$

d) $g(x) = \sqrt{x} - 12$

e) $g(x) = (x - 6)^2$

f) $g(x) = \frac{1}{x} + 5$

g) $g(x) = \sqrt{x + 10}$

h) $g(x) = \frac{1}{x - 2}$

i) $g(x) = \sqrt{x - 9} - 5$ **j)** $g(x) = \frac{1}{x + 3} - 8$

7. Explain why there is more than one possible answer for question 6a) and b) when describing the transformations.

8. Use words and function notation to describe the transformation that can be applied to the graph of $f(x)$ to obtain the graph of $g(x)$. State the domain and range of each function.

Reasoning and Proving

Representing · Selecting Tools

Problem Solving

Connecting · Reflecting

Communicating

a)

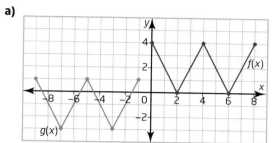

b)

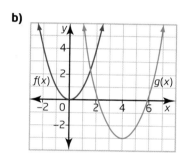

c)

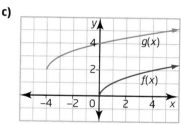

d)

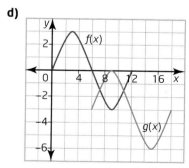

9. The graph of $f(x) = x^2$ is transformed to the graph of $g(x) = f(x + 8) + 12$.

Reasoning and Proving

Representing · Selecting Tools

Problem Solving

Connecting · Reflecting

Communicating

a) Describe the two translations represented by this transformation.

b) Determine three points on the base function. Horizontally translate and then vertically translate the points to determine the image points on $g(x)$.

c) Start with your original points, but this time reverse the order of your translations. Determine whether the order of the translations is important.

d) Confirm your result from parts b) and c) by graphing.

e) Repeat parts a) to d) with a different base function.

10. Given $f(x) = x$, determine if there is a single horizontal translation that has the same effect as a single vertical translation. Justify your answer algebraically (with equations), numerically (with points), and graphically (with sketches).

11. Use the base function $f(x) = x$. Write the equation for each transformed function.

a) $n(x) = f(x - 4) - 6$

b) $r(x) = f(x + 2) + 9$

c) $s(x) = f(x + 6) - 7$

d) $t(x) = f(x - 11) + 4$

12. Repeat question 11 using the base function $f(x) = x^2$.

13. Repeat question 11 using the base function $f(x) = \sqrt{x}$.

14. Repeat question 11 using the base function $f(x) = \frac{1}{x}$. State any restrictions on the variable.

15. Chapter Problem The traffic safety bureau receives data regarding the acceleration of a prototype electric sports car. It can accelerate from 0 to 100 km/h in about 4 s. Its position, d, in metres, at any time t, in seconds, is given by $d(t) = 3.5t^2$. Matthew is comparing the prototype to a hybrid electric car, which has its position given by $d(t) = 1.4t^2$.

a) In a race between the two cars, the hybrid is given a head start. Where would the hybrid have to start so that after 4 s of acceleration, both cars are in the same position?

b) Verify your solution by graphing.

16. The cost to produce x units of a product can be modelled by the function $c(x) = \sqrt{x} + 500$.

Reasoning and Proving

Representing   Selecting Tools

Problem Solving

Connecting   Reflecting

Communicating

a) State and interpret the domain and range of the cost function.

b) Suppose that the cost to make 10 prototype units is to be included in the cost. Write a new function representing the cost of this product.

c) What type of transformation does the change in part b) represent?

d) How does the transformation in part b) affect the domain and range?

C **Extend**

17. Use Technology In this section, you dealt with static translations. In computer animation, dynamic translations are used. Open *The Geometer's Sketchpad®*. Go to the *Functions 11* page on the McGraw-Hill Ryerson Web site and follow the links to Section 2.3. Download the file **2.3_Animation.gsp**. In this sketch, you will be able to change a parameter t that represents time by moving a sliding point.

a) Study the form of the function $g(x)$. What similarities and differences are there compared to a translated function of the form $g(x) = f(x - d) + c$?

b) What happens when you move the slider t?

c) How does changing the parameter function $P(x)$ affect the motion of the base function $f(x)$? Use the following functions to investigate this.

  i) $P(x) = x^2$

  ii) $P(x) = \sqrt{x}$

  iii) $P(x) = \dfrac{1}{x}$

d) How could you change the translated function $g(x)$ so that when you move the slider t the translation is only vertical? horizontal?

e) Click on the **Link to Butterfly** button and move the slider t. Here you can see a very rudimentary example of computer animation. Repeat parts c) and d) for this sketch.

18. Math Contest The roots of $x^3 - 2x^2 - 5x + 6 = 0$ are 3, -2, and 1. The sum of the roots of $(x + 2)^3 - 2(x + 2)^2 - 5(x + 2) + 6 = 0$ is

A 2   **B** 8   **C** 0   **D** -4

19. Math Contest The parabola $y = 2x^2$ is translated to a new parabola with x-intercepts 4 and -3. The y-intercept of the new parabola is

A 12   **B** -12 **C** -0.5 **D** -24

20. Math Contest A lattice point is a point on the Cartesian plane where both coordinates are integers. How many lattice points are there on the line $2x + 3y - 600 = 0$, where $x > 0$ and $y > 0$?

A 98   **B** 99   **C** 100   **D** 200

Reflections of Functions

Teaz Apparel is a local store that sells athletic clothing. The word *Teaz* in their logo is the same whether viewed right-side up or upside down. Think of how **reflections** could be used to make this logo.

reflection

- a transformation in which a figure is reflected over a reflection line

Investigate

Tools

- graphing calculator

How can you determine the line of reflection?

1. Press (Y=) and enter the function $f(x) = \sqrt{x}$ for **Y1**. Press (ZOOM) and select **6:ZStandard** to observe the graph of the function.

2. Enter the function $f(-x) = \sqrt{-x}$ as **Y2**. Press (GRAPH) to observe the graph of the new function.

3. **Reflect** Compare the graph of **Y2** to the graph of **Y1**. In what line can the graph of **Y1** be reflected to create the graph of **Y2**?

4. Enter the function $-f(x) = -$**Y1** as **Y3**. Press (GRAPH) to observe the graph of the new function.

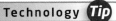

5. **Reflect** Compare the graph of **Y3** to to the graph of **Y1**. In what line can the graph of **Y1** be reflected to create the graph of **Y3**?

6. Enter the function $-f(-x) = -$**Y2** as **Y4**. Press (GRAPH) to observe the graph of the new function.

7. **Reflect** Compare the graph of **Y4** to the graph of **Y1**. In what line(s) can the graph of **Y1** be reflected to create the graph of **Y4**? Compare the graph of **Y4** to the graph of **Y2**. In what line(s) can the graph of **Y2** be reflected to create the graph of **Y4**?

Technology Tip

To enter an existing function in the **Y=** editor, like **Y1**, press (VARS), cursor over to the **Y-VARS** menu, select **1:Function…**, and then select **1:Y1**.

The graph of $g(x) = f(-x)$ is a reflection of the graph of $f(x)$ in the y-axis.

The graph of $h(x) = -f(x)$ is a reflection of the graph of $f(x)$ in the x-axis.

The graph of $q(x) = -f(-x)$ is a reflection of the graph of $f(x)$ in the y-axis and the x-axis.

Example 1

Graph Reflections

Given the function $f(x) = \sqrt{x} + 2$, write an equation to represent each of the following. Then, sketch each graph and state the domain and range of each function.

a) $h(x)$: a reflection in the y-axis

b) $r(x)$: a reflection in the x-axis

c) $s(x)$: a reflection in the y-axis and then a reflection in the x-axis

Solution

a) $h(x) = f(-x)$
$$= \sqrt{-x} + 2$$

Use key points to sketch the graph of $f(x)$.

For a reflection in the y-axis, each image point will be an equal distance from the y-axis but on the other side. The image points will have the same y-coordinates as the original key points but their x-coordinates will have opposite signs. Once the points are plotted, you can sketch the graph of $h(x)$.

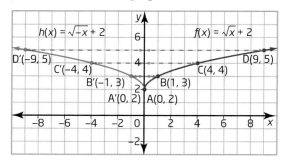

For $f(x)$, the domain is $\{x \in \mathbb{R}, x \geq 0\}$ and the range is $\{y \in \mathbb{R}, y \geq 2\}$.

For $h(x)$, the domain is $\{x \in \mathbb{R}, x \leq 0\}$ and the range is $\{y \in \mathbb{R}, y \geq 2\}$.

b) $r(x) = -f(x)$
$$= -(\sqrt{x} + 2)$$
$$= -\sqrt{x} - 2$$

For a reflection in the x-axis, each image point will be an equal distance from the x-axis but on the other side. The image points will have the same x-coordinates as the key points but their y-coordinates will have opposite signs.

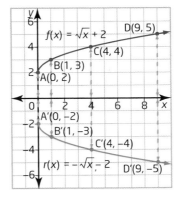

For $f(x)$, the domain is $\{x \in \mathbb{R}, x \geq 0\}$ and the range is $\{y \in \mathbb{R}, y \geq 2\}$.

For $r(x)$, the domain is $\{x \in \mathbb{R}, x \geq 0\}$ and the range is $\{y \in \mathbb{R}, y \leq -2\}$.

c) $s(x) = -f(-x)$

$\quad = -\left(\sqrt{-x} + 2\right)$

$\quad = -\sqrt{-x} - 2$

There are two reflections, first in the y-axis and then in the x-axis. Start with the resulting points from part a), which were reflected in the y-axis, and reflect these in the x-axis. For each image point, first the x-coordinate and then the y-coordinate will have opposite signs.

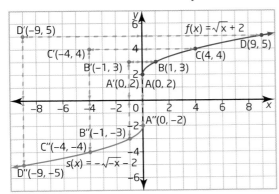

For a reflection in both the y-axis and x-axis, the order of the reflections is not important.

For $f(x)$, the domain is $\{x \in \mathbb{R}, x \geq 0\}$ and the range is $\{y \in \mathbb{R}, y \geq 2\}$.

For $s(x)$, the domain is $\{x \in \mathbb{R}, x \leq 0\}$ and the range is $\{y \in \mathbb{R}, y \leq -2\}$.

Using a TI-Nspire™ CAS graphing calculator, you can view the graph of the function $f(x) = \sqrt{x} + 2$ and the resulting graphs of the three reflections.

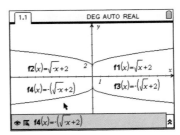

A reflection of a point (x, y) in the y-axis becomes $(-x, y)$. So, any point that lies on the y-axis will not change under this reflection because its x-coordinate is 0.

A reflection of a point (x, y) in the x-axis becomes $(x, -y)$. So, any point that lies on the x-axis will not change under this reflection because its y-coordinate is 0.

Points that do not change under a transformation are said to be invariant.

Example 2

Describe Reflections

For each graph, describe the reflection that transforms $f(x)$ into $g(x)$.

a)

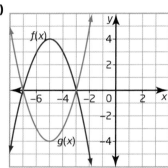

b)

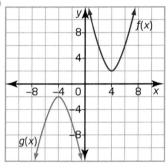

Solution

a) The key points $(-6, 3)$, $(-5, 4)$, and $(-4, 3)$ on the graph of $f(x)$ have image points on the graph of $g(x)$ that are equidistant but on the other side of the x-axis: $(-6, -3)$, $(-5, -4)$, and $(-4, -3)$. This indicates a reflection in the x-axis.

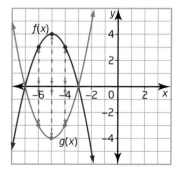

Notice that the two points on the x-axis, $(-7, 0)$ and $(-3, 0)$, are invariant.

b) Reflecting the key points $(2, 6)$, $(4, 2)$, and $(6, 6)$ on the graph of $f(x)$ in the x-axis gives $(2, -6)$, $(4, -2)$, and $(6, -6)$, which are not on $g(x)$. Similar results occur if the points are reflected in the y-axis. However, if the points $(2, -6)$, $(4, -2)$, and $(6, -6)$ are reflected in the y-axis, the image points $(-2, -6)$, $(-4, -2)$, and $(-6, -6)$ are on the graph of $g(x)$. The function $g(x)$ is a reflection of $f(x)$ in both axes.

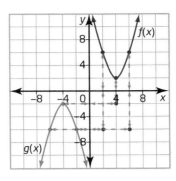

Key Concepts

Reflection	Numerical Representation	Graphical Representation	Algebraic Representation
$y = f(-x)$	A point (x, y) becomes $(-x, y)$.	The graph is reflected in the y-axis.	Replace x with $-x$ in the expression.
$y = -f(x)$	A point (x, y) becomes $(x, -y)$.	The graph is reflected in the x-axis.	Multiply the entire expression by -1.
$y = -f(-x)$	A point (x, y) becomes $(-x, -y)$.	The graph is reflected in one axis and then the other.	First replace x with $-x$ in the expression and then multiply the entire expression by -1.

Communicate Your Understanding

C1 Consider the functions $f(x) = x$, $f(x) = x^2$, $f(x) = \frac{1}{x}$, and $f(x) = \sqrt{x}$. Describe any reflections that leave any of these functions unchanged. Explain.

C2 Determine whether $g(x)$ could be a reflection of $f(x)$. If so, describe the reflection.

a)

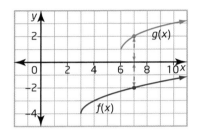

b)

$f(x)$	$g(x)$
(3, 8)	(8, –3)
(5, 12)	(12, –5)
(7, 16)	(16, –7)
(9, 20)	(20, –9)

c) $f(x) = 3(x + 3)^2 + 10$ and $g(x) = 3x^2 - 18x + 37$

C3 A student claims that the graph of $g(x)$ is a reflection of the graph of $f(x)$ in the x-axis because two points, one on each graph, are equidistant from the x-axis. Is the student correct? Explain your answer.

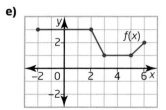

A Practise

For help with questions 1 to 4, refer to Example 1.

1. Copy each graph of $f(x)$ and sketch its reflection in the x-axis, $g(x)$. Then, state the domain and range of each function.

a)

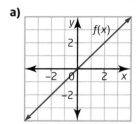

b)

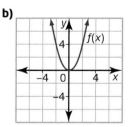

c)

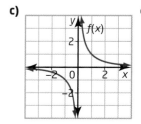

d)

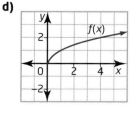

e)

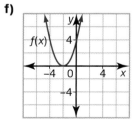

f)

2. For each function $f(x)$ in question 1, sketch the graph of its reflection in the y-axis, $h(x)$. Then, state the domain and range of each function.

3. For each function $f(x)$ in question 1, sketch the graph of the function $k(x) = -f(-x)$. Then, state the domain and range of each function.

4. For each function $f(x)$, determine the equation for $g(x)$.

  a) $f(x) = \sqrt{x + 4} - 4$, $g(x) = -f(x)$

  b) $f(x) = (x + 1)^2 - 4$, $g(x) = f(-x)$

  c) $f(x) = (x - 5)^2 + 9$, $g(x) = -f(-x)$

  d) $f(x) = \dfrac{1}{x - 3} - 6$, $g(x) = -f(-x)$

  e) $f(x) = -\sqrt{x - 2} + 5$, $g(x) = f(-x)$

  f) $f(x) = \sqrt{x + 9} - 1$, $g(x) = -f(-x)$

For help with question 5, refer to Example 2.

5. For each graph, describe the reflection that transforms $f(x)$ into $g(x)$.

a)

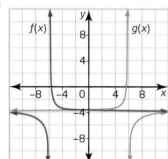

b)

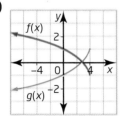

c)

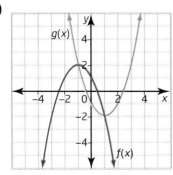

B   Connect and Apply

6. Look at the logo for Teaz Apparel at the beginning of this section. Identify the type of reflection(s) in this logo.

7. Describe any patterns that you notice about how the domain and range are affected by reflections in the x- and y-axes. Use specific examples to support your answer.

8. Use Technology
Use graphing technology for this question.

  a) Determine the invariant points of the function $f(x) = (x - 2)^2 - 9$ when it is reflected in the

    i) x-axis

    ii) y-axis

  b) Give a function that might have an invariant point under the reflection $-f(-x)$. Explain your answer.

9. Determine algebraically whether $g(x)$ is a reflection of $f(x)$ in each case. Verify your answer by graphing.

  a) $f(x) = x^2$, $g(x) = (-x)^2$

  b) $f(x) = \sqrt{x}$, $g(x) = \sqrt{-x}$

  c) $f(x) = \dfrac{1}{x}$, $g(x) = \dfrac{-1}{x}$

  d) $f(x) = (x + 5)^2 + 4$, $g(x) = -(x + 5)^2 - 4$

  e) $f(x) = \sqrt{x - 10} + 3$, $g(x) = -\sqrt{x - 10} + 3$

  f) $f(x) = \dfrac{1}{x + 7}$, $g(x) = \dfrac{1}{-x + 7}$

10. Use Technology Use graphing software to create a logo design using functions and reflections.

11. Use Technology The function $g(x) = -f(-x)$ is also known as a reflection in the origin of the function $f(x)$.

a) Open *The Geometer's Sketchpad®*. Go to the *Functions 11* page on the McGraw-Hill Ryerson Web site and follow the links to Section 2.4. Use the file **Reflect.gsp** to determine what reflection in a point means physically. Describe how you would reflect a function in the origin.

b) Use your method to sketch the graph of the function shown after it is reflected in the origin.

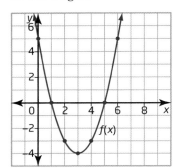

12. Determine whether there are translations and reflections that have equal effects.

a) Graph the function $f(x) = (x - 4)^2$.

b) Graph the reflection of $f(x)$ in the y-axis.

c) Determine a translation that can be applied to $f(x)$ that has the same effect as the reflection in part b).

d) Verify algebraically that the transformations in parts b) and c) are the same.

e) Predict if the same would be true for reflections in the x-axis. Explain.

f) Would the conclusion from steps b) to e) work for any other type of function? Explain.

✓ **Achievement Check**

13. a) State the base function that corresponds to $f(x) = \sqrt{x + 2} + 3$ and describe the transformations that are applied to the base function to obtain $f(x)$.

b) Write the equations for $-f(x)$, $f(-x)$, and $-f(-x)$. Describe the transformation(s) represented by each equation.

c) Sketch the graphs of all four functions on the same set of axes.

d) State the domain and range of each function. Describe any similarities or differences.

e) Are any points invariant? Explain.

C Extend

14. Sketch the graph of $f(x) = \sqrt{x}$ reflected in each line.

a) $x = 4$

b) $y = x$

15. Math Contest The point (m, n) is reflected in the x-axis and then the image is reflected in the y-axis. What is the y-intercept of the line joining the original point and the final reflected point?

16. Math Contest The number of multiples of 2 or 3 but not 6 in the first $6n$ natural numbers is

A $4n$ **B** $6n$ **C** $2n$ **D** $3n$

17. Math Contest Show that $n^3 - n$ is always divisible by 6.

18. Math Contest State the domain and the range of $f(x) = \dfrac{3x}{(x - 3)(x + 2)}$.

19. Math Contest A 4-cm by 4-cm by 4-cm cube is painted red and then sliced into 1-cm by 1-cm by 1-cm cubes. The number of smaller cubes with two sides painted red is

A 37   **B** 27   **C** 24   **D** 0

Stretches of Functions

In Section 2.3, you learned that the graph of a function or shape can be transformed without changing its shape by using a translation. However, in the case of real animation, that movement is usually combined with shape, colour, and orientation changes.

In this section, you will explore how you can control the shape of a function or object.

Investigate

Tools

• graphing calculator

How does stretching the graph of a function affect its shape?

A: Graph Functions of the Form $g(x) = af(x)$

1. Clear any graphed functions and graph the following functions as **Y1**, **Y2**, and **Y3** on the same set of axes. Use a standard window.

   Set 1: $f(x) = x^2$ $\qquad$ $g(x) = 2x^2$ $\qquad$ $h(x) = 5x^2$

   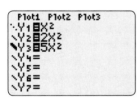 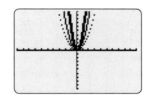

2. Compare the equations of $g(x)$ and $h(x)$ to the equation of $f(x)$. Compare the graphs of $g(x)$ and $h(x)$ to the graph of $f(x)$.

3. Repeat steps 1 and 2 with each set of functions.

   Set 2: $f(x) = \sqrt{x}$ $\qquad$ $g(x) = 2\sqrt{x}$ $\qquad$ $h(x) = 5\sqrt{x}$

   Set 3: $f(x) = \frac{1}{x}$ $\qquad$ $g(x) = 2\left(\frac{1}{x}\right)$ $\qquad$ $h(x) = 5\left(\frac{1}{x}\right)$

4. **Reflect**

   a) Describe how the value of a in $g(x) = af(x)$ changes the graph of $f(x)$.

   b) Are there any invariant points?

   c) How are the domain and range affected?

B: Graph Functions of the Form $g(x) = f(kx)$

1. Clear any graphed functions and graph the following functions as **Y1**, **Y2**, and **Y3** on the same set of axes. Use a standard window.

   Set 1: $f(x) = x^2$ $g(x) = \left(\dfrac{1}{2}x\right)^2$ $h(x) = \left(\dfrac{1}{5}x\right)^2$

2. Compare the equations of $g(x)$ and $h(x)$ to the equation of $f(x)$. Compare the graphs of $g(x)$ and $h(x)$ to the graph of $f(x)$.

3. Repeat steps 1 and 2 with each set of functions.

   Set 2: $f(x) = \sqrt{x}$ $g(x) = \sqrt{\dfrac{1}{2}x}$ $h(x) = \sqrt{\dfrac{1}{5}x}$

   Set 3: $f(x) = \dfrac{1}{x}$ $g(x) = \dfrac{1}{\left(\dfrac{1}{2}x\right)}$ $h(x) = \dfrac{1}{\left(\dfrac{1}{5}x\right)}$

4. **Reflect**

   a) Describe how the value of k in $g(x) = f(kx)$ changes the graph of $f(x)$.

   b) Are there any invariant points?

   c) How are the domain and range affected?

5. **Reflect** Compare the transformations on the functions in parts A and B. Describe any similarities and differences.

The graph of the function $g(x) = af(x)$, $a > 0$, is a vertical stretch or a vertical compression of the graph of $f(x)$ by a factor of a.

- If $a > 1$, the graph is a vertical stretch by a factor of a.
- If $0 < a < 1$, the graph is a vertical compression by a factor of a.

Any points on the x-axis are invariant.

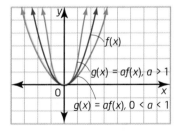

The graph of the function $g(x) = f(kx)$, $k > 0$, is a horizontal stretch or a horizontal compression of the graph of $f(x)$ by a factor of $\dfrac{1}{k}$.

- If $k > 1$, the graph is a horizontal compression by a factor of $\dfrac{1}{k}$.
- If $0 < k < 1$, the graph is a horizontal stretch by a factor of $\dfrac{1}{k}$.

Any points on the y-axis are invariant.

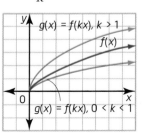

In general, when the graph of a function is elongated in one direction, the word **stretch** is used to describe the transformation. If it is shortened in one direction, the word **compression** is used to describe the transformation.

stretch

- a transformation that results in the distance from the *x*-axis of every point growing by a scale factor greater than 1 (vertical stretch) or the distance from the *y*-axis of every point growing by a scale factor greater than 1 (horizontal stretch)

compression

- a transformation that results in the distance from the *x*-axis of every point shrinking by a scale factor between 0 and 1 (vertical compression) or the distance from the *y*-axis of every point shrinking by a scale factor between 0 and 1 (horizontal compression)

Example 1

Graph Stretches and Compressions

Given the function $f(x) = \sqrt{x}$, write equations to represent $g(x)$ and $h(x)$ and describe the transformations. Then, transform the graph of $f(x)$ to sketch graphs of $g(x)$ and $h(x)$ and state the domain and range of the functions.

a) $g(x) = 2f(x)$ and $h(x) = \frac{1}{2}f(x)$

b) $g(x) = f(2x)$ and $h(x) = f\left(\frac{1}{2}x\right)$

Solution

a) $g(x) = 2f(x)$

$= 2\sqrt{x}$

Since $a = 2$, the graph of $g(x)$ is a vertical stretch by a factor of 2 of the graph of $f(x)$. Each *y*-value of $g(x)$ will be twice as far from the *x*-axis as the corresponding y-value of $f(x)$.

$h(x) = \frac{1}{2}f(x)$

$= \frac{1}{2}\sqrt{x}$

Since $a = \frac{1}{2}$, the graph of $h(x)$ is a vertical compression by a factor of $\frac{1}{2}$ of the graph of $f(x)$. Each *y*-value of $h(x)$ will be $\frac{1}{2}$ as far from the *x*-axis as the corresponding *y*-value of $f(x)$.

x	$f(x) = \sqrt{x}$	$g(x) = 2\sqrt{x}$	$h(x) = \frac{1}{2}\sqrt{x}$
0	0	0	0
1	1	2	$\frac{1}{2}$
4	2	4	1
9	3	6	$\frac{3}{2}$

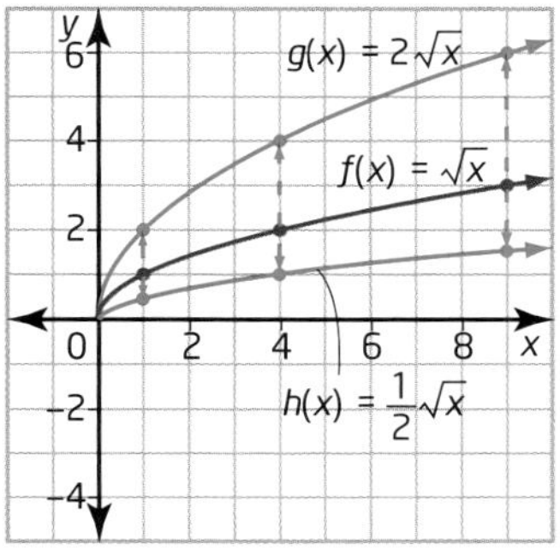

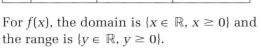

For $f(x)$, the domain is $\{x \in \mathbb{R}, x \geq 0\}$ and the range is $\{y \in \mathbb{R}, y \geq 0\}$.

For $g(x)$, the domain is $\{x \in \mathbb{R}, x \geq 0\}$ and the range is $\{y \in \mathbb{R}, y \geq 0\}$.

For $h(x)$, the domain is $\{x \in \mathbb{R}, x \geq 0\}$ and the range is $\{y \in \mathbb{R}, y \geq 0\}$.

b) $g(x) = f(2x)$

$\qquad = \sqrt{2x}$

Since $k = 2$, the graph of $g(x)$ is a horizontal compression by a factor of $\frac{1}{k}$, or $\frac{1}{2}$, of the graph of $f(x)$. Each x-value of $g(x)$ will be $\frac{1}{2}$ as far from the y-axis as the corresponding x-value of $f(x)$.

$h(x) = f\left(\frac{1}{2}x\right)$

$\qquad = \sqrt{\frac{1}{2}x}$

Since $k = \frac{1}{2}$, the graph of $h(x)$ is a horizontal stretch by a factor of $\frac{1}{k}$, or 2, of the graph of $f(x)$. Each x-value of $h(x)$ will be twice as far from the y-axis as the corresponding x-value of $f(x)$.

x	$f(x) = \sqrt{x}$	$g(x) = \sqrt{2x}$	$h(x) = \sqrt{\frac{1}{2}x}$
0	0	0	0
1	1	$\sqrt{2}$	$\sqrt{\frac{1}{2}}$
2	$\sqrt{2}$	2	1
4	2	$\sqrt{8}$	$\sqrt{2}$
8	$\sqrt{8}$	4	2

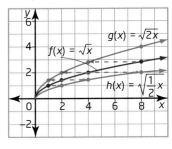

For $f(x)$, the domain is $\{x \in \mathbb{R}, x \geq 0\}$ and the range is $\{y \in \mathbb{R}, y \geq 0\}$.

For $g(x)$, the domain is $\{x \in \mathbb{R}, x \geq 0\}$ and the range is $\{y \in \mathbb{R}, y \geq 0\}$.

For $h(x)$, the domain is $\{x \in \mathbb{R}, x \geq 0\}$ and the range is $\{y \in \mathbb{R}, y \geq 0\}$.

Example 2

Describe Transformations of Given Equations

For each function $g(x)$, describe the transformation from a base function of $f(x) = x$, $f(x) = x^2$, $f(x) = \sqrt{x}$, or $f(x) = \frac{1}{x}$. Then, transform the graph of $f(x)$ to sketch the graph of $g(x)$.

a) $g(x) = 3x$

b) $g(x) = 4x^2$

Solution

a) The function $g(x) = 3x$ represents a transformation of the base function $f(x) = x$. The actual transformation can be described in two ways.

- Thinking of $g(x)$ as $3(x) = 3f(x)$ indicates that it is a vertical stretch by a factor of 3.

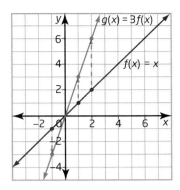

- Thinking of $g(x)$ as $(3x) = f(3x)$ indicates that it is a horizontal compression by a factor of $\frac{1}{3}$.

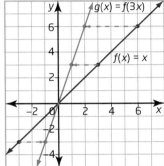

b) The function $g(x) = 4x^2$ represents a transformation of the base function $f(x) = x^2$. The actual transformation can be described in two ways.

- Thinking of $g(x)$ as $4(x^2) = 4f(x)$ indicates that it is a vertical stretch by a factor of 4.

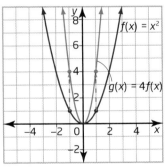

- Thinking of $g(x)$ as $(2x)^2 = f(2x)$ indicates that it is a horizontal compression by a factor of $\frac{1}{2}$.

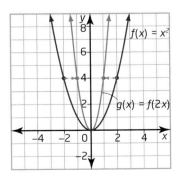

Example 3

Simple Harmonic Motion

A mass on a spring bobs up and down. The period is the amount of time that it takes for the mass to move from its starting position to the top, then to the bottom, and then back to its starting position. The period, T,

in seconds, is given by $T(m) = 2\pi\sqrt{\dfrac{m}{k}}$, where

m is the mass, in kilograms, and k is the spring constant, in newtons per metre (N/m).

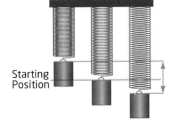

Starting Position

The Ideal Spring Company needs to show how each of their springs performs compared to the others.

a) Graph the period versus the mass for various spring constants.

b) How are the graphs of the Strong and Heavy Duty springs related to the graph of the Basic spring?

Spring Type	Spring Constant (N/m)
Basic	100
Strong	200
Heavy Duty	300

Solution

a)

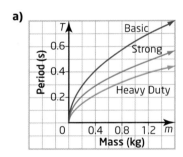

b) Consider the Basic spring to have a function given by $T(m) = 2\pi\sqrt{\dfrac{m}{k}}$ and that the spring constants for the Strong and Heavy Duty springs are multiples of the spring constant for the Basic spring.

Spring	Spring Constant	Formula	Comparison to Basic
Basic	k	$T(m) = 2\pi\sqrt{\dfrac{m}{k}}$	
Strong	$k_{strong} = 2k$	$T(m) = 2\pi\sqrt{\dfrac{m}{2k}} = 2\pi\sqrt{\dfrac{\frac{1}{2}m}{k}}$	This is a horizontal stretch by a factor of 2.
Heavy Duty	$k_{heavy\ duty} = 3k$	$T(m) = 2\pi\sqrt{\dfrac{m}{3k}} = 2\pi\sqrt{\dfrac{\frac{1}{3}m}{k}}$	This is a horizontal stretch by a factor of 3.

Key Concepts

- Stretches and compressions are transformations that cause functions to change shape.

- The graph of $g(x) = af(x)$, $a > 0$, is a vertical stretch or a vertical compression of the graph of $f(x)$ by a factor of a. If $a > 1$, the graph is vertically stretched by a factor of a. If $0 < a < 1$, the graph is vertically compressed by a factor of a.

- The graph of $g(x) = f(kx)$, $k > 0$, is a horizontal stretch or a horizontal compression of the graph of $f(x)$ by a factor of $\frac{1}{k}$. If $k > 1$, the graph is horizontally compressed by a factor of $\frac{1}{k}$. If $0 < k < 1$, the graph is horizontally stretched by a factor of $\frac{1}{k}$.

Communicate Your Understanding

C1 Given that the graph of $g(x)$ is a transformation of the graph of $f(x)$, describe how you know that it is a vertical stretch and not a translation.

C2 Explain why the graph of $g(x) = af(x)$, $a > 0$, stretches the graph of $f(x)$ vertically and not horizontally.

C3 Describe how the graph of the function $g(x) = \frac{3}{x}$ is related to the graph of the base function $f(x) = \frac{1}{x}$.

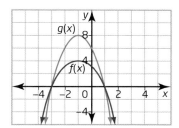

A Practise

For help with questions 1 to 3, refer to Example 1.

1. a) Copy and complete the table of values.

x	$f(x) = x^2$	$g(x) = 5f(x)$	$h(x) = f\left(\frac{1}{4}x\right)$
0			
2			
4			
6			

b) Sketch the graphs of all three functions on the same set of axes.

c) Explain how the points on the graphs of $g(x)$ and $h(x)$ relate to the transformations.

2. Copy each graph of $f(x)$ and then graph and label each related function.

i) $g(x) = 3f(x)$ **ii)** $h(x) = f(4x)$

iii) $m(x) = f(2x)$ **iv)** $r(x) = f\left(\frac{x}{5}\right)$

a)

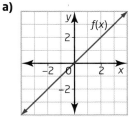

b)

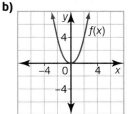

c)

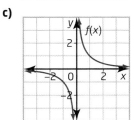

d)

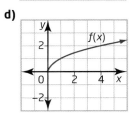

3. For each function $g(x)$, identify the value of a or k and describe how the graph of $g(x)$ can be obtained from the graph of $f(x)$.

a) $g(x) = 10f(x)$ **b)** $g(x) = f(9x)$

c) $g(x) = \frac{1}{5}f(x)$ **d)** $g(x) = f\left(\frac{1}{20}x\right)$

For help with question 4, refer to Example 2.

4. For each function $g(x)$, describe the transformation from a base function of $f(x) = x$, $f(x) = x^2$, $f(x) = \sqrt{x}$, or $f(x) = \frac{1}{x}$. Then, transform the graph of $f(x)$ to sketch the graph of $g(x)$.

a) $g(x) = 10x$ **b)** $g(x) = (5x)^2$

c) $g(x) = \sqrt{\frac{x}{3}}$ **d)** $g(x) = \frac{4}{x}$

e) $g(x) = \sqrt{16x}$ **f)** $g(x) = \frac{x}{4}$

Ⓑ Connect and Apply

For help with question 5, refer to Example 3.

5. Various space agencies have conducted experiments in space. One possible experiment uses pendulums to verify the theoretical values of the acceleration due to gravity on places other than Earth. The period, T, in seconds, of any pendulum is given by $T = 2\pi\sqrt{\frac{\ell}{g}}$, where ℓ is the length of the pendulum, in metres, and g is the acceleration due to gravity, in metres per square second.

Reasoning and Proving · Representing · Selecting Tools · Problem Solving · Connecting · Reflecting · Communicating

Celestial Body	Gravitational Acceleration (m/s²)
Earth	9.8
Mars	3.7
Moon	1.6

a) Graph the period versus length for Earth, the moon, and Mars.

b) If the gravity on a comet is one tenth that of Earth, what will the graph of its period versus its length look like?

6. Describe the transformation that must be applied to the graph of $f(x)$ in order to obtain the graph of $g(x)$.

a)

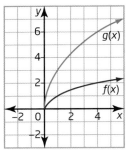

b)

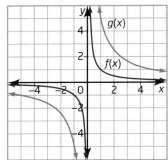

7. a) Determine three key points on the graph of $f(x) = x^2$.

Reasoning and Proving · Representing · Selecting Tools · Problem Solving · Connecting · Reflecting · Communicating

b) Transform the graph of $f(x)$ to obtain the graph of $c(x) = 4f(2x)$ by applying the vertical stretch or compression followed by the horizontal stretch or compression.

c) Transform the graph of $f(x)$ to obtain the graph of $c(x) = 4f(2x)$ by applying the horizontal stretch or compression followed by the vertical stretch or compression.

d) Compare the graphs from parts b) and c).

e) Is there a single stretch that will have the same result as the two original stretches?

f) Repeat parts a) to e) with a different base function.

8. A long ocean wave, such as near the shore or from a tsunami, does not disperse the way a short wave does. The speed of a long wave depends on the depth of the water and can be calculated using the formula $s = \sqrt{gh}$, where g is the acceleration due to gravity, 9.8 m/s^2, and h is the depth of the water, in metres.

a) Sketch the graph of this function.

b) Determine the speed of a wave coming to shore at a depth of 2 m.

c) Determine the speed of a tsunami wave at an ocean depth of 4000 m.

9. Chapter Problem From his work at the traffic safety bureau, Matthew knows that if the length of the skid marks from any vehicle and the road condition are known, then he can estimate the minimum speed the vehicle was going before the brakes were applied. The speed, s, in kilometres per hour, is given by $s = 16.0\sqrt{fd}$, where f is the coefficient of friction for the road surface and d is the average length of all skid marks, in metres.

Type of Surface	f
dry concrete	0.77
wet concrete	0.54
dry asphalt	0.73
wet asphalt	0.54
dry brick	0.65
wet brick	0.34
dirt	0.63

a) Graph the speed for all types of surfaces on the same set of axes.

b) For a skid mark of length 15 m, how much slower would a vehicle have to be travelling on wet brick compared to dry brick to stop in the same distance?

10. Explain why the graph of $g(x) = f(kx)$ stretches horizontally by a factor of $\frac{1}{k}$ and not a factor of k.

11. A ball is dropped from a height of 20 m. The downward acceleration due to gravity is -9.8 m/s^2. The height of the ball is given as $h(t) = -4.9t^2 + 20$.

a) State the domain and range of the function.

b) Write the equation for the height of the ball if it were dropped on a planet with gravity of -12.4 m/s^2.

c) Compare the domain and range of the function in part b) to that of the given function.

C Extend

12. Use Technology In this section, you dealt with static stretches. Computer animation uses dynamic stretches. Open *The Geometer's Sketchpad®*. Go to the *Functions 11* page on the McGraw-Hill Ryerson Web site and follow the links to Section 2.5. Download the file **2.5_Animation.gsp**. In this sketch, you will be able to change a parameter called t by moving a sliding point.

a) Study the form of the function $g(x)$. What similarities and differences are there to a transformed function of the form $g(x) = f(kx)$?

b) What happens when you move the slider t?

c) How does changing the parameter function $P(x)$ affect the motion of the base function $f(x)$? Use the following functions to investigate this.

  i) $P(x) = x^2$

  ii) $P(x) = \sqrt{x}$

  iii) $P(x) = \frac{1}{x}$

d) Click on the **Link to Function 2** button and repeat parts a) to c) using $g(x) = af(x)$.

e) Click on the **Link to Butterfly** button and move the slider t. Here you can see a very rudimentary example of computer animation.

13. **a) Use Technology** Use technology to graph the function $f(x) = x^3 - 3x$.

   b) If $g(x) = 3f(x)$ and $h(x) = f(3x)$, determine the equations for $g(x)$ and $h(x)$.

   c) Without using technology, describe and sketch the graphs of $g(x)$ and $h(x)$.

   d) Is there a vertical transformation that will have the same effect as $h(x)$ does on $f(x)$?

14. **Math Contest** In a high school, the ratio of male to female students is 8:5. When 400 senior males are removed and 300 senior females are removed, the ratio is 8:3. The number of students in the whole school is

   A 1300   **B** 975   **C** 935   **D** 960

15. **Math Contest** The floor function $\lfloor x \rfloor$ returns the value of the greatest integer less than or equal to x. For example, $\lfloor 5.7 \rfloor = 5$ and $\lfloor -3.1 \rfloor = -4$. The value of $\lfloor -4.1 + \lfloor -3.2 \rfloor - \lfloor 3.6 - 4.5 \rfloor + 2 \rfloor$ is

   A -6 **B** -5 **C** 6   **D** 0

16. **Math Contest** Rectangle ABFD has AB = 8 cm and AD = 12 cm. Point C is located inside the rectangle such that AC = BC = EC.

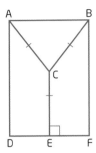

The length of AC is

   A $6\frac{2}{3}$ cm **B** 8 cm   **C** 2π cm **D** 7 cm

17. **Math Contest** Determine the coordinates of the vertex of the quadratic function $y = (2x - 6)^2 + 4(2x - 6) + 5$.

18. **Math Contest** Given the transformation $(x, y) \rightarrow (x, 2x + y)$, determine the equation of the line $3x + 5y - 30 = 0$ after it undergoes this transformation.

Career Connection

Since graduating with a 4-year bachelor of science degree from the University of Ontario Institute of Technology, Teaghan has worked in a forensic laboratory. Here, she is being further trained in the field of ballistics—the science of the flight path of a bullet. Tracing this path is important in a crime investigation, since it will show from which direction the bullet was fired. Teaghan explores various functions involving variables such as the bullet's initial velocity, firing angle, drag, and gravitational constant. Teaghan's research, when presented in a court of law, can be vital in coming to a fair verdict.

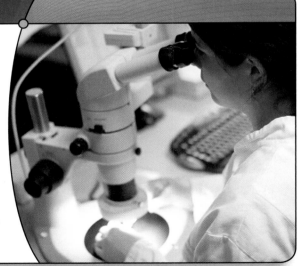

Use *The Geometer's Sketchpad®* to Explore Transformations

A: Translations

Tools

- computer with *The Geometer's Sketchpad®*
- Translations1.gsp
- Translations2.gsp
- Stretches1.gsp
- Stretches2.gsp

1. Open *The Geometer's Sketchpad®*. Go to the *Functions 11* page on the McGraw-Hill Ryerson Web site and follow the links to Section 2.5. Download the file **Translations1.gsp**. In this sketch, you will explore transformations of five different functions, each called $f(x)$. Follow the instructions on each page and click on the **Link to Function** button to move to the next function.

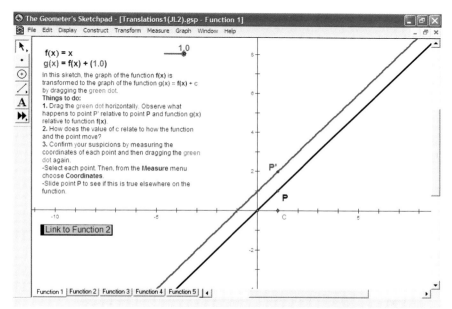

2. Reflect Describe how the value of c in $g(x) = f(x) + c$ changes the graph of $f(x)$.

3. Download the file **Translations2.gsp**. Follow the instructions on each page and click on the **Link to Function** button to move to the next function.

4. Reflect Describe how the value of d in $g(x) = f(x - d)$ changes the graph of $f(x)$.

B: Reflections

1. Open *The Geometer's Sketchpad®*. From the **Graph** menu, choose **Plot New Function**. In the **Edit Function** dialogue box, enter sqrt(x) to represent the base function $f(x) = \sqrt{x}$.

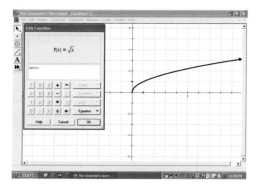

2. Plot a new function. From the **Graph** menu, choose **Plot New Function**, select $f(x)$ on the workspace, and then enter $-x$ in the function to create the new function $g(x) = f(-x)$.

3. Repeat step 2 to create the new functions $h(x) = -f(x)$ and $q(x) = -f(-x)$.

4. **Reflect** Compare each new function to the base function $f(x)$. Describe the mirror line that is used for each reflection. Confirm your hypothesis by repeating steps 1 to 3 for $f(x) = (x - 2)^2$.

C: Stretches and Compressions

1. Open *The Geometer's Sketchpad®*. Go to the *Functions 11* page on the McGraw-Hill Ryerson Web site and follow the links to Section 2.5. Download the file **Stretches1.gsp**. In this sketch, you will explore transformations of five different functions each called $f(x)$. Follow the instructions on each page and click on the **Link to Function** button to move to the next function.

2. **Reflect**
   a) Describe how the value of a in $g(x) = af(x)$ changes the graph of $f(x)$.
   b) Points that do not change under a transformation are said to be invariant. Were there any invariant points?
   c) How were the domain and range affected?

3. Download the file **Stretches2.gsp**. Follow the instructions on each page and click on the **Link to Function** button to move to the next function.

4. **Reflect**
   a) Describe how the value of k in $g(x) = f(kx)$ changes the graph of $f(x)$.
   b) Were there any invariant points?
   c) How were the domain and range affected?

Combinations of Transformations

An anamorphosis is an image that can only be seen correctly when viewed from a certain perspective. For example, the face in the photo can only be seen correctly in the side of the cylindrical mirror. To be viewed correctly, this image requires reflections and stretches to occur simultaneously. In mathematics, situations are rarely described by simple relationships, and so by combining translations, reflections, stretches, and compressions, you can model many different scenarios.

Investigate

Tools
- grid paper

Optional
- graphing calculator

or

- graphing software

Does the order matter when performing transformations?

A: Translations

1. Given the function $f(x) = x^2$, graph each pair of transformed functions on the same set of axes.

   a) $g(x) = f(x) + 3$ and $h(x) = g(x + 6)$

   b) $m(x) = f(x + 6)$ and $r(x) = m(x) + 3$

2. Describe each translation in step 1.

3. Write equations for $h(x)$ and $r(x)$ in terms of $f(x)$.

4. **Reflect** Compare the graphs of $h(x)$ and $r(x)$ and the equations of $h(x)$ and $r(x)$. What does this tell you about whether the order of the translations matters? Explain your reasoning.

B: Stretches

1. Given the function $f(x) = x^2$, graph each pair of transformed functions on the same set of axes.

   a) $b(x) = 5f(x)$ and $p(x) = b\left(\frac{1}{4}x\right)$

   b) $n(x) = f\left(\frac{1}{4}x\right)$ and $s(x) = 5n(x)$

2. Describe each stretch in step 1.

3. Write equations for $p(x)$ and $s(x)$ in terms of $f(x)$.

4. **Reflect** Compare the graphs of $p(x)$ and $s(x)$ and the equations of $p(x)$ and $s(x)$. What does this tell you about whether the order of the stretches matters? Explain your reasoning.

C: Translations and Stretches

1. Given the function $f(x) = x^2$, graph each pair of transformed functions on the same set of axes.

   a) $j(x) = 2f(x)$ and $s(x) = j(x) + 5$

   b) $q(x) = f(x) + 5$ and $t(x) = 2q(x)$

2. Describe each transformation in step 1.

3. Write equations for $s(x)$ and $t(x)$ in terms of $f(x)$.

4. Given the function $f(x) = x^2$, graph each pair of transformed functions on the same set of axes.

   a) $w(x) = f\left(\frac{1}{2}x\right)$ and $u(x) = w(x + 5)$

   b) $v(x) = f(x + 5)$ and $z(x) = v\left(\frac{1}{2}x\right)$

5. Describe each transformation in step 4.

6. Write equations for $u(x)$ and $z(x)$ in terms of $f(x)$.

7. **Reflect** In which order do you think stretches and translations should be done when they are combined? Explain.

Example 1

Combinations of Transformations

Describe the combination of transformations that must be applied to the base function $f(x)$ to obtain the transformed function. Then, write the corresponding equation and sketch its graph.

a) $f(x) = x^2$, $g(x) = \frac{1}{2}f[4(x - 3)] - 2$

b) $f(x) = \sqrt{x}$, $g(x) = -2f(3x + 15) + 4$

Solution

a) Compare the transformed equation to $y = af[k(x - d)] + c$ to determine the values of the parameters a, k, d, and c.

For $g(x) = \frac{1}{2}f[4(x - 3)] - 2$, $a = \frac{1}{2}$, $k = 4$, $d = 3$, and $c = -2$.

The function $f(x)$ is vertically compressed by a factor of $\frac{1}{2}$, horizontally compressed by a factor of $\frac{1}{4}$, and then translated 3 units right and 2 units down.

vertical compression
by a factor of $\frac{1}{2}$

vertical translation of
2 units down

$$g(x) = \frac{1}{2}f[4(x - 3)] - 2$$

horizontal compression
by a factor of $\frac{1}{4}$

horizontal translation of
3 units right

$$g(x) = \frac{1}{2}f[4(x - 3)] - 2$$

$$= \frac{1}{2}[4(x - 3)]^2 - 2$$

$$= \frac{1}{2}(4x - 12)^2 - 2$$

$$= \frac{1}{2}(16x^2 - 96x + 144) - 2$$

$$= 8x^2 - 48x + 72 - 2$$

$$= 8x^2 - 48x + 70$$

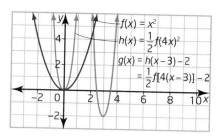

b) First, rewrite $g(x) = -2f(3x + 15) + 4$ in the form $y = af[k(x - d)] + c$.

$$g(x) = -2f(3x + 15) + 4$$

$$= -2f[3(x + 5)] + 4$$

For $g(x) = -2f[3(x + 5)] + 4$, $a = -2$, $k = 3$, $d = -5$, and $c = 4$.
The function $f(x)$ is reflected in the x-axis, vertically stretched by a factor of 2, horizontally compressed by a factor of $\frac{1}{3}$, and then translated 5 units left and 4 units up.

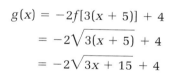

reflection in the x-axis   vertical stretch by a factor of 2   vertical translation of 4 units up

$$g(x) = -2f[3(x + 5)] + 4$$

horizontal compression by a factor of $\frac{1}{3}$ horizontal translation of 5 units left

$$g(x) = -2f[3(x + 5)] + 4$$

$$= -2\sqrt{3(x + 5)} + 4$$

$$= -2\sqrt{3x + 15} + 4$$

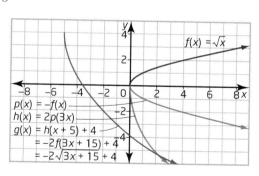

When combining transformations, order matters. To accurately sketch the graph of a function of the form $y = af[k(x - d)] + c$, apply transformations represented by the parameters a and k before transformations represented by the parameters d and c. That is, stretches, compressions, and reflections occur before translations. This is similar to the order of operations, where multiplication and division occur before addition and subtraction.

Example 2

Apply Transformations

During a race in the sportsman category of drag racing, it is common for cars with different performance potentials to race against each other while using a handicap system. For example, Byron is racing against Eve. Since Eve has a faster car, when they race, it appears as though Byron gets a head start. The distance, E, in metres, that Eve's car travels is given by $E(t) = 10t^2$, where t is the time, in seconds, after she starts. The distance, B, in metres, that Byron's car travels is given by $B(t) = 5(t + h)^2$, where t is the time after Eve starts and h is the head start, in seconds.

a) On the same set of axes, graph distance versus time for both drivers for h-values of 1 s, 2 s, 3 s, and 4 s.

b) The standard length of a drag strip is approximately 400 m. How much of a head start can Eve give Byron and still cross the finish line first?

c) Determine the domain and range of each function.

d) The acceleration of each car is represented by the stretch of each equation. Compare the accelerations of the two cars.

Solution

a) There are five curves to graph: one representing Eve and four representing Byron given each head start.

Eve	$E(t) = 10t^2$
Byron with 1-s head start	$B_1(t) = 5(t + 1)^2$
Byron with 2-s head start	$B_2(t) = 5(t + 2)^2$
Byron with 3-s head start	$B_3(t) = 5(t + 3)^2$
Byron with 4-s head start	$B_4(t) = 5(t + 4)^2$

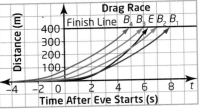

b) Based on the graph, it appears that as long as the head start is no more than about 2.5 s, Eve will still cross the line first.

c) For this situation, the equations given are only valid from the time the car starts moving to the time it crosses the finish line.

Function		Domain	Range
Eve	$E(t) = 10t^2$	$\{t \in \mathbb{R}, t \geq 0\}$	$\{E \in \mathbb{R}, 0 \leq E \leq 400\}$
Byron with 1-s head start	$B_1(t) = 5(t + 1)^2$	$\{t \in \mathbb{R}, t \geq -1\}$	
Byron with 2-s head start	$B_2(t) = 5(t + 2)^2$	$\{t \in \mathbb{R}, t \geq -2\}$	$\{B \in \mathbb{R}, 0 \leq B \leq 400\}$
Byron with 3-s head start	$B_3(t) = 5(t + 3)^2$	$\{t \in \mathbb{R}, t \geq -3\}$	
Byron with 4-s head start	$B_4(t) = 5(t + 4)^2$	$\{t \in \mathbb{R}, t \geq -4\}$	

d) The equation for Eve's car has $a = 10$ while the equations for Byron's car have $a = 5$. Thus, the acceleration of Eve's car is twice that of Byron's car.

Key Concepts

- Stretches, compressions, and reflections can be performed in any order before translations.
- Ensure that the function is written in the form $y = af[k(x - d)] + c$ to identify specific transformations.
- The parameters a, k, d, and c in the function $y = af[k(x - d)] + c$ correspond to the following transformations:

  a corresponds to a vertical stretch or compression and, if $a < 0$, a reflection in the x-axis.

  k corresponds to a horizontal stretch or compression and, if $k < 0$, a reflection in the y-axis.

  d corresponds to a horizontal translation to the right or left.

  c corresponds to a vertical translation up or down.

Communicate Your Understanding

C1 Stretches, compressions, and reflections can be performed in any order. Explain why.

C2 A student describes the function $g(x) = f(3x + 12)$ as a horizontal compression by a factor of $\frac{1}{3}$ followed by a horizontal translation of 12 units left of the base function $f(x)$. Explain the mistake this student has made.

A Practise

For help with questions 1 to 4, refer to Example 1.

1. Compare the transformed equation to $y = af[k(x - d)] + c$ to determine the values of the parameters a, k, d, and c. Then, describe, in the appropriate order, the transformations that must be applied to a base function $f(x)$ to obtain the transformed function.

   a) $g(x) = 4f(x - 3)$ **b)** $g(x) = \frac{1}{3}f(x) + 1$

   c) $g(x) = f(x + 5) + 9$ **d)** $g(x) = f\left(\frac{1}{4}x\right) + 2$

   e) $g(x) = f(5x) - 2$ **f)** $g(x) = 2f(x) - 7$

2. Repeat question 1 for each transformed function $g(x)$.

   a) $g(x) = 3f(2x) - 1$

   b) $g(x) = -2f(x) + 1$

   c) $g(x) = \frac{1}{2}f(x - 4) + 5$

   d) $g(x) = f(-3x) + 4$

   e) $g(x) = -f\left(\frac{1}{2}x\right) - 3$

   f) $g(x) = \frac{1}{4}f(3x) - 6$

3. Describe, in the appropriate order, the transformations that must be applied to the base function $f(x)$ to obtain the transformed function. Then, write the corresponding equation and transform the graph of $f(x)$ to sketch the graph of $g(x)$.

   a) $f(x) = \sqrt{x}$, $g(x) = 4f(3x)$

   b) $f(x) = \frac{1}{x}$, $g(x) = f(x - 1) + 2$

   c) $f(x) = x^2$, $g(x) = f\left[\frac{1}{4}(x + 2)\right]$

   d) $f(x) = x$, $g(x) = -5f(x) - 3$

4. Repeat question 3 for $f(x)$ and the transformed function $g(x)$.

   a) $f(x) = x$, $g(x) = -\frac{1}{2}f[2(x + 1)] - 3$

   b) $f(x) = x^2$, $g(x) = -2f[3(x - 4)] - 1$

   c) $f(x) = \sqrt{x}$, $g(x) = \frac{1}{2}f\left[\frac{1}{2}(x + 3)\right] + 5$

   d) $f(x) = \frac{1}{x}$, $g(x) = 2f[-(x - 3)] + 4$

For help with questions 5 and 6, refer to Example 2.

5. For each function, identify the base function as one of $f(x) = x$, $f(x) = x^2$, $f(x) = \sqrt{x}$, and $f(x) = \frac{1}{x}$. Sketch the graphs of the base function and the transformed function, and state the domain and range of the functions.

a) $b(x) = 10x - 8$

b) $e(x) = 3x^2 - 5$

c) $h(x) = (5x + 20)^2$

d) $j(x) = 2\sqrt{x} - 7$

e) $m(x) = \dfrac{5}{x + 8}$

f) $r(x) = \dfrac{2}{3 - x} + 1$

B **Connect and Apply**

6. Two skydivers jump out of a plane. The first skydiver's motion can be modelled by the function $g(t) = 4000 - 5(t + 10)^2$. The second skydiver jumps out a few seconds later with a goal of catching up to the first skydiver. The motion of the second skydiver can be modelled by $h(t) = 4000 - 5t^2$. For both functions, the distance above the ground is measured in metres and the time is the number of seconds after the second skydiver jumps.

Reasoning and Proving
Representing · *Selecting Tools*
Problem Solving
Connecting · *Reflecting*
Communicating

a) Graph the functions on the same set of axes.

b) Will the second skydiver catch up to the first before they have to open their parachutes at 800 m?

c) State the domain and range of these functions in this context.

7. Copy the graph of the function $f(x)$. Sketch the graph of $g(x)$ after each transformation.

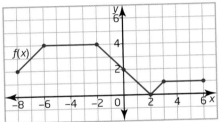

a) $g(x) = 3f(x + 4)$

b) $g(x) = f(4x) + 3$

c) $g(x) = f(2x - 12)$

d) $g(x) = 5f(0.5x + 1) - 6$

8. The siren of an ambulance approaching you sounds different than when it is moving away from you. This difference in sound is called the Doppler effect. The Doppler effect for a 1000-Hz siren can be modelled by the equation

$f = 1000\left(\dfrac{332}{332 \pm v}\right)$, where f is the frequency of the sound, in hertz; v is the speed of the ambulance, in metres per second; and the positive sign (+) is used when the ambulance is moving away from you and the negative sign (−) when it is moving toward you.

a) For an ambulance travelling at a speed of 20 m/s, what is the difference in frequency as the ambulance approaches and passes you?

b) Assuming an ambulance cannot travel faster than 40 m/s, determine the domain and range of this function.

9. Although a transformed function is traditionally written in the form $g(x) = af[k(x - d)] + c$, it can also be written in the form $\frac{1}{a}[g(x) - c] = f[k(x - d)]$. How does this form help explain the seemingly backward nature of the horizontal transformations with respect to the values of d and k?

Reasoning and Proving
Representing · *Selecting Tools*
Problem Solving
Connecting · *Reflecting*
Communicating

10. The value, V, in thousands of dollars, of a certain car after t years can be modelled by the equation $V(t) = \dfrac{35}{t + 3}$.

a) Sketch the graph of this relation.

b) What was the initial value of this car?

c) What is the projected value of this car after

    i) 1 year?

    ii) 2 years?

    iii) 10 years?

✔ **Achievement Check**

11. The base function $f(x) = \sqrt{x}$ is transformed by a reflection in the x-axis, followed by a vertical stretch by a factor of 3, then a horizontal compression by a factor of $\dfrac{1}{2}$, then a vertical translation of 3 units down, and finally a horizontal translation of 6 units right.

a) Determine the equation of the transformed function.

b) Use key points on the base function to determine image points on the transformed function.

c) Sketch the graph of the transformed function.

d) Determine the domain and range of the transformed function.

C Extend

12. a) Given the base function $f(x) = x^3$, use a table of values or a graphing calculator to sketch the graph of $y = f(x)$.

b) Sketch the graph and determine the equation for each transformed function.

    i) $g(x) = 3f(x + 2)$

    ii) $h(x) = -f(4x - 12) + 5$

13. The equation of a circle, centred at the origin and with radius r, is $x^2 + y^2 = r^2$. Describe the transformations needed to graph each of the following. Then, sketch each circle.

a) $(x - 2)^2 + (y - 1)^2 = 25$

b) $(x + 4)^2 + (y - 5)^2 = 9$

14. Use Technology In this section, you dealt with static transformations. In computer animation, dynamic transformations are used. Open *The Geometer's Sketchpad®*. Go to the *Functions 11* page on the McGraw-Hill Ryerson Web site and follow the links to Section 2.6. Download the file **2.6_Animation.gsp**. In this sketch, you will be able to change a parameter called t by moving a sliding point.

a) Study the form of the function $g(x)$. What similarities and differences are there compared to a transformed function of the form $g(x) = f[k(x - d)] + c$?

b) What happens when you move the slider t?

c) How does changing the parameter function $P(x)$ affect the motion of the base function $f(x)$? Use the following functions to investigate this.

    i) $P(x) = x^2$

    ii) $P(x) = \sqrt{x}$

    iii) $P(x) = \dfrac{1}{x}$

d) Click on the **Link to Butterfly** button and move the slider t. Here you can see a very rudimentary example of computer animation. Repeat parts b) and c) for this sketch.

15. Math Contest In a magic square, the sum of each row, column, and major diagonal is the same. For the magic square shown, determine the value of y.

3	y	
6	z	5

A 2   **B** 3   **C** 4   **D** 5

2.7

Inverse of a Function

Engineers have been able to determine the
relationship between the speed of a car and its
stopping distance. A typical function describing this
relationship is $D = 0.006v^2$, where D is the stopping
distance, in metres, and v is the speed, in kilometres per hour. The graph of this function (below left)
shows that as the speed increases, the stopping distance increases faster. Another useful graph is the
inverse (below right), which shows the maximum speed allowed to stop within a given distance.

In this section, you will
learn about the **inverse
of a function** and how
it relates to the idea of
reversing operations.

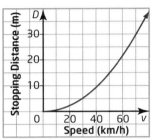

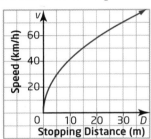

inverse of a function

• The inverse of a function
  f is denoted by f^{-1}.

• The function and
  its inverse have the
  property that if
  $f(a) = b$, then $f^{-1}(b) = a$.

Tools

• grid paper
• ruler

Investigate

How can you determine the inverse of a function?

1. Sketch the graph of the function
$f(x) = x^2$ and its inverse.

a) Start by looking at points on
the graph of the function.
Thinking of an inverse in
terms of a reverse operation,
copy and complete the table
by switching the
x- and y-coordinates of each
point.

Points on the Function	Points on the Inverse of the Function
(–3, 9)	
(–2, 4)	
(–1, 1)	
(0, 0)	
(1, 1)	
(2, 4)	
(3, 9)	

b) Plot the original function
points, draw a smooth curve through them, and label the curve
$f(x)$.

c) Plot the new points on the same set of axes and draw a smooth
curve through them. Label this curve as $f^{-1}(x)$.

2. a) State the domain and range of $f(x)$.

b) State the domain and range of $f^{-1}(x)$.

Connections

The notation $f^{-1}(x)$ is
read as "the inverse of
f at x." Note that the –1
in $f^{-1}(x)$ does not behave
like an exponent, so
$$f^{-1}(x) \neq \frac{1}{f(x)}.$$

3. Reflect

a) Compare the domain and range of $f(x)$ to the domain and range of $f^{-1}(x)$.

b) Is $f^{-1}(x)$ a function? Explain.

4. a) Draw a line segment between each original point and its corresponding inverse point.

b) Locate the midpoint of each line segment.

c) All of these midpoints should lie on a straight line. What is the equation of that line?

5. Reflect Describe a way to draw the inverse of a function using reflections.

6. On the same set of axes, sketch the graphs of $g(x) = -x^2$, $h(x) = 2x - 3$, and $k(x) = \pm\sqrt{x}$. Note that $k(x)$ represents two functions: $k(x) = \sqrt{x}$ and $k(x) = -\sqrt{x}$.

7. Reflect Which of the graphs from step 6 is the same as the graph of the inverse of $f(x)$? Compare its equation to that of $f(x)$. How do you think the notion of "reversing" comes into play when dealing with the equations of a function and its inverse?

Example 1

Determine the Inverse Numerically

The table shows ordered pairs belonging to a function $f(x)$. Determine $f^{-1}(x)$, graph $f(x)$ and its inverse, and then state the domain and range of $f(x)$ and its inverse.

$f(x)$
(−5, 0)
(−4, 2)
(−3, 5)
(−2, 6)
(0, 7)

Solution

Switch the x- and y-coordinates, and then plot the points.

$f(x)$	$f^{-1}(x)$
(−5, 0)	(0, −5)
(−4, 2)	(2, −4)
(−3, 5)	(5, −3)
(−2, 6)	(6, −2)
(0, 7)	(7, 0)

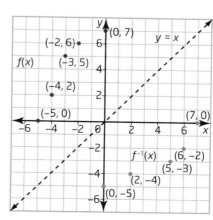

Notice that switching the x- and y-coordinates reflects the graph of $f(x)$ in the line $y = x$.

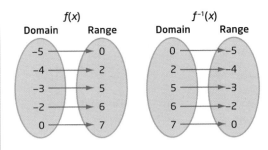

$f(x)$ — Domain, Range

$f^{-1}(x)$ — Domain, Range

Notice that the domain of $f(x)$ is the range of $f^{-1}(x)$, and the range of $f(x)$ is the domain of $f^{-1}(x)$.

Connections

In mathematics, tools exist for manipulating numbers and expressions. Many of these tools come in pairs. Two examples are addition and subtraction and multiplication and division. These are considered to be inverse operations since one "undoes" or "reverses" the other.

The inverse of a function $f(x)$ can be found by reversing the operations that the function specifies. Consider the function $f(x) = 3x + 2$. This function multiplies each x-value by 3 and adds 2 to the result. Reversing the operations then subtracts 2 from each x and divides the result by 3.

So, the inverse of $f(x)$ is $f^{-1}(x) = \dfrac{x - 2}{3}$. The inverse is the "reverse" of the original function.

A systematic method for determining the inverse of a function algebraically can be described by the following steps:

1. Write the equation in "$y =$" form, if it is not already in that form.

2. Interchange x and y in the equation.

3. Solve the new equation for y.

4. Replace y with $f^{-1}(x)$.

Example 2

Determine the Inverse of a Function Algebraically

For each function $f(x)$,
  i) determine $f^{-1}(x)$
  ii) graph $f(x)$ and its inverse
  iii) determine whether the inverse of $f(x)$ is a function
  a) $f(x) = 2x - 3$
  b) $f(x) = 2x^2 + 16x + 29$

Solution

a) i) $f(x) = 2x - 3$

Step 1: $y = 2x - 3$ Replace $f(x)$ with y.

Step 2: $x = 2y - 3$ Interchange x and y.

Step 3: $x + 3 = 2y$ Isolate y. Notice that the inverse operations are

$\dfrac{x + 3}{2} = y$ used.

Step 4: $f^{-1}(x) = \dfrac{x + 3}{2}$ Replace y with $f^{-1}(x)$.

ii) The graphs of the function $f(x)$ and its inverse are reflections of each other in the line $y = x$. Any points that lie on the line $y = x$ are invariant, since their x- and y-coordinates are equal.

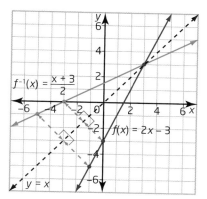

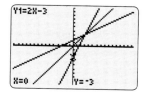 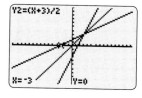

Using a graphing calculator, set the line style of $y = x$ to **Dot**. The window can be adjusted using **ZSquare** from the **ZOOM** menu.

iii) The inverse of $f(x)$ is a function, since there is only one y-value for each x-value. In other words, the graph of $f^{-1}(x)$ passes the vertical line test.

b) i)

$$f(x) = 2x^2 + 16x + 29$$

Step 1: $y = 2x^2 + 16x + 29$ Replace $f(x)$ with y.

Before you interchange x and y, rewrite the quadratic function in vertex form, $y = a(x - h)^2 + k$, by completing the square.

$$y = 2(x^2 + 8x) + 29$$
$$= 2(x^2 + 8x + 16 - 16) + 29$$
$$= 2(x^2 + 8x + 16) - 32 + 29$$
$$= 2(x + 4)^2 - 3$$

Step 2: $x = 2(y + 4)^2 - 3$ Interchange x and y.

Step 3: $x + 3 = 2(y + 4)^2$ Isolate y. Notice that the inverse operations are used.

$$\frac{x + 3}{2} = (y + 4)^2$$

$$\pm\sqrt{\frac{x + 3}{2}} = y + 4$$ Take the square root of both sides. Recall that there is a positive and a negative root.

$$\pm\sqrt{\frac{x + 3}{2}} - 4 = y$$

Step 4: $f^{-1}(x) = \pm\sqrt{\dfrac{x + 3}{2}} - 4$ Replace y with $f^{-1}(x)$.

ii) The graphs of the function $f(x)$ and its inverse are reflections of each other in the line $y = x$.

Reflect key points in the line $y = x$ to help you sketch the graph of the inverse of $f(x)$.

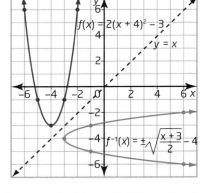

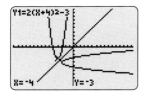 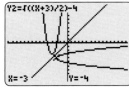 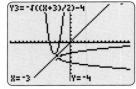

To graph $g^{-1}(x) = \pm\sqrt{\dfrac{x+3}{2}} - 4$, you must enter two equations,

$y = \sqrt{\dfrac{x+3}{2}} - 4$ and $y = -\sqrt{\dfrac{x+3}{2}} - 4$.

iii) The inverse of $f(x)$ is not a function, since there are two y-values for each x-value. In other words, the graph of $f^{-1}(x)$ does not pass the vertical line test.

Example 3

Apply Inverses

The relationship between the speed of a car and its stopping distance can be modelled by the function $D = 0.006v^2$, where D is the stopping distance, in metres, and v is the speed, in kilometres per hour. The graph of this function and its inverse are shown.

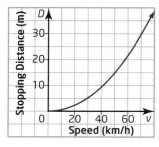 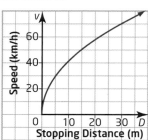

a) State the domain and range of the function D.

b) Determine an equation for the inverse of the function. State its domain and range.

Solution

a) Since the speed must be greater than or equal to zero, the domain is $\{v \in \mathbb{R}, v \geq 0\}$.

Distance cannot be negative, so the range is $\{D \in \mathbb{R}, D \geq 0\}$.

b) For a real-life context, to determine the inverse of the relationship, solve for the dependent variable. This is because the cause-and-effect relationship between speed and stopping distance does not change, so you cannot just switch D and v.

$$D = 0.006v^2$$

$$\frac{D}{0.006} = v^2$$

$$v = \sqrt{\frac{D}{0.006}}$$ Take the square root of both sides. Since speed must be greater than or equal to zero, only the positive root is needed.

The domain is $\{D \in \mathbb{R}, D \geq 0\}$ and the range is $\{v \in \mathbb{R}, v \geq 0\}$.

Key Concepts

- The inverse of a function $f(x)$ is denoted by $f^{-1}(x)$.

- The inverse of a function can be found by interchanging the x- and y-coordinates of the function.

- The graph of $f^{-1}(x)$ is the graph of $f(x)$ reflected in the line $y = x$.

- The inverse of a function can be found by interchanging x and y in the equation of the function and then solving the new equation for y.

- For algebraic inverses of quadratic functions, the functions must be in vertex form.

- The inverse of a function is not necessarily a function.

Communicate Your Understanding

C1 You are asked to solve the equation $3x + 4 = 19$. How is the method used to solve this equation similar to the method used to determine an inverse?

C2 The function $f(x) = 9x - 5$ has inverse $f^{-1}(x) = \dfrac{x + 5}{9}$. Discuss how the idea of inverse or reversed operations relates the function and its inverse.

C3 Explain why a quadratic function needs to be in vertex form in order to determine its inverse algebraically.

A Practise

For help with questions 1 and 2, refer to Example 1.

1. Write the inverse of each function. Then, state the domain and range of the function and its inverse.

   a) $\{(1, 5), (4, 2), (5, -3), (7, 0)\}$

   b) $\{(3, 5), (4, 0), (5, -5), (6, -10)\}$

   c)

   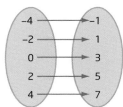

   d)

   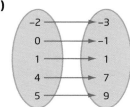

2. Copy each graph. Then, sketch the inverse of each function and state the domain and range of the function and its inverse.

   a)

   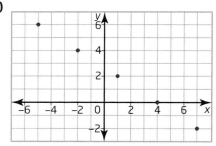

   b)

   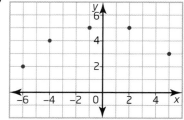

For help with questions 3 to 7, refer to Example 2.

3. Copy each graph of $f(x)$ and then sketch the graph of the inverse of each function. Is the inverse of $f(x)$ a function? Explain.

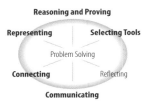

Reasoning and Proving

Representing — Selecting Tools

Problem Solving

Connecting — Reflecting

Communicating

   a)

   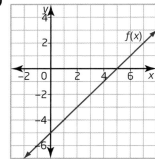

   b)

   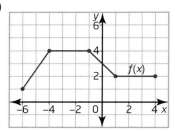

   c)

   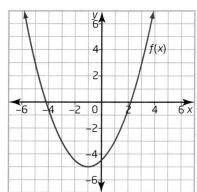

4. Determine the equation of the inverse of each function.

   a) $f(x) = 2x$

   b) $f(x) = 6x - 5$

   c) $f(x) = -x + 10$

   d) $f(x) = \dfrac{2x + 4}{5}$

5. Determine the equation of the inverse of each function.

a) $f(x) = x^2 + 6$ **b)** $f(x) = 4x^2$

c) $f(x) = (x + 8)^2$ **d)** $f(x) = \frac{1}{2}x^2 + 10$

6. For each quadratic function, complete the square and then determine the equation of the inverse.

a) $f(x) = x^2 + 6x + 15$

b) $f(x) = -x^2 + 20x - 99$

c) $f(x) = 2x^2 + 24x - 3$

d) $f(x) = -3x^2 - 36x - 100$

7. For each function $f(x)$,

i) determine $f^{-1}(x)$

ii) graph $f(x)$ and its inverse with or without technology

iii) state whether the inverse of $f(x)$ is a function and explain your reasoning

a) $f(x) = -5x + 6$

b) $f(x) = \frac{1}{3}x - 8$

c) $f(x) = (x - 8)^2 + 16$

d) $f(x) = -x^2 + 20x - 64$

B Connect and Apply

For help with question 8, refer to Example 3.

8. In ballistics, the paths of projectiles are studied. It is known that the greater the speed at which an object is fired, the farther it will travel. For a particular spring-loaded cannon, this relationship can be modelled by $d = \frac{v^2}{10}$, where d is the distance, in metres, travelled by the projectile and v is the muzzle speed, in metres per second. Different speeds can be attained by adjusting the spring.

a) Graph the distance function and state its domain and range.

b) Graph the inverse of the distance function. What does it represent? State its domain and range.

c) Which equation, the original or the inverse, might be more useful for someone using the cannon?

9. In the 2008 Beijing Olympics, Usain "Lightning" Bolt set a new world record in the 100-m dash by smashing his own previous record by 0.03 s. By all accounts, however, he coasted to the finish line. His coach suggested that if he had continued at the speed he had been travelling, he would have run the race in 9.52 s.

Physicists led by Hans Kristian Eriksen investigated this possibility. For the majority of the race, Bolt's position, in metres, could be modelled by the function $d(t) = 11.8t - 12.5$, where t is the time, in seconds.

a) Graph Bolt's position function and state the domain and range.

b) Suggest reasons why the domain of this function should not start at $t = 0$.

c) Determine the inverse of this function and state its domain and range.

d) Use the inverse to determine if Bolt's coach was close to being correct.

Connections

Go to the *Functions 11* page on the McGraw-Hill Ryerson Web site and follow the links to Chapter 2 to read the paper entitled "Velocity Dispersions in a Cluster of Stars: How Fast Could Usain Bolt Have Run?"

10. Explain why $f(x) = f^{-1}(x)$ for any function of the form $f(x) = -x + b$.

11. Determine whether the two relations shown in each graph are inverses of each other. Explain your reasoning.

a)

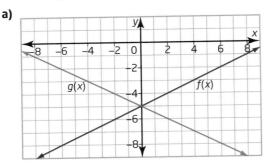

b)

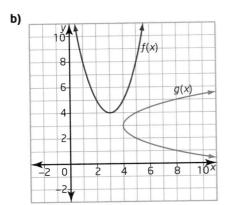

c)

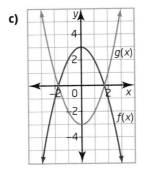

d)

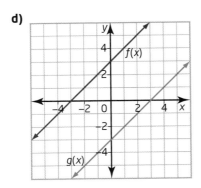

12. The equation $y = \frac{9}{5}x + 32$ can be used to convert between Celsius and Fahrenheit temperatures, where x is the temperature, in degrees Celsius, and y is the temperature, in degrees Fahrenheit.

a) Determine the inverse of this equation. What does it represent? What do the variables represent?

b) Graph the original and inverse equations on the same set of axes.

c) What temperature is the same in Celsius and Fahrenheit? Explain how you know.

13. Chapter Problem At the traffic safety bureau, Matthew determines that for a car travelling at approximately 100 km/h, the stopping distance, in metres, once the brakes are applied is approximately given by $d = -2.8(t - 5)^2 + 70$, where t is the time, in seconds.

a) Determine the inverse of this function. What does this represent in the context of the question?

b) In the context, what should the domain and range of the original function and its inverse be?

c) Compare the distance travelled in the first 20 m of braking, the second 20 m of braking, and the third 20 m of braking.

14. Refer to Example 2 of Section 2.6. Use inverses to calculate the exact time a 400-m drag race would take for each car.

15. For each quadratic function $f(x)$,

   i) determine $f^{-1}(x)$

   ii) graph $f(x)$ and its inverse

   iii) restrict the domain of $f(x)$ to one branch of the parabola so that $f^{-1}(x)$ is also a function

   iv) graph $f(x)$ and its inverse with the restricted domains

a) $f(x) = 2x^2$

b) $f(x) = x^2 + 2$

c) $f(x) = (x - 3)^2$

16. a) Given the function $f(x) = 3x + 7$, determine the inverse.

b) Determine the values of $f(f^{-1})$ and $f^{-1}(f)$. That is, substitute the inverse equation into the original and vice versa.

c) Repeat parts a) and b) for $f(x) = x^2 - 6$.

d) Can you make a general statement about $f(f^{-1})$ and $f^{-1}(f)$?

✔ **Achievement Check**

17. A rock is thrown from the top of a 100-m cliff. Its height, h, in metres, after t seconds can be modelled approximately by the function $h(t) = 100 - 5t^2$.

a) Graph the function and state its domain and range.

b) Determine the inverse of $h(t)$ and state its domain and range. Explain what this inverse represents in the context of the question.

c) A second rock is thrown upward off the cliff. Its height, h, in metres, after t seconds can be modelled approximately by the function $h(t) = 100 + 10t - 5t^2$. Solve for t by finding the inverse. Then, determine at what time the rock will hit the ground.

C **Extend**

18. a) Determine the inverse of the function $f(x) = \sqrt{x + 3}$.

b) State the domain and range of the function and its inverse.

c) Sketch the graphs of the function and its inverse.

19. The volume, V, of a sphere with radius r is given by $V = \frac{4}{3}\pi r^3$.

a) Determine the inverse of the equation. What does it represent?

b) State the domain and range of the function and its inverse in the context of the question.

20. a) Given the function $f(x) = \frac{1}{x}$, determine the inverse.

b) Use the graph of $f(x)$ to explain your answer for part a).

21. a) Given the function $f(x) = \frac{5}{5x - 16}$, determine the inverse.

b) State the domain and range of the function and its inverse.

22. a) Use the property from question 16 to test if f and g are inverses of each other.

i) $f(x) = -5x + 20$
$g(x) = -\frac{x}{5} + 4$

ii) $f(x) = x^2 - 10x + 27$
$g(x) = \sqrt{x - 2} + 5$

iii) $f(x) = (x + 4)^3 + 6$
$g(x) = \sqrt[3]{x - 6} - 4$

iv) $f(x) = \sqrt[4]{x + 10}$
$g(x) = x^4 - 10$

b) **Use Technology** Use graphing technology to verify your answers in part a).

23. Math Contest Given $f(x) = x^2 + 3x - 3$ and $g(x) = f^{-1}(x)$, a possible value for $g(1)$ is

A -4 **B** 0 **C** -1

D cannot be determined

24. Math Contest Given that the function $f(x)$ is the single point $(6, -2)$, then the distance from $f(x)$ to $f^{-1}(x)$ is

A $8\sqrt{2}$ units   **B** 64 units

C 0 units   **D** 16 units

25. Math Contest The point $(5, 1)$ is reflected in the line $y = x + 1$. The image point is

A $(1, 6)$ **B** $(2, 5)$ **C** $(0, 6)$ **D** $(0, 5)$

26. Math Contest Determine the integral ordered pairs that solve the system of equations $x + xy + y = 19$ and $x^2y + xy^2 = 84$.

Chapter 2 Review

2.1 Functions and Equivalent Algebraic Expressions, pages 78 to 87

1. Determine whether the functions in each pair are equivalent.

a) $f(x) = (x + 6)(x - 8) + (x + 16)(x + 3)$,
$g(x) = 3(x^2 + 3x + 5) - (x - 5)(x - 3)$

b) $f(x) = (x + 5)(x - 4) - (x - 8)(x - 1)$,
$g(x) = 2(5x - 28)$

2. Simplify each expression and state all restrictions on x.

a) $\dfrac{x + 7}{x^2 + 10x + 21}$ **b)** $\dfrac{x^2 - 64}{x - 8}$

3. A square piece of cardboard with side length 40 cm is used to create an open-topped box by cutting out squares with side length x from each corner.

a) Determine a simplified expression for the surface area of the box.

b) Determine any restrictions on the value of x.

2.2 Skills You Need: Operations With Rational Expressions, pages 88 to 96

4. Simplify each expression and state the restrictions.

a) $\dfrac{3x^2}{5xy} \times \dfrac{20xy^3}{12xy}$ **b)** $\dfrac{150a^3b^4}{20a^2b} \div \dfrac{6b}{8ab^2}$

c) $\dfrac{1}{3x} + \dfrac{5}{2x^2}$ **d)** $\dfrac{4}{x - 6} - \dfrac{3}{x - 4}$

5. Simplify each expression and state the restrictions.

a) $\dfrac{x^2 + 7x}{3x + 21} \times \dfrac{x^2 + 3x + 2}{x + 2}$

b) $\dfrac{x^2 + 4x - 60}{3x + 30} \div \dfrac{x^2 - 8x + 12}{6x - 12}$

c) $\dfrac{3}{x^2 + 7x + 10} - \dfrac{5x}{x^2 - 4}$

d) $\dfrac{-10x}{x^2 + 18x + 32} + \dfrac{12x}{x^2 + 6x - 160}$

6. For the open-topped box in question 3, determine a simplified expression for the ratio of the volume to the surface area. What are the restrictions on x?

2.3 Horizontal and Vertical Translations of Functions, pages 97 to 104

7. Copy the graph of the function $f(x)$. Sketch the graph of $g(x)$ by determining the image points A′, B′, C′, and D′.

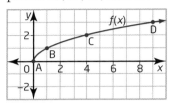

a) $g(x) = f(x) + 6$ **b)** $g(x) = f(x - 3)$

8. For each function $g(x)$, identify the base function as one of $f(x) = x$, $f(x) = x^2$, $f(x) = \sqrt{x}$, and $f(x) = \dfrac{1}{x}$ and describe the transformation first in the form $y = f(x - d) + c$ and then in words. Transform the graph of $f(x)$ to sketch the graph of $g(x)$. Then, state the domain and range of each function.

a) $g(x) = (x + 7)^2 - 8$

b) $g(x) = \sqrt{x - 6} + 3$

c) $g(x) = \dfrac{1}{x + 3} + 1$

2.4 Reflections of Functions, pages 105 to 112

9. Copy the graph of $f(x)$ and sketch each reflection, $g(x)$. State the domain and range of each function.

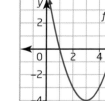

a) $g(x) = f(-x)$

b) $g(x) = -f(x)$

c) $g(x) = -f(-x)$

10. a) Determine the equation of each function, $g(x)$, after a reflection in the x-axis.

    i) $f(x) = \sqrt{x} + 5$ **ii)** $f(x) = \dfrac{1}{x} - 7$

b) Determine the equation of each function in part a), $h(x)$, after a reflection in the y-axis.

2.5 Stretches of Functions, pages 113 to 124

11. Given the function $f(x) = x^2$, identify the value of a or k, transform the graph of $f(x)$ to sketch the graph of $g(x)$, and state the domain and range of each function.

a) $g(x) = 4f(x)$ **b)** $g(x) = f(5x)$

c) $g(x) = f\left(\frac{x}{3}\right)$ **d)** $g(x) = \frac{1}{4}f(x)$

12. For each function $g(x)$, describe the transformation from a base function of $f(x) = x$, $f(x) = x^2$, $f(x) = \sqrt{x}$, or $f(x) = \frac{1}{x}$. Then, transform the graph of $f(x)$ to sketch the graph of $g(x)$.

a) $g(x) = 5x$ **b)** $g(x) = \frac{1}{4x}$

c) $g(x) = (3x)^2$ **d)** $g(x) = \sqrt{9x}$

2.6 Combinations of Transformations, pages 125 to 131

13. Describe, in the appropriate order, the transformations that must be applied to the base function $f(x)$ to obtain the transformed function. Then, write the corresponding equation and transform the graph of $f(x)$ to sketch the graph of $g(x)$.

a) $f(x) = \sqrt{x}$, $g(x) = 3f(x + 6)$

b) $f(x) = x$, $g(x) = -f(6x) - 5$

c) $f(x) = \frac{1}{x}$, $g(x) = \frac{1}{5}f(x) + 4$

d) $f(x) = x^2$, $g(x) = -2f(3x + 12) - 6$

14. For each, identify the base function as one of $f(x) = x$, $f(x) = x^2$, $f(x) = \sqrt{x}$, and $f(x) = \frac{1}{x}$. Sketch the graphs of the base function and the transformed function. State the domain and range of the functions.

a) $g(x) = 2x + 9$ **b)** $g(x) = \frac{3}{x + 4}$

c) $g(x) = -4\sqrt{x} + 1$ **d)** $g(x) = (5x + 20)^2$

2.7 Inverse of a Function, pages 132 to 141

15. For each function $f(x)$:

i) determine $f^{-1}(x)$

ii) graph $f(x)$ and its inverse

iii) state whether or not $f^{-1}(x)$ is a function

a) $f(x) = 7x - 5$

b) $f(x) = 2x^2 + 9$

c) $f(x) = (x + 4)^2 + 15$

d) $f(x) = 5x^2 + 20x - 10$

16. Jai works at an electronics store. She earns $600 a week, plus commission of 5% of her sales.

a) Write a function to describe Jai's total weekly earnings as a function of her sales.

b) Determine the inverse of this function.

c) What does the inverse represent?

d) One week, Jai earned $775. Calculate her sales that week.

Chapter Problem   WRAP-UP

In Sections 2.1, 2.3, 2.5, and 2.7, you explored how functions and transformations relate to the workings of a traffic safety bureau. In general, traffic safety bureaus have a lot to do with civil engineering.

a) Describe how these mathematical concepts relate to civil engineering.

b) Research what is needed to become a civil engineer. How does studying mathematics relate to this field? Be specific.

Chapter 2 Practice Test

For questions 1 to 5, select the best answer.

1. Describe the reflection that transforms $f(x)$ to $g(x)$.

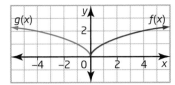

  A a reflection in the x-axis

  B a reflection in the y-axis

  C a reflection in x-axis and then a reflection in the y-axis

  D a reflection in the line $y = x$

2. The graph of $f(x)$ is transformed to obtain the graph of $g(x) = 4f(3x + 21) - 15$. Describe the horizontal translation that occurs.

  A 3 units left   **B** 21 units left

  C 7 units left   **D** 15 units left

3. Describe, in the appropriate order, the transformations that must be applied to the graph of $f(x)$ to obtain the graph of $g(x) = 5f(x - 9) + 7$.

  A vertically stretched by a factor of 5 and then translated 9 units left and 7 units up

  B translated 9 units left and 7 units up and then vertically stretched by a factor of 5

  C translated 9 units right and 7 units up and then vertically stretched by a factor of 5

  D vertically stretched by a factor of 5 and then translated 9 units right and 7 units up

4. State the restrictions on x in the expression $\dfrac{(x + 7)(x - 1)}{(x - 4)(x + 7)}$.

  A $x \neq 4$

  B $x \neq 1, x \neq 4$

  C $x \neq -7, x \neq 4$

  D $x \neq -7, x \neq 1, x \neq 4$

5. If a function is defined by a set of points, then the inverse can be found by

  A reflecting the points in the y-axis

  B interchanging the x- and y-coordinates

  C reflecting the points in the origin

  D taking the reciprocal of each coordinate

6. Are $\dfrac{6x^2 - 27x - 105}{x - 7}$ and $(x + 3)(x + 10) - (x + 3)(x + 5)$ equivalent expressions? Justify your answer.

7. Copy the graph of $f(x)$ and then sketch the graph of the inverse of $f(x)$. State whether or not the inverse is a function.

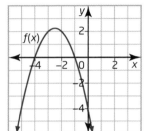

8. Simplify each expression and state any restrictions.

  a) $\dfrac{x - 8}{x + 7} \times \dfrac{x + 15}{x^2 + 12x - 45}$

  b) $\dfrac{x^2 + 12x + 20}{x + 5} \div \dfrac{x^2 + 7x - 30}{x + 10}$

  c) $\dfrac{x + 3}{x - 7} - \dfrac{x + 9}{x - 2}$

  d) $\dfrac{x + 8}{x + 3} + \dfrac{x - 6}{x^2 + 9x + 18}$

9. a) Given the function $g(x) = 4(3x + 6)^2 + 9$, identify the base function as one of $f(x) = x$, $f(x) = x^2$, $f(x) = \sqrt{x}$, and $f(x) = \dfrac{1}{x}$.

  b) Describe, in the appropriate order, the transformations that must be applied to the base function $f(x)$ to obtain the transformed function $g(x)$.

  c) Sketch the graphs of $f(x)$ and $g(x)$.

  d) State the domain and range of the functions.

10. a) Given the function $g(x) = \frac{1}{5}\sqrt{2(x-8)} - 3$, identify the base function as one of $f(x) = x$, $f(x) = x^2$, $f(x) = \sqrt{x}$, and $f(x) = \frac{1}{x}$.

b) Describe, in the appropriate order, the transformations that must be applied to the base function $f(x)$ to obtain the transformed function $g(x)$.

c) Sketch the graphs of $f(x)$ and $g(x)$.

d) State the domain and range of the functions.

11. a) Given the function $g(x) = \frac{2}{0.5x} + 5$, identify the base function as one of $f(x) = x$, $f(x) = x^2$, $f(x) = \sqrt{x}$, and $f(x) = \frac{1}{x}$.

b) Describe, in the appropriate order, the transformations that must be applied to the base function $f(x)$ to obtain the transformed function $g(x)$.

c) Sketch the graphs of $f(x)$ and $g(x)$.

d) State the domain and range of the functions.

12. For each function,

  i) determine $f^{-1}(x)$

  ii) graph $f(x)$ and its inverse

  iii) determine whether the inverse of $f(x)$ is a function

  a) $f(x) = 3x + 8$

  b) $f(x) = 6(x - 9)^2 + 8$

  c) $f(x) = 3x^2 + 36x + 8$

13. A small skateboard company is trying to determine the best price for its boards. When the boards are priced at $80, 120 are sold in a month. After doing some research, the company finds that each increase of $5 will result in selling 15 fewer boards.

  a) Write an equation to represent the revenue, R, in dollars, as a function of x, the number of $5 increases.

  b) State the domain and range of the revenue function.

c) Determine the inverse of the revenue function. What does this equation represent in the context of the question? State the domain and range of the inverse.

d) Determine the number of $5 increases for a revenue of $8100.

14. A small plane is travelling between Windsor and Pelée Island (a distance of approximately 60 km) and is directly affected by the prevailing winds. Thus, the actual speed of the plane with respect to the ground is the speed of the plane (160 km/h) plus or minus the wind speed, w.

  a) Develop a simplified equation for the total time it takes to make a round trip if the wind speed is w. State the domain and range and any restrictions on this relationship.

  b) Graph your relationship from part a).

  c) The pilot thinks that if he has a strong headwind on the way out, then he will be able to make up any lost time on the way back when he has a tailwind. Determine if he is correct.

15. In Canada, fuel efficiency, ℓ, for cars is stated in litres per 100 km. In the United States, fuel efficiency, m, is stated in miles per gallon (mpg). The formula $m = \frac{235}{\ell}$ can be used to convert from the Canadian system to the United States system.

  a) Sketch the graph of the function.

  b) In Canada, cars that have better fuel efficiency have a lower value for ℓ. Is the same true for m? Justify your response.

  c) 1 L equals 0.264 US gallons. 1 L also equals 0.220 Imperial gallons. Determine a new function relating the fuel efficiency in Imperial gallons to litres per 100 km.

  d) How would the graph of your function from part c) compare to the graph in part a)? Explain.

Functions in Design

CD covers and T-shirts often use graphics in their designs. Many of these designs can be defined by mathematical functions.

a) Plot the graphic design defined by the following set of functions, where $x \in \mathbb{R}$.

$$y = \frac{4}{x}, \ -2 \leq x \leq -0.1, \ 0.1 \leq x \leq 2$$

$$y = -\frac{4}{x}, \ -2 \leq x \leq 2$$

$$y = \sqrt{6 - x}, \ x \geq 2$$

$$y = -\sqrt{6 - x}, \ x \geq 2$$

$$y = \frac{2}{3}\sqrt{11 - x}, \ x \geq 2$$

$$y = -\frac{2}{3}\sqrt{11 - x}, \ x \geq 2$$

$$y = \sqrt{2(4 - x)}, \ x \geq 2$$

$$y = -\sqrt{2(4 - x)}, \ x \geq 2$$

$$y = \sqrt{x + 6}, \ x \leq -2$$

$$y = -\sqrt{x + 6}, \ x \leq -2$$

$$y = \frac{2}{3}\sqrt{x + 11}, \ x \leq -2$$

$$y = -\frac{2}{3}\sqrt{x + 11}, \ x \leq -2$$

$$y = \sqrt{2(x + 4)}, \ x \leq -2$$

$$y = -\sqrt{2(x + 4)}, \ x \leq -2$$

b) Explain the significance of $x = 2$.

c) Create and draw your own graphic design using transformations of $y = \frac{1}{x}$ and $y = \sqrt{x}$. You may also use transformations of other functions in your design. List the functions you decide to use, as well as their domains.

Exponential Functions

When you think of exponents, you probably think of repeated multiplication. In this chapter, you will expand your knowledge of exponents and exponential functions. What does a zero exponent mean? What about negative and fractional exponents? What do such number concepts have to do with the planets and our solar system, the growth of living organisms, nuclear power generation, and investments and loans?

In ancient times, now-famous astronomers and mathematicians extended the basic concept of exponents to describe all sorts of scientific phenomena. Eventually, engineers and scientists applied these discoveries in innovative ways to improve our quality of life.

By the end of this chapter, you will

- graph an exponential relation, given its equation in the form $y = a^x$ $(a > 0, a \neq 1)$, define this relation as the function $f(x) = a^x$, and explain why it is a function

- determine the value of a power with a rational exponent

- simplify algebraic expressions containing integer and rational exponents and evaluate numerical expressions containing integer and rational exponents and rational bases

- determine and describe key properties relating to domain and range, intercepts, increasing/decreasing intervals, and asymptotes for exponential functions represented in a variety of ways

- distinguish exponential functions from linear and quadratic functions by making comparisons in a variety of ways

- determine and describe the roles of the parameters $a, k, d,$ and c in functions of the form $y = af[k(x - d)] + c$ in terms of transformations on the graph of $f(x) = a^x$ $(a > 0, a \neq 1)$

- sketch graphs of $y = af[k(x - d)] + c$ by applying one or more transformations to the graph of $f(x) = a^x$ $(a > 0, a \neq 1)$, and state the domain and range of the transformed functions

- determine that the equation of a given exponential function can be expressed using different bases

- represent an exponential function with an equation, given its graph or its properties

- collect data that can be modelled as an exponential function, from primary sources, using a variety of tools, or from secondary sources, and graph the data

- identify exponential functions, including those that arise from real-world applications involving growth and decay, given various representations, and explain any restrictions that the context places on the domain and range

- solve problems using given graphs or equations of exponential functions arising from a variety of real-world applications by interpreting the graphs or by substituting values for the exponent into the equations

Prerequisite Skills

Refer to the Prerequisite Skills Appendix on pages 478 to 495 for examples of the topics and further practice.

Exponent Rules

1. Match each exponent rule with its corresponding method for simplifying.

Rule

a) Product rule: $(x^a)(x^b)$

b) Quotient rule: $\dfrac{x^a}{x^b}$

c) Power of a power rule: $(x^a)^b$

Method

A Subtract the exponents: x^{a-b}

B Multiply the exponents: $x^{a \times b}$

C Add the exponents: x^{a+b}

2. Choose one of the exponent rules. Verify that it holds by using one or more of the following tools:

- numerical examples
- algebraic reasoning
- concrete materials
- diagrams

3. Simplify. Use the exponent rules.

a) $(x^3)(x^2)$

b) $(y^4)(y^2)(y^3)$

c) $m^6 \div m^4$

d) $\dfrac{h^4}{h^3}$

e) $a^3 \times a^4 \times b \times b^5$

f) $\dfrac{x^4 y^3}{x^2 y}$

g) $(ab^2c^3)^4$

h) $(3uv^3)^2$

i) $\left(\dfrac{2ab^2}{2^3}\right)^2$

j) $\left(\dfrac{-3w^2}{4r^3}\right)^3$

4. Evaluate.

a) $2^3 \times 2^4$

b) $(3^2)(3^3)(3)$

c) $5^2 \times 4^2 \times 5 \times 4^2$

d) $(-1)^3(-1)^2(-1)^5$

e) $8^5 \div 8^3$

f) $\dfrac{5^5}{5^4}$

g) $(3^2)^4$

h) $[(-2)^3]^2$

Zero and Negative Exponents

5. Consider the function $y = 2^x$.

a) Copy and complete the table.

x	y
4	$2^4 = 16$
3	$2^3 = 8$
2	$2^2 = $ ▨
1	$2^1 = $ ▨
0	$2^0 = $ ▨

b) Describe the pattern in the column of y-values.

c) Extend the pattern to illustrate the meaning of negative exponents.

x	y
4	$2^4 = 16$
3	$2^3 = 8$
2	$2^2 = $ ▨
1	$2^1 = $ ▨
0	$2^0 = $ ▨
−1	$2^{-1} = \dfrac{1}{2} = \dfrac{1}{2^1}$
−2	$2^{-2} = \dfrac{1}{4} = $ ▨
−3	$2^{-3} = $ ▨
−n	$2^{-n} = $ ▨

6. Evaluate.

a) 5^0

b) 4^{-2}

c) $(-6)^{-3}$

d) $3^{-4} \times 3^2$

e) $(-2)^0$

f) -2^0

g) $\left(\dfrac{4}{5}\right)^{-2}$

h) $9^{-1} \times 9^0$

7. Simplify. Write your answers using only positive exponents.

a) $(x^2)(x^{-3})$

b) $(y^{-2})^3$

c) $\dfrac{u^3 v^{-2}}{u^2 v^{-1}}$

d) $(4a^2b)^{-2}$

Graph Functions

8. Based on the graphs shown, identify the

   i) domain

   ii) range

   iii) x- and y-intercepts, if they exist

a)

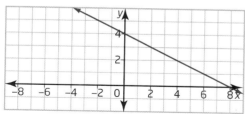

b)

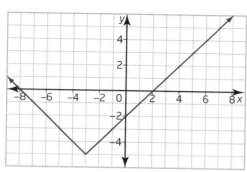

9. Sketch each function. Then, identify the

   i) domain

   ii) range

   iii) x- and y-intercepts, if they exist

   a) $y = x^2 - 9$ **b)** $y = \sqrt{x + 4}$

Transformations of Functions

10. The graph is a transformation of the graph of $y = x^2$. Describe the transformations that were used.

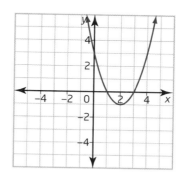

11. Graph each function by applying transformations of the base function $y = \sqrt{x}$.

   a) $y = 3\sqrt{x}$ **b)** $y = \sqrt{2x}$

   c) $y = -\sqrt{x}$ **d)** $y = \sqrt{x} - 5$

   e) $y = 2\sqrt{x - 3}$ **f)** $y = -\sqrt{x - 2} + 4$

Chapter Problem

For millennia, astronomers and other stargazers have been fascinated by the sun, moon, planets, and stars. While it might seem difficult to explore these celestial bodies, advances in science and mathematics allow us to accurately describe how they behave and interact. As you work through this chapter, you will begin to unravel some of the ancient mysteries of the universe and learn some of the ways in which it is possible to describe these fascinating objects.

3.1

The Nature of Exponential Growth

Game shows can be a lot of fun, especially if you are a winning contestant! Have you ever seen a show in which a contestant is faced with a mathematical question?

Suppose that you are the winner of a game show and that you can choose one of three different prizes, each involving a growing pattern. How can your understanding of patterns and mathematical relationships help you pick the best prize? You will see how the concept of exponential growth can be applied in selecting a game show prize in question 8.

Tools

- coloured tiles or linking cubes
- grid paper

or

- graphing calculator

or

- computer with *The Geometer's Sketchpad®*

Investigate

How can you discover the nature of exponential growth?

Consider the three growing patterns shown.

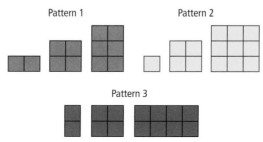

Pattern 1   Pattern 2

Pattern 3

1. Use words to describe how each pattern is growing.

2. Which pattern is growing
   a) fastest?
   b) slowest?
   Explain your reasoning.

3. a) Build or draw the next two terms in each pattern.
   b) Does this confirm your answers in step 2? Explain.

4. a) Copy and complete the table for the pattern 1.

Pattern 1

Term number, n	Number of Squares, t	First Differences	Second Differences
1	2		
		2	
2	4		0
		2	
3	6		
4			
5			

b) Examine the first differences and the second differences. Describe any patterns you see.

c) Is this relationship linear or non-linear? Explain your reasoning.

d) Write an equation to relate the total number of squares, t, to the term number, n.

e) Sketch the graph of this relationship.

5. Repeat step 4 for pattern 2 and for pattern 3.

6. Reflect Refer to steps 4 and 5.

a) Graph the three relationships on the same set of axes.

b) Describe how these relationships are alike. How do they differ?

c) Which colour of tiles are you likely to run out of first, if you continue to build these patterns? Explain why you think so.

Example 1

Model Exponential Growth

A type of bacteria grows so that it triples in number every day. On the day that Roger begins observing the bacteria, a sample has a population of 100.

a) Find the population after each of the first 4 days.

b) Write an equation to model this growth.

c) Graph the relation. Is it a function? Explain why or why not.

d) Assuming this trend continues, predict the population after

  i) 1 week

  ii) 2 weeks

e) Describe the pattern of finite differences for this relationship.

Solution

a) Calculate the population for the first 4 days. Organize the information using a table.

Day	Population
0	100
1	$100 \times 3 = 300$
2	$300 \times 3 = 900$
3	$900 \times 3 = 2700$
4	$2700 \times 3 = 8100$

The initial population is 100.

The population triples each day.

b) To better illustrate the relationship between the day and the total population, express each population calculation in terms of the number of times the initial population is tripled.

Day	Population
0	100
1	$100 \times 3^1 = 300$
2	$100 \times 3^2 = 900$
3	$100 \times 3^3 = 2700$
4	$100 \times 3^4 = 8100$
n	100×3^n

After 1 day, the initial population triples.

After 2 days, the initial population triples again.

After n days, the initial population has tripled n times.

Therefore, an equation relating the population, p, to the number of days, n, is $p(n) = 100 \times 3^n$.

c) A graph of the relation $p(n) = 100 \times 3^n$ is shown. This is a function because each element in the domain corresponds to exactly one element in the range.

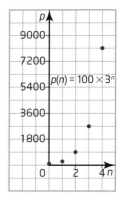

d) Notice that the graph increases steeply as n increases, making it difficult to extrapolate very far. Use the equation $p(n) = 100 \times 3^n$ to find future populations.

i) Substitute $n = 7$ into the equation to find the population after 1 week (7 days).

$$p(7) = 100 \times 3^7$$
$$= 100 \times 2187$$
$$= 218\ 700$$

After 1 week, the bacteria population will be 218 700.

ii) Substitute $n = 14$ into the equation to find the population after 2 weeks.

$$p(14) = 100 \times 3^{14}$$
$$= 100 \times 4\ 782\ 969$$
$$= 478\ 296\ 900$$

After 2 weeks, the bacteria population will be 478 296 900.

e) Add two columns to the table for the first and second differences.

Day	Population	First Differences	Second Differences
0	100		
		300 − 100 = 200	
1	300		600 − 200 = 400
		900 − 300 = 600	
2	900		1800 − 600 = 1200
		2700 − 900 = 1800	
3	2700		5400 − 1800 = 3600
		8100 − 2700 = 5400	
4	8100		

The first differences are not constant. The ratio of successive first differences is the same, as each value after the first is three times the previous value. Similarly, the ratio of successive second differences is the same.

Technology Tip

You can use a graphing calculator to calculate finite differences.

Refer to the Technology Appendix on pages 496 to 516.

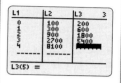

Example 1 illustrates **exponential growth**. This type of growth commonly occurs in science and business.

In the Investigate, you considered exponents with values greater than zero, but you will also see expressions that involve a zero exponent. What is the meaning of a zero exponent? You can explore zero exponents by examining patterns and applying algebraic and graphical reasoning.

exponential growth

- pattern of growth in which each term is multiplied by a constant amount (greater than one) to produce the next term
- produces a graph that increases at a constantly increasing rate

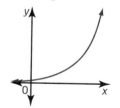

- has a repeating pattern of finite differences: the ratio of successive finite differences is constant

Example 2

Apply a Zero Exponent in a Model

Use the data in Example 1 to demonstrate the meaning of 3^0.

Solution

Look at the table in Example 1 and work backward.

Day	Population
4	$100 \times 3^4 = 8100$
3	$100 \times 3^3 = 2700$
2	$100 \times 3^2 = 900$
1	$100 \times 3^1 = 300$
0	$100 \times 3^0 = 100$

For this pattern to be extended, 3^0 must equal 1, because $100 \times 1 = 100$.

The value of 3^0 can be verified by graphing the function $y = 3^x$ and identifying the y-intercept: When $x = 0$, $y = 1$.

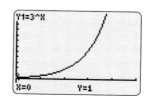

Technology Tip

You can use a graphing calculator to view and analyse this function. To find the y-intercept:

- Press [2nd] [CALC].
- Select **1:value** and enter 0 to identify the y-intercept.

- Exponential growth functions have these properties:
  - As the independent variable increases by a constant amount, the dependent variable increases by a common factor.
  - The graph increases at an increasing rate.
  - The finite differences exhibit a repeating pattern: the ratio of successive finite differences is constant.
- Any non-zero real number raised to the exponent zero is equal to 1:
  $b^0 = 1$ for $b \in \mathbb{R}$, $b \neq 0$.

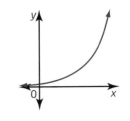

Communicate Your Understanding

C1 An insect colony, with an initial population of 50, triples every day.

a) Which function models this exponential growth?

   A $p(n) = 50 \times 2^n$

   B $p(n) = 150 \times 3n$

   C $p(n) = 50 \times 3^n$

b) For the correct model, explain what each part of the equation means.

C2 Consider these three functions:

   $y = x^2$ $y = 2x$ $y = 2^x$

a) How do the equations differ? How do the graphs differ?

b) Describe the domain and range of each function.

C3 Consider these three functions:

   $y = x^3$ $y = 3x$ $y = 3^x$

Which of these functions is linear? Which is exponential? Justify your choices.

C4 Describe the pattern of finite differences for each type of function. Give an example of each to illustrate your response.

a) a linear function

b) a quadratic function

c) an exponential function

C5 Does $5^0 - 2^0 = 2^0 - 5^0$? Explain.

A Practise

For help with question 1, refer to Example 1.

1. An insect colony, with an initial population of 20, quadruples every day.

   a) Copy and complete the table.

Day	Population	First Differences	Second Differences
0	20		
1	80		
2			
3			
4			
5			

   b) Is the relationship between the insect population and the number of days exponential? Explain how you can tell.

   c) Examine the finite differences. Describe how the first differences and second differences are related.

   d) Will the pattern of first and second differences observed in part c) continue with the third and fourth differences? Write down your conjecture.

   e) Calculate the third and fourth differences. Was your conjecture in part d) correct? Explain.

For help with questions 2 to 4, refer to Example 2.

2. What is the value of 10^0? Use patterns and numerical reasoning to justify your answer.

3. a) Rewrite the expression $\dfrac{a^3}{a^3}$ by expanding both powers.

   b) Divide out common factors in the numerator and denominator. What is the simplified value of this expression?

   c) Write the expression $\dfrac{a^3}{a^3}$ as a single power by applying the quotient rule.

   d) Write a statement that explains how the results of parts b) and c) are related.

4. Evaluate.

   a) 6^0 b) $(-3)^0$ c) $\left(\dfrac{3}{5}\right)^0$ d) x^0

B Connect and Apply

5. a) Use linking cubes, coloured tiles, or tools of your choice to design a growing pattern that can be described by $t(n) = 3^{n-1}$, where n is the term number and $t(n)$ is the number of items in that term.

   b) Draw diagrams to illustrate the first four terms in your pattern, where $t(1)$ is the first term.

   c) How many items would you need to build

   i) the 5th term?   ii) the 10th term?

   d) Suppose that you have 500 items in total to use when constructing a model of this pattern. What is the greatest number of terms you can build at the same time?

   e) Suppose that you have 1000 items in total. What is the greatest number of terms you can build at the same time? How does this answer differ from your answer to part d)? Explain this result.

6. **Use Technology** Use a graphing calculator or graphing software.

   a) Predict the key features of the graph of the function $y = 0^x$:

   i) domain

   ii) range

   iii) shape

   b) Graph the function and check your predictions.

   c) Use a tracing feature to check the value of y when $x = 0$. Does the technology provide the correct answer? Explain.

7. Suppose that there is a rumour going around your school that next year all weekends will be extended to three days. Initially, on day 0, five students know the rumour. Suppose that each person who knows the rumour tells two more students the day after they hear about it. Also assume that no-one hears the rumour more than once.

a) How many people will learn about the rumour

  i) on day 1?   **ii)** on day 2?

b) Estimate your school's student population. How long will it take for this rumour to spread throughout the entire school?

c) Is this an example of exponential growth? Explain your reasoning.

8. Suppose you just won the choice of one of three prizes at a game show:

- Everyday Deal: On day 1, the prize is worth $1. Then, every day for two weeks, the value of the prize is one more dollar than it was the day before.

- Square Deal: On day 1, the prize is worth 1^2, or $1. On day 2, the prize is worth 2^2, or $4, and so on, for two weeks.

- Double Deal: On day 1, the prize is worth $1. On day 2, the prize value doubles to $2 \times \$1$, or $2. On day 3, the value doubles again to $2 \times \$2$, or $4, and so on, for two weeks.

Which prize should you take at the end of the two-week period? Why? Use an algebraic method to justify your choice.

9. A bacterial colony has an initial population of 200. The population triples every week.

Reasoning and Proving
Representing — Selecting Tools
Problem Solving
Connecting — Reflecting
Communicating

a) Write an equation to relate population, p, to time, t, in weeks.

b) Sketch the graph of this relationship for the first month.

c) Determine the approximate population after 10 days. Which tool do you prefer to use for this: the equation or the graph? Explain why.

d) Determine the approximate population after 3 months. Which tool do you prefer to use for this: the equation or the graph? Explain why.

10. Most savings accounts offer compound interest. After each compounding period, interest earned is added to the principal (the initial deposit amount). The amount, A, in dollars, in an account earning interest, compounded annually, with a single deposit can be calculated using the formula $A = P(1 + i)^n$, where P is the principal, in dollars; i is the annual interest rate (expressed as a decimal); and n is the number of years for which the principal earns interest. Marvin deposits $100 into an account that pays interest at 5% per year, compounded annually.

a) Write the annual interest rate as a decimal. Substitute this value into the formula.

b) Copy and complete the table.

Number of Compounding Periods (years)	Amount ($)	
0	100	
1	105	$A = 100(1 + 0.05)^1$
2		$= 100(1.05)^1$
3		$= 105$
4		

c) Calculate the first and second differences.

d) Graph the function.

e) If interest is only paid at the end of each compounding period, do the points between the values in the table have meaning? Explain why or why not.

f) Is this function exponential? Explain.

11. Use the formula for compound interest given in question 10. Sadia deposits a $2000 inheritance into an account that earns 4% per year, compounded annually. Find the amount in the account after each time.

a) 3 years   **b)** 8 years

12. Use the formula for compound interest given in question 10. Heidi invests $500 in an account that earns 7% per year, compounded annually.

a) How long does Heidi need to leave her investment in the account in order to double her money? Explain how you solved this.

b) How much longer would it take if the account paid simple interest, at the same rate? Simple interest does not get added to the principal after each compounding period. Use the formula $I = Prt$, where I is the interest, in dollars; P is the principal, in dollars; r is the interest rate (as a decimal); and t is the time, in years.

C Extend

13. Find an example of exponential growth in a media source, such as a newspaper or the Internet. Identify the source and briefly describe the nature of the relationship.

14. Bacteria A has an initial population of 500 and doubles every day, while bacteria B has an initial population of 50 and triples daily.

a) After how long will the population of B overtake the population of A? What will their populations be at this point?

b) How much faster would B overtake A if A's doubling period were twice as long?

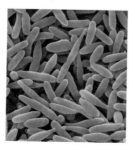

15. Refer to question 8.

a) Suppose the Double Deal is changed so that the prize is worth $0.20 on day 1 instead of $1. On day 2, the value doubles 2 × $0.20, or $0.40. Then, on day 3, the value doubles again to 2 × $0.40, or $0.80, and so on, for two weeks. Which prize should you take at the end of the two-week period? Justify your choice.

b) What is the smallest initial value that makes the Double Deal the best prize option? Explain.

16. Math Contest The doubling period of a type of yeast cell is 3 days. A jar starts off with one yeast cell. After 27 days, there are 512 cells. It takes 30 days to fill the jar. The number of cells in the jar when it is full is

A 512   **B** 4096   **C** 1024   **D** $512(2)^{30}$

17. Math Contest How many terms in the sequence $3^1, 3^2, 3^3, ..., 3^{75}$ have a units digit of 1 when evaluated?

A 0   **B** 25   **C** 19   **D** 18

18. Math Contest Given that $\dfrac{x^2y^6}{z} = 3$ and $\dfrac{x^2z^5}{y^2} = 27$, one possible value of $x^2y^2z^2$ is

A 3   **B** 9   **C** 27   **D** 81

19. Math Contest Paul and Brian are playing a game by throwing a die. Paul throws first. If he throws a 1, a 2, a 3 or a 4, then he wins. If Brian throws a 5 or a 6, then he wins. They continue alternating throws until someone wins. What is the probability that Brian will win?

20. Math Contest A unit fraction is a fraction of the form $\dfrac{1}{n}$, where $n \in \mathbb{N}$. Find all ways to express 1 as the sum of three unit fractions. An example is $\dfrac{1}{3} + \dfrac{1}{3} + \dfrac{1}{3}$.

Use Technology

Use the Lists and Trace Features on a TI-Nspire™ CAS Graphing Calculator

Tools

- TI-Nspire™ CAS graphing calculator

A: Calculate First and Second Differences for the Population Data in Example 1 on pages 151 to 153

1. Open a new document. Open a page using the **Lists & Spreadsheet** application.

2. Set up the table.

- At the top of column A, type the title *day*. Press ⏎.

- At the top of column B, type the title *pop*. Press ⏎.

- Enter the data for the day, starting in cell A1.

- Enter the data for the population, starting in cell B1.

3. Calculate the first differences.

- At the top of column C, type the title *first_diff*.

- In the formula cell below the title, type =.

- Press 📖 and select tab 2.

- Cursor down to **List** and press ⏎.

- Scroll down to **Operations**, and press ⏎.

- Scroll down to **Difference List**, and press ⏎.

- Type *pop* between the brackets, and press ⏎.

  The first differences will be displayed.

- In a similar manner, you can calculate the second differences in column D.

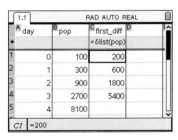

B: Calculate the Population Data in Example 2 on page 153

1. Open a new document. Open a page using the **Lists & Spreadsheet** application.

2. Set up the table.

   - At the top of column A, type the title *day*.

   - At the top of column B, type the title *pop*.

   - Enter the data for the day, starting in cell A1.

   - In the formula cell for column B, type = 100 × 3 ^ a, and press ⏎.

   - The population data will be displayed in column B.

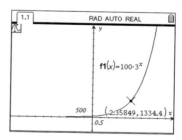

C: Trace the Population Function in Example 2

1. Open a new document. Open a page using the **Graphs & Geometry** application.

2. Graph the function.

   - For function *f1*, type 100 × 3 ^ *x* and press ⏎.

   - Press (menu). Select **4:Window** and then **1:Window Settings**.

   - Set the *x*-range from −5 to 5 and the *y*-range from −100 to 8100.

   - Press (menu). Select **5:Trace** and then **1:Graph Trace**.
     Note that a trace point appears and the coordinates of the point are displayed.

   - Use the cursor to move the trace point along the graph.
     Note that the coordinates of the trace point change as the point is moved.

Exponential Decay: Connecting to Negative Exponents

Nuclear energy provides more than 15% of Canada's electrical power. When atoms of certain elements are split, a tremendous amount of energy is released, which is converted into electricity that we can use. This process is called nuclear fission, and it is one of the key processes involved in nuclear power generation.

Over 50% of Ontario's electric power comes from fission reactors. One of the disadvantages of using nuclear fission to produce energy is the dangerous waste material produced. Scientists and engineers must ensure that such materials are contained and disposed of safely.

Tools

• graphing calculator

half-life

• length of time for an unstable element to spontaneously decay to one half its original amount

Connections

You will learn more about nuclear fission if you study physics in high school or university.
Visit the *Functions 11* page on the McGraw-Hill Ryerson Web site and follow the links to Chapter 3 to find out more about CANDU reactors.

Investigate

How can you explore exponential decay?

Uranium is commonly used as fuel for nuclear reactors. Uranium has several different forms, or isotopes, some of which occur naturally and some of which are produced through nuclear fission. One isotope, uranium-239 (U-239), has a **half-life** of about 2 years. This means that after 2 years, half the U-239 has "decayed," or changed, into a new substance.

Suppose you have a 1000-mg sample of U-239. How can you model the amount remaining over time?

1. Copy and complete the table.

Time (years)	Number of Half-Life Periods (2 years)	Amount of U-239 Remaining (mg)
0	0	1000
2	1	500
4	2	
6	3	
8	4	

2. a) Describe the trend in the table in step 1.

    b) Do you think this relationship between the number of half-life periods and the amount of U-239 remaining is

      • linear?   • quadratic?   • exponential?
      Justify your choice.

3. a) Determine the approximate time it will take for the sample to decay to
  i) 10 mg
  ii) 0.1% of its original amount

b) Will the mass of U-239 in the sample ever reach zero? Explain your reasoning.

4. a) Use a graphing calculator to make a scatter plot of the amount of U-239 remaining versus the number of half-life periods:
  - Press (STAT) and select **EDIT**.
  - Enter the data in lists **L1** and **L2**.
  - Press (2nd) [STAT PLOT] and select **Plot1**.
  - Select the settings shown.
  - Press (ZOOM) and select **9:ZoomStat**.

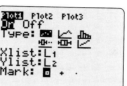

b) Reflect Compare the shape of the scatter plot to the exponential curves you explored in Section 3.1. Describe how they are alike. How do they differ?

5. a) Calculate the first and second differences for this function.

b) Is this relationship exponential? Explain.

6. a) Create an algebraic model for this function using the graphing calculator:
  - From the home screen, press (STAT) and then cursor over to the **CALC** menu.
  - Choose **0:ExpReg**.
  - Press (2nd) [L1] (,) (2nd) [L2] (,). Then press (VARS), select **Y-VARS**, and choose **1:Function**.
  - Choose **1:Y1** and press (ENTER).
  An exponential equation will appear.

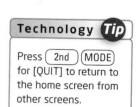

Technology Tip

Press (2nd) (MODE) for [QUIT] to return to the home screen from other screens.

b) Substitute the values given for a and b to write the equation for this relationship in the form $y = ab^x$.

c) Reflect Explain the roles of a and b in the equation you wrote in part b).

7. a) Press (GRAPH) to see the curve of best fit.

b) Does the graph accurately model the relationship? Explain.

8. Reflect Use the **Zoom** and **Trace** operations to check your answers in step 3. Comment on what you notice.

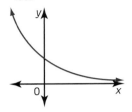
The relationship in the Investigate is an example of **exponential decay**. This type of relationship commonly occurs in such areas of study as science and business.

Example 1

Model Exponential Decay

When U-239 decays, it forms a different material called plutonium-239 (Pu-239). This highly toxic waste material has a much longer half-life of 24 years. Determine approximately how long it will take for a 50-mg sample of Pu-239 to decay to 10% of its original amount.

Solution

10% of 50 mg is 5 mg. You need to find the number of 24-year periods after which 5 mg will remain.

Method 1: Use a Table or a Spreadsheet

Enter the number of half-life periods, years, and amount remaining using three columns.

• Enter 0 in cell A2 and 1 in cell A3. Highlight cells A2 and A3. With the mouse over the bottom right corner of cell A3, click and drag straight down to continue the pattern.

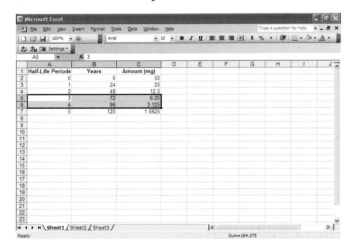

• Enter 0 in cell B2. In cell B3, type = and then click on cell B2, type +24 and press (Enter). Then, highlight B3 and, with the mouse over the bottom left corner, click and drag down.

• Use the same technique for the last column, but enter 50 in cell C2 and use the equation C3 = C2/2.

Read down the last column. The sample will reach a level of 5 mg somewhere between 72 and 96 years from now.

Method 2: Use Systematic Trial

Write an equation to relate the amount of Pu-239 remaining to the number of half-life periods. This gives the equation $A(n) = 50\left(\dfrac{1}{2}\right)^n$, where n is the number of 24-year half-life periods and A is the amount of Pu-239 remaining, in milligrams.

Substitute $A = 5$ and solve for n.

$$A(n) = 50\left(\dfrac{1}{2}\right)^n$$

$$5 = 50\left(\dfrac{1}{2}\right)^n$$

$$0.1 = \left(\dfrac{1}{2}\right)^n \qquad \text{Divide both sides by 50.}$$

Use systematic trial with a calculator to find the value of n that satisfies this equation. For ease of calculation, use 0.5 in place of $\dfrac{1}{2}$.

n	0.5^n	Mathematical Reasoning
5	0.03125	Try 5 half-lives. This gives a value much lower than 0.1. Try a shorter period of time.
2	0.25	Too high. The correct value is between 2 and 5. Try 3 next.
3	0.125	Close, but high.
3.3	0.1015...	This is very close to 0.1. This will give a reasonable approximation.

The number of half-life periods is approximately 3.3. Multiply this by 24 to find the equivalent number of years.

$$3.3 \times 24 = 79.2$$

It will take approximately 79 years for the sample of Pu-239 to decay to 10% of its initial mass.

Method 3: Use a Graphical Model

Write an equation to model the relationship, graph it, and read the information from the graph. The graph of $A(n) = 50\left(\dfrac{1}{2}\right)^n$ is shown.

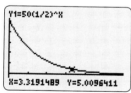
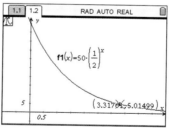

Connections

You will learn how to find exact solutions to equations such as $5 = 50\left(\dfrac{1}{2}\right)^n$ when you study logarithms in grade 12.

Using the **Trace** operation, you can read that the amount has decayed to about 5 mg after approximately 3.3 half-lives. Convert this to years by multiplying by 24.

$$3.3 \times 24 = 79.2$$

It will take approximately 79 years for the sample of Pu-239 to decay to 10% of its initial amount.

In Methods 2 and 3 of Example 1, you considered the function $A(n) = 50\left(\frac{1}{2}\right)^n$, where n is greater than or equal to zero. However, you will sometimes encounter exponential expressions with negative exponents. You can use the following relationship to evaluate expressions involving negative exponents:

$b^{-n} = \dfrac{1}{b^n}$ for any $b \in \mathbb{R}$, $b \neq 0$, and $n \in \mathbb{N}$.

Example 2

Evaluate Expressions Involving Negative Exponents

Evaluate.

a) 3^{-2} **b)** $6^{-2} \times 6^3$ **c)** $(-2)^{-4} + 4^{-2}$ **d)** $(4^{-2})^{-3} \div 4^8$

Solution

a) $3^{-2} = \dfrac{1}{3^2}$

$= \dfrac{1}{9}$

b) $6^{-2} \times 6^3 = 6^{-2+3}$ Apply the product rule. Add the exponents.

$= 6^1$

$= 6$

c) $(-2)^{-4} + 4^{-2} = \dfrac{1}{(-2)^4} + \dfrac{1}{4^2}$

$= \dfrac{1}{16} + \dfrac{1}{16}$

$= \dfrac{2}{16}$

$= \dfrac{1}{8}$

d) $(4^{-2})^{-3} \div 4^8 = 4^{(-2)(-3)} \div 4^8$ Apply the power of a power rule first.

$= 4^6 \div 4^8$ Multiply exponents.

$= 4^{6-8}$ Apply the quotient rule. Subtract exponents.

$= 4^{-2}$

$= \dfrac{1}{4^2}$

$= \dfrac{1}{16}$

Example 3

Simplify Expressions Involving Negative Exponents

Simplify. Express answers using only positive exponents.

a) $(x^{-2})(x^{-3})(x^4)$ **b)** $\dfrac{a^2b^{-3}}{a^{-1}b^2}$ **c)** $(2u^3v^{-2})^{-3}$

Solution

a) $(x^{-2})(x^{-3})(x^4) = x^{-2-3+4}$ Apply the product rule.

$\qquad\qquad\qquad\quad = x^{-1}$

$\qquad\qquad\qquad\quad = \dfrac{1}{x}$

b) $\dfrac{a^2b^{-3}}{a^{-1}b^2} = a^{2-(-1)}b^{-3-2}$ Apply the quotient rule.

$\qquad\quad = a^3b^{-5}$

$\qquad\quad = \dfrac{a^3}{b^5}$

c) $(2u^3v^{-2})^{-3} = 2^{-3}u^{3(-3)}v^{(-2)(-3)}$ Apply the power of a power rule.

$\qquad\qquad\quad = \dfrac{1}{2^3}u^{-9}v^6$

$\qquad\qquad\quad = \dfrac{v^6}{8u^9}$

Example 4

Evaluate Powers Involving Fractional Bases

Simplify.

a) $\left(\dfrac{1}{3}\right)^{-1}$ **b)** $\left(-\dfrac{27}{8}\right)^{-2}$

Solution

a) $\left(\dfrac{1}{3}\right)^{-1} = \dfrac{1}{\left(\dfrac{1}{3}\right)^1}$ Write with a positive exponent.

$\qquad\quad = 1 \div \dfrac{1}{3}$

$\qquad\quad = 1 \times \dfrac{3}{1}$ Multiply by the reciprocal.

$\qquad\quad = 3$

b) $\left(-\dfrac{27}{8}\right)^{-2} = \left(-\dfrac{8}{27}\right)^2$ Apply the property of negative exponents.

$\qquad\qquad\quad = \dfrac{64}{729}$

Connections

The result in Example 4 part a) can be generalized as follows.
$\left(\dfrac{a}{b}\right)^{-n} = \left(\dfrac{b}{a}\right)^n$ for $a, b \in \mathbb{R}, a, b \neq 0$, and $n \in \mathbb{N}$.

- Exponential decay functions have the following properties:
  - As the independent variable increases by a constant amount, the dependent variable decreases by a common factor.
  - The graph decreases at a decreasing rate.
  - They have a repeating exponential pattern of finite differences: the ratio of successive finite differences is constant.

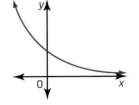

- A power involving a negative exponent can be expressed using a positive exponent:

  $b^{-n} = \dfrac{1}{b^n}$ for $b \in \mathbb{R}$, $b \neq 0$, and $n \in \mathbb{N}$.

- The exponent rules hold for powers involving negative exponents.

- Rational expressions raised to a negative exponent can be simplified:

  $\left(\dfrac{a}{b}\right)^{-n} = \left(\dfrac{b}{a}\right)^{n}$ for $a, b \in \mathbb{R}$, $a, b \neq 0$, and $n \in \mathbb{N}$.

Communicate Your Understanding

C1 Compare exponential growth and exponential decay. Describe how these types of relationships are alike. How are they different?

C2 The equation $A(n) = 50\left(\dfrac{1}{2}\right)^{n}$ from Example 1 gives the amount, A, in milligrams, of Pu-239 remaining after n 24-year half-life periods.

Claudia says, "I can write a simpler form of this equation: $A(n) = 50(2)^{-n}$."

a) Do you think Claudia's model is valid? Explain your thinking.

b) Suggest at least two ways that you could verify the equivalence of these two models.

C3 Explain how you can use a positive exponent to rewrite a power involving a negative exponent. Create an example to illustrate your answer.

C4 Explain how you can use a negative exponent to rewrite a power involving a positive exponent. Create an example to illustrate your answer.

A Practise

For help with questions 1 to 4, refer to Example 2.

1. Write each as a power with a positive exponent.

a) 3^{-1} **b)** x^{-1} **c)** y^{-2}

d) $(ab)^{-1}$ **e)** $-x^{-2}$ **f)** $(-x)^{-2}$

2. Write each as a power with a negative exponent.

a) $\dfrac{1}{5^2}$ **b)** $\dfrac{1}{k^3}$

3. Evaluate. Express as a fraction in lowest terms.

a) 6^{-2} **b)** 2^{-5} **c)** 10^{-4}

d) 9^{-3} **e)** $2^{-2} + 4^{-1}$ **f)** $6^{-1} + 3^{-1} + 2^{-3}$

4. Apply the exponent rules to evaluate.

a) $(4^{-2})^{-1}$

b) $(2^{-4})^2$

c) $\dfrac{10^4}{10^{-1}}$

d) $5^{-3} \div 5^{-2}$

e) $(7^{-2})(7^4)$

f) $4^{-3} \times 4^{-5} \times 4^6 \times 4^0$

g) $\dfrac{3(3^4)}{3^3}$

h) $\dfrac{(4^5)(4^{-2})}{4^2}$

For help with question 5, refer to Example 3.

5. Simplify. Express your answers using only positive exponents.

a) $m^{-2} \times m^3$

b) $(3v^{-3})(-2v^{-6})$

c) $p^4 \div p^{-3}$

d) $\dfrac{6w^{-4}}{2w^{-2}}$

e) $(k^{-3})^{-4}$

f) $(2ab^{-3})^{-2}$

For help with questions 6 and 7, refer to Example 4.

6. Evaluate.

a) $\left(\dfrac{1}{8}\right)^{-2}$

b) $\left(\dfrac{3}{10}\right)^{-6}$

c) $\left(\dfrac{9}{4}\right)^{-2}$

d) $\left(-\dfrac{5}{2}\right)^{-3}$

e) $\left(\dfrac{1}{2}\right)\left(-\dfrac{1}{4}\right)^{-2}$

f) $\left[\left(\dfrac{1}{4}\right)^2\left(\dfrac{2}{5}\right)\right]^{-2}$

7. Simplify. Express your answers using only positive exponents.

a) $\left(\dfrac{1}{ab}\right)^{-2}$

b) $\left(\dfrac{1}{8u}\right)^{-3}$

c) $\left(\dfrac{g^4}{w^2}\right)^{-2}$

d) $\left(\dfrac{4a^3}{3b^2}\right)^{-3}$

e) $\left(\dfrac{3a^2}{b^3}\right)^{-3}$

f) $\left(\dfrac{x^{-2}}{y^{-1}}\right)^{-2}$

B Connect and Apply

8. Tungsten-187 (W-187) is a radioactive isotope that has a half-life of 1 day. Suppose you start with a 100-mg sample.

a) Make a table of values that gives the amount of W-187 remaining at the end of each day for the next 4 days.

Reasoning and Proving

Representing — Selecting Tools

Problem Solving

Connecting — Reflecting

Communicating

b) Write an equation in the form $f(x) = ab^x$ to relate the amount of W-187 remaining and time. Identify what each variable in the equation represents and give the appropriate unit for each variable.

c) Sketch the graph of the relation. Describe the shape of the curve.

d) How much W-187 will remain after 1 week?

e) How long will it take for the amount of W-187 to decay to 5% of its initial amount? Describe the tools and strategies you used to solve this.

f) Write a different function to model the same situation. Explain why the two functions are equivalent.

9. a) Evaluate each expression. Express your answers as fractions.

  i) 3^{-2}

  ii) 3^{-3}

b) Multiply your answers from part a) together.

c) Apply the product rule of exponents to the expression $3^{-2} \times 3^{-3}$. Write the result with a positive exponent and evaluate.

d) Compare your answers to parts b) and c). What does this illustrate about powers with negative exponents?

e) Create another example to illustrate this property.

10. Use two numerical examples to verify that the quotient rule holds for expressions involving negative exponents.

11. Use numerical or algebraic reasoning to verify that the power of a power rule holds for expressions involving negative exponents.

12. Shylo is very excited about her brand new car!

Although she paid $20 000 for the car, its resale value will depreciate (decrease) by 30% of its current value every year. The equation relating the car's depreciated value, v, in dollars, to the time, t, in years, since her purchase is $v(t) = 20\,000(0.7)^t$.

a) Explain the significance of each part of this equation.

b) How much will Shylo's car be worth in

   i) 1 year?   **ii)** 2 years?

c) Graph the depreciation function. Is it an example of exponential decay? Explain how you can tell.

d) How long will it take for Shylo's car to depreciate to 10% of its original price?

13. Consider Example 1. Suppose that the original sample of Pu-239 was larger than the 50 mg present at the beginning of the study.

a) Explain how you can use the exponential model in Example 1 to describe decay that happened before the beginning of the study.

Reasoning and Proving

Representing   Selecting Tools

Problem Solving

Connecting   Reflecting

Communicating

b) Find the mass of this sample

   i) 1 half-life before the beginning of the study

   ii) 3 half-lives before the beginning of the study

14. Use algebraic reasoning to prove the general result $\left(\dfrac{a}{b}\right)^{-n} = \left(\dfrac{b}{a}\right)^{n}$ for $a, b \in \mathbb{R}$, $a, b \neq 0$, and $n \in \mathbb{N}$.

15. Use algebraic reasoning to show how the formula $A = P(1 + i)^n$ can be expressed in the form $P = A(1 + i)^{-n}$.

✔ Achievement Check

16. The formula $P(n) = A(1 + i)^{-n}$ is used to calculate the principal, $P(n)$, invested in an account that has been accumulating interest, compounded annually. A is the current amount in the account, in dollars; i is the annual interest rate (as a decimal); and n is the number of years the principal has been earning interest.

a) Oscar deposited some money into an account that pays 3% per year, compounded annually. Today the account balance is $660. How much was in the account

   i) 1 year ago?

   ii) 5 years ago?

b) Does this formula represent exponential growth or decay? Explain.

c) Rewrite the formula to isolate A. Does this form of the formula represent exponential growth or decay? Explain.

17. Refer to question 16. Lydia wants to invest some money that will grow to $1000 in 6 years. If her account pays 4.5% interest, compounded annually, how much should Lydia invest today?

18. Chapter Problem There is a gravitational force of attraction between every pair of objects in the universe. The strength of this force depends on the mass of each object and the distance that separates the objects.

The formula $F = GMmr^{-2}$ relates this force to the mass of each of the objects and the distance between them, where G is a constant equal to 6.7×10^{-11}; M and m are the masses of the two objects, in kilograms; and r is the distance separating them, in metres.

The mass of Earth, M, is 6.0×10^{24} kg; the mass of the moon, m, is 7.4×10^{22} kg; and Earth and the moon are 380 000 km apart. Use this information to determine the force, F, in newtons (N), of attraction between the moon and Earth.

C Extend

19. Refer to question 18.

a) Rewrite the formula $F = GMmr^{-2}$ in its more usual form, with a positive exponent.

b) This relationship between force and distance is an example of an inverse square relationship. Explain what this means.

c) Research to find another example of an inverse square relationship. Describe the variables that are related, and provide a sample calculation.

20. Refer to question 18. Compare the strength of this force to the force of attraction between

a) the moon and your body

b) Earth and your body, using $r = 6400$ km (the radius of Earth)

21. Math Contest If $f(x) = 3^{2 - 3x}$, then the value of $[f(1 + x)][f(1 - x)]$ is

A $\dfrac{1}{9}$ **B** 9   **C** 27   **D** 1

22. Math Contest The y-intercept of the function $y = -2\left(\dfrac{1}{3}\right)^{2x - 1} + 2$ is

A 2   **B** 0   **C** 8   **D** -4

23. Math Contest Consider the following system of equations.

$x_1 + x_2 = 120$
$x_2 + x_3 = 160$
$x_3 + x_4 = 140$
$x_4 + x_5 = 125$
$x_1 + x_3 + x_5 = 215$

What is the value of $x_1 + x_5$?

A 160   **B** 125   **C** 120   **D** 140

Career Connection

Sinthujan studied medical radiation technology at a Canadian college for $2\frac{1}{2}$ years. Radiation therapy is one of the most common ways to treat cancer. In his job, under the direction of an oncologist, Sinthujan uses high-energy external beam radiation to stop cancers from multiplying. He exposes the patient to radiation from a machine a number of times over a period of weeks. To reach the right spot in the body, Sinthujan completes calculations to optimize the beam angle, beam size, and distance from the cancer. The goal is not only to successfully radiate the entire cancerous growth but also to minimize the side effects for the patient.

3.3

Rational Exponents

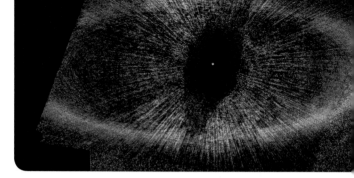

Is there life on other planets? Are planets like Fomalhaut b, shown here, similar to Earth? Will we ever be able to travel through space to find out? These questions have been asked for generations and have formed the basis for countless science fiction books and movies. How are such stories related to the mathematics of exponential functions?

Investigate

How can you find the meaning of a rational exponent?

Somewhere far, far away...

The corrupt Galactic Empire is taking over the universe at an exponential rate! How long will it be before planet Earth falls under the rule of the Empire? Meanwhile, rumours of a Rebel Alliance are beginning to spread. Will the Rebel Alliance be able to break the Empire's dominion before the fall of Earth?

Currently, the Galactic Empire controls 100 planets. However, the number of captured planets is quadrupling every decade. This growth is modelled by the graph and equation shown.

1. Look at the equation. Explain what each variable represents and state its units of measure.

2. Look at the graph.

   a) Identify the coordinates at the P-intercept. Explain their significance.

   b) How many planets will fall under the control of the Empire after

      i) 1 decade?

      ii) 2 decades?

      Explain how you can use the graph to find this information.

   c) Use the equation to check these answers.

3. a) Explain how you can use the graph to estimate the number of planets controlled by the Empire after 5 years. How many planets will it control after 5 years?

   b) Enter $t = \dfrac{1}{2}$ into the equation and use a calculator to evaluate $P(t)$. Does this answer agree with your answer in part a)? Explain.

The graph is labelled with P on the vertical axis marked at 400, 800, 1200, 1600, 2000, and t on the horizontal axis marked at 2 and 4. The curve is labelled $P(t) = 100(4)^t$.

4. a) Evaluate the expression $100 \times \sqrt{4}$.

b) How does this compare to $100 \times 4^{\frac{1}{2}}$?

c) **Reflect** What does this suggest about the expressions $\sqrt{4}$ and $4^{\frac{1}{2}}$?

5. a) Begin with the equation $4 = 2^2$. Raise each side to the exponent $\frac{1}{2}$ and use the power of a power rule to simplify the expression on the right side.

b) **Reflect** Since $\sqrt{4} = 2$, does the result in part a) confirm that $4^{\frac{1}{2}} = \sqrt{4}$? Explain.

6. a) **Reflect** Does the result of step 5b) hold for powers involving bases other than 4? Write down your prediction.

b) Choose several different bases and use a calculator to evaluate each base raised to the exponent $\frac{1}{2}$.

c) Compare these to the square root of each base. Comment on what you notice.

In the Investigate, you discovered a method that can be used to show that $b^{\frac{1}{2}} = \sqrt{b}$ for $b \in \mathbb{R}$, $b \geq 0$. Similar reasoning can be applied to evaluate powers involving other rational exponents.

Example 1

Powers With Rational Exponents of the Form $\frac{1}{n}$

Evaluate.

a) $8^{\frac{1}{3}}$

b) $(-32)^{\frac{1}{5}}$

c) $-16^{\frac{1}{4}}$

d) $\left(\dfrac{16}{81}\right)^{\frac{1}{4}}$

e) $(-27)^{-\frac{1}{3}}$

Solution

a) $8^{\frac{1}{3}}$

Apply the product rule of exponents to find the value of $8^{\frac{1}{3}}$:

$$8^{\frac{1}{3}} \times 8^{\frac{1}{3}} \times 8^{\frac{1}{3}} = 8^{\frac{1}{3} + \frac{1}{3} + \frac{1}{3}}$$
$$= 8^1$$
$$= 8$$

Taking cube roots of both sides, it follows that

$$8^{\frac{1}{3}} = \sqrt[3]{8} \qquad \text{The cube of } 8^{\frac{1}{3}} \text{ is equal to 8, so } 8^{\frac{1}{3}} \text{ is equal to the cube root of 8.}$$
$$= 2$$

Connections

$\sqrt[3]{8}$ is read as "the cube root of eight."

$\sqrt[4]{16}$ is read as "the fourth root of sixteen."

The terminology used for this type of expression is as follows:

- $\sqrt[4]{16}$ is called a radical.
- 16 is the radicand.
- 4 is the index.

Connections

The result in Example 1a) can be generalized as follows.

$b^{\frac{1}{n}} = \sqrt[n]{b}$ for any $n \in \mathbb{N}$. If n is even, b must be greater than or equal to 0.

b) $(-32)^{\frac{1}{5}} = \sqrt[5]{-32}$ Think: What number raised to the exponent 5 produces -32?

$$= -2 \qquad \sqrt[5]{-32} = -2, \text{ because } (-2)(-2)(-2)(-2)(-2) = -32.$$

c) $-16^{\frac{1}{4}} = -\sqrt[4]{16}$

$$= -2$$

Note that, unlike in part b), the negative sign is not part of the base of the power.

d) $\left(\dfrac{16}{81}\right)^{\frac{1}{4}} = \sqrt[4]{\dfrac{16}{81}}$ $\sqrt[4]{\dfrac{16}{81}} = \dfrac{2}{3}$, because $\left(\dfrac{2}{3}\right)^4 = \left(\dfrac{2}{3}\right)\left(\dfrac{2}{3}\right)\left(\dfrac{2}{3}\right)\left(\dfrac{2}{3}\right)$

$$\qquad\qquad = \dfrac{2}{3} \qquad\qquad\qquad\qquad\qquad = \dfrac{2 \times 2 \times 2 \times 2}{3 \times 3 \times 3 \times 3}$$

$$\qquad\qquad\qquad\qquad\qquad\qquad\qquad\qquad = \dfrac{16}{81}$$

e) $(-27)^{-\frac{1}{3}} = \dfrac{1}{(-27)^{\frac{1}{3}}}$ Rewrite the power with a positive exponent.

$$= \dfrac{1}{\sqrt[3]{-27}}$$

$$= \dfrac{1}{-3} \qquad\qquad \text{Evaluate the cube root in the denominator.}$$

$$= -\dfrac{1}{3}$$

You can apply the exponent rules to interpret rational exponents in which the numerator is not one.

Example 2

Powers With Rational Exponents of the Form $\dfrac{m}{n}$

Evaluate each expression.

   a) $8^{\frac{2}{3}}$ **b)** $81^{\frac{5}{4}}$ **c)** $\left(\dfrac{49}{81}\right)^{-\frac{3}{2}}$

Solution

a) $8^{\frac{2}{3}} = 8^{\frac{1}{3} \times 2}$ Express the exponent as a product: $\dfrac{2}{3} = \dfrac{1}{3} \times 2$

$$= \left(8^{\frac{1}{3}}\right)^2 \qquad \text{Use the power of a power rule.}$$

$$= \left(\sqrt[3]{8}\right)^2 \qquad \text{Write } 8^{\frac{1}{3}} \text{ as a cube root.}$$

$$= 2^2$$

$$= 4$$

b) $81^{\frac{5}{4}} = \left(81^{\frac{1}{4}}\right)^5$

$$= \left(\sqrt[4]{81}\right)^5$$

$$= 3^5 \qquad \text{Evaluate the fourth root of 81.}$$

$$= 243$$

c) $\left(\dfrac{49}{81}\right)^{-\frac{3}{2}} = \left(\dfrac{81}{49}\right)^{\frac{3}{2}}$ Rewrite the power with a positive exponent.

$= \left(\sqrt{\dfrac{81}{49}}\right)^{3}$

$= \left(\dfrac{\sqrt{81}}{\sqrt{49}}\right)^{3}$

$= \left(\dfrac{9}{7}\right)^{3}$

$= \dfrac{729}{343}$

The reasoning used in part a) of Example 2 can be applied to obtain the general result $b^{\frac{m}{n}} = \left(\sqrt[n]{b}\right)^{m}$ for any non-zero real number b, where $m \in \mathbb{Z}$, $n \in \mathbb{N}$. Notice that b must be greater than or equal to 0 if n is even.

Example 3

Apply Exponent Rules

Simplify. Express your answers using only positive exponents.

a) $\dfrac{\left(x^{\frac{2}{3}}\right)\left(x^{\frac{2}{3}}\right)}{x^{\frac{1}{3}}}$ **b)** $\left(y^{\frac{1}{4}}\right)^{2} \times \left(y^{-\frac{1}{3}}\right)^{2}$ **c)** $\left(5x^{\frac{1}{2}}\right)^{2} \times 4x^{-\frac{1}{2}}$

Solution

a) $\dfrac{\left(x^{\frac{2}{3}}\right)\left(x^{\frac{2}{3}}\right)}{x^{\frac{1}{3}}} = \dfrac{x^{\frac{4}{3}}}{x^{\frac{1}{3}}}$ Apply the product rule.

$= x^{\frac{4}{3} - \frac{1}{3}}$ Apply the quotient rule.

$= x^{\frac{3}{3}}$

$= x$

b) $\left(y^{\frac{1}{4}}\right)^{2} \times \left(y^{-\frac{1}{3}}\right)^{2} = y^{\frac{1}{2}} \times y^{-\frac{2}{3}}$ Apply the power of a power rule.

$= y^{\frac{3}{6}} \times y^{-\frac{4}{6}}$ Write the exponents with common denominators.

$= y^{\frac{3}{6} - \frac{4}{6}}$ Apply the product rule.

$= y^{-\frac{1}{6}}$

$= \dfrac{1}{y^{\frac{1}{6}}}$ Express with a positive exponent.

c) $\left(5x^{\frac{1}{2}}\right)^{2} \times 4x^{-\frac{1}{2}} = 25x \times 4x^{-\frac{1}{2}}$ Apply the power of a power rule.

$= 100x^{\frac{1}{2}}$ Apply the product rule.

> **Connections**
>
> Note that $\dfrac{1}{y^{\frac{1}{6}}}$ can also be expressed as $\dfrac{1}{\sqrt[6]{y}}$.

Example 4

Solve a Problem Involving a Rational Exponent

The following formula relates the volume, V, and surface area, S, of a sphere.

$$V(S) = \frac{(4\pi)^{-\frac{1}{2}}}{3} \times S^{\frac{3}{2}}$$

Find the volume, to the nearest cubic metre, of a spherical holding tank with surface area 100 m².

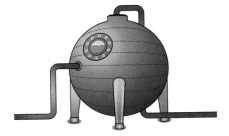

Solution

Substitute $S = 100$ into the formula and evaluate for V:

$$V(100) = \frac{(4\pi)^{-\frac{1}{2}}}{3} \times 100^{\frac{3}{2}}$$

Use a calculator to evaluate $(4\pi)^{-\frac{1}{2}}$.

Use algebraic reasoning to evaluate $100^{\frac{3}{2}}$:

$$100^{\frac{3}{2}} = \left(\sqrt{100}\right)^3$$
$$= 10^3$$
$$= 1000$$

$$V(100) \doteq \frac{0.282}{3} \times 1000$$
$$= 94$$

The volume of the holding tank is approximately 94 m³.

Communicate Your Understanding

C1 a) What is a cube root? Provide an example to illustrate your explanation.

b) Repeat part a) for the fourth root of a number.

C2 a) Explain how you can write the fifth root of a number

  i) as a radical

  ii) as a power

b) Create an example to illustrate your answers.

C3 Consider the following simplification. For each step, explain the rule being applied.

Step **Explanation**

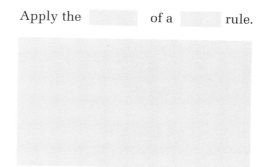

$(x^{-\frac{1}{2}})^3(x^{\frac{1}{3}})^2 = (x^{-\frac{3}{2}})(x^{\frac{2}{3}})$

$= x^{-\frac{3}{2} + \frac{2}{3}}$

$= x^{-\frac{9}{6} + \frac{4}{6}}$

$= x^{-\frac{5}{6}}$

$= \dfrac{1}{x^{\frac{5}{6}}}$

$= \dfrac{1}{(\sqrt[6]{x})^5}$

Apply the ▢ of a ▢ rule.

A Practise

For help with questions 1 and 2, refer to Example 1.

1. Evaluate each cube root.

a) $\sqrt[3]{64}$

b) $(-1000)^{\frac{1}{3}}$

c) $\sqrt[3]{\dfrac{1}{8}}$

d) $\left(\dfrac{8}{27}\right)^{\frac{1}{3}}$

2. Evaluate each root.

a) $81^{\frac{1}{4}}$

b) $\sqrt[4]{\dfrac{16}{625}}$

c) $64^{\frac{1}{6}}$

d) $\sqrt[5]{-100\,000}$

For help with questions 3 and 4, refer to Example 2.

3. Evaluate.

a) $8^{\frac{2}{3}}$

b) $32^{\frac{4}{5}}$

c) $(-64)^{\frac{5}{3}}$

d) $\left(\dfrac{1}{10\,000}\right)^{\frac{3}{4}}$

4. Evaluate.

a) $16^{-\frac{1}{4}}$

b) $25^{-\frac{3}{2}}$

c) $\left(\dfrac{1}{8}\right)^{-\frac{7}{3}}$

d) $\left(-\dfrac{1}{32}\right)^{-\frac{2}{5}}$

e) $\left(\dfrac{10\,000}{81}\right)^{-\frac{3}{4}}$

f) $\left(-\dfrac{8}{27}\right)^{-\frac{2}{3}}$

For help with questions 5 and 6, refer to Example 3.

5. Simplify. Express your answers using only positive exponents.

a) $x^{\frac{1}{4}} \times x^{\frac{1}{4}}$

b) $(m^{\frac{1}{3}})(m^{\frac{3}{4}})$

c) $\dfrac{w^{\frac{1}{2}}}{w^{\frac{1}{3}}}$

d) $\dfrac{ab^2}{a^{\frac{1}{2}}b^{\frac{1}{3}}}$

e) $(y^{\frac{1}{2}})^{\frac{2}{3}}$

f) $(u^{\frac{3}{4}}v^{\frac{1}{2}})^{\frac{2}{9}}$

6. Simplify. Express your answers using only positive exponents.

a) $k^{\frac{3}{4}} \div k^{-\frac{1}{4}}$

b) $\dfrac{p^{-\frac{2}{3}}}{p^{\frac{5}{6}}}$

c) $(y^{\frac{2}{3}})^{-3}$

d) $(w^{-\frac{8}{9}})^{-\frac{3}{4}}$

e) $(8x)^{\frac{2}{3}}(27x)^{-\frac{1}{3}}$

f) $5(7y^{-\frac{2}{3}})^{-2}$

For help with question 7, refer to Example 4.

7. The surface area, S, of a sphere can be expressed in terms of its volume, V, using the formula $S(V) = (4\pi)^{\frac{1}{3}}(3V)^{\frac{2}{3}}$. A beach ball has volume 24 000 cm³. Find its surface area, to the nearest hundred square centimetres.

B Connect and Apply

8. What is the square-cube law? Consider the following sequence of cubes.

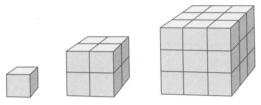

a) Write a formula to express the area, A, of one face in terms of the side length, ℓ.

b) Write a formula to express the side length, ℓ, in terms of the area, A, using a rational exponent.

c) What is the side length of a cube for which each square face has an area of
   i) 36 m²? **ii)** 169 cm²? **iii)** 80 m²?

d) Modify your answers to parts a) and b) to relate the total surface area, S, and the side length, ℓ.

e) Use the results of part d) to calculate the side length of a cube with a surface area of
   i) 150 m² **ii)** 600 cm² **iii)** 250 m²

Connections

The square-cube law is important in many areas of science. It can be used to explain why elephants have a maximum size and why giant insects cannot possibly exist, except in science fiction! Why do you think this is so?

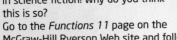

Go to the *Functions 11* page on the McGraw-Hill Ryerson Web site and follow the links to Chapter 3 to find out more about the square-cube law and its impact on humans and other creatures.

---

9. Refer to question 8.

a) Write a formula to express the volume of the cube, V, in terms of the side length, ℓ.

b) Write a formula to express the side length, ℓ, in terms of the volume, V, using a rational exponent.

c) What is the side length of a cube with a volume of
   i) 64 m³? **ii)** 343 cm³? **iii)** 15.4 m³?

10. Refer to question 8.

a) Which formula correctly relates the surface area and volume of a cube?

  A $S = 6V^{\frac{3}{2}}$ **B** $S = 6V^{\frac{2}{3}}$

  C $V = \left(\dfrac{S}{6}\right)^{\frac{3}{2}}$ **D** $V = 6S^{\frac{3}{2}}$

b) Is there more than one correct formula? Use algebraic and geometric reasoning to support your answer.

c) Why is this relationship called the square-cube law?

11. a) Use one of the formulas from question 10 to find the surface area of a cube with a volume of
   i) 1000 cm³   **ii)** 200 m³

b) Which formula did you select, and why?

c) Use one of the formulas from question 10 to find the volume of a cube with a surface area of
   i) 294 m²   **ii)** 36.8 cm²

d) Is the formula you used in part c) the same as the formula you used in part b)? Explain why or why not.

12. Chapter Problem One of Kepler's laws of planetary motion states that the square of a planet's period of revolution (its "year"), T, is related to the cube of its mean radial distance, r, from the sun. This can be expressed using the equation

$T = kr^{\frac{3}{2}}$, where k is a constant. The radius of Earth's orbit around the sun is 1.5×10^{11} m, and $T = 1$ year.

a) Find the value of the constant, k.

b) Mars is approximately 2.3×10^{11} m from the sun. How long is Mars's year, compared to Earth's?

c) The planet Venus takes approximately 0.62 Earth years to orbit the sun. What is the approximate radius of Venus's orbit?

Connections

Johannes Kepler lived in the late 16th and early 17th centuries in Europe. He made some of science's most important discoveries about planetary motion.

13. Refer to question 12.

a) Use algebraic reasoning to rewrite $T = kr^{\frac{3}{2}}$ with r in terms of T.

b) Jupiter's period of revolution around the sun is approximately equal to 12 Earth years. What is Jupiter's average distance from the sun?

✔ **Achievement Check**

14. The formulas $h = 241m^{-\frac{1}{4}}$ and $r = \dfrac{107}{2}m^{-\frac{1}{4}}$ give the heartbeat frequency, h, in beats per minute, and respiratory frequency, r, in breaths per minute, for a resting animal with mass m, in kilograms.

a) Determine the heartbeat frequency and respiratory frequency for each animal.

i) killer whale: 6400 kg

ii) dog: 6.4 kg

iii) mouse: 0.064 kg

b) Describe what happens to each frequency as the mass of the animal decreases.

c) Use the formula $B = \dfrac{1}{100}m^{\frac{2}{3}}$ to determine the brain mass, B, for each animal in part a).

C Extend

15. a) What is the formula for the volume of a cylinder?

b) Rewrite this formula to express the radius as a function of the volume and height of the cylinder.

16. Refer to question 15.

Reasoning and Proving

Representing — Selecting Tools

Problem Solving

Connecting — Reflecting

Communicating

a) What is the formula for the surface area of a cylinder?

b) Substitute the result of question 15b) into this formula.

c) Simplify the result to express the surface area of a cylinder with a height of 10 m in terms of its volume.

d) Find the surface area of a cylindrical storage tank with height 10 m and volume 1000 m³.

17. In the expansion of a particular gas, the relation between the pressure, P, in kilopascals (kPa), and the volume, V, in cubic metres, is given by $P^2V^3 = 850$.

a) Solve the equation for V.

b) What is the volume of gas when the pressure is 10 kPa?

c) Plot the graph of this relation.

d) Is this relation a function?

18. Math Contest A new operation * is defined as $a*b = (b + 1)^{a + 1}$. The value of $[(-2)*3]*15$ is

A 32 **B** 216

C −90 **D** 65 536

19. Math Contest Without using a calculator, determine the value of $\dfrac{25^{\frac{3}{5}}}{\sqrt[5]{5}}$.

3.4

Properties of Exponential Functions

Capacitors are used to store electric potential energy. When a capacitor in a resistor-capacitor (RC) circuit is discharged, the electric potential across the capacitor decays exponentially over time. This sort of circuit is used in a variety of electronic devices, such as televisions, computers, and MP3 players. Engineers and technicians who design and build such devices must have a solid understanding of exponential functions.

Many situations can be modelled using functions of the form $f(x) = ab^x$, where $a \neq 0$ and $b > 0$, $b \neq 1$. How do the values of a and b affect the properties of this type of function?

Tools

- computer with *The Geometer's Sketchpad®*

or

- grid paper

or

- graphing calculator

interval

- an unbroken part of the real number line
- is either all of $\mathbb{R}$ or has one of the following forms: $x < a$, $x > a$, $x \leq a$, $x \geq a$, $a < x < b$, $a \leq x \leq b$, $a < x \leq b$, $a \leq x < b$, where $a, b \in \mathbb{R}$, and $a < b$

Connections

It is important to be careful around discarded electrical equipment, such as television sets. Even if the device is not connected to a power source, stored electrical energy may be present in the capacitors.

Investigate

How can you discover the characteristics of the graph of an exponential function?

A: The Effect of b on the Graph of $y = ab^x$

Start with the function $f(x) = 2^x$. In this case, $a = 1$.

1. a) Graph the function.

b) Describe the shape of the graph.

2. Use algebraic and/or graphical reasoning to justify your answers to the following.

a) What are the domain and the range of the function?

b) What is the y-intercept?

c) Is there an x-intercept?

d) Over what **interval** is the function

i) increasing?

ii) decreasing?

3. Change the value of b. Use values greater than 2.

a) Compare each graph to the graph of $y = 2^x$. Describe how the graphs are alike. How do they differ?

b) Describe how the value of b has affected the characteristics listed in step 2.

c) Explain why a value of b greater than 2 has this effect on the graph.

If you are using *The Geometer's Sketchpad®*, you can set b as a parameter whose value you can change dynamically:

- From the **Graph** menu, choose **New Parameter**. Set the name as b and its initial value to 2. Click **OK**.
- From the **Graph** menu, choose **Plot New Function**. Click on the parameter b, and then click on ^ **x** and **OK**.

You can change the value of b in three ways:

- Click on parameter b and press (+) and (−) on the keyboard to increase or decrease the value of b in 1-unit increments.
- Right-click on parameter b and choose **Edit Parameter** to enter a specific value.
- Right-click on parameter b and choose **Animate Parameter**. Use the buttons on the **Motion Controller** to see the effects of changing b continuously.

4. Change the value of b again. This time, use values between 0 and 1.

 a) How has the graph changed?

 b) Describe how the values of b affect the characteristics listed in step 2.

 c) Explain why a value of b between 0 and 1 has this effect on the graph.

5. What happens to the graph when you set $b = 1$? Explain this result.

6. Reflect Summarize how the values of b affect the shape and characteristics of the graph of $f(x) = b^x$.

B: The Effect of a on the Graph of $y = ab^x$

Use the function $f(x) = a \times 2^x$. In this part of the Investigate, keep $b = 2$, and explore what happens as you change the value of a.

1. Set $a = 1$. This gives the original graph of $f(x) = 2^x$. Explore what happens when

 a) $a > 1$

 b) $0 < a < 1$

 c) $a < 0$

2. Reflect Write a summary of the effects of various values of a on the graph of the function $f(x) = a \times 2^x$. Include the following characteristics: domain, range, x- and y-intercepts, and intervals of increase and decrease. Explain why changing the value of a has these effects. Sketch diagrams to support your explanations.

Connections

In Section 3.3, you saw how to deal with rational exponents. The definition of an exponent can be extended to include real numbers, and so the domain of a function like $f(x) = 2^x$ is all real numbers. Try to evaluate 2^π using a calculator.

Technology Tip

With a graphing calculator, you can vary the line style to see multiple graphs simultaneously. Refer to the Technology Appendix on pages 496 to 516.

One of the interesting features of an exponential function is its asymptotic behaviour. Consider the function $f(x) = 2^x$. If you keep looking left at decreasing values of x, you will see that the corresponding y-value of the function gets closer and closer to, but never reaches, the x-axis. In this case, the x-axis is an asymptote.

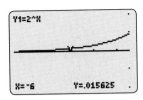
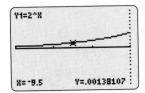

Example 1

Analyse the Graph of an Exponential Function

Graph each exponential function. Identify the

- domain
- range
- x- and y-intercepts, if they exist
- intervals of increase/decrease
- asymptote

a) $y = 4\left(\dfrac{1}{2}\right)^x$

b) $y = -3^{-x}$

Solution

a) $y = 4\left(\dfrac{1}{2}\right)^x$

Method 1: Use a Table of Values

Select negative and positive values of x that will make it easy to compute corresponding values of y.

x	y
−2	16
−1	8
0	4
1	2
2	1
3	$\dfrac{1}{2}$
4	$\dfrac{1}{4}$

$$4\left(\frac{1}{2}\right)^{-2} = 4\left(\frac{2}{1}\right)^2$$
$$= 16$$

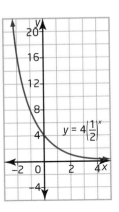

Use the table of values to graph the function.

Method 2: Use a Graphing Calculator

Use a graphing calculator to explore the graph of this function.

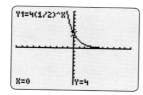

The function is defined for all values of x. Therefore, the domain is $\{x \in \mathbb{R}\}$.

The function has positive values for y, but y never reaches zero. Therefore, the range is $\{y \in \mathbb{R}, y > 0\}$.

The graph never crosses the x-axis, which means there is no x-intercept.

The graph crosses the y-axis at 4. Therefore, the y-intercept is 4.

The graph falls to the right throughout its domain, so the y-values decrease as the x-values increase. Therefore, the function is decreasing over its domain.

As the x-values increase, the y-values get closer and closer to, but never reach, the x-axis. Therefore, the x-axis, or the line $y = 0$, is an asymptote.

b) $y = -3^{-x}$

 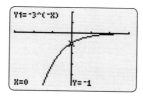

The domain is $\{x \in \mathbb{R}\}$.

All function values are negative. Therefore, the range is $\{y \in \mathbb{R}, y < 0\}$.

There is no x-intercept.

The y-intercept is -1.

The graph rises throughout its domain. Therefore, the function is increasing for all values of x.

The x-axis, whose equation is $y = 0$, is an asymptote.

Connections

Could you use transformations to quickly sketch the graph of $y = -3^{-x}$? You will explore this option in Section 3.5.

Example 2

Write an Exponential Equation Given Its Graph

Write the equation in the form $y = ab^x$ that describes the graph shown.

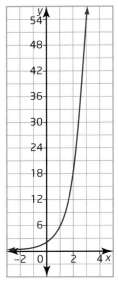

> **Solution**

Read some ordered pairs from the graph.

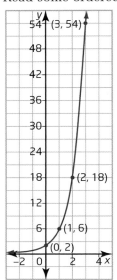

Note that as x changes by 1 unit, y increases by a factor of 3, confirming that this function is an exponential function.

x	y	Change in y
0	2	
		× 3
1	6	
		× 3
2	18	
		× 3
3	54	

Since each successive value increases by a factor of 3, this function must have $b = 3$. Since all points on this graph must satisfy the equation $y = ab^x$, substitute the coordinates of one of the points, and the value of b, to find the value of a.

Pick a point that is easy to work with, such as (1, 6). Substitute $x = 1$, $y = 6$, and $b = 3$:

$y = ab^x$

$6 = a \times 3^1$

$6 = a \times 3$

$a = 2$

Therefore, the equation that describes this curve is $y = 2 \times 3^x$.

Example 3

Write an Exponential Function Given Its Properties

A radioactive sample has a half-life of 3 days. The initial sample is 200 mg.

a) Write a function to relate the amount remaining, in milligrams, to the time, in days.

b) Restrict the domain of the function so that the mathematical model fits the situation it is describing.

Solution

a) This exponential decay can be modelled using a function of the form $A(x) = A_0\left(\dfrac{1}{2}\right)^x$, where x is the time, in half-life periods; A_0 is the initial amount, in milligrams; and A is the amount remaining, in milligrams, after time x.

Start with 200 mg. After every half-life, the amount is reduced by half.

Substituting $A_0 = 200$ into this equation gives $A(x) = 200\left(\dfrac{1}{2}\right)^x$. This expresses A as a function of x, the number of half-lives. To express A as a function of t, measured in days, replace x with $\dfrac{t}{3}$.

The half-life of this material is 3 days. Therefore, the number of elapsed half-lives at any given point is the number of days divided by 3.

$$A(t) = 200\left(\frac{1}{2}\right)^{\frac{t}{3}}$$

This equation relates the amount, A, in milligrams, of radioactive material remaining to time, t, in days.

b) A graph of this function reveals a limitation of the mathematical model.

The initial sample size, at $t = 0$, was 200 mg. It is not clear that the function has any meaning before this time. Since it is only certain that the mathematical model fits this situation for non-negative values of t, it makes sense to restrict its domain:

$A(t) = 200\left(\dfrac{1}{2}\right)^{\frac{t}{3}}$ for

$\{t \in \mathbb{R}, t \geq 0\}$.

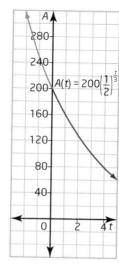
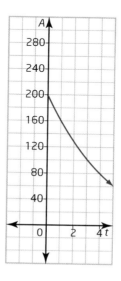

- The graph of an exponential function of the form $y = ab^x$ is

  - increasing if $a > 0$ and $b > 1$
  - decreasing if $a > 0$ and $0 < b < 1$
  - decreasing if $a < 0$ and $b > 1$
  - increasing if $a < 0$ and $0 < b < 1$

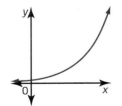 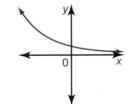 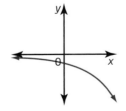 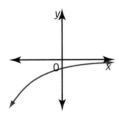

- The graph of an exponential function of the form $y = ab^x$, where $a > 0$ and $b > 0$, has
  - domain $\{x \in \mathbb{R}\}$
  - a horizontal asymptote at $y = 0$
  - range $\{y \in \mathbb{R}, y > 0\}$
  - a y-intercept of a

- The graph of an exponential function of the form $y = ab^x$, where $a < 0$ and $b > 0$, has
  - domain $\{x \in \mathbb{R}\}$
  - a horizontal asymptote at $y = 0$
  - range $\{y \in \mathbb{R}, y < 0\}$
  - a y-intercept of a

- You can write an equation to model an exponential function if you are given enough information about its graph or properties.

- Sometimes it makes sense to restrict the domain of an exponential model based on the situation it represents.

Communicate Your Understanding

C1 **a)** Is an exponential function either always increasing or always decreasing? Explain.

  b) Is it possible for an exponential function of the form $y = ab^x$ to have an x-intercept? If yes, given an example. If no, explain why not.

C2 Consider the exponential functions $f(x) = 100\left(\frac{1}{2}\right)^x$ and $g(x) = -10(2)^x$.

  a) Which function has a graph with range

  i) $\{y \in \mathbb{R}, y < 0\}$?   **ii)** $\{y \in \mathbb{R}, y > 0\}$?

  Explain how you can tell by inspecting the equations.

  b) Which function is

  i) increasing?   **ii)** decreasing?

  Explain how you can tell by inspecting the equations.

C3 Describe what is meant by "asymptotic behaviour." Support your explanation with one or more sketches.

A Practise

For help with questions 1 to 3, refer to Example 1.

1. Match each graph with its corresponding equation.

a)

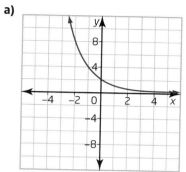

b)

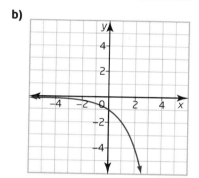

c)

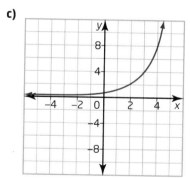

d)

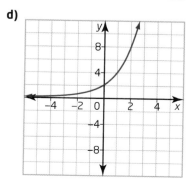

A $y = 2 \times 2^x$

B $y = 2 \times \left(\dfrac{1}{2}\right)^x$

C $y = \dfrac{1}{2} \times 2^x$

D $y = -2^x$

2. a) Sketch the graph of an exponential function that satisfies all of these conditions:
- domain $\{x \in \mathbb{R}\}$
- range $\{y \in \mathbb{R}, y > 0\}$
- y-intercept 5
- function increasing

b) Is this the only possible graph? Explain.

3. a) Sketch the graph of an exponential function that satisfies all of these conditions:
- domain $\{x \in \mathbb{R}\}$
- range $\{y \in \mathbb{R}, y < 0\}$
- y-intercept -2
- function decreasing

b) Is this the only possible graph? Explain.

For help with questions 4 and 5, refer to Example 2.

4. Write an exponential equation to match the graph shown.

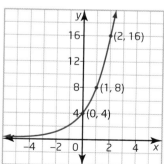

5. Write an exponential equation to match the graph shown.

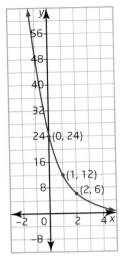

For help with question 6, refer to Example 3.

6. A radioactive sample with an initial mass of 25 mg has a half-life of 2 days.

   a) Which equation models this exponential decay, where t is the time, in days, and A is the amount of the substance that remains?

   A $A = 25 \times 2^{\frac{t}{2}}$

   B $A = 25 \times \left(\frac{1}{2}\right)^{2t}$

   C $A = 25 \times \left(\frac{1}{2}\right)^{\frac{t}{2}}$

   D $A = 2 \times 25^{\frac{t}{2}}$

   b) What is the amount of radioactive material remaining after 7 days?

B Connect and Apply

7. Graph each function and identify the

   i) domain

   ii) range

   iii) x- and y-intercepts, if they exist

   iv) intervals of increase/decrease

   v) asymptote

   a) $f(x) = \left(\frac{1}{2}\right)^x$

   b) $y = 2 \times 1.5^x$

   c) $y = -\left(\frac{1}{3}\right)^x$

8. a) Graph each function.

   i) $f(x) = 2^x$

   ii) $r(x) = \frac{2}{x}$

   b) Describe how the graphs are alike. How do they differ?

   c) Compare the asymptotes of these functions. What do you observe?

9. a) Graph each function.

   i) $g(x) = \left(\frac{1}{2}\right)^x$ **ii)** $r(x) = \frac{2}{x}$

   b) Describe how the graphs are alike. How do they differ?

   c) Compare the asymptotes of these functions. What do you observe?

10. a) Predict how the graphs of the following functions are related.

   i) $f(x) = 3^{-x}$ **ii)** $g(x) = \left(\frac{1}{3}\right)^x$

   b) Graph both functions and check your prediction from part a).

   c) Use algebraic reasoning to explain this relationship.

11. The graph shows the voltage drop across a capacitor over time while discharging an RC circuit. At $t = 0$ s, the circuit begins to discharge.

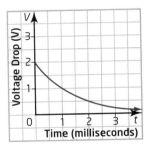

   a) What is the domain of this function?

   b) What is the range?

   c) What is the initial voltage drop across the capacitor?

   d) What value does the voltage drop across the capacitor approach as more time passes?

   e) Approximately how long will it take the voltage drop to reach 50% of the initial value?

12. A flywheel is rotating under friction. The number, R, of revolutions per minute after

Reasoning and Proving
Representing — *Selecting Tools*
Problem Solving
Connecting — *Reflecting*
Communicating

t minutes can be determined using the function $R(t) = 4000(0.75)^{2t}$.

a) Explain the roles of the numbers 0.75 and 2 in the equation.

b) Graph the function.

c) Which value in the equation indicates that the flywheel is slowing?

d) Determine the number of revolutions per minute after

    i) 1 min   **ii)** 3 min

Ⓒ Extend

13. Use Technology Refer to question 11. The equation that models this situation is given by $V = V_0 b^{\frac{t}{RC}}$, where V is the voltage drop, in volts; V_0 is the initial voltage drop; t is the time, in seconds; R is the resistance, in ohms (Ω); and C is the capacitance, in farads (F).

For this circuit, $R = 2000\ \Omega$ and $C = 1\ \mu\text{F}$. Note that $1\ \mu\text{F} = 0.000\ 001$ F.

a) Determine the value of the base, b.

b) Explain your method.

c) Graph the function using a graphing calculator or graphing software. Use the window settings shown.

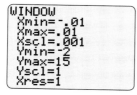

```
WINDOW
 Xmin=-.01
 Xmax=.01
 Xscl=.001
 Ymin=-2
 Ymax=15
 Yscl=1
 Xres=1
```

d) What are the domain and range of this function?

e) Explain how and why the domain and range are restricted, as illustrated in the graph of question 11.

14. Suppose a square-based pyramid has a fixed height of 25 m.

a) Write an equation, using rational exponents where appropriate, to express the side length of the base of a square-based pyramid in terms of its volume.

b) How should you limit the domain of this function so that the mathematical model fits the situation?

c) What impact does doubling the volume have on the side length of the base? Explain.

15. Suppose that a shelf can hold cylindrical drums with a fixed height of 1 m.

a) Write a simplified equation, using rational exponents where appropriate, to express the surface area in terms of the volume for drums that will fit on the shelf.

b) Find the surface area and diameter of a drum with a volume of 0.8 m³.

c) What are the restrictions on the domain of the function used in this model?

d) Graph the function for the restricted domain.

16. Math Contest Find all solutions to $3x - 2^x - 1 = 0$.

17. Math Contest Consider the function $y = 12\left(\dfrac{1}{2}\right)^x - 3$. The y-intercept is b and the x-intercept is a. The sum of a and b is

  A 11   **B** 6   **C** 7   **D** 18

18. Math Contest A number is between 20 and 30. When this number is subtracted from its cube, the result is 13 800. When the same number is added to its cube, the answer is

  A 13 848   **B** 13 852

  C 13 846   **D** 13 844

3.5

Transformations of Exponential Functions

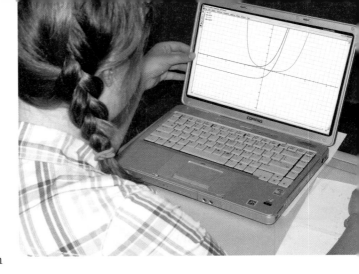

Once you understand the basic shape of an exponential function, you can apply your understanding of transformations to easily graph a variety of related curves.

You should be familiar with the following types of transformations:

- $f(x) \rightarrow f(x) + c$
- $f(x) \rightarrow f(x - d)$
- $f(x) \rightarrow af(x)$
- $f(x) \rightarrow f(kx)$

What type of transformation does each of these represent? Do these same transformations apply to exponential functions?

Tools

- computer with *The Geometer's Sketchpad*®

or

- graphing calculator

Investigate

How can you transform an exponential function?

1. a) Make a conjecture about what happens when you transform the function $y = 2^x$ to the function $y = 2^x + 3$.

   b) Use a graphing calculator or graphing software to test your prediction. Describe what you notice.

   c) Repeat parts a) and b) for the following:

   i) $y = 2^x \rightarrow y = 2^x - 4$

   ii) two other transformations of this type

   d) Summarize your observations.

2. a) Consider the transformation $y = 2^x \rightarrow y = 2^{x + 3}$. How do you think this will compare to the transformation in step 1a)?

   b) Test your prediction. Repeat for two other transformations of this type.

   c) Describe the effects of this type of transformation.

3. a) Predict what will happen to the graph of $y = 2^x$ when you transform it to $y = 2(2^x)$.

   b) Test your prediction. Repeat for two other transformations of this type. Include at least one negative value. Describe what you notice.

4. a) Do you think the transformation $y = 2^x \rightarrow y = 2^{2x}$ will produce the same effect as that in step 3a)? Explain your reasoning.

b) Test your prediction.

c) Carry out two other transformations of this type. Use at least one negative value. Summarize your observations.

5. Choose a different base and repeat the analysis in steps 1 to 4. Do you get similar results using different bases?

6. Reflect Write a brief summary of
- horizontal and vertical translations of exponential functions
- horizontal and vertical stretches of exponential functions
- horizontal and vertical reflections of exponential functions

Use diagrams to support your explanations.

7. a) Reflect Can you express the function $y = 2^{2x}$ in another form? Use algebraic reasoning to explain.

b) Use graphing technology to verify that the two functions are equivalent.

Example 1

Horizontal and Vertical Translations

Sketch graphs of the following functions using the graph of $y = 3^x$ as the base. Describe the effects, if any, on the

- asymptote
- domain
- range

a) $y = 3^x - 4$

b) $y = 3^{x-2}$

c) $y = 3^{x+1} + 3$

Solution

a) $y = 3^x - 4$

This translation will shift $y = 3^x$ down 4 units. Start with the graph of $y = 3^x$ and then apply the translation.

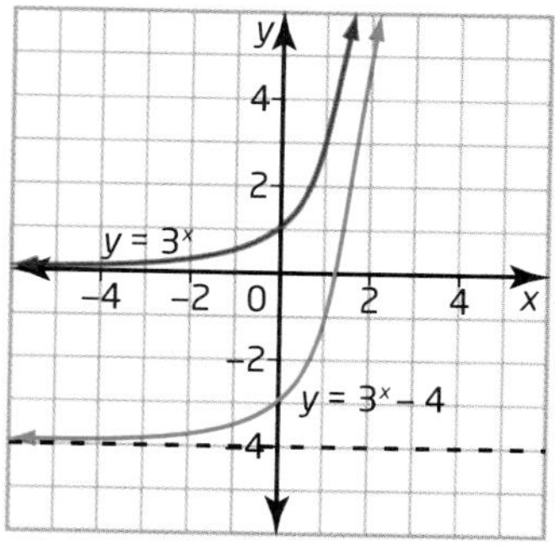

Note that the asymptote has shifted down 4 units.

The graph extends indefinitely to the right and left, so the domain remains $\{x \in \mathbb{R}\}$.

The graph shows that the function has values above the line $y = -4$, so the range is $\{y \in \mathbb{R}, y > -4\}$.

b) $y = 3^{x-2}$

This translation will shift $y = 3^x$ to the right 2 units. Start with the graph of $y = 3^x$ and then apply the translation.

The asymptote has not changed: it remains the line $y = 0$.

The horizontal shift has not changed the domain of $\{x \in \mathbb{R}\}$.

The range also remains unchanged: $\{y \in \mathbb{R}, y > 0\}$.

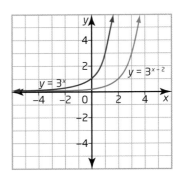

c) $y = 3^{x+1} + 3$

This compound translation includes both a horizontal and a vertical shift. Translate the curve of $y = 3^x$ left 1 unit and up 3 units.

The horizontal asymptote has shifted 3 units upward to the line $y = 3$.

The domain remains $\{x \in \mathbb{R}\}$.

The range is $\{y \in \mathbb{R}, y > 3\}$.

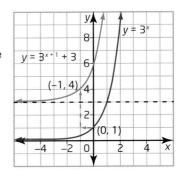

You can check your results using a graphing calculator.

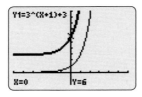
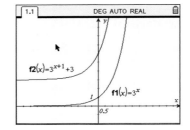

Example 2

Stretches, Compressions, and Reflections

Graph each function using transformations of the base function $y = 4^x$.

a) $y = 4^{2x}$

b) $y = -2(4^x)$

c) $y = 4^{-\frac{1}{2}x}$

Solution

a) $y = 4^{2x}$

Start with $y = 4^x$. Then, compress the graph horizontally by a factor of $\frac{1}{2}$.

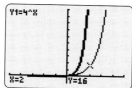
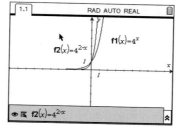

b) $y = -2(4^x)$

This compound transformation involves a stretch and a reflection:

$$y = -2(4^x)$$

Reflect in the x-axis. ⟵   Stretch vertically by a factor of 2.

Start with the graph of $y = 4^x$. Then, apply the vertical stretch.

Now reflect $y = 2(4^x)$ in the x-axis.

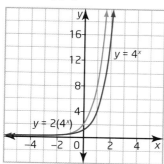
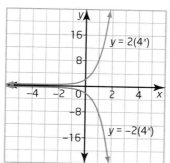

c) $y = 4^{-\frac{1}{2}x}$

This compound transformation also involves a stretch and a reflection:

$$y = 4^{-\frac{1}{2}x}$$

Reflect in the y-axis. ⟵   Stretch horizontally by a factor of 2.

Start with the graph of $y = 4^x$ and apply the horizontal stretch.

Now reflect this curve in the y-axis.

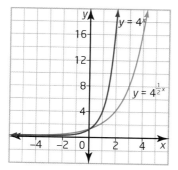
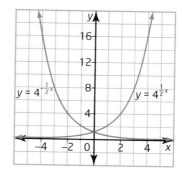

Example 3

Graph $y = ab^{k(x-d)} + c$

Graph the function $y = -2^{2(x-3)} + 5$.

Solution

Start with $y = 2^x$. Identify the transformations that will produce the graph of the equation given above:

$$y = -2^{2(x-3)} + 5$$

Reflect in the x-axis.   Compress horizontally by a factor of $\frac{1}{2}$.   Shift right 3 units and up 5 units.

Start with the graph of $y = 2^x$. To show $y = 2^{2x}$, compress horizontally.

Next, reflect the curve in the x-axis to show $y = -2^{2x}$.

Finally, perform the horizontal and vertical translations.

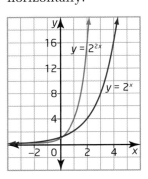
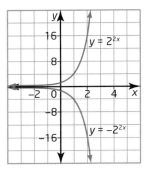
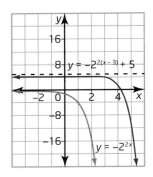

Example 4

Circuit Analysis

In a particular circuit, the current, I, in amperes (A), after t seconds can be found using the formula $I(t) = 0.9(1 - 10^{-0.044t})$.

a) Graph this function using graphing technology. What is the appropriate domain for the function modelling the current?

b) What is the current in the circuit after
   i) 2 s?   **ii)** 5 s?

c) Describe what is happening to the current over the chosen domain.

Connections

You explored compound transformations of functions in Chapter 2.

Solution

Method 1: Use a Graphing Calculator

a) Use systematic trial to set an appropriate viewing window. Note that the appropriate domain must not allow negative values for the current. The domain is $\{t \in \mathbb{R}, t > 0\}$.

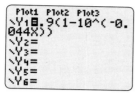 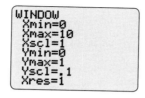 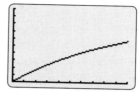

b) i) To determine the current at 2 s:

- Press (2nd) [CALC] and then select **1:value**.
- Enter 2 when prompted and press (ENTER).

 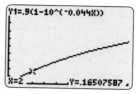

At $t = 2$ s, the current is approximately 0.17 A.

ii) Use the same process to determine the current after 5 s.

At $t = 5$ s, the current is approximately 0.36 A.

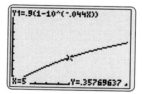

c) The function is increasing over $\{t \in \mathbb{R}, t > 0\}$, and the rate of increase is decreasing.

Method 2: Use *The Geometer's Sketchpad®*

a) Start a new sketch. From the **Graph** menu, choose **Plot New Function**. Enter the function as shown, and click **OK**.

From the **Graph** menu, click on the **Grid Form** menu and choose **Rectangular Grid**. Click and drag the origin and scales to obtain a clear view of the graph. Note that the appropriate domain must not allow negative values for the current. The domain is $\{t \in \mathbb{R}, t > 0\}$.

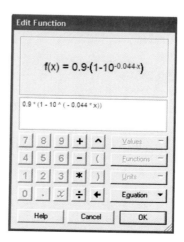

b) i) To determine the current at 2 s, determine the value of I when $t = 2$:

- Select the graph. From the **Construct** menu, choose **Point On Function Plot**.
- From the **Measure** menu, choose **Coordinates**.
- Click and drag the point as close as you can to $t = 2$. Then, read the corresponding I-value.

At $t = 2$ s, the current is approximately 0.17 A.

ii) Use the same process to determine the current after 5 s.

At $t = 5$ s, the current is approximately 0.36 A.

c) The function is increasing over $\{t \in \mathbb{R}, t > 0\}$, and the rate of increase is decreasing.

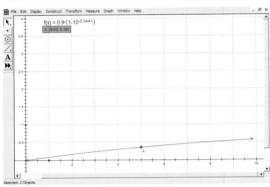

Key Concepts

- Exponential functions can be transformed in the same way as other functions.
- The graph of $y = ab^{k(x - d)} + c$ can be found by performing the following transformations on the graph of the base $y = b^x$:

Horizontal and Vertical Translations

- If $d > 0$, translate right d units; if $d < 0$, translate left.
- If $c > 0$, translate up c units; if $c < 0$, translate down.

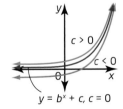

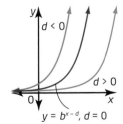

Vertical Stretches, Compressions, and Reflections

- If $a > 1$, stretch vertically by a factor of a.
- If $0 < a < 1$, compress vertically by a factor of a.
- If $a < 0$, reflect in the x-axis and stretch or compress.

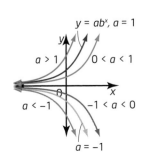

Horizontal Stretches, Compressions, and Reflections

– If $k > 1$, compress horizontally by a factor of $\frac{1}{k}$.

– If $0 < k < 1$, stretch horizontally by a factor of $\frac{1}{k}$.

– If $k < 0$, reflect in the y-axis and stretch or compress.

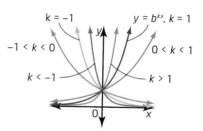

- Some exponential functions can easily be written using different bases. For example, $y = 2^{4x}$ is equivalent to $y = 16^x$.

Communicate Your Understanding

C1 Match each transformation with the corresponding equation, using the function $y = 10^x$ as the base. Give reasons for your answers. Not all transformations will match an equation.

Transformation

a) horizontal stretch by a factor of 3

b) shift 3 units up

c) shift 3 units left

d) vertical compression by a factor of $\frac{1}{3}$

e) vertical stretch by a factor of 3

f) shift 3 units right

g) reflect in the x-axis

A $y = 10^x + 3$

B $y = 10^{x + 3}$

C $y = -10^x$

D $y = 10^x - 3$

E $y = 10^{3x}$

F $y = 10^{-x}$

G $y = \left(\frac{1}{3}\right)10^x$

C2 Give a corresponding equation for each unmatched transformation in question C1.

C3 **a)** Describe how you could sketch the graph of $y = 5^{2x}$ using a transformation.

b) Describe how you could sketch the graph of $y = 5^{2x}$ by applying an exponent rule.

C4 Describe the effect of each constant, a, k, c, and d, when the graph of the function $y = b^x$ is transformed to $y = ab^{k(x - d)} + c$.

C5 Refer to Example 4.

a) How could you determine whether or not the current increases indefinitely?

b) Carry out the method described in part a) to determine if the current does increase indefinitely.

A Practise

For help with questions 1 to 3, refer to Example 1.

1. Describe the transformation that maps the function $y = 4^x$ onto each function given.

a) $y = 4^x + 2$ **b)** $y = 4^{x-3}$

c) $y = 4^{x+4}$ **d)** $y = 4^{x-1} - 5$

2. Sketch the graph of each function in question 1. Use the graph of $y = 4^x$ as the base.

3. Write the equation for the function that results from each transformation applied to the base function $y = 5^x$.

a) translate down 3 units

b) shift right 2 units

c) translate left $\frac{1}{2}$ unit

d) shift up 1 unit and left 2.5 units

For help with questions 4 to 6, refer to Example 2.

4. Describe the transformations that map the function $y = 8^x$ onto each function.

a) $y = \left(\frac{1}{2}\right)8^x$ **b)** $y = 8^{4x}$

c) $y = -8^x$ **d)** $y = 8^{-2x}$

5. Sketch the graph of each function in question 4. Use the graph of $y = 8^x$ as the base. Be sure to choose appropriate scales for your axes.

6. Write the equation for the function that results from each transformation applied to the base function $y = 7^x$.

a) reflect in the x-axis

b) stretch vertically by a factor of 3

c) stretch horizontally by a factor of 2.4

d) reflect in the y-axis and compress vertically by a factor of 7

For help with question 7 and 8, refer to Example 3.

7. Sketch the graph of $y = \left(-\frac{1}{2}\right)2^{x-4}$ by using $y = 2^x$ as the base and applying transformations.

8. Sketch the graph of $y = 3^{-0.5x - 1} - 5$ by using $y = 3^x$ as the base and applying transformations.

B Connect and Apply

For help with question 9, refer to Example 4.

9. The temperature, T, in degrees Celsius, of a cooling metal bar after t minutes is given by $T(t) = 20 + 100(0.3)^{0.2t}$.

a) Sketch the graph of this relation.

b) What is the asymptote of this function? What does it represent?

c) How long will it take for the temperature to be within 0.1 °C of the value of the asymptote?

10. a) Graph the function $f(x) = \left(\frac{1}{2}\right)^{\frac{1}{2}(x+3)} - 1$.

b) Identify the following properties.

   i) domain

   ii) range

   iii) equation of the asymptote

11. a) Sketch the graph of $y = 9^x$.

b) Rewrite $y = 9^x$ using a base of 3. Describe how you can graph this function by transforming the graph of $y = 3^x$.

c) Rewrite $y = 9^x$ using a base of 81. Describe how you can graph this function by transforming the graph of $y = 81^x$.

d) Explain why all three of these functions are equivalent.

Reasoning and Proving

Representing — Selecting Tools

Problem Solving

Connecting — Reflecting

Communicating

12. a) Rewrite the function $y = 8^x$ in two different ways, using a different base in each case.

b) Explain why all three functions are equivalent.

13. a) Write the equation for a transformed exponential function whose asymptote is $y = 4$, with a y-intercept of 6.

b) Is the function you produced in part a) the only possible answer? Use transformations to help explain your answer.

14. a) Write the equation for a transformed exponential function with a base of 2 that passes through the point $(0, 2)$.

b) Write two different equations that satisfy these criteria.

c) Use algebraic and/or graphical reasoning to explain why each equation is a solution.

15. Does it matter in which order transformations are applied?

a) Start with a base function of the form $y = b^x$ and create a new exponential function by applying at least one of each of the following types of transformations to your base function:
- translation
- stretch or compression
- reflection

b) Predict whether or not the order in which you carry out the transformations will affect the final graph.

c) Graph the function by applying the transformations in any order you choose.

d) Repeat part c) by applying the transformations in several different orders.

e) Repeat parts a) to d) for a different function of your choice.

f) Compare your results with the predictions you made. Describe your findings.

16. Examine the growing pattern shown.

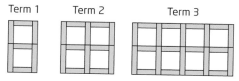

a) Build or draw the next term in this pattern.

b) Is the pattern of white squares growing exponentially? Explain how you know.

c) Write an equation to express the number of squares, s, as a function of the term number, n.

d) How many squares are in the

i) 5th term?

ii) 10th term?

17. Refer to question 16. Suppose that you built this model using toothpicks. Focus on the number of toothpicks needed to build each stage of the model.

a) Make a table that compares the term number, n, with the number of toothpicks, t, in each term.

b) Explore the patterns in the finite differences.

c) Graph the data.

d) Is the function that expresses t in terms of n an exponential function? Explain.

e) Write an equation to express t as a function of n.

f) Use transformations to describe how this function is related to the exponential function you found in question 16c).

18. Use Technology Does a vertical stretch of factor a of an exponential function produce the same effect as a horizontal compression of factor $\frac{1}{a}$?

a) Write a conjecture about this claim.

b) Use graphing technology to explore several cases, using various values of a and various bases.

c) Write a brief report of your findings.

19. Use Technology For exponential functions, does a horizontal translation of *d* units produce the same effect as a vertical stretch?

a) Write a conjecture about this claim.

b) Use graphing technology to explore several cases, using various values of *d* and various bases.

c) Write a brief report of your findings.

✓ Achievement Check

20. a) Describe the transformations that must be applied to the graph of $y = 3^x$ to obtain the graph of $y = -\left(\frac{1}{3}\right)^{12-3x} + 2$.

b) Graph the function $y = -\left(\frac{1}{3}\right)^{12-3x} + 2$.

c) Identify the following properties.

  i) domain

  ii) range

  iii) equation of the asymptote

  iv) intercept(s), if they exist

C Extend

21. Refer to question 16. Another interpretation of the model is that it consists of white square pieces and yellow rectangular pieces of three sizes, arranged in the patterns shown.

a) How many pieces of of each size are used in the first term of the pattern?

b) Are the growing patterns for the numbers of each of these pieces all exponential in nature? Explain.

c) Write an equation to describe the total number of pieces as a function of the term number.

d) Describe how the function you found in part c) is related to the functions you found in questions 16 and 17, using transformations, if possible.

22. Use Technology The curve in which a rope or wire hangs under its own weight is called a catenary. A telephone wire hanging between two poles has the shape of a catenary. The equation of the path of a certain telephone wire is $y = 0.2\left(2^{\frac{x}{4}} + 2^{-\frac{x}{4}}\right)$, where all measurements are in metres.

a) Graph this relation using a graphing calculator.

b) What other function does this resemble?

c) Select seven points and use an appropriate regression feature to determine an equation to model this curve, using your answer in part b) as your model.

d) Graph both functions on the same set of axes.

e) How do the graphs compare?

f) Zoom out a couple of times and repeat the comparison.

23. Math Contest If $f(x) = 3^x$ and $f(x + 2) + f(x + 3) + f(x + 4) = kf(x)$, what is the value of *k*?

24. Math Contest If $4^y = 7$, then the value of $4^{3y} + 2$ is

A 23   **B** 345   **C** $\sqrt[3]{7} + 2$ **D** 2189

25. Math Contest What is the range of the function $y = 12\left(\frac{1}{2}\right)^x - 3$?

26. Math Contest In the diagram, AD = 6 cm, and B and C trisect AD. The ratio of the area between the green curves to the area of the blue circle is

A 1:3   **B** 4:9   **C** 2:9   **D** 1:2

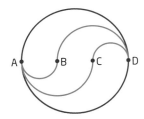

Making Connections: Tools and Strategies for Applying Exponential Models

Are Canadians getting wealthier? Every home buyer knows that house prices and construction costs usually go up, but are earnings keeping up? How do the earnings of Ontarians compare with the earnings in the rest of Canada?

Example 1

Construct a Model of Exponential Growth

The table gives the average weekly earnings, rounded to the nearest dollar, for Canadians over a 5-year period.

Year	Earnings ($)
2002	679
2003	688
2004	702
2005	725
2006	747

a) Construct an exponential function to model the data.

b) Predict the average Canadian's weekly earnings in 2010.

c) Predict when the average Canadian might expect to earn $1000 per week.

Solution

Method 1: Use a Graphing Calculator

a) Make a scatter plot of the data. For simplicity, renumber the years from 0 to 4.

- Press (STAT) and select **1:Edit**.

- Enter the data in lists **L1** and **L2**.

- Press (Y=). Clear any functions in the equation section. Then, turn on **Plot1** only.

- Press (2nd) [STATPLOT] and select **Plot1**.

- Use the settings shown.

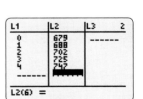

Press (ZOOM) and select **9:ZoomStat**. A scatter plot of the data will appear.

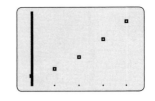

The trend appears to be exponential. Use exponential regression to find a curve of best fit.

- Press (2nd) [QUIT] to return to the home screen.
- Press (STAT). Cursor over to **CALC** and select **0:ExpReg**.
- Press (2nd) [L1] (,) (2nd) [L2] (,), and then press (VARS). Select **Y-VARS**, and then select **1:Function**.
- Select **1:Y1** and press (ENTER).

An exponential equation will appear.

Round the calculated values of a and b and substitute into the equation $y = ab^x$ to obtain the approximate equation of the curve of best fit.

$$y = 674 \times 1.025^x$$

Replace x and y with variables that make sense for the problem. Let n represent the number of years following 2002 and E represent the average Canadian's weekly earnings in year n.
Then, the equation is $E(n) = 674 \times 1.025^n$.

Press (GRAPH) to see the curve of best fit drawn through the scatter plot. Use the window settings shown.

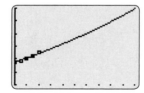

b) To predict the average Canadian's weekly earnings in 2010, find the value of E when $n = 8$.

- Press (2nd) [CALC].
- Select **1:value** and enter 8 when prompted.

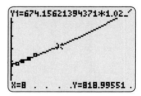

Therefore, assuming that the trend continues, the average Canadian will earn approximately $819 per week in 2010.

c) To find when the average Canadian might expect to earn $1000 per week, find the intersection of the graph with the graph of $y = 1000$.

- Press (2nd) [CALC].
- Select **5:intersect**.

From the graph, you can see that the average Canadian can expect to earn $1000 per week in approximately 16.2 years after 2002, or in 2018.

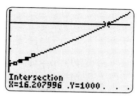

Method 2: Use *Fathom*™

a) Enter the data in a Case Table.

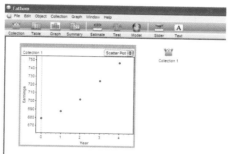

Make a scatter plot of Earnings versus Year by clicking and dragging these attributes to the vertical and horizontal axes.

Construct a curve of best fit of the form $y = ab^x$:

- Create two sliders and name them a and b.

Note that placing the cursor over different parts of a slider scale allows you to adjust the scale by clicking and dragging. Consider the domain and range of the given points when adjusting the slider windows.

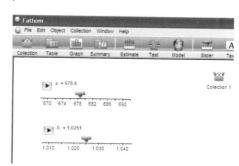

- a is the initial value, or vertical intercept. Its value appears to be between 670 and 690.

- b is the multiplier that gives each successive value of Earnings. Compare the ratios of successive terms in the data.

$688 \div 679 = 1.01\ldots$

$702 \div 688 = 1.02\ldots$

$725 \div 702 = 1.03\ldots$

$747 \div 725 = 1.03\ldots$

The value of b for the curve of best fit will likely be between 1.01 and 1.04.

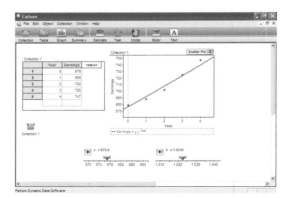

• Select the graph. From the **Graph** menu, choose **Plot Function**.

• Enter $a \times b^{\text{Year}}$ and click **OK**.

An exponential curve will appear. Adjust the sliders to find the curve of best fit.

Let n represent the number of years following 2002 and E represent the average Canadian's weekly earnings in year n. Then, the equation for this curve is $E(n) = 677 \times 1.023^n$.

b) Use the equation to predict the average weekly earnings in 2010. Since this is 8 years after the initial value, substitute $n = 8$ into the equation.

$$E(n) = 677 \times 1.023^n$$
$$E(8) = 677 \times 1.023^8$$
$$\doteq 812$$

This model predicts that the average Canadian will earn approximately $812 per week in 2010.

c) To predict the year in which the average Canadian can expect to earn $1000 per week, extrapolate the curve of best fit:

• Click and drag one of the corners of the graph to enlarge it.

• Place the cursor over the vertical scale and adjust it so that 1000 appears.

• Place the cursor over the horizontal scale and adjust it so that you can read the corresponding year.

• From the **Graph** menu, choose **Moveable Line**. Adjust this to be a horizontal line crossing the vertical axis at 1000.

Construct a second moveable line and adjust it to read the corresponding year.

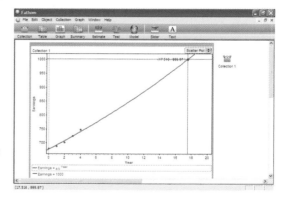

According to the curve of best fit, the average Canadian can expect to earn $1000 per week approximately 17.5 years after 2002, or some time in the year 2019.

The choice of methods and tools in a given situation can depend on a number of factors, including
• accuracy required
• preference of the user
• availability

Notice from Example 1 that each method and technology tool can produce slight variations in the exponential model that is generated. This, in turn, produces slight variations in the predictions that are made. It is important to realize that such models are often limited in their accuracy.

Example 2

Choose a Model of Depreciation

The value of a computer n years after it is purchased is given in the table.

Number of Years, n	Value ($)
1	1200
2	960
3	768
4	614
5	492
6	393

a) Enter the data in a table using a graphing calculator. Determine the first differences and describe the trend and what it means.

b) Make a scatter plot and construct each of the following types of models to represent this relationship:
• linear
• quadratic
• exponential
Assess the usefulness of each model.

c) Determine the most likely purchase price of the computer.

Solution

a) Enter the data in **L1** and **L2** using the **Table Editor**. To calculate the first differences:
• Move the cursor to the top of the **L3** column.
• Press (2nd) [LIST]. Cursor over to **OPS**.
• Select **7:ΔList(** and press (2nd) [L2].
• Press ( )) and then press (ENTER).

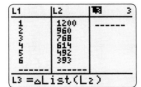 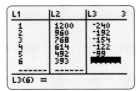

The first differences are decreasing at a decreasing rate, suggesting that the computer depreciates most quickly in the early years following purchase and less quickly as it ages.

b) Linear Model

Perform a linear regression and store the equation as **Y1**.

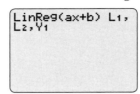 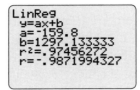

The line of best fit corresponds approximately to the equation $v(n) = -160n + 1297$, where v is the value of the computer, in dollars, n years after purchase.

To view the scatter plot and line of best fit, ensure that **Plot1** and **Y1** are turned on. From the **ZOOM** menu, choose **9:ZoomStat**.

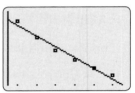

Although the line of best fit passes near most of the data points, it does not reflect the curved nature of the trend, which indicates a decreasing rate of depreciation. This may not be the best model for this situation.

Quadratic Model

Perform a quadratic regression and store the equation as **Y2**.

 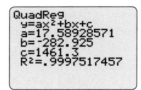

The quadratic curve of best fit corresponds approximately to the equation $v(n) = 17.6n^2 - 283n + 1461$, where v is the value of the computer, in dollars, n years after purchase.

To view the scatter plot and quadratic curve of best fit, turn **Y1** off and ensure that **Plot1** and **Y2** are turned on. From the ZOOM menu, select **9:ZoomStat**.

 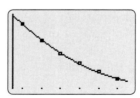

The quadratic curve of best fit models the data trend well for the domain shown. However, this quadratic function does not indicate continuing depreciation. This can be observed by extrapolating beyond the data set. Press ZOOM, select **3:Zoom Out**, and press ENTER.

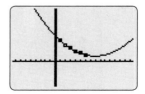

According to the graph, the value function will reach a minimum and then begin to increase, which makes no sense in this situation. Therefore, the quadratic model is not effective for extrapolating beyond the given set of data for this scenario.

Exponential Model

Perform an exponential regression and store the equation as **Y3**.

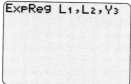 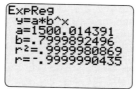

The exponential curve of best fit corresponds approximately to the equation $v(n) = 1500 \times 0.8^n$, where v is the value of the computer, in dollars, n years after purchase.

To view the scatter plot and exponential curve of best fit, turn **Y1** and **Y2** off and ensure that **Plot1** and **Y3** are turned on. From the (ZOOM) menu, select **9:ZoomStat**.

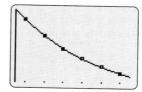

The exponential curve of best fit models the data trend well for the domain shown, and beyond. This can be illustrated by extrapolating beyond the data set. Press (ZOOM), select **3:Zoom Out**, and press (ENTER).

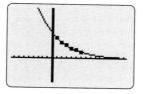

The exponential model correctly reflects the continuous depreciation of the computer. It is the best model for this scenario.

c) Apply the exponential model to determine the purchase price of the computer by evaluating the function when $n = 0$.

Method 1: Use the Graph

Press (2nd) [CALC] and select **1:value**. When prompted, enter 0 and press (ENTER). The corresponding function value will be given.

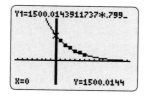

Method 2: Use the Equation

$v(n) = 1500 \times 0.8^n$

$v(0) = 1500 \times 0.8^0$

$ = 1500 \times 1$

$ = 1500$

Both the graph and the equation indicate that the purchase price of the computer was $1500.

- You can use a variety of tools to construct algebraic and graphical models, including
  - a graphing calculator
  - dynamic statistics software such as *Fathom*™
  - a spreadsheet
- Various types of regression (e.g., linear, quadratic, exponential) can be used to model a relationship. The best choice will effectively describe the trend between and beyond the known data values.
- Exponential functions are useful in modelling situations involving continuous growth or decay/depreciation.

Communicate Your Understanding

C1 What type of regression curve would you choose to model each set of data? Explain your choices.

a)

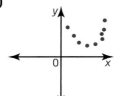

b)

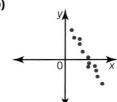

c)

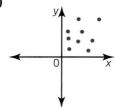

d)

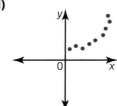

C2 a) Two different technological tools were used to solve Example 1. List the advantages and disadvantages of each tool.

b) Explain why there may be slight variations in finding an exponential model to fit real data.

C3 a) How can you tell if a set of data might be modelled by an exponential function by considering

  i) the numerical data?

  ii) a scatter plot?

b) Describe two situations in which you might expect to see an exponential relationship.

A Practise

For help with questions 1 to 4, refer to Example 1.

1. Match each exponential scatter plot with the corresponding equation of its curve of best fit. Not all equations will match one of the graphs.

a)

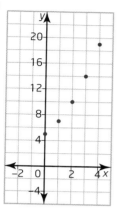

A $y = 20 \times 0.85^x$

B $y = 5 \times 1.8^x$

C $y = 2 \times 1.8^x$

D $y = 5 \times 1.4^x$

E $y = 20 \times 1.4^x$

F $y = 2 \times 1.4^x$

b)

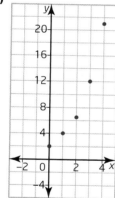

c)

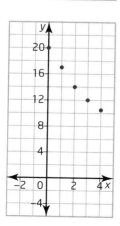

2. Pick one of the unmatched equations from question 1. Sketch a scatter plot that the equation could fit.

3. Annette has invested some money. The scatter plot shows the value of her investment after the first few years.

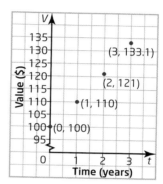

a) Do the data appear to have an exponential trend? Explain your reasoning.

b) Estimate values of a and b to develop an exponential model for the data of the form $V(n) = a \times b^n$. Explain how you arrived at your estimated values.

c) Use the tool of your choice to find an exponential model for these data.

d) Use the exponential model you produced in part c) to predict the value of Annette's investment after 10 years.

e) Approximately how long it will take for Annette's investment to double in value?

Connections

Data from investment earnings can look linear, but often involve an exponential relationship. You will learn more about investment and loan calculations in Chapter 7 Financial Applications.

For help with questions 4 and 5, refer to Example 2.

4. At 9 a.m., Gina finds out that she has been promoted to vice-president of sales. By 9:30 a.m., she has told two people in the office about it. By 10 a.m., each person who heard the news at 9:30 has told two other people in the office the news. The news about Gina's promotion continues to spread this way throughout the company.

a) Make a table of values to relate the number of people who have just heard the news to time, in half-hour intervals.

b) Make a scatter plot. Describe the trend.

c) What type of function represents the spread of this news? Justify your answer.

d) Determine an equation to model this relation. Explain how you determined the equation.

B Connect and Apply

5. Refer to question 4.

a) Do you think the trend will continue indefinitely? Explain why or why not.

b) Sketch the graph of this relation for the 24-h period immediately following the moment Gina first heard her news. Assume that 250 people work at Gina's company. Explain each part of the graph.

6. Visit the Statistics Canada Web site at http://www.statcan.gc.ca/edu/edu05_0018c-eng.htm to research data on the farm value of potatoes from 1908 to 2004.

a) Construct a table with the headings Year, Year Number, and Value of Potatoes. Record the data for every 4 years, starting with 1908 (year number 0) and ending with 2004 (year number 24).

b) Make a scatter plot that relates Value of Potatoes to Year Number.

c) Determine the equation of the exponential function that best represents the data.

d) Graph the curve of best fit.

7. Refer to question 6. Pose and answer two questions using the exponential model you created.

8. The table shows the koala population in a natural park reserve over a number of years.

Reasoning and Proving
Representing · Selecting Tools
Problem Solving
Connecting · Reflecting
Communicating

a) Make a scatter plot for the data. Does the trend suggest an exponential relationship? Explain.

Year	Population
0	800
1	830
2	870
3	900
4	940
5	970

b) Construct a curve of best fit and find an exponential equation to model the data.

c) Predict the koala population after 12 years.

d) How long will it take for the koala population to reach 2000? Describe how you found your answer and discuss any assumptions you must make.

9. The Consumer Price Index (CPI) is a measure of the cost of living. It is found by tracking the average family's typical living expenses. An upward trend in CPI is called inflation. The table gives the CPI for Canadians over a 7-year period.

Year	CPI ($)
2002	100
2003	102.8
2004	104.7
2005	107
2006	109.1
2007	111.8
2008	115.6

a) Construct an exponential function to model the data.

b) Compare this model to the one in Example 1. Which is growing faster: the average Canadian's earnings or the CPI? Explain your reasoning.

10. The E-STAT Web site at http://www. statcan.gc.ca contains a vast array of data. Navigate to the E-STAT table of contents and explore some topics of interest to you.

a) Find a set of data that exhibits an exponential relationship. Describe the variables being compared.

b) Make a scatter plot of the data.

c) Find the curve of best fit and its corresponding equation.

d) Pose and answer two questions using the exponential model you created.

11. The earnings data from Example 1 can be found on E-STAT. Visit http://www40. statcan.gc.ca/l01/cst01/labr79-eng.htm to view the data. The data used in the example were for all Canadians. Examine the other data. How do the earnings of Ontarians compare with those of

a) all Canadians?

b) residents of other individual provinces?

Write a brief report of your findings.

12. How long does it take for a cup of coffee to get cold? For this activity you will need

- a cup of coffee or other hot liquid
- a stir stick
- a thermometer or a temperature probe and graphing calculator

a) Use the thermometer or temperature probe to measure the initial temperature. Record this value along with time, $t = 0$.

b) Take temperature readings each minute for several minutes, stirring the coffee or hot liquid before each measurement. Record the time and temperature data in a table.

c) Make a scatter plot of temperature versus time. Describe the shape of the curve.

d) Find the equation of the curve of best fit.

e) Determine an approximate value for the elapsed time before the temperature reaches the ideal drinking temperature of coffee of 71 °C.

f) How long will it be before the temperature drops to a lukewarm temperature of 30 °C?

13. Refer to question 12.

a) Describe the effects on the coffee-cooling curve if cream and sugar are added. Sketch graphs to support your explanation.

Reasoning and Proving

Representing — Selecting Tools

Problem Solving

Connecting — Reflecting

Communicating

b) How would the curve change if a person took sips of the beverage at regular intervals? Sketch graphs to help explain your reasoning.

C Extend

14. Do human populations grow exponentially over time? Find data for Canada, another country, or the world. Find one or more examples of exponential population growth and build models to describe them. Write a brief report of your findings.

15. Math Contest In the diagram, X is the midpoint of AB, Y divides BC in the ratio 1:2, and Z divides AC in the ratio 1:3. Show that the area of △XBY equals the area of △ZCY.

Chapter 3 Review

3.1 The Nature of Exponential Growth, pages 150 to 157

1. A bacterial colony with an initial population of 300 doubles every day. Which equation models this exponential growth?

   A $P = 2 \times 300^n$ **B** $P = 300 \times \left(\frac{1}{2}\right)^n$

   C $P = 200 \times 3^n$ **D** $P = 300 \times 2^n$

2. a) Use concrete materials or sketches to illustrate an exponential growing pattern that triples from term to term. Draw the first three terms.

   b) Make a table of values for the first five terms that relates the number of objects to the term number.

   c) Find the first and second differences. How are these patterns related?

   d) Write an equation to model your growing pattern.

   e) How many objects would you need to build the 10th term?

3. a) What is the value of a non-zero number raised to the exponent zero?

   b) Use algebraic reasoning to explain why this is true.

3.2 Exponential Decay: Connecting to Negative Exponents, pages 160 to 169

4. A radioactive substance with an initial mass of 250 mg has a half-life of 1 year.

   a) Write an equation to relate the mass of radioactive material remaining to time.

   b) What mass will remain after 10 years?

   c) How long will it take for the sample to decay to 20% of its initial mass? Explain how you arrived at your answer.

5. Refer to question 4.

   a) Show how you can write the equation from part a) in another way.

   b) Explain why the two equations are equivalent.

6. Evaluate. Express as a fraction in lowest terms.

   a) 10^{-1} b) 4^{-2} c) $3^{-2} + 9^{-1}$

   d) $5^{-3} + 5^0$ e) $\left(\frac{1}{5}\right)^{-1}$ f) $\left(\frac{3}{4}\right)^{-3}$

7. Simplify. Express your answers using only positive exponents.

   a) $(x^{-2})(x^{-1})(x^0)$ b) $(3km^2)(2k^{-2}m^{-2})$

   c) $w^{-3} \div w^{-2}$ d) $\dfrac{u^{-2}v^3}{u^{-3}v^{-2}}$

   e) $(z^{-3})^{-2}$ f) $(2ab^{-1})^{-2}$

3.3 Rational Exponents, pages 170 to 177

8. Evaluate.

   a) $\sqrt[3]{64}$ b) $\sqrt[4]{625}$ c) $\sqrt[5]{-3125}$

   d) $\left(\dfrac{1}{64}\right)^{\frac{1}{6}}$ e) $27^{\frac{2}{3}}$ f) $(-1000)^{\frac{4}{3}}$

   g) -4^{-3} h) $\left(\dfrac{3}{4}\right)^{-2}$ i) $\left(-\dfrac{27}{125}\right)^{-\frac{2}{3}}$

9. The length, x, in centimetres, by which a spring with spring constant k is stretched or compressed from its rest position is related to its stored potential energy, U, in joules (J), according to the equation $x = (2Uk^{-1})^{\frac{1}{2}}$.

   a) Use the power of a power rule to write this equation in a different form.

   b) Write the equation in radical form, using a single radical.

   c) A spring with spring constant 10 has 320 J of stored energy. By how much is this spring stretched?

3.4 Properties of Exponential Functions, pages 178 to 187

10. a) Graph the function $y = 27\left(\dfrac{1}{3}\right)^x$.

    b) Identify the

       i) domain   ii) range

       iii) x- and y-intercepts, if they exist

       iv) intervals of increase/decrease

       v) equation of the asymptote

11. Determine the equation for the exponential graph shown.

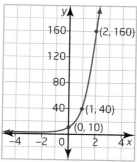

3.5 Transformations of Exponential Functions, pages 188 to 198

12. a) Sketch the function $y = 2^{x-3} + 4$.

b) Identify the

   i) domain

   ii) range

   iii) equation of the asymptote

13. Describe the transformation or transformations that map the base function $y = 5^x$ onto each given function.

a) $y = 2(5^x)$ **b)** $y = 5^{2x}$

c) $y = -5^{-x}$ **d)** $y = 5^{-5x-10}$

3.6 Making Connections: Tools and Strategies for Applying Exponential Models, pages 199 to 209

14. The height, h, in centimetres, of a bouncing ball after n bounces is given.

Number of Bounces, n	Height, h (cm)
0	100
1	76
2	57
3	43
4	32
5	24

a) Calculate the first and second differences and describe the trend.

b) Make a scatter plot of height versus number of bounces. Describe the shape of the curve.

c) Perform an appropriate regression analysis on the data. Write the equation of the curve of best fit. Justify your choice of the type of regression curve.

d) Will the ball ever stop bouncing? Discuss this with respect to

   i) the mathematical model

   ii) the real situation

e) Why might your answers in part d) differ?

Chapter Problem   WRAP-UP

In this chapter, you explored some of the forces that affect celestial bodies. How is it possible to observe these forces in action? One tool that scientists have available is the telescope. The power of modern telescopes is quite impressive compared to those that were first invented.

a) Research the history of the telescope. Answer the following questions.
- When was it first invented, and by whom?
- How is magnifying power measured?
- What were the magnifying powers of the first telescopes?
- What are the magnifying powers of some modern telescopes?

b) How has the magnifying power of the most powerful telescopes changed over time? Can the increase in magnifying power be modelled by an exponential function? Justify your answer, using words, graphs, and equations.

For questions 1 to 4, select the best answer.

1. One day, 5 friends started a rumour. They agreed that they would each tell the rumour to two different friends the next day. On each day that followed, every person who just heard the rumour would tell another two people who had not heard the rumour. Which equation describes the relation between the number of days that have elapsed, d, and the number of people, P, who hear the rumour on that day?

   A $P = 2 \times 5^d$　　　**B** $P = 5 \times 2^d$

   C $P = 5 \times \left(\frac{1}{2}\right)^d$　　　**D** $P = 2 \times \left(\frac{1}{5}\right)^d$

2. What is the value of $4^{-\frac{1}{2}}$?

   A -2　　**B** $-\frac{1}{2}$　　**C** $\frac{1}{2}$　　**D** $\frac{1}{16}$

3. Which is the correct equation when $y = 5^x$ is translated 3 units down and 4 units left?

   A $y = 5^{x+4} - 3$　　　**B** $y = 5^{x-4} - 3$

   C $y = 5^{x+3} - 4$　　　**D** $y = 5^{x-3} - 4$

4. Which is correct about exponential functions?

   A The ratio of successive first differences is constant.

   B The first differences are constant.

   C The first differences are zero.

   D The second differences are constant.

5. Evaluate. Express your answers as integers or fractions in lowest terms.

   a) $49^{\frac{1}{2}}$　　　**b)** 5^{-3}　　　**c)** $(-4)^0$

   d) $16^{\frac{1}{4}}$　　　**e)** $(-8)^{\frac{5}{3}}$　　　**f)** $\left(\frac{3}{4}\right)^{-4}$

   g) $\left(\frac{27}{64}\right)^{-\frac{1}{3}}$　　**h)** $\left(-\frac{8}{125}\right)^{-\frac{4}{3}}$

6. Simplify. Express your answers using only positive exponents.

   a) $(x^{-2})(x^3)(x^{-4})$　　　**b)** $\dfrac{p^{-3}}{p^2}$

   c) $(2k^4)^{-1}$　　　**d)** $(a^{\frac{1}{2}})(a^{\frac{2}{3}})$

   e) $(y^{\frac{2}{3}})^{-6}$　　　**f)** $(u^{\frac{1}{2}}v^{-3})^{-2}$

7. Build or sketch a model that shows an exponential growing pattern that is doubling from one term to the next.

   a) Sketch the first three terms of the model.

   b) Make a table of values that relates the number of objects to the term number.

   c) Graph the relation.

   d) Find the first and second differences.

   e) Write an equation for this model.

   f) Give at least three reasons that confirm that the pattern is exponential in nature.

8. Match each graph with its corresponding equation.

   a)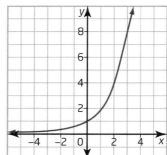

   b)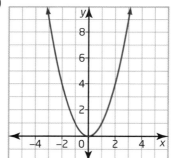

   c)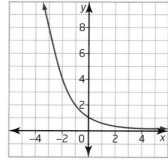

d)

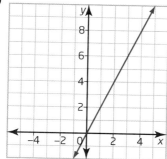

A $y = x^2$

B $y = 2x$

C $y = 2^x$

D $y = \left(\dfrac{1}{2}\right)^x$

9. a) Sketch the graph of the function $y = 2^{x-5} + 3$.

b) Identify the

    i) domain

    ii) range

    iii) equation of the asymptote

10. Describe the transformation(s) that map the base function $y = 8^x$ onto each function.

a) $y = \dfrac{1}{3}(8^x)$ **b)** $y = 8^{4x}$

c) $y = -8^{-x}$ **d)** $y = 8^{-3x-6}$

11. A radioactive substance with an initial mass of 80 mg has a half-life of 2.5 days.

a) Write an equation to relate the mass remaining to time.

b) Graph the function. Describe the shape of the curve.

c) Limit the domain so that the model accurately describes the situation.

d) Find the amount remaining after

    i) 10 days

    ii) 15 days

e) How long will it take for the sample to decay to 5% of its initial mass?

12. a) Sketch the function $y = \left(-\dfrac{1}{2}\right)2^{x+3} - 1$ by applying transformations to the graph of the base function $y = 2^x$.

b) For the transformed function, find the

    i) domain

    ii) range

    iii) equation of the asymptote

13. The height, h, of a square-based pyramid is related to its volume, V, and base side length, b, by the equation $h = 3Vb^{-2}$. A square-based pyramid has a volume of 6250 m³ and a base side length of 25 m. Find its height.

14. The population of Pebble Valley over a period of 5 years is shown.

Year	Population
0	2000
1	2150
2	2300
3	2500
4	2700
5	2950

a) Make a scatter plot for this relationship. Do the data appear to be exponential in nature? Explain your reasoning.

b) Find the equation of the curve of best fit.

c) Limit the domain of the function so that it accurately models this situation.

d) Predict the population of Pebble Valley 7 years after the first table entry. State any assumptions you must make.

e) How long will it take for the town to double in size? State any assumptions you must make.

Chapters 1 to 3 Review

Chapter 1 Functions

1. State the domain and the range of each relation. Is each relation a function? Justify your answer.

   a)

   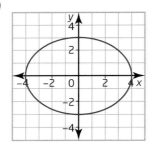

   b) {(−2, 1), (−1, 4), (0, 9), (1, 16), (2, 25)}

   c) $y = 0.5x^2 - 4$

2. Write each function in mapping notation. Then, for each function, determine $f(-1)$.

   a) $f(x) = \sqrt{1 - 3x}$

   b) $f(x) = \dfrac{2x + 1}{x^2 - 4}$

3. The amount, A, in dollars, to be invested at an interest rate i to have $1500 after 1 year is given by the relation $A(i) = \dfrac{1500}{1 + i}$. Note that i must be expressed as a decimal.

   a) Determine the domain and the range for this relation.

   b) Graph the relation.

   c) How much money needs to be invested at 3%?

   d) What rate of interest is required if $1000 is invested?

4. a) Draw the mapping diagram for the given data.

      {(2, 4), (5, 0), (6, 4), (3, 3), (4, −2)}

   b) Is this relation a function? Explain.

5. A farmer has 4000 m of fencing to enclose a rectangular field and subdivide it into three equal plots of land. Determine the dimensions of each plot of land so that the total area is a maximum.

6. A store sells T-shirts with logos on them. Last year, the store sold 600 of these T-shirts at $15 each. The sales manager is planning to increase the price. A survey indicates that for each $1 increase in the price, 30 fewer T-shirts will be sold per year.

   a) What price will maximize the yearly revenue?

   b) What is the maximum yearly revenue?

7. Solve each quadratic equation. Give exact answers.

   a) $2x^2 - 4x - 3 = 0$

   b) $3x^2 - 12x + 4 = 0$

8. Use the discriminant to determine the number of roots for each equation.

   a) $4x^2 + 3x - 2 = 0$

   b) $-3x^2 + 10x - 7 = 0$

   c) $5x^2 - 8x + 1 = 0$

9. The length of a rectangle is 2 m more than three times its width. If the area is 20 m², find the dimensions of the rectangle to the nearest hundredth of a metre.

10. Determine the equation in standard form for each quadratic function.

    a) x-intercepts −3 and 4, containing the point (1, −4)

    b) x-intercepts $2 \pm \sqrt{3}$, y-intercept 2

11. Water shoots out of a decorative fountain, making an arc in the shape of a parabola. The arc spans a distance of 6 m from one side of the fountain to the other. The height of the arc at a horizontal distance of 1 m from the starting point is 5 m.

    a) Sketch the quadratic function that represents the arc such that the vertex of the parabola is on the y-axis and the horizontal distance from one side to the other is along the x-axis.

    b) Determine the equation for the function.

    c) Find the maximum height of the arc.

12. Determine the exact point(s) of intersection of each pair of functions.

a) $f(x) = 2x^2 - 3x + 4$ and $g(x) = 2x + 5$

b) $f(x) = -x^2 + 8x + 3$ and $g(x) = -0.5x + 1$

13. For what value of k will the line $y = -5x + k$ be tangent to the graph of the function $f(x) = -4x^2 + 3x + 1$?

Chapter 2 Transformations of Functions

14. Determine whether the functions in each pair are equivalent.

a) $f(x) = (2x + 1)(x - 3) - (x + 2)(x - 4)$,
$g(x) = 3(x - 1)^2 - (2x + 1)(x - 2)$

b) $f(x) = (x + 3)(x - 2) + 2(x - 5)(x + 1)$,
$g(x) = -(x - 2)(x + 3) + 2x(1 - x)$

15. Given the graph of a function $f(x)$, sketch the graph of $g(x)$ by determining the image points A′, B′, C′, D′, and E′.

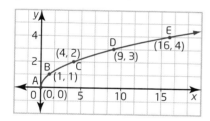

a) $g(x) = f(x) + 4$

b) $g(x) = f(x - 2)$

c) $g(x) = f(x - 6) + 3$

d) $g(x) = f(x + 5) - 1$

16. Copy the graph of $f(x)$ and sketch each reflection, $g(x)$. Then, state the domain and range of each function.

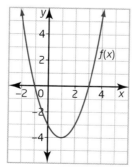

a) $g(x) = f(-x)$

b) $g(x) = -f(x)$

c) $g(x) = -f(-x)$

17. For each function $g(x)$,

i) identify the base function as one of $f(x) = x$, $f(x) = x^2$, $f(x) = \sqrt{x}$, or $f(x) = \dfrac{1}{x}$

ii) describe the transformation in the form $y = f(x - d) + c$ and in words

iii) transform the graph of $f(x)$ to sketch the graph of $g(x)$

iv) state the domain and range of the base function and the transformed function

a) $g(x) = (x + 2)^2 - 1$

b) $g(x) = \sqrt{x + 3} - 4$

c) $g(x) = \dfrac{1}{x - 4} + 6$

d) $g(x) = (x - 7)^2 + 3$

18. David and his friend Shane are in a 20-km bike race. David bikes 1.5 km/h faster than Shane. The time, in hours, to complete the race is given by $t = \dfrac{d}{v}$, where d is the distance, in kilometres, and v is the speed, in kilometres per hour.

a) If v represents Shane's speed, determine a function to represent David's time. What are the domain and range?

b) Determine a function to represent Shane's time. What are the domain and range?

c) Graph both functions on the same set of axes.

d) Use the graph to determine what would be true about Shane's time if it took David 45 min to complete the race.

19. Determine the equation of each function after

i) a reflection in the x-axis, giving $g(x)$

ii) a reflection in the y-axis, giving $h(x)$

a) $f(x) = 2x^2 - 7x + 3$

b) $f(x) = \sqrt{x} - 3$

c) $f(x) = \dfrac{1}{x + 2}$

20. Given the function $f(x) = x^2$, identify the value of a or k, transform the graph of $f(x)$ to sketch the graph of $g(x)$, and state the domain and range of $g(x)$.

a) $g(x) = 2f(x)$ **b)** $g(x) = f(3x)$

c) $g(x) = f\left(\dfrac{x}{4}\right)$ **d)** $g(x) = \dfrac{1}{3}f(x)$

21. For each function $g(x)$, describe the transformation from a base function of $f(x) = x$, $f(x) = x^2$, $f(x) = \sqrt{x}$, or $f(x) = \dfrac{1}{x}$. Then, transform the graph of $f(x)$ to sketch the graph of $g(x)$.

a) $g(x) = 7x$ **b)** $g(x) = \dfrac{1}{5x}$

c) $g(x) = (3x)^2$ **d)** $g(x) = \sqrt{6x}$

22. Describe, in the appropriate order, the transformations that must be applied to the base function $f(x)$ to obtain the transformed function. Then, write the corresponding equation and transform the graph of $f(x)$ to sketch the graph of $g(x)$.

a) $f(x) = \sqrt{x}$, $g(x) = 4f(x + 3)$

b) $f(x) = x$, $g(x) = -f(5x) - 2$

c) $f(x) = x^2$, $g(x) = -3f(2x + 9) - 4$

23. For each function $f(x)$,

   i) determine $f^{-1}(x)$

   ii) graph $f(x)$ and its inverse

   iii) determine whether $f^{-1}(x)$ is a function

a) $f(x) = 11x - 3$

b) $f(x) = 3x^2 + 4$

c) $f(x) = (x + 8)^2 + 19$

d) $f(x) = 2x^2 - 3x + 14$

24. Issa works at a furniture store. She earns $450 per week, plus commission of 6% of her sales.

a) Write a function to describe Issa's total weekly earnings as a function of her sales.

b) Determine the inverse of this function.

c) What does the inverse represent?

d) One week, Issa earned $1020. Calculate her sales that week.

Chapter 3 Exponential Functions

25. Match each graph with one of these equations.

$$y = x^2 \qquad y = 3x \qquad y = 3^x \qquad y = \left(\dfrac{1}{3}\right)^x$$

a)

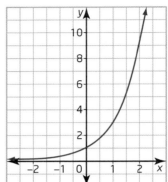

b)

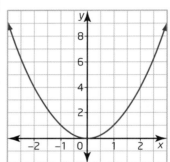

c)

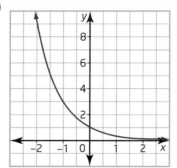

d)

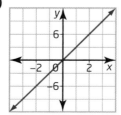

26. A bacterial colony with an initial population of 150 triples every day. Which equation models this exponential growth?

A $P = 3 \times 150^n$

B $P = 150 \times \left(\dfrac{1}{3}\right)^n$

C $P = 150 \times 3^n$

D $P = 150 \times 2^n$

27. A particular radioactive substance has a half-life of 3 years. Suppose an initial sample has a mass of 200 mg.

a) Write the equation that relates the mass of radioactive material remaining to time.

b) How much will remain after one decade?

c) How long will it take for the sample to decay to 10% of its initial mass? Explain how you arrived at your answer.

d) Show how you can write the equation from part a) in another way.

e) Explain why the two equations are equivalent.

28. Evaluate. Express as a fraction in lowest terms.

a) 9^{-1} **b)** 5^{-2} **c)** $4^{-2} + 16^{-1}$

d) $3^{-3} + 3^0$ **e)** $\left(-\dfrac{1}{5}\right)^{-2}$ **f)** $\left(\dfrac{2}{3}\right)^{-5}$

29. Simplify. Express your answers using only positive exponents.

a) $(x^{-3})(x^{-2})(x^0)$ **b)** $(2nm^2)^{-3}(4n^{-2}m^{-2})$

c) $a^{-4} \div a^{-5}$ **d)** $\dfrac{m^{-3}n^{-4}}{m^{-2}b^{-1}}$

e) $(s^{-4})^{-5}$ **f)** $(3ab^{-3})^{-2}$

30. Evaluate. Express any fractions in lowest terms.

a) $\sqrt[4]{81}$ **b)** $\sqrt[3]{-1000}$ **c)** $\sqrt[9]{-512}$

d) $343^{\frac{1}{3}}$ **e)** $\left(\dfrac{125}{216}\right)^{\frac{1}{3}}$ **f)** $81^{\frac{3}{4}}$

g) $128^{\frac{4}{7}}$ **h)** -5^{-4} **i)** $\left(\dfrac{2}{3}\right)^{-5}$

31. a) Graph the function $y = 64\left(\dfrac{1}{4}\right)^x$.

b) Identify the

  i) domain **ii)** range

  iii) x- and y-intercepts, if they exist

  iv) intervals of increase/decrease

  v) equation of the asymptote

c) Show how you can write the equation from part a) in another way. Explain why the two equations are equivalent.

32. The population of Astro Hill over a period of 6 years is shown.

Year	Population
0	1500
1	1575
2	1654
3	1736
4	1823
5	1914
6	2010

a) Make a scatter plot for the data. Does the relation appear to be exponential? Explain your reasoning.

b) Find the equation of the curve of best fit.

c) Limit the domain of the function so that it accurately models this situation.

d) Predict the population of Astro Hill 9 years after the first table entry. State any assumptions you must make.

e) How long will it take for the town's population to double? State any assumptions you must make.

33. A radioactive substance with an initial mass of 100 mg has a half-life of 1.5 days.

a) Write an equation to relate the mass remaining to time.

b) Graph the function. Describe the shape of the curve.

c) Limit the domain so that the model accurately describes the situation.

d) Find the amount remaining after

  i) 8 days **ii)** 2 weeks

e) How long will it take for the sample to decay to 3% of its initial mass?

Radioactive Isotopes

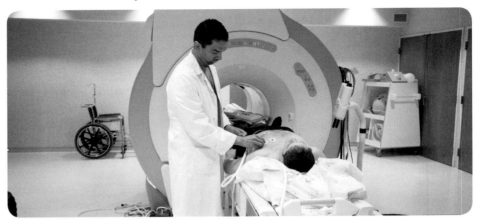

Radioactive isotopes are used in nuclear medicine to allow physicians to explore bodily structures in patients. Very small quantities of these isotopes, such as iodine-131 (I-131; half-life 8.065 days), are injected into patients. The isotopes are traced through the body so a medical diagnosis can be made. These elements have a very short half-life, so the label on the bottle will state the radioactivity of the element (the amount of the element that remains) at a particular moment in time.

a) A bottle of I-131 is delivered to a hospital on September 5. It states on the label that the radioactivity at 12:00 p.m. on September 10 will be 380 megabecquerels (MBq).

  i) Write a defining equation for the relationship between the amount of radioactivity and the time since the bottle was delivered.

  ii) What is the radioactive activity at

   • 12:00 p.m. on the delivery day?

   • 6:00 a.m. on September 25?

  iii) Sketch the graph of this relationship.

b) Effective half-life is the time required for a radioactive isotope contained in a body to reduce its radioactivity by half, due to a combination of radioactive decay and the natural elimination of the isotope from the body. In patients with Graves disease, the effective half-life of I-131 is 62.5% of the normal half-life. In patients with a disease called toxic nodular goitre, the effective half-life is 75% of the normal half-life. Compare these results to the standard rate of decay for I-131 numerically, graphically, and algebraically.

c) Research one of the topics below and write a short report on your findings.
   • other radioactive isotopes that are used in medical diagnoses or treatments
   • diseases that can be treated with radioactive isotopes
   • the production and transport of radioactive isotopes
   • the training required for medical personnel to use radioactive isotopes

Trigonometry

Airports are often surrounded by mountains, trees, buildings, power lines, and other obstructions. Pilots need accurate information about these objects to safely steer clear of them. This information is particularly important when weather and lighting conditions force pilots to navigate using instruments alone. A challenge for aviation and air traffic control authorities is that the distances and heights for these obstructions are often difficult, if not impossible, to measure directly. In this chapter, you will learn how trigonometry can be used to overcome these types of challenges.

By the end of this chapter, you will

- determine the exact values of the sine, cosine, and tangent of the special angles: 0°, 30°, 45°, 60°, and 90°

- determine the values of the sine, cosine, and tangent of any angle from 0° to 360°, through investigation using a variety of tools and strategies

- determine the measures of two angles from 0° to 360° for which the value of a given trigonometric ratio is the same

- define the secant, cosecant, and cotangent ratios for angles in a right triangle in terms of the sides of the triangle, and relate these ratios to the cosine, sine, and tangent ratios

- prove simple trigonometric identities, using the Pythagorean identity $\sin^2 x + \cos^2 x = 1$; the quotient identity $\tan x = \dfrac{\sin x}{\cos x}$; and the reciprocal identities $\sec x = \dfrac{1}{\cos x}$, $\csc x = \dfrac{1}{\sin x}$, and $\cot x = \dfrac{1}{\tan x}$

- pose and solve problems involving right triangles and oblique triangles in two-dimensional settings, using the primary trigonometric ratios, the cosine law, and the sine law (including the ambiguous case)

- pose and solve problems involving right triangles and oblique triangles in three-dimensional settings, using the primary trigonometric ratios, the cosine law, and the sine law

Prerequisite Skills

Refer to the Prerequisite Skills Appendix on pages 478 to 495 for examples of the topics and further practice.

Classify Triangles

1. Measure the sides and angles of each triangle. Classify each as completely as possible, using terms such as equilateral, isosceles, scalene, and right.

a)    **b)**

c)   **d)**

Angle Sum of a Triangle

2. Sketch each triangle using pencil and paper or geometry software. Then, determine the indicated values by measuring.

a) In $\triangle ABC$, $\angle A = 50°$ and $\angle B = 70°$. Determine the value of $\angle C$.

b) $\triangle DEF$ is isosceles such that $DE = DF$ and $\angle D = 40°$. Determine the measures of the other two angles.

c) $\triangle GHI$ is equilateral. Find the measures of all angles.

d) $\triangle JKL$ is isosceles and $\angle K = 90°$. Find the measures of the other two angles.

Use the Pythagorean Theorem

3. Determine the measure of the unknown side in each triangle. Round your answer to one decimal place, if necessary.

a) 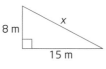   **b)**

Use Similar Triangles

4. Use similar triangles to determine the unknown value in each figure.

a)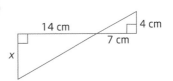

b)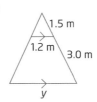

Find Primary Trigonometric Ratios

5. In each triangle, determine the primary trigonometric ratios for $\angle A$ and $\angle C$.

a) 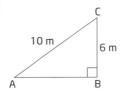   **b)**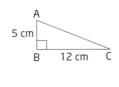

6. Use a calculator to find the approximate primary trigonometric ratios for each angle. Round your answers to four decimal places, if necessary. Be sure to set your calculator to degrees, rather than radians.

a) 30°   **b)** 45°   **c)** 60°

Determine an Angle Given a Trigonometric Ratio

7. Find each angle measure, to the nearest degree.

a) $\angle A$ given that $\sin A = 0.5299$

b) $\angle B$ given that $\cos B = \dfrac{3}{4}$

c) $\angle C$ given that $\tan C = \dfrac{1}{\sqrt{3}}$

> **Technology Tip**
>
> To access the functions $\sin^{-1}$, $\cos^{-1}$, and $\tan^{-1}$ on your calculator, you may need to press another key, such as [2nd], [SHIFT], or [INV].

Apply Trigonometric Ratios to Problems

8. In △ABC, ∠A = 50°, ∠B = 90°, and a = 8 cm.

a) Sketch the triangle, labelling all given measurements. Which trigonometric ratio would you use to determine the value of c? Justify your choice.

b) Determine c, to the nearest centimetre.

c) Determine ∠C.

9. A ladder of length 6.0 m is leaning against a building to reach a window 5.8 m above the ground. Safety instructions for the ladder indicate that a safe angle to erect the ladder is between 70° and 80° with the ground.

a) Use a protractor and a ruler to draw an accurate scale diagram of this situation.

b) Predict whether this setup is safe. Justify your prediction.

c) Select and use a trigonometric ratio to check your prediction.

Apply the Sine Law and the Cosine Law

10. Determine the length of the unknown side b in △ABC. Round your answer to one decimal place, if necessary.

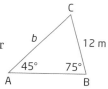

11. Determine the length of the unknown side d in △DEF, to the nearest tenth of a centimetre.

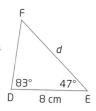

12. In △PQR, q = 18 m, r = 14 m, and ∠P = 48°.

a) Select the appropriate trigonometric tool to find the measure of p. Justify your selection.

b) Determine the measure of p, to the nearest metre.

c) Find, to the nearest degree, the measure of ∠Q.

Connections

A trigonometric tool is an equation used to solve for an unknown. Examples of trigonometric tools are the primary trigonometric ratios, the sine law, and the cosine law.

13. You are given △ABC such that a = 15 cm, ∠A = 35°, and ∠C = 55°. You want to find the measure of c. Select the most appropriate trigonometric tool to use. Justify your selection.

Chapter Problem

Chantal is a member of an orienteering club. Orienteering is an activity in which participants make their way around a course, stopping at checkpoints along the way. At the starting point, racers are given a map, a compass to measure direction, and a pedometer to measure distance. They use these tools to find their way through the course.

For a mathematics project, Chantal created an orienteering course. Her directions require participants to use trigonometry to determine directions and distances between checkpoints.

Only paper and pencil are allowed for the first three legs, but participants are given a calculator at checkpoint #3. As a participant in Chantal's race, you will use the trigonometry you learn throughout this chapter to make your way around the course.

Special Angles

Aircraft pilots often cannot see other nearby planes because of clouds, fog, or visual obstructions. Air Traffic Control uses software to track the location of aircraft to ensure that they are kept a safe distance from one another. The software uses trigonometry to make these calculations. The radar screen here shows an aircraft, identified by GZW, 10 km east of the control tower, and another, identified as TGL, 8 km southwest of the tower. To find the distance between the two aircraft, the software can use the cosine law, but it needs the cosine of an obtuse angle. Are there trigonometric ratios for angles greater than 90°? If so, how are they calculated?

In this section, you will learn how to find the primary trigonometric ratios for any angle from 0° to 360°.

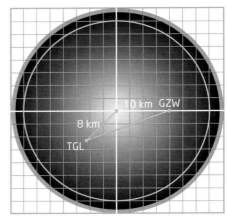

Tools

- computer with *The Geometer's Sketchpad®*

or

- grid paper

unit circle

- a circle with centre at the origin and a radius of 1 unit

Technology Tip

In *The Geometer's Sketchpad®*, you can drag the unit point on the *x*-axis to make the circle a convenient size. When measuring distances using the **Measure** menu, be sure to select **Coordinate Distance** to apply the proper scale factor.

Investigate A

How can you find exact trigonometric ratios?

Some triangles contain known angles and sides. You can use these triangles to find exact trigonometric ratios for special angles.

1. Draw a set of axes. Using the origin as the centre, draw a circle. The radius of this circle will represent 1 unit. This circle is known as a **unit circle**.

If you are using grid paper for this investigation, create a unit circle of workable size to help with accuracy.

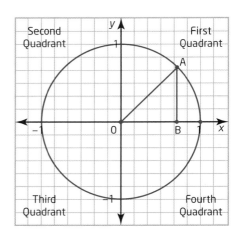

2. a) Draw a 45° angle in the first quadrant by placing the **initial arm** on the x-axis. Extend the **terminal arm** of the angle until it meets the circle at point A, such that OA is a radius of the circle. This representation is known as an **angle in standard position**.

b) Draw a vertical line from point A to the x-axis, and label the intersection point B.

c) Draw a line from the origin to point B to form △OAB.

3. Reflect Classify △OAB. Be as specific as you can.

4. Use the Pythagorean theorem to find the side lengths of △OAB. Leave your answers in radical form. Do not convert to a decimal.

5. a) Use the side lengths to find exact expressions for sin 45°, cos 45°, and tan 45°.

b) Use a calculator to evaluate these expressions to 4 decimal places.

6. Use a calculator to determine the values of sin 45°, cos 45°, and tan 45°.

7. a) Reflect How do the trigonometric ratios obtained from the triangle compare to those obtained from the calculator?

b) What is the relationship between cos 45° and the measure of side OB of △OAB?

c) What is the relationship between sin 45° and the measure of side AB of △OAB?

d) Find the coordinates of point A. How do the two relationships in parts b) and c) relate to the coordinates of point A?

initial arm
- first arm, or ray, of an angle drawn on a Cartesian plane that meets the other (terminal) arm of the angle at origin

terminal arm
- the arm of an angle that meets the initial arm at the origin and rotates around the origin counterclockwise to form a positive angle or clockwise to form a negative angle

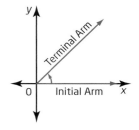

angle in standard position
- the position of an angle when its initial arm is on the positive x-axis and its vertex is at the origin

Investigate B

How can you find trigonometric ratios for angles greater than 90°?

1. Line segment OA from Investigate A forms an angle of 45° with the x-axis. Reflect point A in the y-axis to obtain point C, and join point C to the origin. What is the measure of the angle between OC and the negative x-axis? This angle is referred to as a **reference angle**. The significance of knowing the reference angle is that the values of the six trigonometric functions for any angle greater than 90° are the same as the corresponding values for its reference angle— with a possible change in sign.

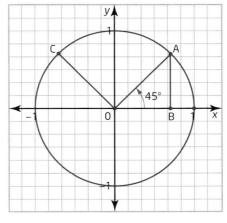

Technology

In *The Geometer's Sketchpad*®, you can use the **Transform** menu to rotate the terminal arm about the origin to form an exact angle. For help with *The Geometer's Sketchpad*®, refer to the Technology Appendix on pages 496 to 516.

reference angle
- the acute angle between the terminal arm and the x-axis of an angle in standard position

2. What are the coordinates of point C?

3. Look back at the relationships found in step 7d) of Investigate A. Use the coordinates of point C to determine cos 135° and sin 135°.

4. Reflect How can you use the coordinates of point C to represent tan 135°?

5. a) Find tan 135°.

   b) Find the slope of the terminal arm OC. How does this slope relate to tan 135°?

6. Use a calculator to compare the trigonometric ratios that you found in steps 3 and 5 with the calculator values of sin 135°, cos 135°, and tan 135°.

Connections

How does a calculator find trigonometric ratios for angles? The sine of an angle x can be expressed as a series of values involving powers of x and various coefficients. The calculator adds the terms of the series to find the sine, using enough terms to obtain the desired accuracy. Similar series exist for cosine and tangent. These are known as Taylor series. Visit the McGraw-Hill Ryerson Web site and follow the links to learn more about Taylor series.

Investigate C

How can you use a unit circle to find the trigonometric ratios for any angle?

1. Starting from the x-axis, plot a point D such that the line OD forms an angle of 230° measured counterclockwise from the positive x-axis.

2. To find the coordinates of point D, draw a vertical line to meet the x-axis at point E. The angle EOD is the reference angle for the angle in standard position.

3. Measure OE and ED. Use the measurements to determine the coordinates of point D. Record the coordinates of point D.

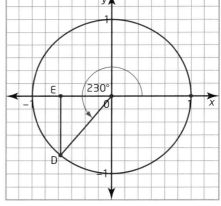

4. Find sin 230°, cos 230°, and tan 230°.

5. Reflect Explain why sin 230° and cos 230° are negative, but tan 230° is positive.

Example 1

Determine the Primary Trigonometric Ratios for 30° and 60°

Another triangle whose side lengths and angles are known is an equilateral triangle.

a) Draw an equilateral triangle with side length 2 units such that the base is horizontal. From the top vertex, draw a vertical line to form two congruent right triangles.

b) What are the measures of the angles in these triangles?

c) Find the side lengths of the base and height of one of these triangles. Leave answers in radical form where appropriate.

d) Use the side lengths and angle measures to find exact values of the trigonometric ratios for 30° and 60°.

Solution

a)

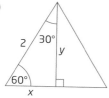

b) The altitude of the triangle bisects the top angle into two 30° angles. The angles in each triangle are 30°, 60°, and 90°.

c) Let x represent the base of one of the triangles. x is half the length of one side, or 1 unit.

Let y represent the height of the triangle. Since the triangle is a right triangle, the Pythagorean theorem applies.

$$x^2 + y^2 = 2^2$$
$$1^2 + y^2 = 4$$
$$y^2 = 3$$
$$y = \sqrt{3} \qquad \text{Since lengths are positive, discard the negative value for } y.$$

d) Since the adjacent side to the 60° angle measures 1 unit, the opposite side measures $\sqrt{3}$ units, and the hypotenuse measures 2 units,

$$\sin 60° = \frac{\sqrt{3}}{2}, \cos 60° = \frac{1}{2}, \text{ and}$$

$$\tan 60° = \frac{\sqrt{3}}{1}$$
$$= \sqrt{3}$$

Similarly,

$$\sin 30° = \frac{1}{2}, \cos 30° = \frac{\sqrt{3}}{2}, \text{ and } \tan 30° = \frac{1}{\sqrt{3}}$$

Technology

A computer algebra system (CAS) can display either exact or approximate values of the trigonometric ratios for special angles. You will learn more about how to use a CAS in the Use Technology section following Section 4.2.

Example 2

Trigonometric Ratios for 0°, 90°, 180°, and 270°

Use a unit circle to find exact values of the trigonometric ratios for 0°, 90°, 180°, and 270°.

Solution

Choose a point on the terminal arm of each angle in the unit circle.

For an angle of 0°, the required point is on the x-axis at $(1, 0)$.

$$\sin \theta = y \qquad \cos \theta = x \qquad \tan \theta = \frac{y}{x}$$

$$\sin 0° = 0 \quad \cos 0° = 1 \quad \tan 0° = \frac{0}{1}$$
$$= 0$$

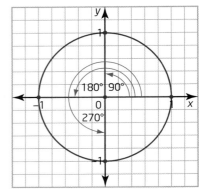

For an angle of 90°, the required point is on the y-axis at $(0, 1)$.

$$\sin \theta = y \qquad \cos \theta = x \qquad \tan \theta = \frac{y}{x}$$

$$\sin 90° = 1 \quad \cos 90° = 0 \quad \tan 90° = \frac{1}{0} \qquad \text{Division by 0 is undefined.}$$

$$\tan 90° \text{ is undefined.}$$

For an angle of 180°, the required point is on the x-axis at $(-1, 0)$.

$$\sin \theta = y \qquad \cos \theta = x \qquad \tan \theta = \frac{y}{x}$$

$$\sin 180° = 0 \quad \cos 180° = -1 \quad \tan 180° = \frac{0}{-1}$$
$$\tan 180° = 0$$

For an angle of 270°, the required point is on the y-axis at $(0, -1)$.

$$\sin \theta = y \qquad \cos \theta = x \qquad \tan \theta = \frac{y}{x}$$

$$\sin 270° = -1 \quad \cos 270° = 0 \quad \tan 270° = \frac{-1}{0}$$
$$\tan 270° \text{ is undefined.}$$

Example 3

Apply Trigonometric Ratios

An air traffic controller observes that a ValuAir flight is 20 km due east of the control tower, while a First Class Air flight is 25 km in a direction 10° west of north from the control tower.

a) What is the angle of separation of the two aircraft as seen from the tower?

b) Construct a unit circle to determine the cosine of the angle in part a).

Connections

θ is the lowercase form of the Greek letter theta. Greek letters are often used to represent variable quantities in science and mathematics. Other letters often used for angles are α, β, and ϕ (alpha, beta, and phi).

Connections

To represent 10° west of north, start from north and turn 10° toward the west.

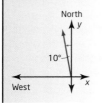

Solution

a) From east to north is an angle of 90°. A further angle of 10° results in an angle of separation of 100°.

b) Use geometry software or grid paper to construct a unit circle, and plot the point A required for an angle of 100°. Draw a vertical line to meet the x-axis at point B to complete the triangle. Measure the sides of the triangle to determine the coordinates of point A.

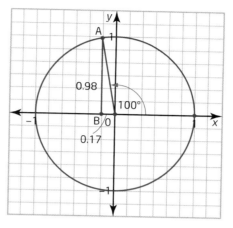

Reminder: If you are using grid paper, apply an appropriate scale factor.

The coordinates of point A are approximately $(-0.17, 0.98)$. Therefore, $\cos 100° \doteq -0.17$.

Technology Tip

You can obtain accuracy to about one decimal place when using grid paper. Using geometry software generally allows more accuracy. With *The Geometer's Sketchpad®*, for example, you can set the **Preferences** under the **Edit** menu to measure up to five decimal places.

Key Concepts

- Using a unit circle is one way to find the trigonometric ratios for angles greater than 90°.

- Any point on a unit circle can be joined to the origin to form the terminal arm of an angle. The angle θ is measured starting from the initial arm along the positive x-axis, proceeding counterclockwise to the terminal arm.

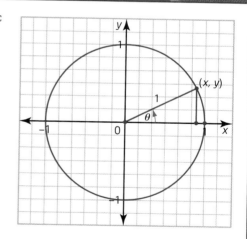

- The coordinates of the point (x, y) on a unit circle are related to θ such that $x = \cos \theta$ and $y = \sin \theta$.

- $\tan \theta = \dfrac{y}{x}$

- Exact trigonometric ratios for special angles can be determined using special triangles.

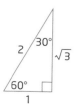 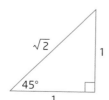

- The exact trigonometric ratios for 45° are $\sin 45° = \dfrac{1}{\sqrt{2}}$, $\cos 45° = \dfrac{1}{\sqrt{2}}$, and $\tan 45° = 1$.

Communicate Your Understanding

C1 As the terminal arm moves counterclockwise from the positive x-axis around the circle, trace what happens to the sign of $\cos \theta$ as you move from $0°$ to $360°$. Explain why this happens in terms of coordinates. Then, do the same trace for $\sin \theta$. Finally, trace what happens for $\tan \theta$.

C2 Some trigonometric ratios for certain angles are undefined. Give two examples. Explain why they are undefined.

C3 Which trigonometric ratios are positive in the fourth quadrant? Which are negative? Explain why.

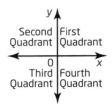

Ⓐ Practise

For help with questions 1 to 4, see Investigate A and Examples 1 and 2.

1. Compare the exact values of the trigonometric ratios for $30°$ and $60°$ to the trigonometric ratios calculated by a calculator.

2. Compare the exact values of the trigonometric ratios from Example 2 to the trigonometric ratios calculated by a calculator.

3. a) Use a unit circle to represent an angle of $30°$. Draw a triangle and use it to write the three primary trigonometric ratios in exact form for $30°$.

b) Use a unit circle to represent an angle of $60°$. Draw a triangle and use it to determine the exact primary trigonometric ratios for $60°$.

4. In a table, summarize the exact trigonometric ratios for the angles $0°$, $30°$, $45°$, $60°$, and $90°$. Add and complete a column for the ratios as given by a calculator, correct to 4 decimal places.

For help with questions 5 and 6, see Investigate B.

5. a) When using a unit circle to find trigonometric ratios for $135°$, a reference angle of $45°$ is used. What reference angle should you use to find the trigonometric ratios for $120°$?

b) Construct a unit circle to find the exact values of the three primary trigonometric ratios for $120°$.

6. Construct a unit circle to find the exact values of the three primary trigonometric ratios for $315°$.

For help with questions 7 and 8, see Investigate C and Example 3.

7. Use a unit circle to find the approximate primary trigonometric ratios for $40°$. Measure any side lengths needed. Compare your answers to those generated by calculator, correct to 4 decimal places.

8. Use a unit circle to find the approximate primary trigonometric ratios for $310°$. Measure any side lengths needed. Compare your answers to those generated by calculator.

9. Create a table to summarize the exact values of the primary trigonometric ratios for $0°$, $90°$, $180°$, $270°$, and $360°$.

10. a) Which trigonometric ratios are positive for angles in the first quadrant? second quadrant? third quadrant? fourth quadrant?

b) One way to remember the signs of trigonometric ratios is called the CAST rule, as shown (the letters spell CAST, moving counterclockwise, beginning in the fourth quadrant. What do the letters in each quadrant stand for?

B Connect and Apply

11. A pine tree that is 10 m tall is damaged in a windstorm such that it leans sideways to make an angle of 60° with the ground.

a) Represent this situation with a diagram.

b) Find an exact expression for the length of the shadow of the tree when the sun is directly overhead.

12. A sailboat is 12 km north of a lighthouse. A motor cruiser is 12 km east of the same lighthouse.

a) Use trigonometry to find an exact expression for the distance between the two boats.

b) Check your answer using another method.

13. Tall structures are sometimes stabilized with ropes or cables attached to the ground. These stabilizers are known as guy wires. A flagpole is stabilized by two guy wires attached to the top of the pole. On one side, a 25-m-long wire makes an angle of 60° with the ground. The sine of the angle formed by the second wire and the ground equals the cosine of the angle of the first guy wire.

Reasoning and Proving

Representing   Selecting Tools

Problem Solving

Connecting   Reflecting

Communicating

a) Represent this situation with a diagram.

b) Determine the length, to the nearest tenth of a metre, of the second guy wire without calculating any angles.

c) Why is it not necessary to find the angle that the second guy wire makes with the ground to solve the problem?

d) Determine the angle made by the second guy wire with the ground.

14. Use Technology Use a calculator for this question.

a) Copy and complete the table.

θ	sin θ	Quadrant	Sign
30°			
150°			
210°			
330°			

b) Relate the sign of sin θ with the quadrant. Are the signs as you expected?

c) Now, work backward. Find the angle that satisfies

i) sin $\theta = 0.5$ **ii)** sin $\theta = -0.5$

The calculator will give you only one answer for each, despite the fact that there are two angles between 0° and 360° that have each value. Note also that the calculator expressed the second angle as $-30°$ and not 330°. For angles between 180° and 360°, the calculator starts at the positive x-axis and proceeds in a clockwise direction. Angles measured in this direction are defined as negative.

d) Construct a similar table for cos θ, using the angles 60°, 120°, 240°, and 300°. Then, start with the cosine, and find the angle for both positive and negative values. Note the answers provided by the calculator.

e) Select suitable angles to test tan θ. Note how the calculator presents the angles when you work backward.

15. a) Pose a real-world problem that can be solved using trigonometric ratios for special angles without using a calculator. Solve your problem to ensure that there is a solution.

Reasoning and Proving

Representing — Selecting Tools

Problem Solving

Connecting — Reflecting

Communicating

b) Trade your problem with a classmate. Solve each other's problem.

c) Trade solutions. Judge the mathematical correctness of the solution. Look for proper form and careful use of mathematical symbols.

16. Chapter Problem You are about to begin Chantal's trigonometric orienteering course. Prepare a set of axes on grid paper to make a map of your progress, labelling the Start position at the origin. All coordinates for the course will be positive. You may not use a calculator to help you until you reach checkpoint #3. Use the instructions below to calculate the direction and distance to checkpoint #1. Draw this leg on your map and label the angle and distance. Choose and record a suitable scale.

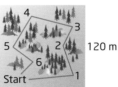

120 m

120 m

Checkpoint #1

Direction: North of east

Use the angle in the first quadrant that has a sine of $\frac{1}{2}$.

Distance: The result of evaluating $-40(\cos 150° \times \tan 135° \times \sin 300°)$

17. Stefan has set up a right $\triangle EFG$ on one side of a river such that FG measures 20 m and $\angle DEF$ measures 60°. EG bisects $\angle DEF$. Without using a calculator, determine the width, DG, of the river.

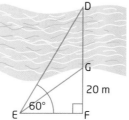

D

G

20 m

60°

E   F

✔ **Achievement Check**

18. In $\triangle PQR$, $\angle Q = 90°$, $\angle P = 60°$, and $\angle R = 30°$. PR = 1 unit. Extend side QR to T such that PR = RT. Join PT.

a) Draw a diagram to represent this situation.

b) Calculate the exact measure of $\angle T$. Justify your answer.

c) What lengths do you need to know to find tan T? Explain.

d) Determine the exact value of the unknown lengths in part c). Do not use a calculator. Justify your reasoning.

e) Find the exact value for tan T.

C **Extend**

19. Consider an angle of 30° in standard position on a unit circle. Join A to B and to C as shown. Show that the lengths of the sides of $\triangle ABC$ satisfy the Pythagorean theorem and that $\angle CAB = 90°$.

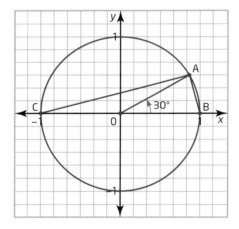

20. Refer to question 19. Let $\angle AOB$ be any angle in the first quadrant, and let the coordinates of A be (x, y). Show that the sides of $\triangle ABC$ satisfy the Pythagorean theorem and that $\angle CAB = 90°$.

21. The town of Dainfleet is planning to build a municipal swimming pool in the shape of a regular hexagon. The projected cost of the pool depends on its area. Without using a calculator, show that the side length, ℓ, of the pool is related to its area, A, by the formula

$$\ell = \sqrt{\frac{2A}{3\sqrt{3}}}$$

22. Math Contest An equilateral triangle has a height of $3\sqrt{3}$ cm. Its perimeter is

A 12 cm   **B** 18 cm

C 6 cm   **D** $9\sqrt{3}$ cm

E $18 + 3\sqrt{3}$ cm

23. Math Contest The parallel sides of a trapezoid have lengths of 7 cm and 15 cm. The two lower base angles are 30° and 60°. The area of the trapezoid is

A $22\sqrt{3}$ cm²   **B** $14\sqrt{3}$ cm²

C 22 cm²   **D** $30\sqrt{3}$ cm²

E $8\sqrt{3}$ cm²

24. Math Contest A circle has an inscribed isosceles triangle with one side as the diameter. What is the ratio of the area of the triangle to the area of the circle?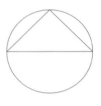

A π:2   **B** 1:2π

C 1:π   **D** 2:π

E 1:4

Career Connection

Building codes exist to ensure that structures are properly built with suitable building materials. As a building inspector, Christopher visits sites during all phases of the construction to make sure regulations are being followed. Initially, a site must be able to support the type of building planned and blueprints have to be checked for the structure's stability. As the building goes up, Christopher checks the stability, wiring, and safety features. A good knowledge of trigonometry is important when buildings are meant to last and when people's safety is at stake. To prepare for his job academically, Christopher completed a three-year diploma in architecture and construction engineering technology at Conestoga College.

4.2

Co-terminal and Related Angles

Trigonometric ratios can be used to model quantities such as the alternating-current electricity that powers electric motors, among other electrical devices. When solving problems involving trigonometric quantities, there is almost always more than one solution—sometimes an infinite number of solutions. It is important to find all possible solutions and then select which solutions are appropriate for the problem.

In this section, you will learn how to identify different angles that have the same trigonometric ratio, as well as learn how they are related.

Tools

• grid paper

Investigate

How can you find different angles with the same trigonometric ratios?

1. a) In the first quadrant, $45°$ has a sine of $\dfrac{1}{\sqrt{2}}$. Explain why.

   b) Draw a unit circle. Add a terminal arm to represent $45°$. Label the angle.

2. Label the x- and y-coordinates of the point where the terminal arm intersects the unit circle.

3. Find another point on the unit circle that has the same y-coordinate. What is the x-coordinate of this point?

4. a) Draw a second angle in standard position with its terminal arm through the point you found in step 3.

   b) What is the measure of this second angle?

5. Which of the trigonometric ratios for the two angles are the same? Which are different?

6. Reflect For any chosen point on the unit circle, how many other points will have the same y-coordinate? Explain why.

7. a) Which angle in the first quadrant has a cosine of $\dfrac{1}{2}$?

   b) Draw a unit circle and plot the point where the terminal arm of the angle intersects the circle. Then, draw the terminal arm of this angle.

8. Label the x- and y-coordinates of the point in step 7.

9. Find another point on the unit circle that has the same x-coordinate. What is the y-coordinate of this point?

10. a) Draw a second angle in standard position with its terminal arm through the point you found in step 9.

b) What is the measure of this second angle?

11. Which of the trigonometric ratios for the two angles are the same? Which are different?

12. Reflect For any chosen point on the unit circle, how many other points will have the same x-coordinate? Explain how they are related.

13. Suppose that the circle being used is not a unit circle, but rather a circle with radius r. The coordinates (x, y) of a point on the circle are no longer the cosine and sine of the angle, but are related to the cosine and sine. Study the circle shown. Write expressions for $\sin \theta$, $\cos \theta$, and $\tan \theta$ in terms of x, y, and r.

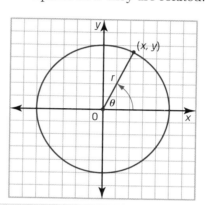

Example 1

Find Primary Trigonometric Ratios and Angles Using Any Circle

a) Given that $\sin A = \frac{3}{5}$ and that $\angle A$ lies in the first quadrant, determine exact values for $\cos A$ and $\tan A$.

b) Determine the primary trigonometric ratios for another angle between $0°$ and $360°$ that has the same sine value.

c) Draw a diagram showing the locations of the two angles. How are the two angles related?

d) Use a calculator to help you find the two angles, to the nearest degree.

Solution

a) Since $\sin A = \frac{3}{5}$, possible values of y and r are 3 and 5. Therefore, let $y = 3$ and $r = 5$.

$$x^2 + y^2 = r^2$$ Use the Pythagorean theorem to find the value of x.
$$x^2 + 3^2 = 5^2$$
$$x^2 = 16$$
$$x = \pm 4$$

Since ∠A lies in the first quadrant, $x = 4$.

$$\cos A = \frac{x}{r} \qquad \tan A = \frac{y}{x}$$
$$= \frac{4}{5} \qquad\qquad = \frac{3}{4}$$

b) The sine ratio is positive in the first and second quadrants. The point that defines an angle with the same sine is $(-4, 3)$. Let ∠B represent the angle.

$$\sin B = \frac{y}{r} \qquad \cos B = \frac{x}{r} \qquad \tan B = \frac{y}{x}$$
$$= \frac{3}{5} \qquad\qquad = \frac{-4}{5} \qquad\qquad = \frac{3}{-4}$$
$$\qquad\qquad\qquad = -\frac{4}{5} \qquad\qquad = -\frac{3}{4}$$

c) From the diagram, $∠B = 180° - ∠A$.

d) Ensure that the calculator is set to degree measure.

$$\sin A = \frac{3}{5}$$
$$∠A = \sin^{-1}\left(\frac{3}{5}\right)$$
$$\doteq 37°$$

$$∠B = 180° - ∠A$$
$$\doteq 180° - 37°$$
$$= 143°$$

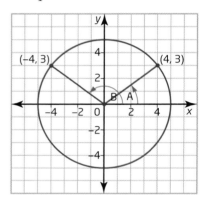

Example 2

Relations for the Cosine and Tangent Ratios

a) Determine another angle between 0° and 360° that has the same cosine as ∠A in Example 1. What is the relationship between this angle and ∠A?

b) Determine another angle between 0° and 360° that has the same tangent as ∠A in Example 1. What is the relationship between this angle and ∠A?

Solution

a) Determine another angle, α, such that $\cos \alpha = \frac{4}{5}$. Since the cosine ratio is positive in the fourth quadrant, the coordinates of the required point are $(4, -3)$. From the diagram,
$$∠\alpha = 360° - ∠A$$
$$\doteq 360° - 37°$$
$$= 323°$$

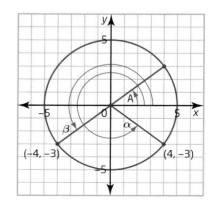

b) Determine another angle, β, such that $\tan \beta = \frac{3}{4}$. Since the tangent ratio is positive in the third quadrant, the coordinates of the required point are $(-4, -3)$.

From the diagram,

$$\beta = 180° + \angle A$$
$$\doteq 180° + 37°$$
$$= 217°$$

Example 3

Solve a Map Problem

The city plan of Port Foghorn uses a Cartesian grid, with each grid mark representing a distance of 1 km. The plan places City Hall at the origin of the grid. Ted's house is at grid point $(-6, 2.5)$.

a) The angle of rotation for Suzette's house has the same tangent ratio as the angle of rotation for Ted's house. Where is Suzette's house?

b) Find the angles in standard position if the lines drawn from City Hall to each of the two houses are terminal arms. Round your answers to the nearest degree.

Solution

a) Ted's house is in the second quadrant, so the tangent is negative. If Suzette's house has the same tangent ratio, it must be in the fourth quadrant at $(6, -2.5)$.

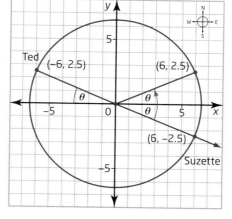

b) Ted's house is at a reflection of $(6, 2.5)$ in the y-axis. Suzette's house a reflection of $(6, 2.5)$ in the x-axis. The reference angle associated with these points is θ, where

$$\tan \theta = \frac{2.5}{6}$$
$$\theta \doteq 23°$$

Ted's house is at approximately $180° - 23° = 157°$.

Suzette's house is at approximately $360° - 23° = 337°$.

Example 4

co-terminal angles

- angles in standard position that have the same terminal arm

Co-terminal Angles

a) Find three other positive angles that have the same terminal arm as 30°.

b) Find three negative angles that have the same terminal arm as 30°.

Solution

a) Turn in a counterclockwise direction from 30°. If you continue for 360°, you arrive back at the same terminal arm. $30° + 360° = 390°$, so 30° and 390° are co-terminal angles.

Two other positive angles that are co-terminal with 30° are as follows:

$30° + 2(360°) = 750°$

$30° + 3(360°) = 1110°$

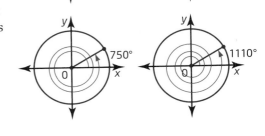

Connections

A positive angle is generated when the terminal arm moves in a counterclockwise direction. A negative angle is generated when the terminal arm moves in a clockwise direction.

b) Starting at the positive x-axis and proceeding in a clockwise direction defines a negative angle. You will reach the terminal arm of 30° after a rotation of −330°. Hence, −330° is co-terminal with 30°.

Two other negative angles that are co-terminal with 30° are as follows:

$30° - 2(360°) = -690°$

$30° - 3(360°) = -1050°$

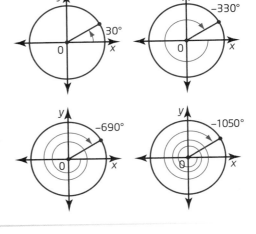

- The primary trigonometric ratios for the angle θ in standard position that has a point (x, y) on its terminal arm can be calculated as

$$\sin \theta = \frac{y}{r}, \cos \theta = \frac{x}{r}, \text{ and } \tan \theta = \frac{y}{x}, \text{ where } r = \sqrt{x^2 + y^2}.$$

- For any given sine ratio, two distinct angles between $0°$ and $360°$ have this sine ratio.

- For any given cosine ratio, two distinct angles between $0°$ and $360°$ have this cosine ratio.

- For any given tangent ratio, two distinct angles between $0°$ and $360°$ have this tangent ratio.

- Pairs of related angles can be found using the coordinates of the endpoints of their terminal arms. Use a reference angle in the first quadrant.

- Co-terminal angles are angles with the same terminal arm. They can be positive or negative.

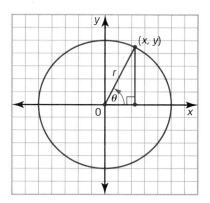

Communicate Your Understanding

C1 Explain why there are exactly two angles between $0°$ and $360°$ that have a given sine ratio.

C2 The terminal arm of an angle is in the first quadrant. What kind of reflection will give the terminal arm of an angle that has the same sine ratio? the same cosine ratio? the same tangent ratio?

C3 How many co-terminal angles can you find for an angle of $30°$? Explain.

C4 How do the trigonometric ratios for $30°$ relate to the trigonometric ratios for $390°$? Is this true for all co-terminal angles? Explain.

Ⓐ Practise

Note: Unless otherwise specified, assume that all angles are between $0°$ and $360°$.

For help with questions 1 and 2, refer to Example 1.

1. The coordinates of a point on the terminal arm of an angle θ are shown. Determine the exact primary trigonometric ratios for θ.

a) A(5, 12)

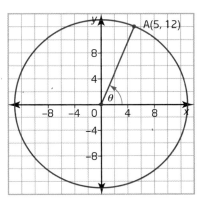

b) B(−3, 4)

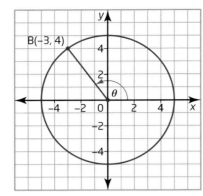

c) C(−6, −8)

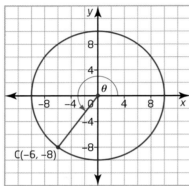

d) D(2, 5)

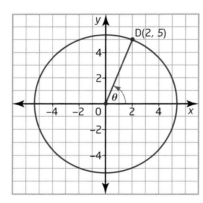

e) E(−1, −3)

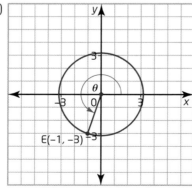

2. The coordinates of a point on the terminal arm of an angle θ are given. Determine the exact primary trigonometric ratios for θ.

   a) G(−8, 6)   **b)** H(3, −4)

   c) I(−15, −8)   **d)** J(3, −5)

   e) K(1, 2)   **f)** L(6, −2)

For help with questions 3 and 4, refer to Examples 1 and 2.

3. One of the primary trigonometric ratios for an angle is given, as well as the quadrant in which the terminal arm lies. Find the other two primary trigonometric ratios.

   a) $\sin A = \dfrac{8}{17}$, first quadrant

   b) $\cos B = \dfrac{3}{5}$, fourth quadrant

   c) $\tan C = -\dfrac{5}{12}$, second quadrant

   d) $\sin D = -\dfrac{2}{3}$, third quadrant

   e) $\cos E = -\dfrac{5}{6}$, second quadrant

   f) $\tan F = \dfrac{12}{7}$, first quadrant

4. Determine another angle that has the same trigonometric ratio as each given angle. Draw a sketch with both angles labelled.

   a) cos 45°   **b)** sin 150°

   c) tan 300°   **d)** sin 100°

   e) cos 230°   **f)** tan 350°

For help with questions 5 and 6, refer to Example 4.

5. a) Determine any three positive angles that are co-terminal with 120°.

   b) Determine any three negative angles that are co-terminal with 330°.

6. Determine the exact primary trigonometric ratios for each angle. You may wish to use a unit circle to help you.

   a) $\angle A = -45°$ **b)** $\angle B = -120°$

   c) $\angle C = 540°$ **d)** $\angle D = -315°$

   e) $\angle E = 420°$ **f)** $\angle F = -270°$

B Connect and Apply

7. Without using a calculator, determine two angles between $0°$ and $360°$ that have a cosine of $-\dfrac{\sqrt{3}}{2}$.

8. Two angles between $0°$ and $360°$ have a tangent of -1. Without using a calculator, determine the angles.

9. The cosine of each of two angles between $0°$ and $360°$ is $\dfrac{1}{\sqrt{2}}$. Without using a calculator, determine the angles.

10. Two angles between $0°$ and $360°$ have a tangent that is undefined. What are the angles? Why is the tangent undefined for each of these?

11. The point $P(-4, 9)$ is on the terminal arm of $\angle A$.

a) Determine the primary trigonometric ratios for $\angle A$ and $\angle B$, such that $\angle B$ has the same sine as $\angle A$.

b) Use a calculator and a diagram to determine the measures of $\angle A$ and $\angle B$, to the nearest degree.

12. The point $R(-3, -5)$ is on the terminal arm of $\angle E$.

Reasoning and Proving / Representing / Selecting Tools / Problem Solving / Connecting / Reflecting / Communicating

a) Determine the primary trigonometric ratios for $\angle E$ and $\angle F$ such that $\angle F$ has the same tangent as $\angle E$.

b) Use a calculator and a diagram to determine the measures of $\angle E$ and $\angle F$, to the nearest degree.

13. Use Technology Open *The Geometer's Sketchpad®*.

a) Draw a circle with a radius of 5 grid units. Plot a point A on the circle in the first quadrant.

b) Measure the coordinate distance between point A and the origin. Change the label to r. Measure the x- and y-coordinates of point A.

c) Construct formulas to calculate the sine, cosine, and tangent of $\angle A$ defined by terminal arm OA, using the measures of x, y, and r.

d) Right-click on point A and select **Animate Point**. Observe the values of the trigonometric ratios as A moves around the circle. Pause the animation at selected points at which you know the ratios, and compare the values on the screen to your knowledge.

e) Try the controls in the **Motion Controller**. Determine what each of them does. You can also control the animation from the **Display** menu.

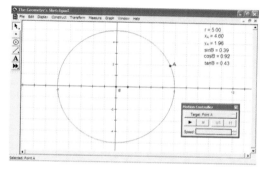

f) As the sine increases in the first quadrant, what happens to the cosine? What happens to the tangent? What happens in the second quadrant?

14. An acute angle θ has the point $A(p, q)$ on its terminal arm.

Reasoning and Proving / Representing / Selecting Tools / Problem Solving / Connecting / Reflecting / Communicating

a) Find an expression for the distance OA in terms of p and q.

b) Write exact expressions for the primary trigonometric ratios for θ.

c) Locate the angle $90° - \theta$. Sketch the terminal arm for this angle. Determine the coordinates of a point B on the terminal arm of $90° - \theta$ in terms of p and q.

d) Write exact expressions for the primary trigonometric ratios for $90° - \theta$.

e) Compare the expressions that you found in parts b) and d).

15. Chapter Problem For the second leg of your orienteering course, calculate the direction and distance. Carefully draw the leg on your map, and label all distances and angles. Note: You may not use a calculator.

Direction: Face south. Turn left through an angle with a cosine of 0 and a sine of 1.

Distance: Find two angles between 0° and 360° with a sine of $-\dfrac{1}{\sqrt{2}}$. Subtract the smaller angle from the larger angle. Find the sine of the resulting angle. Multiply by 40 to obtain the distance.

✔ **Achievement Check**

16. Consider $\angle C$ such that $\sin C = \dfrac{7}{25}$.

a) What are the possible quadrants in which $\angle C$ may lie?

b) If you know that $\cos C$ is negative, how does your answer to part a) change?

c) Sketch a diagram to represent $\angle C$ in standard position, given that the condition in part b) is true.

d) Find the coordinates of a point P on the terminal arm of $\angle C$.

e) Write exact expressions for the other two primary trigonometric ratios for $\angle C$.

C Extend

17. The side length of a rhombus is s. One of its diagonals has the same length. Determine an exact expression for the length of the other diagonal.

18. A regular octagon has side length ℓ. A line segment is drawn joining two of its vertices to form a triangle and an irregular heptagon. Determine an expression for the exact length of this line segment.

19. Use Technology How can you use a graphing calculator to check answers when determining two angles with the same trigonometric ratio? For example, suppose you are asked to determine the values of θ such that $\sin \theta = 0.5$.

a) Set the window variables as shown. Enter the left side as **Y1** and the right side as **Y2**.

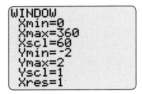

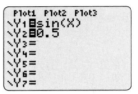

b) Press (GRAPH). Press (2nd) [CALC]. Select **5:intersect**. Use the **Intersect** operation twice to determine the values that satisfy the condition.

20. Math Contest A clock face is in the form of a coordinate system with the origin at the centre of the face. The minute hand passes through the point $\left(1, \sqrt{3}\right)$. The hour hand is somewhere between the 4 and the 5. The time is

A 4:05 **B** 4:10 **C** 4:15

D 4:07 **E** 4:12

21. Math Contest Given A(0, 0), B(3, $3\sqrt{3}$), and C($2\sqrt{3}$, 2), what is the area, in square units, of $\triangle$ABC?

A 12 **B** $\dfrac{5\sqrt{3}}{2}$ **C** 6

D $3\sqrt{3}$ **E** 3

22. Math Contest If $4x = 7 - 5y$, what is the value of $12x + 15y$?

A 3 **B** 7 **C** 21

D 27 **E** 31

Use a Computer Algebra System to Find Exact Trigonometric Ratios and Angles

A computer algebra system (CAS) found on calculators such as the TI-Nspire™ CAS graphing calculator can display exact values of the trigonometric ratios for the special angles you learned about in Section 4.1. With its equation-solving power, a CAS can also find all angles that satisfy a given function, unlike an ordinary calculator that gives only one answer.

This activity is written for the CAS on a TI-Nspire™ CAS graphing calculator. Other systems can be used.

Tools

• TI-Nspire™ CAS graphing calculator

A: Display Exact Values

1. Turn on the TI-Nspire™ CAS graphing calculator.
   • Press ⌂ and select **8:System Info**.
   • Select **2:System Settings…**.
   • Use the (tab) key to scroll down to **Angle**, and ensure that it is set to **Degree**.

   Continue on to **Auto or Approx** and ensure that it is set to **Auto**. Continue down to **OK**, and press ⊚ twice.

2. Press ⌂ and select **6:New Document**. Select **1:Add Calculator**.

3. Enter sin(30) and press ⊚. Notice how the result is displayed. Investigate cos(30) and tan(30). Do you see anything unusual about the display? Explain why this is equivalent to the value that you determined using a unit circle.

   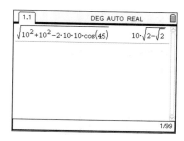

4. You can use a CAS to obtain exact answers to trigonometric problems. For example, in △ABC, $b = 10$ cm, $c = 10$ cm, and $\angle A = 45°$. Find the exact measure of c using the cosine law.

B: Find Angles

1. When you use an ordinary calculator to find an angle θ such that $\sin \theta = 0.5$, you only get one answer. If you use the **sin⁻¹** operation on the TI-Nspire™ CAS graphing calculator, the same thing happens. Try it.

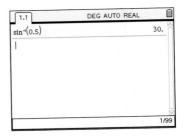

2. Now, use the equation-solving power of the CAS.

   - Press (menu).
   - Select **3:Algebra**.
   - Select **1:solve**.
   - Type sin(x) = 0.5, x)|0≤x≤360.
   - Press (enter).

   Notice that the CAS has found the angles between 0° and 360° that have a sine of 0.5. The domain of the solution needs to be restricted to answers between 0° and 360°. This is done with the expression following the "with" operator (|).

Technology Tip

To obtain the ≤ sign, press (ctrl) and then (<).

3. Try the same thing with the equation $\cos \theta = 0.5$. Before using the CAS, predict the answers. Then, use the CAS to see if your predictions are correct.

   Notice that, unlike an ordinary calculator, the CAS does not use a negative angle for the fourth quadrant.

Technology Tip

You can force the calculator to give you an approximate answer without resetting the mode by pressing (ctrl) before pressing (enter).

4. The CAS can also solve more complex trigonometric equations. Are there any angles between 0° and 360° that satisfy the equation $\sin \theta + \cos \theta = 1$? Write down your prediction, and justify why you think you are correct. Then, use the CAS to check your prediction.

5. Write a trigonometric equation that you think has a solution. Trade equations with a classmate and solve each other's equation. Discuss the results.

Reciprocal Trigonometric Ratios

The primary trigonometric ratios have many uses, from solving triangles in surveying and navigation to working with music theory and electronics, especially in connection with music synthesizers. The **reciprocal** trigonometric ratios are related to the primary trigonometric ratios and have many applications, including radar antenna design.

In this section, you will learn what the reciprocal trigonometric ratios are, how to calculate them, and how they behave.

reciprocals

• two expressions that have a product of 1

(e.g., 4 and $\frac{1}{4}$ or x and $\frac{1}{x}$)

Investigate

How can you use a calculator to calculate the reciprocal trigonometric ratios?

1. The reciprocal of the sine ratio is called the **cosecant ratio**. It is defined in a right triangle as

   $$\csc \theta = \frac{\text{hypotenuse}}{\text{opposite}}$$

   a) What is the exact value of sin 30°? Predict the exact value of csc 30°.

   b) Use a calculator to determine sin 30°. Then, press the reciprocal key. The key is usually labelled $\frac{1}{x}$ or x^{-1}. Does the result confirm your prediction?

cosecant ratio

• reciprocal of the sine ratio: $\csc \theta = \frac{1}{\sin \theta}$

2. The reciprocal of the cosine ratio is called the **secant ratio**. It is defined in a right triangle as

   $$\sec \theta = \frac{\text{hypotenuse}}{\text{adjacent}}$$

   a) What is the exact value of cos 60°? Predict the exact value of sec 60°.

   b) Use the calculator to determine cos 60°. Then, press the reciprocal key. Does the result confirm your prediction?

secant ratio

• reciprocal of the cosine ratio: $\sec \theta = \frac{1}{\cos \theta}$

3. The reciprocal of the tangent ratio is called the **cotangent** ratio. It is defined in a right triangle as

   $$\cot \theta = \frac{\text{adjacent}}{\text{opposite}}$$

   a) What is the exact value of tan 30°? Predict the exact value of cot 30°.

   b) Use the calculator to determine tan 30°. Then, press the reciprocal key. Does the result agree with your prediction?

cotangent ratio

• reciprocal of the tangent ratio:

$\cot \theta = \frac{1}{\tan \theta}$

4. Use your knowledge of special angles to copy and complete the table. Use exact values.

θ	$\sin \theta$	$\csc \theta$	$\cos \theta$	$\sec \theta$	$\tan \theta$	$\cot \theta$
0°						
30°						
45°						
60°						
90°						

5. Reflect As the measure of angle θ increases, how does the value of $\sin \theta$ compare to the value of $\csc \theta$? How does the value of $\cos \theta$ compare to the value of $\sec \theta$? How does the value of $\tan \theta$ compare to the value of $\cot \theta$?

Example 1

Determine Reciprocal Trigonometric Ratios Using a Triangle

Consider a right triangle with sides of length 3 units, 4 units, and 5 units. Determine the six trigonometric ratios for $\angle A$. Then, determine the six trigonometric ratios for $\angle B$.

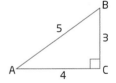

Solution

$$\sin A = \frac{\text{opposite}}{\text{hypotenuse}} \qquad \cos A = \frac{\text{adjacent}}{\text{hypotenuse}} \qquad \tan A = \frac{\text{opposite}}{\text{adjacent}}$$
$$= \frac{3}{5} \qquad\qquad\qquad = \frac{4}{5} \qquad\qquad\qquad = \frac{3}{4}$$

$$\csc A = \frac{\text{hypotenuse}}{\text{opposite}} \qquad \sec A = \frac{\text{hypotenuse}}{\text{adjacent}} \qquad \cot A = \frac{\text{adjacent}}{\text{opposite}}$$
$$= \frac{5}{3} \qquad\qquad\qquad = \frac{5}{4} \qquad\qquad\qquad = \frac{4}{3}$$

$$\sin B = \frac{\text{opposite}}{\text{hypotenuse}} \qquad \cos B = \frac{\text{adjacent}}{\text{hypotenuse}} \qquad \tan B = \frac{\text{opposite}}{\text{adjacent}}$$
$$= \frac{4}{5} \qquad\qquad\qquad = \frac{3}{5} \qquad\qquad\qquad = \frac{4}{3}$$

$$\csc B = \frac{\text{hypotenuse}}{\text{opposite}} \qquad \sec B = \frac{\text{hypotenuse}}{\text{adjacent}} \qquad \cot B = \frac{\text{adjacent}}{\text{opposite}}$$
$$= \frac{5}{4} \qquad\qquad\qquad = \frac{5}{3} \qquad\qquad\qquad = \frac{3}{4}$$

Example 2

Determine the Angle Given the Reciprocal Trigonometric Ratio

Each angle is in the first quadrant. Determine the measure of each angle, to the nearest degree.

a) $\csc A = 8$ **b)** $\sec B = \dfrac{5}{2}$ **c)** $\cot C = \dfrac{5}{16}$

Solution

a) $\csc A = 8$

$\sin A = \dfrac{1}{8}$

$\angle A \doteq 7°$

b) $\sec B = \dfrac{5}{2}$

$\cos B = \dfrac{2}{5}$

$\angle B \doteq 66°$

c) $\cot C = \dfrac{5}{16}$

$\tan C = \dfrac{16}{5}$

$\angle C \doteq 73°$

```
                    Done
sin⁻¹(1/8)
          7.180755781
```

> **Technology Tip**
>
> Use the function $\sin^{-1}$ to determine $\angle A$. You may need to press another key, such as [2nd], to access this function.

Example 3

Determine Angles in the Unit Circle That Have a Given Reciprocal Trigonometric Ratio

Determine two angles between $0°$ and $360°$ that have a cosecant of -2.

Solution

$\csc \theta = -2$

Take the reciprocal of both sides.

$\sin \theta = \dfrac{1}{-2}$

$\qquad = -\dfrac{1}{2}$

Since $\sin 30° = \dfrac{1}{2}$, the reference angle is $30°$.

The sine ratio is negative in the third and fourth quadrants. Look for reflections of $30°$ that lie in these quadrants.

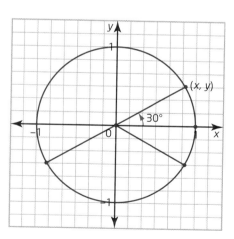

One possible value of θ is
$180° + 30° = 210°$. The other possible value of θ is $360° - 30° = 330°$.

Two angles between $0°$ and $360°$ that have a cosecant of -2 are $210°$ and $330°$.

- The reciprocal trigonometric ratios are defined as follows:

$$\csc\theta = \frac{\text{hypotenuse}}{\text{opposite}} \qquad \sec\theta = \frac{\text{hypotenuse}}{\text{adjacent}} \qquad \cot\theta = \frac{\text{adjacent}}{\text{opposite}}$$

$$= \frac{1}{\sin\theta} \qquad\qquad = \frac{1}{\cos\theta} \qquad\qquad = \frac{1}{\tan\theta}$$

Communicate Your Understanding

C1 For angles restricted to the first quadrant, what are the maximum and minimum values that $\sin\theta$ may have? What are the maximum and minimum values that $\csc\theta$ may have?

C2 Write expressions for $\csc\theta$, $\sec\theta$, and $\cot\theta$ in terms of x, y, and r if the terminal arm of angle θ intersects a circle of radius r at the point (x, y).

C3 Are there any values of θ, $0° \leq \theta \leq 90°$, for which $\sec\theta$ is undefined? If so, determine them. If not, explain why not.

A Practise

For help with question 1, refer to the Investigate.

1. Use a calculator to determine the six trigonometric ratios for each angle, to three decimal places.

   a) $20°$ **b)** $42°$ **c)** $75°$

   d) $88°$ **e)** $153°$ **f)** $289°$

For help with questions 2 to 4, refer to Example 1.

2. Determine exact expressions for the six trigonometric ratios for $315°$. Hint: Draw a diagram of the angle in standard position. Then, use special triangles to determine the exact values.

3. Determine exact expressions for the six trigonometric ratios for $120°$.

4. Determine exact expressions for the six trigonometric ratios for $270°$.

For help with question 5, refer to Example 2.

5. Find the measure, to the nearest degree, of an angle in the first quadrant that satisfies each ratio.

Reasoning and Proving

Representing — Selecting Tools

Problem Solving

Connecting — Reflecting

Communicating

If there is no such angle, explain why.

   a) $\sin A = \frac{2}{3}$ **b)** $\cos B = \frac{3}{5}$

   c) $\tan C = \frac{12}{5}$ **d)** $\csc D = \frac{9}{8}$

   e) $\sec E = \frac{4}{3}$ **f)** $\cot F = \frac{3}{4}$

   g) $\csc G = -\frac{4}{3}$ **h)** $\sec H = \frac{2}{5}$

For help with questions 6 and 7, refer to Example 3.

6. Determine two angles between $0°$ and $360°$ that have a secant of $-\sqrt{2}$. Use a unit circle to help you. Do not use a calculator.

7. Determine two angles between $0°$ and $360°$ that have a cotangent of -1. Use a unit circle to help you. Do not use a calculator.

8. Each point lies on the terminal arm of an angle in standard position. Determine exact expressions for the six trigonometric ratios for the angle.

   a) $P(-5, 12)$ **b)** $Q(-4, -3)$

   c) $R(-8, 15)$ **d)** $S(24, -7)$

   e) $T(9, 40)$ **f)** $U(-2, -3)$

   g) $V(5, -3)$ **h)** $W(-2, 7)$

B Connect and Apply

9. △PQR has a right angle at Q. If $q = 17$ cm and $p = 15$ cm, determine exact expressions for the six trigonometric ratios for ∠P.

For questions 10 to 13, round your answers to the nearest degree.

10. Determine two angles between 0° and 360° that have a cosecant of 5.

11. Determine two angles between 0° and 360° that have a secant of −5.

12. Determine two angles between 0° and 360° that have a cotangent of −3.

13. An angle has a cosecant of 1.2. The secant of the same angle is negative. Determine a value for the angle between 0° and 360°.

14. Use Technology Open *The Geometer's Sketchpad®.*

a) Draw a circle with a radius of 5 grid units. Plot a point A on the circle in the first quadrant.

b) Measure the coordinate distance between point A and the origin. Change the label to *r*. Measure the *y*-coordinate of point A.

c) Construct formulas to calculate the sine and the cosecant of ∠A, defined by terminal arm OA.

d) Animate point A, and observe the values of the sine and cosecant as A moves around the circle.

e) Use the **Motion Controller** to reverse the direction of motion of point A in such a way that it stays in the first quadrant. What happens to the values of sine and cosecant as ∠A increases? as ∠A decreases?

f) Add calculations for cos A and sec A. Repeat the animation while observing these values. Explain why this happens.

g) Add calculations for tan A and cot A. Repeat the animation while observing these values. Explain why this happens.

15. Chapter Problem You are leaving checkpoint #2 on the orienteering course and are on your way to checkpoint #3. Draw this leg of your orienteering challenge on your map. Label all distances and directions.

Direction: Face west. Turn right through an angle with a cosecant of 1.

Distance: The result of evaluating $12(\csc 30° + \sec 300° + \cot 225°)$, rounded to the nearest metre, if necessary.

✔ Achievement Check

16. An angle θ satisfies the relation $\csc \theta \cos \theta = -1$.

a) Use the definition of the reciprocal trigonometric ratios to express the left side in terms of $\sin \theta$ and $\cos \theta$.

b) What is the relation between $\sin \theta$ and $\cos \theta$ for this angle?

c) Determine two possible values for θ. Do not use a calculator.

d) Give an example of other information needed to determine a unique value for θ.

e) If $\sec \theta$ is known to be negative, what is the $\csc \theta$ and value of θ?

C Extend

17. Use expressions for the reciprocal trigonometric ratios in terms of x, y, and r to show that $1 + \tan^2 \theta = \sec^2 \theta$, regardless of the value of θ.

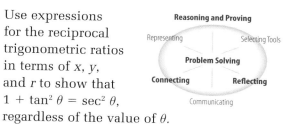

Reasoning and Proving

Representing · Selecting Tools · Problem Solving · Connecting · Reflecting · Communicating

18. Given that $\cot B = -\dfrac{c}{d}$ and ∠B is in the second quadrant, determine expressions, in terms of c and d, for the other five trigonometric ratios for B. State any restrictions on the values of c and d.

19. Given that $\sec A = \dfrac{t+1}{t-1}$ and $\angle A$ is in the fourth quadrant, determine an expression for sin A. State any restrictions on the value of t.

20. Parking regulations of a municipality require that each parking space be 3 m wide and 7 m long. Parking along a city block measuring 100 m can be set up for parallel or angle parking.

a) How many parking spaces can be made along the street using parallel parking?

b) How many parking spaces can be made along the street using angle parking at 45°?

c) What area of the roadway is lost to parking if parallel parking is used?

d) Compared to the area of roadway used for parallel parking, predict the area of roadway lost if angle parking is used. Give reasons for your prediction.

e) Calculate the area of roadway lost if angle parking is used. Compare your answer to your prediction in part d) and account for any differences.

21. One of the first recorded attempts to measure the radius of Earth was made by Eratosthenes of Alexandria, who lived from about 276 B.C.E. to 194 B.C.E. He was a Greek mathematician living in what is now Egypt. Eratosthenes' method of measurement was to observe the position of the sun in relation to Earth. He noted that at noon on the summer solstice, the sun was directly overhead the present-day city of Aswan. No shadows were cast. However, at Alexandria, about 800 km north, the sun cast shadows at an angle of 7.2° from the vertical.

a) Represent this problem using a diagram, labelling all information. State any assumptions that you make, and justify why they are reasonable.

b) Use trigonometry to determine a relation among the data given. Then, use the relation to calculate a value for the radius of Earth.

c) Find the accepted value for the radius of Earth using a library or the Internet and compare it to the value that you calculated in part b).

d) Since the sun was directly overhead on the summer solstice, what must the latitude of Aswan be? Use an atlas or the Internet to check.

Connections

In the northern hemisphere, December 21 is usually the shortest day of the year and June 21 is usually the longest. These days are known as the winter and summer solstices. Because of the inclination of Earth's axis, the apparent position of the sun changes as Earth orbits the sun. On the winter solstice, the sun is directly overhead at noon along the Tropic of Capricorn, at 23.5° south latitude. On the summer solstice, the sun is directly overhead at noon along the Tropic of Cancer, at 23.5° north latitude. On the two days of the year when day and night are about equal in duration (usually March 21 and September 21), the sun is directly overhead along the equator at noon. These days are known as the vernal and autumnal equinoxes. Visit the *Functions 11* page on the McGraw-Hill Ryerson Web site and follow the links to Chapter 4 to find out more about solstices and equinoxes.

22. Math Contest In $\triangle PQR$, sec Q = 2.5, PQ = 3, and QR = 5. Without using a calculator, find PR.

23. Math Contest Find the smallest natural number that when divided by 3 leaves a remainder of 1, when divided by 4 leaves a remainder of 2, and when divided by 5 leaves a remainder of 3.

24. Math Contest Three ports, Ashtra, Bretha, and Cratha, form a right triangle at Bretha. A ship sailing at 10 km/h makes the trip from Bretha to Ashtra in 2.5 h. The trip from Bretha to Cratha takes 6 h at the same speed. How far is it from Ashtra to Cratha?

Problems in Two Dimensions

Land surveyors use primary trigonometric ratios, the cosine law, and the sine law to determine distances that are not easily measured directly. For example, a surveyor may need to measure the distance across a river at the location planned for a new bridge. Obstructions on the shore may make it necessary to use a triangle that contains an obtuse angle. Care must be taken when using the sine law when two sides and one opposite angle are given. Sometimes, there are two answers, but only one of them is the desired answer. This is known as the **ambiguous case**.

In this section, you will solve problems involving triangles that contain an obtuse angle and deal with the possibility of two answers for the same problem.

ambiguous case

• a problem that has two or more solutions

Tools

• compasses
• protractor

Optional

• computer with *The Geometer's Sketchpad*®
• grid paper

Investigate

How can you identify the ambiguous case?

A surveyor measures two of the sides and one angle in $\triangle ABC$. She determines that $b = 600$ m, $c = 700$ m, and $\angle B = 45°$. Notice that two sides and one opposite angle are given. This is known as the side-side-angle, or SSA, case. Follow the directions below to construct $\triangle ABC$.

1. Draw a horizontal line segment. Label the left endpoint B.

2. Measure an angle of 45° upward from the line segment, with its vertex at B.

3. Use a suitable scale to draw line segment BA along the terminal arm of the 45° angle. Label point A.

4. Set your compasses to represent the length of the line segment b. With centre A, draw an arc below A such that it cuts the first horizontal line segment in two points. Label these C_1 and C_2, from left to right. Join A to C_1 and C_2.

5. **Reflect** What is the relationship between $\angle AC_1B$ and $\angle AC_2B$?

6. **Reflect** Identify two triangles that have side lengths of $b = 600$ m and $c = 700$ m, and $\angle B = 45°$. Which triangle is an acute triangle? Which triangle is an obtuse triangle? Draw these as separate triangles.

7. Reflect In $\triangle ABC$, consider that you are given b, c, and $\angle B$.

a) In what circumstances can only one triangle be drawn?

b) When is no triangle possible?

Whenever you are given two sides and one opposite angle and want to use the sine law, you must check for the ambiguous case. Sketch the possible triangles, and calculate an answer for each. Sometimes there are two possible triangles, sometimes there is one possible triangle, and sometimes it is not possible to draw a triangle to match a given set of measurements.

Example 1

Solve a Problem Using Primary Trigonometric Ratios

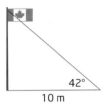

Basiruddin needs a new rope for his flagpole but is unsure of the length required. He measures a distance of 10 m away from the base of the pole. From this point, the angle of elevation to the top of the pole is 42°.

a) What is the height of the pole, to the nearest tenth of a metre?

b) How much rope should Basiruddin buy? Justify your answer.

Solution

a) It is reasonable to assume that the flagpole is perpendicular to the ground. You can use primary trigonometric ratios. Let h represent the height, in metres, of the flagpole.

$$\tan 42° = \frac{\text{opposite}}{\text{adjacent}}$$

$$\tan 42° = \frac{h}{10}$$

$$h = 10 \tan 42°$$

$$\doteq 9.0$$

The height of the flagpole is about 9.0 m.

b) Basiruddin should buy about 19 m of rope. The rope must be attached to the flagpole in a loop so that the flag can be lowered and raised. Allow some extra rope for knots and winding around pulleys.

Example 2

Solve an Oblique Triangle Problem

Patina, Quentin, and Romeo are standing on a soccer field. Quentin is
23 m from Romeo. From Quentin's point of view, the others are separated
by an angle of 72°. From Patina's point of view, the others are separated
by an angle of 55°.

a) Sketch a diagram for this situation. Why is the triangle that is formed
an **oblique triangle**?

b) Is it necessary to consider the ambiguous case? Justify your answer.

c) Determine the distance from Patina to Romeo, to the nearest tenth of
a metre. If there are two answers, determine both.

oblique triangle

• a triangle with no right
angle

Solution

a) $\angle R = 180° - 72° - 55°$

$= 53°$

Since the triangle has no right angle, it is an
oblique triangle.

b) It is not necessary to consider the ambiguous case.
Two angles and a side are given, not two sides and
one opposite angle.

c) Use the sine law.

$$\frac{q}{\sin Q} = \frac{p}{\sin P}$$

$$\frac{q}{\sin 72°} = \frac{23}{\sin 55°}$$

$$q = \frac{23 \sin 72°}{\sin 55°}$$

$$\doteq 26.7$$

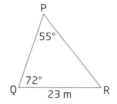

Romeo is about 26.7 m from Patina.

Example 3

Use the Sine Law

A lighthouse at point L is 10 km from a yacht at point Y and 8 km from
a sailboat at point B. From the yacht, the lighthouse and the sailboat are
separated by an angle of 48°.

a) Is it necessary to consider the ambiguous case? Explain.

b) Sketch possible diagrams for this situation.

c) Determine the distance from the yacht to the sailboat, to the nearest tenth of a kilometre. If there are two answers, determine both. If there are no answers, explain why.

Solution

a) Two sides and one opposite angle are given, so it is necessary to consider the ambiguous case.

b)

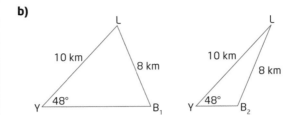

c) Use the sine law in $\triangle LPB_1$ to determine $\angle B_2$.

$$\frac{\sin B_1}{b} = \frac{\sin P}{p}$$

$$\frac{\sin B_1}{10} = \frac{\sin 48°}{8}$$

$$\sin B_1 = \frac{10 \sin 48°}{8}$$

$$\doteq 0.9289$$

$$\angle B_1 \doteq 68°$$

$$\angle L \doteq 180° - 48° - 68°$$

$$= 64°$$

Use the sine law to determine the length of ℓ.

$$\frac{\ell}{\sin L} = \frac{y}{\sin Y}$$

$$\frac{\ell}{\sin 64°} = \frac{8}{\sin 48°}$$

$$\ell = \frac{8 \sin 64°}{\sin 48°}$$

$$\doteq 9.7$$

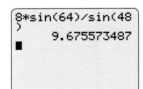

Using acute $\triangle LYB_1$, the two ships are about 9.7 km apart.

Now use $\triangle LYB_1$.

$$\angle B_2 = 180° - \angle B_1$$

$$\doteq 180° - 68°$$

$$= 112°$$

$$\angle L \doteq 180° - 48° - 112°$$
$$= 20°$$

$$\frac{\ell}{\sin L} = \frac{y}{\sin Y}$$

$$\frac{\ell}{\sin 20°} = \frac{8}{\sin 48°}$$

$$\ell = \frac{8 \sin 20°}{\sin 48°}$$

$$\doteq 3.7$$

Using the obtuse triangle, the ships are about 3.7 km apart.
There are two possible answers to this problem.

```
8*sin(20)/sin(48
)
          3.681867992
■
```

Example 4

Use the Cosine Law

The radar screen at an air traffic control tower shows a Piper Cherokee
15 km from the tower in a direction 30° east of north, and a Cessna
Skyhawk 16 km from the tower in a direction 40° east of north, at their
closest approach to each other. If the two aircraft are less than 2 km
apart, the controller must file a report.

a) Sketch a diagram showing the tower and the two aircraft. Label the
given distances and angles.

b) From the tower, what is the angle separating the aircraft?

c) Is it necessary to consider the ambiguous case? Justify your answer.

d) Will the controller need to file a report? Explain.

> **Solution**

a)

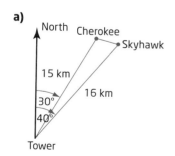

b) From the tower, the aircraft are 40° − 30° = 10° apart.

c) Two sides and a contained angle are given. Since the angle is
contained, and not opposite, the ambiguous case need not be
considered.

Connections

When driving a car, a
"near miss" is considered
as coming within less
than 1 m of another
vehicle. In aviation,
because of the speed of
jet aircraft, a near miss
can often mean coming
within 1 km of another
aircraft horizontally, or
300 m vertically. Two
jetliners at normal cruise
approach each other at
a combined speed of
nearly 2000 km/h. At a
distance of 1 km, they
could collide in less than
2 s.

d) Let d represent the distance between the two planes. Use the cosine law.

$$d^2 = 15^2 + 16^2 - 2(16)(15) \cos 10°$$

$$\doteq 8.3$$

$$d \doteq 2.9 \qquad \text{Since } d \text{ is a distance, only the positive square root applies.}$$

The aircraft are approximately 2.9 km apart at their closest approach. Because the aircraft are more than 2 km apart, the controller does not need to file a report.

Key Concepts

- Primary trigonometric ratios are used to solve triangles that contain a right angle.

- The sine law is used to solve oblique triangles when two angles and a side are given. In the case when two sides and an opposite angle are given, there may be two possible solutions, one solution, or no solution. This is known as the ambiguous case.

- The cosine law is used to solve oblique triangles when two sides and a contained angle or three sides and no angles are given.

Communicate Your Understanding

C1 If two angles and the side between them are given in a triangle, in how many ways can you draw the triangle? Explain why, using a diagram.

C2 Is it possible to have an ambiguous case using the cosine law? If so, show an example. If not, explain why not.

C3 Is it possible to have a triangle such that an unknown side can be determined either with the sine law or the cosine law? If so, show an example. If not, explain why not.

A Practise

For help with questions 1 and 2, see Examples 1, 2, and 4.

1. For each of the following, select the most appropriate trigonometric tool among primary trigonometric ratios, the sine law, and the cosine law. Justify your choice. Do not solve.

   a) In $\triangle ABC$, $\angle A = 90°$, $\angle B = 39°$, and $a = 10$ cm. Determine b.

   b) In $\triangle PQR$, $\angle P = 35°$, $\angle R = 65°$, and $p = 3$ m. Determine q.

   c) In $\triangle DEF$, $\angle D = 60°$, $\angle F = 50°$, and $d = 12$ cm. Determine f.

   d) In $\triangle XYZ$, $\angle X = 42°$, $y = 25$ km, and $z = 20$ km. Determine x.

2. Determine the indicated unknown quantity for each triangle in question 1. Round each answer to one decimal place.

For help with questions 3 and 4, see Example 1.

3. The shadow of a tree that is 12 m tall measures 9 m in length. Determine the angle of elevation of the sun.

4. There is a water hazard between a golfer's ball and the green. The golfer has two choices. He can hit the ball alongside the water hazard to a point left of the green and play the next shot from there. Or, he can hit directly over the water hazard to the green. The golfer can usually hit an approach shot at least 60 m. Should he attempt the direct shot, or go around the hazard?

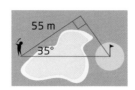

For help with question 5, see Example 2.

5. Yolanda flies her ultra-light airplane due east for 100 km. She turns right through an angle of 130°, and flies a second leg. Then, she turns right 110° and returns to her starting point.

a) Represent the flight path using an appropriate diagram, labelling all information.

b) Determine the total length of the flight, to the nearest kilometre.

For help with question 6, see Example 3.

6. For each of the following, draw possible diagrams that match the given measurements. Then, calculate the length of side *c*. If the calculation cannot be made, explain why.

a) In △ABC, $a = 13$ cm, $b = 21$ cm, and ∠A = 29°.

b) In △ABC, $a = 24$ m, $b = 21$ m, and ∠A = 75°.

For help with question 7, see Example 4.

7. Bill and Nadia live across a ravine from each other. Bill walked 180 m to the end of the ravine, turned right through an angle of 45°, and walked another 200 m to Nadia's house. Determine an exact expression for the distance between the two houses.

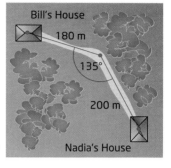

B **Connect and Apply**

8. A radio antenna is stabilized by two guy wires. One guy wire is 100 m in length and is attached to the top of the antenna. The wire makes an angle of 60° with the ground. One end of the second guy wire is attached to the ground at the same point as the first guy wire. The other end is attached to the antenna such that the wire makes an angle of 45° with the ground. Determine an exact expression for the distance between the points where the two guy wires are attached to the antenna.

9. A decorative pottery bowl with a diameter of 30 cm is used as a garden ornament. A rain shower fills it with water to a maximum depth of 7 cm. The bowl is slowly tipped to remove the water. What angle will the rim of the bowl make with the horizontal when the water begins to spill out?

10. A Ferris wheel has a radius of 20 m, with 10 cars spaced around the circumference at equal distances. If the cars are numbered in order, how far is it directly from the first car to the fifth car?

11. Charles leaves the marina and sails his boat 10° west of north for 1.5 h at 18 km/h. He then makes a starboard (right) turn to a heading of 60° east of north, and sails for 1.2 h at 20 km/h.

Reasoning and Proving
Representing · Selecting Tools
Problem Solving
Connecting · Reflecting
Communicating

a) At the end of that time, how far is Charles from his starting point to the nearest kilometre?

b) What is the course required for Charles to return directly to the marina?

12. Giulia unreels her kite string until the kite is flying on a string of length 50 m. A light breeze holds the kite such that the string makes an angle of 60° with the ground. After a few minutes, the wind picks up speed. The wind now pushes the kite until the string makes an angle of 45° with the ground. What distance has the kite changed position horizontally over the ground. Determine an exact expression.

13. Use Technology There are several applets available on the Internet to calculate answers using the sine law and the cosine law. Perform a search using the key phrase "sine law calculator" or "cosine law calculator." Use the calculators to check your answers to some of the questions in this exercise.

14. In △ABC, ∠A is 40°, $a = 10$ cm, and $b = 12$ cm. Determine c, to the nearest tenth of a centimetre.

a) Explain why the ambiguous case must be considered for this triangle.

b) Sketch diagrams to represent the two possible triangles that match these measurements.

c) Solve for side c in both triangles. How many valid solutions are there?

d) If side a is 12 cm rather than 10 cm, how many solutions are there? Explain why.

e) Determine any solutions in part d).

15. a) Refer to your answer to question 14d). If side a is 7 cm rather than 10 cm, how many solutions are there? Explain why.

b) Determine the minimum value of a that results in at least one solution. Calculate your answer to four decimal places.

16. a) Create an ambiguous triangle problem that has two solutions. Determine the solutions to ensure that the question is valid.

b) Trade problems with a classmate, and solve.

c) Trade solutions. Write a short critique of your partner's solution, including any comments about proper form.

17. Chapter Problem You receive a scientific calculator at checkpoint #3. Determine the direction and distance to checkpoint #4 from the information below. Draw the leg on your map. Include all angles and distances.

Direction: North of west

Use ∠A from △ABC. In △ABC, ∠B = 85°, $a = 41$ m, and $c = 32$ m. Round to the nearest degree, if necessary.

Distance: The measure of b, in △ABC, to the nearest metre

18. A shade tree that is 20 m tall is located 30 m from Wok's apartment building, which is 10 m in height. By mid morning, the shadow of the tree falls directly toward the building. The angle of elevation of the sun increases by 15° per hour. Determine the length of time that at least part of the shadow of the tree falls on Wok's building.

19. Many buildings are now designed to use energy as efficiently as possible. One approach involves putting awnings on south-facing windows so that the summer sunlight is shaded from the window but the winter sunlight shines in. The maximum angle of elevation, θ, of the sun at a latitude of L degrees above the equator is given by $\theta = (90° - L) + 23.5°$ for latitudes north of the Tropic of Cancer.

Reasoning and Proving
Representing — Selecting Tools
Problem Solving
Connecting — Reflecting
Communicating

a) Explain why this equation includes the angle 23.5°.

b) Consider a south-facing window that is 1.5 m high in a house built at a latitude of 45° north of the equator. Use a diagram to model an awning that extends a distance d over the window so that the entire window is shaded at noon on the summer solstice.

c) Determine the value of d required in part b).

d) How much of the window receives sunlight at noon on the winter solstice?

20. Albert and Bieta live on the same side of Main Street, 200 m apart. Charmayne lives directly across the street from Albert, and Daniel lives directly across the street from Bieta. From Albert's house, the angle between Bieta's house and Daniel's house is 31°. From Bieta's house, the angle between Albert's house and Charmayne's house is 25°.

a) Represent the positions of the four houses using a diagram. Label all given angles and distances.

b) Outline a method you can use to determine the distance from Charmayne's house to Daniel's house.

c) Use your method to determine the distance.

✔ **Achievement Check**

21. During a canoe trip, Enrico stops at a point along the south side of a river that flows from east to west. From here he can see a forest lookout tower, located 2.5 km away at a point on the north side of the river. As Enrico continues his trip, he stops at another point on the south side of the river that is 1.8 km from the lookout tower. The angle between the lookout tower, Enrico's first stop, and his second stop is 35°.

a) Explain why there are two possible locations for Enrico's second stop. Draw a diagram to represent each possible location. Label all angles and distances.

b) Determine the possible angles between the lookout tower, Enrico's second stop, and his first stop.

c) Without performing calculations, predict which angle found in part b) will result in the longer distance between Enrico's first and second stops. Explain.

d) Determine the possible distances between Enrico's first and second stops.

e) Suppose the given 35° represents the angle between Enrico's first stop, the lookout tower, and his second stop. How does the solution to the problem change? Solve this new problem.

C Extend

22. A clinometer for measuring angles of elevation for real-world objects can be made using simple materials.

    a) Search the Internet for a simple plan for a clinometer.

    b) Use the plan to make a clinometer.

    c) Select a height in your neighbourhood that is difficult to measure directly. Use the clinometer to help you make this measurement.

    d) Write a short report on your methods and calculations.

23. The grand ballroom of a hotel is on the third floor, 15 m above the lobby. It is reached by a spiral staircase that ascends a cylindrical hall of diameter 72 m in one complete turn. Determine the angle of elevation of the staircase.

24. While exploring a flat, desert-like plain on Mars, an astronaut sees a rock column, M, shaped like a mitten, and another rock column, T, shaped like a toy top. He is interested to know how far apart the columns are, but does not have enough oxygen to walk over to find out. The astronaut starts at point A, 600 m from a rock column, B, shaped like a banana. He measures ∠MAB as 155° and ∠TAB as 32°. He walks 600 m to column B. From here, he measures ∠MBA as 20° and ∠TBA as 146°.

    a) Sketch a diagram to model these data.

    b) Explain how you can use trigonometric tools to determine the distance MT.

    c) Determine the distance MT.

25. On the vernal equinox (March 21 or 22 in the northern hemisphere), assume that the sun rises at 6:00 a.m., sets at 6:00 p.m., and is directly overhead at noon.

    a) A flagpole is 10 m high. At what time will its shadow be 5 m long?

    b) Explain why there is more than one answer to part a).

26. Show that the area of △PQR can be calculated using the formula
    $A = \frac{1}{2}pq \sin R$.

27. **Math Contest** Three circles of equal radius are drawn tangent to each other. An equilateral triangle is drawn to circumscribe the three circles. If the radius, r, of each circle is 2 cm, what is the length of one side of the triangle, to the nearest centimetre?

    A 10 cm **B** 11 cm **C** 12 cm

    D 9 cm **E** 8 cm

    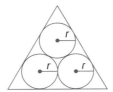

28. **Math Contest** A plane is flying at 500 km/h. The angle of depression to a lighthouse on an island in the distance is 6°. After 12 min, as the plane continues to approach the lighthouse, the angle of depression is 15°. How long will it take for the plane to be directly above the lighthouse?

29. **Math Contest** A regular pentagon is inscribed in a circle of diameter 10 cm. What is the area, to the nearest square centimetre, of the part of the circle outside the pentagon?

    A 59 cm^2 **B** 19 cm^2

    C 79 cm^2 **D** 20 cm^2

    E 18 cm^2

Use Geometry Software to Test for the Ambiguous Case

A pipeline is to be drilled from point A to point B through a rock outcrop. To determine the length of pipe needed, a surveyor sends an apprentice to take measurements. The apprentice takes a sighting from A to B and turns left through a measured angle of 40°. He walks along this line for 200 m until he is past the rock outcrop at point C. He then walks directly to B, measuring CB as 150 m. When the apprentice presents the measurements to the surveyor, the surveyor tells him that she does not have enough information.

a) Show why the surveyor's statement is true.

b) Write a note to the apprentice advising him how he might have taken his measurements to avoid this problem.

Use the following steps to model the problem using *The Geometer's Sketchpad®.*

- Open *The Geometer's Sketchpad®*. Plot a point A. Draw a line segment such that A is the left endpoint.

- Double-click on point A to mark it as a centre. Use a suitable scale. A scale of 1cm:50 m is used here. From the **Transform** menu, select **Translate**. Ensure that the Polar radio button is selected.

Tools

- computer with *The Geometer's Sketchpad®*

Technology Tip

The **Polar** button lets you describe a translation as a distance and an angle. The **Rectangular** button lets you describe a translation as a horizontal distance and a vertical distance.

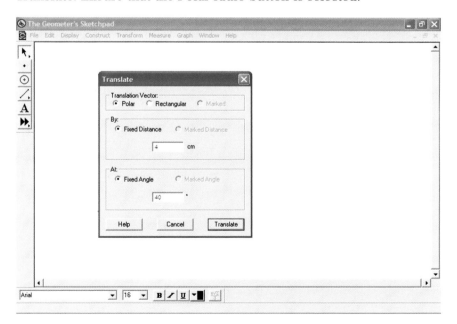

- Enter 4 cm and 40° in the **Distance** and **Angle** boxes.

- Using the scale, point C will be at a fixed distance of 4 cm and a fixed angle of 40°. Press **Translate**. Right-click on the translated point, and use the menu to label it C.

- Use the **Transform** menu again to translate point C a scale distance of 3 cm at an angle of 0°.

- Select point C and then point C′. From the **Construct** menu, select **Circle by Center+Point**.

- Extend the line segment if necessary so that the circle intersects it at two points. Select the circle and the line segment. From the **Construct** menu, select **Intersections**. These points show the possible locations of point B. Relabel them B_1 and B_2. Draw line segments to form $\triangle AB_1C$ and $\triangle AB_2C$. Use your sketch to help you answer part b) above. What angle(s) and length(s) does the apprentice need to measure so the surveyor can calculate the length of the pipeline, B_1B_2?

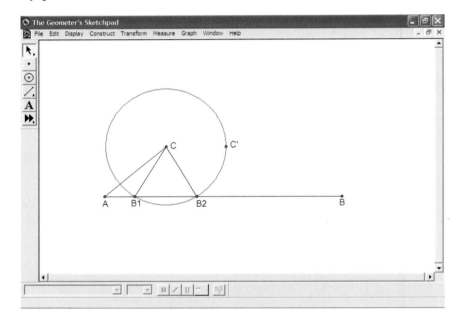

Problems in Three Dimensions

Some airports have obstructions such as towers, hills, or tall buildings within a few kilometres of the end of their runways. The elevation of such obstructions often cannot be measured directly. When flying under instrument-only flight rules (for example, when visibility is obscured by fog or snow), the pilot of a departing aircraft cannot see these obstructions. In order to be certified for instrument departures, airports must publish the minimum rate of climb required to clear any possible obstructions.

In this section, you will learn to solve problems in three dimensions using the primary trigonometric ratios, the sine law, and the cosine law.

Investigate

How can you use trigonometry to solve a three-dimensional problem?

1. A hill of unknown height and at an unknown distance is located directly off the departure end of runway 09 (takeoff to the east) at City Airport. From the departure end, the angle of elevation of the hill is 7°. From a point 200 m south of the departure end, the angle formed by the base of the hill and the departure end is 87°. Draw a diagram of this situation.

2. Select the appropriate trigonometric tool to determine the distance from the departure end of the runway to the base of the hill. Determine this distance to the nearest metre.

3. Determine the height of the hill, rounded up to the nearest 10 m.

4. The required rate of climb can be expressed in metres per kilometre, measured from the departure end. What rate of climb is required for an aircraft to just clear the hill?

5. For safety reasons, the rate of climb actually required by regulation must allow the aircraft to clear the obstruction by a specified margin, usually about 330 m. Under this rule, what rate of climb is required?

6. **Reflect** Suggest another context that results in a problem in three dimensions that can be solved using trigonometry.

Connections

Airport runways are formally identified by angle directions, using three digits. Starting from north at 000°, turn toward east at 090°, south at 180°, and west at 270°. On airfields, runways are numbered by the first two digits of the runway direction angle, or bearing. Hence, a runway that is landed on facing east is numbered 09. If you landed on this runway from the other end, what number would you see?

Example 1

Use Primary Trigonometric Ratios to Solve a Problem in Three Dimensions

A radio antenna lies due north of Sam's house. Sam walks to Elena's house, a distance of 1200 m, 50° east of north. From Elena's house, the antenna appears due west, with an angle of elevation of 12°. Determine the height of the antenna, to the nearest metre.

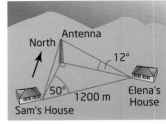

Solution

Since Sam's house is south of the antenna and Elena's house is east of the antenna, the triangle formed by the two houses and the base of the antenna is a right triangle. Use primary trigonometric ratios.

Let d represent the distance, in metres, from Elena's house to the base of the antenna.

$$\sin 50° = \frac{d}{1200}$$
$$d = 1200 \sin 50°$$
$$\doteq 919$$

Elena's house is about 919 m from the base of the antenna.

Let h represent the height of the antenna. Use the tangent ratio.

$$\tan 12° = \frac{h}{919}$$
$$h = 919 \tan 12°$$
$$\doteq 195$$

The height of the antenna is about 195 m.

Example 2

Use the Sine Law to Solve a Problem in Three Dimensions

A surveyor is on one side of a river. On the other side is a cliff of unknown height that she wants to measure. The surveyor lays out a baseline AB of length 150 m. From point A, she selects point C at the base of the cliff and measures ∠CAB to be 51°. She selects point D on top of the cliff directly above C and measures an angle of elevation of 32°. She moves to point B and measures ∠CBA as 62°.

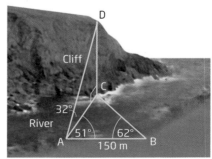

a) Are any of the triangles in this problem right triangles? Justify your answer.

b) Which length would you determine first? Select the appropriate trigonometric tool to determine this length. Determine the length, to the nearest metre.

c) Which tool can you use to determine the height of the cliff? Justify your choice. Determine the height of the cliff, to the nearest metre.

Solution

a) Since point C is directly below point D, △ACD is a right triangle.

b) Determine AC in △ABC first. Two angles and a side are given for △ABC. Use the sine law to determine AC. Then, you can use △ACD to determine the height of the cliff CD.

In △ABC,

$$\angle C = 180° - 51° - 62°$$ 　　The sum of the angles in a triangle is 180°.
$$= 67°$$

$$\frac{b}{\sin B} = \frac{c}{\sin C}$$ 　　Use the sine law.

$$\frac{b}{\sin 62°} = \frac{150}{\sin 67°}$$ 　　Substitute the given values.

$$b = \frac{150 \sin 62°}{\sin 67°}$$ 　　Solve for the unknown value.

$$\doteq 144$$

The length AC is 144 m, to the nearest metre.

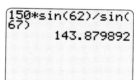
```
150*sin(62)/sin(
67)
          143.879892
```

Connections

By convention, the side opposite ∠A is called a, the side opposite ∠B is called b, and the side opposite ∠C is called c.

c) Since △ACD is a right triangle, the most appropriate tool is primary trigonometric ratios. Let h represent the height, in metres, of the cliff and use b from △ABC.

$$\tan 32° = \frac{h}{b}$$

$$= \frac{h}{144}$$

$$h = 144 \tan 32°$$

$$\doteq 90$$

The height of the cliff is approximately 90 m.

Example 3

Use the Cosine Law to Solve a Problem in Three Dimensions

Justine is flying her hot-air balloon. She reports that her position is over a golf course located halfway between Emerytown and Fosterville, at an altitude of 1500 m. Fosterville is 16.0 km east of Danburg, and Emerytown is 16.5 km from Danburg, in a direction 42° south of east. What is the angle of elevation of Justine's balloon as seen from Danburg, to the nearest degree?

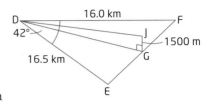

When solving three-dimensional problems, it is often helpful to draw two-dimensional triangles for each step in the solution.

Solution

Determine the distance from Emerytown to Fosterville.

Since two sides and a contained angle are given, use the cosine law.

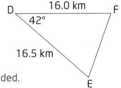

$$d^2 = e^2 + f^2 - 2ef \cos D$$
$$= 16.0^2 + 16.5^2 - 2(16.0)(16.5) \cos 42°$$
$$\doteq 135.87$$
$$d \doteq 11.66 \qquad \text{Distance is positive, so the negative root is excluded.}$$

The distance from Emerytown to Fosterville is approximately 11.7 km.

The golf course is $\frac{11.7}{2}$ or 5.85 km from Emerytown.

Use the sine law in △DEF to determine the measure of ∠E.

$$\frac{\sin E}{16.0} = \frac{\sin 42°}{11.7}$$
$$\sin E = \frac{16.0 \sin 42°}{11.7}$$
$$\sin E \doteq 0.9151$$
$$\angle E \doteq 66°$$

Use the cosine law in △DEG to determine the measure of DG.

$$e^2 = g^2 + d^2 - 2(g)(d) \cos E$$
$$= 16.5^2 + 5.85^2 - 2(16.5)(5.85) \cos 66°$$
$$\doteq 227.95$$
$$DG \doteq 15.1$$

DG measures approximately 15.1 km.

The altitude of Justine's balloon above the golf course is 1500 m, or 1.5 km. Use primary trigonometric ratios to determine the angle of elevation from Danburg, ∠D in right △DJG.

$$\tan D = \frac{1.5}{15.1}$$
$$\angle D \doteq 6°$$

The angle of elevation of the balloon as seen from Danburg is about 6°.

- Three-dimensional problems involving triangles can be solved using one or more of the following: the Pythagorean theorem, the six trigonometric ratios, the sine law, and the cosine law.

- The method chosen to solve a triangle depends on the known information.

Communicate Your Understanding

C1 Why are three-dimensional problems more difficult to deal with than two-dimensional problems, given that you are using the same trigonometric tools?

C2 Pieter is visiting the Taj Mahal, in Agra, India. Describe a method he could use to determine the height of the building that could be carried out from the garden area in front, without approaching the building itself. What is the minimum number of measurements that Pieter would need to make? Justify your answer.

Connections

The Taj Mahal was built as a mausoleum to contain the crypt of one person, the beloved wife of emperor Shah Jahan. It now contains three crypts. To find out more about the Taj Mahal, visit the *Functions 11* page on the McGraw-Hill Ryerson Web site and follow the links to Chapter 4.

A Practise

For help with questions 1 to 3, refer to Example 1.

1. The bases on a baseball diamond are 27.4 m apart. The pitcher pitches, and the batter hits a fly ball straight up 15 m. What is the maximum angle of elevation of the ball, to the nearest degree, as seen by the pitcher if he is standing at the centre of the diamond?

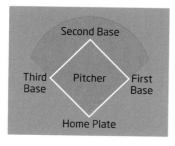

2. A square-based tent has the cross-sectional shape shown. The side wall goes up at an angle of elevation of 60° for 2 m, then continues at an angle of elevation of 30° for another 2 m to the peak.

a) Determine an exact value for the height of the tent.

b) Determine an exact value for the side length of the base.

c) Determine an exact value for the length of one of the diagonals of the base.

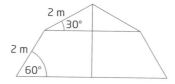

3. The Great Pyramid of Cheops at Giza in Egypt has a square base of side length 230 m. The angle of elevation of one triangular face is 52°. Determine the measure of the angle θ between the height and one of the edges where two triangular faces meet.

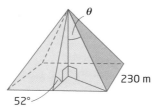

B Connect and Apply

For help with question 4, refer to Example 2.

4. A grass airstrip runs from north to south. Dave notes that there are trees off the southern end at an unknown distance and an unknown height. He would like to determine the height of the trees. From the departure point of the runway, the angle of elevation of the tallest tree is 4°. Dave walks 100 m west and notes that the base of the tree and the departure point of the runway are separated by an angle of 83°.

Reasoning and Proving
Representing   Selecting Tools
Problem Solving
Connecting   Reflecting
Communicating

a) Draw a diagram to model this situation, labelling all measurements.

b) What will you calculate first? What tool will you use? Perform the calculation.

c) Determine the height of the tallest tree.

d) Dave consults his aircraft's operating manual and, taking air temperature into account, calculates that his plane can climb at a rate of 75 m per kilometre of horizontal distance flown. Is it safe for Dave to attempt a takeoff and climb out straight ahead? Justify your answer.

5. A box in the shape of a square-based prism has a base of side length 10 cm and a height of 20 cm. A rod dropped into the box lies exactly from one of the bottom corners to the opposite top corner. Determine the angle between the rod and the vertical edge of the box, rounded to one decimal place.

For help with questions 6 and 7, refer to Example 3.

6. The island of Santorini in Greece is a partially sunken volcanic crater, or caldera. Nicos starts at point A and walks 4 km in a straight line to point B. From point A, the volcanic cone at point C makes $\angle$CAB measuring 53°.

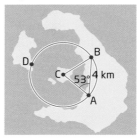

a) Determine the approximate average radius of the central lagoon using the circle shown.

b) How far is it from point C to point D on the nearby smaller island, to the nearest tenth of a kilometre?

c) Santos is at point C, looking up at an angle of elevation of 3° above point D to the edge of a cliff. What is the height of the cliff, to the nearest metre?

d) What assumptions must you make to solve the problem? Justify whether they are reasonable.

Connections

The island of Santorini suffered a cataclysmic volcanic explosion around 1600 B.C.E. Some writers postulate that this eruption, and the damage it caused to other islands by way of tsunamis, led to the legend of the lost continent of Atlantis.

7. Jodi and Leanna are on top of a cliff at point D, 100 m above the base. They decide to race to a picnic table at A, where lunch is waiting. Jodi runs, at a constant speed of 5 m/s, down the hill from D to C and then directly to A. Leanna climbs down the cliff to B at a constant rate of 1 m/s, and then runs as fast as Jodi to A. Who reaches lunch first?

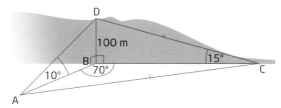

8. A three-part race consists of swimming, climbing, and zipping. You begin at point A. The finish is at point D, which is 200 m from A in a direction 65° west of north. The first leg is a 600-m swim to an island B due west of A. The second leg is a climb up a vertical cliff to point C. Point C has an angle of elevation of 10°, as seen from point A. The third leg is a zip down a zip line from point C to the finish at point D. You can swim at 1.5 m/s, climb at 0.75 m/s, and zip at 15 m/s.

Reasoning and Proving

Representing

Selecting Tools

Problem Solving

Connecting

Reflecting

Communicating

a) Sketch a diagram to represent this problem, labelling all given measurements on the diagram.

b) How long does it take you to complete the race?

9. A methane molecule, CH_4, consists of four hydrogen atoms at the corners of a tetrahedron and one carbon atom in the centre of the tetrahedron. Use drinking straws and marshmallows, toothpicks and gumdrops, or other suitable manipulatives to make a model of the methane molecule.

a) Explain how you ensured that your "carbon atom" is in the middle of the tetrahedron.

b) Measure the angle formed using two of the hydrogen atoms with the carbon molecule as the vertex.

c) Use the Internet to find a model of the methane atom. What is the exact angle?

d) Suggest ways to refine your model to obtain a more accurate answer.

Connections

Chemists often make three-dimensional models of molecules to help them visualize chemical bonds among atoms. The angles between the atoms can be measured from the models and used to formulate hypotheses. Trigonometry is used to construct mathematical models of molecular structures. The calculations are complicated, but you can use simple manipulatives to obtain reasonable estimates of angles in a molecule.

10. Ranjeet parks his car in a lot on the corner of Park Lane and Main Street. He walks 80 m east to First Avenue, turns 30° to the left, and follows First Avenue for 100 m to the Metro Building, where he takes the elevator to his office on the 15th floor. Each floor in the building is 4 m in height. From his office window, Ranjeet can see his car in the lot.

a) Sketch a diagram to represent this problem, labelling all given measurements on the diagram.

b) How far is Ranjeet from his car, in a direct line?

11. Chapter Problem It is time to move onward to checkpoint #5. Determine the direction and distance from the information given. Draw the leg on your map. Label all angles and distances.

Direction: West of South

Determine two angles between 0° and 360° whose cosecant is $-\dfrac{2}{\sqrt{3}}$. Add their degree measures, and divide by 12. Use this angle.

Distance: The height of the tree in the following:

William stands some distance from the base of a tree. From his position, the angle of elevation of the top of the tree is 30°. William then moves 40 m in a direction perpendicular to the line from his original position to the base of the tree. At this second point, William observes that his original position and the base of the tree are separated by an angle of 65°. Determine the height of the tree, rounded to the nearest metre, if necessary.

12. A scuba diver drops into the water from a dive boat and descends to a coral reef at a depth of 20 m. She follows the reef in a westerly direction. She estimates that she has travelled 30 m along the reef. The diver continues to follow the reef, which turns 30° to the right, swimming for another 25 m without changing depth. At this point, how far is she from the dive boat?

13. a) Pose a problem involving three dimensions. The solution must include at least one use of the sine law or cosine law and require at least three calculations of unknown values. Solve your problem to ensure that it works.

b) Trade your problem with a classmate. Solve each other's problem.

c) Trade solutions, and discuss the validity of the methods used.

C Extend

14. A regular tetrahedron has sides of length s. Show that the surface area, A, of the tetrahedron can be determined using the formula $A = \sqrt{3}\,s^2$.

15. The paper cup for a snow cone has a radius of R and a vertical angle of 60°. When a ball of radius r is dropped into the cup, the top of the ball is even with the top of the cup. Determine an expression for the distance from the bottom of the ball to the vertex of the cone in terms of R and r.

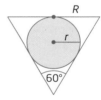

16. A regular tetrahedron has sides of length s. Determine an expression for the height, h, in terms of s.

17. A pyramid has a base in the shape of a rhombus with side length s. The height of the pyramid is equal to the side length. One diagonal of the rhombus is also equal to the side length. Determine the angle of elevation from the end of the other diagonal to the top of the pyramid.

18. Anwar lives in central Canada. His friend, Bill, lives in the southern United States. Chantal, another friend, lives in France. Each friend determines the exact location of their own house using a Global Positioning System (GPS) unit. Anwar then plots each location on a globe and draws three lines in a triangular shape to connect the locations.

a) When Anwar adds the three angles in the triangle on the globe, the sum is not 180°. Explain why this is so.

b) Is the sum more or less than 180°? Justify your answer.

19. The Global Positioning System (GPS) tracks satellites in orbit around Earth to determine your position on Earth's surface. There are 24 satellites in the GPS constellation, and most GPS receivers will track up to 12 at one time. How many are actually needed to determine a position using trigonometry?

a) When a GPS receiver locks on to a signal from a satellite, the receiver locates itself somewhere on a sphere with that satellite at the centre. When it locks on to the signal of a second satellite, the GPS unit locates itself on the intersection of two spheres. What does the intersection of two spheres look like? Explain.

b) When the GPS receiver locks on to the signal of a third satellite, the receiver locates itself on the intersection of the third sphere with the intersection found in part a). What does this third possible intersection look like? Explain.

c) Why is a fourth satellite necessary to give a precise fix on a location?

20. Math Contest A ship is stranded at sea. Also at sea are a Coast Guard cutter and an ocean liner. A helicopter is 2000 m above the Coast Guard cutter. The angle of depression from the helicopter to the stranded ship is 13°. The angle of elevation of the helicopter from the ocean liner is 23°. The angle formed at the cutter between the other two boats is 55°. If the cutter travels at 25 km/h and the liner at 20 km/h, what is the shortest time in which the stranded vessel will be reached by either the cutter or the liner?

21. Math Contest The product $990y$ is a perfect cube. The least natural number that y can be is

A 980 100   **B** 36 300

C 12 100   **D** 110

E 31 575

22. Math Contest How many routes are there from A to B if you can only move right or down?

A 460   **B** 30

C 462   **D** 450

E 475

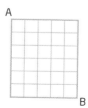

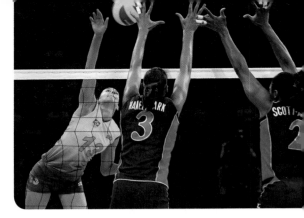

Trigonometric Identities

Solutions to equations that arise from real-world problems sometimes include trigonometric terms. One example is a trajectory problem. If a volleyball player serves a ball at a speed of 10 m/s, at an angle of θ with respect to the horizontal, the horizontal distance x that the ball will fly before hitting the ground can be modelled by the relation $x = 20 \tan \theta \cos^2 \theta$. The complexity of this equation makes it difficult to determine anything about the flight of the volleyball.

Some relations among trigonometric ratios are always true, regardless of what the angle is. These relations are known as **identities**. In this case, two identities can be used to simplify the above equation to $x = 10 \sin 2\theta$. This form is easier to work with.

identity
- an equation that is always true, regardless of the value of the variable

For example, suppose that you want to know the angle of serve that will send the volleyball the greatest distance. The sine ratio has a maximum value of 1 at an angle of 90°. If $2\theta = 90°$, then $\theta = 45°$. Therefore, you should serve the ball at an angle of 45° to send it the greatest distance.

In this section, you will learn the basic trigonometric identities and how to use them to prove other identities.

Investigate

How can you use relationships from a circle to prove an identity?

Earlier in this chapter, you used a circle to relate the trigonometric ratios for an angle θ to a point (x, y) on the terminal arm and the radius, r, of the circle.

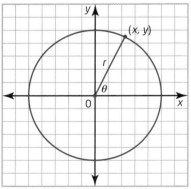

1. Write the three primary trigonometric ratios for angle θ in terms of x, y, and r.

2. a) In the expression $\dfrac{\sin \theta}{\cos \theta}$, substitute the applicable expressions from step 1 and simplify.

   b) **Reflect** What trigonometric ratio is equivalent to this simplified expression?

   c) This ratio and the original expression in part a) are equal. Write this equation.

3. **Reflect** Use your calculator to verify the identity in step 2 for several angles. Select at least one angle from each of the four quadrants.

4. a) In the expression $\sin^2 \theta + \cos^2 \theta$, substitute the applicable expressions from step 1 and simplify.

   b) The original expression and the simplified expression form another identity. Write this equation.

5. Reflect Use a calculator to verify the identity in step 4 for several angles. Select at least one angle from each of the four quadrants. If you determine that it works for a finite number of angles, does that constitute a proof? Justify your answer.

6. The identity in step 4 is known as the Pythagorean identity. Explain why it is called this.

The basic identities that you will be using are summarized here:

Pythagorean Identity $\sin^2 \theta + \cos^2 \theta = 1$

Quotient Identity $\dfrac{\sin \theta}{\cos \theta} = \tan \theta$

Reciprocal Identities $\csc \theta = \dfrac{1}{\sin \theta}$ $\sec \theta = \dfrac{1}{\cos \theta}$ $\cot \theta = \dfrac{1}{\tan \theta}$

If it appears that two expressions are always equal, you can form a conjecture that they are an identity. To prove an identity, write down the left side and the right side as shown in Example 1. Work with the left side (L.S.), the right side (R.S.), or both sides until you arrive at the same expression on both sides.

Example 1

Use Basic Identities to Prove an Identity From One Side

Prove that $\tan^2 \theta + 1 = \sec^2 \theta$.

Solution

L.S. $= \tan^2 \theta + 1$ R.S. $= \sec^2 \theta$

$= \dfrac{\sin^2 \theta}{\cos^2 \theta} + 1$ Use the quotient identity.

$= \dfrac{\sin^2 \theta}{\cos^2 \theta} + \dfrac{\cos^2 \theta}{\cos^2 \theta}$ Use a common denominator.

$= \dfrac{\sin^2 \theta + \cos^2 \theta}{\cos^2 \theta}$

$= \dfrac{1}{\cos^2 \theta}$ Use the Pythagorean identity.

$= \sec^2 \theta$ Use a reciprocal identity.

L.S. = R.S.

Therefore, $\tan^2 \theta + 1 = \sec^2 \theta$.

One possible strategy is to use the identities to transform one side into terms involving only sines and cosines. Then, simplify.

Connections

$\tan A = \dfrac{\sin A}{\cos A}$, so squaring both sides gives $(\tan A)^2 = \left(\dfrac{\sin A}{\cos A} \right)^2$ or $\tan^2 A = \dfrac{\sin^2 A}{\cos^2 A}$.

Example 2

Use Known Identities to Prove an Identity Using Both Sides

Prove that $1 - \cos^2 \theta = \sin \theta \cos \theta \tan \theta$.

Connections

The Pythagorean Identity can be written in different forms.
$\sin^2 \theta + \cos^2 \theta = 1$
$\sin^2 \theta = 1 - \cos^2 \theta$
$\cos^2 \theta = 1 - \sin^2 \theta$

Solution

It is more convenient to work from both sides in this example.

$$\text{L.S.} = 1 - \cos^2 \theta \qquad\qquad\qquad\qquad \text{R.S.} = \sin \theta \cos \theta \tan \theta$$

$$= \sin^2 \theta \quad \text{Use the Pythagorean identity.} \qquad = \sin \theta \cos \theta \frac{\sin \theta}{\cos \theta} \quad \text{Use the quotient identity.}$$

$$= \sin^2 \theta$$

Therefore, $1 - \cos^2 \theta = \sin \theta \cos \theta \tan \theta$.

Example 3

Work With Rational Expressions Involving Trigonometric Ratios

Prove that $\dfrac{\sin \theta}{1 + \cos \theta} = \dfrac{1 - \cos \theta}{\sin \theta}$.

Solution

Inspect both sides. Since there are no squared terms, you cannot use the Pythagorean identity directly. However, you can use your knowledge of the difference of squares to create the squared terms. Multiply the numerator and denominator on the left side by $1 - \cos \theta$.

Connections

The earliest development of trigonometric identities is traced to Claudius Ptolemy, a Greek astronomer and mathematician who lived about 130 B.C.E. Unlike the trigonometry we do today, which is based on relations in right triangles, the trigonometry Ptolemy worked with involved circles, arcs, and chords.

$$\text{L.S.} = \frac{\sin \theta}{1 + \cos \theta} \qquad\qquad\qquad\qquad \text{R.S.} = \frac{1 - \cos \theta}{\sin \theta}$$

$$= \frac{\sin \theta}{1 + \cos \theta} \times \frac{1 - \cos \theta}{1 - \cos \theta}$$

$$= \frac{\sin \theta(1 - \cos \theta)}{(1 + \cos \theta)(1 - \cos \theta)}$$

$$= \frac{\sin \theta(1 - \cos \theta)}{1 - \cos^2 \theta}$$

$$= \frac{\sin \theta(1 - \cos \theta)}{\sin^2 \theta} \qquad \text{Use the Pythagorean identity.}$$

$$= \frac{1 - \cos \theta}{\sin \theta} \qquad \text{Simplify.}$$

$$\text{L.S} = \text{R.S.}$$

Therefore, $\dfrac{\sin \theta}{1 + \cos \theta} = \dfrac{1 - \cos \theta}{\sin \theta}$.

Key Concepts

- A trigonometric identity is a relation among trigonometric ratios that is true for all angles for which both sides are defined.

- The basic identities are the Pythagorean identity, the quotient identity, and the reciprocal identities:

  Pythagorean Identity $\qquad \sin^2 \theta + \cos^2 \theta = 1$

  Quotient Identity $\qquad \dfrac{\sin \theta}{\cos \theta} = \tan \theta$

  Reciprocal Identities $\qquad \csc \theta = \dfrac{1}{\sin \theta} \qquad \sec \theta = \dfrac{1}{\cos \theta} \qquad \cot \theta = \dfrac{1}{\tan \theta}$

- The basic identities can be used to prove more complex identities.

- Identities can be used to simplify solutions to problems that result in trigonometric expressions.

Communicate Your Understanding

C1 Sabariah says that she has discovered the trigonometric identity $\sin 3\theta = 2 \sin \theta$. As a proof, she points out that the left side equals the right side when $\theta = 30°$. Verify that her solution solves the equation. Does this prove that $\sin 3\theta = 2 \sin \theta$? Justify your answer.

C2 Consider the claimed identity in question C1. What is the difference between an equation and an equation that is an identity?

C3 You can show that an equation is not an identity by finding at least one counterexample. A counterexample is a value of the variable for which the equation is not true. Determine a counterexample for the equation in question C1.

A Practise

For help with question 1, refer to the Investigate.

1. Prove the Pythagorean identity using trigonometric definitions involving the opposite side, adjacent side, and hypotenuse of an angle in a right triangle.

2. Use a graphing calculator or grid paper to plot a graph of the relation $y = \sin^2 x + \cos^2 x$. Explain the shape of the graph.

For help with questions 3 and 4, refer to Example 1.

3. Prove each identity.

   a) $\sin \theta = \cos \theta \tan \theta$

   b) $\csc \theta = \sec \theta \cot \theta$

   c) $\cos \theta = \sin \theta \cot \theta$

   d) $\sec \theta = \csc \theta \tan \theta$

4. Prove each identity.

   a) $1 + \csc A = \csc A(1 + \sin A)$

   b) $\cot B \sin B \sec B = 1$

   c) $\cos C(\sec C - 1) = 1 - \cos C$

   d) $1 + \sin D = \sin D(1 + \csc D)$

For help with questions 5 and 6, refer to Example 2.

5. Prove that $1 - \sin^2 \theta = \sin \theta \cos \theta \cot \theta$.

6. Prove that $\csc^2 \theta = \cot^2 \theta + 1$.

B Connect and Apply

For help with questions 7 and 8, refer to Example 3.

7. Prove that $\dfrac{\cos \theta}{1 + \sin \theta} = \dfrac{1 - \sin \theta}{\cos \theta}$.

8. Prove that $\dfrac{\cos \theta}{1 - \sin \theta} + \dfrac{\cos \theta}{1 + \sin \theta} = \dfrac{2}{\cos \theta}$.

9. Prove that $\csc^2 \theta \cos^2 \theta = \csc^2 \theta - 1$.

10. **Use Technology** The identity in question 8 can be broken into two relations, one for the left side and one for the right side. Use a graphing calculator.

   a) Enter the left side in **Y1** and the right side in **Y2**. With your calculator in degree mode, set the window as shown. Set the line style to heavy for **Y2**.

   The graph of **Y1** will appear first. Then, the graph of **Y2** will be drawn. Since it is drawn using a thick line, you can see whether it matches the graph of **Y1**.

   b) Compare the graphs. Explain your results.

   > **Technology Tip**
   >
   > Another way to compare two graphs is to toggle them on and off. In the **Y=** editor, move the cursor over the equal sign and press (ENTER). When the equal sign is highlighted, the graph is displayed. When the equal sign is not highlighted, the graph is not displayed.

11. Consider the graphing approach used in question 10. Does this constitute a proof of the identity? Justify your answer.

12. Prove that $\tan \theta + \cot \theta = \dfrac{\sec \theta}{\sin \theta}$. Use a graphing calculator to illustrate the identity.

13. Prove that $\cot^2 \theta\,(1 + \tan^2 \theta) = \csc^2 \theta$. Use a graphing calculator to illustrate the identity.

14. **Chapter Problem** You are on the last leg of the orienteering course. Determine the direction and distance from the information given. Draw the leg on your map. Label all angles and distances.

   Direction: East of south

   Determine the two angles between 0° and 360° such that $\dfrac{\csc \theta}{\sec \theta} = \cot \theta \tan \theta$. Add their degree measures and divide by 9. Use this angle. Hint: Use identities to simplify each side of the equation first.

   Distance: The result of evaluating $20(\sec^2 \theta \sin^2 \theta + \sec^2 \theta \cos^2 \theta - \tan^2 \theta \sin^2 \theta - \tan^2 \theta \cos^2 \theta)$, rounded to the nearest metre if necessary.

15. Draw a right angle. Using the vertex as the centre, draw a quarter-circle that intersects the two arms of the angle. Select any point A on the quarter-circle, other than a point on one of the arms. Draw a tangent line to the quarter-circle at A such that the line intersects one arm at point B and the other arm at point C. Label $\angle AOC$ as θ. Show that the measure of BA divided by the radius of the quarter-circle equals the cotangent of $\angle \theta$.

16. A student writes the following proof for the identity $\cos \theta = \sin \theta \cot \theta$. Critique it for form, and rewrite it in proper form.

$$\cos \theta = \sin \theta \cot \theta$$
$$\cos \theta = \sin \theta \frac{1}{\tan \theta}$$
$$\tan \theta \cos \theta = \sin \theta$$
$$\frac{\sin \theta}{\cos \theta} \cos \theta = \sin \theta$$
$$\sin \theta = \sin \theta$$
$$\text{L.S.} = \text{R.S.}$$

✔ **Achievement Check**

17. Consider the equation
$\tan^2 \theta - \sin^2 \theta = \sin^2 \theta \tan^2 \theta$.

a) **Use Technology** Use a graphing calculator to graph each side of the equation. Does it appear to be an identity? Justify your answer.

b) Which of the basic identities will you use first to simplify the left side?

c) Simplify the left side as much as possible. Explain your steps and identify any other identities that you use.

d) Is it necessary to simplify the right side? Explain. If so, simplify it.

e) If the two sides are not the same, go back and try another approach.

C Extend

18. Some trigonometric equations involve multiples of angles. One of these is $\sin 2\theta = 2 \sin \theta \cos \theta$.

a) Use a graphing calculator to graph each side of this equation. Does it appear to be an identity?

b) Show that the equation is true for $\theta = 30°$, $45°$, and $90°$.

c) Evaluate each side for an angle from each of the other quadrants.

d) Review the example of the volleyball serve at the beginning of this section (page 270). Assuming the identity to be true, use it to show that $20 \tan \theta \cos^2 \theta = 10 \sin 2\theta$.

19. Some trigonometric identities involve complements of angles. For example, the complement of θ is $90° - \theta$. Consider the equation $\cos \theta = \sin (90° - \theta)$.

a) Use a graphing calculator to graph each side of this equation. Does it appear to be an identity?

b) Show that the equation is true for $\theta = 30°$, $45°$, and $90°$.

c) Use a unit circle to show where this identity comes from.

d) Make a conjecture concerning an identity for $\cos (90° - \theta)$ and an identity for $\tan (90° - \theta)$. Test each conjecture by using a graphing calculator.

20. Some trigonometric identities involve supplements of angles. For example, the supplement of θ is $180° - \theta$. Consider the equation $\sin \theta = \sin (180° - \theta)$.

a) Use a graphing calculator to graph each side of this relation. Does it appear to be an identity?

b) Show that the equation is true for $\theta = 30°$, $45°$, and $90°$.

c) Use a unit circle to show where this identity comes from.

d) Make a conjecture concerning an identity for $\cos (180° - \theta)$. Test your conjecture by graphing. If necessary, adjust your conjecture and retest.

21. **Math Contest** If $\sin^2 \theta + \sin^2 2\theta + \sin^2 3\theta = 1$, what does $\cos^2 3\theta + \cos^2 2\theta + \cos^2 \theta$ equal?

A 1   **B** 1.5   **C** 2   **D** 2.5   **E** 3

22. **Math Contest** Given $\sin \theta \cot \theta = \dfrac{\sqrt{3}}{2}$, a possible value for $\sin \theta$ is

A $\dfrac{\sqrt{3}}{2}$ **B** 30   **C** -0.5

D $-\dfrac{\sqrt{3}}{2}$ **E** $\dfrac{1}{\sqrt{3}}$

23. **Math Contest** Given $\cos \theta = 3 \sin \theta$, a possible value for $\cos^2 \theta$ is

A 0.25   **B** 0.7071   **C** 0.5   **D** 0.9   **E** 1

Chapter 4 Review

4.1 Special Angles, pages 220 to 231

1. Use a unit circle to determine exact values for the primary trigonometric ratios for 210°. Check your results using a calculator.

2. A ship is tied to a dock with a rope of length 10 m. At low tide, the rope is stretched tight, forming an angle of 45° with the horizontal. At high tide, the stretched rope makes an angle of 30° with the horizontal. How much closer to the dock, horizontally, is the ship at low tide than at high tide? Determine an exact expression. Then, use a calculator to determine an approximate answer, correct to the nearest tenth of a metre.

4.2 Co-terminal and Related Angles, pages 232 to 240

3. The coordinates of a point on the terminal arm of an angle θ are shown. Determine the exact primary trigonometric ratios for θ.

   a) A(−5, 12)   b) B(3, −4)   c) C(6, −8)

   d) D(−2, −3)   e) E(1, −5)   f) F(−7, 4)

4. One of the primary trigonometric ratios for an angle is given, as well as the quadrant that the terminal arm lies in. Determine the other two primary trigonometric ratios.

   a) $\sin A = \frac{4}{5}$, first quadrant

   b) $\cos B = \frac{8}{17}$, fourth quadrant

   c) $\tan C = -\frac{12}{5}$, second quadrant

   d) $\sin D = -\frac{4}{7}$, third quadrant

5. Round your answers in question 5 to the nearest degree.

   a) Solve the equation $\sin \theta = -0.25$ for $0° \le \theta \le 360°$.

   b) Solve the equation $\cos \theta = \frac{4}{5}$ for $0° \le \theta \le 360°$

   c) Solve the equation $\tan \theta = \frac{5}{8}$ for $0° \le \theta \le 360°$.

4.3 Reciprocal Trigonometric Ratios, pages 243 to 248

6. Each point lies on the terminal arm of an angle. Determine the six trigonometric ratios for the angle, rounded to four decimal places.

   a) A(−5, −12)   b) B(−4, 3)

   c) C(8, 15)   d) D(7, −24)

7. Determine two angles between 0° and 360° that have a secant of −4. Round your answers to the nearest degree.

8. An angle between 0° and 360° has a cosecant of −1.

   a) Is this enough information to determine a unique solution? If yes, explain why. If no, what other information is required?

   b) Determine the angle or angles.

4.4 Problems in Two Dimensions, pages 249 to 258

9. Marko rides 10 km north of his home on his mountain bike. He reaches an abandoned railroad, turns through an angle of 120° onto the railroad, and then rides another 20 km.

   a) Draw a diagram to model this situation, labelling all distances and angles.

   b) Select the most appropriate trigonometric tool to determine Marko's distance from home. Justify your selection.

   c) Determine an exact value for Marko's distance from home. Then, use a calculator to find the approximate distance.

10. In $\triangle ABC$, $\angle A = 32°$, $a = 15$ m, and $b = 18$ m.

a) Use drawing tools or geometry software to illustrate why the ambiguous case applies to this situation.

b) Sketch diagrams to represent the two possible triangles that match these measurements.

c) Solve for side c in both triangles, to the nearest metre.

4.5 Problems in Three Dimensions,
pages 261 to 269

11. An asymmetric pyramid has a base in the shape of a kite, with the longer sides of the base measuring 150 m and the shorter sides measuring 120 m. The angle between the two longer sides measures 70°. The angle of elevation of the top of the pyramid, as seen from the vertex between the longer and shorter sides, is 75°. Determine the height of the pyramid to the nearest tenth of a kilometre.

12. Cate is sailing her boat off the coast, which runs straight north and south. Her GPS confirms that she is 8 km from Haytown and 10 km from Beeville, two towns on the coast. The towns are separated by an angle of 80°, as seen from the boat. A helicopter is hovering at an altitude of 1000 m halfway between Haytown and Beeville.

a) Determine the distance between Haytown and Beeville, to the nearest tenth of a kilometre.

b) Determine the angle of elevation of the helicopter, as seen from the sailboat, to the nearest tenth of a degree.

4.6 Trigonometric Identities,
pages 270 to 275

13. Prove that $\dfrac{\cot \theta}{\csc \theta} = \cos \theta$.

14. Prove that $\sin^4 \theta - \cos^4 \theta = \sin^2 \theta - \cos^2 \theta$.

15. Prove that
$\cot \theta = \cos \theta \sin \theta + \cos^3 \theta \csc \theta$.

Chapter Problem   WRAP-UP

As you worked through this chapter, you completed six legs of an orienteering course based on trigonometry. It is time to head back to the starting point and finish the course.

a) Refer to your map. Create a problem that involves trigonometry to model the direction back to the starting point from checkpoint #6, similar to the problems that you solved to complete the six legs.

b) Trade your problem with a classmate. Solve each other's problem. Do you both finish back at the starting point?

c) Use Technology Select a suitable scale and set up a map of the orienteering course using *The Geometer's Sketchpad®*. Select appropriate tools from the **Transform** menu to draw each of the six legs. Measure the direction and distance back to the starting point from checkpoint #6. How does it compare with the direction and distance that you measured from your map?

For questions 1 to 5, select the best answer.

1. An angle in the first quadrant has a sine of $\dfrac{1}{\sqrt{2}}$. The tangent of this angle is

  A $\dfrac{1}{\sqrt{2}}$ **B** 1   **C** $\dfrac{1}{\sqrt{3}}$ **D** $\sqrt{3}$

2. A 25-m-high pine tree is growing in soft ground. After a storm, the tree leans at an angle of 60° with the ground. A pine cone falls from the top of the tree to the ground. Determine an expression for the exact distance that the pine cone falls.

  A $25\sqrt{3}$ m   **B** $\dfrac{25}{2}$ m

  C $\dfrac{\sqrt{3}}{2}$ m   **D** $\dfrac{25\sqrt{3}}{2}$ m

3. An angle θ in the third quadrant has a sine of -0.6133. In which quadrant is another angle with the same sine?

  A first quadrant   **B** second quadrant

  C third quadrant   **D** fourth quadrant

4. An angle in the second quadrant has a tangent of $-\dfrac{3}{4}$. Another angle with the same tangent measures about

  A 37°   **B** 53°   **C** 127°   **D** 323°

5. In $\triangle$PQR, $\angle$P = 25°, $\angle$R = 65°, and $q = 12$ cm. To determine the length of p, what is the most appropriate trigonometric tool?

  A the sine law

  B the cosine law

  C primary trigonometric ratios

  D reciprocal trigonometric ratios

6. a) $\angle$A lies in the second quadrant and has a cotangent of $-\dfrac{5}{7}$. Sketch a diagram showing the position of $\angle$A, including a triangle with the lengths of the sides labelled.

  b) Determine expressions for the other five trigonometric ratios for $\angle$A.

7. A hot-air balloon is used to give rides to visitors at a summer fair. The balloon is tethered to the ground by a long cable. The cable is extended to its maximum length of 300 m, and the wind is blowing the balloon such that the cable makes an angle of 60° with the ground. The cable is pulled in to 200 m, but the wind strengthens, decreasing the angle to 45°.

a) Sketch the two positions of the balloon, including distances and angles.

b) Find an exact expression for the horizontal distance that the balloon moves between the two positions.

c) Use a calculator to help you determine whether the balloon moves horizontally toward or away from the tether point.

8. Tanis leaves home and rides her bicycle 12 km north. She turns east and rides another 5 km. Then, she turns onto a forest bicycle path that runs 45° south of east and rides for another 5 km.

   a) Sketch a diagram of Tanis's journey.

   b) What is the most appropriate trigonometric tool to use in determining her distance from home? Justify your answer.

   c) How far is Tanis from home at this point?

   d) Which direction will take her directly home?

9. Antonio parks his car in the parking lot of a mountain-biking area and then bikes 1.4 km along a level trail in a direction 20° east of north. He turns right through an angle of 140° and rides up a sloping trail with an angle of elevation of 15°. When Antonio reaches the top of a hill, his odometer indicates that he has come another 1.2 km. He notices that there is a path sloping downward directly back to the parking lot. Antonio takes this path, returning to his car. Determine the total distance that he rode his bike, to the nearest tenth of a kilometre.

10. While visiting relatives in the Azores Islands, Juan sails from their home on Sao Jorge to Faial, a 45-km ferry ride. From Faial, he measures the angle of elevation to the Pico volcano as 5.8° and the angle of separation between the base of the volcano and Sao Jorge as 80°. When he returns to Sao Jorge, Juan measures the angle of separation of Faial and the base of the Pico volcano as 29°. Use this information to determine the height of the volcano, to the nearest metre.

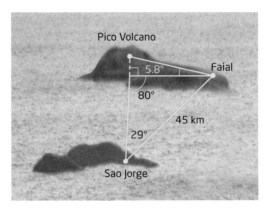

11. Use a unit circle to show that $\cos \theta = \cos (360° - \theta)$ is an identity.

12. Prove that $\dfrac{\csc \theta}{\sec \theta} = \cot \theta$.

13. Prove that $\dfrac{\sin \theta}{1 - \cos \theta} = \csc \theta(1 + \cos \theta)$.

Pyramids and Angles of Elevation

Use eight drinking straws to build a square-based pyramid with equilateral triangular faces.

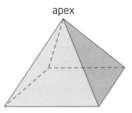

apex

a) Determine the height of the pyramid.

b) Imagine that you are standing at the midpoint of one of the edges of the base. Calculate the angle of elevation to the apex.

c) Now, imagine walking to one of the vertices of the base. Predict whether the angle of elevation to the apex will change. Use words to justify your prediction.

d) Verify your prediction in part c) mathematically.

e) Develop an algebraic model to calculate the angle of elevation of the apex from any point on the edge of the base.

Trigonometric Functions

Trigonometric ratios can be used to extend the concept of functions to include trigonometric functions. These functions and their transformations can be used to model many real-world phenomena, such as tidal action or the number of hours of daylight in a particular location at various times throughout the year. In this chapter, you will investigate the basic trigonometric functions and learn how to transform them. You will learn to choose the parameters of the transformation to develop models for real-world applications. You will also use these models to pose and answer questions and make predictions.

By the end of this chapter, you will

- describe key properties of periodic functions arising from real-world applications, given a numerical or graphical representation

- predict, by extrapolating, the future behaviour of a relationship modelled using a numeric or graphical representation of a periodic function

- make connections between the sine ratio and the sine function and between the cosine ratio and the cosine function by graphing the relationship between angles from 0° to 360° and the corresponding sine ratios or cosine ratios, with or without technology, defining this relationship as the function $f(x) = \sin x$ or $f(x) = \cos x$, and explaining why the relationship is a function

- sketch the graphs of $f(x) = \sin x$ and $f(x) = \cos x$ for angle measures expressed in degrees, and determine and describe key properties

- determine, through investigation using technology, and describe the roles of the parameters a, k, d, and c in functions of the form $y = af[k(x - d)] + c$ in terms of transformations of the graphs of $f(x) = \sin x$ and $f(x) = \cos x$ with angles expressed in degrees

- determine the amplitude, period, phase shift, domain, and range of sinusoidal functions whose equations are given in the form $f(x) = a \sin [k(x - d)] + c$ or $f(x) = a \cos [k(x - d)] + c$

- sketch graphs of $y = af[k(x - d)] + c$ by applying one or more transformations to the graphs of $f(x) = \sin x$ and $f(x) = \cos x$, and state the domain and range of the transformed functions

- represent a sinusoidal function with an equation, given its graph or its properties

- collect data that can be modelled as a sinusoidal function from primary sources or from secondary sources, and graph the data

- identify sinusoidal functions, including those that arise from real-world applications involving periodic phenomena, given various representations, and explain any restrictions that the context places on the domain and range

- determine, through investigation, how sinusoidal functions can be used to model periodic phenomena that do not involve angles

- predict the effects on a mathematical model of an application involving sinusoidal functions when the conditions in the application are varied

- pose and solve problems based on applications involving a sinusoidal function by using a given graph or a graph generated with technology from its equation

Prerequisite Skills

Refer to the Prerequisite Skills Appendix on pages 496 to 516 for examples of the topics and further practice.

Use the Cosine Law

1. A circle of radius 5 cm has a point on its circumference every 30°.

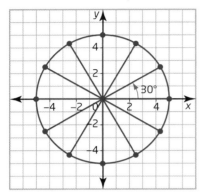

a) Find the distance between two adjacent points. Round your answer to one decimal place.

b) Find the distance between two points separated by 60°.

c) What is the distance between two points separated by 180°?

Find Trigonometric Ratios of Special Angles

2. Use a unit circle to determine the exact sine and cosine ratios of the angles in each set.

a) 30° and 60°

b) 120°, 150°, 210°, 240°, 300°, and 330°

c) 45°, 135°, 225°, and 315°

d) 0°, 90°, 180°, and 270°

Determine the Domain and Range of a Function

3. Consider the function $f(x) = x^2$. Write the domain and range using set notation.

4. Write the equation of a function with domain $\{x \in \mathbb{R}, -5 \le x \le 5\}$ and range $\{y \in \mathbb{R}, 0 \le y \le 5\}$.

Shift Functions

5. a) Graph the following functions on the same set of axes.

   i) $y = x^2$

   ii) $y = x^2 + 3$

   iii) $y = x^2 - 2$

b) Describe the transformations of the second and third functions with respect to the first.

6. a) Graph the following functions on the same set of axes.

   i) $y = x^2$

   ii) $y = (x - 3)^2$

   iii) $y = (x + 2)^2$

b) Describe the transformations of the second and third functions with respect to the first.

7. a) The parabola $y = x^2$ is translated 5 units to the left and 3 units down. Write the equation of the transformed function.

b) The parabola $y = x^2$ is translated 4 units to the right and 7 units up. Write the equation of the transformed function.

8. The parabola $y = x^2$ is translated horizontally and vertically so that its vertex passes through (2, 2). Describe the translations and verify your answer.

Stretch Functions

9. a) Graph the following functions on the same set of axes.

   i) $y = x^2$

   ii) $y = 2x^2$

   iii) $y = \dfrac{1}{2}x^2$

b) Describe the transformations of the second and third functions with respect to the first.

10. a) Graph the following functions on the same set of axes.

   i) $y = (x - 3)^2$

   ii) $y = 2(x - 3)^2$

   iii) $y = \frac{1}{2}(x - 3)^2$

b) Describe the transformations of the second and third functions with respect to the first.

11. The parabola $y = x^2$ is stretched vertically so that it passes through the point (2, 16). What is the equation of the stretched parabola? Verify your answer.

12. The parabola $y = (x - 4)^2$ is stretched horizontally so that it passes through the point (2, 36). What is the equation of the stretched parabola? Verify your answer.

Reflect Functions

13. a) Graph the following functions on the same set of axes.

   i) $y = (x + 2)^2$

   ii) $y = -(x + 2)^2$

b) Use a reflection to describe the transformation of the second function with respect to the first.

14. a) Determine an equation for each of the functions shown.

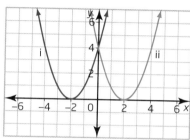

b) Use a reflection to describe the transformation of function ii) with respect to function i).

Combine Transformations

15. a) The graph of $y = x^2$ is translated 4 units to the left, stretched horizontally by a factor of 2, and then translated 1 unit up. Write the equation of the transformed function.

b) Graph the original and transformed functions on the same set of axes.

16. Describe the transformations applied to $y = x^2$ to produce the graph defined by $y = -3(x - 4)^2 + 8$.

Solve Equations Involving Rational Expressions

17. Solve $\dfrac{360}{k} = 30$.

18. Solve $\dfrac{360}{k} = \dfrac{1}{30}$.

Chapter Problem

All the sounds that you hear are made up of waves of pressure passing through the air and vibrating on your eardrums. Sound waves can be represented using trigonometric functions. These representations can be used for diverse purposes, such as voice recognition, as well as the design of concert halls and noise-cancelling headphones.

In this chapter, you will learn how sound can be modelled by trigonometric functions and how transformations of the functions affect the characteristics of sounds, including loudness, pitch, and quality. You will learn how trigonometric functions are used in music synthesis, from the sounds of your favourite band to soundtracks for motion pictures.

Modelling Periodic Behaviour

What do the sounds of your favourite band, the idling of a car engine, the phases of the moon, and your heartbeat all have in common? All are examples of processes that repeat in a regular pattern. Your heart, when you are at rest, follows the same cycle each time it beats. A car engine has moving parts that repeat the same motions over and over. In the lunar cycle, the moon grows from a tiny sliver, to a beautiful full moon, and then wanes until it disappears, only to reappear at the beginning of the next cycle. Your favourite band plays instruments that create repetitive pressure patterns in the air that your ears interpret as music. Periodic patterns can be modelled by trigonometric functions.

Tools

- grid paper
- protractor
- ruler
- compasses

or

- graphing calculator

Investigate

How can you model periodic behaviour mathematically?

Antique carousels featuring intricately painted horses and other animals are still popular attractions. Several towns in Ontario feature them, as do many amusement parks.

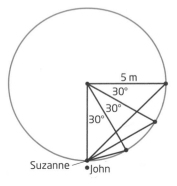

Suppose that a carousel has a diameter of 10 m. John is standing at the edge of the carousel, watching his sister Suzanne on a horse on the carousel's outer edge. How does the distance between John and Suzanne change as the carousel completes a full turn? Predict the shape of a graph that represents distance versus angle for one revolution.

1. Draw a circle to represent the carousel. Mark a point just outside the circle to represent John. Mark a point on the circumference to represent Suzanne at the point where she passes John.

2. Assume that the carousel turns in a counterclockwise direction and that the distance between John and the edge of the carousel can be ignored. Mark points on the circle to represent Suzanne's position at 30° intervals for one complete revolution. For each position, determine the distance between John and Suzanne using appropriate trigonometric tools. (The diagram illustrates the first three distances to measure.) Record your results in a table with angle in the first column and distance, in metres, in the second column.

3. Reflect Predict the values for Suzanne's position as the carousel continues to rotate through 360° to 720°. Justify your predictions.

4. Use the values in your table to sketch the graph of distance versus angle of revolution. Record distance along the vertical axis and the angle of revolution from 0° to 720° along the horizontal axis.

5. Reflect Compare the graph to your predicted graph. How are the graphs similar? How are they different?

6. a) Inspect the graph for two revolutions of the carousel. Predict the total angle of revolution that Suzanne moves through in five revolutions.

b) If a ride consists of 12 revolutions, what is the total angle of revolution that Suzanne moves through?

7. a) Use the graph to estimate two angles during the first revolution when the distance between John and Suzanne is 8 m. Locate these angles on your diagram of the carousel.

b) In the third revolution, predict the angles when the distance between John and Suzanne is 8 m.

8. How many **cycles** are shown in the graph?

9. The **period** of a pattern is measured in units appropriate to the problem. What is the period of this pattern?

10. Reflect How does a **periodic function** differ from a linear function or a quadratic function?

11. What is the minimum distance between John and Suzanne during the first revolution? What is the maximum distance?

12. What is the **amplitude** of this function?

13. Reflect Suppose that Suzanne is on a horse that is 2 m from the centre of the carousel. Predict how the graph will change from the one that you drew in step 4. Sketch your prediction of the graph of distance versus angle of revolution for two revolutions of the carousel.

cycle
- one complete repetition of a pattern

period
- the horizontal length of one cycle on a graph

periodic function
- a function that has a pattern of *y*-values that repeats at regular intervals

amplitude
- half the distance between the maximum and minimum values of a periodic function

Example 1

Classify Functions

a) Examine each graph. Determine whether the function is periodic. If it is, determine the period.

i)

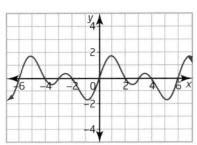

ii)

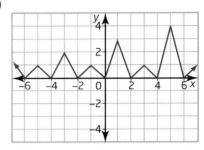

b) Examine the graph. Determine whether the function is periodic. If it is, determine the amplitude.

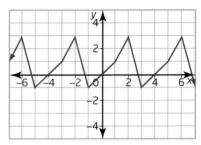

Solution

a) i) A periodic function has a pattern of y-values that repeats at regular intervals. The period is the length of the interval. In this example, the pattern of y-values in one section of the graph repeats in the next section. Therefore, the function is periodic.

To determine the period, select a convenient starting point and note the x-coordinate. In this case, choose $(-6, 0)$. Move to the right, and estimate the x-coordinate where the next cycle begins. This appears to be at the origin. Subtract the two x-coordinates. The period is $0 - (-6)$, or 6 units.

ii) In this example, the pattern of y-values in one section of the graph does not repeat in the next section. Therefore, the function is not periodic.

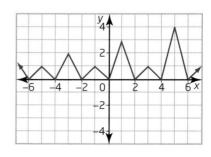

b) The function illustrated in the graph is periodic because there is a repeating pattern of y-values on a regular basis. A periodic function usually has a maximum value and a minimum value every cycle. The amplitude is

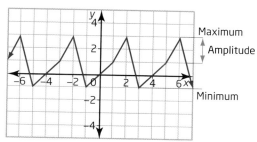

half the difference between the maximum and minimum values. In the graph shown, the maximum is 3 and the minimum is −1.

Therefore, the amplitude is $\dfrac{3 - (-1)}{2}$, or 2 units.

Example 2

Predicting With Periodic Functions

Consider the periodic function shown.

a) What is the period of the function?

b) Determine $f(2)$ and $f(5)$.

c) Predict $f(8)$, $f(-10)$, and $f(14)$.

d) What is the amplitude of the function?

e) Determine four x-values such that $f(x) = 2$.

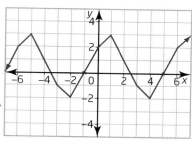

Solution

a) Select a convenient starting point, such as $(-7, 0)$. Move to the right until the pattern begins to repeat. This occurs at $(-1, 0)$. The period is equal to the horizontal length of this cycle, calculated by subtracting the x-coordinates. Thus, the period is $-1 - (-7)$, or 6 units.

b) Read values from the graph: $f(2) = 1$ and $f(5) = 0$.

c)
$f(8) = f(2 + 6)$	$f(-10) = f(-10 + 6 + 6)$	$f(14) = f(14 - 6 - 6)$
$= f(2)$	$= f(2)$	$= f(2)$
$= 1$	$= 1$	$= 1$

From part a), the period of the function is 6. The value of the function at x is the same as the value at x plus or minus any multiple of 6.

d) The maximum value is 3. The minimum value is −2. The amplitude is $\dfrac{3 - (-2)}{2}$, or 2.5 units.

e) From the graph, the value of $f(0)$ is 2. Determine other x-values by adding the period to or subtracting the period from $x = 0$. Two possible answers are $x = 6$, $x = 12$, and $x = 18$, or $x = -6$, $x = -12$, and $x = -18$.

Example 3

Natural Gas Consumption in Ontario

The graph shows residential natural gas consumption in Ontario per month, beginning in January 2001. Data are obtained from Statistics Canada through its online E-STAT interactive tool.

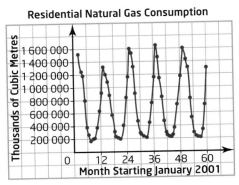

Residential Natural Gas Consumption

a) Explain why the graph has this shape.

b) Do the data appear to be periodic? Justify your answer.

c) Assume that the consumption of natural gas in Ontario can be modelled using a periodic function. Determine the approximate maximum value, minimum value, and amplitude of this function.

d) Estimate the period of this function. Does this value make sense? Explain why.

e) Estimate the domain and range of the function.

f) Explain how the graph can be used to estimate the natural gas consumption in February 2011.

Solution

a) The consumption of natural gas in Ontario varies with the season. One expects consumption to be high in the winter months and low in the summer months.

b) The data are approximately periodic. The values do not exactly match from cycle to cycle.

c) A reasonable estimate for the maximum is 1 600 000 thousand cubic metres (1 600 000 000 m³). The minimum is about 200 000 thousand cubic metres (200 000 000 m³).

$$\text{Amplitude} = \frac{1\ 600\ 000 - 200\ 000}{2}$$

$$= \frac{1\ 400\ 000}{2}$$

$$= 700\ 000$$

The amplitude is about 700 000 thousand cubic metres (700 000 000 m³).

d) From the graph, the period is about 12 months. This is reasonable. One expects the seasonal cycle for consumption of natural gas to be yearly.

e) Let t represent the time, in months, and let g represent the consumption of natural gas, in thousands of cubic metres. The domain is $\{t \in \mathbb{R}, 1 \le t \le 60\}$. Note that the lower bound of the domain is not 0. The data begin in January, which is the first month. The range is approximately $\{g \in \mathbb{R}, 200\,000 \le g \le 1\,600\,000\}$.

f) To obtain a reasonable estimate of gas consumption during the month of February, use the graph to find the consumption for each February shown. Take the average of these values. This is a reasonable estimate of the consumption predicted for February 2011.

Key Concepts

- A pattern that repeats itself regularly is periodic.
- A periodic pattern can be modelled using a periodic function.
- One repetition of a periodic pattern is called a cycle.
- The horizontal length of a cycle on a graph is called the period. The period may be in units of time or other units of measurement.

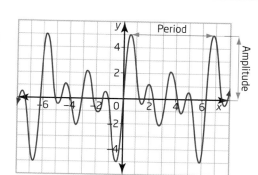

- A function is periodic if there is a positive number, p, such that $f(x + p) = f(x)$ for every x in the domain of $f(x)$. The least value of p that works is the period of the function.
- $f(x + np) = f(x)$, where p is the period and n is any integer.
- The amplitude of a periodic function is half the difference between the maximum value and the minimum value in a cycle.

Communicate Your Understanding

C1 The population of a mining town has increased and decreased several times in the past few decades. Do you expect the population as a function of time to be periodic? Justify your answer.

C2 a) Consider a function such that $f(x + q) = -f(x)$. Sketch the graph of a simple function that follows this kind of relationship.

b) Is the function in part a) periodic? Justify your answer.

C3 Consider the decimal expansion of the fraction $\frac{1}{7}$. If you graph each digit in the expansion on the vertical axis versus its decimal place on the horizontal axis, is the pattern periodic? Use a graph to support your answer.

A Practise

For help with questions 1 to 5, refer to Example 1.

1. Classify each graph as periodic or not periodic. Justify your answers.

a)
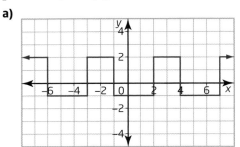

b)
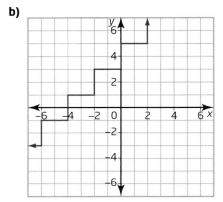

c)
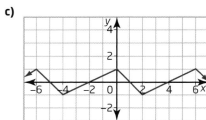

d)
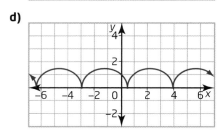

2. Determine the amplitude and period for any graph in question 1 that is periodic.

3. Sketch four cycles of a periodic function with an amplitude of 5 and a period of 3.

4. Sketch four cycles of a periodic function with an amplitude of 4 and a period of 6.

5. Do your graphs in questions 3 and 4 match those of your classmates? Explain why or why not.

For help with questions 6 to 8, refer to Example 2.

6. A periodic function $f(x)$ has a period of 8. The values of $f(1)$, $f(5)$, and $f(7)$ are -3, 2, and 8, respectively. Predict the value of each of the following. If a prediction is not possible, explain why not.

Reasoning and Proving

Representing   Selecting Tools

Problem Solving

Connecting   Reflecting

Communicating

a) $f(9)$ b) $f(29)$

c) $f(63)$ d) $f(40)$

7. a) Sketch the graph of a periodic function, $f(x)$, with a maximum value of 7, a minimum value of -1, and a period of 5.

b) Select a value a for x, and determine $f(a)$.

c) Determine two other values, b and c, such that $f(a) = f(b) = f(c)$.

B Connect and Apply

8. Sunita draws a periodic function so that $f(p) = f(q)$. Can you conclude that the period of the function is the difference between p and q? Justify your answer, including a diagram.

9. A navigation light on a point in a lake flashes 1 s on and 1 s off. After three flashes, the light stays off for an extra 2 s.

a) Let 1 represent "on" and 0 represent "off." Sketch a graph with time on the horizontal axis to represent the flashing of the light. Include three cycles.

b) Explain why this pattern is periodic.

c) What is the period of the pattern?

d) What is the amplitude?

10. The people mover at an airport shuttles between the main terminal and a satellite terminal 300 m away. A one-way trip, moving at a constant speed, takes 1 min, and the car remains at each terminal for 30 s before leaving.

   a) Sketch a graph to represent the distance of the car from the main terminal with respect to time. Include four complete cycles.

   b) What is the period of the motion?

   c) What is the amplitude of the motion?

11. Which of the following values do you expect to follow a periodic pattern? Justify your answer for each case.

Reasoning and Proving

Representing — Selecting Tools

Problem Solving

Connecting — Reflecting

Communicating

   a) the cost of 1 kg of tomatoes at the local supermarket at different times of the year

   b) the interest rate offered on an investment by a bank over a term of 5 years

   c) the percent of the moon's face that is illuminated over several months

   d) the volume of air in your lungs during several minutes of normal breathing

12. Use Technology Sunspots are huge storms that take place on the sun. They can produce electromagnetic waves that interfere with radio, television, and other communication systems on Earth. Is the number of sunspots at any particular time random, or does the number follow a periodic pattern? Use the Internet to find a graph or table of sunspot activity over several decades. Inspect the data and decide whether the number of sunspots over time may be considered periodic. Justify your answer.

13. Is it possible for a periodic function to be either continuously increasing or continuously decreasing? Justify your answer, including a diagram.

14. While visiting the east coast of Canada, Ranouf notices that the water level at a town dock changes during the day as the tides come in and go out. Markings on one of the piles supporting the dock show a high tide of 3.3 m at 6:30 a.m., a low tide of of 0.7 m at 12:40 p.m., and a high tide again at 6:50 p.m.

   a) Estimate the period of the fluctuation of the water level at the town dock.

   b) Estimate the amplitude of the pattern.

   c) Predict when the next low tide will occur.

15. The city of Quito, Ecuador, is located on the equator, about 6400 km from the centre of Earth. As Earth turns, Quito rotates about Earth's axis. Consider midnight local time as the starting time and the position of Quito at that hour as the starting location. Let d represent the distance in a straight line from the starting location at time t.

Reasoning and Proving

Representing — Selecting Tools

Problem Solving

Connecting — Reflecting

Communicating

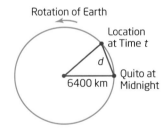

Rotation of Earth

Location at Time t

d

6400 km — Quito at Midnight

   a) Explain why the graph of d versus t will show a periodic pattern.

   b) What is the period of this motion?

   c) What is the amplitude of this motion?

   d) Suppose that you want to generate a table of values for d as a function of t. Determine an appropriate trigonometric tool to use. Explain why it is the most appropriate tool for this problem. Describe how you would use the tool to generate the table of values.

16. The average monthly temperatures over 1 year in a given location usually follow a periodic pattern.

   a) Estimate the maximum value, minimum value, and amplitude of this pattern for where you live.

   b) What is the period of this pattern? Explain.

17. Describe a real-world pattern that you think might be periodic. Do not use a pattern that has already been used in this section. Trade patterns with a classmate. Perform an investigation to determine whether the pattern is periodic. If you determine that the pattern is periodic, determine the period and the amplitude. If it is not, explain why not.

18. Chapter Problem Randy connects his synthesizer to an oscilloscope and plays a B key that he knows produces a sound with frequency close to 500 cycles every second, or 500 Hz (hertz). The pattern is shown. Time, in seconds, is shown on the horizontal axis.

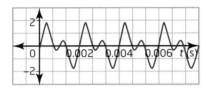

   a) Explain how you know that the pattern is periodic.

   b) What is the period?

   c) Determine a relation between the period and the frequency of the note being played.

Connections

One of the oldest purely electronic instruments is the theremin, invented in 1919 by Leon Theremin, a Russian engineer. Players control the instrument's sound by moving their hands toward or away from the instrument's two antennas. One antenna controls the pitch of the sound; the other controls the volume. You have probably heard the eerie, gliding, warbling sounds of a theremin in science fiction or horror films.

19. Use Technology Use dynamic geometry software to sketch a model of the carousel in the Investigate on page 284. Animate the point that represents Suzanne, and note how the measurements of angle and distance change during a revolution.

20. The hours and minutes of daylight on the first of each month of 2006 in Windsor, Ontario, are shown in the table.

Date	Daylight (Hours:Minutes)
Jan. 1	9:09
Feb. 1	10:00
Mar. 1	11:14
Apr. 1	12:43
May 1	14:04
Jun. 1	15:04
Jul. 1	15:14
Aug. 1	14:28
Sep. 1	13:10
Oct. 1	11:45
Nov. 1	10:21
Dec. 1	9:19

   a) Explain why these data will show a periodic pattern over several years.

   b) Predict the number of hours of daylight on May 1, 2010.

   c) Predict the number of hours of daylight on September 15, 2008.

✔ **Achievement Check**

21. At the doctor's office for a routine physical examination, Armand has his blood pressure checked. He notices that the pressure reaches a high value (systolic pressure) of 120 and a low value (diastolic pressure) of 80, measured in millimetres of mercury (mmHg). The doctor counts 18 pulse beats in 15 s. Is the blood pressure pattern periodic? Justify your answer.

C Extend

22. A lighthouse beacon rotates through 360° every 12 s. The lighthouse is located 100 m off the shore of an island with a coastline of steep cliffs running north and south. As the light beam sweeps clockwise, starting from north (direction of 0°), it strikes some part of the cliff.

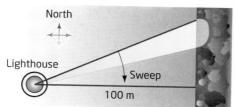

a) How long does it take the light beam to reach an angle of 30°? What is the distance travelled by the beam to the cliff at that time? Record time and distance in a table.

b) Repeat part a) for 60°, 90°, 120°, and 150°.

c) What happens to the distance as the beam approaches 180°?

d) After passing 180°, how long does it take until the beam strikes the cliff again at some point?

e) Use your table to sketch the graph of distance versus time for one revolution of the light.

f) Explain why your graph shows a periodic pattern. What is the period?

g) What is the amplitude of the pattern? Explain.

23. In some cases, the amplitude of a function decreases with time. An example is a function used to model the sound of a plucked guitar string. As time goes on, the sound becomes fainter and dies. This is known as a damped periodic function. An example is shown.

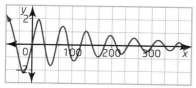

a) Construct a table of values of y versus x, recording the maximum value for each cycle in the y column.

b) Draw a scatter plot for y versus x.

c) What kind of model do the data appear to follow?

d) Use your knowledge from a previous chapter to construct the model.

e) Graph the model on your scatter plot. Comment on the fit.

24. Math Contest If the fraction $\frac{5}{7}$ is written in expanded decimal form, what is the 100th digit after the decimal point?

A 1   **B** 4   **C** 2   **D** 8

25. Math Contest A number has the pattern 978675...0. How many digits does this number have?

A 14   **B** 16   **C** 18   **D** 20

26. Math Contest A sequence is created using the following rules.

- If the number is odd, the next number is found by adding 1 to the number and then dividing by 2.

- If the number is even, the next number is the number divided by 2.

If you start with the number 211, what is the 53rd number in the sequence?

A 27   **B** 3   **C** 1   **D** 100

27. Math Contest Of 50 students surveyed. 30 say they like algebra, 21 say they like trigonometry, and 8 say they like both. How many students do not like either algebra or trigonometry?

A 7   **B** 0   **C** 12   **D** 1

5.2

The Sine Function and the Cosine Function

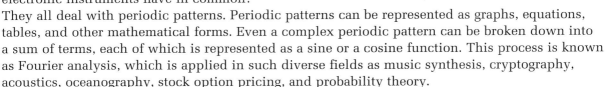

What do an oceanographer, a stock analyst, an audio engineer, and a musician playing electronic instruments have in common?

They all deal with periodic patterns. Periodic patterns can be represented as graphs, equations, tables, and other mathematical forms. Even a complex periodic pattern can be broken down into a sum of terms, each of which is represented as a sine or a cosine function. This process is known as Fourier analysis, which is applied in such diverse fields as music synthesis, cryptography, acoustics, oceanography, stock option pricing, and probability theory.

In this section, you will use your knowledge of the sine and cosine ratios to develop sine and cosine functions. You will investigate the properties of these functions and become familiar with the characteristics of their graphs.

Tools

- calculator
- grid paper

Investigate A

How can you use a table and grid paper with the sine ratio to construct a function?

In this chapter, you will consider wider applications of the trigonometric ratios, including applications where the independent variable does not represent an angle. In these applications, it is appropriate to use x rather than θ to represent the variable and to think of sine and cosine as functions of x: $f(x) = \sin x$ and $g(x) = \cos x$.

1. Use a unit circle to find exact values for $\sin x$. Use a calculator to determine approximate values for $\sin x$. Begin at 0° and continue every 30° until you reach 360°. Copy and complete the table.

	sin x	
x	Exact Value	Rounded to One Decimal Place
0°	0	0.0
30°	$\frac{1}{2}$	0.5
⋮	⋮	⋮
⋮	⋮	⋮
360°		

2. a) Plot the ordered pairs $(x, \sin x)$ on a graph, from $x = 0°$ to $x = 360°$. Use the decimal values for $\sin x$. Place the graph beside the unit circle.

b) Draw a smooth curve through the points.

3. Reflect Why do you think that this graph is often called a sine wave?

4. Continue your table past 360° for several more rows. What do you notice about the entries?

5. a) Predict the shape of the graph past 360°. Justify your prediction.

b) Verify your prediction.

6. Use your table and graph to copy and complete the table of properties for $y = \sin x$ for 0° to 360°. Leave the third column blank for now. You will use the third column in Investigate C.

Property	$y = \sin x$	
maximum		
minimum		
amplitude		
period		
domain		
range		
y-intercept		
x-intercepts		
intervals of increase		
intervals of decrease		

7. Reflect Explain why the graph of $y = \sin x$ is periodic.

8. How can you verify that $y = \sin x$ is a function? Perform the verification. Write the function using function notation.

Many periodic patterns follow a **sinusoidal** relation and can be represented as a simple sine or cosine function. One of these patterns is the alternating current of electricity that provides energy for lights and appliances in your home. Other patterns can be modelled using combinations of two or more sine and cosine functions, or transformations of these functions. You will see some of these later in this chapter.

sinusoidal
- having the curved form of a sine wave

Investigate B

How can you use technology with the sine ratio to construct a function?

Method 1: Use a Graphing Calculator

1. Press (2nd) [TBLSET] to access the **TABLE SETUP** screen. This screen allows you to specify the starting value and the increment for a table of values. Set **TblStart** to 0 and △**Tbl** to 10, as shown. Make sure **Indpnt** and **Depend** are set to **AUTO**.

```
TABLE SETUP
 TblStart=0
 ⌂Tbl=30
Indent: Auto Ask
Depend: Auto Ask
```

2. Press (MODE) and ensure that your calculator is in **DEGREE** mode. Ensure that all plots are turned off. Access the **Y=** editor, and enter the expression sin (X) in **Y1**.

3. Adjust the window settings such that X is plotted from 0 to 360 with a scale of 30 and Y is plotted from −2 to +2 with a scale of 0.5. Press (GRAPH).

4. **Reflect** Compare the graph shown by the graphing calculator to the graph that you sketched in Investigate A. Use the scale on each axis to help you compare several points. Press (2nd) [CALC]. Select **1: value** to evaluate y for your selection of x.

5. Press (2nd) [TABLE] to access the table of values. Scroll down and compare the table to the one you constructed in Investigate A.

6. Continue scrolling past 360 to find the next maximum. How does it compare to your prediction in step 5a) of Investigate A? Predict where the next maximum will occur. Scroll down to check your answer.

7. Scroll back up and continue past 0. Predict where the next maximum will occur in this direction. Continue scrolling to check your answer.

8. **Reflect** Suppose that you can see the graph of $f(x) = \sin x$ from $x = -720$ to $x = 720$. How many cycles would you expect to see? Where would the maximum values occur? Where would the minimum values occur?

9. Adjust your window variables so that you can see the graph of $f(x) = \sin x$ from $x = -720$ to $x = 720$. Check your predictions from step 8.

Method 2: Use a TI-Nspire™ CAS Graphing Calculator

1. a) Press ⌂ and select **8:System Info**. Select **2:System Settings....** Use the ⇥ key to scroll down to **Angle**, and ensure that it is set to **Degree**. Continue on to **Auto or Approx** and ensure that it is set to **Auto**. Continue down to **OK** and press ↵ twice.

b) Press ⌂ and select **6:New Document**. Select **2:Add Graphs & Geometry**.

c) Type sin(x) for function **f1**. Press ↵.

d) Press ▣. Select **4:Window**. Select **1:Window Settings**. Set **XMin** to −360, **XMax** to 360, **Ymin** to −2, and **YMax** to 2. Tab down to **OK** and press ↵. The graph will be displayed as shown.

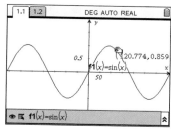

2. Reflect Compare the graph shown by the graphing calculator to the graph that you sketched in Investigate A.

b) Press ▣. Select **6:Points & Lines**. Select **2:Point On**. Move the cursor to the graph, and press ↵.

c) Press ⌃ ↵ to grab the point. Use the cursor keys to move the point along the graph. Compare the displayed values to those in your table from Investigate A.

3. a) Press ⌂. Add a **Lists & Spreadsheet** page.

b) Press ▣. Select **5:Function Table**. Select **1:Switch to Function Table**. Press ↵. A table will appear.

c) Press ▣. Select **5:Function Table**. Select **3:Edit Function Table Settings**. Set **Table Start** to 0. Set **Table Step** to 10. Tab down to **OK** and press ↵. The function table will be displayed as shown.

4. Scroll down and compare the table to the one you constructed in Investigate A.

5. Continue scrolling past 360 to find the next maximum. How does it compare to your prediction in step 5a) of Investigate A? Predict where the next maximum will occur. Scroll down to check your answer.

6. Scroll back up and continue past 0. Predict where the next maximum will occur in this direction. Continue scrolling to check your answer.

7. a) Press ⓒᵗʳˡ and the left cursor key to return to the graph display.

   b) Suppose that you could see the graph of $f(x) = \sin x$ from $x = -720$ to $x = 720$. How many cycles would you expect to see? Where would the maximum values occur? Where would the minimum values occur?

8. Reflect Adjust your window settings so that you can see the graph of $f(x) = \sin x$ from $x = -720$ to $x = 720$. Check your predictions from step 7.

Investigate C

How can you use the cosine ratio to construct a function?

The cosine curve has similarities to the sine curve, as well as some differences. Follow the steps of Investigate A and Investigate B to investigate the cosine curve. When you finish, complete the third column of the table in step 6 of Investigate A to summarize the properties of the cosine function.

Key Concepts

- The sine and cosine ratios, along with the unit circle, can be used to construct sine and cosine functions.
- Both the sine and cosine functions have a wave-like appearance, with a period of 360°.

Properties	$y = \sin x$	$y = \cos x$
sketch of graph		
maximum value	1	1
minimum value	−1	−1
amplitude	1	1
domain	$\{x \in \mathbb{R}\}$	$\{x \in \mathbb{R}\}$
range	$\{y \in \mathbb{R}, -1 \leq y \leq 1\}$	$\{y \in \mathbb{R}, -1 \leq y \leq 1\}$
x-intercepts	0°, 180°, and 360° over one cycle	90° and 270° over one cycle
y-intercept	0	1
intervals of increase (over one cycle)	$\{x \in \mathbb{R}, 0° \leq x \leq 90°, 270° \leq x \leq 360°\}$	$\{x \in \mathbb{R}, 180° \leq x \leq 360°\}$
intervals of decrease (over one cycle)	$\{x \in \mathbb{R}, 90° \leq x \leq 270°\}$	$\{x \in \mathbb{R}, 0° \leq x \leq 180°\}$

Communicate Your Understanding

C1 Without a graph, predict the values of x for which the graphs of $y = \sin x$ and $y = \cos x$ will intersect in the interval from $0°$ to $360°$. Justify your answer. Then, use graphs and tables to verify your answer.

C2 Review the x-intercepts for the sine and cosine functions. Write an expression for each graph, involving an integer n, that yields the x-intercepts when different values of n are substituted.

C3 Consider a point on the unit circle that is rotating around the circle in a counterclockwise direction.

  a) Which function represents the horizontal displacement of the point with respect to the origin?

  b) Which function represents the vertical displacement of the point with respect to the origin?

  c) Justify your choices of functions in parts a) and b).

B Connect and Apply

1. You are in a car of a Ferris wheel. The wheel has a radius of 8 m and turns counterclockwise. Let the origin be at the centre of the wheel. Begin each sketch in parts a) and b) when the radius from the centre of the wheel to your car is along the positive x-axis.

  a) Sketch the graph of your horizontal displacement versus the angle through which you turn for one rotation of the wheel. Which function models the horizontal displacement? Justify your choice.

  b) Sketch the graph of your vertical displacement versus the angle through which you turn for one rotation of the wheel. Which function models the vertical displacement? Justify your choice.

2. **Chapter Problem** Sounds can be modelled using sinusoidal functions. A simple instrument such as a flute produces a sound that can be modelled very closely using the function $y = \sin x$. As sounds become more complex, the model must become more complex. For example, the sound from a stringed instrument can be modelled closely using a more complex function such as $y = \sin x + \sin 2x$.

  a) Use technology or grid paper to sketch the graphs of $y = \sin x$ and $y = \sin x + \sin 2x$.

  b) How do the graphs differ? How are they similar?

Connections

In musical terms, you have added the second harmonic, sin 2x, to the fundamental, sin x. An electronics engineer can mimic the sounds of conventional instruments electronically by adding harmonics, or overtones. This process is known as music synthesis and is the basic principle behind the operation of synthesizers. To learn more about how the addition of harmonics changes a sound, go to the *Functions 11* page of the McGraw-Hill Ryerson Web site and follow the links to Chapter 5.

  c) Add the third harmonic, sin 3x, to your model and sketch the graph. Compare the graph to the simple sine wave and to the sine wave together with the second harmonic.

3. The hour hand on a clock has a length of 12 cm. Let the origin be at the centre of the clock.

Reasoning and Proving

Representing · Selecting Tools · Problem Solving · Connecting · Reflecting · Communicating

a) Sketch the graph of the vertical position of the tip of the hour hand versus the angle through which the hand turns for a time period of 72 h. Assume that the hour hand starts at 9.

b) Sketch the graph of the horizontal position of the tip of the hour hand versus the angle through which the hand turns for a time period of 72 h. Assume that the hour hand starts at 3.

c) How many cycles appear in the graph in part a)?

d) How many cycles will appear in the graph in part a) if you use the minute hand rather than the hour hand? Explain your prediction.

C Extend

4. What does the graph of $y = \tan x$ look like? Use a calculator to investigate. Round values of tan x to three decimal places.

a) Construct a table of values for x and tan x. Use 10° increments up to 70°. Then, use 5° increments up to 85°. Change to 1° increments up to 89°.

b) What happens to the value of tan x as x approaches 90°? Review the unit circle and explain why this happens. What is the value of tan 90°?

c) Continue your table of values up to 360°. Adjust the increment as required.

d) Use your table of values to draw a graph of $y = \tan x$. To keep the scale manageable, use y-values from -10 to 10. Allow space on the horizontal axis x-values from $-720°$ to 720°.

e) Draw the asymptotes as vertical dashed lines at $x = 90°$ and $x = 270°$ on this graph. The graph of the tangent function approaches, but never reaches, each of these asymptotes.

f) Predict what the graph will look like if it is extended past $x = 360°$ to $x = 720°$. Where will the asymptotes be drawn? Use the calculator to check a few points. Then, sketch the graph from $x = 360°$ to $x = 720°$.

g) Predict what the graph will look like if it is extended left past $x = 0°$. Where will the asymptotes be drawn? Use the calculator to check a few points. Then, sketch the graph from $x = -720°$ to $x = 0°$.

h) Is the graph of $y = \tan x$ periodic? Justify your answer. If the function is periodic, determine the period.

5. a) Show that $y = \tan x$ is a function.

Reasoning and Proving

Representing · Selecting Tools · Problem Solving · Connecting · Reflecting · Communicating

b) Is it possible to identify the amplitude of the function? Justify your answer.

c) For what interval(s) of values for x from 0° to 360° is the function increasing? For what interval(s) is it decreasing?

d) **Use Technology** Use a graphing calculator to plot the tangent function from $x = -360°$ to $x = 360°$. Compare the graph on the calculator to the graph that you sketched in question 4.

e) You can add asymptotes at appropriate values of x. Return to the home screen. Press (2nd) [DRAW]. Select **4:Vertical**, and type 90. Return to the graph. Note that a vertical line appears at $x = 90°$. Add other asymptotes as appropriate.

f) What is the domain of the tangent function? What is the range? Write each using set notation.

6. a) Sketch the function $f(x) = \sin x$ from $x = 0°$ to $x = 360°$.

b) Review the definition of cosecant. Using your graph from part a), determine the shape of the graph of $y = \csc x$.

c) Use grid paper and a scientific calculator, or a graphing calculator, to check your answer to part b). Add asymptotes where appropriate.

d) Show that $y = \csc x$ is a function.

e) What is the domain of the function? What is the range?

7. Use a method similar to that in question 6 to analyse the graph of $y = \sec x$.

8. Use a method similar to that in question 6 to analyse the graph of $y = \cot x$.

9. Consider the function $y = \sin x + \cos x$.

a) Predict the y-intercept of the function.

b) Predict the x-intercepts from $0°$ to $360°$. Justify your answer.

c) Use a graph or a graphing calculator to verify your answers to parts a) and b).

10. Math Contest For $0° \leq \theta \leq 360°$, over what intervals is $\sin \theta \leq \cos \theta$?

11. Math Contest For $-90° \leq \theta \leq 90°$, for what value(s) of θ does $\tan \theta = \cot \theta$?

12. Math Contest From a list of five numbers, a pair are chosen and then totalled. The sums of all possible pairs are 4, 8, 10, 12, 14, 18, 20, 22, 26, and 30. What is the sum of all five numbers?

A 164   **B** 82

C 41   **D** not possible to determine

Career Connection

Mariah completed a three-year diploma in respiratory therapy at Canadore College and then accumulated three years of experience. Now she is a perfusionist, where she assists during open-heart surgery by operating the heart-lung machine. This machine functions in place of a patient's heart and lungs while they are being operated on; it takes the patient's blood, oxygenates it, and pumps it back into the body. This allows the doctor to stop the patient's heart so that it can be worked on. Mariah is operating the patient's lifeline—she must monitor vital signs and make necessary adjustments to the heart-lung machine as well as administer drugs, intravenous fluids, and blood.

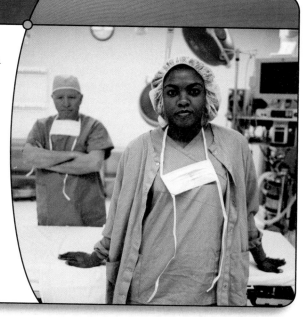

Use Technology

Dynamically Unwrap the Unit Circle

Tools

- graphing calculator

Draw a graph of the unit circle and plot a point at (1, 0). Recall that the coordinates of a point on the unit circle can be expressed as (cos θ, sin θ), where θ is an angle in standard position. Imagine the point moving counterclockwise around the circle. As the point moves, the angle θ increases from 0° to 360°. At the same time, the y-coordinate of the point follows the sine function. You can use a graphing calculator to plot the unit circle and the sine function simultaneously.

1. Press (MODE). Set the fourth line to parametric mode **PAR** and the sixth line to simultaneous mode **SIMUL**.

Technology *Tip*

When you are in parametric mode, pressing (X, T, θ, n) will return a T.

2. In parametric mode, you can enter a separate equation for each of x and y in terms of a third parameter. The calculator assigns the variable T to the third parameter. The **SIMUL** mode will plot the two graphs at the same time, rather than one after the other. Press (Y=). Notice that the list looks somewhat different from what you are used to. Enter the expression cos(T) for **X1T** and sin(T) for **Y1T**.

3. **Reflect** Compare these expressions to the coordinates of a point on the unit circle.

4. Plot the unit circle and the sine function on the same set of axes. The unit circle has a radius of 1 and the sine function needs an interval of 0° to 360° for one cycle. These scales are not compatible. To compensate, adjust the scale for the sine function by dividing by 60. This allows you to use a window that can accommodate both graphs. Enter T/60 for **X2T** and sin(T) for **Y2T**.

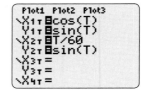

5. Press (WINDOW). The window variables will also look a little different from what you are used to. Set the T interval from 0 to 360 with a scale of 1, the X interval from −2 to 8 with a scale of 1, and the Y interval from −3 to 3 with a scale of 1.

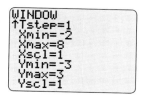

6. Press (GRAPH). Watch how the unit circle and the sine function are drawn in step with each other. **Note:** Keep in mind that the scales are different for the two graphs so that you can display them on the same screen. For the unit circle, each mark on the *x*-axis represents 1 unit. For the sine function, each mark on the *x*-axis represents 60°.

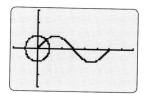

7. Reflect The instructions direct you to operate the graphing calculator in a mode that is probably new to you. Review each step to ensure that you understand what is being done in that step. Explain the role of T in the functions being graphed.

8. Modify steps 1 to 6 to plot the unit circle along with the cosine curve. What changes do you need to make? Explain why these changes are necessary.

Extend

9. Suppose that you want to plot the unit circle along with the tangent, cosecant, secant, and cotangent curves, one at a time.

   a) Explain which of steps 1 to 6 need to be changed and which do not.

   b) Make the changes that you identified in part a). Then, plot the four graphs.

> **Technology Tip**
>
> If you want to watch the graphs be drawn again, you cannot just press (QUIT) and then press (GRAPH). The graphing calculator remembers the last graph that you asked for, and will just display it, provided that you have not made any changes that affect the graph. There are several ways to get around this feature. One is to select **PlotsOn** from the **STATPLOT** menu and then select **PlotsOff**. When you press (GRAPH), the unit circle and sine function will be drawn again.

5.3

Investigate Transformations of Sine and Cosine Functions

Many real-world processes can be modelled with sinusoidal functions. However, the basic sine function usually requires one or more transformations to fit the parameters of the process. One example is the position of the sun above the horizon north of the Arctic Circle in summer. Because the sun does not set during this time, there is no negative value for its position relative to the horizon. As a result, the basic sine function must be adjusted so that the range has no negative values.

In this section, you will learn how to transform the sine and cosine functions so that you can use them as models for real-world applications later in the chapter.

Tools

- graphing calculator

Optional

- graphing software

Investigate

How can you investigate transformations of sine and cosine functions using technology?

A: Graph $y = a \sin x$

1. **a)** Use a graphing calculator or graphing software to graph $y = \sin x$ and $y = 2 \sin x$ on the same set of axes, from $x = 0°$ to $x = 360°$.

   b) How are the graphs similar? How are they different?

2. **a)** Add the graph of $y = 3 \sin x$ to the same set of axes.

   b) What is the effect of multiplying the sine function by a constant factor?

3. **a)** Hide the graphs of $y = 2 \sin x$ and $y = 3 \sin x$. Predict the shape of the graph of $y = \frac{1}{2} \sin x$. Justify your prediction.

   b) Graph $y = \frac{1}{2} \sin x$ and compare the graph to the graph of $y = \sin x$. Was your prediction correct?

4. **a)** Hide the graph of $y = \frac{1}{2} \sin x$. Predict the shape of the graph of $y = -\sin x$. Justify your prediction.

   b) Graph $y = -\sin x$ and compare the graph to the graph of $y = \sin x$. Was your prediction correct?

   c) Predict the shape of the graph of $y = -2 \sin x$. Verify your prediction by graphing.

5. Reflect Consider the transformation of the sine function that results from multiplying the function by a factor a: $y = a \sin x$. Describe the transformation under the following conditions.

a) $a > 1$ **b)** $0 < a < 1$

c) $a < -1$ **d)** $-1 < a < 0$

B: Graph $y = \sin kx$

1. a) Graph the functions $y = \sin x$ and $y = \sin 2x$ on the same set of axes from $x = 0°$ to $x = 360°$.

b) How are the graphs similar? How are they different?

c) How are the periods related?

2. a) Hide the graph of $y = \sin 2x$. Predict the period of the graph of $y = \sin 3x$.

b) Graph $y = \sin 3x$ to verify your prediction.

3. a) Hide the graph of $y = \sin 3x$. Predict the period of the graph of
$y = \sin \frac{1}{2}x$.

b) Graph $y = \sin \frac{1}{2}x$ to verify your prediction. You may need to
adjust your window to accommodate one full cycle of $y = \sin \frac{1}{2}x$.

4. Reflect Consider the transformation of the sine function that results from multiplying the variable x by a factor k: $y = \sin kx$.

a) How is the period of $y = \sin kx$ related to the period of $y = \sin x$?

b) Describe the transformation that occurs when $k > 1$ and when
$0 < k < 1$.

c) Describe the transformation that occurs when $k < -1$ and when
$-1 < k < 0$. Graph to check your conjectures.

C: Graph $y = \sin (x - d)$

1 a) Graph the functions $y = \sin x$ and $y = \sin (x - 30°)$ on the same
set of axes from $x = 0°$ to $x = 360°$.

b) How are the graphs similar? How are they different?

2. a) Predict what the graph of $y = \sin (x - 60°)$ will look like. Justify
your prediction.

b) Graph $y = \sin (x - 60°)$ to verify your prediction.

3. a) Predict what the graph of $y = \sin (x + 30°)$ will look like. Justify
your prediction.

b) Graph $y = \sin (x + 30°)$ to verify your prediction.

4. Reflect Consider the transformation of the sine function that results from subtracting a parameter d from the variable x: $y = \sin (x - d)$. Describe the transformation under the following conditions.

a) $d > 0$ **b)** $d < 0$

D: Graph $y = \sin x + c$

1. a) Graph the functions $y = \sin x$ and $y = \sin x + 1$ on the same set of axes from $x = 0°$ to $x = 360°$.

   b) How are the graphs similar? How are they different?

2. a) Predict what the graph of $y = \sin x - 1$ will look like. Justify your prediction.

   b) Graph $y = \sin x - 1$ to verify your prediction.

3. a) Predict what the graph of $y = \sin x + 3$ will look like. Justify your prediction.

   b) Graph $y = \sin x + 3$ to verify your prediction. You may need to adjust your window variables to display the graph properly.

4. **Reflect** Consider the transformation of the sine function that results from adding a parameter c to the function: $y = \sin x + c$. Describe the transformation under the following conditions.

   a) $c > 0$ b) $c < 0$

5. **Reflect** Review your reflections from parts A, B, C, and D. Copy and complete a table similar to the one shown to summarize the effect that the value of each of these factors has on the form of the graph. The first line of the table is filled in for you.

Factor	Value	Effect
	$a > 1$	amplitude is greater than 1
a	$0 < a < 1$	
	$-1 < a < 0$	
	$a < -1$	
	$k > 1$	
k	$0 < k < 1$	
	$-1 < k < 0$	
	$k < -1$	
d	$d > 0$	
	$d < 0$	
c	$c > 0$	
	$c < 0$	

Example 1

Functions of the Form $y = a \sin kx$

Consider the function $y = 3 \sin 4x$.

   a) What is the amplitude?

   b) What is the period?

   c) How many cycles will occur between $x = 0°$ and $x = 360°$?

   d) Graph the function from $x = 0°$ to $x = 360°$.

Solution

Compare $y = 3 \sin 4x$ to $y = a \sin kx$.

a) $a = 3$; the y-values of the sine function are multiplied by a factor of 3. The amplitude is 3 units.

b) $k = 4$; to determine the period, divide $360°$ by k: $\dfrac{360°}{4} = 90°$.

The period is $90°$.

c) Since the period is $90°$ and $k = 4$, four cycles will occur between $0°$ and $360°$.

d)

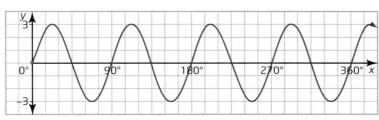

Example 2

Functions of the Form $y = a \sin (x - d) + c$

Consider the function $y = \sin (x - 45°) + 2$.

a) What is the amplitude?

b) What is the period?

c) Describe the phase shift, or horizontal translation.

d) Describe the vertical shift, or vertical translation.

e) Graph the function from $x = 0°$ to $x = 720°$.

Solution

Compare $y = \sin (x - 45°) + 2$ to $y = a \sin (x - d) + c$.

a) $a = 1$; the amplitude of the function is 1.

b) $k = 1$; the period of the function is $360°$.

c) $d = 45°$; the phase shift is $45°$ to the right.

d) $c = 2$; the vertical shift is 2 units up.

e)

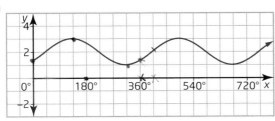

Example 3

Functions of the Form $y = a \sin [k(x - d)] + c$

Consider the function $y = -2 \sin [3(x + 30°)] - 1$.

a) What is the amplitude?

b) What is the period?

c) Describe the phase shift.

d) Describe the vertical shift.

e) Graph the function from $x = 0°$ to $x = 360°$.

Solution

Compare $y = -2 \sin [3(x + 30°)] - 1$ to $y = a \sin [k(x - d)] + c$.

a) $a = -2$; the amplitude of the function is 2.

b) $k = 3$; the period of the function is $\dfrac{360°}{3} = 120°$.

The value of *d* is negative. This indicates a horizontal translation to the left.

c) $d = -30°$; the phase shift is 30° to the left.

d) $c = -1$; the vertical shift is 1 unit down.

e)

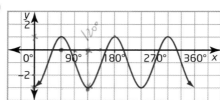

Communicate Your Understanding

C1 Consider the graph of $y = 5 \sin 2x + c$. What values of c are required so that the graph has only positive y-values? Explain how you found your answer.

C2 Compare the following graphs. Explain how a horizontal reflection can be used to transform graph a) into graph b).

a)

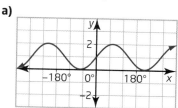

b)

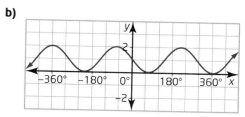

C3 Consider the graphs of $y = \sin x$ and $y = \cos x$. Determine two ways in which the graph of the cosine function can be expressed as a horizontal translation of the sine function.

A Practise

For help with questions 1 to 3, refer to Example 1.

1. Sketch one cycle for each function. Include an appropriate scale on each axis. State the vertical stretch and amplitude of the function.

a) $y = 4 \sin x$

b) $y = \frac{3}{2} \sin x$

c) $y = -5 \sin x$

d) $y = -\frac{5}{4} \sin x$

2. Sketch one cycle for each function. Include an appropriate scale on each axis. State the vertical stretch and then the amplitude of the function.

a) $y = 3 \cos x$

b) $y = \frac{1}{2} \cos x$

c) $y = -2 \cos x$

d) $y = -\frac{2}{3} \cos x$

3. Determine the horizontal stretch and the period of each function.

a) $y = 2 \sin 5x$

b) $y = -3 \sin \frac{2}{3}x$

c) $y = 8 \sin \frac{1}{6}x$

d) $y = \frac{1}{2} \sin \frac{1}{2}x$

e) $y = 4 \cos x$

f) $y = -2 \cos 8x$

g) $y = \frac{1}{2} \cos 12x$

h) $y = -\frac{5}{4} \cos \frac{3}{4}x$

For help with Questions 4 to 8, refer to Examples 2 and 3.

4. Write two equations, one in the form $y = a \sin kx$ and one in the form $y = a \cos [k(x - d)]$, to match each graph.

a)

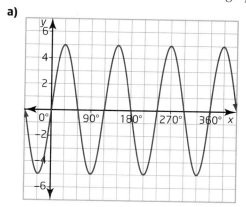

b)

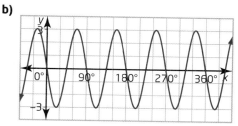

5. Write two equations, one in the form $y = a \cos kx$ and one in the form $y = a \sin [k(x - d)]$, to match each graph.

a)

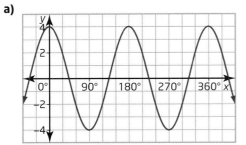

b)

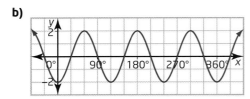

6. Determine the phase shift and the vertical shift with respect to $y = \sin x$ for each function.

a) $y = \sin (x - 50°) + 3$

b) $y = 2 \sin (x + 45°) - 1$

c) $y = -5 \sin (x - 25°) + 4$

d) $y = 3 \sin [2(x + 60°)] - 2$

7. Determine the phase shift and the vertical shift with respect to $y = \cos x$ for each function.

a) $y = \cos (x + 30°)$

b) $y = 4 \cos (x - 32°) + 6$

c) $y = -9 \cos (x + 120°) - 5$

d) $y = 12 \cos [5(x - 150°)] + 7$

8. a) State the phase shift and the vertical shift of each sinusoidal function.

i) $y = \sin (x + 100°) + 1$

ii) $y = 2 \sin x + 3$

iii) $y = \sin (x + 45°) - 2$

iv) $y = 3 \sin (x - 120°) + 2$

b) Sketch two cycles of the graph of each function. Include an appropriate scale on each axis.

9. a) State the vertical shift and the amplitude of each sinusoidal function.

i) $y = \cos (x - 70°)$

ii) $y = 3 \cos x - 1$

iii) $y = \cos (x + 35°) + 2$

iv) $y = 4 \cos (x - 120°) - 3$

b) Sketch two cycles of the graph of each function. Include an appropriate scale on each axis.

B Connect and Apply

10. The vertical position, y, in centimetres, of a point on the rim of the wheel of a stationary exercise bicycle after time, t, in seconds, can be modelled by the equation $y = 40 \sin 720t + 50$.

a) What is the lowest vertical position that the point reaches?

b) What is the highest vertical position that the point reaches?

c) What is the period of rotation of the wheel, in seconds?

d) Suppose that the period of the rotation of the wheel triples. How does the equation change? Justify your answer.

11. a) Determine the amplitude, the period, the phase shift, and the vertical shift of each function.

i) $y = 5 \sin [4(x + 60°)] - 2$

ii) $y = 2 \cos [2(x + 150°)] - 5$

iii) $y = \frac{1}{2} \sin \left[\frac{1}{2}(x - 60°) \right] + 1$

iv) $y = 0.8 \cos [3.6(x - 40°)] - 0.4$

b) **Use Technology** Graph each function using technology. Compare the graph to the characteristics you expected.

12. The theory of biorhythms seeks to explain why people have "good" days and "bad" days. According to the theory, three periodic functions begin at birth and stay with you throughout your life. The physical cycle has a period of 23 days, the emotional cycle has a period of 28 days, and the intellectual cycle has a period of 33 days. As a person moves through life, the cycles lose phase with each other, but return now and then to the same phase, such that all three maximum values coincide. Whenever a rhythm crosses the time axis, a critical day occurs.

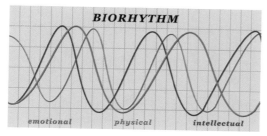

BIORHYTHM

emotional   physical   intellectual

a) Assuming an amplitude of 1, model each biorhythm—physical, emotional, and intellectual—with a sine function that begins at birth.

b) Use grid paper or technology to plot all three functions on the same set of axes for the first 150 days of life.

c) Identify good days (when two or more biorhythms reach a maximum or close to a maximum).

d) Identify bad days (when two or more biorhythms reach a minimum or close to a minimum).

13. Chapter Problem The human ear interprets the amplitude of a sound wave as loudness. Thus, a sound wave modelled by $y = 2 \sin kt$ is louder than a sound wave modelled by $y = \sin kt$. Because the human ear does not operate on a linear scale, the perceived loudness ratio is not actually 2:1. When an instrument is played, the sound wave spreads out in a spherical pattern. The amplitude decreases as the square of the distance. Suppose that a sound wave can be modelled as $y = 64 \sin kt$ at a distance of 1 m from its source. At a distance of 2 m,

$$a = \frac{64}{2^2}$$

$$= 16$$

The modelling equation becomes $y = 16 \sin kt$.

a) Write the modelling equation at a distance of 4 m from the source.

b) Write the modelling equation at a distance of 8 m from the source.

c) How far from the source does the modelling equation become

$$y = \frac{1}{4} \sin kt?$$

14. The graph of $y = \sin x$ is transformed so that it has an amplitude of 4 and x-intercepts that coincide with the minimum values. The period is 360° and the phase shift is 0.

Reasoning and Proving

Representing   Selecting Tools

Problem Solving

Connecting   Reflecting

Communicating

a) Write the equation of the transformed function.

b) What phase shift is needed for the transformed function from part a) to have a y-intercept of 2? Draw a graph to show that your answer is correct.

c) Can the required y-intercept in part b) be achieved by altering the period rather than the phase shift? Justify your answer.

15. a) Write the equation of a transformed sine function that includes at least three transformations. Generate a minimum number of clues about the transformation. Ensure that the clues can be used to determine the transformation.

b) Trade clues with a classmate. Determine the transformations required to match the clues. If more than one answer is possible, explain why.

c) Trade equations and discuss any observations or concerns.

16. a) Write the equation of a transformed cosine function that includes at least three transformations. Do not use the same three transformations you used in question 15. Generate a minimum number of clues about the transformation.

b) Trade clues with a classmate. Determine the transformations required to match the clues. If more than one answer is possible, explain why.

c) Trade equations and discuss any observations or concerns.

✓ **Achievement Check**

17. a) Determine each of the following for the function $y = 6 \cos [5(x + 45°)] - 3$. Justify your answer.

   i) the amplitude

   ii) the period

   iii) the phase shift

   iv) the vertical shift of the function

b) Sketch the function in part a) on grid paper without using a table of values. Explain your reasoning.

C Extend

18. A sine function has half the period of $y = \sin x$. All other parameters of the two functions are the same.

a) Predict the number of points of intersection if the two functions are graphed from $x = 0°$ to $x = 360°$. Justify your prediction.

b) Determine the number of points of intersection if the two functions are graphed from $x = 0°$ to $x = 360°$. Was your prediction correct? If not, explain why.

c) Determine the coordinates of the first point to the right of the origin where the graphs of the two functions intersect.

d) Suppose that the graph is continued to $x = 720°$. How many points of intersection do you expect in the new section of the graph? Justify your thinking.

e) Extend the graph and check your prediction in part d). Was your prediction correct? If not, explain why not.

f) Suppose that the second function had a period of one-third the first. How does your answer to part a) change?

19. Consider the function $y = \tan x$ and its transformation $y = a \tan [k(x - d)] + c$. Use a graphing calculator to investigate the effects of a, k, d, and c on the graph of $y = \tan x$. Write a brief report of your findings.

20. Math Contest The sum of eight consecutive positive integers is 404. What is the sum of the least and greatest numbers in this sequence?

  A 50.5   **B** $2\sqrt{101}$

  C 101   **D** 25.25

21. Math Contest Two circles are tangent to each other. A line segment drawn from the centre, D, of the larger circle is tangent to the smaller circle at A. Another line segment drawn from the centre, B, of the smaller circle is tangent to the larger circle at C. Prove that AD is longer than BC.

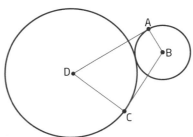

Graphing and Modelling With $y = a \sin [k(x - d)] + c$ and $y = a \cos [k(x - d)] + c$

In order to model a real-world situation using a sine or a cosine function, you must analyse the situation and then transform the amplitude, period, vertical shift, and phase shift accordingly. For example, tides in the ocean can be modelled using a sine function with a period of about 12 h.

In this section, you will learn how to use a graph or a list of properties of the desired function to write a corresponding equation.

Example 1

Determine the Characteristics of a Sinusoidal Function From an Equation

An engineer uses the function $y = 3 \cos [2(x - 5)] + 4$ to model the vertical position, y, in metres, of a rod in a machine x seconds after the machine is started.

a) What are the amplitude, period, phase shift, and vertical shift of the position function?

b) What are the lowest and highest vertical positions that the rod reaches?

c) Use Technology Use technology to graph the function. Check your answers in part b) using the graph.

d) State the domain and range of the original cosine function and the transformed function.

Solution

a) Comparing the given equation $y = 3 \cos [2(x - 5)] + 4$ to the general equation $y = a \cos [k(x - d)] + c$ gives $a = 3$, $k = 2$, $d = 5$, and $c = 4$.

Since $a = 3$, the amplitude is 3 m.

Determine the period.

$$\frac{360}{k} = \frac{360}{2}$$
$$= 180$$

The period is 180 s.

Since $d = 5$, the phase shift is 5 s to the right.

Since $c = 4$, the vertical shift is 4 m upward.

b) The least value of the basic cosine function is -1. Since the amplitude is 3, this stretches down to -3. The vertical shift of 4 m upward pushes this to 1. So, the lowest vertical position is 1 m.

The greatest value of the basic cosine function is 1. Since the amplitude is 3, this stretches up to 3. The vertical shift of 4 upward pushes this to 7. The highest vertical position is 7 m.

c) Method 1: Use a Graphing Calculator

The graph is shown. Press $\boxed{\text{2nd}}$ [CALC]. Use **4:maximum** to determine the maximum value and **3:minimum** to determine the minimum value.

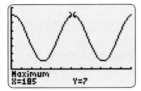 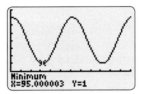

Method 2: Use a TI-Nspire™ CAS Graphing Calculator

Refer to the instructions for graphing in Section 5.2. Graph the function. Plot a point on the function. Grab the point and drag it toward the maximum. When you reach the maximum, the word "maximum" will appear, along with the coordinates.

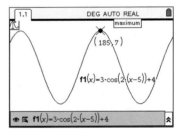

Similarly, you can drag the point toward the minimum. When you have reached the minimum, the word "minimum" will appear, along with the coordinates.

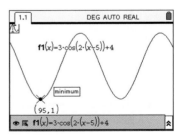

d) For the function $y = \cos x$, the domain is $\{x \in \mathbb{R}\}$.

The range is $\{y \in \mathbb{R}, -1 \le y \le 1\}$.

For the function $y = 3 \cos [2(x - 5)] + 4$, the domain is $\{x \in \mathbb{R}\}$.

The range is $\{y \in \mathbb{R}, 1 \le y \le 7\}$.

Example 2

Sketch a Graph

a) Describe the transformations that must be applied to the graph of $f(x) = \sin x$ to obtain the graph of $g(x) = 4 \sin 3x + 1$. Apply these transformations to sketch the graph of $g(x)$.

b) State the domain and range of $f(x)$ and $g(x)$.

c) Modify the equation for $g(x)$ to include a phase shift of 30° to the right. Call this function $h(x)$. Apply the phase shift to the graph of $g(x)$ and transform it to $h(x)$.

Solution

a) Start with the graph of $f(x) = \sin x$, curve i).

Apply the amplitude of 4 to get curve ii).

Apply the vertical shift of 1 unit upward to get curve iii). You may include a horizontal reference line at $y = 1$ to help you.

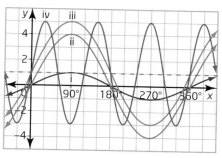

Apply the horizontal compression by a factor of 3 to get curve iv).

b) For the function $f(x) = \sin x$, the domain is $\{x \in \mathbb{R}\}$. The range is $\{y \in \mathbb{R}, -1 \leq y \leq 1\}$. For the function $g(x) = 4 \sin 3x + 1$, the domain is $\{x \in \mathbb{R}\}$. The range is $\{y \in \mathbb{R}, -3 \leq y \leq 5\}$.

c) The equation with a phase shift of 30° to the right is $h(x) = 4 \sin [3(x - 30°)] + 1$. The graphs of $g(x)$ and $h(x)$ are shown.

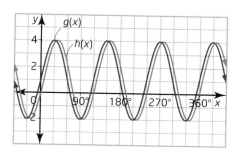

When graphing a transformed sine or cosine function, follow these steps:

1. Sketch the basic function.

2. Apply the vertical stretch or compression to achieve the desired amplitude.

3. Apply the vertical shift. Use a horizontal reference line to help you.

4. Apply the horizontal stretch or compression to achieve the desired period.

5. Apply the phase shift.

Example 3

Represent a Sinusoidal Function Given Its Properties

a) A sinusoidal function has an amplitude of 3 units, a period of 180°, and a maximum at (0, 5). Represent the function with an equation in two different ways.

b) Use grid paper or a graphing calculator to verify that your two models represent the same graph.

Solution

a) Method 1: Use a Cosine Function

The amplitude is 3, so $a = 3$.

The period is 180°.

$$\frac{360°}{k} = 180°$$

$$k = 2$$

A maximum occurs at (0, 5). When $x = 0$, cos $x = 1$, which is its maximum value. The amplitude has already placed the maximum at 3. The additional vertical shift required is upward 2 units to 5. Therefore, $c = 2$.

The function can be modelled by the equation $f(x) = 3 \cos 2x + 2$.

Method 2: Use a Sine Function

Use the same values of a, k, and c as in Method 1. Then, apply the appropriate phase shift to bring the maximum to (0, 5).

The maximum of the sine function normally occurs at $x = 90°$. However, the period in this case is 180°, so the maximum occurs at $\frac{90°}{2} = 45°$. To move the maximum to the y-axis, a phase shift of 45° to the left is required.

The sine function is $g(x) = 3 \sin [2(x + 45°)] + 2$.

b) Enter the cosine model in **Y1** and the sine model in **Y2**. Change the line style for **Y2** to heavy. When you press (GRAPH), the cosine model will be drawn first. Then, the sine model will be drawn. You can pause the graphing process by pressing (ENTER) while the graph is being drawn. Press (ENTER) again to resume.

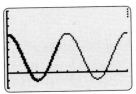

Example 4

Determine a Sinusoidal Function Given a Graph

Determine the equation of a
sinusoidal function that represents
the graph. Check your equation using
a graphing calculator.

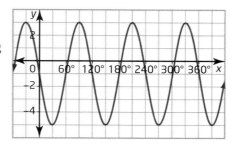

Solution

From the graph, the maximum value
of y is 3 and the minimum value is
-5.

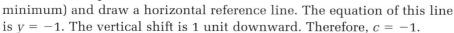

$$a = \frac{3 - (-5)}{2}$$

$$= 4$$

The amplitude is 4.

Count down 4 units from the
maximum (or up 4 units from the
minimum) and draw a horizontal reference line. The equation of this line
is $y = -1$. The vertical shift is 1 unit downward. Therefore, $c = -1$.

Use either a sine function or a cosine function to construct the model.
For this example, use a sine function. Determine the start of the first sine
wave to the right of the y-axis, moving along the horizontal reference
line. This occurs at $x = 60°$. The phase shift is 60° to the right. Therefore,
$d = 60°$.

Continue along the reference line to determine the end of the first cycle.
This occurs at $x = 180°$. The period is $180° - 60° = 120°$.

$$\frac{360°}{k} = 120°$$

$$k = 3$$

Substitute the parameters $a = 4$, $k = 3$, $d = 60°$, and $c = -1$ into the
general equation $y = a \sin [k(x - d)] + c$.

$y = 4 \sin [3(x - 60°)] - 1$.

Check using a graphing calculator. The graph on the calculator matches
the given graph.

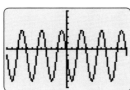
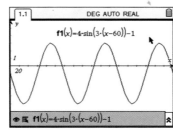

Key Concepts

- The amplitude, period, phase shift, and vertical shift of sinusoidal functions can be determined when the equations are given in the form
  $f(x) = a \sin [k(x - d)] + c$ or $f(x) = a \cos [k(x - d)] + c$.

- The domain of a sinusoidal function is $\{x \in \mathbb{R}\}$. The range extends from the minimum value to the maximum value of the function. Any cycle can be used to determine the minimum and the maximum.

- Transformations can be used to adjust the basic sine and cosine functions to match a given amplitude, period, phase shift, and vertical shift.

- The equation of a sinusoidal function can be determined given its properties.

- The equation of a sinusoidal function can be determined given its graph.

Communicate Your Understanding

C1 The equation of a sine function is $y = 5 \sin (3x - 60°) + 2$. Explain why the phase shift is not 60°. Determine the phase shift.

C2 The equation of a cosine function is $y = \cos [2(x + 60°)]$.

a) Start with the basic cosine function. Make a rough sketch of the effect of applying the horizontal compression first and then make a second sketch of the effect of applying the phase shift.

b) Start with the basic cosine function. Make a rough sketch of the effect of applying the phase shift first and then make a second sketch of the effect of applying the horizontal compression.

c) Compare the graphs in parts a) and b). In particular, compare the location of the first maximum to the left of the y-axis. Explain any differences.

d) Which describes the correct procedure, part a) or part b)? Justify your answer. Use a graphing calculator to check your prediction.

C3 In Example 3, the desired function can be represented using either a sine function or a cosine function. Is this always the case? Justify your answer.

A Practise

For help with questions 1 and 2, refer to Example 1.

1. Determine the amplitude, the period, the phase shift, and the vertical shift of each function with respect to $y = \sin x$.

a) $y = 5 \sin [4(x - 25°)] + 3$

b) $y = -2 \sin [18(x + 40°)] - 5$

c) $y = 3 \sin [120(x - 30°)] + 2$

d) $y = \frac{3}{4} \sin \left[\frac{2}{3}(x - 60°) \right] + \frac{1}{2}$

2. Determine the amplitude, the period, the phase shift, and the vertical shift of each function with respect to $y = \cos x$.

a) $y = -3 \cos [5(x - 45°)] + 4$

b) $y = 2 \cos [24(x + 80°)] - 1$

c) $y = 3 \cos [72(x - 10°)] + 3$

d) $y = \frac{5}{2} \cos \left[\frac{3}{4}(x - 40°) \right] + \frac{1}{2}$

For help with questions 3 and 4, refer to Example 2.

3. a) Describe the transformations that must be applied to the graph of $f(x) = \sin x$ to obtain the graph of $g(x) = 3 \sin 2x - 1$. Apply each transformation, one step at a time, to sketch the graph of $g(x)$.

b) State the domain and range of $f(x)$ and $g(x)$.

c) Modify the equation for $g(x)$ to include a phase shift of 60° to the left. Call this function $h(x)$. Apply the phase shift to the graph of $g(x)$ and transform it to $h(x)$.

4. a) Transform the graph of $f(x) = \cos x$ to $g(x) = 4 \cos 3x - 2$ by applying transformations to the graph one step at a time.

b) State the domain and range of $f(x)$ and $g(x)$.

c) Modify the equation for $g(x)$ to include a phase shift of 60° to the right. Call this function $h(x)$. Apply the phase shift to the graph of $g(x)$ and transform it to $h(x)$.

For help with questions 5 and 6, refer to Example 3.

5. A sinusoidal function has an amplitude of 5 units, a period of 120°, and a maximum at (0, 3).

a) Represent the function with an equation using a sine function.

b) Represent the function with an equation using a cosine function.

6. A sinusoidal function has an amplitude of $\frac{1}{2}$ units, a period of 720°, and a maximum at $\left(0, \frac{3}{2}\right)$.

a) Represent the function with an equation using a sine function.

b) Represent the function with an equation using a cosine function.

For help with question 7, refer to Example 4.

7. a) Determine the equation of a cosine function to represent the graph in Example 4.

b) Check your equation using a graphing calculator.

B **Connect and Apply**

8. Consider the function $f(x) = 10 \sin (x - 45°) + 10$.

a) Determine the amplitude, the period, the phase shift, and the vertical shift of the function with respect to $y = \sin x$.

b) What are the maximum and minimum values of the function?

c) Determine the first three x-intercepts to the right of the origin.

d) Determine the y-intercept of the function.

9. Consider the function $g(x) = 5 \cos [2(x - 30°)]$.

a) Determine the amplitude, the period, the phase shift, and the vertical shift of the function with respect to $y = \cos x$.

b) What are the maximum and minimum values of the function?

c) Determine the first three x-intercepts to the right of the origin.

d) Determine the y-intercept of the function.

10. Use Technology Use a graphing calculator or graphing software to verify your answers to questions 8 and 9.

11. a) Transform the graph of $f(x) = \sin x$ to $g(x) = 5 \sin [6(x - 120°)] - 4$. Show each step in the transformation.

b) State the domain and range of $f(x)$ and $g(x)$.

c) **Use Technology** Use a graphing calculator to check your final graph.

12. a) Transform the graph of $f(x) = \cos x$ to $g(x) = 6 \cos [5(x + 60°)] + 2$. Show each step in the transformation.

b) State the domain and range of $f(x)$ and $g(x)$.

c) Use Technology Use a graphing calculator to check your final graph.

13. a) Represent the graph of $f(x) = 2 \sin [3(x - 30°)]$ with an equation using a cosine function.

b) Use Technology Use a graphing calculator to check your graph.

14. a) Determine the equation of a sine function that represents the graph shown. Check your equation using a graphing calculator.

Reasoning and Proving

Representing · Selecting Tools

Problem Solving

Connecting · Reflecting

Communicating

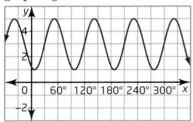

b) Use Technology Determine the equation of a cosine function that represents the graph. Check your equation using a graphing calculator.

15. Chapter Problem Suppose that two trumpet players play the same note. Does the result sound like one trumpet playing twice as loud or like two trumpets playing together? You have probably noticed that two instruments of the same kind playing the same note always sound like two instruments, and not like one instrument played louder. The same effect occurs for people singing. The reason is that the two notes will always differ by a phase shift. To see how this works, let the equation $y = \sin x$ represent one instrument playing a note.

a) If the second instrument could play perfectly in phase with the first, the two sounds would be represented by

$$y = \sin x + \sin x$$
$$= 2 \sin x$$

Graph this representation and $y = \sin x$ on the same set of axes. How are the two related?

b) In reality, the two instruments will be out of phase. Pick an arbitrary phase difference of 90°. The function that represents the two instruments playing together is $y = \sin x + \sin (x - 90°)$. Graph this function. How does it compare to $y = 2 \sin x$?

c) A music synthesizer can make electronic circuits that simulate instruments playing in phase with each other. This is generally not very interesting, since the sound is the same as a single instrument playing louder. Electronic engineers purposely change the phase of each instrument to achieve a "chorus" effect of several instruments playing together. Choose different phase shifts and write a function that represents four instruments playing together. Graph the function and describe the graph.

Connections

Robert Moog invented the electronic synthesizer in 1964. Although other electronic instruments existed before this time, Moog was the first to control the electronic sounds using a piano-style keyboard. This allowed musicians to make use of the new technology without first having to learn new musical skills. Visit the *Functions 11* page on the McGraw-Hill Ryerson Web site and follow the links to Chapter 5 to find out more about the Moog synthesizer.

16. At the end of a dock, high tide of 14 m is recorded at 9:00 a.m. Low tide of 6 m is recorded at 3:00 p.m. A sinusoidal function can model the water depth versus time.

Reasoning and Proving

Representing — Selecting Tools

Problem Solving

Connecting — Reflecting

Communicating

a) Construct a model for the water depth using a cosine function, where time is measured in hours past high tide.

b) Construct a model for the water depth using a sine function, where time is measured in hours past high tide.

c) Construct a model for the water depth using a sine function, where time is measured in hours past low tide.

d) Construct a model for the water depth using a cosine function, where time is measured in hours past low tide.

e) Compare your models. Which is the simplest representation if time is referenced to high tide? low tide? Explain why there is a difference.

✓ Achievement Check

17. a) Describe the transformations that must be applied to the graph of $f(x) = \sin x$ to obtain the graph of $g(x) = 2 \sin [4(x - 40°)] - 3$.

b) Sketch the graph of $g(x)$ by applying the transformations described in part a).

c) State the domain and range of $g(x)$. Justify your answer.

C Extend

18. Suppose that you are given the coordinates, (p, q), of a point. Can you always determine a value of a such that the graph of $y = a \sin x$ will pass through the point? If so, explain why, providing a diagram. If not, explain why, and indicate the least amount of information that needs to be added.

19. Consider the relation $y = \sqrt{\sin x}$.

a) Sketch the graph of the function $y = \sin x$ over two cycles.

b) Use the graph from part a) to sketch a prediction for the shape of the graph of $y = \sqrt{\sin x}$.

c) Use technology or grid paper and a table of values to check your prediction. Resolve any differences.

d) How do you think the graph of $y = \sqrt{\sin x + 1}$ will differ from the graph of $y = \sqrt{\sin x}$?

e) Graph $y = \sqrt{\sin x + 1}$ and compare it to your prediction. Resolve any differences.

20. a) Determine the minimum number of transformations that can be applied to $y = \sin x$ such that the maximum values of the transformed function coincide with the x-intercepts of $y = \cos x$. If this is not possible, explain why, including a diagram.

b) Determine the minimum number of transformations that can be applied to $y = \sin x$ such that the maximum values of the transformed function coincide with the x-intercepts of $y = \tan x$. If this is not possible, explain why, including a diagram.

21. Math Contest Given the function $y = 3 \sin [2(x - 30°)]$, find the smallest positive value for x that gives a maximum value for y.

22. Math Contest The period of $y = |4 \cos (3x - 30°)|$ is

A 360°   **B** 90°   **C** 60°   **D** 120°

23. Math Contest When a number is divided by 21, the remainder is 17. What is the remainder when the number is divided by 7?

A 1   **B** 3   **C** 5   **D** 6

5.5

Data Collecting and Modelling

One of the real-world applications of sinusoidal models is the motion of a pendulum. A Foucault pendulum is used to measure the rotation of Earth. As Earth turns, the axis of swing of the pendulum rotates with it.

In this section, you will learn to collect data that can be modelled with sinusoidal functions and then construct a suitable model using transformations.

Tools

- graphing calculator
- motion sensor
- pendulum

Technology

These instructions assume the use of a CBR™ motion sensor with a TI-83 Plus or TI-84 Plus graphing calculator. If you are using different technology, refer to the manual.

Technology Tip

The motion sensor cannot measure distances less than about 0.5 m. Ensure that your pendulum is never closer than this. The maximum distance that it can measure is about 4 m, but your pendulum may be too small a target to return a usable signal from this distance.

Investigate

How can you collect data on the motion of a pendulum and use the data to construct a sinusoidal model?

1. Set up a pendulum. Use a large object as the bob (at least the size of a basketball) so it can be detected by the motion sensor. Use a string or rope long enough to give the pendulum a period of more than 1 s.

2. **a)** Connect the CBR™ motion sensor to the graphing calculator using the cable provided.

   b) Press (APPS) and select **2:CBL/CBR**. Note that the application on your calculator may have a different number.

   c) At the **CBL/CBR** screen, press (ENTER). Select **3:Ranger** and press (ENTER). Note that the Ranger program on your calculator may have a different number.

   d) Select **1:SETUP/SAMPLE** from the main menu. Move the cursor up to **START NOW**. Press (ENTER).

3. Start the pendulum swinging. Point the motion sensor at the bob of the pendulum such that the bob swings directly toward and away from the sensor. Press (ENTER) and collect data for 15 s. At the end of the collection time, a graph of distance versus time is shown.

4. **Reflect** Inspect the graph. Does it appear sinusoidal? Are there any spikes or other sudden jumps that indicate a misalignment of the pendulum and motion sensor during the data collection process? If so, adjust your physical setup. Press (ENTER) and select **REPEAT SAMPLE**. Continue refining your experimental arrangement until you have a smooth graph.

5. a) Press (ENTER) and select **SHOW PLOT**. Confirm that the graph is a smooth function that appears sinusoidal.

b) Press (ENTER) and select **QUIT**. The time data will be stored in list **L1** and the distance data will be stored in list **L2**.

6. a) Press (GRAPH) and then (TRACE). Use the cursor keys to determine the maximum and minimum of your graph. Determine the amplitude, a.

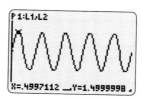

b) Add the amplitude to the minimum to determine the vertical shift, c. Use the **Y=** editor to plot a horizontal reference line using this value. Alternatively, you can use the **DRAW** menu and select **3:Horizontal**.

c) Return to the graph. Use the reference line to help you trace the start of the first sine wave to the right of the vertical axis. Read the phase shift, d.

d) Continue to the end of the first cycle. Use the start and end to determine the period. Once you have the period, determine the value of k.

Connections

For help in determining an equation given a graph, refer to Example 4 in Section 5.4.

7. a) Use the values of a, c, d, and k to write the equation to model the motion of the pendulum.

b) Enter this equation using the **Y=** editor. Plot the curve and verify that it closely matches the graph drawn by the Ranger software. If there are major discrepancies, check your calculations.

8. Reflect Start the pendulum swinging and estimate the amplitude and period. Review the amplitude and period of the pendulum that you calculated in parts a) and d) of step 6. Compare the two sets of values.

9. a) Predict the effect that each of the following will have on your graph. Consider each one separately.

i) the length of the pendulum is shortened

ii) the amplitude is increased

b) Check your predictions in part a) using the pendulum and the motion sensor.

Example 1

Retrieve Data from Statistics Canada

Using data from Statistics Canada, determine if there is a period of time over which changes in the population of Canadians aged 20 to 24 can be modelled using a sinusoidal function.

Solution

Visit www.statcan.gc.ca/edu/edu05_0018c-eng.htm.

Select **Sinusoidal**.

Select **table 051-0001**.

Under **Geography**, select **Canada**.

Under **Sex**, select **Both sexes**.

Under **Age group**, select **20 to 24 years**.

Set the reference period to **from 1976 to 2005**.

Select **Retrieve as individual Time Series**. If you plan to analyse the data with a spreadsheet or other software, select the downloadable file format as **CSV (comma-separated values)**, with **Time as rows**.

Otherwise, you can select the screen output as an HTML table, with **Time as rows**. Select **Retrieve Now**. The table is shown.

Population of Canada, Aged 20 to 24 Years, Both Sexes, By Year					
Year	Population	Year	Population	Year	Population
1976	2 253 367	1986	2 446 250	1996	2 002 036
1977	2 300 910	1987	2 363 227	1997	2 008 307
1978	2 339 362	1988	2 257 415	1998	2 014 301
1979	2 375 197	1989	2 185 706	1999	2 039 468
1980	2 424 484	1990	2 124 363	2000	2 069 868
1981	2 477 137	1991	2 088 165	2001	2 110 324
1982	2 494 358	1992	2 070 089	2002	2 150 370
1983	2 507 401	1993	2 047 334	2003	2 190 876
1984	2 514 313	1994	2 025 846	2004	2 224 652
1985	2 498 510	1995	2 009 474	2005	2 243 341

Source: Statistics Canada

Graph the data.

The population of people in Canada aged 20 to 24 from 1976 to 2005 appears to follow a sinusoidal model.

Population Aged 20 to 24 in Canada, 1976 to 2005

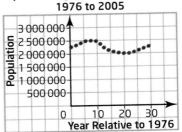

Example 2

Make Predictions

The relationship between the height above the ground of a person riding a Ferris wheel and time can be modelled using a sinusoidal function.

a) Describe the effect on this function if the platform from which the person enters the ride is raised by 1 m.

b) Describe the effect on this function if the Ferris wheel turns twice as fast.

Solution

a) Because the platform is not at the lowest point of the wheel, a phase shift is introduced. The rider does not reach the lowest point until the wheel turns through the phase shift. If the platform used to enter the ride is raised by 1 m, the phase shift increases and it takes longer for the rider to reach the lowest point in the ride. The graph will shift to the right.

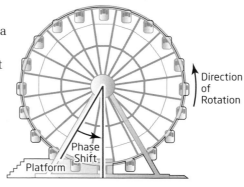

b) If the wheel turns twice as fast, the period will be half as long.

The graph will be compressed horizontally by a factor of $\frac{1}{2}$.

Example 3

Use a Sinusoidal Model to Determine Values

The height, h, in metres, above the ground of a rider on a Ferris wheel after t seconds can be modelled by the sine function $h(t) = 10 \sin [3(t - 30)] + 12$.

a) Graph the function using graphing technology.

b) Determine each of the following.

   i) the maximum and minimum heights of the rider above the ground

   ii) the height of the rider above the ground after 30 s

   iii) the time required for the Ferris wheel to complete one revolution

Solution

a)

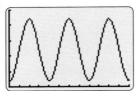 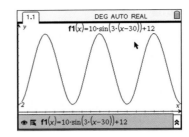

b) The values can be determined either by calculation or by using technology.

Method 1: Use the Equation

i) The amplitude is 10 m and the vertical shift is 12 m. Therefore, the maximum height of the rider above the ground is 10 m + 12 m, or 22 m. The minimum height is −10 m + 12 m, or 2 m.

ii) To determine the height of the rider above the ground after 30 s, substitute 30 for t in the equation.

$$h(t) = 10 \sin [3(t - 30)] + 12$$
$$= 10 \sin [3(30 - 30)] + 12$$
$$= 10 \sin 0 + 12$$
$$= 0 + 12$$
$$= 12$$

The height of the rider above the ground after 30 s is 12 m.

iii) The value of k is 3.

$$\frac{360}{k} = \frac{360}{3}$$
$$k = 120$$

The period is 120 s. The time required for the Ferris wheel to complete one revolution is 120 s.

Method 2: Use the Graph

i) Press $\boxed{\text{2nd}}$ [CALC]. Use the **maximum** operation from the **CALCULATE** menu.

The maximum height of the rider above the ground is 22 m.

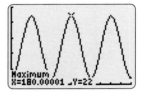

Technology *Tip*

If you are using a TI-Nspire™ CAS graphing calculator, refer to the instructions on page 33 to determine the maximum and minimum values and the period.

Similarly, use the **minimum** operation from the **CALCULATE** menu to determine the minimum.

The minimum height is 2 m.

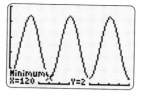

ii) Use the **value** operation from the **CALCULATE** menu to determine the height after 30 s.

The height after 30 s is 12 m.

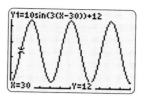

Connections

A maximum and an adjacent minimum are half a cycle apart. To obtain the value of the full period, it is necessary to multiply by 2.

iii) To determine the period, subtract the coordinates of the adjacent maximum and minimum and multiply by 2. The period is 2(180 s − 120 s), or 120 s.

Key Concepts

- Data can be collected from physical models using tools such as a motion sensor.
- Data can be downloaded from statistical sources such as Statistics Canada.
- Data can sometimes be modelled using a sinusoidal function.
- Use a graph or a table to build a model to determine the amplitude, phase shift, period, and vertical shift of a sinusoidal function.
- Predictions about the behaviour of an altered model can be made by considering the effect of changing a parameter on the graph of the original equation.
- The graph or equation can be used to determine values.

Communicate Your Understanding

C1 Consider the model you constructed in the Investigate. How does your analysis change if you decide to model the motion with a cosine function rather than a sine function?

C2 Consider the population graph for people in Canada aged 20 to 24. What kind of model is appropriate for the period from 1976 to 1980? from 1981 to 1988? Give reasons for your answers.

C3 Suppose that the entire Ferris wheel in Example 3 is moved upward 1 m and the phase shift is decreased to 20°. What changes do you expect to see in the graph? Justify your answer.

A Practise

For help with questions 1 and 2, refer to the Investigate.

1. A sensor is used to gather data on the motion of a pendulum. Data are recorded on a graph 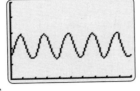 with time, in seconds, from 0 s to 10 s, on the horizontal axis and distance, in metres, from 0 m to 5 m, on the vertical axis.

   a) Use the graph to estimate the maximum and minimum values. Then, use these values to find the amplitude, a.

   b) Copy the graph and sketch a horizontal reference line. Estimate the vertical shift, c.

   c) Use the horizontal reference line to estimate the phase shift, d.

   d) Use the horizontal reference line to estimate the period. Use the period to find the value of k.

   e) Construct a model for the motion by writing an equation using a sinusoidal function.

   f) **Use Technology** Use technology to graph your model. Compare your model to the graph shown. If you see any significant differences, check and adjust your model.

2. A motion sensor is used to gather data on the motion of a pendulum. The table of values is exported to a computer, and graphing software is used to draw the graph shown. Time, in seconds, is on the horizontal axis. Distance, in metres, is on the vertical axis.

Reasoning and Proving

Representing — Selecting Tools

Problem Solving

Connecting — Reflecting

Communicating

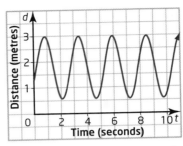

a) Use the graph to estimate the maximum and minimum values. Then, use these values to find the approximate amplitude, a.

b) Copy the graph and sketch a horizontal reference line. Estimate the vertical shift, c.

c) Use the horizontal reference line to estimate the phase shift, d.

d) Use the horizontal reference line to estimate the period. Use the period to find the value of k.

e) Construct a model for the motion by writing an equation using a sinusoidal function.

f) **Use Technology** Use technology to graph your model. Compare your model to the graph shown. If you see any significant differences, check and adjust your model.

For help with questions 3 and 4, refer to Example 3.

3. The height, h, in metres, of the tide in a given location on a given day at t hours after midnight can be modelled using the sinusoidal function
$h(t) = 5 \sin [30(t - 5)] + 7$.

   a) Find the maximum and minimum values for the depth, h, of the water.

   b) What time is high tide? What time is low tide?

   c) What is the depth of the water at 9:00 a.m.?

   d) Find all the times during a 24-h period when the depth of the water is 3 m.

4. The population, P, of a lakeside town with a large number of seasonal residents can be modelled using the function $P(t) = 5000 \sin [30(t - 7)] + 8000$, where t is the number of months after New Year's Day (January is month 1).

a) Find the maximum and minimum values for the population over a whole year.

b) When is the population a maximum? When is it a minimum?

c) What is the population on September 30?

d) When is the population about 10 000?

For help with question 5, refer to Example 1.

5. a) The owner of an ice-cream shop kept records of average daily sales for each month for the past year, as shown, beginning in January. Construct a sinusoidal function to model the average daily sales versus the month.

b) Over what domain and range is your model valid?

Month	Daily Sales ($)	Month	Daily Sales ($)
1	45	7	355
2	115	8	285
3	195	9	205
4	290	10	105
5	360	11	42
6	380	12	18

For help with Questions 6 and 7, refer to Example 2.

6. A Ferris wheel has a diameter of 20 m and is 4 m above ground level at its lowest point. Assume that a rider enters a car from a platform that is located 30° around the rim before the car reaches its lowest point.

a) Model the rider's height above the ground versus angle using a transformed sine function.

b) Model the rider's height above the ground versus angle using a transformed cosine function.

c) Suppose that the platform is moved to 60° around the rim from the lowest position of the car. How will the equations in parts a) and b) change? Write the new equations.

7. Suppose that the centre of the Ferris wheel in question 6 is moved upward 2 m, but the platform is left in place at a point 30° before the car reaches its lowest point. How do the equations in parts a) and b) of question 6 change? Write the new equations.

8. The movement of a piston in an automobile engine can be modelled by the function $y = 50 \sin 10\ 800t + 20$, where y is the distance, in millimetres, from the crankshaft and t is the time, in seconds.

a) What is the period of the motion?

b) Determine the maximum, minimum, and amplitude.

c) When do the maximum and minimum values occur?

d) What is the vertical position of the piston at $t = \dfrac{1}{120}$ s?

B Connect and Apply

9. The period, T, in seconds, of a pendulum is related to the length, ℓ, in metres, according to the relation

$$T = 2\pi\sqrt{\frac{\ell}{g}},$$

where g is the acceleration due to gravity, about 9.8 m/s², near the surface of Earth.

a) If the length is doubled, by what factor does the period increase?

b) If you want a pendulum with half the period of the given pendulum, what must you do to the length?

c) Suppose that you make a pendulum with half the period of the pendulum used in the Investigate. Modify the equation that models the motion of the pendulum to reflect the new period.

d) Suppose that you take the pendulum in the Investigate to the moon, where the rate of acceleration due to gravity is about $\frac{1}{6}$ that of the rate at Earth's surface. Predict the effect on the period of the pendulum.

e) Modify the equation that models the motion of the pendulum so that it is accurate for lunar gravity.

10. A double pendulum can be made by connecting a second pendulum to the bob of the first. Make a model of a double pendulum using any materials available, and set it in motion.

a) Watch the bob of the first pendulum. Describe the motion. Would it be possible to model it using a sinusoidal function?

b) Watch the bob of the second pendulum. Describe the motion. Would it be possible to model it using a sinusoidal function?

c) Try different relative lengths between the two pendulum strings. Can you determine a ratio that results in sinusoidal motion?

11. How closely can deep breathing be modelled using a sinusoidal function?

a) Practise slow, deep breathing, filling your lungs to capacity, and then exhaling until you cannot expel any more air. Keep the rate slow, such that inhaling and exhaling each take at least 5 s.

b) Fill a 2-L plastic bottle with water. Invert the bottle in a sink half full of water. Exhale through a tube such as a flexible straw, and capture the exhaled air in the bottle. Use the amount of water displaced to estimate the volume of air that you breathed out. If you have a large lung capacity, you may need to use more than one bottle. Use a felt pen to mark the level each second.

c) Make a table of values of volume exhaled versus time. Use the table to sketch a graph.

d) Use your table and graph to construct a sinusoidal function to model the data.

e) Graph the model on the same set of axes. How closely does the actual exhalation follow a sinusoidal model?

Connections

You cannot actually expel all of the air from your lungs. Depending on the size of your lungs, 1 L to 2 L of air remains even when you think your lungs are empty.

12. Smog is a generic term used to describe pollutants in the air. A smog alert is usually issued when the air quality index is greater than 50. Air quality can vary throughout the day, increasing when more cars are on the road. Consider a model of the form $I = 30 \sin [15(t - 4)] + 25$, where I is the value of the air quality index and t measures the time after midnight, in hours.

a) What is the period of the modelled function? Explain why this makes sense.

b) Determine the maximum, minimum, and amplitude.

c) When do the maximum and minimum occur?

d) During what time interval would a smog alert be issued, according to this model?

13. a) Find your pulse. Use a watch to determine how many times your heart beats in 1 min. Use this measurement to calculate the period of one heartbeat.

b) Assuming an amplitude of 1 unit, use a sine function to construct a model of your heartbeat versus time.

c) Use the library or the Internet to obtain a tracing from a medical heart monitor. How good is a sinusoidal function as a model for a human pulse?

14. Chapter Problem Your voice is as unique as a fingerprint, and your voice pattern can be used to identify you. Even if you have a complex voice, a computer can be programmed to analyse your voice pattern and break it into a sum of sinusoidal functions of varying periods, amplitudes, and phase shifts. This process is known as Fourier analysis.

a) To see how this process works, start with the model $y = \sin x$. Pick three different pairs of amplitudes and periods. Apply each pair to the basic sine function and add to form the voice model. An example is

$$y = \sin x + 0.5 \sin 2x + 0.75 \sin 3x + 0.25 \sin 5x$$

Graph the model. Add another term to your model, and graph it again. What changes do you notice?

b) Borrow a microphone and oscilloscope from the physics department at your school. Sing a single note and see your own voice pattern. Compare patterns with others in your class.

15. Visit www.statcan.gc.ca/edu/edu05_0018c-eng.htm. Select **Sinusoidal**.

Select **International travellers into Canada**, table 387-0004.

Select **table 075-0013**.

Under **Geography**, select **Canada**.

Under **Travel category**, select **Inbound international travel**.

Under **Sex**, select **Both sexes**.

Under **International Travellers**, select **Total travel**.

Under **Seasonal adjustment**, select **Unadjusted**.

Set the reference period to **from Mar 1986 to Mar 2006**.

If you want to see the data on your computer screen, select **Retrieve as a Table** and then **Retrieve Now**.

If you plan to analyse the data with a spreadsheet or other software, select **Retrieve as individual Time Series**. Select the downloadable file format as **CSV (comma-separated values)**, with **Time as rows**.

a) Select a recent year. Construct a sinusoidal model to represent the number of international travellers to Canada for that year.

b) Inspect the data from other years. Does your model apply to any year? Justify your answer.

c) Make a graph of the maximum values versus year for each year that you have data for. Explain why the long-term trend among the maximum values appears to be periodic.

d) Construct a sinusoidal model to represent the variation in maximum values from year to year. What is the apparent period of this long-term variation?

16. Visit www.statcan.gc.ca/edu/edu05_0018c-eng.htm Select **Sinusoidal**.

a) Select a table of interest and download the data.

b) Pose a question that can be answered by constructing a sinusoidal model of the data.

c) Solve your question to ensure that it works.

d) Exchange questions with a classmate. Solve each other's question.

e) Exchange solutions, and discuss whether they are correct.

✔ Achievement Check

17. Bungee jumping is thought to have originated in Queenstown, New Zealand, during the 1980s. Data for a bungee jumper are shown. Timing begins when the bungee cord is fully extended. The vertical height of the jumper above  the ground for 15 s is shown. Use a sine function to model the jump.

Time, t (s)	Height, y (m)	Time, t (s)	Height, y (m)
0	110	8	35
1	103	9	60
2	85	10	85
3	60	11	103
4	35	12	110
5	17	13	103
6	10	14	85
7	17	15	60

C Extend

18. Consider a 10-m-tall tree. On a certain day, the sun rises at 6:00 a.m., is directly overhead at noon, and sets at 6:00 p.m. From 6:00 a.m. until noon, the length, s, in metres, of the tree's shadow can be modelled by the relation $s = 10 \cot 15t$, where t is the time, in hours, past 6:00 a.m.

a) Modify the model so that it is valid from noon until 6:00 p.m.

b) Graph the model and the modified model in part a) on the same set of axes.

19. Math Contest A cube with sides of 6 cm has each side increased to 18 cm. How many of the smaller cubes will fit in the larger cube?

  A 3   **B** 27   **C** 9   **D** 81

20. Math Contest A glass container is filled with 50 L of water. 10 L of water is removed and replaced with 10 L of grape juice. The mixture is shaken well. Then, 20 L of the mixture is removed and replaced with 20 L of grape juice. How many litres of grape juice are now in the container?

  A 20   **B** 24   **C** 25   **D** 26

21. Math Contest If the number 3000 is written in the form $2^x 3^y 5^z$, what is the value of $x + y + z$?

  A 3   **B** 4   **C** 6   **D** 7

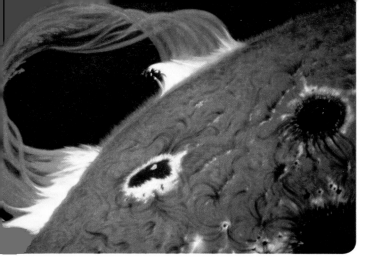

Use Sinusoidal Functions to Model Periodic Phenomena Not Involving Angles

You have worked with sinusoidal applications that do not involve angles, for example, the heights of tides versus time. In this section, you will work with other real-world situations that can be modelled by sinusoidal functions but do not necessarily involve an angle as the independent variable. Sunspot activity is an example. Sunspots are huge solar storms. Their activity appears to follow a periodic pattern that can be modelled by a sinusoidal function. The model is used to predict disruptions to radio-based communications on Earth.

Investigate

How can you use sinusoidal functions to model the tides?

1. The function $h(t) = 5 \sin [30(t + 3)]$ can be used to model the relationship between the height, in metres, of the tides in a certain place above or below mean sea level, and the time of day, in hours past midnight. Graph the model over a period of 24 h.

2. Use your graph to determine when the first high tide occurs. What is the height of the tide above mean sea level?

3. At what time does the first low tide occur? What is the height of the tide? Explain why the answer is negative.

4. At what times do the next high and low tides occur?

5. What is the period of the function?

6. Reflect Use your answers to explain why the phase shift is 3.

Tools

- graphing calculator

Optional

- graphing software or other graphing tools

Connections

Tides are caused principally by the gravitational pull of the moon on Earth's oceans. The physics of rotating systems predicts that one high tide occurs when the water is facing the moon and another occurs when the water is on the opposite side of Earth, away from the moon. This results in two tide cycles each day. To learn more about tides, visit the *Functions 11* page on the McGraw-Hill Ryerson Web site and follow the links to Chapter 5.

Example 1

Model Alternating Electric Current (AC)

The electricity used in most of the world is alternating current. Unlike the electricity from a battery, which always flows in the same direction, AC electricity reverses direction in a cyclical fashion. The number of cycles per second is not the same in all countries. In Canada, the United States, and some other countries, the frequency standard is 60 Hz (hertz), which means 60 complete cycles per second. The maximum voltage is about 170 V. The voltage can be modelled as a function of time using a sine function: $V = a \sin [k(t - d)] + c$.

a) What is the period of 60-Hz AC?

b) Determine the value of k.

c) What is the amplitude of the voltage function?

d) Model the voltage with a suitably transformed sine function.

e) Use Technology Use technology to graph the voltage function over two cycles. Explain what the scales on the axes represent.

Solution

a) Since there are 60 complete cycles every second, the period is $\dfrac{1}{60}$ s.

b) $\dfrac{360}{k} = \dfrac{1}{60}$

$\quad k = 21\ 600$

The value of k is 21 600.

c) The amplitude is 170 V.

d) The voltage function is $V = 170 \sin 21\ 600t$.

e) To graph the voltage function over two cycles, set the range of x from 0 s to $\dfrac{1}{30}$ s and the x-scale to $\dfrac{1}{120}$ s. Each tick on the x-axis represents $\dfrac{1}{120}$ s.

Set the range of y from -200 V to 200 V and the y-scale to 50 V. Each tick on the y-axis represents 50 V.

The graph is shown.

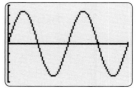

Example 2

Model the Angle of the Sun Above the Horizon on the Summer Solstice in Inuvik

The table shows the angle of the sun above the horizon for each hour on the summer solstice in Inuvik, Northwest Territories.

Hour Past Midnight	0	1	2	3	4	5	6	7	8	9	10	11
Angle Above the Horizon (°)	2.4	1.8	2.4	4.2	7.2	11	16	22	27	33	38	42
Hour Past Midnight	12	13	14	15	16	17	18	19	20	21	22	23
Angle Above the Horizon (°)	45	46	45	42	38	33	27	22	17	12	7.5	4.3

a) Use the table to determine a sinusoidal model for the angle of the sun above the horizon.

b) Graph the points in the table on the same set of axes as your model to verify the fit.

c) Is the fit as expected? Explain any discrepancies.

Solution

a) From the table, the maximum angle of elevation is 46° and the minimum angle is 1.8°. The amplitude is $\dfrac{46 - 1.8}{2} = 22.1$. Therefore, the value of a is 22.1.

The vertical shift is $1.8 + 22.1 = 23.9$. Therefore, the value of c is 23.9.

The sine wave starts at 23.9. This is about 7.5 h past midnight. Therefore, $d \doteq 7.5$.

The period is 24 h.

$$\dfrac{360}{k} = 24$$
$$k = 15$$

The angle above the horizon can be modelled with the equation

$$h(t) = 22.1 \sin [15(t - 7.5)] + 23.9.$$

b) The graph is shown, superimposed over the data points.

c) The fit is good at first, but begins to depart from the data points as the day progresses. Earth's movement around the sun may account for the departure from a purely sinusoidal model. The real period is not exactly 24 h.

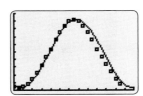

Example 3

Predator-Prey Populations

When two animals have a predator/prey relationship, the population of each over time can be modelled with a sinusoidal function. If the population of prey is large, the population of predators increases since there is an adequate food supply. As the population of predators increases, the population of prey decreases. Eventually, there is not enough food for the predators, and they also begin to die off. As the number of predators declines, more prey survive, and the population of prey increases again.

Suppose that the number, N, of prey in a given area can be modelled by the function $N(t) = 250 \sin 90t + 500$, where t is the number of years since a base year of 1990.

a) What was the population of prey in 1990?

b) When did the population reach a maximum?

c) What was the maximum population at this time?

d) When did the population reach a minimum?

e) What was the minimum population at that time?

f) How many years passed between maximum populations?

Solution

a) Substitute 0 for t. Since $\sin 0 = 0$, the population in 1990 was 500.

b) **Use Technology** Use a graphing calculator to graph the function over at least two cycles. Adjust the window variables accordingly. Then, use the **maximum** operation from the **CALCULATE** menu to determine the first maximum. It occurred after 1 year, in 1991.

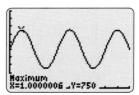

c) The population of prey in 1991 was 750.

d) Use the **minimum** operation from the **CALCULATE** menu to determine the first minimum. It occurred at the end of 3 years, in 1993.

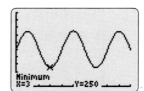

e) The population of prey in 1993 was 250.

f) The next maximum occurred in 1995. Four years passed between maximum populations.

Key Concepts

- Sinusoidal functions can be used to model periodic phenomena that do not involve angles as the independent variable.
- The amplitude, phase shift, period, and vertical shift of the basic sine or cosine function can be adjusted to fit the characteristics of the phenomenon being modelled.
- Technology can be used to quickly draw and analyse the graph modelled by the equation.
- The graph can be used to solve problems related to the phenomenon.

Communicate Your Understanding

C1 A situation modelled by a sinusoidal function has no x-intercepts. What conclusions can you draw about the relation between a and c?

C2 A situation can be modelled by the sinusoidal function $y = a \sin [k(x - d)] + c$. If the graph passes through the origin, can you conclude that the phase shift, d, is 0? Justify your answer, including a diagram.

C3 The period of a sinusoidal function is greater than 360° but less than 720°. What restrictions does this condition place on the value of k? Justify your answer.

A Practise

For help with questions 1 and 2, refer to the Investigate.

1. In the Investigate, the sinusoidal function $h(t) = 5 \sin [30(t + 3)]$ is used to model the height of tides in a particular location on a particular day. On a different day, the maximum height is 8 m, the minimum height is –8 m, and high tide occurs at 5:30 a.m.

   a) Modify the function such that it matches the new data.

   b) Predict the times for the next high and low tides.

2. Suppose that a cosine function is chosen to model the tides in the Investigate.

   a) Modify the function so that a cosine function is used but all predictions of tides remain the same.

   b) Verify that the cosine model correctly predicts the low and high tides for the day.

For help with question 3, refer to Example 1.

3. Sometimes demand for electricity becomes so great that suppliers such as Ontario Power Generation cannot maintain the desired maximum voltage on the electricity grid. This creates a condition known as a brownout. In a brownout, incandescent lamps dim and some appliances do not work at all. How does the graph of voltage versus time change during a brownout? Sketch the new graph and justify your changes.

For help with question 4, refer to Example 3.

4. The population of prey in a predator-prey relation is shown. Time is in years since 1985.

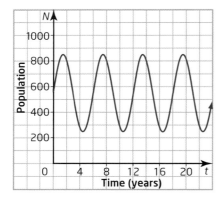

a) Determine the maximum and minimum values of the population, to the nearest 50. Use these to find the amplitude.

b) Determine the vertical shift, c.

c) Determine the phase shift, d.

d) Determine the period. Use the period to determine the value of k.

e) Model the population versus time with a sinusoidal function.

f) Graph your function. Compare it to the graph shown.

B Connect and Apply

5. The depth, d, in metres, of water in a seaplane harbour on a given day can be modelled using the function
$d = 12 \sin [30(t - 5)] + 14$, where t is the time past midnight, in hours.

a) Determine the maximum and minimum depths of the water in the harbour.

b) What is the period of the function?

c) Graph the water level over 24 h.

d) If the water is less than 3 m deep, landing a seaplane is considered unsafe. During what time intervals, between midnight and midnight the following day, is it considered unsafe to land a seaplane?

e) What other factors are important in deciding whether it is safe to land?

6. At another time of year in the same harbour as in question 5, the maximum water depth is 22 m and the minimum depth is 6 m. The first high tide occurs at 5:00 a.m.

a) Modify the model in question 5 to match the new data.

b) Graph the water level over 24 h.

c) During what time intervals, between midnight and midnight the following day, is it considered unsafe to land a seaplane?

7. The electricity standard used in Europe and many other parts of the world is alternating current (AC) with a frequency of 50 Hz

and a maximum voltage of 240 V. The voltage can be modelled as a function of time using a sine function.

a) What is the period of 50-Hz AC?

b) Determine the value of k.

c) What is the amplitude of the voltage function?

d) Model the voltage with a suitably transformed sine function.

e) **Use Technology** Use technology to graph the voltage function over two cycles. Explain what the scales on the axes represent.

8. Julia constructs a model AC generator in physics class and cranks it by hand at 3 revolutions per second. She is able to light up a flashlight bulb that is rated for 6 V.

a) What is the period of the AC produced?

b) Determine the value of k.

c) What is the amplitude of the voltage function?

d) Model the voltage with a suitably transformed sine function.

e) **Use Technology** Graph the voltage function over two cycles. Explain what the scales on the axes represent.

9. The table shows annual average sunspot activity from 1970 to 2006.

Year (since 1970)	Sunspots (Annual Average)	Year (since 1970)	Sunspots (Annual Average)
0	107.4	19	162.2
1	66.5	20	145.1
2	67.3	21	144.3
3	36.7	22	93.5
4	32.3	23	54.5
5	14.4	24	31.0
6	11.6	25	18.2
7	26.0	26	8.4
8	86.9	27	20.3
9	145.8	28	61.6
10	149.1	29	96.1
11	146.5	30	123.3
12	114.8	31	123.3
13	64.7	32	109.4
14	43.5	33	65.9
15	16.2	34	43.3
16	11.0	35	30.2
17	29.0	36	15.4
18	100.9		

a) Use the table to determine a sinusoidal model for the number of sunspots.

b) Graph the points in the table on the same axes as your model to verify the fit.

c) Is the fit as you expected? Explain any discrepancies.

10. Refer to your model in question 9.

a) Predict the next three occurrences of maximum sunspot activity after 2006.

b) Predict the next three occurrences of minimum sunspot activity after 2006.

c) What is the variation in the maximum and minimum values over the data in the table?

Connections

Sunspots were observed as early as 165 B.C.E. Like many phenomena in the sky, they were thought to have a mystical significance to humans.

11. In Example 3, the population of prey can be modelled with the function $N(t) = 250 \sin 90t + 500$. Research shows that the population of predators follows the period of the population of prey, with a phase shift of $\frac{1}{4}$ of a cycle to the right. Suppose that the predators have a minimum population of 50 and a maximum population of 100.

a) Construct a model for the population of predators using a sine function.

b) Graph the population of prey and predators on the same set of axes over a period of 12 years from the base year.

c) Suggest reasons why there is a phase shift to the right.

12. **Use Technology** Search the Internet for a predator-prey simulation game.

a) Play the game in a small group and generate a table of data.

b) Graph the data for prey and predators.

c) Use the graph and the table to construct a model for the population of prey and the population of predators.

d) Graph the models on the same set of axes as the data. How well do the models represent the data?

13. The graph represents monthly residential natural gas consumption in Ontario from January 2001 to December 2005.

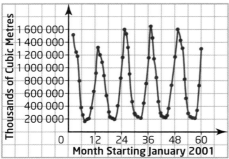

Residential Natural Gas Consumption

a) Use the graph to construct a sinusoidal model for natural gas consumption.

b) Graph the model for a period of 5 years, starting in January 2001.

c) Use the model to predict residential natural gas consumption in December 2008.

14. The number of hours of daylight on the 15th of each month, beginning in January, is shown for any point on Earth with a latitude of 50° north.

Reasoning and Proving

Representing — Selecting Tools

Problem Solving

Connecting — Reflecting

Communicating

Month	Hours of Daylight
1	8:30
2	10:07
3	11:48
4	13:44
5	15:04
6	16:21
7	15:38
8	14:33
9	12:42
10	10:47
11	9:06
12	8:05

a) Graph the data.

b) Use the graph and the table to construct a model for the number of hours of daylight.

c) Graph the model on the same set of axes as the data. Comment on the fit.

d) Use your model to predict the number of hours of daylight on January 31.

15. Use Technology The U.S. Naval Observatory calculates daylight tables for any location on Earth. Go to the *Functions 11* page of the McGraw-Hill Ryerson Web site and follow the links to access the observatory's Web site.

a) Use an atlas or the Internet to determine the latitude and longitude of your location.

b) On the Naval Observatory's site, select **Duration of Daylight Table for One Year**. Enter your location data and obtain the table. Record the data for the 15th of each month to make a table of values.

c) Graph the data.

d) Use the graph and the table to construct a model for the number of hours of daylight at your location.

e) Graph the model on the same set of axes as the data. Comment on the fit.

f) Use your model to predict the number of hours of daylight on any convenient day. Check your prediction by direct observation.

16. The propeller of a small airplane has an overall length of 2.0 m. The propeller clears the ground by a distance of 40 cm and spins at 1200 revolutions per minute while the airplane is taxiing.

a) Model the height of one of the propeller tips above the ground as a function of time using a sinusoidal function.

b) Graph the function over four cycles.

c) Determine all times in the first cycle when the tip is 1.0 m above the ground.

17. **Chapter Problem** Sound synthesis can include special effects. For example, a sine wave of one frequency can be used to control the amplitude of a sine wave of a higher frequency by multiplication. The result is a throbbing effect called tremolo. The effect first became popular when electric guitars became available in the 1950s. To see how tremolo works, use sin x to control the amplitude of sin $10x$ by multiplication: $y = (\sin x)(\sin 10x)$.

a) **Use Technology** On a graphing calculator, set the window such that x runs from -360 to 360 with a scale of 30, and y runs from -2 to 2 with a scale of 1. Enter and graph the function.

b) Observe the change in the amplitude of one function as it is controlled by the other. Are the sound bursts identical? Look carefully for reflections. Explain why they occur.

c) Tremolo is one of many special effects that can be added to sounds by manipulating the basic sinusoidal function models. Investigate other effects, such as vibrato, wah-wah, pitch bend, ping-pong, chorus, distortion, and attack delay. Many Web sites include sample sounds in a format that you can listen to. Listen for these same effects in your favourite music.

18. Refer to question 12 on page 311 about the theory of biorhythms.

a) Calculate the number of days that you have been alive. Be sure to account for the extra day in leap years.

b) The physical cycle has a period of 23 days. Divide your answer in part a) by 23 and determine the remainder. This tells you how long ago the current physical cycle began.

c) Use a method similar to part b) to determine when your current emotional cycle began. Recall that the period is 28 days. Repeat for the intellectual cycle, with a period of 33 days.

d) Use a long piece of grid paper to plot all three biorhythms. Use a suitable amplitude and a different colour for each.

e) Model each biorhythm with a sinusoidal function.

f) **Use Technology** Enter the models into a graphing calculator. Adjust the window variables appropriately and determine when your next "good" days and "bad" days will occur.

19. The wind turbine at Exhibition Place in Toronto is 94 m tall and has three blades, each measuring 24 m in length. The blades turn at a frequency of 27 revolutions per minute.

a) Use a sinusoidal function to model the height above the ground of one of the blade tips as a function of time.

b) Graph the function over four cycles.

c) Determine all times in the first cycle when the tip of the blade is 100 m above the ground.

C Extend

20. Non-reflective coating on eyeglasses is a very thin layer applied to the outside of the lenses. Light reflects from the front and back of the coating almost simultaneously, and the two reflections combine. The reflection from the front undergoes a phase shift, while that from the back does not.

The light reflected from the coating can be modelled with the sinusoidal function $P(x) = \sin x + \sin (x - 180°)$, where x is the phase of the light wave when it hits the coating, and $P(x)$ is the proportion of the light wave that is reflected.

a) Graph this function over two cycles.

b) Inspect the function carefully and explain why the graph has the form that it does. Why is a thin coating non-reflective?

c) The second term in the reflection function can also be expressed in terms of a cosine function. Determine a cosine function that has the same effect as the sine function shown.

Connections

Reflection from a film that is much thinner than the wavelength of the light being used forms a "perfect window." No light is reflected; it is all transmitted. This is why images viewed through non-reflective eyeglasses appear brighter than when viewed through lenses without the coating. You can use a soap bubble kit to see another example of this perfect window. Dip the bubble blower into the solution, and hold it so that the soap film is vertical. Orient the film to reflect light. You will see a series of coloured bands as the soap drains to the bottom. Then, you will see what looks like a break in the film forming at the top. This is the perfect window. You can test to see if there is still soap there by piercing the window with a pin or a sharp pencil.

21. Polaris, also known as the North Star, is the star closest to being directly overhead if you view it from the North Pole. However, Earth's axis is not always pointing in the same direction. The axis is moving in a slow circle, a motion similar to that of a spinning top. The effect is called precession. Because of this movement, Vega, the bright star to the right of centre in the photograph, will eventually become the North Star. As Earth's axis continues to move, Polaris will return as the North Star.

a) Use the library or the Internet to determine the period of precession of Earth's axis. Do you expect to see Vega as the North Star during your lifetime?

b) Model the precession of Earth as a sinusoidal function.

c) **Use Technology** Determine the window settings needed to graph this function on a graphing calculator. Then, graph the function.

22. Math Contest The notation $n!$ means to multiply all the natural numbers from the number n down to 1. For example, $5! = 5 \times 4 \times 3 \times 2 \times 1$. When 50! is expanded, how many zeros are at the end of the number?

A 10   **B** 5   **C** 50   **D** 12

23. Math Contest If $y = \sqrt{x}$, what is the value of $x^{25} + 121 - y^{50}$?

Create a Scatter Plot and a Function Using a TI-Nspire™ CAS Graphing Calculator

Refer to Example 2 on page 335.

Hour Past Midnight	0	1	2	3	4	5	6	7	8	9	10	11
Angle Above the Horizon (°)	2.4	1.8	2.4	4.2	7.2	11	16	22	27	33	38	42
Hour Past Midnight	12	13	14	15	16	17	18	19	20	21	22	23
Angle Above the Horizon (°)	45	46	45	42	38	33	27	22	17	12	7.5	4.3

Tools

- TI-Nspire™ CAS graphing calculator

1. Open a new document. Create a page using the **Lists & Spreadsheet** application.

2. Enter the hour data in column A.

3. Enter the angle data in column B.

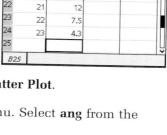

4. Open a new **Graphs & Geometry** page. Press (menu) and change the graph type to **Scatter Plot**.

5. Select **hour** from the x-axis dropdown menu. Select **ang** from the y-axis dropdown menu.

6. Press (menu). Set the **Window** settings from −5 to 25 for the x-axis and from −10 to 50 for the y-axis.

   A scatter plot will appear as shown.

7. Change the graph type back to **Function**.

8. Refer to the function derived in Example 2: $h(t) = 22.1 \sin [15(t − 7.5)] + 23.9$. Type the function as **f1**. Press (enter).

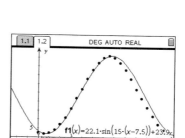

9. The graph is shown, superimposed over the data points. The fit is good at first but begins to depart from the data points as the day progresses. Earth's movement around the sun may account for the departure from a purely sinusoidal model. The real period is not exactly 24 h.

Chapter 5 Review

5.1 Modelling Periodic Behaviour, pages 284 to 293

1. Consider the graph shown.

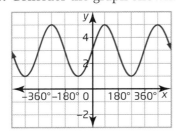

a) Explain why the function represented is periodic.

b) How many cycles are shown?

c) What are the maximum and minimum values?

d) What is the amplitude?

e) What is the period?

2. A shuttle bus takes passengers from a remote parking lot to the airport terminal 1.5 km away. The bus runs continually, completing a cycle in 10 min, which includes a 1-min stop at the parking lot and a 1-min stop at the terminal.

a) Sketch a graph to represent the position of the bus with respect to the parking lot as a function of time. Include two cycles.

b) What is the amplitude of the pattern?

c) Suppose that the bus increases its speed. Explain how this affects the graph.

5.2 The Sine Function and the Cosine Function, pages 294 to 301

3. Without using technology, sketch a graph of the sine function for values of x from $-540°$ to $540°$. Label the axes with an appropriate scale.

4. Without using technology, sketch a graph of the cosine function for values of x from $-540°$ to $540°$. Label the axes with an appropriate scale.

5.3 Investigate Transformations of Sine and Cosine Functions, pages 304 to 312

5. Consider the function $y = \cos(x + 60°) + 3$.

a) What is the amplitude?

b) What is the period?

c) Describe the phase shift.

d) Describe the vertical shift.

e) Graph the function for values of x from $0°$ to $360°$.

f) How does the equation change if the phase shift and vertical shift are both in the opposite direction from the original function? Justify your answer.

5.4 Graphing and Modelling With $y = a \sin[k(x - d)] + c$ and $y = a \cos[k(x - d)] + c$, pages 313 to 321

6. A robot arm is used to cap bottles on an assembly line. The vertical position, y, in centimetres, of the arm after t seconds can be modelled by the function $y = 30 \sin[360(t - 0.25)] + 45$.

a) Determine the amplitude, period, phase shift, and vertical shift.

b) What is the lowest vertical position that the arm reaches?

c) State the domain and range of the original sine function and the transformed function in set notation.

d) Suppose that the assembly line receives new bottles that require a lowest vertical position of 20 cm. How does the equation modelling the robot arm change?

5.5 Data Collecting and Modelling, pages 322 to 332

7. Sunrise times for 1 year in Fort Erie, Ontario, measured on the 21st of each month, starting in January, are shown using Eastern Standard Time (EST).

Month (21st day)	Time (EST)
1	7:40
2	7:04
3	6:17
4	5:25
5	4:47
6	4:37
7	4:55
8	5:28
9	6:01
10	6:36
11	7:15
12	7:43

a) Convert the times to decimal format. Round each value to two decimal places. Create a scatter plot, with the month on the horizontal axis and the time on the vertical axis.

b) Construct a model of the sunrise times using a sine function. State the amplitude, period, phase shift, and vertical shift.

c) Graph the model on the same axes as the data. Comment on the fit.

8. Use your model from question 7 to predict the sunrise time on January 7 and July 7.

5.6 Use Sinusoidal Functions to Model Periodic Phenomena Not Involving Angles, pages 333 to 341

9. The volume of blood in the left ventricle of an average-sized human heart varies from a minimum of about 50 mL to a maximum of about 130 mL. Ken has an average-sized heart and a resting pulse of 60 beats per minute. Assume that one heart beat represents the period.

a) Using a sine function, model the volume of blood in Ken's left ventricle with respect to time.

b) Sketch a graph of volume in relation to time for four cycles.

c) How much blood is pumped from the left ventricle every minute?

d) How does the function change if you use a cosine function?

e) When Ken runs, his heart rate rises to 120 beats per minute. Adjust your model from part a) to reflect Ken's heart rate while running.

f) Explain why the amplitude does not change in part c).

Chapter Problem WRAP-UP

You have seen how applications in music synthesis, voice pattern recognition, and special effects sounds can be modelled using sinusoidal functions.

a) How does the amplitude of the modelling function relate to the sound that you hear? Give examples.

b) How does the period of the modelling function relate to the sound that you hear? Give examples.

c) What is the phase shift's role in music played on traditional instruments, songs sung by a choir, and music synthesis?

For questions 1 to 8, select the best answer.

For questions 1 to 3, refer to the graph of the periodic function shown.

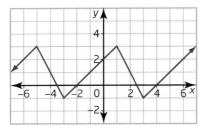

1. The period of the function is

A 1   **B** 2   **C** 3   **D** 6

2. The amplitude of the function is

A 1   **B** 2   **C** 3   **D** −1

3. The value of $f(12)$ is

A −1   **B** 0   **C** 2   **D** 3

For questions 4 to 7, consider the function
$y = \frac{3}{8} \cos [5(x - 30°)] + \frac{3}{4}.$

4. The period of the function is

A 72°   **B** 180°   **C** 360°   **D** 1800°

5. The minimum value of the function is

A $-\frac{3}{8}$ **B** 0   **C** $\frac{3}{8}$ **D** $\frac{3}{4}$

6. With respect to $y = \cos x$, the phase shift of the function is

A 30° left   **B** 30° right

C 60° left   **D** 60° right

7. With respect to $y = \cos x$, the vertical shift of the function is

A $\frac{3}{8}$ up   **B** $\frac{3}{8}$ down

C $\frac{3}{4}$ up   **D** $\frac{3}{4}$ down

8. Consider the function
$y = 2 \cos (3x + 120°)$. What is the phase shift of the function?

A 40° left   **B** 40° right

C 120° left   **D** 120° right

9. Consider the function
$y = 3 \sin [4(x + 60°)] - 2.$

a) What is the amplitude of the function?

b) What is the period of the function?

c) Describe the phase shift of the function.

d) Describe the vertical shift of the function.

e) Graph the function one step at a time. Label each step according to the transformation taking place.

f) State the domain and range of the transformed function. Use set notation.

10. A sinusoidal function has an amplitude of 4 units, a period of 90°, and a maximum at (0, 2).

a) Represent the function with an equation using a cosine function.

b) Represent the function with an equation using a sine function.

11. A sinusoidal function has an amplitude of $\frac{1}{4}$ units, a period of 720°, and a maximum point at $\left(0, \frac{3}{4}\right)$.

a) Represent the function with an equation using a sine function.

b) Graph the function over two cycles.

12. Consider the function
$f(x) = 2 \cos [3(x - 120°)].$

a) Determine the amplitude, period, phase shift, and vertical shift with respect to $y = \cos x$.

b) What are the maximum and minimum values?

c) Find the first three x-intercepts to the right of the origin.

d) Find the y-intercept.

13. a) Determine the equation of the sine function shown.

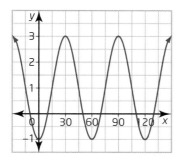

b) Suppose that the maximum values on the graph are half as far apart. How does the equation in part a) change? Justify your answer.

14. A summer resort town often shows seasonal variations in the percent of the workforce employed. The table lists the percent employed on the first of each month, starting in January, for 1 year.

Month	Employment (%)
1	62
2	67
3	75
4	80
5	87
6	92
7	96
8	93
9	89
10	79
11	72
12	65

a) Construct a model for these data using either a sine function or a cosine function. State the amplitude, period, phase shift, and vertical shift.

b) Graph the model on the same set of axes as the data. Comment on the fit.

c) Use your model to predict the employment level on June 15.

d) Economic forecasters predict a mild recession for the following year that will decrease employment levels for each month by 10%. Describe the effect that this will have on the graph of the function.

15. The Ferris wheel at a carnival has a diameter of 18 m and descends to 2 m above the ground at its lowest point. Assume that a rider enters a car at this point and rides the wheel for two revolutions.

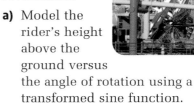

a) Model the rider's height above the ground versus the angle of rotation using a transformed sine function.

b) Suppose that the rider enters the car from a platform located 45° along the rim of the wheel before the car reaches its lowest point. Adjust your model in part a) to reflect this situation.

c) Graph the equations from parts a) and b) on the same set of axes. How are they similar? How are they different? Explain the differences.

Chapter 4 Trigonometry

Where necessary, round angles to the nearest degee and trigonometric ratios to four decimal places.

1. a) Use the unit circle to determine exact values for the primary trigonometric ratios of 315°.

   b) Check your results using a calculator.

2. a) Use the unit circle to determine approximate values for the primary trigonometric ratios for 255°.

   b) Check your results using a calculator.

3. The coordinates of a point on the terminal arm of an angle θ are (3, −1). Determine the exact trigonometric ratios of θ.

4. Angle Q is in the second quadrant, and $\sin Q = \frac{15}{17}$. Determine values for $\cos Q$ and $\tan Q$.

5. Solve the equation $\tan \theta = -\frac{3}{8}$ for $0° \le \theta \le 360°$.

6. Determine two angles between 0° and 360° that have a cosecant of −8.

7. Margit flies her small plane due west at 200 km/h for one hour. She turns right through an angle of 45°, and continues at the same speed for half an hour.

   a) Sketch a diagram to illustrate this problem.

   b) At the end of her flight, how far is Margit from her starting point?

8. Given △ABC, such that $a = 2.4$ cm, $c = 3.2$ cm, and $\angle A = 28°$.

   a) Draw two possible diagrams that match the given measurements.

   b) Calculate the length of side b and the degree measure of the other two angles.

9. Detectors for subatomic particles known as neutrinos must be built far below ground to minimize interference from external sources of radiation. To reach such an underground laboratory, visitors start at an elevator building on the surface, descend straight down for 2.1 km, and walk east for 1.9 km to enter the lab. To reach the detector, the visitors turn left through an angle of 30°, and walk another 300 m. What is the straight-line distance, to the nearest tenth of a kilometre, from the elevator building to the detector?

10. In △PQR, $\angle P$ is 29°, $p = 16$ m, and $q = 25$ m. Determine all possible values for side r, to the nearest tenth of a metre.

11. Prove: $\sec \theta = \csc \theta \tan \theta$.

12. Prove: $\csc \theta = \sin \theta + \cos^2 \theta \csc \theta$.

Chapter 5 Trigonometric Functions

13. Consider the graph shown.

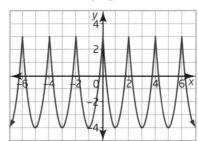

   a) Explain why the function represented is periodic.

   b) How many complete cycles are shown?

   c) What are the maximum and minimum values?

   d) What is the amplitude?

   e) What is the period?

14. a) Use a graph to determine the values of x for which $\sin x = \cos x$ from $-180°$ to $180°$.

b) Check your answers using a calculator.

15. Consider the function
$y = 3 \sin[2(x - 45°)] - 1$.

a) What is the amplitude?

b) What is the period?

c) Describe the phase shift.

d) Describe the vertical shift.

e) Graph the function for values of x from $0°$ to $360°$.

f) How would the equation change if the period were $90°$?

16. A sinusoidal function has an amplitude of $\frac{1}{2}$ units, a period of $1080°$, and a maximum point at $\left(0, \frac{3}{4}\right)$.

a) Represent the function with an equation using a sine function.

b) Draw a graph of the function over two cycles.

17. Consider the function
$f(x) = \frac{1}{4} \cos [2(x - 90°)]$.

a) Determine the amplitude, period, phase shift, and vertical shift with respect to $y = \cos x$.

b) What are the maximum and minimum values?

c) Find the first three x-intercepts to the right of the origin.

d) Find the y-intercept.

18. In some countries, water wheels are used to pump water to a higher level. An Egyptian water wheel pumps water from a level of -1.3 m up to 1.7 m. It completes a full turn in 15 s.

a) Use a sinusoidal function to model the height of the water as a function of time.

b) For your model, state the amplitude, period, phase shift, and vertical shift.

c) What is the height of the water at a time of 20 s?

19. The Snowbirds air demonstration team performs a vertical loop. The altitude and time data for the loop are shown in the table.

Time (s)	Altitude (m)
0	3000
1	4000
2	4732
3	5000
4	4732
5	4000
6	3000
7	2000
8	1268
9	1000
10	1268
11	2000
12	3000

a) Use a sine function to model the altitude with respect to time.

b) Sketch a graph of your model for 4 cycles.

c) How does the function change if you use a cosine function?

Modelling a Rotating Object

Tools

- string
- large paper clip
- tape measure
- grid paper

Work with a partner. One partner performs the actions in parts a) and b), and the other partner makes the measurements.

a) Attach a large paper clip to the end of a string. Holding the opposite end of the string, let your arm and the string hang down toward the floor. Measure the distance from the pivot point of your shoulder to

- the floor
- the end of the paper clip
- the wall in front of you

b) Rotate your arm vertically at a constant speed, enough to keep the string taut. Measure the period of the rotation.

c) Determine an equation for a sine function that gives the height of the paper clip relative to the angle of rotation, starting from the rest position.

d) Determine an equation for the height of the paper clip relative to time, beginning from the rest position.

e) Determine an equation for the distance from the paper clip to the wall relative to the angle of rotation, starting from the rest position.

f) Determine an equation for the distance from the paper clip to the wall relative to time, beginning from the rest position.

g) Sketch the graph of each relation.

h) Describe how each equation would change if you reversed the direction of rotation. Justify your answer.

i) How would the equation in part c) change if you were relating the rotational distance travelled, instead of the height, to the angle of rotation? Justify your answer.

Discrete Functions

In this chapter, you will explore a wide variety
of number patterns called sequences. You will
learn that sequences have many applications
in fields such as medicine, biology, finances, and
construction.

A fractal, such as the one shown, is the result of a pattern
formed by performing a recursive process to generate a set
of points. You will explore this special type of pattern in this
chapter's Chapter Problem.

By the end of this chapter, you will

- make connections between sequences and discrete
  functions, represent sequences using function
  notation, and distinguish between a discrete function
  and a continuous function
- determine and describe a recursive procedure for
  generating a sequence, given the initial terms,
  and represent sequences as discrete functions in a
  variety of ways
- connect the formula for the nth term of a sequence
  to the representation in function notation, and
  write terms of a sequence given one of these
  representations or a recursion formula
- represent a sequence algebraically using a recursion
  formula, function notation, or the formula for the
  nth term, and describe the information that can be
  obtained by inspecting each representation
- determine, through investigation, recursive patterns
  in the Fibonacci sequence, in related sequences, and
  in Pascal's triangle, and represent the patterns in a
  variety of ways

- determine, through investigation, and describe
  the relationship between Pascal's triangle and the
  expansion of binomials, and apply the relationship to
  expand binomials raised to whole-number exponents
- identify sequences as arithmetic, geometric, or
  neither, given a numeric or algebraic representation
- determine the formula for the general term of an
  arithmetic sequence or geometric sequence, through
  investigation using a variety of tools and strategies,
  and apply the formula to calculate any term in a
  sequence
- determine the formula for the sum of an arithmetic
  or geometric series, through investigation using
  a variety of tools and strategies, and apply the
  formula to calculate the sum of a given number of
  consecutive terms
- solve problems involving arithmetic and geometric
  sequences and series, including those arising from
  real-world applications

Prerequisite Skills

Refer to the Prerequisite Skills Appendix on pages 478 to 495 for examples of the topics and further practice.

Identify Patterns

1. Determine the next three items in each pattern.

a)

b)

c) A, BB, CCC, DDDD, …

d) P, PQ, PQR, PQRS, …

e) 3, 6, 9, 12, …

f) $-5, 10, -15, 20, …$

g) $7, 3, -1, -5, …$

h) $\dfrac{1}{2}, \dfrac{1}{3}, \dfrac{1}{4}, \dfrac{1}{5}, …$

i) $x, 2x, 3x, 4x, …$

Evaluate Functions

2. For $f(x) = 3x - 1$, determine

a) $f(1)$ **b)** $f(-3)$

c) $f\left(\dfrac{1}{2}\right)$ **d)** $f\left(\dfrac{3}{m + 2}\right)$

3. For $f(x) = 2^x$, determine

a) $f(1)$ **b)** $f(-2)$

c) $f\left(\dfrac{1}{3}\right)$ **d)** $f\left(\dfrac{t - 1}{3}\right)$

4. For $f(x) = x^2 - 3x + 1$, determine

a) $f(3)$ **b)** $f(-1)$

c) $f(t - 2)$ **d)** $f(2t)$

Graph Functions

5. The domain of each function is $\{x \in \mathbb{R}\}$. Sketch the graph of each function.

a) $y = 2x + 3$

b) $f(x) = -\dfrac{1}{2}x - 1$

c) $y = x^2$

d) $f(x) = x^2 + 1$

e) $f(x) = (x - 3)^2$

f) $y = 2^x$

g) $f(x) = 2^x + 1$

h) $f(x) = 3^{x - 1}$

Solve Equations

6. Solve each equation and check your solutions.

a) $3 - 2y = 5y + 6$

b) $3t + 8 = t + 8$

c) $6a + 4(3 - a) = 15$

d) $\dfrac{x}{4} - 5 = 6$

e) $\dfrac{x}{6} - \dfrac{2x}{3} = -3$

Evaluate Expressions

7. Evaluate.

a) 8% of 60 **b)** 15% of 700

c) 12% of 4 **d)** 125% of 16

e) 85% of 0.06 **f)** 70% of 1400

8. Evaluate.

a) $\dfrac{3}{5} - \left(-\dfrac{1}{5}\right)$ **b)** $\dfrac{1}{2} \times \left(-\dfrac{3}{7}\right)$

c) $-\dfrac{4}{5} \div \left(-\dfrac{1}{6}\right)$ **d)** $\dfrac{13}{6} \times (-9)$

e) $-\dfrac{4}{3} - \left(-\dfrac{3}{2}\right)$ **f)** $-\dfrac{11}{3} \div \left(-\dfrac{5}{3}\right)$

Finite Differences

9. Use finite differences to determine whether each relation is linear, quadratic, or neither.

a)

x	y
1	3
2	9
3	17
4	27
5	39

b)

x	y
1	5
2	7
3	9
4	11
5	13

c)

x	y
1	2
2	4
3	8
4	16
5	32

10. Using the linear function $y = 3x - 1$ as an example, explain how the first differences relate to the slope of a line.

11. Using the quadratic function $y = 2x^2 - 5x - 3$ as an example, explain how the second differences relate to the value of a in an equation of the form $y = ax^2 + bx + c$.

Solve Linear Systems of Equations

12. Solve each system of equations.

a) $2x + y = 7$

$x + y = 4$

b) $3x + 3y = 41$

$4x + 5y = 71$

c) $4x - 3y = 96$

$2x + 5y = -8$

d) $\frac{1}{2}x - \frac{2}{5}y = \frac{9}{10}$

$\frac{1}{3}x - \frac{1}{4}y = \frac{2}{3}$

Chapter Problem

Fractals are amazing and beautiful shapes that can be found in mathematics, art, and nature. They are characterized by patterns and relationships that give them their fascinating shapes. These geometric shapes exhibit greater and greater complexity as they are enlarged. Mathematicians began studying fractals in the 17th century. Today, fractals have a wide range of applications in many fields, including music, environmental science, medicine, and video game design. For example, a biomedical engineer might need to know the total surface area of the bronchial tubes in the human lung or an environmental scientist might be concerned about the total length of coastline to be affected by an oil spill.

Go to the *Functions 11* page on the McGraw-Hill Ryerson Web site and follow the links to Chapter 6 to see more examples of fractals.

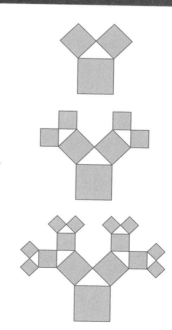

Sequences as Discrete Functions

The word *sequence* is used in everyday language. In a sequence, the order in which events occur is important. For example, builders must complete work in the proper sequence to construct safe, strong houses.

In mathematics, a **sequence** is a set of numbers, usually separated by commas, arranged in a particular order. Some sequences have very specific patterns and can be represented by mathematical rules or functions. Many natural phenomena, such as the spiral patterns seen in seashells, sunflowers, and galaxies, can be represented by sequences.

sequence
- an ordered list of numbers identified by a pattern or rule that may stop at some number or continue indefinitely
  3, 7, 11, 15
  2, 6, 18, 54, ...
- a function whose domain is the set, or a subset, of the natural numbers and whose range is the terms of the sequence

Tools

- square dot paper
- ruler

Investigate

How can you relate each number of a sequence to its position in the list?

The pattern of floor tiles in a new hotel is designed using nested squares. Explore the sequence formed by the number of enclosed regions created.

Method 1: Use Pencil and Paper

1. Construct a 16-unit by 16-unit square.

2. Locate the midpoint of each side. Connect consecutive midpoints to form a new square.
   Continue constructing midpoints and smaller squares until the squares are too small to work with.

3. Copy and complete the table for the pattern you created.

Number of Squares, n	Number of Regions, t
1	1
2	5
3	9

4. Refer to your completed table.

a) Reflect Describe the pattern in the Number of Regions column.

b) Write the values in this column as a sequence of **terms**. Use the pattern to write the next three terms of the sequence.

5. Graph the sequence using ordered pairs of the form (number of squares, number of regions). Should you join the points with a smooth curve or line or leave them as distinct points? Explain your thinking.

6. Reflect Determine an **explicit formula** to describe the number of regions, t_n, according to the number of squares, n.

term (of a sequence)

- a single value or object in a sequence

explicit formula

- a formula that represents any term in a sequence relative to the term number, n, where $n \in \mathbb{N}$

Method 2: Use *The Geometer's Sketchpad*®

Tools

- computer with *The Geometer's Sketchpad*®

1. Open *The Geometer's Sketchpad*®. From the **Graph** menu, choose **Grid Form** and then **Rectangular Grid**. Right-click on each axis and choose **Hide Axis** from the drop-down menu.

2. From the **Graph** menu, choose **Snap Points**. Draw a 16-unit by 16-unit square.

3. Select the sides of the square. From the **Construct** menu, choose **Midpoints**. Join the midpoints with line segments to form a square. Continue constructing midpoints and smaller squares until the squares are too small to work with.

4. Copy and complete the table for the pattern you created.

Number of Squares, *n*	Number of Regions, *t*
1	1
2	5
3	9

5. Refer to your completed table.

a) Reflect Describe the pattern in the Number of Regions column.

b) Write the values in this column as a sequence of **terms**. Use the pattern to write the next three terms of the sequence.

6. Graph the sequence using ordered pairs of the form (number of squares, number of regions). Should you join the points with a smooth curve or line or leave them as distinct points? Explain your thinking.

7. Reflect Determine an **explicit formula** to describe the number of regions, t_n, according to the number of squares, n.

Example 1

Use the Explicit Formula to Write Terms in a Sequence

Write the first three terms of each sequence, given the explicit formula for the nth term of the sequence, $n \in \mathbb{N}$.

a) $t_n = 3n^2 - 1$　　　　　　　　　**b)** $t_n = \dfrac{n-1}{n}$

Technology Tip

See the Use Technology feature at the end of this section for a TI-Nspire™ graphing calculator solution.

Solution

a) Method 1: Use Pencil and Paper

To determine the value of the first three terms, substitute the term numbers 1, 2, and 3 for n.

$t_n = 3n^2 - 1$

$$t_1 = 3(1)^2 - 1 \qquad\qquad t_2 = 3(2)^2 - 1 \qquad\qquad t_3 = 3(3)^2 - 1$$
$$ = 2 \qquad\qquad\qquad = 11 \qquad\qquad\qquad = 26$$

The first three terms of the sequence are 2, 11, and 26.

Method 2: Use a Graphing Calculator

The terms of a sequence can be generated using a graphing calculator.

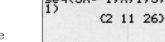

- Press (2nd) [LIST] and cursor over to the **OPS** menu.
- Select **5:seq(** and enter $3x^2 - 1$, x, 1, 3, 1).
- Press (ENTER).

The first three terms of the sequence are 2, 11, and 26.

Technology Tip

When using the **sequence** function of a graphing calculator to generate the terms of a sequence, you need to specify five things. For example, to generate the first three terms of the sequence $t_n = 3n^2 - 1$, you need

- the expression for the xth term of the sequence, $3x^2 - 1$
- the variable, x
- the starting term number, 1
- the ending term number, 3
- the increment value for the term numbers, 1

b) Substitute the term numbers 1, 2, and 3 for n.

$t_n = \dfrac{n-1}{n}$

$$t_1 = \dfrac{1-1}{1} \qquad\qquad t_2 = \dfrac{2-1}{2} \qquad\qquad t_3 = \dfrac{3-1}{3}$$
$$ = 0 \qquad\qquad\qquad = \dfrac{1}{2} \qquad\qquad\qquad = \dfrac{2}{3}$$

The first three terms of the sequence are 0, $\dfrac{1}{2}$, and $\dfrac{2}{3}$.

Example 2

Determine Explicit Formulas in Function Notation

For each sequence, make a table of values using the term number and term and calculate the finite differences. Then, graph the sequence using the ordered pairs (term number, term) and determine an explicit formula for the nth term, using function notation.

a) 7, 12, 17, 22, …　　　　　　　　**b)** 1, 10, 25, 46, …

Solution

a) Patterns in finite differences tables can be used to help determine a formula for the terms in a sequence.

Term Number, n	Term, t_n	First Differences
1	7	
		5
2	12	
		5
3	17	
		5
4	22	

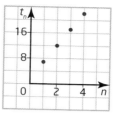

The graph models a function since there is exactly one value of t_n for each value of n. This function is linear since the first differences are constant. The rate of change, or the slope, is the first difference, 5.

$f(n) = 5n + b$

By inspection, $b = 2$. Then, an explicit formula to determine the terms in the sequence is $f(n) = 5n + 2$, where $n \in \mathbb{N}$.

b) Find the first and second differences.

Term Number, n	Term, t_n	First Differences	Second Differences
1	1		
		9	
2	10		6
		15	
3	25		6
		21	
4	46		

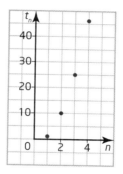

Since the second differences are constant, this function is quadratic. Half the value of the second difference corresponds to the value of a in a quadratic function of the form $f(n) = an^2 + bn + c$.

$f(n) = 3n^2 + bn + c$

To determine the values of b and c, substitute the coordinates of two points and solve a linear system of equations.

For (1, 1), $1 = 3(1)^2 + b + c$, or $-2 = b + c$.

For (2, 10), $10 = 3(2)^2 + 2b + c$, or $-2 = 2b + c$.

$$-2 = b + c \qquad ①$$
$$\underline{-2 = 2b + c \qquad ②}$$
$$0 = -b \qquad ① - ②$$
$$b = 0$$

Substitute $b = 0$ into equation ① and solve for c.

$$-2 = b + c$$
$$-2 = 0 + c$$
$$c = -2$$

An explicit formula to determine the terms in the sequence is $f(n) = 3n^2 - 2$, where $n \in \mathbb{N}$.

Example 3

Types of Functions

a) The charge in a battery decreases by about 2% per day and can be modelled by the function $C(d) = 100(0.98)^d$, where d is the time, in days, and C is the level of the charge, as a percent. How much charge is left after 10 days? Is this a **continuous function** or a **discrete function**? Explain.

b) A certain bacterial culture starts with 200 bacteria and doubles every hour. Its growth can be modelled by the function $N(t) = 200(2)^t$, where t is the time, in hours, and N is the number of bacteria. How many bacteria will there be after 10 h? Is this function continuous or discrete? Explain.

continuous function

- a function that maps real numbers to real numbers and has a graph that is a curve with no holes or jumps

discrete function

- a function whose graph is made up of separate points that are not connected

> **Solution**

a) To determine the charge level after 10 days, substitute $d = 10$ into $C(d) = 100(0.98)^d$.

$$C(10) = 100(0.98)^{10}$$
$$\doteq 81.7$$

After 10 days, the charge level of the battery is approximately 81.7%.

The table of values and graph show how the battery charge changes over time.

Time (days), d	Charge Level (%), C
0	100.0
1	98.0
2	96.0
3	94.1
4	92.2

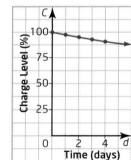

This is a continuous function since the charge level will be continuously changing over time. It does not drop 2% suddenly at the end of every day, but gradually decreases as time goes by.

b) To determine the number of bacteria after 10 h, substitute $t = 10$ into $N(t) = 200(2)^t$.

$$N(10) = 200(2)^{10}$$
$$= 204\ 800$$

After 10 h, there will be 204 800 bacteria.

The table of values and graph show the number of bacteria over time.

Time (h), t	Number of Bacteria, N
0	200
1	400
2	800
3	1600
4	3200

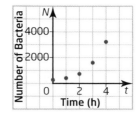

Since you cannot have part of a bacterium, this function is discrete. After each hour, the number of bacteria is double the number of the previous hour.

Example 4

Determine the Value of a Car

The value of a new car purchased for \$78 000 depreciates at a rate of 15% in the first year and 4% every year after that.

a) Determine the value of the car at the end of the first year, the second year, and the third year. Write these values as a sequence.

b) Determine an explicit formula for the value of the car at the end of year n.

c) What is the value of the car at the end of year 20? Is this realistic? Explain your thinking.

Connections

When an item *depreciates*, its value decreases over time. Some examples of items that depreciate are vehicles, electronics, computers, and clothing.

Solution

a) The value of the car when it is new is \$78 000. At the end of the first year, the car depreciates by 15%, so it is worth \$78 000 × 0.85, or \$66 300.

At the end of the second year, the car value decreases by 4%, so it is worth 96% of its value at the start of that year.

0.96 × \$66 300 = \$63 648

At the end of year 3, the car value again decreases by 4%.

$$0.96 \times (0.96 \times \$66\ 300) = 0.96 \times \$63\ 648$$
$$= \$61\ 102.08$$

The sequence that represents the value of the car at the end of each year is 66 300, 63 648, 61 102.08, … or
66 300, 0.96(66 300), 0.96^2(66 300), ….

b) The explicit formula for the value of the car at the end of year n is
$t_n = 66\ 300(0.96)^{n-1}$.

c) Substitute $n = 20$ to find the value of the car at the end of year 20.

$$t_n = 66\ 300(0.96)^{n-1}$$
$$t_{20} = 66\ 300(0.96)^{20-1}$$
$$= 66\ 300(0.96)^{19}$$
$$\doteq 30\ 525.79$$

At the end of year 20, the value of the car is $30 525.79.

It is possible that the car will be worth more than this if the owner looks after it carefully. It could also be worth much less if it has been involved in a collision, has a high odometer reading, or has a lot of rust. There are many factors that can affect the value of a used car.

Key Concepts

- A sequence of numbers can be represented by a discrete function. The graph of a discrete function is a distinct set of points, not a smooth curve.

- The domain of a function representing a sequence is the set or a subset of the natural numbers, $\mathbb{N}$.

- Given the explicit formula for the nth term, t_n or $f(n)$, of a sequence, the terms can be written by substituting the term numbers for n. Examples of explicit formulas are $t_n = 3n + 2$ and $f(n) = 5n + 3$.

- An explicit formula for the nth term of a sequence can sometimes be determined by finding a pattern among the terms.

Communicate Your Understanding

C1 Graph the sequence of numbers represented by the ordered pairs $(1, 1), (2, -1), (3, -3), (4, -5), \dots$. On the same set of axes, graph the function $f(x) = -2x + 3$, $x \in \mathbb{R}$. Describe the similarities and differences between the two graphs. Write the formula for the sequence using function notation and specify the domain.

C2 Consider the domain of a continuous and of a discrete function. What are the similarities between the domains? How are they different?

C3 Describe two situations in which it might be important to know a specific term in a sequence.

A Practise

For help with questions 1 and 2, refer to Example 1.

1. Write the first three terms of each sequence, given the explicit formula for the nth term of the sequence.

a) $t_n = 3n - 1$

b) $t_n = 2 - 5n$

c) $t_n = 3^{n-1}$

d) $f(n) = 2^{-n}$

e) $t_n = \dfrac{n+1}{n} - 1$

f) $f(n) = 3(2)^{n+2}$

2. Write the 12th term, given the explicit formula for the nth term of the sequence.

a) $f(n) = 1 - 3n$

b) $t_n = 2n + 5$

c) $f(n) = n^2 - 2$

d) $t_n = \dfrac{n+1}{n}$

e) $t_n = n^2 + 2n$

f) $f(n) = (-2)^{n-1}$

*For help with questions 3 to 5, refer to
Example 2.*

3. Describe the pattern in each sequence.
Write the next three terms of each
sequence.

a) 4, 16, 64, 256, …

b) 7, 6, 5, 4, …

c) $-3, -6, -9, -12, …$

d) 100, 10, 1, 0.1, …

e) 5, -10, 15, -20, …

f) $\dfrac{1}{3}, \dfrac{1}{9}, \dfrac{1}{27}, \dfrac{1}{81}, …$

g) $x, 3x, 5x, 7x, …$

h) 4, 8, 12, 16, …

i) $a, ar, ar^2, ar^3, …$

j) 0.2, -0.4, 0.6, -0.8, …

4. For each sequence, make a table of values
using the term number and term and
calculate the finite differences. Then,
determine an explicit formula in function
notation and specify the domain.

a) 2, 4, 6, 8, …

b) 2, 1, 0, -1, …

c) 3, 6, 9, 12, …

d) 0, 3, 8, 15, …

e) 3, 6, 11, 18, …

f) $-10, -9, 0, 17, …$

5. The graphs show the terms in a sequence.
Write each sequence in function notation
and specify the domain.

a)

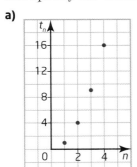

b)

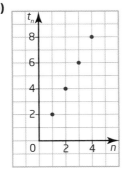

c)

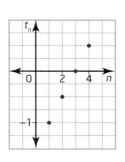

d)

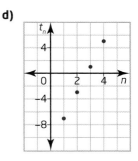

For help with question 6, refer to Example 3.

6. For each graph, specify whether the
function is discrete or continuous and
explain your choice.

a)

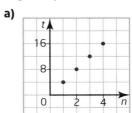

b)

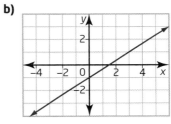

c)

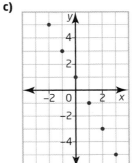

B **Connect and Apply**

7. Describe the pattern in each sequence and
write the next three terms.

a) 1, 1, 1, 2, 1, 3, 1, 4, 1, …

b) 1, 5, 2, 10, 3, 15, …

c) 3, $3\sqrt{5}$, 15, $15\sqrt{5}$, 75, …

d) $\dfrac{1}{2}, \dfrac{1}{4}, \dfrac{1}{8}, \dfrac{1}{16}, …$

8. Consider the sequence 7, 14, 21, 28, ... Determine whether or not each of the following numbers is part of this sequence. Explain your thinking.

a) 98   **b)** 110   **c)** 378   **d)** 575

9. Use Technology

The world population in 1995 was 5.7 billion. Since then the growth rate has been approximately 1.2% per year.

a) Graph the equation $y = 5.7(1.012)^x$ using a graphing calculator with the window settings shown.

```
WINDOW
 Xmin=0
 Xmax=50
 Xscl=5
 Ymin=5
 Ymax=10
 Yscl=.5
 Xres=1
```

b) Describe the shape of the graph. How would the graph change if the growth rate were greater? Use the graphing calculator to verify your description.

c) Assume the trend continues. Determine the population in each year from 2007 to 2015. Write these numbers as a sequence.

10. Use Technology A new car valued at $35 000 will depreciate at an average rate of 20% per year over the next several years.

a) Enter the following information in a spreadsheet.

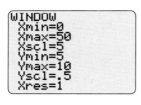

	A	B
1	Year	Value
2	0	35000
3	=A2+1	=0.8*B2

b) Use **Fill Down** to calculate the value of the car for the next 15 years.

c) Make an **XY (Scatter)** plot of this data.

d) Use function notation to write an explicit formula to represent the value of the car at the end of year n.

e) Is this a continuous or a discrete function? Explain your thinking.

11. If two resistors, A and B, are in parallel, then the combined resistance, R, in ohms (Ω), is found by the formula

$$\frac{1}{R} = \frac{1}{R_A} + \frac{1}{R_B}$$

Assume each resistor has a resistance of 1 Ω. Use the formula to determine the value of the resistance for 2, 3, 4, 5, and 6 resistors in parallel. Write these numbers as a sequence.

12. Chapter Problem The Koch snowflake was one of the earliest fractals to be described. The snowflake starts as an equilateral triangle. At each stage, the middle third of each side is replaced by two line segments, each equal in length to the line segment they replace.

Stage 1   Stage 2   Stage 3

a) Work with a partner and use isometric dot paper to draw the diagrams shown. Use the pattern to draw the next diagram.

b) Copy and complete the table.

Stage Number	Line Segment Length	Number of Line Segments	Perimeter of the Snowflake
1	1	3	3
2	$\frac{1}{3}$	12	4
3	$\frac{1}{9}$		
4			
5			
6			

c) Determine an explicit formula for the nth term in columns two, three, and four of the table.

d) Use your formulas to calculate the values for stage 24.

13. Determine an explicit formula for the nth term of each sequence. Use the formula to write the 15th term.

a) $-4, 8, -16, 32, \ldots$ b) $1, \frac{2}{3}, \frac{3}{5}, \frac{4}{7}, \ldots$

c) $1, \sqrt{2}, \sqrt{3}, 2, \ldots$ d) $1, 2, 4, 8, \ldots$

e) $1, \frac{1}{2}, \frac{1}{3}, \frac{1}{4}, \ldots$ f) $1, -1, 1, -1, \ldots$

14. Create two different sequences that start with 1, 2, 3. Write an explicit formula for the nth term of each sequence in function notation. Graph each sequence.

15. A new small business plans to double its sales every day for its first 2 weeks. Sales on the first day are $50.

Reasoning and Proving
Representing   **Selecting Tools**
Problem Solving
Connecting   Reflecting
Communicating

a) Write the sequence that represents the sales for the first 6 days according to the plan.

b) Write an explicit formula to determine the sales on any of the first 14 days.

c) Use your formula to determine the sales on the 14th day. Is this reasonable? Why or why not?

16. A high school is experiencing declining enrolment. This year the enrolment was 2100, and it has been predicted that every year there will be 110 fewer students. Write an explicit formula to determine the number of students in any given year. After how long will the enrolment drop below 800 students?

C Extend

17. a) Use a calculator to determine approximate values for the first three terms of the sequence

$$\sqrt{3}, \sqrt{\sqrt{3}}, \sqrt{\sqrt{\sqrt{3}}}, \sqrt{\sqrt{\sqrt{\sqrt{3}}}}, \ldots$$

b) Describe the pattern in the sequence.

c) Use the pattern to predict the value of the 50th term in this sequence.

18. Determine an explicit formula for the total number of squares in an n by n square.

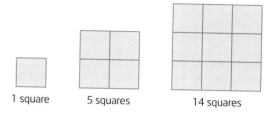

1 square   5 squares   14 squares

19. Math Contest The multiples of 5 are printed in the columns of a Bingo game card as shown.

B	I	N	G	O
5	10	15	20	
	40	35	30	25
45	50	55	60	
	80	75	70	65
85	90	95	100	

If the numbers continue in this pattern, in which column will the number 5555 occur?

A B   **B** N   **C** G   **D** O

20. Math Contest The crown jewels are missing. Scotland Yard has four suspects, Albert, Bob, Cecilia, and Dwight. Albert says, "Cecilia is the thief." Bob says, "I am not the thief." Cecilia says, "Dwight is the thief." Dwight says, "Cecilia lied." If only one of these statements is true, who is the real thief?

A Albert   **B** Bob   **C** Cecilia   **D** Dwight

21. Math Contest A bag contains two balls. The value of one ball is 4. The value of the other is 9. A ball is chosen and the value of the ball is added to a running total. The number of different sums that are not possible to attain is

A 6

B 12

C 11

D Not possible to determine

Use a TI-Nspire™ CAS Graphing Calculator to Write Terms in a Sequence

Write the first three terms of each sequence, given the explicit formula for the nth term of the sequence, $n \in \mathbb{N}$.

Tools

- TI-Nspire™ CAS graphing calculator

$$A: t_n = 3n^2 - 1 \qquad\qquad B: t_n = \frac{n - 1}{n}$$

Connections

Example 1 on page 356 is used to model the steps needed to find the first three terms of a sequence, given the explicit formula for the nth term of the sequence.

Solution

Open a new document. Open a page using the **Lists & Spreadsheet** application.

Enter the headings for columns A, B, and C.

- At the top of column A, type n and press ⏎.

- At the top of column B, type a_t_n and press ⏎.

- At the top of column C, type b_t_n and press ⏎.

Enter the values 1, 2, and 3 for n, starting in cell A1.

Enter the explicit formulas for the sequences.

- In the formula cell for column B,
  type $= 3a^2 - 1$ and press ⏎.

- In the formula cell for column C, type $= (a - 1) \div a$ and press ⏎.

The first three terms for each sequence will be displayed.

Technology Tip

To type an underscore (_), use the symbol palette.

- Press ⌃ 🔣 .

- Use the cursor keys to move to _.

- Press ⏎.

1.1		RAD AUTO REAL		
A n	**B** a_t_n	**C** b_t_n	**D**	
◆	=3*a[]^2-1	=(a[]-1)/a[		
1	1	2	0	
2	2	11	1/2	
3	3	26	2/3	
4				
5				
C1	=0			

Recursive Procedures

In Section 6.1, you used function notation to write an explicit formula to determine the value of any term in a sequence. Sometimes it is easier to calculate one term in a sequence using the previous terms.

Computer programmers use sequences of code to create instructions for computers. Often these sequences tell the computer to use a previous value to find the next one. This is known as a recursive procedure.

Investigate

Tools
• grid paper

Optional
• computer with *The Geometer's Sketchpad®*

How can you model the relationship between consecutive terms of a sequence?

The first three diagrams in a pattern are shown. Model the pattern.

1. a) For Diagram 1, draw a square with side length 1 unit.

Diagram 1   Diagram 2   Diagram 3

b) For Diagram 2, start with Diagram 1 and draw a square with side length 1 unit adjacent to the first square. This creates a rectangle.

c) For Diagram 3, draw a larger rectangle. Start with Diagram 2 and draw a square with side length 2 units adjacent to and directly above the two smaller squares.

2. Diagram 4 will contain a square with side length 3 units. Where should this square be drawn in order to continue the pattern? Draw Diagram 4.

3. Copy and complete the table for the pattern of diagrams.

Diagram Number	Side Length of Square (units)
1	1
2	1
3	2
4	
5	
6	

4. a) Write the side lengths of the squares as a sequence.

  b) **Reflect** Determine the relationship between consecutive terms in the sequence and write a formula for the nth term, t_n, in terms of the $(n-1)$th term, t_{n-1}, and the $(n-2)$th term, t_{n-2}.

Fibonacci sequence

- the sequence of numbers 1, 1, 2, 3, 5, 8, ...
- Each number, after the first two numbers, is the sum of the preceding two numbers.

recursion formula

- a formula by which each term of a sequence is generated from the preceding term or terms

The sequence formed by the side lengths of the squares in the Investigate is a famous sequence known as the **Fibonacci sequence**.

A sequence is said to be recursive if a new term is found using a previous term or terms. For example, the Fibonacci sequence 1, 1, 2, 3, 5, 8, 13, ... is a recursive sequence because each term beginning with the third term is the result of adding the two previous terms. The **recursion formula** for this sequence can be written as $t_1 = 1$, $t_2 = 1$, $t_n = t_{n-1} + t_{n-2}$, where t_1 is the first term, t_2 is the second term, t_n is the nth term, and so on.

Connections

The Fibonacci sequence is named after Leonardo Fibonacci (c. 1175–1250), who discovered the sequence while studying the reproductive nature of rabbits. Fibonacci is also credited with introducing the decimal number system to Europe.
Go to the *Functions 11* page on the McGraw-Hill Ryerson Web site and follow the links to Chapter 6 to learn more about the Fibonacci sequence.

Example 1

Write the Terms of a Sequence Given the Recursion Formula

Write the first four terms of each sequence.

a) $t_1 = 3$, $t_n = t_{n-1} - 2$

b) $f(1) = -\dfrac{1}{2}$, $f(n) = f(n-1) + \dfrac{3}{2}$

Solution

a) The first term is given as 3. Use the equation $t_n = t_{n-1} - 2$ to determine the next three terms in the sequence.

$$
\begin{aligned}
t_2 &= t_1 - 2 & t_3 &= t_2 - 2 & t_4 &= t_3 - 2 \\
&= 3 - 2 & &= 1 - 2 & &= -1 - 2 \\
&= 1 & &= -1 & &= -3
\end{aligned}
$$

The first four terms of the sequence are 3, 1, -1, -3.

b) The first term is given as $-\dfrac{1}{2}$. Use the equation $f(n) = f(n-1) + \dfrac{3}{2}$ to determine the next three terms in the sequence.

$$
\begin{aligned}
f(2) &= f(1) + \frac{3}{2} & f(3) &= f(2) + \frac{3}{2} & f(4) &= f(3) + \frac{3}{2} \\
&= -\frac{1}{2} + \frac{3}{2} & &= 1 + \frac{3}{2} & &= \frac{5}{2} + \frac{3}{2} \\
&= 1 & &= \frac{5}{2} & &= 4
\end{aligned}
$$

The first four terms of the sequence are $-\dfrac{1}{2}$, 1, $\dfrac{5}{2}$, 4.

Example 2

Write a Recursion Formula

Determine a recursion formula for each sequence.

a) $-3, 6, -12, 24, \ldots$

b)

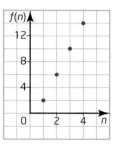

c) $3, 5, 8, 12, \ldots$

Solution

a) Look for a pattern in the terms.

$t_1 = -3$
$t_2 = t_1 \times (-2)$
$t_3 = t_2 \times (-2)$
$t_4 = t_3 \times (-2)$

The recursion formula is $t_1 = -3$, $t_n = -2t_{n-1}$.

b) Look for a pattern in the y-coordinates.

$f(1) = 2$
$f(2) = 6$
$f(3) = 10$
$f(4) = 14$

Each term is 4 more than the previous term. The recursion formula is
$f(1) = 2$, $f(n) = f(n-1) + 4$.

c) Look for a pattern in the terms.

$t_1 = 3$
$t_2 = t_1 + 2$
$t_3 = t_2 + 3$
$t_4 = t_3 + 4$

The recursion formula is $t_1 = 3$, $t_n = t_{n-1} + n$.

Example 3

Medication in the Human Body

A runner injures her knee in a race. Her doctor prescribes physiotherapy along with 500 mg of an anti-inflammatory medicine every 4 h for 3 days.

The half-life of the anti-inflammatory medicine is approximately 4 h. This means that after 4 h, about half of the medicine is still in the body.

a) Make a table of values showing the amount of medicine remaining in the body after each 4-h period of time.

b) Write the amount of medicine remaining after each 4-h period as a sequence. Write a recursion formula for the sequence.

c) Graph the sequence.

d) Describe what happens to the medicine in the runner's body over time.

Solution

Technology Tip

To calculate the amount of medicine in the body using a spreadsheet, insert the formula =0.5*B2+500, and then fill down.

a) This can be done using pencil and paper or a spreadsheet. Round your answers to the nearest tenth of a milligram, where necessary.

4-h Interval	Amount of Medicine (mg)
0	500
1	$\frac{1}{2}(500) + 500 = 750$
2	$\frac{1}{2}(750) + 500 = 875$
3	937.5
4	968.8
5	984.4
6	992.2
7	996.1
8	998.0
9	999.0
10	999.5
11	999.8
12	999.9

1.1		RAD AUTO REAL	
interval	amount_mg	C	D
=seqn(u(n			
0.	500		
1.	750.		
2.	875.		
3.	937.5		
4.	968.75		

A | interval

b) The sequence representing the amount of medicine remaining in the body after each 4-h period is 500, 750, 875, 937.5, 968.8, ..., 999.9. The recursion formula is $t_1 = 500$, $t_n = 500 + 0.5t_{n-1}$.

c)

Amount of Medicine in the Body

d) From the graph, the amount of medicine in the body increases until it appears to reach a constant level of about 1000 mg.

Key Concepts

- A recursive procedure is one where a process is performed on an initial object or number and then the result is put through the steps of the process again. This is repeated many times over.

- A sequence can be defined recursively if each term can be calculated from the previous term or terms.

- A recursion formula shows the relationship between the terms of a sequence.

- A sequence can be represented by a pattern, an explicit formula, or a recursion formula. Formulas can also be written using function notation.

  For example:

  Pattern: 1, 3, 5, 7, ...

  Explicit formula: $t_n = 2n - 1$ or $f(n) = 2n - 1$

  Recursion formula: $t_1 = 1$, $t_n = t_{n-1} + 2$, or $f(1) = 1$, $f(n) = f(n-1) + 2$

- In an explicit or a recursion formula for a sequence, n is a natural number because it is a term number. To find the terms of a sequence using a recursion formula, begin with the next natural number that is not used in the formula.

Communicate Your Understanding

C1 What do you need to know about a sequence in order to write a recursion formula to describe the terms in the sequence?

C2 **a)** The recursion formula $t_1 = 5$, $t_n = 2t_{n-1} + 1$, has two parts. Describe the two parts.

   b) Why does a recursion formula have at least two parts?

   c) What characteristic of a sequence is needed for the formula to have more than two parts?

C3 A sequence has the recursion formula $t_1 = 4$, $t_n = -2t_{n-1} + 5$. Use words to describe how this formula is used to determine consecutive terms in the sequence.

C4 The explicit formula for the nth term of a sequence is $t_n = 6(2^{n-1}) - 1$, while the recursion formula for the same sequence is $t_1 = 5$, $t_n = 2t_{n-1} + 1$. When might it be more convenient to use one form of the formula instead of the other? Explain.

A Practise

For help with questions 1 and 2, refer to Example 1.

1. Write the first four terms of each sequence, where $n \in \mathbb{N}$.
   a) $t_1 = 4, t_n = t_{n-1} + 3$
   b) $t_1 = 7, t_n = 2t_{n-1} - 1$
   c) $t_1 = -3, t_n = 0.2t_{n-1} - 1.2$
   d) $t_1 = 50, t_n = \dfrac{t_{n-1}}{2}$
   e) $t_1 = 8, t_n = 2n - 3t_{n-1}$
   f) $t_1 = 100, t_n = \dfrac{5t_{n-1}}{0.1}$

2. Write the first four terms of each sequence, where $n \in \mathbb{N}$.
   a) $f(1) = 9, f(n) = f(n-1) - 2$
   b) $f(1) = -1, f(n) = -3f(n-1)$
   c) $f(1) = 3, f(n) = \dfrac{f(n-1)}{n}$
   d) $f(1) = 18, f(n) = f(n-1) + 2$
   e) $f(1) = 0.5, f(n) = -f(n-1)$
   f) $f(1) = 25, f(n) = -0.5f(n-1)$

For help with questions 3 and 4, refer to Example 2.

3. Determine a recursion formula for each sequence.
   a) 5, 11, 17, 23, ...
   b) 4, 1, −2, −5, ...
   c) 4, 8, 16, 32, ...
   d) $-4, -2, -1, -\dfrac{1}{2}, \dots$
   e) −5, 15, −45, 135, ...

4. For each graph, write the sequence of terms and determine a recursion formula using function notation.

   a)
   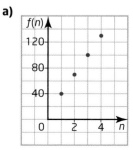

   b)
   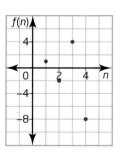

5. An example of a constant sequence is 206, 206, 206, ... Write a recursion formula for this sequence. Write another constant sequence and its recursion formula.

B Connect and Apply

For help with questions 6 and 7, refer to Example 3.

6. A new theatre is being built for a youth orchestra. This theatre has 50 seats in the first row, 54 in the second row, 62 in the third row, 74 in the next row, and so on.
   a) Represent the number of seats in the rows as a sequence.
   b) Describe the pattern in the number of seats per row.
   c) Write a recursion formula to represent the number of seats in any row.

7. Sacha and Marghala paid $250 000 for their first home. The real estate agent told them that the house will appreciate in value by 3% per year.
   a) Copy and complete the table to show the value of the house for the next 10 years.

Year	House Value ($)
0	250 000
1	250 000 + 0.03 × 250 000 = 257 500

   b) Write the value of the house for the first 10 years as a sequence.
   c) Write a recursion formula to represent the value of the house. Use your formula to predict the value after 15 years.

8. Write the first four terms of each sequence.
   a) $t_1 = 1, t_n = (t_{n-1})^2 + 3n$
   b) $f(1) = 8, f(n) = \dfrac{f(n-1)}{2}$
   c) $t_1 = 3, t_n = 2t_{n-1}$
   d) $t_1 = -5, t_n = 4 - 2t_{n-1}$
   e) $t_1 = \dfrac{1}{2}, t_n = 4t_{n-1} + 2$
   f) $f(1) = a + 3b, f(n) = f(n-1) + 4b$

9. Use the given recursion formula to determine the first four terms of each sequence. Then, use words to describe the rule for determining terms in the sequence.

a) $f(1) = 2$, $f(2) = 2$,
$f(n) = f(n - 1) + 2f(n - 2)$

b) $f(1) = 1$, $f(2) = 2$, $f(n) = f(n - 1)f(n - 2)$

c) $t_1 = 5$, $t_2 = 7$, $t_n = t_{n - 2} - t_{n - 1}$

d) $t_1 = -2$, $t_2 = 3$, $t_n = 3t_{n - 2} + t_{n - 1}$

e) $t_1 = 1$, $t_2 = -4$, $t_n = t_{n - 2} \times t_{n - 1}$

f) $t_1 = 3$, $t_2 = 1$, $t_3 = 7$,
$t_n = t_{n - 3} + t_{n - 2} - t_{n - 1}$

10. The diagrams show the diagonals in regular polygons with n sides. Write the sequence for the number of diagonals and determine the recursion formula for this sequence.

11. A square-based pyramid with height 7 m is constructed with cubic blocks measuring 1 m on each side.

Write a recursion formula for the sequence that represents the number of blocks used at each level from the top down.

12. A sequence has a first term of -8. Each succeeding term is 4 more than twice the previous term.

a) Write the first four terms of this sequence.

b) Define the sequence using a recursion formula and then graph the sequence.

13. Given the explicit formula of a sequence, write the first four terms and then determine a recursion formula for each sequence.

Reasoning and Proving
Representing • Selecting Tools
Problem Solving
Connecting • Reflecting
Communicating

a) $t_n = (2n - 1)^2$

b) $t_n = \dfrac{n^2 + 1}{n}$

c) $f(n) = 3^{-n}$

d) $t_n = 3n + 1$

e) $f(n) = (n - 2)(n + 2)$

f) $f(n) = 2(4)^{n - 1}$

14. Given the recursion formula, write the first four terms of the sequence and then determine the explicit formula for the sequence.

a) $t_1 = 3$, $t_n = 2t_{n - 1} + 1$

b) $t_1 = 1$, $t_n = \dfrac{1}{2}t_{n - 1}$

c) $t_1 = 10$, $t_n = t_{n - 1} - 10$

d) $t_1 = -2$, $t_n = t_{n - 1} - \dfrac{1}{n(n - 1)}$

15. **Chapter Problem** The Sierpinski triangle was described by Waclaw Sierpinski in 1915. This now famous fractal was also seen in Italian art in the 13th century.

a) Use isometric dot paper or *The Geometer's Sketchpad*® to construct a large equilateral triangle. Consider the area of this triangle to be 1 square unit.

b) Locate and join the midpoints to make a new triangle. Shade in all but the centre triangle. Determine the area of the shaded regions.

c) Continue to draw triangles formed by the midpoints of the sides of the smaller and smaller shaded triangles. Always leave the centre triangle unshaded and determine the area of the shaded regions.

d) Write the area of the shaded regions at each stage as a sequence. Write a formula for this sequence. Is your formula explicit or recursive?

Stage 1   Stage 2   Stage 3

16. Write a recursion formula for each sequence.

a) 2, 6, 12, 20, 30, ...   **b)** 3, 7, 16, 32, ...

c) 2, 5, 26, 677, ...   **d)** −1, 0, 3, 12, ...

✔ **Achievement Check**

17. Canadian checkers is played on a checkerboard that has 12 squares per side. What would happen if you placed a penny on the first square, two pennies on the second square, four on the third square, eight on the fourth square, and so on?

a) Write the numbers of pennies on the first 12 squares as a sequence.

b) Write a recursion formula to represent the number of pennies on any square. Use your formula to determine the number of pennies on square 20.

c) Write an explicit formula, in function notation, to represent the number of pennies on any square. Use this formula to verify your answer to part b).

d) Is this function discrete or continuous? Explain.

C Extend

18. Write the first five terms of each sequence, starting at $f(1)$.

a) $f(2) = -3, f(n) = -2f(n - 1)$

b) $f(3) = 9, f(n) = f(n - 1) + n^2$

19. Create three different sequences that start with 2, 3, 4. Write recursion formulas for these sequences. Write the next two terms of each of your sequences and challenge your classmates to determine the recursive rule that you used.

Reasoning and Proving
Representing · Selecting Tools
Problem Solving
Connecting · Reflecting
Communicating

20. a) Write a new sequence using the terms of the Fibonacci sequence. Start with the first two terms of the Fibonacci sequence. Then, divide the third term in the Fibonacci sequence by the second term to get the next term in the new sequence. Continue dividing the next term in the Fibonacci sequence by the previous term to get the next term in the new sequence. Describe the pattern in the new sequence.

b) The sequence in part a) converges to a value close to 1.618. This is the number φ (phi), which is also known as the golden ratio. Research the golden ratio and prepare a poster for the classroom.

21. The golden spiral is constructed from the rectangle diagram you constructed in the Investigate.

a) In each square, construct an arc with radius equal to the side length of the square.

b) Determine the area under the spiral for each square. Write the areas as a sequence of numbers. Calculate the total area under the spiral.

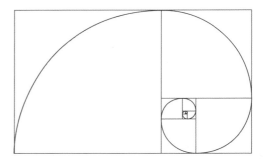

22. Math Contest The Lucas numbers are similar to the Fibonacci numbers but the first two terms are $t_1 = 2$ and $t_2 = 1$. The sequence is 2, 1, 3, 4, 7, 11, ... Let L_n be the nth Lucas number and F_n be the nth Fibonacci number. For $n > 2$, show that $L_n - F_n = F_{n-2}$.

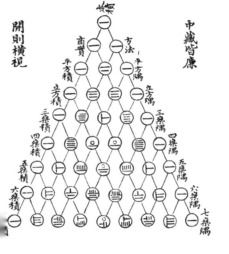

Pascal's Triangle and Expanding Binomial Powers

It is widely believed that some time during the 11th century, both the Chinese and the Persians discovered an unusual array of numbers. However, the triangle representing the array of numbers was named after Blaise Pascal (1623–1662), a French mathematician who lived and worked in the mid-1600s. Pascal is credited with the discoveries of many of the triangle's special properties and applications, as well as with many other important contributions to the field of mathematics.

The triangular arrangement of numbers known as **Pascal's triangle** can be built using a recursive procedure. Each term in Pascal's triangle is the sum of the two terms immediately above it. The first and last terms in each row are 1 since the only term immediately above them is always a 1.

Pascal's triangle

- a triangular arrangement of numbers with 1 in the first row, and 1 and 1 in the second row
- Each number in the succeeding rows is the sum of the two numbers above it in the preceding row.

```
                    1
                1       1
            1       2       1
        1       3       3       1
    1       4       6       4       1
  1     5       10      10      5       1
1       6       15      20      15      6       1
```

Investigate

How can you use patterns to expand a power of a binomial?

1. Expand each power of a binomial using the distributive property and simplifying or by using a CAS.

   a) $(a + b)^1$

   b) $(a + b)^2$

   c) $(a + b)^3$

   d) $(a + b)^4$

2. **Reflect** Examine the pattern in the coefficients of the terms in each expansion. Describe how the pattern relates to Pascal's triangle.

3. **Reflect** Study the variables in the terms of each expansion. Describe how the degree of each term relates to the power of the binomial.

4. Predict the terms in the expansion of $(a + b)^5$.

Tools

Optional
- Computer Algebra System (CAS)

Technology

You can use the CAS engine of a TI-Nspire™ CAS graphing calculator to expand a power of a binomial.

- Open a new calculator page.
- Press (menu), select **3:Algebra**, and then select **3:Expand**.
- Enter the power of a binomial. For example, type $(a + b)^3$ and press (enter).

The expansion will be displayed.

Example 1

Patterns in Pascal's Triangle

a) Write the first seven rows of Pascal's triangle and label the rows.

b) The powers of 2 can be found by looking for a pattern in the triangle. Find the pattern.

Solution

a)

row 0							1						
row 1						1		1					
row 2					1		2		1				
row 3				1		3		3		1			
row 4			1		4		6		4		1		
row 5		1		5		10		10		5		1	
row 6	1		6		15		20		15		6		1

b) If the terms in each row are added, the sequence formed is the powers of 2.

Row 0 sum: $1 = 2^0$

Row 1 sum: $2 = 2^1$

Row 2 sum: $4 = 2^2$

Row 3 sum: $8 = 2^3$

and so on.

Example 2

Position of Terms in Pascal's Triangle

A term in Pascal's triangle can be represented by $t_{n,\, r}$, where n is the horizontal row number and r is the diagonal row number.

$n = 0$				1 $r = 0$				$t_{0,\,0}$
$n = 1$			1	1 $r = 1$				$t_{1,\,0}\ t_{1,\,1}$
$n = 2$		1	2	1 $r = 2$				$t_{2,\,0}\ t_{2,\,1}\ t_{2,\,2}$
$n = 3$	1	3	3	1 $r = 3$				$t_{3,\,0}\ t_{3,\,1}\ t_{3,\,2}\ t_{3,\,3}$
$n = 4$	1	4	6	4	1 $r = 4$			$t_{4,\,0}\ t_{4,\,1}\ t_{4,\,2}\ t_{4,\,3}\ t_{4,\,4}$
$n = 5$	1	5	10	10	5	1 $r = 5$		$t_{5,\,0}\ t_{5,\,1}\ t_{5,\,2}\ t_{5,\,3}\ t_{5,\,4}\ t_{5,\,5}$
$n = 6$	1	6	15	20	15	6	1 $r = 6$	$t_{6,\,0}\ t_{6,\,1}\ t_{6,\,2}\ t_{6,\,3}\ t_{6,\,4}\ t_{6,\,5}\ t_{6,\,6}$

Each term is equal to the sum of the two terms immediately above it, which can be represented as $t_{n,\,r} = t_{n-1,\,r-1} + t_{n-1,\,r}$.

Express $t_{5,\,3} + t_{5,\,4}$ as a single term from Pascal's triangle in the form $t_{n,\,r}$.

Solution

Any term in Pascal's triangle is the sum of the terms immediately above it.

$t_{5,3} + t_{5,4} = t_{6,4}$

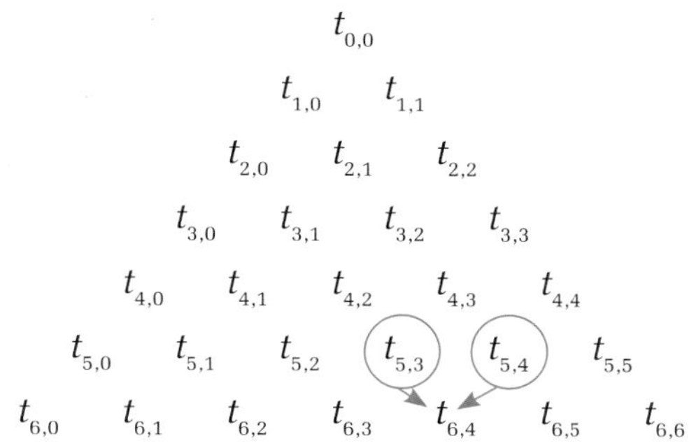

$t_{0,0}$

$t_{1,0} \quad t_{1,1}$

$t_{2,0} \quad t_{2,1} \quad t_{2,2}$

$t_{3,0} \quad t_{3,1} \quad t_{3,2} \quad t_{3,3}$

$t_{4,0} \quad t_{4,1} \quad t_{4,2} \quad t_{4,3} \quad t_{4,4}$

$t_{5,0} \quad t_{5,1} \quad t_{5,2} \quad \boxed{t_{5,3}} \quad \boxed{t_{5,4}} \quad t_{5,5}$

$t_{6,0} \quad t_{6,1} \quad t_{6,2} \quad t_{6,3} \quad t_{6,4} \quad t_{6,5} \quad t_{6,6}$

Example 3

Relate Other Patterns to Pascal's Triangle

The diagrams represent the triangular numbers.

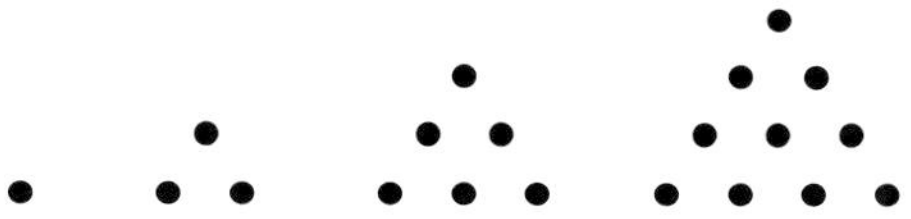

a) Write the number of dots in each diagram as a sequence.

b) Locate these numbers in Pascal's triangle. Describe their position.

c) Write an explicit formula and a recursion formula for the triangular numbers.

Solution

a) The sequence of triangular numbers is 1, 3, 6, 10, ….

b) The numbers are located in diagonal row 2 of Pascal's triangle.

c) Calculate the finite differences.

Term Number, n	Term, $f(n)$	First Differences	Second Differences
1	1		
		2	
2	3		1
		3	
3	6		1
		4	
4	10		

Since the second differences are constant, this function is quadratic. Half the value of the second difference corresponds to the value of a in a quadratic function of the form $f(n) = an^2 + bn + c$.

$f(n) = \dfrac{1}{2}n^2 + bn + c$

To determine the values of b and c, substitute the coordinates of two points, say $(1, 1)$ and $(2, 3)$, and solve the linear system of equations.

$$\frac{1}{2} = b + c$$

$$1 = 2b + c$$

This gives $b = \frac{1}{2}$ and $c = 0$.

The explicit formula for the nth term is $f(n) = \frac{1}{2}n^2 + \frac{1}{2}n$.

The recursion formula is $f(1) = 1$, $f(n) = f(n - 1) + n$.

Connections

If you take Mathematics of Data Management in grade 12, you will see how Pascal's triangle and expansions of $(a + b)^n$ are connected to probability.

Powers of binomials can be expanded by using patterns. The coefficients in the expansion of $(a + b)^n$ can be found in row n of Pascal's triangle.

Value of n	$(a + b)^n$
0	$(a + b)^0 = 1$
1	$(a + b)^1 = a + b$
2	$(a + b)^2 = a^2 + 2ab + b^2$
3	$(a + b)^3 = a^3 + 3a^2b + 3ab^2 + b^3$
4	$(a + b)^4 = a^4 + 4a^3b + 6a^2b^2 + 4ab^3 + b^4$

There is also a pattern in the powers of a and b. In each expansion, the power of a decreases, the power of b increases, and the degree of each term is always equal to the exponent of the binomial power.

Example 4

Expand a Power of a Binomial

Use Pascal's triangle to expand each power of a binomial.

a) $(a + b)^7$　　**b)** $(m - n)^5$　　**c)** $(2x + 1)^6$　　**d)** $\left(\dfrac{y}{2} - y^2\right)^4$

Solution

a) Since the exponent is 7, the coefficients occur in row 7 of Pascal's triangle. The powers of a will decrease and the powers of b will increase.

$$(a + b)^7 = 1a^7b^0 + 7a^6b^1 + 21a^5b^2 + 35a^4b^3 + 35a^3b^4$$
$$+ 21a^2b^5 + 7a^1b^6 + 1a^0b^7$$
$$= a^7 + 7a^6b + 21a^5b^2 + 35a^4b^3 + 35a^3b^4 + 21a^2b^5 + 7ab^6 + b^7$$

Note that you can use the CAS engine of a TI-Nspire™ CAS graphing calculator to check your answer.

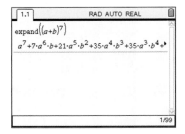

b) The coefficients occur in row 5 of Pascal's triangle. Let $a = m$ and $b = -n$ and apply the pattern of powers.

$$(m - n)^5 = 1(m)^5(-n)^0 + 5(m)^4(-n)^1 + 10(m)^3(-n)^2 + 10(m)^2(-n)^3$$
$$+ 5(m)^1(-n)^4 + 1(m)^0(-n)^5$$
$$= m^5 - 5m^4n + 10m^3n^2 - 10m^2n^3 + 5mn^4 - n^5$$

c) The coefficients occur in row 6 of Pascal's triangle. Let $a = 2x$ and $b = 1$ and apply the pattern of powers.

$$(2x + 1)^6 = 1(2x)^6(1)^0 + 6(2x)^5(1)^1 + 15(2x)^4(1)^2 + 20(2x)^3(1)^3$$
$$+ 15(2x)^2(1)^4 + 6(2x)^1(1)^5 + 1(2x)^0(1)^6$$
$$= 64x^6 + 192x^5 + 240x^4 + 160x^3 + 60x^2 + 12x + 1$$

d) The coefficients occur in row 4 of Pascal's triangle. Let $a = \dfrac{y}{2}$ and $b = -y^2$ and apply the pattern of powers.

$$\left(\frac{y}{2} - y^2\right)^4 = 1\left(\frac{y}{2}\right)^4(-y^2)^0 + 4\left(\frac{y}{2}\right)^3(-y^2)^1 + 6\left(\frac{y}{2}\right)^2(-y^2)^2 + 4\left(\frac{y}{2}\right)^1(-y^2)^3$$
$$+ 1\left(\frac{y}{2}\right)^0(-y^2)^4$$
$$= \frac{y^4}{16} - \frac{y^5}{2} + \frac{3y^6}{2} - 2y^7 + y^8$$

Key Concepts

- Pascal's triangle is a triangular array of natural numbers in which the entries can be obtained by adding the two entries immediately above.

  $t_{n, r} = t_{n-1, r-1} + t_{n-1, r}$, where n is the horizontal row number and r is the diagonal row number; $n, r \in \mathbb{N}$ and $r \le n$

- Many number patterns can be found in Pascal's triangle. For example, the sums of the terms of the rows form a sequence of the powers of 2 and the terms in diagonal row 2 are triangular numbers.

- The coefficients of the terms in the expansion of $(a + b)^n$ correspond to the terms in row n of Pascal's triangle.

Communicate Your Understanding

C1 Look at Pascal's triangle. What is the value of $t_{6, 3}$? Does $t_{3, 6}$ have the same value?

C2 Describe how to determine a term in Pascal's triangle if you know the row and diagonal row numbers.

C3 Explore Pascal's triangle for other patterns. Write sequences to represent the patterns you found and describe how to determine the terms in these sequences.

C4 Describe how you would use Pascal's triangle to expand $(a + b)^8$.

A Practise

For help with questions 1 and 2, refer to Example 1.

1. The hockey stick pattern is one of many found in Pascal's triangle. Start on any of the 1s along the side. Select any number of entries along a diagonal to this 1, ending inside the triangle. Determine the sum of these numbers. Turn at the bottom, as shown in the example. How is the number not on the diagonal related to the sum? On a copy of Pascal's triangle, outline five hockey stick patterns of your own.

2. Determine the sum of the terms in each row of Pascal's triangle.

a) row 8　　　　　　**b)** row 12

c) row 20　　　　　　**d)** row n

For help with questions 3 and 4, refer to Example 2.

3. Express as a single term from Pascal's triangle in the form $t_{n, r}$.

a) $t_{4, 3} + t_{4, 4}$　　　　**b)** $t_{8, 5} + t_{8, 6}$

c) $t_{25, 17} + t_{25, 18}$　　**d)** $t_{a, b} + t_{a, b + 1}$

4. Write each as the sum of two terms, each in the form $t_{n, r}$.

a) $t_{4, 2}$　**b)** $t_{12, 9}$　**c)** $t_{28, 14}$　**d)** $t_{17, x}$

For help with questions 5 to 7, refer to Example 3.

5. Use Pascal's triangle to expand each power of a binomial.

a) $(x + 2)^5$　　**b)** $(y - 3)^4$　　**c)** $(4 + t)^6$

d) $(1 - m)^5$　　**e)** $(2x - 3y)^4$　**f)** $(a^2 + 4)^5$

6. How many terms are in each expansion?

a) $(3a + 5)^0$　　　　**b)** $(x + 2)^{25}$

c) $(t - 6)^{15}$　　　　**d)** $(5b + 6a)^n$

7. Use patterns in the terms of the expansion to determine the value of k in each term of $(x + y)^{12}$.

Reasoning and Proving
Representing — Selecting Tools
Problem Solving
Connecting — Reflecting
Communicating

a) ky^{12}　　　　　　**b)** $792x^k y^5$

c) $495x^8 y^k$　　　　**d)** $kx^4 y^8$

B Connect and Apply

8. What row number of Pascal's triangle has each row sum?

a) 256　　　　　　**b)** 2048

c) 16 384　　　　　**d)** 65 536

9. Write each as the difference of two terms in the form $t_{n, r}$.

a) $t_{4, 2}$　**b)** $t_{6, 3}$　**c)** $t_{12, 9}$　**d)** $t_{28, 14}$

10. Look for patterns in Pascal's triangle. What are the missing numbers in each diagram?

a)
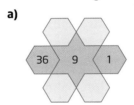

b)
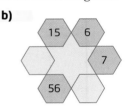

c)
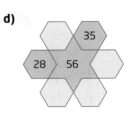

d)
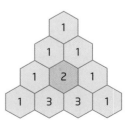

11. Chapter Problem

You can find fractal qualities in Pascal's triangle.

Use a copy of Pascal's triangle and colour all even numbers one colour and all odd numbers another colour. Describe the pattern that emerges.

12. Find the Fibonacci sequence in Pascal's triangle. Describe the position of these numbers.

Hint: Write Pascal's triangle as a right triangle and look diagonally.

C Extend

13. Determine the sum of the squares of the terms in the horizontal rows of Pascal's triangle. Write these numbers as a sequence and then locate the sequence in the triangle. Write a formula for the sequence.

Reasoning and Proving
Representing — Selecting Tools
Problem Solving
Connecting — Reflecting
Communicating

14. In the expansion of $(1 + x)^n$, the first three terms are 1, -18, and 144. Determine the values of x and n.

15. Describe the process used to generate the terms in the triangular array shown. Write this in a recursive form. Write the next three rows of this triangular array.

$$\frac{1}{1}$$

$$\frac{1}{2} \qquad \frac{1}{2}$$

$$\frac{1}{3} \qquad \frac{1}{6} \qquad \frac{1}{3}$$

$$\frac{1}{4} \qquad \frac{1}{12} \qquad \frac{1}{12} \qquad \frac{1}{4}$$

$$\frac{1}{5} \qquad \frac{1}{20} \qquad \frac{1}{30} \qquad \frac{1}{20} \qquad \frac{1}{5}$$

16. Locate a row in Pascal's triangle where the first term after the 1 is a prime number. Look for a relationship between that number and the other terms in the row. Describe this relationship. Locate another row where the first term after the 1 is prime. Do you see the same relationship? Ask a classmate which row they tried and see if they came to the same conclusion.

17. Determine the number of pathways for the checker from the top to the bottom of the checkerboard if the checker can be moved diagonally down only.

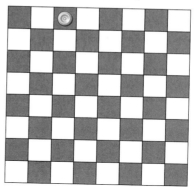

18. Math Contest A school hallway contains 50 lockers numbered 1 to 50. One student ensures they are closed. A second student opens every even-numbered locker. A third student changes the state of the lockers that are a multiple of 3. (To change the state of a locker means an open locker will be closed and a closed locker will be opened.) A fourth student changes the state of all lockers that are a multiple of 4. This pattern continues for 50 students. After the last student, what is the sum of the numbers on the lockers that are closed?

A 100 **B** 765 **C** 140 **D** 50

19. Math Contest The value of the constant in the expansion of $\left(2x^3 - \dfrac{3}{x^2}\right)^5$ is

A 0 **B** -1080 **C** 1080 **D** -243

20. Math Contest Every day at midnight, a ship leaves New York for London at the same time a ship leaves London for New York. It takes exactly 5 days to complete this journey. How many New York–bound ships will a London-bound ship pass on its journey?

A 11 **B** 9 **C** 10 **D** 5

6.4

Arithmetic Sequences

The Great Pyramid of Giza, built in honour of the Egyptian pharaoh Khufu, is believed to have taken 100 000 workers about 20 years to build. Over 2.3 million stones with an average mass of approximately 2300 kg each were used. One example of a sequence that can be found in the Great Pyramid of Giza is the number of stones used to build each level of the pyramid.

Many sequences have very specific patterns. One such pattern occurs when a constant is added to each term to get the next term. This is called an **arithmetic sequence**.

arithmetic sequence

• a sequence where the difference between consecutive terms is a constant

Investigate

How can you identify an arithmetic sequence?

A wall is to be constructed along the 1-km boundary between a city park and a busy street. The wall will be built using cinder blocks measuring 20 cm in height and 40 cm in length. Each row in the wall will contain 100 fewer blocks than the previous row, and the wall will be 3.6 m in height at the centre.

Tools

• grid paper

Method 1: Use Pencil and Paper

1. a) Copy and complete the table.

Row Number	Number of Blocks in the Row	Row Length (cm)
1	2500	100 000
2	2400	96 000
3		
4		
5		

b) How many table rows would you need to determine the number of blocks in the top row of the wall? How did you determine this?

2. a) Write the numbers of blocks in the rows as a sequence.

b) Graph the sequence.

c) Write an explicit formula to represent the number of blocks in row n.

d) What is the value of n for the top row of the wall? Use the formula to determine the number of blocks in the top row of the wall.

3. a) Write the row lengths as a sequence.

   b) Graph the sequence.

   c) Write an explicit formula to determine the length of row n.

   d) Use the formula to determine the length of the top row of the wall.

4. Reflect The sequences from steps 2 and 3 are arithmetic sequences.

   a) Compare the graphs of the sequences. Is an arithmetic sequence a discrete or a continuous function? Explain.

   b) Compare the formulas of the sequences. Describe any similarities or differences.

Method 2: Use a Spreadsheet

1. a) Enter the information in the cells as shown. From the **Edit** menu, use **Fill Down** to complete the next three rows of the spreadsheet.

	A	B	C
1	Row	Number of Blocks in the Row	Row Length (cm)
2	1	2500	100000
3	=A2+1	=B2-100	=C2-4000

Note that if you are using the **Lists & Spreadsheet** application on a TI-Nspire™ CAS graphing calculator, change the formulas to refer to cells A1, B1, and C1.

To fill down, press (menu), select **3:Data**, and then select **3:Fill Down**. Use the cursor keys to fill the desired number of cells.

   b) How many table rows would you need to determine the number of blocks in the top row of the wall? How did you determine this?

2. a) Write the numbers of blocks in a row as a sequence.

   b) Make an **XY (Scatter)** plot of these data.

   c) Write an explicit formula to represent the number of blocks in row n.

   d) What is the value of n for the top row of the wall? Use the formula to determine the number of blocks in the top row of the wall.

3. a) Write the row lengths as a sequence.

   b) Make an **XY (Scatter)** plot of these data.

   c) Write an explicit formula to determine the length of row n.

   d) Use the formula to determine the length of the top row of the wall.

4. Reflect The sequences from steps 2 and 3 are arithmetic sequences.

   a) Compare their graphs. Is an arithmetic sequence a discrete or a continuous function? Explain.

   b) Compare their formulas. Describe any similarities or differences.

Tools

- computer with spreadsheet software

or

- TI-Nspire™ CAS graphing calculator

common difference

- the difference between any two consecutive terms in an arithmetic sequence

An arithmetic sequence can be written as $a, a + d, a + 2d, a + 3d, \ldots,$ where a is the first term and d is the **common difference**. Then, the formula for the general term, or the nth term, of an arithmetic sequence is $t_n = a + (n - 1)d$, where $n \in \mathbb{N}$.

Example 1

Arithmetic Sequences

For each arithmetic sequence, determine the values of the first term, a, and the common difference, d.

a) $-4, 0, 4, 8, \ldots$

b) $\dfrac{1}{3}, \dfrac{5}{6}, \dfrac{4}{3}, \dfrac{11}{6}, \ldots$

c) $t_n = 2n + 3$

Solution

a) Since a is the first term of the sequence, $a = -4$.

The value of d, the common difference, is found by subtracting consecutive terms.

$$\begin{aligned} d &= t_2 - t_1 \qquad \text{Choose any two consecutive terms.} \\ &= 0 - (-4) \\ &= 4 \end{aligned}$$

b) The first term is $a = \dfrac{1}{3}$. Calculate the common difference, d.

$$\begin{aligned} d &= t_2 - t_1 \\ &= \frac{5}{6} - \frac{1}{3} \\ &= \frac{5}{6} - \frac{2}{6} \\ &= \frac{3}{6} \\ &= \frac{1}{2} \end{aligned}$$

c) Use the formula $t_n = 2n + 3$ to write the first few terms.

$$\begin{aligned} t_1 &= 2(1) + 3 & t_2 &= 2(2) + 3 & t_3 &= 2(3) + 3 \\ &= 5 & &= 7 & &= 9 \end{aligned}$$

The first term is 5, so $a = 5$.
The value of d is 2.

Example 2

Determine a Formula for the General Term

Consider the sequence $-13, -19, -25, ...$.

a) Is this sequence arithmetic? Explain how you know.

b) Determine an explicit formula for the general term.

c) Write the value of the 15th term.

d) Determine a recursion formula for the sequence.

Solution

a) This is an arithmetic sequence. By observing the terms, you can see that the first term is -13 and that consecutive terms are decreasing by 6.

b) For this sequence, $a = -13$ and $d = -6$.
$$t_n = a + (n - 1)d$$
$$= -13 + (n - 1)(-6)$$
$$= -13 - 6n + 6$$
$$= -6n - 7$$

An explicit formula for the general term is $t_n = -6n - 7$ or, using function notation, $f(n) = -6n - 7$.

c) $t_{15} = -6(15) - 7$
$$= -97$$

d) Since an arithmetic sequence can be written as
$a, a + d, a + 2d, a + 3d, ...,$

$t_1 = a$
$t_2 = a + d$, or $t_2 = t_1 + d$
$t_3 = t_2 + d$
$\vdots$
$t_n = t_{n-1} + d$

For the sequence $-13, -19, -25, ...$, the recursion formula is
$t_1 = -13, t_n = t_{n-1} - 6$.

Example 3

Length of Ownership

Anna paid $5000 for an antique guitar. The guitar appreciates in value by $160 every year. If she sells the guitar for a little over $7000, how long has she owned it?

Solution

Since the value of the guitar increases by a constant amount each year, the value at the end of each year forms an arithmetic sequence.

The first term in the sequence is 5160 since this is the value at the end of the first year.

Substitute $a = 5160$, $d = 160$, and $t_n = 7000$ into the formula for the general term of an arithmetic sequence and solve for n.

$$t_n = a + (n - 1)d$$
$$7000 = 5160 + (n - 1)(160)$$
$$7000 = 5160 + 160n - 160$$
$$2000 = 160n$$
$$n = 12.5$$

Anna owned the guitar for 12.5 years.

Example 4

Determine a and d Given Two Terms

In an arithmetic sequence, $t_{11} = 72$ and $t_{21} = 142$. What is the value of the first term and of the common difference?

Solution

Substitute the given values into the formula for the general term, $t_n = a + (n - 1)d$, to form a system of equations. Then, solve the system for a and d.

For t_{11}, $72 = a + 10d$.

For t_{21}, $142 = a + 20d$.

$$
\begin{array}{lr}
72 = a + 10d & ① \\
\underline{142 = a + 20d} & ② \\
-70 = -10d & ① - ② \\
d = 7 &
\end{array}
$$

Substitute $d = 7$ into equation ① and solve for a.

$$72 = a + 10d$$
$$72 = a + 10(7)$$
$$72 = a + 70$$
$$a = 2$$

The first term is 2 and the common difference is 7.

Key Concepts

- An arithmetic sequence is a sequence in which the difference between consecutive terms is a constant.

- The difference between consecutive terms of an arithmetic sequence is called the common difference.

- The formula for the general term of an arithmetic sequence is $t_n = a + (n - 1)d$, where a is the first term, d is the common difference, and n is the term number.

Communicate Your Understanding

C1 Compare these two sequences.

A: 1, 3, 5, 7, 9, ...   B: 2, 1, 3, 2, 4, ...

Is each an arithmetic sequence? Explain your reasoning.

C2 How can the first term and the common difference be used to determine any term in an arithmetic sequence? Use a specific example to model your answer.

A Practise

For help with questions 1 to 5, refer to Examples 1 and 2.

1. For each arithmetic sequence, determine the values of a and d. Then, write the next four terms.

a) 12, 15, 18, ...   **b)** 6, 4, 2, ...

c) 0.2, 0.35, 0.5, ...   **d)** −30, −24, −18, ...

e) 5, −1, −7, ...   **f)** $\frac{1}{2}$, 1, $\frac{3}{2}$, ...

2. State whether or not each sequence is arithmetic. Justify your answer.

a) 3, 5, 7, 9, ...   **b)** 2, 5, 9, 14, ...

c) 4, −6, 8, −10, ...   **d)** 13, 7, 1, −5, ...

e) −12, −5, 2, 9, ...   **f)** 0, 1.5, 3, 4.5, ...

3. Given the values of a and d, write the first three terms of the arithmetic sequence. Then, write the formula for the general term.

a) $a = 5$, $d = 2$ **b)** $a = -2$, $d = -4$

c) $a = 9$, $d = -3.5$ **d)** $a = 0$, $d = -\frac{1}{2}$

e) $a = 100$, $d = 10$ **f)** $a = \frac{3}{4}$, $d = \frac{1}{2}$

g) $a = 10$, $d = t$ **h)** $a = x$, $d = 2x$

4. Given the formula for the general term of an arithmetic sequence, determine t_{12}.

a) $t_n = 3n + 4$ **b)** $f(n) = 1 - 4n$

c) $t_n = \frac{1}{2}n + \frac{3}{2}$ **d)** $f(n) = 20 - 1.5n$

5. Given the formula for the general term of an arithmetic sequence, write the first three terms. Then, graph the discrete function that represents each sequence.

a) $t_n = 2n - 3$ **b)** $f(n) = -n - 1$

c) $f(n) = 2(2 - n)$ **d)** $t_n = -2n - 5$

e) $f(n) = \frac{2n + 1}{4}$ **f)** $t_n = 0.2n + 0.1$

For help with questions 6 and 7, refer to Example 3.

6. Which term in the arithmetic sequence 9, 4, −1, ... has the value −146?

7. Determine the number of terms in each arithmetic sequence.

a) 5, 10, 15, ..., 200

b) 38, 36, 34, ..., −20

c) −5, −8, −11, ..., −269

d) −7, −4, −1, ..., 95

B Connect and Apply

8. Verify that the sequence determined by the recursion formula

Reasoning and Proving
Representing · Selecting Tools · Problem Solving · Connecting · Reflecting · Communicating

$t_1 = 8$, $t_n = t_{n-1} - 2$, is arithmetic.

9. For each sequence, determine the values of a and d and write the next three terms.

a) $\dfrac{5}{2}, 2, \dfrac{3}{2}, \ldots$

b) $-6, -\dfrac{7}{2}, -1, \ldots$

c) $2a, 2a - b, 2a - 2b, \ldots$

For help with question 10, refer to Example 4.

10. Determine a and d and then write the formula for the nth term of each arithmetic sequence with the given terms.

a) $t_8 = 33$ and $t_{14} = 57$

b) $t_{10} = 50$ and $t_{27} = 152$

c) $t_5 = -20$ and $t_{18} = -59$

d) $t_7 = 3 + 5x$ and $t_{11} = 3 + 23x$

11. Write a recursion formula for each sequence in question 10.

12. For each graph of an arithmetic sequence, determine the formula for the general term.

a)

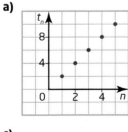

b)

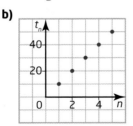

c)

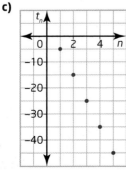

d)

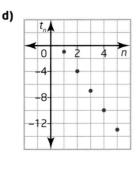

13. In a lottery, the owner of the first ticket drawn receives $10 000. Each successive winner receives $500 less than the previous winner.

a) How much does the 10th winner receive?

b) How many winners are there in total? Explain.

14. An engineer's starting salary is $87 000. The company has guaranteed a raise of $4350 every year with satisfactory performance. What will the engineer's salary be after 10 years?

15. At the end of the second week after opening, a new fitness club has 870 members. At the end of the seventh week, there are 1110 members. If the increase is arithmetic, how many members were there in the first week?

16. A number, m, is called an arithmetic mean of a and b if a, m, and b form an arithmetic sequence. If there are two arithmetic means, m and n, then a, m, n, and b form an arithmetic sequence. Determine two arithmetic means between 9 and -45.

17. How many multiples of 8 are there between -58 and 606?

18. Investigate the sequences with the following recursion formulas. Which are arithmetic? Provide a general observation about how to identify an arithmetic sequence from a recursion formula.

Reasoning and Proving
Representing · Selecting Tools · Problem Solving · Connecting · Reflecting · Communicating

a) $t_n = t_{n-1} + 3$

b) $t_n = 4t_{n-1} + t_{n-2}$

c) $t_n = (t_{n-1})^2$

d) $t_n = -2t_{n-1} - 5$

C Extend

19. Refer to question 16. The pattern continues for any number of arithmetic means. Determine the three arithmetic means between $x + 2y$ and $4x + 4y$.

20. Determine x so that x, $\frac{1}{2}x + 7$, and $3x - 1$ are the first three terms of an arithmetic sequence.

21. The sum of the first two terms of an arithmetic sequence is 15 and the sum of the next two terms is 43. Write the first four terms of the sequence.

22. a) Solve the system of equations
   $x + 2y = 3$ and $5x + 3y = 1$.

   b) Solve the system of equations
   $9x + 5y = 1$ and $2x - y = -4$.

   c) Make and prove a conjecture about the solution to a system of equations $ax + by = c$ and $dx + ey = f$, where a, b, c and d, e, f are separate arithmetic sequences.

23. Math Contest Sam starts at 412 and counts aloud backward by 6s (412, 406, 400, …). A number that she will say is

  A 32   **B** 12   **C** 58   **D** 104

24. Math Contest Show that for any triangle that contains a 60° angle, the three angles form an arithmetic sequence.

25. Math Contest Without using a calculator, determine the next number in the sequence
$\frac{1}{36}, \frac{1}{18}, \frac{1}{12}, \frac{1}{9}, \dots$

  A $\frac{1}{6}$ **B** $\frac{5}{36}$ **C** $\frac{1}{4}$ **D** $\frac{1}{7}$

26. Math Contest The fifth term of a sequence is 7 and the seventh term is 5. Each term in the sequence is the sum of the previous two terms. What is the ninth term in this sequence?

  A 3   **B** 1   **C** 8   **D** -5

27. Math Contest A number is rewritten in its single-digit sum when all the digits are added together. If the sum is not a single digit, then add the digits again, continuing this process until there is a single digit. For example, 23 454 has a single-digit sum of 9, since $2 + 3 + 4 + 5 + 4 = 18$ and $1 + 8 = 9$. A term in a sequence is defined by squaring the previous term and then determining the single-digit sum of this square. If the first term of this sequence is 5, what is the 101st term?

  A 7   **B** 13   **C** 25   **D** 4

Career Connection

After completing a 4-year bachelor's degree at the University of Western Ontario, where he studied computer science and biology, Stephen works in the field of bioinformatics. Bioinformaticians derive knowledge from computer analysis of biological data. When scientists study organisms, large amounts of data are generated about their cells, proteins, genes, and other characteristics. Stephen uses analytical techniques and computer algorithms to document biological data. He also uses his computer and math skills to help other researchers analyse the information stored in the database. Their goal is to detect, prevent, and cure diseases.

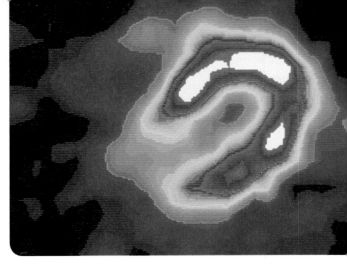

6.5

Geometric Sequences

Radioactive substances are used by doctors for diagnostic purposes. For example, thallium-201 (Tl-201) is a radioactive substance that can be injected into the bloodstream and then its movement in the patient's bloodstream and heart viewed by a special camera. Since radioactive substances are harmful, doctors need to know how long such substances remain in the body. **Geometric sequences** can be used as models to predict the length of time that radioactive substances remain in the body.

Scientists and other professionals may also use geometric sequences to make predictions about levels of radioactivity in the soil or atmosphere.

geometric sequence

• a sequence where the ratio of consecutive terms is a constant

Tools

• grid paper

Connections

The becquerel (Bq) is used to measure the rate of radioactive decay. It equals one disintegration per second. Commonly used multiples of the becquerel are kBq (kilobecquerel, 10^3 Bq), MBq (megabecquerel, 10^6 Bq), and GBq (gigabecquerel, 10^9 Bq). This unit was named after Henri Becquerel, who shared the Nobel Prize with Pierre and Marie Curie for their work in discovering radioactivity.

Investigate

How can the terms in a geometric sequence be determined?

A patient is injected with 50 MBq of Tl-201 before undergoing a procedure to take an image of his heart. Tl-201 has a half-life of 73 h.

1. Copy and complete the table to determine the amount of Tl-201 remaining in the body after approximately 2 weeks (or five 73-h periods).

Time (73-h periods)	Amount of Tl-201 (MBq)	First Differences
0	50	
1		
2		
3		
4		
5		

2. Write the amount of Tl-201 at the end of each 73-h period as a sequence using 50 as the first term.

3. **Reflect** Is this an arithmetic sequence? Explain your answer.

4. Describe the pattern in the first differences.

5. Graph the sequence and describe the pattern in the points.

6. Divide each term after the first by the previous term. What do you notice?

7. Write each term of the sequence as an expression in terms of the original amount of Tl-201 and the value you found in step 6. Use the expressions to develop a formula for the general term of this sequence.

8. Reflect After how long will the amount of Tl-201 in the body be less than 0.01 MBq?

The terms of a geometric sequence are obtained by multiplying the first term, a, and each subsequent term by a **common ratio**, r. A geometric sequence can be written as a, ar^2, ar^3, ar^4, ... Then, the formula for the general term, or the nth term, of a geometric sequence is $t_n = ar^{n-1}$, where $r \neq 0$ and $n \in \mathbb{N}$.

common ratio
- the ratio of any two consecutive terms in a geometric sequence

Example 1

Determine the Type of Sequence

Determine whether each sequence is arithmetic, geometric, or neither. Justify your answer.

a) 2, 5, 10, 17, ...

b) 0.2, 0.02, 0.002, 0.0002, ...

c) $a + 2$, $a + 4$, $a + 6$, $a + 8$, ...

Solution

a) $\frac{5}{2} = 2.5$, $\frac{10}{5} = 2$, $\frac{17}{10} = 1.7$

There is no common ratio.

Divide each term by the previous term to check for a common ratio.

$5 - 2 = 3$, $10 - 5 = 5$, $17 - 10 = 7$

There is no common difference.

Subtract consecutive terms to check for a common difference.

This sequence is neither arithmetic nor geometric.

b) $\frac{0.02}{0.2} = 0.1$, $\frac{0.002}{0.02} = 0.1$, $\frac{0.0002}{0.002} = 0.1$

There is a common ratio, so this sequence is geometric.

c) $(a + 4) - (a + 2) = 2$, $(a + 6) - (a + 4) = 2$, $(a + 8) - (a + 6) = 2$

This sequence has a common difference, so it is an arithmetic sequence.

Example 2

Write Terms in a Geometric Sequence

Write the first three terms of each geometric sequence.

a) $f(n) = 5(3)^{n-1}$

b) $t_n = 16\left(\dfrac{1}{4}\right)^{n-1}$

c) $a = 125$ and $r = -2$

Solution

a) $f(n) = 5(3)^{n-1}$

$$f(1) = 5(3)^{1-1} \qquad\qquad f(2) = 5(3)^{2-1} \qquad\qquad f(3) = 5(3)^{3-1}$$
$$= 5(3)^0 \qquad\qquad\qquad = 5(3)^1 \qquad\qquad\qquad = 5(3)^2$$
$$= 5 \qquad\qquad\qquad\quad = 15 \qquad\qquad\qquad = 45$$

The first three terms are 5, 15, and 45.

b) $t_n = 16\left(\dfrac{1}{4}\right)^{n-1}$

$$t_1 = 16\left(\frac{1}{4}\right)^{1-1} \qquad\qquad t_2 = 16\left(\frac{1}{4}\right)^{2-1} \qquad\qquad t_3 = 16\left(\frac{1}{4}\right)^{3-1}$$
$$= 16\left(\frac{1}{4}\right)^0 \qquad\qquad\quad = 16\left(\frac{1}{4}\right)^1 \qquad\qquad\quad = 16\left(\frac{1}{4}\right)^2$$
$$= 16 \qquad\qquad\qquad\quad = 4 \qquad\qquad\qquad\quad = 1$$

The first three terms are 16, 4, and 1.

Connections

When the common ratio of a geometric sequence is negative, the result is an alternating sequence. This is a sequence whose terms alternate in sign.

c) Given that $a = 125$ and $r = -2$, the formula for the general term is $t_n = 125(-2)^{n-1}$.

$$t_1 = 125(-2)^{1-1} \qquad\qquad t_2 = 125(-2)^{2-1} \qquad\qquad t_3 = 125(-2)^{3-1}$$
$$= 125(-2)^0 \qquad\qquad\quad = 125(-2)^1 \qquad\qquad\quad = 125(-2)^2$$
$$= 125 \qquad\qquad\qquad = -250 \qquad\qquad\qquad = 500$$

The first three terms are 125, -250, and 500.

Example 3

Determine the Number of Terms

Determine the number of terms in the geometric sequence 4, 12, 36, ..., 2916.

Solution

For the given sequence, $a = 4$, $r = 3$, and $t_n = 2916$. Substitute these values into the formula for the general term of a geometric sequence and solve for n.

$$t_n = ar^{n-1}$$
$$2916 = 4(3)^{n-1}$$
$$\frac{2916}{4} = 3^{n-1}$$
$$729 = 3^{n-1}$$
$$3^6 = 3^{n-1} \qquad \text{Write 729 as a power of 3.}$$

Since the bases are the same, the exponents must be equal.

$$n - 1 = 6$$
$$n = 7$$

There are seven terms in this sequence.

Example 4

Highway Accidents

Seatbelt use became law in Canada in 1976. Since that time, the number of deaths due to motor vehicle collisions has decreased. From 1984 to 2003, the number of deaths decreased by about 8% every 5 years. The number of deaths due to motor vehicle collisions in Canada in 1984 was approximately 4100.

Connections

According to Transport Canada, 93% of Canadians used their seatbelts in 2007. The 7% of Canadians not wearing seatbelts accounted for almost 40% of fatalities in motor vehicle collisions.

a) Determine a formula to predict the number of deaths for any fifth year following 1984.

b) Write the number of deaths as a sequence for five 5-year intervals.

Solution

a) The number of deaths can be represented by a geometric sequence with $a = 4100$ and $r = 0.92$. Then, the formula is $t_n = 4100(0.92)^{n-1}$ where n is the number of 5-year periods since 1984.

b) $t_1 = 4100$, $t_2 = 4100(0.92)$, $t_3 = 4100(0.92)^2$, $t_4 = 4100(0.92)^3$, $t_5 = 4100(0.92)^4$

The numbers of deaths for five 5-year intervals are 4100, 3772, 3470, 3193, and 2937.

Key Concepts

- A geometric sequence is a sequence in which the ratio of consecutive terms is a constant.

- The ratio between consecutive terms of a geometric sequence is called the common ratio.

- The formula for the general term of a geometric sequence is $t_n = a(r)^{n-1}$, where a is the first term, r is the common ratio, and n is the term number.

Communicate Your Understanding

C1 How can you determine if a sequence is arithmetic, geometric, or neither? Give an example of each type of sequence.

C2 Describe how to determine the formula for the general term, t_n, of the geometric sequence 5, −10, 20, −40, ...

C3 Consider the graphs of the sequences shown. Identify each sequence as arithmetic or geometric. Explain your reasoning.

a)

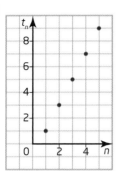

b)

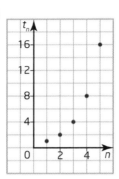

A Practise

For help with question 1, refer to Example 1.

1. Determine whether the sequence is arithmetic, geometric, or neither. Give a reason for your answer.

a) 5, 3, 1, −1, ...

b) 5, −10, 20, −40, ...

c) 4, 0.4, 0.04, 0.004, ...

d) $\frac{1}{2}, \frac{1}{6}, \frac{1}{18}, \frac{1}{54}, \ldots$

e) 1, $\sqrt{2}$, $\sqrt{3}$, 2, $\sqrt{5}$, ...

f) 1, 5, 2, 5, ...

For help with questions 2 to 4, refer to Example 2.

2. State the common ratio for each geometric sequence and write the next three terms.

a) 1, 2, 4, 8, ...

b) −3, 9, −27, 81, ...

c) $\frac{2}{3}, -\frac{2}{3}, \frac{2}{3}, -\frac{2}{3}, \ldots$

d) 600, −300, 150, −75, ...

e) −15, −15, −15, −15, ...

f) 0.3, 3, 30, 300, ...

g) 72, 36, 18, 9, ...

h) x, x^3, x^5, x^7, ...

3. For each geometric sequence, determine the formula for the general term and then write t_9.

a) 54, 18, 6, ...

b) 4, 20, 100, ...

c) $\frac{1}{6}, \frac{1}{5}, \frac{6}{25}, \ldots$

d) 0.0025, 0.025, 0.25, ...

4. Write the first four terms of each geometric sequence.

a) $t_n = 5(2)^{n-1}$

b) $a = 500, r = -5$

c) $f(n) = \frac{1}{4}(-3)^{n-1}$

d) $f(n) = 2(\sqrt{2})^{n-1}$

e) $a = -1, r = \frac{1}{5}$

f) $t_n = -100(-0.2)^{n-1}$

For help with question 5, refer to Example 3.

5. Determine the number of terms in each geometric sequence.

a) 6, 18, 54, …, 4374

b) 0.1, 100, 100 000, …, 10^{14}

c) 5, −10, 20, …, −10 240

d) 3, $3\sqrt{3}$, 9, …, 177 147

e) 31 250, 6250, 1250, …, 0.4

f) 16, −8, 4, …, $\frac{1}{4}$

B Connect and Apply

6. Determine if each sequence is arithmetic, geometric, or neither. If it is arithmetic, state the values of a and d. If it is geometric, state the values of a and r.

a) x, $3x$, $5x$, …

b) $1, \frac{x}{2}, \frac{x^2}{4}, …$

c) $\frac{m^2}{n}, \frac{m^3}{2n}, \frac{m^4}{3n}, …$

d) $\frac{5x}{10}, \frac{5x}{10^3}, \frac{5x}{10^5}, …$

7. Which term of the geometric sequence 1, 3, 9, … has a value of 19 683?

8. Which term of the geometric sequence $\frac{3}{64}, -\frac{3}{16}, \frac{3}{4}, …$ has a value of 192?

9. *Listeria monocytogenes* is a bacteria that rarely causes food poisoning. At a temperature of 10 °C, it takes about 7 h for the bacteria to double. If the bacteria count in a sample of food is 100, how long will it be until the count exceeds 1 000 000?

10. In 1986, a steam explosion at a nuclear reactor in Chernobyl released radioactivity into the air, causing widespread death; disease; and contamination of soil, water, and air that continues today. One of the radioactive components released, cesium-137 (Cs-137), is very dangerous to human life as it accumulates in the soil, the water, and the body. It is believed by scientists that a contamination of Cs-137 of over 1 Ci/km² (curie per square kilometre) is dangerous.

Reasoning and Proving

Representing — Selecting Tools

Problem Solving

Connecting — Reflecting

Communicating

a) Determine the amount of Cs-137 per square kilometre if about 1.5×10^6 Ci of this radioactive substance was released into the environment and spread over an area of about 135 000 km².

b) The half-life of Cs-137 is 30 years. Write an explicit formula to represent the level of Cs-137 left after n years. How long will it take for the contamination to reach safe levels?

c) Research this tragedy to discover more about the long-term effects on the environment and the people of the contaminated region.

Connections

The curie (Ci) is a unit of radioactivity, named after Pierre and Marie Curie, that has since been replaced by the becquerel (Bq).
1 Ci = 3.7×10^{10} Bq

11. A chain e-mail starts with one person sending out six e-mail messages. Each of the recipients sends out six messages, and so on. How many e-mail messages will be sent in the sixth round of e-mailing?

12. Chapter Problem A square with area 1 square unit is partitioned into nine squares and then all but the middle square are shaded. This process is repeated with the remaining shaded squares to produce a fractal called the Sierpinski carpet.

Stage 1

Stage 2

a) Use grid paper to produce the first five stages of the fractal.

b) Write a formula to determine the shaded area at each stage.

c) Use the formula to determine the shaded area at stage 20.

d) Research this fractal. When was it first explored?

13. In a certain country, elections are held every 4 years. Voter turnout at elections increases by 2.6% each time an election is held. In 1850, when the country was formed, 1 million people voted.

Reasoning and Proving

Representing · Selecting Tools

Problem Solving

Connecting · Reflecting

Communicating

a) Determine an equation to model the number of voters at any election. Graph the equation.

b) Is this function continuous or discrete? Explain your answer.

c) How many people vote in the 2010 election?

14. The geometric mean of a set of n numbers is the positive nth root of the product of the numbers. For example, given two non-consecutive terms of a geometric sequence, 6 and 24, their product is 144 and the geometric mean is $\sqrt{144}$, or 12. The numbers 6, 12, and 24 form a geometric sequence.

a) Determine the geometric mean of 5 and 125.

b) Insert three geometric means between 4 and 324.

✔ **Achievement Check**

15. Aika wanted to test her dad's knowledge of sequences so she decided to offer him two different options for her allowance for one year. In option 1, he would give her $25 every week. In option 2, he would give her $0.25 the first week and then double the amount every following week.

a) Which option represents an arithmetic sequence? Determine the general term for the sequence.

b) Which option represents a geometric sequence? Determine the general term for the sequence.

c) Which plan should her dad pick? Explain.

C **Extend**

16. Determine the value(s) of y if $4y + 1$, $y + 4$, and $10 - y$ are consecutive terms in a geometric sequence.

17. Determine x and y for each geometric sequence.

a) 3, x, 12, y, …   **b)** -2, x, y, 1024, …

18. Refer to question 14. Determine three geometric means between $x^5 + x^4$ and $x + 1$.

19. The population of a city increases from 12 000 to 91 125 over 10 years. Determine the annual rate of increase, if the increase is geometric.

20. The first three terms of the sequence -8, x, y, 72 form an arithmetic sequence, while the second, third, and fourth terms form a geometric sequence. Determine x and y.

21. Math Contest Three numbers form an arithmetic sequence with a common difference of 7. When the first term of the sequence is decreased by 3, the second term increased by 7, and the third term doubled, the new numbers form a geometric sequence. What is the original first term?

A 7   **B** 16   **C** 20   **D** 68

22. Math Contest A geometric sequence has the property that each term is the sum of the previous two terms. If the first term is 2, what is one possibility for the second term?

A $-4 + \sqrt{3}$ **B** $1 - \sqrt{5}$

C $4 - \sqrt{3}$ **D** $-1 + \sqrt{5}$

23. Math Contest Film speed is the measure of a photographic film's sensitivity to light. The ISO (International Organization of Standardization) film-speed scale forms a geometric sequence. If the first term in the sequence is 25 and the fourth term is 50, what is the fifth term?

Arithmetic Series

Dar Robinson was a famous stuntman. In 1979, Dar was paid $100 000 to jump off the CN Tower in Toronto. During the first second of the jump, Dar fell 4.9 m; during the next second, he fell 14.7 m; and, during the third second, the drop was another 24.5 m. This pattern continued for 12 s. The total distance of his jump can be found by adding the terms of this sequence together.

Investigate

How can a long sequence of numbers be added quickly?

1. Copy and complete the table to determine the sum of the first 10 even natural numbers.

Number of Terms	Indicated Sum	Sum	Mean of All Terms	Mean of First and Last Terms
1	2	2	2	2
2	2 + 4	6	3	3
3	2 + 4 + 6	12	4	4
4	2 + 4 + 6 + 8	20	5	5

Connections

Recall that the mean is the sum of a set of values divided by the number of values in the set.

2. **Reflect** How is the sum of the terms related to the number of terms in the sum and to the mean of the terms? How is the mean of the first and last terms related to the mean of all the terms?

3. **a)** Write a formula to represent the sum of a **series** when the first and last terms are known.

   b) Use your formula to determine the sum of the first 100 even natural numbers.

series
• the indicated sum of the terms of a sequence

4. Verify that your formula works for another series, $1 + 3 + 5 + 7 + 9 + 11$.

5. Suppose that the sum of the first six even numbers is written in order and then in reverse order.

$$2 + \ \ 4 + 6 + 8 + 10 + 12$$
$$\underline{12 + 10 + 8 + 6 + \ \ 4 + \ \ 2}$$

Add these two series of numbers together and divide the result by 2.

6. **Reflect** Compare the result from step 5 with your formula.

The method shown in step 5 of the Investigate can be used to derive a formula for the sum, S_n, of the first n terms of an **arithmetic series**.

For any arithmetic sequence, the terms can be written as $a, (a + d), (a + 2d), \ldots, (t_n - d), t_n$, where n is the number of terms, a is the first term, d is the common difference between the terms, and t_n is the last term.

The corresponding arithmetic series is

$$S_n = a + (a + d) + (a + 2d) + \cdots + (t_n - d) + t_n$$
$$+\ S_n = t_n + (t_n - d) + (t_n - 2d) + \cdots + (a + d) + a \qquad \text{Write the series in reverse.}$$

$$\overline{2S_n = (a + t_n) + (a + t_n) + (a + t_n) + \cdots + (a + t_n) + (a + t_n)} \quad \text{Add.}$$

$$2S_n = n(a + t_n)$$

$$S_n = \frac{n}{2}(a + t_n) \qquad \qquad \text{①} \qquad\qquad \text{Divide both sides by 2.}$$

By substituting $t_n = a + (n - 1)d$ for t_n in formula ①, you can represent the sum of an arithmetic series with a different formula, formula ②:

$$S_n = \frac{n}{2}[a + a + (n - 1)d]$$

$$S_n = \frac{n}{2}[2a + (n - 1)d] \qquad \text{②}$$

Formula ② can be used to determine the sum, S_n, of the first n terms of an arithmetic series when the value of the last term, t_n, is not known.

Example 1

Determine the Sum of an Arithmetic Series

Determine the sum of the first 10 terms of each arithmetic series.

a) $a = 2$, $d = 4$, $t_{10} = 38$

b) $a = -4$, $d = -3$

Solution

a) Method 1: Use Pencil and Paper

Use formula ①:

$$S_n = \frac{n}{2}(a + t_n)$$

$$S_{10} = \frac{10}{2}(2 + 38)$$

$$= 5(40)$$

$$= 200$$

Use formula ②:

$$S_n = \frac{n}{2}[2a + (n - 1)d]$$

$$S_{10} = \frac{10}{2}[2(2) + (10 - 1)4]$$

$$= 5(40)$$

$$= 200$$

The sum of the first 10 terms of the arithmetic series is 200.

Method 2: Use a Graphing Calculator

Start by listing the first 10 terms and storing them in **L1**.

- Press 2ND [LIST] and cursor over to the **OPS** menu.
- Select **5:seq(** and enter $2 + (x - 1) \times 4$, x, 1, 10, 1).
- Press (STO▶) (2nd) [L1] (ENTER).

Now, determine the sum.

- Press (2nd) [LIST] and cursor over to the **MATH** menu.
- Select **5:sum(** and enter **L1**).
- Press (ENTER).

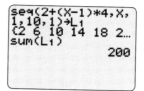

The sum of the first 10 terms of the arithmetic series is 200.

b) Method 1: Use Pencil and Paper

Use formula ②:

$$S_n = \frac{n}{2}[2a + (n - 1)d]$$

$$S_{10} = \frac{10}{2}[2(-4) + (10 - 1)(-3)]$$

$$= 5(-35)$$

$$= -175$$

The sum of the first 10 terms of the arithmetic series is -175.

Method 2: Use a Graphing Calculator

Using the **sequence** function, enter $-4 + (x - 1) \times -3$, x, 1, 10, 1). Store the list in **L1**. Then, use the **sum** function.

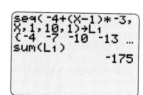

The sum of the first 10 terms of the arithmetic series is -175.

Example 2

Sum of an Arithmetic Series Given the First Few Terms

Determine the specified sum for each arithmetic series.

a) S_{15} for $-12 - 8 - 4 - \cdots$

b) S_{20} for $-11m - 2m + 7m + \cdots$

Solution

a) For the arithmetic series $-12 - 8 - 4 - ...$, $a = -12$, $d = 4$, and $n = 15$.

Use formula ②:

$$S_n = \frac{n}{2}[2a + (n - 1)d]$$

$$S_{15} = \frac{15}{2}[2(-12) + (15 - 1)(4)]$$

$$= \frac{15}{2}(32)$$

$$= 240$$

b) For the arithmetic series $-11m - 2m + 7m + ...$, $a = -11m$, $d = 9m$, and $n = 20$.

Use formula ②:

$$S_n = \frac{n}{2}[2a + (n - 1)d]$$

$$S_{20} = \frac{20}{2}[2(-11m) + (20 - 1)(9m)]$$

$$= 10(149m)$$

$$= 1490m$$

Example 3

Sum of an Arithmetic Series Given the First Three Terms and the Last Term

Determine the sum of the arithmetic series.

$3 + 8 + 13 + \cdots + 58$

Solution

To use either formula, first determine the number of terms.

For this series, $a = 3$, $d = 5$, and $t_n = 58$.

$$t_n = a + (n - 1)d$$
$$58 = 3 + (n - 1)(5)$$
$$58 = 5n - 2$$
$$60 = 5n$$
$$n = 12$$

Use formula ①:

$$S_n = \frac{n}{2}(a + t_n)$$

$$S_{12} = \frac{12}{2}(3 + 58)$$

$$= 6(61)$$

$$= 366$$

Use formula ②:

$$S_n = \frac{n}{2}[2a + (n - 1)d]$$

$$S_{12} = \frac{12}{2}[2(3) + (12 - 1)5]$$

$$= 6(61)$$

$$= 366$$

The sum of the arithmetic series is 366.

Example 4

Compare Wages

A student is offered a job with a math teacher that will last 20 h. The first option pays $4.75 for the first hour, $5 for the second hour, $5.25 for the next hour, and so on. The second option pays $7/h for all hours worked. Which option pays more?

Solution

The first method of payment is an arithmetic series with $a = 4.75$, $d = 0.25$, and $n = 20$. To determine the total amount earned, calculate the sum of the series.

$$S_n = \frac{n}{2}[2a + (n - 1)d]$$

$$S_{20} = \frac{20}{2}[2(4.75) + (20 - 1)(0.25)]$$

$$= 10(14.25)$$

$$= 142.5$$

The amount earned by the first option is $142.50. The amount earned by the second option is $7 × 20, or $140. So, the first option pays more.

Key Concepts

- An arithmetic series is the indicated sum of the terms of an arithmetic sequence. For example, 4, 9, 14, 19, ... is an arithmetic sequence, while $4 + 9 + 14 + 19 + \cdots$ is an arithmetic series.

- Given the first term, the last term, and the number of terms of an arithmetic series, the sum of the series can be found using the formula $S_n = \frac{n}{2}(a + t_n)$ or the formula $S_n = \frac{n}{2}[2a + (n - 1)d]$.

- Given the first terms of an arithmetic series, the sum of the first n terms can be found using the formula $S_n = \frac{n}{2}[2a + (n - 1)d]$.

Communicate Your Understanding

C1 Describe how an arithmetic series is related to an arithmetic sequence. Use an example to model your answer.

C2 Describe when it is easier to use the formula $S_n = \frac{n}{2}(a + t_n)$ and when the formula $S_n = \frac{n}{2}[2a + (n - 1)d]$ is a better choice.

C3 Describe a real-life situation that could be defined by an arithmetic series.

C4 The word *series* is often used in the English language. For example, a TV program with a different episode every week is called a series. Describe some other everyday uses of the word *series*.

A Practise

For help with question 1, refer to Example 1.

1. Determine the sum of each arithmetic series.

 a) $a = 4$, $t_n = 9$, $n = 6$

 b) $a = 10$, $d = -2$, $n = 12$

 c) $a = 7$, $t_n = -22$, $n = 12$

 d) $a = -4$, $t_n = 17$, $n = 20$

 e) $a = \frac{1}{3}$, $d = -\frac{1}{2}$, $n = 7$

 f) $a = 3x$, $t_n = 21x$, $n = 15$

For help with questions 2 and 3, refer to Example 2.

2. For each arithmetic series, state the values of a and d. Then, determine the sum of the first 20 terms.

 a) $5 + 9 + 13 + \cdots$

 b) $20 + 25 + 30 + \cdots$

 c) $45 + 39 + 33 + \cdots$

 d) $2 + 2.2 + 2.4 + \cdots$

 e) $\frac{1}{2} + \frac{3}{4} + 1 + \cdots$

 f) $-5 - 6 - 7 - \cdots$

3. The first and last terms in each arithmetic series are given. Determine the sum of the series.

 a) $a = \frac{1}{2}$, $t_8 = 4$

 b) $a = 19$, $t_{12} = 151$

 c) $a = -5$, $t_{45} = 17$

 d) $a = 11$, $t_{20} = 101$

For help with questions 4 and 5, refer to Example 3.

4. Determine the sum of each arithmetic series.

 a) $6 + 13 + 20 + \cdots + 69$

 b) $4 + 15 + 26 + \cdots + 213$

 c) $5 - 8 - 21 - \cdots - 190$

 d) $100 + 90 + 80 + \cdots - 100$

5. Determine the sum of each arithmetic series.

 a) $-1 + 2 + 5 + \cdots + 164$

 b) $2 - 5 - 12 - \cdots - 222$

 c) $21.5 + 14.2 + 6.9 + \cdots - 715.8$

 d) $\frac{5}{3} + \frac{11}{3} + \frac{17}{3} + \cdots + \frac{53}{3}$

B Connect and Apply

6. The 15th term in an arithmetic sequence is 43 and the sum of the first 15 terms of the series is 120. Determine the first three terms of the sequence.

7. In an arithmetic sequence of 50 terms, the 17th term is 53 and the 28th term is 86. Determine the sum of the first 50 terms of the corresponding arithmetic series.

Reasoning and Proving

Representing — Selecting Tools

Problem Solving

Connecting — Reflecting

Communicating

8. Determine the sum of each arithmetic series.

 a) $2\sqrt{7} + 5\sqrt{7} + 8\sqrt{7} + \cdots + 83\sqrt{7}$

 b) $x - 2x - 5x - \cdots - 56x$

 c) $(5a - 3b) + (4a - 2b) + (3a - b) + \cdots$
 $\qquad + (-5a + 7b)$

 d) $\frac{2}{x} + \frac{4}{x} + \frac{6}{x} + \cdots + \frac{18}{x}$

9. Which are arithmetic series? Justify your answers.

 a) $-2 - 8 - 11 - 17 - \cdots$

 b) $2x^2 + 3x^2 + 4x^2 + \cdots$

 c) $a + (a + 2b) + (a + 4b) + \cdots$

 d) $\frac{17}{20} + \frac{11}{20} + \frac{27}{20} + \cdots$

10. In a grocery store, apple juice cans are stacked in a triangular display. There are 5 cans in the top row and 12 cans in the bottom row. Each row has 1 can less than the previous row. How many cans are in the display?

11. A toy car is rolling down an inclined track and picking up speed as it goes. The car travels 4 cm in the first second, 8 cm in the second second, 12 cm in the next second, and so on. Determine the total distance travelled by the car in 30 s.

12. A snowball sentence is constructed so that each word has one more letter than the previous word. An example is, "I am not cold today."

a) Determine the total number of letters in the sentence.

b) Write your own snowball sentence and determine the number of letters in your sentence.

13. Determine an expression for the sum of the terms of an arithmetic series where the terms are represented by $t_n = 3n - 2$.

14. a) Determine x so that $2x$, $3x + 1$, and $x^2 + 2$ are the first three terms of an arithmetic sequence.

Reasoning and Proving

Representing — Selecting Tools

Problem Solving

Connecting — Reflecting

Communicating

b) Determine the sum of the first 10 terms of the sequence.

✔ **Achievement Check**

15. Icy Treats finds that its profit increases by $200 per week throughout the 16-week summer season. Icy Treat's profit is $1200 in the first week.

a) Explain why the total profit for the season is represented by an arithmetic series.

b) Determine the total profit for the season.

ⓒ Extend

16. If $S(n)$ is a function representing the sum of an arithmetic series, determine the series with $S(13) = 507$ and $S(25) = 2025$. Graph this function.

17. How many terms in the series $5 + 9 + 13 + \cdots + t_n$ are less than 500? How many terms are needed for a sum of less than 500?

18. In an arithmetic series, the sum of the first 9 terms is 162 and the sum of the first 12 terms is 288. Determine the series.

19. Math Contest Two arithmetic sequences, 3, 9, 15, 21, … and 4, 11, 18, 25, …, share common terms. For example, 81 is a term in both sequences. What is the sum of the first 20 terms that these sequences have in common?

A 8760

B 8750

C 8740

D 8770

20. Math Contest The sum of the series $1 + 2 + 4 + 5 + 7 + 8 + 10 + 11 + \cdots + 2999$ is

A 2 999 500

B 2 999 000

C 3 000 000

D 4 500 000

21. Math Contest What is the value of $(1^2 + 3^2 + \cdots + 171^2) - (2^2 + 4^2 + 6^2 + \cdots + 170^2)$?

22. Math Contest Solve $6^{x-3} - 6^{x-4} = 1080$.

23. Math Contest A geometric sequence has 1 as its first term and $2n$ as its last. Show that if there are $2n$ terms, then the product of the terms of the sequence is $(2n)^n$.

24. Math Contest Without using a calculator, determine the sum of the first 20 terms of the sequence $\frac{1}{2}, \frac{1}{6}, \frac{1}{12}, \frac{1}{20}, \ldots$

6.7

Geometric Series

The Canadian Open is an outdoor tennis tournament. The tournament started in 1881, and the men's and women's events alternate between Toronto and Montreal every other year. In the first round of the men's singles event, 32 matches are played. In the second round, 16 matches are played. In the third round, 8 matches are played, and so on. These numbers form the terms of a geometric sequence. To determine the total number of matches played in this event, you need to add these terms together. When the terms of a geometric sequence are added together, the result is called a **geometric series**.

geometric series

• the indicated sum of the terms of a geometric sequence

Tools

• computer with spreadsheet software

Investigate

How can you develop a formula for the sum of the terms in a geometric sequence?

A nickel is placed on a game board with 32 squares. On each succeeding square, the number of nickels is doubled. How much money will be on the last square? How much money will be on the board when it is full?

Method 1: Use a Spreadsheet

1. Enter the following information in a spreadsheet. From the **Edit** menu, use **Fill Down** to complete the next 30 rows of the spreadsheet.

	A	B	C
1	Number of Squares	Number of Nickels	Total Number of Nickels
2	1	1	1
3	=A2+1	=B2*2	=B3+C2

2. How many nickels are on the last square? How many nickels are on the entire game board?

3. Determine a formula for the total number of nickels on the board. Use your formula to calculate the total number of nickels on the game board.

4. **Reflect** Is the function that represents the total number of nickels on the game board continuous or discrete? How do you know?

5. Write the total number of nickels as a series. Is this series arithmetic? Explain your thinking.

Method 2: Use Pencil and Paper

Tools

- grid paper
- counters

1. Draw an 8 by 4 grid of squares. The squares should be large enough to stack counters on.

2. Let each counter represent 1 nickel. Place one counter on a square, two counters on the next square, four counters on the next square, and so on. Use a table similar to the one shown to record your results.

Number of Squares	Number of Nickels on the Square	Total Number of Nickels
1	1	1
2	2	3

3. Determine a formula for the total number of nickels on the board. Use your formula to calculate the total number of nickels on the game board.

4. **Reflect** Is the function that represents the total number of nickels on the game board continuous or discrete? How do you know?

5. Write the total number of nickels as a series. Is this series arithmetic? Explain your thinking.

When the terms of a geometric sequence are added, the resulting expression is called a geometric series. The sum, S_n, of the first n terms of a geometric series is $S_n = a + ar + ar^2 + \cdots + ar^{n-1}$. This can be used to derive a formula for S_n.

$$S_n = a + ar + ar^2 + \cdots + ar^{n-1} \quad \text{①} \quad \text{Write the series.}$$

$$rS_n = \quad\quad ar + ar^2 + \cdots + ar^{n-1} + ar^n \quad \text{②} \quad \text{Multiply both sides by } r \text{ and align}$$

$$rS_n - S_n = -a + ar^n \quad\quad \text{②} - \text{①} \quad \text{like terms.}$$

$$rS_n - S_n = ar^n - a \quad\quad \text{Rearrange the right side.}$$

$$S_n(r - 1) = a(r^n - 1) \quad\quad \text{Factor both sides.}$$

$$S_n = \frac{a(r^n - 1)}{r - 1}, r \neq 1 \quad\quad \text{Divide both sides by } r - 1.$$

Example 1

Identify a Geometric Series

Determine if each series is geometric. Justify your answer.

a) $2 + 6 + 18 + 54 + \cdots$

b) $2 + 8 - 12 + 16 - \cdots$

Solution

a) The series $2 + 6 + 18 + 54 + \cdots$ is geometric if consecutive terms have a common ratio.

$$\frac{6}{2} = 3, \frac{18}{6} = 3, \frac{54}{18} = 3$$

Since the ratio of consecutive terms is 3, this series is geometric.

b) Check $2 + 8 - 12 + 16 - \cdots$ for a common ratio.

$$\frac{8}{2} = 4, \frac{-12}{8} = -1.5, \frac{-16}{-12} = 1.\overline{3}$$

Since the ratio of consecutive terms is not constant, this series is not geometric.

Example 2

Sum of a Geometric Series

Determine the sum of the first 10 terms of each geometric series.

a) $f(1) = 20, r = -3$ **b)** $a = 5, r = 4$

Solution

a) Method 1: Use Pencil and Paper

Substitute $a = 20$, $r = -3$, and $n = 10$ into the formula.

$$S_n = \frac{a(r^n - 1)}{r - 1}$$

$$S_{10} = \frac{20[(-3)^{10} - 1)]}{-3 - 1}$$

$$= \frac{20(59\ 048)}{-4}$$

$$= -295\ 240$$

The sum of the first 10 terms of the geometric series is $-295\ 240$.

Method 2: Use a Graphing Calculator

Start by listing the first 10 terms and storing them in **L1**.

- Press (2nd) [LIST] and cursor over to the **OPS** menu.
- Select **5:seq(** and enter $20 \times (-3)^{x-1}$, x, 1, 10, 1).
- Press (STO▶) (2nd) [L1] (ENTER).

Now, determine the sum.

- Press (2nd) [LIST] and cursor over to the **MATH** menu.
- Select **5:sum(** and enter **L1**).
- Press (ENTER).

The sum of the first 10 terms of the geometric series is $-295\ 240$.

b) Method 1: Use Pencil and Paper

Substitute $a = 5$, $r = 4$, and $n = 10$ into the formula.

$$S_n = \frac{a(r^n - 1)}{r - 1}$$

$$S_{10} = \frac{5(4^{10} - 1)}{4 - 1}$$

$$= \frac{5(1\ 048\ 575)}{3}$$

$$= 1\ 747\ 625$$

The sum of the first 10 terms of the geometric series is 1 747 625.

Method 2: Use a Graphing Calculator

Using the **sequence** function, enter $5 \times 4^{x-1}$, x, 1, 10, 1). Store the list in **L1**. Then, use the **sum** function.

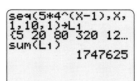

The sum of the first 10 terms of the geometric series is 1 747 625.

Example 3

Sum of a Geometric Series Given the First Three Terms and the Last Term

Determine the sum of each geometric series.

a) $32 + 16 + 8 + \cdots + \dfrac{1}{8}$

b) $1 - 3 + 9 - \cdots - 243$

Solution

a) For this series, $a = 32$, $r = \dfrac{1}{2}$, and $t_n = \dfrac{1}{8}$. Use the formula for the general term of a geometric sequence to determine the value of n.

$$t_n = ar^{n-1}$$

$$\frac{1}{8} = 32\left(\frac{1}{2}\right)^{n-1}$$

$$\frac{1}{256} = \left(\frac{1}{2}\right)^{n-1}$$

$$\left(\frac{1}{2}\right)^8 = \left(\frac{1}{2}\right)^{n-1} \qquad \text{Write } \frac{1}{256} \text{ as a power of } \frac{1}{2}.$$

$$8 = n - 1 \qquad \text{Since the bases are the same, the exponents must be equal.}$$

$$n = 9$$

Now, use the formula for S_n.

$$S_n = \frac{a(r^n - 1)}{r - 1}$$

$$S_9 = \frac{32\left[\left(\frac{1}{2}\right)^9 - 1\right]}{\frac{1}{2} - 1}$$

$$= \frac{32\left(-\frac{511}{512}\right)}{-\frac{1}{2}}$$

$$= \frac{511}{8}$$

b) Substitute $a = 1$, $r = -3$, and $t_n = -243$ into the formula for the general term of a geometric sequence and solve for n.

$$t_n = ar^{n-1}$$
$$-243 = 1(-3)^{n-1}$$
$$(-3)^5 = (-3)^{n-1} \qquad \text{Write } -243 \text{ as a power of } -3.$$
$$5 = n - 1 \qquad \text{Since the bases are the same, the exponents must be equal.}$$
$$n = 6$$

Use the formula for S_n.

$$S_n = \frac{a(r^n - 1)}{r - 1}$$

$$S_6 = \frac{1[(-3)^6 - 1]}{-3 - 1}$$

$$= \frac{728}{-4}$$

$$= -182$$

Example 4

Tennis Tournament

A tennis tournament has 128 entrants. A player is dropped from the competition after losing one match. Winning players go on to another match. What is the total number of matches that will be played in this tournament?

Solution

This situation can be represented by a geometric series. Since there are two players per match, the first term, a, is $128 \div 2$, or 64. After each round of matches, half the players drop out because they lost, so the common ratio, r, is $\frac{1}{2}$. Since there will be a single match played at the end of the tournament, the last term, t_n, is 1.

First, determine the total number of games played by the winner of the tournament. This is the value of n.

$$t_n = ar^{n-1}$$

$$1 = 64\left(\frac{1}{2}\right)^{n-1}$$

$$\frac{1}{64} = \left(\frac{1}{2}\right)^{n-1}$$

$$\left(\frac{1}{2}\right)^6 = \left(\frac{1}{2}\right)^{n-1} \qquad \text{Write } \frac{1}{64} \text{ as a power of } \frac{1}{2}.$$

$$6 = n - 1 \qquad \text{Since the bases are the same, the exponents must be equal.}$$

$$n = 7$$

Now, determine the total number of matches played in the tournament.

$$S_n = \frac{a(r^n - 1)}{r - 1}$$

$$S_7 = \frac{64\left[\left(\frac{1}{2}\right)^7 - 1\right]}{\frac{1}{2} - 1}$$

$$= \frac{64\left(-\frac{127}{128}\right)}{-\frac{1}{2}}$$

$$= 127$$

A total of 127 matches will be played in this tournament.

Connections

Geometric series have many important applications in the financial field. For example, you can determine the amount of money you will have after 50 years if you save $1000 every year. This type of application will be explored in detail in Chapter 7.

Key Concepts

- A geometric series is the sum of the terms in a geometric sequence. For example, $-3 + 6 - 12 + 24 - \cdots$ is a geometric series.

- The formula for the sum of the first n terms of a geometric series with first term a and common ratio r is $S_n = \frac{a(r^n - 1)}{r - 1}, r \neq 1$.

Communicate Your Understanding

C1 Describe the similarities and differences between an arithmetic series and a geometric series.

C2 Andre missed the lesson on determining the sum of a geometric series given the first and last terms as well as the common ratio. Describe the process for him.

C3 Explain why $r \neq 1$ when using the formula $S_n = \frac{a(r^n - 1)}{r - 1}$.

A Practise

For help with question 1, refer to Example 1.

1. Determine whether each series is geometric. Justify your answer.

a) $4 + 20 + 100 + 500 + \cdots$

b) $-150 + 15 - 1.5 + 0.15 - \cdots$

c) $3 - 9 + 18 - 54 + \cdots$

d) $256 - 64 + 16 - 4 + \cdots$

For help with questions 2 and 3, refer to Example 2.

2. For each geometric series, determine the values of a and r. Then, determine the indicated sum.

a) S_8 for $2 + 6 + 18 + \cdots$

b) S_{10} for $24 - 12 + 6 - \cdots$

c) S_{15} for $0.3 + 0.003 + 0.000\,03 + \cdots$

d) S_{12} for $1 - \dfrac{1}{3} + \dfrac{1}{9} - \cdots$

e) S_9 for $2.1 - 4.2 + 8.4 - \cdots$

f) S_{40} for $8 - 8 + 8 - \cdots$

3. Determine S_n for each geometric series.

a) $a = 6$, $r = 2$, $n = 9$

b) $f(1) = 2$, $r = -2$, $n = 12$

c) $f(1) = 729$, $r = -3$, $n = 15$

d) $f(1) = 2700$, $r = 10$, $n = 8$

e) $a = \dfrac{1}{2}$, $r = 4$, $n = 8$

f) $a = 243$, $r = \dfrac{1}{3}$, $n = 10$

For help with questions 4 and 5, refer to Example 3.

4. Determine the sum of each geometric series.

a) $27 + 9 + 3 + \cdots + \dfrac{1}{243}$

b) $7 + 3.5 + 1.75 + \cdots + 0.109\,375$

c) $1200 + 120 + 12 + \cdots + 0.0012$

d) $\dfrac{1}{3} + \dfrac{2}{9} + \dfrac{4}{27} + \dfrac{8}{81} + \cdots + \dfrac{128}{6561}$

5. Determine the sum of each geometric series.

a) $5 - 15 + 45 - \cdots + 3645$

b) $6 - 12 + 24 - 48 + \cdots - 768$

c) $96\,000 - 48\,000 + 24\,000 - \cdots + 375$

d) $1 - \dfrac{2}{3} + \dfrac{4}{9} - \cdots + \dfrac{64}{729}$

B Connect and Apply

6. Determine the specified sum for each geometric series.

a) S_{10} for $\sqrt{3} - 3 + 3\sqrt{3} + \cdots$

b) S_{12} for $\sqrt{2}x + 2x + 2\sqrt{2}x + \cdots$

c) S_{15} for $3 + 3x + 3x^2 + \cdots$

7. Determine the sum of each geometric series.

a) $10 + 5 + \dfrac{5}{2} + \cdots + \dfrac{5}{64}$

b) $2\sqrt{5} + 10 + 10\sqrt{5} + \cdots + 31\,250$

c) $1 + x + x^2 + x^3 + \cdots + x^k$

8. The sum of $4 + 12 + 36 + 108 + \cdots + t_n$ is 4372. How many terms are in this series?

9. The third term of a geometric series is 24 and the fourth term is 36. Determine the sum of the first 10 terms.

10. In a geometric series, $t_1 = 3$ and $S_3 = 21$. Determine the common ratio and an expression for the sum of the first k terms.

11. In a lottery, the first ticket drawn wins a prize of $25. Each ticket drawn after that receives a prize that is twice the value of the preceding prize.

Reasoning and Proving

Representing — Selecting Tools

Problem Solving

Connecting — Reflecting

Communicating

a) Write a function to model the total amount of prize money given away.

b) Graph the function to determine how many prizes can be given out if the total amount of prize money is $2 million.

12. A bouncy ball bounces to $\frac{2}{3}$ of its height when dropped on a hard surface. Suppose the ball is dropped from 20 m.

Reasoning and Proving
Representing   Selecting Tools
Problem Solving
Connecting   Reflecting
Communicating

a) What height will the ball bounce back up to after the sixth bounce?

b) What is the total distance travelled by the ball after 10 bounces?

13. Chapter Problem The Peano curve is a space-filling fractal. The first stage is a line segment of length 1 unit. The second stage is constructed by replacing the original line segment with nine line segments each of length $\frac{1}{3}$ unit. This process continues as each line segment is replaced by nine line segments that are $\frac{1}{3}$ the length of the line segments in the previous stage.

Stage 1   Stage 2   Stage 3

a) Construct as many stages of the Peano curve as you can. Use a table similar to the one shown to record the lengths of the line segments and the total length for each stage.

Stage	Line Segment Length	Total Length
1	1	1
2	$\frac{1}{3}$	3
3	$\frac{1}{9}$	9
4		
5		
6		

b) Determine a formula to represent the length of the line segments at each stage. Use this to determine the length of the line segment at Stage 6.

c) Determine a formula to represent the total length of the line segments. Use your formula to determine the total length after Stage 6.

d) Look for other patterns in this fractal and describe them using formulas, rules, or words.

✓ **Achievement Check**

14. The air in a hot-air balloon cools as the balloon rises. If the air is not reheated, the balloon's rate of ascent will decrease.

a) A hot-air balloon rises 40 m in the first minute. After that, the balloon rises 75% as far as it did in the previous minute. How far does it rise in each of the next 3 min? Write these distances as a sequence.

b) Determine a function to represent the height of the balloon after n minutes. Is this function continuous or discrete? Explain your reasoning and write the domain of the function.

c) Use the function to determine the height of the balloon after 10 min.

C **Extend**

15. Three numbers, a, b, and c, form a geometric series so that $a + b + c = 35$ and $abc = 1000$. Determine the values of a, b, and c.

16. For a geometric series, $\dfrac{S_4}{S_8} = \dfrac{1}{17}$. Determine the first three terms of the series if the first term is 3.

17. The sum of the first five terms of a geometric series is 186 and the sum of the first six terms is 378. If the fourth term is 48, determine a, r, t_{10}, and S_{10}.

18. Determine n if $3 + 3^2 + 3^3 + \cdots + 3^n = 9840$.

19. If $2b - 2$, $2b + 2$, and $5b + 1$ are the first three terms of a geometric sequence, determine the sum of the first five terms.

Chapter 6 Review

6.1 Sequences as Discrete Functions, pages 354 to 364

1. Given the explicit formula, determine the first four terms in each sequence.

a) $t_n = 4 + 2n^2$, $n \in \mathbb{N}$

b) $f(n) = \dfrac{2n - 1}{n}$, $n \in \mathbb{N}$

2. For each sequence, make a table of values using the term number and term and calculate the finite differences. Then, graph the sequence using the ordered pairs (term number, term) and determine an explicit formula for the nth term, using function notation.

a) $-8, -11, -14, -17, \ldots$

b) $3, 2, -3, -12, \ldots$

6.2 Recursive Procedures, pages 365 to 372

3. Write the first four terms of each sequence, where $n \in \mathbb{N}$.

a) $f(1) = 5$, $f(n) = f(n - 1) - 4$

b) $t_1 = 3$, $t_n = 2t_{n-1} - n$

4. Determine a recursion formula for each sequence.

a) $-2, 7, 16, 25, \ldots$

b) $1, -3, 9, -27, \ldots$

6.3 Pascal's Triangle and Expanding Binomial Powers, pages 373 to 379

5. Use Pascal's triangle to expand each power of a binomial.

a) $(x + 4)^5$

b) $(y - 6)^4$

c) $(m + 2n)^4$

d) $(3p - q)^6$

6. Recall that the sequence of triangular numbers 1, 3, 6, 10, 15, ... can be found in Pascal's triangle. Tetrahedral numbers are the sums of consecutive triangular numbers 1, 4, 10, 20, ...

a) Write the next two terms of the sequence representing tetrahedral numbers.

b) Locate these numbers in Pascal's triangle. Describe their position.

6.4

7. Arithmetic (+ / −)

$T_n = a + (n-1)d$

$S_n = \frac{n}{2}[2a + (n-1)d]$

Geometric (× / ÷)

$T_n = ar^{n-1}$

8. $S_n = \dfrac{a(r^n - 1)}{r - 1}$

打小数点、→ 分数

Math → enter → enter

b) $f(n) =$ ...

9. A theatre has 40 rows of seats. Each row has five more seats than the previous row. If the first row has 50 seats, how many seats are in the

a) 20th row?

b) last row?

6.5 Geometric Sequences, pages 388 to 394

10. Determine whether each sequence is arithmetic, geometric, or neither. Justify your answers.

a) $-1, 9, 19, 29, \ldots$

b) $3, 12, 19, 44, \ldots$

c) $-2, 6, -18, 54, \ldots$

11. Write the first three terms of each geometric sequence.

a) $f(n) = 2(-1)^n$

b) $t_n = -3(2)^{n+1}$

12. Angelica ran in a half-marathon. The length of the race was 21.1 km. She ran 1700 m in the first 10 min of the race. In each 10-min interval after the first one, her distance decreased by 4%. How far did she run in the tenth 10-min interval?

6.6 Arithmetic Series, pages 395 to 401

13. For each arithmetic series, state the values of a and d. Then, determine the sum of the first 20 terms.

a) $50 + 45 + 40 + \cdots$

b) $-27 - 21 - 15 - \cdots$

14. On his 12th birthday, Enoch's grandparents deposited $25 into a savings account for him. Each month after that up to and including his 20th birthday, they deposit $10 more than the previous month. How much money will Enoch have on his 20th birthday, excluding interest?

15. Determine the sum of each arithmetic series.

a) $-6 - 13 - 20 - \cdots - 139$

b) $-23 - 17 - 11 - \cdots + 43$

6.7 Geometric Series, pages 402 to 409

16. For each geometric series, determine the values of a and r. Then, determine the sum of the first 10 terms.

a) $2 + 14 + 98 + \cdots$

b) $8 - 16 + 32 - 64 + \cdots$

17. Determine the sum of each geometric series.

a) $245 + 24.5 + 2.45 + \cdots + 0.000\ 245$

b) $6561 + 2187 + 729 + \cdots + \dfrac{1}{6561}$

18. The first four diagrams in a pattern are shown. Each shape is made of small squares with an area of 0.5 cm². Determine the total area of the first 10 diagrams.

Chapter Problem   WRAP-UP

Throughout this chapter, you explored a variety of fractals and sequences related to fractals. This sequence has fractal properties.

1, 1, 2, 1, 3, 2, 4, 1, 5, 3, 6, 2, 7, 4, 8, 1, 9, 5, 10, 3, 11, 6, 12, 2, 13, 7, 14, 4, 15, 8, …

a) Copy the sequence and write the next 20 terms.

Hint: Look for patterns in the term number for each natural number in the sequence.

b) Delete the first occurrence of each natural number. Write the remaining sequence. Describe this sequence in words and write a formula to represent it.

c) Repeat this procedure and describe the pattern that emerges.

d) How is the procedure like constructing a fractal?

Chapter 6 Practice Test

For questions 1 to 5, select the best answer.

1. Which is a recursion formula for the sequence shown?

   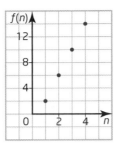

   A $f(n) = f(n - 1) + 4$

   B $f(n) = 4n - 2$

   C $f(n) = 2 + (n - 1)(4)$

   D $f(1) = 2,$
   $f(n) = f(n - 1) + 4$

2. Which expressions represent the missing terms in the binomial expansion shown?
   $(x + y)^7 = x^7 + 7x^6y + + 35x^4y^3 + 35x^3y^4$
   $+ 21x^2y^5 + + y^7$

   A $21y^5x^2, 7yx^6$

   B $21x^5y^2, 7xy^6$

   C $-21x^5y^2, -7xy^6$

   D x^5y^2, xy^6

3. What is the formula for the general term of an arithmetic sequence with $a = 8$ and $d = 2$?

   A $t_n = 2 + (n + 1)(8)$

   B $t_n = 8 + (n - 1)(2)$

   C $t_n = 8 + (n + 1)(2)$

   D $t_n = 2 + (n - 1)(8)$

4. What are the first three terms of a geometric sequence with $a = 3$ and $r = 2$?

   A 3, 5, 7

   B 2, 6, 18

   C 3, 6, 12

   D 2, 5, 8

5. Which series is neither arithmetic nor geometric?

   A $9 + 15 + 21 + 27 + \cdots$

   B $1 + 8 + 27 + 64 + \cdots$

   C $64 - 32 + 16 - 8 + \cdots$

   D $-3 - 2.7 - 2.4 - 2.1 - \cdots$

6. Determine the first five terms of each sequence. Graph the sequence and state whether it is arithmetic, geometric, or neither.

   a) $t_n = 9 - 5n$

   b) $f(n) = 2n^2 + 3n - 4$

   c) $f(n) = \frac{1}{8}(4)^{n-1}$

   d) $t_n = 0.2n + 0.8$

   e) $t_n = \frac{n + 4}{2}$

   f) $f(n) = -3(2)^n$

7. Write an explicit formula and a recursion formula for each sequence.

   a) 64, 32, 16, 8, ...

   b) $-20, -17, -14, -11, \ldots$

   c) 80, 76, 72, 68, ...

   d) $-4000, 1000, -250, 62.5, \ldots$

   e) $-3, -6, -12, -24, \ldots$

   f) $-12\sqrt{2}, -10\sqrt{2}, -8\sqrt{2}, -6\sqrt{2}, \ldots$

8. Write t_{11} for each sequence.

   a) 6, 10, 14, 18, ...

   b) $-3, -6, -12, -24, \ldots$

   c) $5, -10, 20, -40, \ldots$

   d) $-5, -10, -15, -20, \ldots$

9. Given the explicit formula, write t_{15} for each sequence.

   a) $f(n) = 2(-3)^{n+1}$

   b) $t_n = 25n + 50$

   c) $t_n = 10(0.1)^{2n}$

   d) $f(n) = \frac{-3n}{4}$

10. Determine the number of terms in each sequence.

   a) 5, 8, 11, ..., 62

   b) $-4, 12, -36, \ldots, -19\ 131\ 876$

11. A new lake is being excavated. One day, 1.6 t of material is removed from the lake bed. On each of 10 days after that, 5% more is removed.

a) Write the first three excavation amounts as a sequence.

b) Write a recursion formula to represent the amount removed each day. Use this to determine the amount removed on the fifth day.

12. Determine the specified sum for each series.

a) S_{10} for $200 + 100 + 50 + \cdots$

b) S_{18} for $12 + 5 - 2 + \cdots$

13. Determine the sum of each arithmetic series.

a) $120 + 110 + 100 + \cdots - 250$

b) $8 + 24 + 40 + \cdots + 280$

14. Determine the sum of each geometric series.

a) $\dfrac{2}{81} + \dfrac{4}{27} + \dfrac{8}{9} + \cdots + 6912$

b) $5 + 10 + 20 + \cdots + 2560$

15. Use Pascal's triangle to help you expand each expression.

a) $(b - 3)^5$ **b)** $(2x - 5y)^6$

16. The sum of the first three terms of a series is 32. Determine the fourth term if the sum of the first four terms is

a) 40   **b)** 25

17. Determine the sum of the first 15 terms of an arithmetic series if the middle term is 92.

18. Which is greater, A or B? Explain your reasoning.

A = $50^2 - 49^2 + 48^2 - 47^2 + \cdots + 2^2 - 1^2$

B = $50 + 49 + 48 + 47 + \cdots + 2 + 1$

19. In the arrangement of letters shown, starting from the top, proceed to the row below by moving diagonally to the immediate right or left. Determine the number of different paths that will spell the name PASCAL.

```
            P
          A   A
        S   S   S
      C   C   C   C
    A   A   A   A   A
  L   L   L   L   L   L
```

20. A new wood stain loses 6.5% of its colour every year in a city that experiences a lot of hot, sunny days. What percent of colour will a fence in this city have 6 years after being stained?

21. In an arithmetic series, the 4th term is 62 and the 14th term is 122. Determine the sum of the first 30 terms.

22. A sailboat worth $140 000 depreciates 18% in the first year and 10% every year after that. How much will it be worth 8 years after it is bought?

23. A magic square is an arrangement of numbers in which all rows, columns, and diagonals have the same sum. Using the magic square shown, substitute each number with the corresponding term from the Fibonacci sequence.

2	7	6
9	5	1
4	3	8

Show that the sum of the products of the rows is equal to the sum of the products of the columns.

Mathematics in Media Studies

For a media studies project, Khatija wants to produce an image that appears to have a vanishing point. Photocopiers and photoediting software will increase or decrease an image by a chosen percent. Khatija is working with an original image that has dimensions 320 mm by 240 mm. She increased the original by 50% and then decreased the image by 50%, repeating this process several times.

a) Plot a graph of the length versus step number. Show at least five steps of the process.

b) Determine a recursion formula for the end result after each step.

c) Determine an explicit formula for the end result after each step.

d) What will the length of the image be after 10 steps of this process? Give exact answers.

e) Will the length of the image ever reach 0 mm? Explain.

f) Is this relationship linear, quadratic, exponential, or reciprocal? Justify your answer.

g) For the same project, Calvin used repetitive addition of a specific number of millimetres followed by subtraction of a different number of millimetres. Use your own choices of lengths to add and subtract and repeat steps a) to f) for Calvin's process. Compare your results to your results from Khatija's process.

Financial Applications

As you move through high school and on to post-secondary studies, financial mathematics will become increasingly important. If you decide to go to university or college, you may need to understand the concepts and terminology of loans and interest payments. Similarly, once you enter the world of work, you may decide to invest some of your earnings to save for a car, a mortgage, or, eventually, your retirement.

Many of the concepts you have learned in previous chapters will be useful when you explore new financial concepts such as simple and compound interest, present value, and annuities.

By the end of this chapter, you will

- make and describe connections between simple interest, arithmetic sequences, and linear growth, through investigation with technology
- make and describe connections between compound interest, geometric sequences, and exponential growth, through investigation with technology
- solve problems, using a scientific calculator, that involve the calculation of the amount, A; the principal, P; or the interest rate per compounding period, i, using the compound interest formula in the form $A = P(1 + i)^n$
- determine, through investigation using technology, the number of compounding periods, n, using the compound interest formula in the form $A = P(1 + i)^n$; describe strategies for calculating this number; and solve related problems

- explain the meaning of the term *annuity*, and determine the relationships between ordinary simple annuities, geometric series, and exponential growth, through investigation with technology
- determine, through investigation using technology, the effects of changing the conditions of ordinary simple annuities
- solve problems, using technology, that involve the amount, the present value, and the regular payment of an ordinary simple annuity

Prerequisite Skills

Refer to the Prerequisite Skills Appendix on pages 478 to 495 for examples of the topics and further practice.

Linear and Exponential Growth

1. a) Graph the equation $y = 40x + 400$. What type of relationship is this?

   b) Identify the slope and the y-intercept.

   c) Make a table of values using x-values of 0, 1, 2, 3, and 4.

   d) Calculate the first differences and describe their pattern.

2. a) Graph the equation $y = 100(1.05)^x$. What type of relationship is this?

   b) Identify the y-intercept.

   c) Make a table of values using x-values of 0, 1, 2, 3, and 4.

   d) Calculate the first and second differences and describe any patterns you see.

   e) Calculate the common ratios by dividing consecutive y-values, and describe their pattern.

3. Determine whether each table of values represents an exponential function. Justify your reasoning using finite differences, a graph, or common ratios.

a)

x	y
−2	0
1	4.5
0	9.0
1	13.5
2	18.0

b)

x	y
0	100
1	90
2	81
3	72.9
4	65.61

Direct Variation and Partial Variation

4. Identify each relation as a direct variation, a partial variation, or neither. Justify your answer.

   a) $y = 2x$ **b)** $y = 3x + 1$

   c) $C = 5n + 25$ **d)** $d = 4t$

5. The cost of a taxi ride is $3 plus $1 per kilometre.

   a) Write an equation to relate the total cost, C, in dollars, of the ride to the trip distance, d, in kilometres.

   b) Identify the fixed part and the variable part of this relation.

   c) Graph the relation.

   d) Determine the slope and the vertical intercept of the graph.

   e) Explain how your answers to parts b) and d) are related.

Arithmetic Sequences and Series

6. a) Explain why the sequence 7, 10, 13, 16, 19, … is arithmetic.

   b) Determine the first term, a, and the common difference, d.

   c) Write the formula for the general term, or nth term, t_n.

7. The formula for the general term of an arithmetic sequence is $t_n = 5n - 7$.

   a) Write the first four terms of the sequence.

   b) Determine the first term, a, and the common difference, d.

8. Determine the sum of the first 100 terms of the series $3 + 8 + 13 + 18 + \cdots$.

Geometric Sequences and Series

9. a) Explain why the sequence 3, 6, 12, 24, 48, … is geometric.

   b) Determine the first term, a, and the common ratio, r.

   c) Write a formula for the general term, or nth term, t_n.

10. The formula for the general term of a geometric sequence is $t_n = -2(3)^{n-1}$.

   a) Write the first four terms of the sequence.

   b) Determine the first term, a, and the common ratio, r.

11. Determine the sum of the first 15 terms of the series $1 + 1.05 + 1.1025 + 1.157\ 625 + \cdots$.

12. The sum of the first 10 terms of a geometric series is 699 050. The common ratio is 4. Determine the first term.

Solve Equations

13. Solve for each variable.

a) $600 = 40 + 7n$

b) $840 = I + 5(12)$

c) $250 = P[1 + 0.08(4)]$

d) $496.50 = 300(1 + i)^8$

14. Solve for x. Round answers to four decimal places, if necessary.

a) $200 = x(1 + 0.045)^6$

b) $500 = \dfrac{40}{x + 1}$

c) $300 = \dfrac{320}{(1 + x)^2}$

d) $240 = 200x^6$

Time

15. Convert each time to the unit specified.

a) 3 years to months

b) 15 weeks to years

c) 130 days to years

d) 9 months to weeks

e) 100 days to months

f) 25 weeks to months

16. How many intervals are in each time?

a) weekly intervals in 2 years

b) annual intervals in 4 years

c) monthly intervals in 3.5 years

d) quarterly intervals in 3 years

e) semi-annual intervals in 2 years

f) semi-annual intervals in 3.5 years

Chapter Problem

Chloe, a student just entering high school, has inherited $10 000. She decides to invest the money until she is ready for university. To help her make wise decisions, she and her parents hire a financial advisor. The advisor recommends that she invest her money in a diversified portfolio, in other words, put her money into a balanced mix of investment options.

You will encounter problems related to Chloe's investments throughout this chapter.

Simple Interest

Whether you are investing or borrowing, there is almost always a fee charged to the borrower, typically referred to as *interest*. Interest can be either paid or earned.

When you take out a loan, *you* are the borrower and you *pay* interest. When you deposit money at a financial institution, the *bank* is the borrower and you *earn* interest.

simple interest
- interest calculated only on the original principal using the formula $I = Prt$, where I is the interest, in dollars; P is the principal, in dollars; r is the annual rate of interest, as a decimal; and t is the time, in years

principal
- amount of money initially invested or borrowed

annual rate of interest
- rate at which interest is charged, as a percent, per year
- expressed as a decimal for calculations

amount
- the value of an investment or loan at the end of a time period
- calculated by adding the principal and interest

Tools
- graphing calculator

or
- computer with graphing or spreadsheet software

or
- grid paper

The simplest form of interest is called **simple interest**. Simple interest, I, can be calculated by multiplying the **principal**, P, by the **annual rate of interest**, r, expressed as a decimal, and by the time, t, for which the money is lent, in years.

$$I = Prt$$

At the end of the lending period, the **amount**, A, repaid by the borrower to the lender is the sum of the principal and the interest.

$$A = P + I$$

While simple interest is rarely used in bank accounts and loans today, it is important to understand its fundamental nature before learning the more advanced concepts to be introduced in the next section.

Investigate

How can you represent simple interest mathematically?

Alexis receives a $1000 gift for her grade 8 graduation. She decides to invest the money at 5% per year, simple interest.

1. a) Copy and complete the table, which relates the amount of the investment to time.

Time, n (years)	Amount, A ($)	First Differences
1	1050	1100 – 1050 = 50
2	1100	
3	1150	
4		
5		

b) Is this relationship linear? Explain how you know.

2. a) Graph the amount versus time. Describe the trend.

b) Does this support your answer to step 1b)? Explain.

3. a) Determine the slope and the vertical intercept of the graph.

b) Write an equation to relate the amount, A, to the time, n.

c) Is this an example of direct variation or is it an example of partial variation? Explain.

4. a) Examine the values in the Amount column of the table. Explain why this is an arithmetic sequence.

b) Identify the first term, a, and the common difference, d.

c) Write a simplified equation for the nth term of this sequence, using the formula $t_n = a + (n - 1)d$.

d) Compare your equation in part c) to the one from step 3b). How are they alike? different?

5. Reflect Summarize the different mathematical ways that simple interest can be represented.

Example 1

Calculate Simple Interest

a) How much interest is earned if $1200 is invested at 5% per year simple interest for 3 years?

b) How much interest is paid if $400 is borrowed at 8% per annum simple interest for 7 months?

c) How much interest is earned if $900 is invested at 4.25% annual simple interest for 90 days?

Connections

Per year, per annum, yearly, and *annually* are all commonly used terms with the same meaning—per year.

Solution

Use the formula $I = Prt$. Express the interest rate as a decimal and the time in years.

a) $I = Prt$
$= 1200(0.05)(3)$
$= 180$

The interest earned is $180.

b) $I = Prt$
$= 400(0.08)\left(\dfrac{7}{12}\right)$ Seven months represents $\dfrac{7}{12}$ of a year.
$\doteq 18.67$ Round money values to the nearest cent.

The interest paid is $18.67.

c) $I = Prt$
$= 900(0.0425)\left(\dfrac{90}{365}\right)$ There are 365 days in a year.
$\doteq 9.43$

The interest earned is $9.43.

Example 2 —————————————————————○

Develop a Linear Model for Simple Interest

Robert deposits $500 into a guaranteed investment certificate (GIC) that earns 6% per year, simple interest.

a) Develop a linear model to relate the amount to time. Identify the fixed part and the variable part. Graph the function.

b) How long will it take, to the nearest month, for the investment to double?

c) What annual rate of interest must be earned so that the investment doubles in 8 years?

Connections

The linear model representing the amount in an account earning simple interest can also be written using slope y-intercept form, $y = mx + b$, as $A = 30t + 500$.

Solution

a) The amount varies partially with time.

$A = P + I$

The fixed part is the principal, $500. The variable part is the interest, which can be found by substituting the known values into the formula $I = Prt$.

$$I = Prt$$
$$= 500(0.06)t$$
$$= 30t$$

Therefore, the amount is given by $A = 500 + 30t$.

The graph is a straight line with slope 30 and vertical intercept 500.

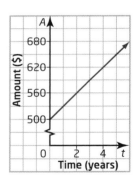

b) Method 1: Apply Graphical Analysis

To determine how long it will take for the amount to double from $500, use graphing technology to locate the point where the graph of $A = 500 + 30t$ intersects the graph of $A = 1000$.

Use a graphing calculator to graph the functions as **Y1** and **Y2**. Apply number sense and systematic trial to set reasonable window settings.

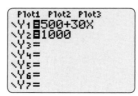

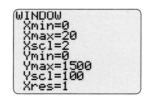

Use the **Intersect** operation to identify the coordinates of the point of intersection.

- Press (2nd) [CALC] to display the **CALCULATE** menu, and select **5:intersect**.
- Press (ENTER) when prompted for the first curve, second curve, and guess.

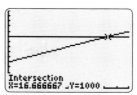

The solution to this linear system indicates that it will take $16\frac{2}{3}$ years for the investment to double.

To express the time in years and months, convert the fraction part of the answer to months:

$$\frac{2}{3} \times 12 = 8$$

The time required for this investment to double is 16 years 8 months.

Method 2: Apply Algebraic Reasoning

To determine how long it will take for the amount to double from $500, substitute $A = 1000$ and solve for t.

$$1000 = 500 + 30t$$
$$500 = 30t$$
$$t = 16\frac{2}{3}$$

It will take $16\frac{2}{3}$ years, or 16 years 8 months, for the investment to double.

c) **Method 1: Apply Graphical Analysis**

To determine the rate of interest for $500 to double in 8 years, substitute $P = 500$ and $t = 8$ into the amount equation to express A in terms of r.

$$A = P + I$$
$$= P + Prt$$
$$= 500 + 500r(8)$$
$$= 500 + 4000r$$

Use the **Intersect** operation on a graphing calculator to locate the point where this function intersects the graph of $A = 1000$.

 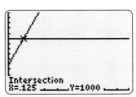

The solution to this linear system indicates that for the amount to double after 8 years, the annual rate of interest must be 0.125, or 12.5%.

Connections

Note that in part b) the independent variable in the graphing calculator, X, represents time, t. In part c), X represents the interest rate, r. It is important to understand the variables being compared in each situation.

Method 2: Apply Algebraic Reasoning

To determine the rate of interest to double $500 in 8 years, substitute $A = 1000$, $P = 500$, and $t = 8$ into the equation $A = P + Prt$ and solve for r.

$$A = P + Prt$$
$$1000 = 500 + 500r(8)$$
$$500 = 4000r$$
$$r = 0.125$$

For the amount to double after 8 years, the annual rate of interest must be 12.5%.

Example 3

Analyse a Simple Interest Scenario

The graph shows the amount of an investment earning simple interest.

a) What is the principal?

b) What is the annual interest rate?

c) Write an equation to relate the amount of the investment to time.

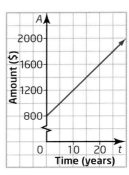

> **Solution**

a) The principal is the amount of the initial investment. This occurs when $t = 0$. From the graph, the vertical intercept is 800. So, the principal is $800.

b) Determine the interest rate from the slope of the line.

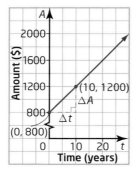

$$m = \frac{\Delta A}{\Delta t} \qquad \text{Use the slope formula.}$$

$$= \frac{1200 - 800}{10 - 0}$$

$$= \frac{400}{10}$$

$$= 40$$

The slope is 40, which means that $40 interest is earned each year. Express this as a percent of the principal.

$$i = \frac{40}{800}$$

$$= 0.05$$

Therefore, the annual interest rate is 5%.

c) This is the graph of a partial variation, so its equation is of the form $A = mt + b$.

The equation for the amount of the investment as a function of time is $A = 40t + 800$.

Key Concepts

- Simple interest, I, in dollars, can be calculated by multiplying the principal, P, in dollars, by the annual interest rate, r, expressed as a decimal, and by the time, t, in years.

$I = Prt$

- The amount, A, of an account earning simple interest is the sum of the principal, P, and the interest, I.

$A = P + I$

- The amount in an account earning simple interest can be represented using
  - a table of values
  - a partial variation equation
  - a linear graph
  - an arithmetic sequence

Communicate Your Understanding

C1 Explain how you can represent each time period in terms of years.

a) 4 months

b) 75 days

c) 15 weeks

C2 The table shows the amount in a simple interest account.

a) Look at the values in the Amount column. Is this an arithmetic sequence? Explain.

b) What is the annual rate of simple interest? How do you know?

C3 An account with an initial value of $600 earns 5% simple interest annually.

a) Describe the shape of the graph of amount versus time.

b) Determine the slope and vertical intercept of the graph. What do they represent?

Time (years)	Amount ($)
0	100
1	108
2	116
3	124
4	132

A Practise

For help with question 1, refer to Example 1.

1. Determine the simple interest earned on each investment.

   a) $450 is deposited for 4 years and earns 6.5% per year simple interest.

   b) $750 is deposited for 5 months at 7% per year simple interest.

   c) $500 is invested at 4.75% annual simple interest for 35 weeks.

   d) $1100 is invested at 7.8% per year, simple interest, for 60 days.

For help with questions 2 to 4, refer to Example 2.

2. Connor deposits $200 into an account that earns 6% simple interest annually.

   a) Determine the amount of the investment after 1, 2, 3, 4, and 5 years.

   b) Identify the first term, a, and the common difference, d, of this arithmetic sequence.

   c) Write an equation to represent the nth term of this sequence. What is the significance of the nth term?

3. The table shows the amount of a simple interest GIC over a period of several years.

Time (years)	Amount ($)
1	689
2	728
3	767
4	806
5	845

   a) Calculate the first differences. What do these values represent?

   b) What is the principal of this investment? How do you know?

   c) What is the annual rate of simple interest?

4. Refer to the table in question 3.

   a) Develop a linear model to represent the amount in the GIC versus time.

   b) Explain why the model from part a) is a partial variation. Identify the fixed part and the variable part.

   c) How long will it take, to the nearest month, for this investment to double from its initial value?

For help with questions 5 and 6, refer to Example 3.

5. The graph shows the amount of an investment earning simple interest.

   a) What is the principal?

   b) What is the annual interest rate?

   c) Write an equation to relate the amount to time.

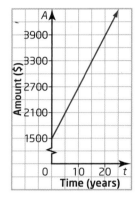

   d) Use your equation from part c) to determine how long it will take, to the nearest month, for the original investment to double.

B Connect and Apply

6. Refer to question 5.

   a) Write an equation to relate the interest to time.

   b) Use your equation from part a) to determine how long it will take for the original investment to double. Compare this result with your answer to question 5d).

7. To save for a new pair of skis, Sven deposits $250 into a savings bond that earns 4.5% per year, simple interest.

a) Write an equation to relate the amount of the investment to time.

b) Graph the function.

c) How long will it take, to the nearest month, for the amount to reach $300?

d) What interest rate is required for the amount to reach $300 in 2 years less than your answer in part c)?

8. Rita borrows $500 at an annual rate of 8.25% simple interest to enrol in a driver's education course. She plans to repay the loan in 18 months.

a) What amount must she pay back?

b) How much interest will she pay?

c) How much sooner should Rita repay the loan if she wants to pay no more than $50 in interest charges?

9. José borrows $1400 to buy a road racing bicycle. He repays the loan 2 years later in the amount of $1700. What annual rate of simple interest was José charged?

10. Chapter Problem Chloe's financial advisor has recommended that she invest at least 20% of her money in treasury bonds, at a fixed rate of return, or interest rate. Following this recommendation, she invests $2000 in a treasury bond for 4 years at a rate of 3.5% per year simple interest. Chloe cannot access this money before the end of the 4 years without paying a financial penalty.

a) Determine the interest earned over the term of the bond.

b) Determine the amount of the investment at the end of 4 years.

11. Tamara took out a loan for $940 at an annual rate of 11.5% simple interest. When she repaid the loan, the amount was $1100. How long did Tamara hold this loan?

12. Dmitri wants to borrow $5500 to buy a used car. He is considering two options:

- Borrow from the bank at 12.4% per year simple interest.
- Borrow from the car dealership at 11% per year simple interest, plus a $200 administration fee due upon the repayment date.

a) For each option, write an equation to relate the amount, A, to time, t, in years.

b) Graph the amount payable versus time for each option on the same set of axes.

c) Which option is the better deal? Explain.

C Extend

13. a) Use algebraic reasoning to derive an equation to express the annual simple interest rate, r, in terms of the principal, P; the amount, A; and the time, t, of a simple interest investment.

b) Use your formula from part a) to determine the annual simple interest rate earned by an account that grows from $860 to $1000 in 3 years.

c) Verify your result in part b) using another method of your choice.

14. a) Use algebraic reasoning to derive an equation to express the time, t, in years, of an investment, in terms of the principal, P; the amount, A; and the annual rate of simple interest, r.

b) Pose and solve a problem related to the formula you developed.

7.2

Compound Interest

Gaston is a talented young musician who earns a living by playing at coffee houses, university campuses, and special events such as weddings. Before he buys a new guitar, Gaston wants to compare various borrowing options that are available to him.

In Section 7.1, you learned that when simple interest is earned, the amount grows linearly as a function of time. However, most investments and loans are based on **compound interest**. This means that at the end of each **compounding period**, the interest is added to the principal for the next compounding period so that interest is then paid on this new total amount.

compound interest

• interest that is calculated at regular compounding periods

• added to the principal for the following compounding period

compounding period

• time interval after which compound interest is calculated

Tools

• graphing calculator

or

• computer with graphing software

Investigate

How can you calculate compound interest?

Recall from the Investigate in Section 7.1 that Alexis receives $1000 for her grade 8 graduation. Under the simple interest scenario, the interest earned at 5% per year for 5 years is $250.

Suppose that Alexis deposits the money into an account that pays the same annual interest rate of 5%, but compounded annually. How does this affect the amount of interest she will earn?

1. Copy the table. Calculate the interest using the formula $I = Prt$ and complete the table. Leave room for two more columns to the right.

Year	Balance at Start of Year ($)	Interest Earned During the Year ($)	Balance at End of Year ($)
1	1000	1000(0.05)(1) = 50	1000 + 50 = 1050
2	1050	1050(0.05)(1) = 52.50	1050 + 52.50 = 1102.50
3			
4			
5			

2. a) Look at the values in the Interest Earned column. Describe what you notice.

b) **Reflect** What is an advantage of compound interest over simple interest?

3. a) Add a column to the right of your table from step 1. Label the column "First Differences." Calculate the first differences by subtracting successive balances at the end of the year. Record the values in the table.

b) What do the first differences represent?

c) Is the balance at the end of the year versus time a linear relationship? Explain.

4. a) Add a column to the right of your table from step 3. Label the column "Common Ratios." Calculate the common ratios by dividing successive balances at the end of the year. For example, calculate 1102.50 ÷ 1050. Record these values in the table.

b) What do you notice about the pattern of common ratios?

c) What type of function does this represent? Explain how you can tell.

5. a) Graph the Balance at the End of Year versus Year, from step 1, using graphing technology.

b) Does the shape of the graph support your answer to step 4c)? Explain.

c) Graph the amount in the simple interest investment given by the equation $A = 1000 + 50t$ on the same set of axes as your graph in part a). How are these graphs alike? different?

d) What happens to these graphs after a long period of time? Why does this happen?

6. Reflect

a) Is the interest earned per year the same for every year under simple interest conditions? under compound interest conditions? Explain.

b) Suppose that Alexis decides to use her investment to help her buy a car when she graduates from university. How much more interest will she have earned in the compound interest account than in the simple interest account, assuming that the money is invested for 8 years?

The amount of a compound interest investment or loan can be found recursively as follows.

Let i represent the annual interest rate per compounding period. The amount after one compounding period can be determined by adding the principal to the interest for that compounding period.

$$A = P + I$$
$$= P + Pit$$
$$= P + Pi(1) \qquad \text{After one compounding period, } t = 1.$$
$$= P + Pi$$
$$= P(1 + i) \qquad \text{Factor the expression.}$$

Connections

You studied recursive relationships in Chapter 6 Discrete Functions.

Therefore, the amount after the first compounding period is the product of the principal at the beginning of the period and the factor $(1 + i)$. This amount becomes the new principal for the second compounding period. This process can be continued, as shown in the table.

Compounding Period	Principal for the Period	Amount Calculation	Amount at End of Period
1	P	$A = P(1 + i)$	$P(1 + i)$
2	$P(1 + i)$	$A = P(1 + i)(1 + i) = P(1 + i)^2$	$P(1 + i)^2$
3	$P(1 + i)^2$	$A = P(1 + i)^2(1 + i) = P(1 + i)^3$	$P(1 + i)^3$
4	$P(1 + i)^3$	$A = P(1 + i)^3(1 + i) = P(1 + i)^4$	$P(1 + i)^4$
$\vdots$	$\vdots$	$\vdots$	$\vdots$

Examine the pattern of terms in the last column.

$P(1 + i)$, $P(1 + i)^2$, $P(1 + i)^3$, $P(1 + i)^4$, ...

This is a geometric sequence with first term $a = P(1 + i)$ and common ratio $r = 1 + i$. Substitute these into the formula for the nth term of a geometric sequence.

$$\begin{aligned} t_n &= ar^{n-1} \\ &= [P(1 + i)](1 + i)^{n-1} \\ &= P(1 + i)^{1 + (n-1)} \qquad \text{Apply the product rule of exponents.} \\ &= P(1 + i)^n \end{aligned}$$

Note that the nth term corresponds to the amount, A, at the end of the nth compounding period. So, replace t_n with A.

$A = P(1 + i)^n$

This result is the compound interest formula.

The amount, A, of a compound interest investment or loan can be determined using the formula $A = P(1 + i)^n$.

P represents the principal.

i represents the interest rate per compounding period, expressed as a decimal.

n represents the number of compounding periods.

Example 1

Calculate Compound Interest

To buy a new guitar, Gaston borrows $650, which he plans to repay in 5 years. The bank charges 12% per annum, compounded annually.

a) Determine the amount that Gaston must repay.

b) How much interest will Gaston have to pay?

c) Compare this to the amount of interest he would have to pay if the bank charged simple interest.

Solution

a) List the given information. Then, apply the compound interest formula.

$P = 650$
$i = 0.12$
$n = 5$

$A = P(1 + i)^n$
$ = 650(1 + 0.12)^5$
$ = 650(1.12)^5$ **650** (×) **1.12** (y^x) **5** (=)
$ \doteq 1145.52$

Gaston must repay $1145.52 after 5 years.

b) To calculate the interest paid, subtract the principal from the amount.

$I = A - P$
$ = 1145.52 - 650$
$ = 495.52$

Gaston will pay $495.52 in interest charges.

c) If the bank charges 12% simple interest, then the interest can be found by applying the simple interest formula.

$I = Prt$
$ = 650(0.12)(5)$
$ = 390$

Gaston would pay only $390 in simple interest, compared to $495.52 in compound interest.

Connections

Securing a simple interest loan for a significant period of time is rare in today's financial institutions.

Example 2

Vary the Compounding Period

Financial institutions often use other compounding periods rather than annual. For example, semi-annual compounding means every 6 months, while quarterly compounding means every 3 months, and so on. Refer to Example 1. What will be the impact on the interest Gaston pays if the interest is compounded

a) semi-annually?

b) monthly?

Solution

a) When interest is charged semi-annually (twice a year), the number of compounding periods is doubled and the interest rate per compounding period is halved.

$P = 650$

$i = \dfrac{0.12}{2}$ Divide by the number of compounding periods in a year, 2.

    $= 0.06$

$n = 5 \times 2$ Multiply by the number of compounding periods in a year, 2.

    $= 10$

Substitute the known values into the compound interest formula.

$A = P(1 + i)^n$

   $= 650(1 + 0.06)^{10}$

   $= 650(1.06)^{10}$

   $\doteq 1164.05$

Calculate the interest paid.

$I = A - P$

   $= 1164.05 - 650$

   $= 514.05$

Gaston will pay \$514.05 in interest charges if interest is compounded semi-annually.

b) When interest is charged monthly, the number of compounding periods and the interest rate per compounding period can be calculated as follows.

$P = 650$

$i = \dfrac{0.12}{12}$ Divide by the number of compounding periods in a year, 12.

    $= 0.01$

$n = 5 \times 12$ Multiply by the number of compounding periods in a year, 12.

    $= 60$

$A = P(1 + i)^n$

   $= 650(1 + 0.01)^{60}$

   $= 650(1.01)^{60}$

   $\doteq 1180.85$

Calculate the interest paid.

$I = A - P$

   $= 1180.85 - 650$

   $= 530.85$

Gaston will pay \$530.85 in interest charges if interest is compounded monthly.

The table summarizes the effects of the various compounding periods.

Compounding Period	Amount, A ($)	Interest, I ($)
annual	1145.52	495.52
semi-annual	1164.05	514.05
monthly	1180.85	530.85

Note that as the compounding period becomes shorter, the interest charges increase.

Example 3

Determine the Interest Rate

Nina is starting a small business. She applies for an $8000 loan, which she plans to repay in 4 years. She is told by the loan officer that the amount payable when the loan is due is $11 501.24. What rate of interest, compounded annually, is Nina being charged?

Solution

List the given information. Then, apply the compound interest formula.

$P = 8000$
$A = 11\ 501.24$
$n = 4$

$$A = P(1 + i)^n$$
$$11\ 501.24 = 8000(1 + i)^4$$
$$\frac{11\ 501.24}{8000} = (1 + i)^4$$
$$1.437\ 655 = (1 + i)^4$$

Method 1: Apply Graphical Analysis

To determine when $(1 + i)^4 = 1.437\ 655$, graph each side of this equation as a separate function using a graphing calculator. Then, use the **Intersect** operation.

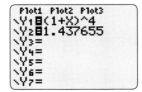 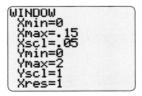 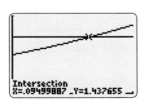

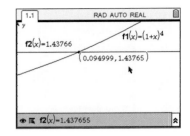

Technology Tip

To use the **Intersection Point(s)** operation on a TI-Nspire™ CAS graphing calculator:

• Press (menu). Select **6:Points & Lines**.

• Select **3:Intersection Point(s)**. Move the cursor to the first graph and press (enter). Move the cursor to the second graph and press (enter).

The coordinates of the intersection point will be displayed.

Similarly, you can use the **Intersection Point(s)** operation on a TI-Nspire™ CAS graphing calculator.

The solution is approximately (0.095, 1.437 655), which indicates that the interest rate is 9.5%, compounded annually.

Method 2: Apply Algebraic Reasoning

To solve the equation $1.437\ 655 = (1 + i)^4$ for i, apply the opposite operations to isolate the variable.

$$\sqrt[4]{1.437\ 655} = \sqrt[4]{(1 + i)^4}$$ Take the fourth root of both sides.

$$\sqrt[4]{1.437\ 655} = 1 + i$$ Apply the properties of powers and roots.

$$\sqrt[4]{1.437\ 655} - 1 = i$$ **1.437655** (2nd) $[\sqrt[x]{y}]$ **4** (−) **1** (=)

$$0.095 \doteq i$$

The interest rate is approximately 9.5%, compounded annually.

Key Concepts

● Compound interest investments or loans add the interest from one compounding period to the previous principal and use the sum as the principal for the next compounding period.

● The compounding effect causes an amount to grow exponentially over time. The amounts after each compounding period produce a geometric sequence.

● The compound interest formula $A = P(1 + i)^n$ can be used to calculate the amount, A, if the principal, P; the interest rate per compounding period, i; and the number of compounding periods, n, are known.

● The table shows common methods of compounding.

Frequency of Compounding	Number of Times Interest Is Added During a Year
annual	1 (every year)
semi-annual	2 (every 6 months)
quarterly	4 (every 3 months)
monthly	12 (every month)
bi-weekly	26 (every 2 weeks)
daily	365 (every day)

Communicate Your Understanding

C1 Explain the advantage of compound interest over simple interest, from an investor's point of view. Use an example to illustrate your answer.

C2 The table shows the amount in an annually compounded interest account over time.

Time (years)	Amount ($)
0	400.00
1	416.00
2	432.64
3	449.95
4	467.94

a) Look at the values in the Amount column. Is this an arithmetic or a geometric sequence? Explain.

b) What is the annual rate of compound interest? How do you know?

C3 An account with an initial value of $800 earns 6% interest per year, compounded annually.

a) Describe the shape of the graph of amount versus time.

b) What is the vertical intercept of the graph? What does it represent?

c) Describe what happens to the slope of the graph.

Ⓐ Practise

For help with questions 1 and 2, refer to Example 1.

1. Darlene invests $500 for 6 years at 4% interest per year, compounded annually.

a) Determine the amount in the account after 6 years.

b) How much interest will Darlene earn?

2. Wes borrows $850 at a rate of 9.5% interest per year, compounded annually, for 4 years.

a) Determine the amount to be repaid after 4 years.

b) How much interest will Wes have to pay?

For help with questions 3 to 7, refer to Example 2.

3. For each compounding condition, determine the interest rate per compounding period, expressed as a decimal.

a) 9% per year, compounded monthly

b) 8% per annum, compounded quarterly

c) 6% annual interest, compounded semi-annually

d) 13% per year, compounded bi-weekly

4. For each compounding condition, determine the number of compounding periods.

a) quarterly compounding for 3 years

b) semi-annual compounding for 4 years

c) monthly compounding for $\frac{3}{4}$ of a year

d) daily compounding for 2 weeks

e) annual compounding for 6 years

5. Determine the total number, n, of compounding periods and the interest rate, i, as a decimal, per compounding period for each scenario.

a) 8.75% per year, compounded annually, for 6 years

b) 6% per annum, compounded quarterly, for 3 years

c) 2.4% per year, compounded monthly, for 2 years

d) 4.5% per annum, compounded, semi-annually for 7.5 years

6. Manjinder invests $1400 in a GIC that earns 5.75% interest per year, compounded quarterly, for 3 years.

a) Determine the amount in the account after 3 years.

b) How much interest was earned?

c) Compare this to the amount of interest that would have been earned if simple interest had been earned at the same rate.

7. Susan's chequing account earns 1.25% interest per year, compounded daily. How much interest will she earn if she has $2000 in the account for 30 days?

Ⓑ Connect and Apply

8. Karin borrows $600 for 5 years at 12% interest per year.

Reasoning and Proving
Representing — Selecting Tools
Problem Solving
Connecting — Reflecting
Communicating

a) Compare the interest charges under each condition. Then, rank these scenarios from best to worst from Karin's perspective.

  i) simple interest

  ii) annual compounding

  iii) quarterly compounding

  iv) monthly compounding

b) Explain the effect of the compounding period on this loan.

For help with questions 9 and 10, refer to Example 3.

9. Ramone borrows $10 000 as start-up capital for his new business. He plans to repay the loan in 4 years, at which point he will owe $15 180.70. What rate of interest is Ramone being charged, assuming that it is compounded annually?

10. Pat borrows $350 for 4 years at an interest rate that is compounded quarterly. At the end of the 4 years, she repays $480.47. What annual interest rate, compounded quarterly, was Pat charged?

11. Suppose you have $1500 to invest for 5 years. Two options are available:

Reasoning and Proving
Representing — Selecting Tools
Problem Solving
Connecting — Reflecting
Communicating

- First Provincial Bank: earns 5% per year, compounded semi-annually

- Northern Credit Union: earns 4.8% per year, compounded monthly

Which investment would you choose and why?

12. Chapter Problem Chloe places $2000 in a chequing account that earns 1.8% interest per year, compounded monthly, for 4 years. Chloe can access this money at any time with no penalty except lost interest.

a) Determine the amount in this account after 4 years, assuming no other transactions take place.

b) How much interest was earned?

c) Compare this with the interest earned by Chloe's investment in question 10 in Section 7.1. Why might Chloe open this chequing account?

13. The Rule of 72 states that the number of years required for an investment to double when interest is compounded annually can be estimated by dividing 72 by the annual interest rate.

a) Use the Rule of 72 to determine how many years it will take for an amount to double for each interest rate, compounded annually.

  i) 8%   **ii)** 9%   **iii)** 12%

b) Verify your results in part a) using the compound interest formula. Is the Rule of 72 exact? Explain.

14. Pavel invested $720 in an account that earned 7.25% interest per year, compounded quarterly. When he closed the account, it contained $985. For how long did Pavel invest his money?

✔ **Achievement Check**

15. Consider these investment options:

Option A: $800 invested at 10% per year, simple interest

Option B: $800 invested at 7% interest per year, compounded annually

a) Write an equation to represent the amount of each investment as a function of time.

b) Graph both equations on the same set of axes.

c) Which is the better investment option? Explain.

d) How does your answer change if the compounding period in Option B changes? Provide a detailed explanation.

C **Extend**

16. Refer to question 13. Is the Rule of 72 valid for compounding periods other than annual compounding? Explore this question and use mathematical reasoning to justify your response.

Connections

Go to the *Functions 11* page on the McGraw-Hill Ryerson Web site and follow the links to Chapter 7 to learn more about the Rule of 72, doubling your money, and more.

17. There are several compound interest calculators available on the Internet. Go to the *Functions 11* page on the McGraw-Hill Ryerson Web site and follow the links to Chapter 7 to see one such calculator. Use this compound interest calculator or an alternative one to answer the following.

a) Why is the online calculator useful?

b) Explain what each field means.

c) Perform a sample calculation using the online tool.

d) Verify the accuracy of the result using the compound interest formula.

e) Discuss the advantages and the disadvantages of the online tool.

18. Math Contest The nominal interest rate is the rate quoted. The effective rate is the actual rate charged if it was simple interest. Some credit cards charge 19% per annum, compounded daily. What is the effective rate, to two decimal places?

A 20.92   **B** 28.00

C 69.35   **D** 19.00

19. Math Contest Sumeet invested $1200 for 5 years. He put part of the money into a high-yielding risky investment at 18% per annum, compounded semi-annually. He put the rest into another investment at 7% per annum, compounded annually. At the end of 5 years, he had earned $869 in interest. In which interval does the interest, I, earned at 18% per annum, compounded semi-annually, fall?

A $I < 530$ **B** $530 < I < 540$

C $540 < I < 550$ **D** $I > 550$

20. Math Contest The constant π is used in many applications in mathematics. Another mathematical constant is e. One of the applications for e is continuous compounding. This means the compounding period is infinitely small. The formula for continuous compounding is $A = Pe^{rt}$, where A represents the amount; P represents the principal; $e \doteq 2.718\ 281\ 828\ 459$; r represents the annual rate of interest, as a decimal; and t represents the number of years. Determine the amounts for $1000 invested for 5 years at 10% for each compounding period.

a) annual   **b)** monthly

c) daily   **d)** continuous

Present Value

Do you plan to buy a car some day?
Having your own vehicle can provide
tremendous freedom and independence.
On the downside, owning a vehicle has all
sorts of costs associated with it. Aside from
the purchase price, you must consider costs such as fuel, insurance, and repairs. It is important to
choose the right time to buy, and even to decide whether you should buy a car at all.

Suppose that you have some money to invest today to buy a car at some future date. If you know
how much money you need in the future, you can decide how much to invest today at a given
interest rate, compounding frequency, and duration.

Investigate

How can you determine the principal that must be invested today to have a known amount in the future?

Eric's parents plan to invest some money so that they can buy a car for
their son in 5 years. They estimate that, 5 years from now, they will need
$10 000 to buy a good used car.

1. One bank offers 6% interest, compounded annually. Which of the
   variables in the compound interest formula $A = P(1 + i)^n$ are known?

2. a) Substitute the known information into the formula and simplify
   the equation, if possible.

   b) Identify the unknown variable. Describe a strategy to solve for the
   variable.

   c) Solve for the unknown variable.

3. Reflect How much should Eric's parents invest under the given
   conditions, and why?

When the principal, P, needed to generate a known future amount is
unknown, the compound interest formula can be rearranged to isolate P.

$$A = P(1 + i)^n$$

$$\frac{A}{(1 + i)^n} = P \qquad \text{Divide both sides by } (1 + i)^n.$$

$$P = \frac{A}{(1 + i)^n}$$

In this form of the formula, the principal is referred to as the **present value** and the amount is referred to as the **future value**. The formula can be rewritten to include these terms.

The present value, PV, of a compound interest account or loan is related to its future value, FV, by the formula $PV = \dfrac{FV}{(1 + i)^n}$, where i represents the interest rate, as a decimal, per compounding period and n represents the number of compounding periods.

present value

• the principal invested or borrowed today to result in a given future amount, with given interest and time conditions

future value

• the amount that a principal invested or borrowed will grow to, with given interest and time conditions

Example 1

Calculate Present Value

Sahar wants to invest money today to have $1000 in 6 years. If she invests her money at 5.75% per year, compounded quarterly, how much does she need to invest?

Connections

The present value formula can also be written with a negative exponent, as either $P = A(1 + i)^{-n}$ or $PV = FV(1 + i)^{-n}$.

Solution

Method 1: Use a Scientific Calculator

Identify the given information.

$FV = 1000$

$i = \dfrac{0.0575}{4}$ Divide by the number of compounding periods in a year, 4.

$ = 0.014\ 375$

$n = 6 \times 4$ Multiply by the number of compounding periods in a year, 4.

$ = 24$

Substitute the known information into the formula for the present value.

$PV = \dfrac{FV}{(1 + i)^n}$

$ = \dfrac{1000}{(1 + 0.014\ 375)^{24}}$

$ = \dfrac{1000}{1.014\ 375^{24}}$ $\boxed{1000}\ \boxed{\div}\ \boxed{1.014375}\ \boxed{y^x}\ \boxed{24}\ \boxed{=}$

$ \doteq 709.96$

Sahar must invest $709.96 today to have $1000 in 6 years.

Method 2: Use a TVM Solver

To access the Time Value of Money (TVM) Solver on a graphing calculator, press (APPS), select **1:Finance**, and then select **1:TVM Solver...**. Enter the values in the fields as shown.

```
N=6
I%=5.75
PV=0
PMT=0
FV=1000
P/Y=1
C/Y=4
PMT:END BEGIN
```

- N represents the time period of the investment (or loan), in years.

- I% represents the annual interest rate, as a percent.

- PV represents the present value.   Do not enter a value, since it is unknown.

- PMT represents the payment.   PMT = 0 because there are no additional payments after the initial investment.

- FV represents the future value.

- P/Y represents the number of payments per year.   P/Y = 1 because the investment is one time only.

- C/Y represents the number of compounding periods per year.

To solve for the unknown present value, move the cursor to the **PV** field and press (ALPHA) (ENTER) for [SOLVE]. The present value will be calculated.

```
N=6
I%=5.75
▪PV=-709.9620061
PMT=0
FV=1000
P/Y=1
C/Y=4
PMT:END BEGIN
```

Note that the present value is negative. This means that the initial amount is paid out, as opposed to received.

Sahar must invest $709.96 today to have $1000 in 6 years.

Technology Tip

Notice that in the TVM Solver you enter the number of years, N, and the annual interest rate, I, as a percent. The TVM Solver automatically converts these using the number of compounding periods per year, C/Y.

Connections

The fields for PMT and P/Y are not required for this type of calculation. You will use them when you learn about annuities in Sections 7.4 and 7.5.

Example 2

Determine the Number of Compounding Periods

Tamara received $250 for her 14th birthday, which she invested at 6% per year. On Tamara's 18th birthday, her investment is worth $317.62. How frequently was the interest compounded?

Solution

Method 1: Apply Graphical Analysis

Let x represent the number of compounding periods per year. Identify the given information.

$PV = 250$

$FV = 317.62$

$i = \dfrac{0.06}{x}$

$n = 4x$

Substitute these values and expressions into the present value formula.

$$PV = \frac{FV}{(1 + i)^n}$$

$$250 = \frac{317.62}{\left(1 + \frac{0.06}{X}\right)^{4x}}$$

This equation is difficult to solve for x using standard algebraic techniques. Solve for x graphically. Graph each side of this equation as a separate function using a graphing calculator, and use the **Intersect** operation.

 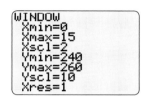 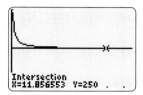

The point of intersection is approximately (12, 250), which means that when interest is compounded 12 times per year, the present value of this account is $250. Therefore, interest in this account was compounded monthly.

Method 2: Use a TVM Solver and Systematic Trial

Access the TVM Solver and enter the values in the fields as shown. The number of compounding periods per year is unknown, so try different values for C/Y and see which gives a present value, PV, closest to $250.

Start with annual compounding and use a systematic approach. With C/Y set to 1, move the cursor to the **PV** field and press (ALPHA) (ENTER) for [SOLVE].

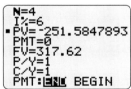

This present value, $251.58, is more than $250, which suggests that interest was earned faster. Try daily interest.

Daily interest means 365 compounding periods per year.

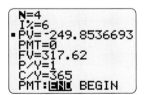

This is very close. Try monthly compounding.

Monthly interest means 12 compounding periods per year.

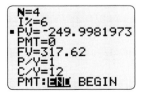

Monthly compounding gives a present value of $250.00, correct to the nearest cent. Therefore, the interest in this account was compounded monthly.

Method 3: Use a Spreadsheet

Set up a table using a spreadsheet, as shown. Include the most common compounding scenarios (annual, semi-annual, quarterly, monthly, and daily) in column A. To calculate the present value for each scenario, enter the present value formula
=317.62/((1+0.06/A2)^(4*A2)) in cell B2. Use **Fill Down** to calculate the remaining present values.

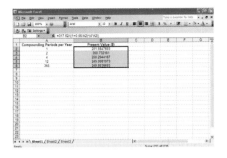

Monthly compounding gives a present value of $250.00, correct to the nearest cent. Therefore, the interest in this account was compounded monthly.

Example 3

Choose a Loan

Lamar wants to borrow some money now to buy a motorcycle and some riding gear. He estimates that in 5 years he can pay back an amount of $12 000. Which of the two loan options should he choose, and why?

Regal Bank: charges 8.9% interest, compounded semi-annually
Suburbia Credit Union: charges 8.4% interest, compounded monthly

Solution

At a glance, the Suburbia Credit Union loan seems to charge a lower interest rate, but the interest is compounded more frequently than with the Regal Bank loan. Calculate and compare the present values of the loans to decide which is the better option.

Regal Bank:

$FV = 12\ 000$

$i = \dfrac{0.089}{2}$

$\quad = 0.0445$

$n = 5 \times 2$

$\quad = 10$

Substitute these values into the present value formula.

$PV = \dfrac{12\ 000}{(1 + 0.0445)^{10}}$

$\quad \doteq 7764.20$

Suburbia Credit Union:

$FV = 12\ 000$

$i = \dfrac{0.084}{12}$

$\quad = 0.007$

$n = 5 \times 12$

$\quad = 60$

Substitute these values into the present value formula.

$PV = \dfrac{12\ 000}{(1 + 0.007)^{60}}$

$\quad \doteq 7896.11$

The Suburbia Credit Union loan has a greater present value than the Regal Bank loan. For Lamar's situation, the Suburbia Credit Union loan is the better option.

- Present value refers to the principal that must be invested today to grow to a known future amount under specified interest and time conditions.
- The formula $PV = \dfrac{FV}{(1 + i)^n}$ can be used to calculate the present value, PV, if the future value, FV; number of compounding periods, n; and interest rate, i, as a decimal, per compounding period are known.

Communicate Your Understanding

C1 Explain how the following terms are related. Include examples to illustrate.

a) principal and amount

b) principal and present value

c) present value, future value, and interest

C2 An investment earns 9% annual interest, compounded semi-annually, for 4 years, at which point it is worth $284.42. Which equation will give the correct present value, and why? Explain what is wrong with each of the other equations.

A $PV = 284.42(1 + 0.045)^8$

B $PV = \dfrac{284.42}{(1 + 0.09)^4}$

C $PV = \dfrac{284.42}{(1 + 0.18)^2}$

D $PV = \dfrac{284.42}{(1 + 0.045)^8}$

A Practise

For help with questions 1 to 4, refer to Example 1.

1. Determine the present value of each future amount for the given conditions.

   a) In 5 years, an investment earning 5% per year, compounded annually, will have a value of $700.

   b) In 3 years, an investment earning 4.8% annual interest, compounded quarterly, will have a value of $1021.86.

2. In 4 years, an investment will be worth $504.99. If interest is earned at a rate of 6% per year, compounded annually, what is the present value of this investment?

3. In 6 years, money invested at 7.5% per annum, compounded quarterly, will grow to $807.21.

   a) How much money was invested?

   b) How much interest will be earned in 6 years?

4. Pina receives a financial gift from her grandparents, which she invests at 8% annual interest, compounded semi-annually. She is advised that the investment will be worth $3421.40 in 4 years.

   a) What is the amount of the gift?

   b) How much interest will Pina's investment earn?

B Connect and Apply

For help with questions 5 and 6, refer to Example 2.

5. A bond will be worth $500 when it becomes due in 5 years. If the bond was purchased today for $450 at 2.13% per year, determine how frequently the interest was compounded.

6. Serge invests $700 at 5.75% per year, compounded quarterly. When the account is closed, its value will be $950. How long will Serge's money be invested?

For help with questions 7 and 8, refer to Example 3.

7. Tracey would like to have $10 000 in 4 years to use as a down payment for a house. She is considering two investment options:

Investment A: 6.6% annual interest, compounded semi-annually

Investment B: 6.2% annual interest, compounded monthly

a) Compare the present values of the two options.

b) Which investment is the better choice for Tracey? Explain your reasoning.

8. Jacques needs to borrow money to buy dress clothes for his new sales job. He estimates that he can repay $1600 in 6 months. He is considering two bank offers:

Reasoning and Proving

Representing   Selecting Tools

Problem Solving

Connecting   Reflecting

Communicating

Bank A: 8.5% annual interest, compounded monthly

Bank B: 9% simple interest

Which bank should Jacques borrow from, and why?

9. Five years ago, money was invested at 7% per year, compounded annually. Today the investment is worth $441.28.

a) How much money was originally invested?

b) How much interest was earned?

10. Four and a half years ago, some money was deposited into an account that paid an annual interest rate of 3.2%, compounded semi-annually. Today, the account has a value of $821.36. What was the amount of the original deposit?

11. Lydia borrows $500 to buy a television. She agrees to repay $610 in a year and a half. What annual rate of interest, compounded monthly, is Lydia being charged?

12. a) An investment reaches a future value of $2500 in 5 years. Explore and compare the effects of varying the compounding period on the present value under each condition.

  i) annual compounding

  ii) semi-annual compounding

  iii) quarterly compounding

  iv) monthly compounding

b) What implication do your results have from an investor's perspective?

13. A loaf of bread costs $3.50 in 2009.

a) What was the price of a similar loaf of bread in 1990, assuming an average inflation rate of 3% per year, compounded annually?

b) How much did a similar loaf cost in 1900?

Connections

The consumer price index (CPI) provides a broad measure of the cost of living in Canada. The CPI measures the average price of consumer goods and services bought by households, including food, housing, transportation, furniture, clothing, and recreation.

14. The future value of a loan due to a financial institution in 10 years is $50 000. The financial institution is willing to sell the debt today discounted at 6% per year, compounded semi-annually. What is the value of the debt today?

Connections

A financial institution considers money owed to it an investment. When a financial institution discounts an investment, it sells the investment to another creditor at a discounted value that is equal to the present value.

15. Chapter Problem Chloe has $6000 in her portfolio left to invest. On the advice of her advisor, she puts the money into a moderate-risk mutual fund. She is hoping that the total future value of her investments will be $12 000 at the end of 4 years.

a) Refer to Section 7.1, question 10, and Section 7.2, question 12. What are the future values of Chloe's other investments?

b) Subtract these from $12 000. What does this answer represent?

c) Determine the minimum interest rate that the mutual fund must earn for Chloe to achieve her goal, assuming that interest is compounded annually.

16. Explore the concept of present value as a function of time. Suppose an account earning 6% per year, compounded annually, has a future value of $800.

Reasoning and Proving
Representing — *Selecting Tools*
Problem Solving
Connecting — *Reflecting*
Communicating

a) Write an equation to represent the present value of the account as a function of time.

b) Use Technology Graph the function. Describe the shape of the graph.

c) Interpret the horizontal scale of the graph.

d) Describe what information the graph provides for $t > 0$.

e) Does the graph have meaning for $t < 0$? If it does, explain what it means. If it does not, explain why not.

✔ **Achievement Check**

17. Tanya wants to have $1200 in 2.5 years to go to Mexico.

a) How much money must she invest today at 6.4% annual interest, compounded semi-annually, to have enough money?

b) Tanya only has $970 today. What interest rate must she obtain to have enough money for her vacation?

c) Suppose that Tanya cannot find a better rate than 6.4%. What other options does she have?

C **Extend**

18. Refer to question 16. Discuss the effects of reflecting this function in the vertical axis, from a geometric perspective and a time-line perspective.

19. Use algebraic reasoning to develop a formula for the present value, PV, of a simple interest account, in terms of its future value, FV; the simple annual rate of interest, r; and time, t, in years.

20. Math Contest A debt can be paid off in three equal instalments: $1000 now, $1000 in 3 years, and $1000 in 6 years. What single payment can pay off the loan 4 years from now, if interest is 10% per annum, compounded semi-annually?

21. Math Contest A circle passes through the points A(5, 7) and B(−3, 11). Which of the following is not a possible centre for the circle?

A (1, 9)   **B** (0, 7)

C (11, 29)   **D** (−2, 11)

Annuities

How would you like to be a millionaire without working all your life to earn it? Perhaps if you were lucky enough to win a lottery or have an amazing run on a television game show, it would happen. For most people, however, fantasies such as these are not likely to come true. However, what if you saved money from a very early age? Is it possible to accumulate a million dollars in your lifetime?

When people invest, they usually do not simply deposit one lump sum and wait several years for it to earn interest. Most wise investors make **regular payments**, often deducted directly from their paycheques. Investments of this type are called **annuities**. In this chapter, you will encounter only **ordinary simple annuities**.

regular payments
• payments of equal value made at equal time periods

annuity
• a sum of money paid as a series of regular payments

ordinary annuity
• an annuity for which the payments are made at the end of each payment period

simple annuity
• an annuity for which the compounding and payment periods are the same

Investigate

How can you determine the amount of an annuity?

Colin is awarded $500 per year as long as he maintains a certain average mark for each of his 4 years of high school. Colin plans to deposit his award at the end of each school year into an account that pays 4% per year, compounded annually.

1. a) Assuming that Colin maintains the necessary average, how many times will he receive $500?

   b) Will each of these $500 deposits earn the same interest, in dollars? Explain.

2. a) Determine a method of calculating the total amount of Colin's investment at graduation.

   b) Carry out the method. How much will be in Colin's account when he graduates?

3. Reflect Consider the method that you used to solve this problem. Would your method be efficient if the number of regular payments was very large? Why or why not?

Situations like the one described in the Investigate can be represented using a **time line**.

The time line shows that a regular payment, R, in dollars, is deposited into an account at the end of each compounding period, for n periods. Because these deposits are made at different times, they will each earn different amounts of interest. For example, the last payment will earn no interest, because it will be received at the end of the annuity. To determine the amount that each of the other deposits will earn, apply the compound interest formula $A = P(1 + i)^n$ to each payment individually.

time line

• a diagram used to illustrate the cash flow of an annuity

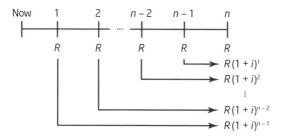

The amount, A, of the annuity can be determined by adding the amounts of all the payments.

$$A = R + R(1 + i) + R(1 + i)^2 + \cdots + R(1 + i)^{n-2} + R(1 + i)^{n-1}$$

Since this is a geometric series with first term $a = R$ and common ratio $r = 1 + i$, use the formula for the sum of a geometric series.

$$S_n = \frac{a(r^n - 1)}{r - 1}$$

$$= \frac{R[(1 + i)^n - 1]}{(1 + i) - 1}$$

$$= \frac{R[(1 + i)^n - 1]}{i}$$

Connections

You studied geometric series in Chapter 6 Discrete Functions.

The total amount, A, at the time of the last payment of an annuity can be determined using the formula $A = \dfrac{R[(1 + i)^n - 1]}{i}$, where

R represents the regular payment, in dollars; i represents the interest rate per compounding period, as a decimal; and n represents the number of compounding periods.

Connections

In this course, you will study only ordinary simple annuities. You will study more complex annuities with, for example, different compounding and payment periods, if you choose to study business at university or college.

This equation can also be written in terms of future value as

$$FV = \frac{R[(1 + i)^n - 1]}{i}.$$

Example 1

Amount of an Annuity

At the end of every month, Hoshi deposits $100 in an account that pays 6% per year, compounded monthly. He does this for 3 years.

a) Draw a time line to represent this annuity.

b) Determine the amount in the account after 3 years.

c) How much interest will the annuity have earned?

Solution

a) Determine the interest per compounding period and the number of compounding periods before drawing the time line.

$$i = \frac{0.06}{12}$$
$$= 0.005$$
$$n = 3 \times 12$$
$$= 36$$
$$R = 100$$

Time (months)

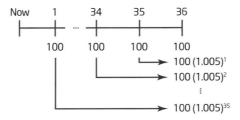

b) Method 1: Use a Scientific Calculator

Substitute the known values into the formula for the amount of an annuity and evaluate.

$$A = \frac{R[(1 + i)^n - 1]}{i}$$
$$= \frac{100[(1 + 0.005)^{36} - 1]}{0.005}$$
$$= \frac{100(1.005^{36} - 1)}{0.005}$$

100 $\boxed{\times}$ $\boxed{(}$ 1.005 $\boxed{y^x}$ 36 $\boxed{-}$ 1 $\boxed{)}$ $\boxed{\div}$ 0.005 $\boxed{=}$

$$\doteq 3933.61$$

The amount in Hoshi's account after 3 years will be $3933.61.

Method 2: Use a TVM Solver

Access the TVM Solver on a graphing calculator and enter the values, as shown.

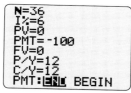

When solving for an annuity, enter the number of payments for N.

The negative sign indicates that payments are being paid, not received.

Both the number of payments and the compounding periods per year are 12.

Move the cursor to the **FV** field and press (ALPHA) [SOLVE].

The future value of the sum of Hoshi's payments is $3933.61. This is the amount in his account after 3 years.

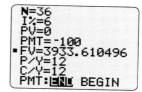

c) To determine the interest earned, calculate the difference between the actual dollar sum of Hoshi's payments and the future value of the annuity. Hoshi made 36 payments of $100, for a total of $3600.

Interest = 3933.61 − 3600
$$= 333.61$$

Hoshi's annuity earned $333.61 in interest.

Example 2

Determine the Regular Payment

Sadia needs $4000 for university tuition when she graduates in 2 years. She plans to make deposits into an account that earns 6.5% per year, compounded bi-weekly.

a) Draw a time line to represent this annuity.

b) How much should she deposit bi-weekly?

Solution

a) Bi-weekly means every 2 weeks. Since there are 52 weeks in a year, the number of compounding periods per year is 52 ÷ 2, or 26.

$$i = \frac{0.065}{26}$$
$$= 0.0025$$

$$n = 2 \times 26$$
$$= 52$$

The regular payment, R, is unknown, but the total future value of the annuity, A, is \$4000. A time line representing this annuity is shown.

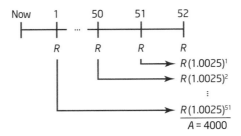

b) Use the formula for the amount of an annuity to solve for the regular payment, R.

Method 1: Substitute and Then Rearrange

$$A = \frac{R[(1 + i)^n - 1]}{i}$$

$$4000 = \frac{R[(1 + 0.0025)^{52} - 1]}{0.0025} \qquad \text{Substitute the known values.}$$

$$10 = R(1.0025^{52} - 1) \qquad \text{Multiply both sides by 0.0025.}$$

$$R = \frac{10}{1.0025^{52} - 1} \qquad \text{Divide both sides by } 1.0025^{52} - 1.$$

$$R \doteq 72.13$$

Sadia should deposit \$72.13 bi-weekly to have \$4000 in 2 years.

Method 2: Rearrange and Then Substitute

$$A = \frac{R[(1 + i)^n - 1]}{i}$$

$$Ai = R[(1 + i)^n - 1] \qquad \text{Multiply both sides by } i.$$

$$R = \frac{Ai}{(1 + i)^n - 1} \qquad \text{Divide both sides by } (1 + i)^n - 1.$$

$$R = \frac{4000(0.0025)}{(1 + 0.0025)^{52} - 1} \qquad \text{Substitute the known values.}$$

$$R \doteq 72.13$$

Sadia should deposit \$72.13 every 2 weeks to have \$4000 in 2 years.

Example 3

Determine the Interest Rate

Oliver plans to invest $2000 quarterly for 5 years. His financial advisor informs him that his investment will grow to $45 682.40 after the 5 years. What annual rate of interest, compounded quarterly, is Oliver's annuity earning?

Solution

List the known information for this ordinary simple annuity.

$A = 45\ 682.40$

$R = 2000$

$n = 5 \times 4$ Payments are made 4 times a year for 5 years.

   $= 20$

Substitute the known values into the equation for the amount of an annuity and solve for i.

$$45\ 682.40 = \frac{2000[(1 + i)^{20} - 1]}{i}$$

This equation is difficult to solve using standard algebraic techniques. A method of systematic trial could be used, but it would be time-consuming.

Method 1: Apply Graphical Analysis

Graph each side of the equation $45\ 682.40 = \dfrac{2000[(1 + i)^{20} - 1]}{i}$ as a

separate function using a graphing calculator, and use the **Intersect** operation.

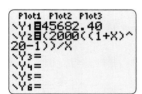 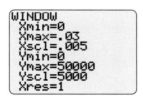 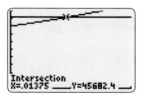

The point of intersection is (0.013 75, 45 682.4), which means that the account will grow to $45 682.40 at the end of the annuity when the interest rate per compounding period is 0.013 75, or 1.375%. To determine the annual interest rate, multiply by the number of compounding periods per year.

$1.375\% \times 4 = 5.5\%$

Oliver's annuity is earning interest at a rate of 5.5%, compounded quarterly.

Method 2: Use a TVM Solver

Access the TVM Solver on a graphing calculator and enter the values, as shown.

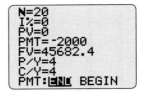

Move the cursor to the **I%** field and press (ALPHA) [SOLVE].

Recall that I% represents the annual interest rate, as a percent. Oliver's annuity is earning interest at a rate of 5.5%, compounded quarterly.

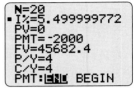

Method 3: Use a TI-Nspire™ CAS Graphing Calculator

Use the **solve** function of the TI-Nspire™ CAS graphing calculator to solve for the interest rate.

- From the home screen, select
  6:New Document.Then, select
  1:Add Calculator.
- Press (menu). Select **3:Algebra**, and then select **1:Solve**.
- Type the equation, and then press
  ⊙ ① (enter).

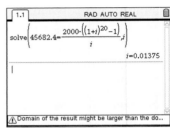

The interest rate per compounding period is 0.013 75, or 1.375%. To determine the annual interest rate, multiply by the number of compounding periods per year.

1.375% × 4 = 5.5%

Therefore, Oliver's annuity is earning interest at a rate of 5.5%, compounded quarterly.

Example 4

Vary the Conditions of an Annuity

Felicia plans to invest $2600 at 6% per year, compounded annually, for the next 15 years. Compare the effects on the final amount if the deposits are made and compounding periods are

- annual
- quarterly
- monthly
- weekly

Solution

Method 1: Use a Graphing Calculator

Use a table to organize the values of the variables needed to use the formula for the amount of an annuity $A = \dfrac{R[(1 + i)^n - 1]}{i}$. Note that the regular payment, R, must be divided by the number of payments per year in each scenario.

Compounding Period	R	i	n
annual	2600	0.06	15
quarterly	650	0.015	60
monthly	216.67	0.005	180
weekly	50	0.001 154	780

Calculate the amount for the first scenario, annual compounding, using a graphing calculator.

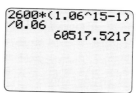

Felicia will have $60 517.52 at the end of 15 years if interest is compounded annually.

Repeat the calculation for the other scenarios.

- Press (2nd) [ENTRY] to recall the previous calculation.
- Use the cursor keys, the **DEL** key, and the **INS** key to modify the equation to fit each scenario.
- Press (ENTER) to perform the new calculation.

Technology *Tip*

Press (CLEAR) to start each calculation with a new window screen.

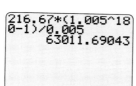

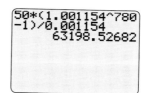

The results of these calculations are summarized in the table.

Compounding Period	Amount ($)
annual	60 517.52
quarterly	62 539.52
monthly	63 011.69
weekly	63 198.53

The amount of the annuity increases as the compounding interval becomes more frequent. The difference between weekly and annual compounding is $63 198.53 − $60 517.52, or $2681.01.

Method 2: Use a Spreadsheet

Set up a table in a spreadsheet.

- Type the headings C/Y (compounding periods per year), n (number of compounding periods or payments), i (interest rate per compounding period), R (regular payment), and A (amount).
- Enter the values 1, 4, 12, and 52 in the C/Y column, to represent the number of compounding periods in each scenario.
- Enter the formulas, starting in cell B2 and working to the right:

B2 =A2*15   n = 15 × number of payments per year

C2 =0.06/A2   i = 0.06 ÷ number of payments per year

D2 =2600/A2   R = $2600 ÷ number of payments per year

E2 =(D2*((1+C2)^B2-1))/C2   Calculate the amount using the formula
$A = \dfrac{R[(1 + i)^n - 1]}{i}$.

- Use **Fill Down** to evaluate the remaining calculations.

The results of these calculations are summarized in the table.

Compounding Period	Amount ($)
annual	60 517.52
quarterly	62 539.52
monthly	63 010.72
weekly	63 194.18

The amount of the annuity increases as the compounding interval becomes more frequent. The difference between weekly and annual compounding is $63 194.18 − $60 517.52, or $2676.66.

Technology Tip

To enter a mathematical expression in a cell in Microsoft® Excel, click on the equal sign and type the expression.

Connections

Some of the amounts are slightly different in Method 1 and Method 2. This is due to rounding in the calculation entry steps. Discrepancies such as this become increasingly important when large sums of money are involved. In general, rounding errors can be avoided or minimized by leaving rational values in fraction form or carrying additional decimal places in the calculation process.

Key Concepts

- An annuity is an investment in which regular payments are deposited into an account.
- An ordinary simple annuity is one in which payments are made at the end of every payment period and interest is compounded at the end of the same payment period.
- The amount, A, of an annuity can be calculated using the formula $A = \dfrac{R[(1 + i)^n - 1]}{i}$, where R represents the regular payment; i represents the interest rate per compounding period, as a decimal; and n represents the number of compounding periods.

Communicate Your Understanding

C1 The time line shows an annuity with an annual interest rate of 8%.

a) How often is interest compounded? How can you tell?

b) What is the duration of the annuity? How can you tell?

c) Explain why this annuity can be represented as a geometric series.

d) Identify the first term, a, and the common ratio, r, of the geometric series.

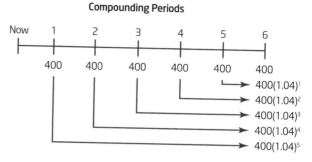

Compounding Periods

C2 The graphing calculator screen of a solution using the TVM Solver is shown.

a) What is the duration of the annuity? How can you tell?

b) Why is the payment value negative?

c) Why is the future value positive?

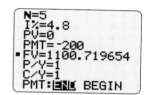

A Practise

For help with questions 1 to 3, refer to Example 1.

1. Calculate the amount of the annuity shown in the time line.

Compounding Periods

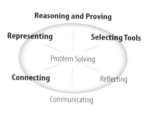

2. To help her granddaughter with university costs, Sasha's grandmother puts $250 into an account that earns 4.5% per year, compounded annually, at the end of every year for 6 years.

a) Draw a time line to represent this annuity.

b) Determine the amount of the annuity.

c) How much interest was earned?

3. At the end of every week, for 2 years, Carlo puts $35 into an account that earns 5.2% per year, compounded weekly.

Reasoning and Proving
Representing · Selecting Tools · Problem Solving · Connecting · Reflecting · Communicating

a) Draw a time line to represent this annuity.

b) Determine the amount of the annuity.

c) How much interest was earned?

For help with questions 4 and 5, refer to Example 2.

4. How much must be invested at the end of each year, for 4 years, to achieve an amount of $10 000, if interest is earned at a rate of 6.25% per year, compounded annually?

5. Lucy wants to have $18 000 in her account 3 years from now to buy a car. How much must she invest per month, if her account earns 7.2% annual interest, compounded monthly?

B Connect and Apply

For help with questions 6 and 7, refer to Example 3.

6. Donna invests $75 every 2 weeks in an account that earns compound interest bi-weekly. If she does this for 7 years, she will end up with $16 939.83 in the account.

   a) How much total interest will have been earned?

   b) Determine the annual rate of interest, compounded bi-weekly.

7. Refer to question 6. By how much must the interest rate be increased for the amount to grow to $18 000 after 7 years?

For help with questions 8 to 10, refer to Example 4. Use the following information. Maurice is planning to deposit $160 per month into an account that earns 4.8% annual interest, compounded monthly, for 15 years.

8. a) Determine the amount in the account at the end of this annuity.

   b) How much interest will have been earned?

9. Maurice's financial advisor suggests that he would improve the value of his annuity if he changed his payments to $40 per week, at the same interest rate, compounded weekly. Do you agree or disagree with the financial advisor? Justify your response with mathematical reasoning.

10. A competing bank offers Maurice 5% per annum, compounded monthly, for his monthly deposits of $160. Which option should Maurice choose? Justify your answer with mathematical reasoning.

- Stick with his current arrangement.
- Follow his financial advisor's suggestion about increasing the frequency of his deposits.
- Switch to the competing bank.

11. Lee would like to retire at age 60 and is considering two investment options:
Option A: Invest $500 per month beginning at age 20.
Option B: Invest $1000 per month beginning at age 40.
In both cases, the interest is 6% per annum, compounded monthly. Which option pays more interest, and by how much?

12. Pinder wants to be a millionaire before he retires. He plans to save a certain amount every week for 40 years.

   a) If he puts money in an investment that earns 7% annual interest, compounded weekly, what amount must Pinder deposit weekly?

   b) What other strategies could Pinder use to achieve his goal? Discuss any assumptions you must make.

C Extend

13. Use Technology Use a graphing calculator or graphing software.

   a) Graph the function $A = \dfrac{100(1.05^n - 1)}{0.05}$. Describe the shape of the graph.

   b) Interpret this function, assuming that it is related to the amount of an annuity.

   c) Assuming that interest is compounded annually, identify the regular payment and the annual interest rate.

   d) Pose and solve two problems related to this function.

14. In question 13, the function

$A = \dfrac{100(1.05^n - 1)}{0.05}$ represents the amount

of an annuity.

a) Write a function to describe the total principal invested after n compounding periods.

b) Graph the amount and the principal functions on the same set of axes. Describe the shape of the principal function.

c) Describe how the graphs of these two functions represent the interest earned over time. Write a function to represent the interest earned after n compounding periods.

15. Math Contest Bethany starts investing $300 per month at 6% per annum, compounded monthly, for 5 years. After 3 years, the interest increases to 9% per annum, compounded monthly. Determine the amount of her investment after 5 years.

A $19 657.37   **B** $21 975.21

C $21 453.45   **D** $3975.21

16. Math Contest In $\triangle ABC$, $a = 10$ mm, $b = 26$ mm, and $c = 24$ mm. If D is the midpoint of AC and BC is extended to E such that DE $= 24$ mm, determine the measure of $\angle CED$ without using a calculator.

A 30°   **B** 60°   **C** 45°   **D** 67°

17. Math Contest Given that $a^2 + (a + b)^2 = 100$ and a and b are whole numbers, determine all possible ordered pairs (a, b) that solve this equation.

18. Math Contest Given $x^2 - y^2 = 2311$, $2311 = (2)(3)(5)(7)(11) + 1$, and $x > y > 0$, where x and y are integers, which of the following is true?

A only x is divisible by 11

B only y is divisible by 11

C both are divisible by 11

D neither is divisible by 11

Career Connection

Felicity is an investment trader for a large firm in Toronto. She uses her company's money to buy and sell stocks, bonds, and shares to make a profit. Because the stock market is so volatile, Felicity must always have access to the newest information from around the world. Success in her job depends on the use of computers that can perform fast mathematical calculations. Waiting too long to make a trade could cost her company a lot of money. Felicity trained for her career by taking a 4-year bachelor of administrative studies degree at York University.

Present Value of an Annuity

Owen and Anna are approaching retirement and are putting their finances in order. They have worked hard and invested their earnings so that they now have a large amount of money on which to live. They hire a financial advisor, and together they consider whether Owen and Anna have enough money to allow them to live comfortably for the rest of their lives by making **regular withdrawals** from an account. To do this, they calculate the **present value of an annuity** based on Owen and Anna's projected living expenses.

regular withdrawals
- withdrawals of equal value drawn at equal periods

present value of an annuity
- the amount of money needed to finance a series of regular withdrawals

Investigate

How can you determine the present value of an annuity?

Owen and Anna have estimated that they will need to withdraw $1000 per month for living expenses for the next 20 years, and wonder if they will have enough to finance this. The amount in their account will earn 9% annual interest, compounded monthly.

1. a) How many withdrawals have Owen and Anna planned for? How do you know?

b) Multiply the total number of withdrawals by $1000. Do Owen and Anna need to have this much in their life savings account on the day they retire? Explain why or why not.

2. Suppose Owen and Anna retire at the end of December. They will make their first withdrawal from their life savings account at the end of January.

a) Determine the present value of this first withdrawal, using the formula $PV = \dfrac{FV}{(1 + i)^n}$.

b) Determine the present value of the second withdrawal, which Owen and Anna will make at the end of February.

c) Are the present values of each withdrawal equal? Explain why or why not.

d) Predict whether the present value of the third withdrawal will be greater than or less than these values. Explain your prediction. Check your prediction by calculating.

3. Will the pattern of present values observed in step 2 continue? Explain your thinking.

4. Reflect Suggest a method to determine the sum of the present values of all of the withdrawals that Owen and Anna plan to make after they retire.

In Section 7.4, problems were posed in which regular payments are made into an account that grows to a large future amount.

In this section, problems will be posed in which regular withdrawals will be made from an account that begins with a large balance.

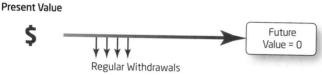

To determine the present value required to finance a retirement plan such as the one in the Investigate, it is necessary to calculate the present value of each withdrawal using the present value formula

$$PV = \frac{FV}{(1 + i)^n}.$$

The present value of the annuity can be determined by adding the present values of all the withdrawals.

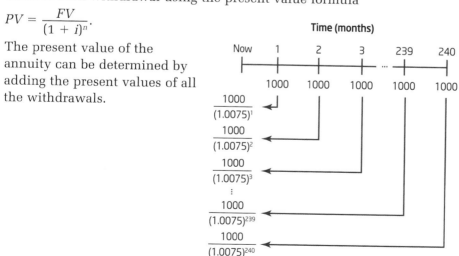

$$PV = \frac{1000}{1.0075^1} + \frac{1000}{1.0075^2} + \frac{1000}{1.0075^3} + \cdots + \frac{1000}{1.0075^{239}} + \frac{1000}{1.0075^{240}}$$

Since this is a geometric series with first term $a = \dfrac{1000}{1.0075^1}$ and common ratio $r = \dfrac{1}{1.0075}$, the formula for the sum of the first n terms of a geometric series $S_n = \dfrac{a(r^n - 1)}{r - 1}$ can be used.

This process can be generalized to produce a simplified result for the present value of an annuity. You can derive this result in question 15.

The present value, PV, of an annuity can be determined using the formula $PV = \dfrac{R[1 - (1 + i)^{-n}]}{i}$, where R represents the regular withdrawal; i represents the interest rate per compounding period, as a decimal; and n represents the number of compounding periods.

Example 1

Present Value of an Annuity

Josh is putting his summer earnings into an annuity from which he can draw living expenses while he is at university. He will need to withdraw $900 per month for 8 months. Interest is earned at a rate of 6%, compounded monthly.

a) Draw a time line to represent this annuity.

b) How much does Josh need to invest at the beginning of the school year to finance the annuity?

Solution

a) Represent the known information on a time line.

$R = 900$
$n = 8$
$i = \dfrac{0.06}{12}$
$\quad = 0.005$

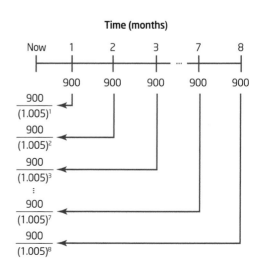

b) Method 1: Use a Scientific Calculator

Substitute the known values into the formula for the present value of an annuity and evaluate.

$$PV = \frac{R[1 - (1 + i)^{-n}]}{i}$$

$$= \frac{900[1 - (1 + 0.005)^{-8}]}{0.005}$$

$$= \frac{900(1 - 1.005^{-8})}{0.005}$$

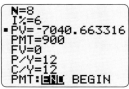

$\doteq 7040.66$

Calculator key strokes may vary.

Josh needs to invest $7040.66 at the beginning of the school year to finance the annuity.

Method 2: Use a TVM Solver

Access the TVM Solver on a graphing calculator and enter the values, as shown.

```
N=8
I%=6
PV=0
PMT=900
FV=0
P/Y=12
C/Y=12
PMT:END BEGIN
```

Move the cursor to the **PV** field and press (ALPHA) [SOLVE].

The present value of this annuity is $7040.66, which is the amount that Josh must invest at the beginning of the school year.

```
N=8
I%=6
•PV=-7040.663316
PMT=900
FV=0
P/Y=12
C/Y=12
PMT:END BEGIN
```

Example 2

Determine the Regular Withdrawal

Fiona's life savings total $300 000 when she decides to retire. She plans an annuity that will pay her quarterly for the next 30 years. If her account earns 5.2% annual interest, compounded quarterly, how much can Fiona withdraw each quarter?

Solution

Determine the number of compounding periods and the interest rate per compounding period.

$n = 30 \times 4$ $\qquad\qquad i = \dfrac{0.052}{4}$ $\qquad\qquad PV = 300\,000$

$\quad = 120$ $\qquad\qquad\qquad\quad = 0.013$

Use the formula for the present value of an annuity to solve for the regular withdrawal, R.

Method 1: Substitute and Then Rearrange

$$PV = \frac{R[1 - (1 + i)^{-n}]}{i}$$

$$300\,000 = \frac{R[1 - (1 + 0.013)^{-120}]}{0.013}$$ Substitute the known values.

$$3900 = R(1 - 1.013^{-120})$$ Multiply both sides by 0.013.

$$R = \frac{3900}{(1 - 1.013^{-120})}$$ Divide both sides by $1 - 1.013^{-120}$.

$$R \doteq 4950.87$$

Fiona can withdraw \$4950.87 every quarter for 30 years.

Method 2: Rearrange and Then Substitute

$$PV = \frac{R[1 - (1 + i)^{-n}]}{i}$$

$$i(PV) = R[1 - (1 + i)^{-n}]$$ Multiply both sides by i.

$$R = \frac{i(PV)}{1 - (1 + i)^{-n}}$$ Divide both sides by $1 - (1 + i)^{-n}$.

$$R = \frac{0.013(300\,000)}{1 - (1 + 0.013)^{-120}}$$ Substitute the known values.

$$R \doteq 4950.87$$

Fiona can withdraw \$4950.87 every quarter for 30 years.

Method 3: Use a TVM Solver

Access the TVM Solver on a graphing calculator and enter the values, as shown. Note that the present value is negative, indicating that this amount is paid into the account.

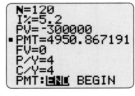

Move the cursor to the **PMT** field and press (ALPHA) [SOLVE].

The amount of the regular withdrawals is \$4950.87. Note that this value is positive, indicating that Fiona will receive these payments.

Technology Tip

When working with annuities using a TVM Solver, you must specify the actual number of payments or withdrawals, N. The graphing calculator software does not automatically assume that this coincides with the number of compounding intervals.

Key Concepts

- The present value of an annuity is the total amount that can finance a series of regular withdrawals over a specific period of time.

- The present value, PV, of an annuity can be calculated using the formula $PV = \dfrac{R[1 - (1 + i)^{-n}]}{i}$, where R represents the regular withdrawal; i represents the interest rate per compounding period, as a decimal; and n represents the number of compounding periods.

Communicate Your Understanding

C1 The time line shows an annuity from which semi-annual withdrawals are made for 10 years. Interest is compounded semi-annually.

a) What is the annual rate of interest? How can you tell?

b) How many withdrawals will be made, in total? How can you tell?

c) Explain why this annuity can be represented as a geometric series.

d) Identify the first term, a, and the common ratio, r, of the geometric series.

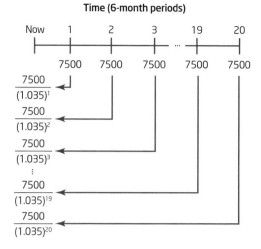

C2 The graphing calculator screen of a solution using the TVM Solver is shown.

Describe this annuity fully.

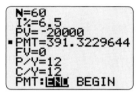

A Practise

For help with questions 1 to 3, refer to Example 1.

1. Calculate the present value of the annuity shown.

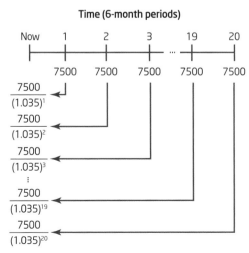

2. Brandon plans to withdraw $1000 at the end of every year, for 4 years, from an account that earns 8% interest, compounded annually.

a) Draw a time line to represent this annuity.

b) Determine the present value of the annuity.

3. Lauren plans to withdraw $650 at the end of every 3 months, for 5 years, from an account that earns 6.4% interest, compounded quarterly.

a) Draw a time line to represent this annuity.

b) Determine the present value of the annuity.

c) How much interest is earned?

For help with questions 4 and 5, refer to Example 2.

4. An annuity has an initial balance of $8000 in an account that earns 5.75% interest, compounded annually. What amount can be withdrawn at the end of each of the 6 years of this annuity?

5. After graduating from high school, Karen works for a few years to save $40 000 for university. She deposits her savings into an account that will earn 6% interest, compounded quarterly. What quarterly withdrawals can Karen make for the 4 years that she will be at university?

B Connect and Apply

6. How much should be in an account today so that withdrawals in the amount of $15 000 can be made at the end of each year for 20 years, if interest in the account is earned at a rate of 7.5% per year, compounded annually?

7. Julie just won $200 000 in a lottery! She estimates that to live comfortably she will need to withdraw $5000 per month for the next 50 years. Her savings account earns 4.25% annual interest, compounded monthly.

   a) Can Julie afford to retire and live off her lottery winnings?

   b) What is the minimum amount that Julie must win to retire in comfort immediately? Discuss any assumptions you must make.

8. An annuity has an initial balance of $5000. Annual withdrawals are made in the amount of $800 for 9 years, at which point the account balance is zero. What annual rate of interest, compounded annually, was earned over the duration of this annuity?

9. Shen has invested $15 000 into an annuity from which she plans to withdraw $500 per month for the next 3.5 years. If at the end of this time period the balance of the annuity is zero, what annual rate of interest, compounded monthly, did this account earn?

10. Jordan has $6000 to invest in an annuity from which he plans to make regular withdrawals over the next 3 years. He is considering two options:

Option A: Withdrawals are made every quarter and interest is earned at a rate of 8%, compounded quarterly.

Option B: Withdrawals are made every month and interest is earned at a rate of 7.75%, compounded monthly.

   a) Determine the regular withdrawal for each option.

   b) Determine the total interest earned for each option.

   c) Discuss the advantages and disadvantages of each option from Jordan's perspective.

11. Ronald and Benjamin need to take out a small loan to help expand their pet-grooming business, Fluff 'n' Shine. They estimate that they can afford to pay back $250 monthly for 3 years. If interest is 6%, compounded monthly, how much of a loan can Ronald and Benjamin afford?

12. **Chapter Problem** Chloe has achieved her initial financial goal of growing her investments to $12 000 after 4 years. She deposits this amount into a new account that earns 5% per year, compounded quarterly. Now her intention is to make regular withdrawals from this account every 3 months for the next 2 years. How much will Chloe's regular withdrawals be?

13. Josie plans to invest $10 000 at the end of each year for the 25 years leading up to her retirement. After she retires, she plans to make regular withdrawals for 25 years. Assume that the interest rate over the next 50 years remains constant at 7% per year, compounded annually.

a) Once she retires, which amount do you predict that Josie will be able to withdraw per year?
  - less than $10 000
  - $10 000
  - more than $10 000

Explain your answer.

b) Estimate how much she will be able to withdraw. Provide reasoning for your estimate.

c) Determine the amount of Josie's investment annuity on the day she retires.

d) Use this amount to determine the regular withdrawal she can make at the end of each year for 25 years after retirement.

e) Compare your answer in part d) to your estimate in part b). How close was your estimate?

✔️ **Achievement Check**

14. Abraham's grandparents plan to set up an annuity to help him when he moves into an apartment to attend college. Abraham will be able to withdraw $3000 at the end of each year for 4 years. The first withdrawal will be made 1 year from now, when Abraham begins college. If the annuity earns 7% interest, compounded annually, how much should Abraham's grandparents invest now to finance the annuity? Use two different methods to solve this problem.

C **Extend**

15. For a simple annuity with regular payment R and interest rate, i, as a decimal, per compounding period, use the formula for the sum of a geometric series,

$S_n = \dfrac{a(r^n - 1)}{r - 1}$, to derive the formula

for the present value of the annuity,

$PV = \dfrac{R[1 - (1 + i)^{-n}]}{i}$.

16. By law, mortgage interest rates must be stated as an annual rate compounded semi-annually. However, payments are usually made monthly, so the interest rate must be converted to a monthly rate. A $200 000 mortgage has an amortization period of 25 years, at an interest rate of 5%, compounded semi-annually.

a) Use the compound interest formula to determine the equivalent interest rate compounded monthly.

b) Determine the monthly payment required to pay off this mortgage over 25 years.

Connections

A mortgage is a type of loan by which a house or other real estate property is used as a guarantee of repayment of the debt. The total time over which the loan is repaid is called the amortization period.

17. A mortgage of $150 000 is amortized over 25 years with an interest rate of 6.7%, compounded semi-annually.

a) What is the monthly payment?

b) Suppose you choose to make weekly payments instead of monthly payments. What is the weekly payment?

c) Calculate the total interest paid with the weekly payments.

Chapter 7 Review

7.1 Simple Interest, pages 418 to 425

1. Louise borrows $720, which she plans to repay in a year and a half. She is charged 9.5% simple interest.

   a) How much interest must Louise pay?

   b) What is the total amount that she must pay back?

2. Yuri deposits $850 into an account that earns 6.25% per year simple interest. How long will it take for the amount in this account to reach $1000?

3. Nicola borrowed $750 for 4 years. The amount she repaid was $945.

   a) Use the given information to draw a graph of the amount in the account as a function of time.

   b) Explain why the relationship is linear.

   c) Determine the vertical intercept of the graph and explain what it means.

   d) Determine the slope of the graph and explain what it means.

7.2 Compound Interest, pages 426 to 435

4. Steve deposits $835 into an account that earns 8.25% per year, compounded annually.

   a) Determine the amount in the account after 5 years.

   b) How much interest will have been earned?

5. An account with an initial value of $1000 earns 3% interest per year, compounded semi-annually.

   a) Describe the shape of the graph of amount versus time.

   b) What is the vertical intercept of the graph? What does it represent?

   c) Describe what happens to the slope of the graph.

6. Elise deposits $500 into an account that earns 6.5% annual interest, compounded quarterly.

   a) How long will it take, to the nearest month, for this amount to double?

   b) Does the doubling time change if the principal changes? Explain.

7.3 Present Value, pages 436 to 443

7. What amount should be invested today so that there will be $1000 in an account in 3 years, if interest is earned at a rate of 7% per annum, compounded annually?

8. Dwayne needs $45 000 in 6 years to buy a new car. His investment earns interest at a rate of 4.8% per year, compounded monthly.

   a) Determine the present value needed in the account so that Dwayne can afford the car.

   b) How much interest will be earned?

9. The present value of an account worth $3823 in 4 years is $3000. If interest is compounded semi-annually, determine the annual rate of interest.

10. The future value of a $200 deposit in an account that earns 6.25% annual interest is $272.71 after 5 years. Determine the compounding period for this investment.

7.4 Annuities, pages 444 to 455

11. At the end of every year for 4 years, Jacqueline deposits $2400 into an account that earns 4.3% per annum, compounded annually.

    a) Draw a time line to illustrate this annuity.

    b) Explain why this annuity can be represented as a geometric series.

    c) Determine the amount of the annuity.

    d) How much interest will be earned?

12. Marko deposits $400 into an account at the end of every month for 8 years. Interest is earned at a rate of 5.5%, compounded monthly.

  a) Determine the amount of the annuity.

  b) How much interest will be earned?

13. Latisha decides to make regular deposits every 2 weeks into an account that earns 7.8% annual interest, compounded bi-weekly. She hopes to have $30 000 at the end of 3 years. Determine the amount of the regular payment that she will need to make.

7.5 Present Value of an Annuity,
pages 456 to 463

14. Examine the time line for the annuity shown.

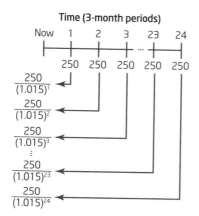

Time (3-month periods)

| Now | 1 | 2 | 3 | 23 | 24 |

250 250 250 250 250

$\dfrac{250}{(1.015)^1}$

$\dfrac{250}{(1.015)^2}$

$\dfrac{250}{(1.015)^3}$

$\vdots$

$\dfrac{250}{(1.015)^{23}}$

$\dfrac{250}{(1.015)^{24}}$

  a) What is the duration of this annuity? How can you tell?

  b) Determine the annual rate of interest and the number of compounding periods per year.

  c) Determine the present value of this annuity.

  d) Determine the total interest earned.

15. Suki would like to withdraw $800 per month for the next 20 years. The interest in her account is 6.25% per year, compounded monthly. How much must Suki deposit today to finance this annuity?

16. Mario has saved $250 000 for his retirement, which he has deposited into an account that earns 7.2% per year, compounded monthly. He plans to make regular monthly withdrawals for the next 25 years. What is the maximum monthly amount that Mario can withdraw?

Chapter Problem   WRAP-UP

In Section 7.1, question 10; Section 7.2, question 12; and Section 7.3, question 15, you explored Chloe's investment portfolio.

  a) What was the interest rate earned by each investment?

  b) What is the total interest earned by all of Chloe's investments, assuming that she just met her financial goal?

  c) The effective rate of return is the annual simple interest rate earned on all investments. Divide the total interest earned by the total principal and by the number of years to determine the effective rate of return of Chloe's investment portfolio.

  d) How much more money could Chloe have earned had she invested her entire principal in the highest-yield investment?

  e) Why do you suppose Chloe's advisor did not recommend the strategy in part d)?

Chapter 7 Practice Test

For questions 1 to 5, select the best answer.

1. Karl borrows $500 for 4 years at an annual simple interest rate of 12% per year. What is the amount that must be repaid?

   A $60

   B $240

   C $560

   D $740

2. Jasmine invests $400 at 8% annual interest, compounded annually. How much interest will be earned after 5 years?

   A $160

   B $187.73

   C $560

   D $587.73

3. If an amount is invested at 6.5% per year, compounded semi-annually, for 3 years, determine the number of compounding periods and the interest rate per compounding period.

   A $n = 3$, $i = 0.065$

   B $n = 6$, $i = 0.0325$

   C $n = 1.5$, $i = 0.13$

   D $n = 12$, $i = 0.01625$

4. If the annual interest rate is 3.9% and the interest per compounding period is 0.975%, what is the compounding period?

   A weekly

   B monthly

   C quarterly

   D semi-annual

5. An amount is deposited into an account that earns 9% per year, compounded quarterly. After 6 years, the amount in the account is $597.02. What is the present value?

   A $350.00

   B $355.98

   C $404.24

   D $421.36

6. After 1 year, Nadia's investment is worth $256.80. After 2 years, the amount has reached $290.40.

   a) How much simple interest is Nadia's investment earning per year?

   b) What is the principal?

   c) What is the annual simple interest rate per year?

7. Deanna invests $500 at 8% per year simple interest. She puts money in the bank on July 1 and takes it out December 3. How much money does she take out?

8. The time line for an annuity is shown.

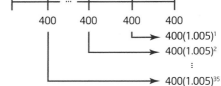

   a) What is the duration of this annuity? How can you tell?

   b) Determine the annual rate of interest and the number of compounding periods per year.

   c) Determine the amount of this annuity.

   d) Determine the total interest earned.

9. Leon has $3000 that he wants to invest for 6 years. Which option should he choose, and why?

   Option A: 5.2% annual interest, compounded quarterly

   Option B: 5% annual interest, compounded monthly

10. Colette takes out a loan for $2800 to buy a scooter. She plans to repay the loan in 3 years. The amount payable when the loan is due is $3420.51. What rate of interest, compounded annually, is Colette being charged?

11. You invest $1000 at 6% per year, compounded quarterly, for 3 years. What interest rate, compounded monthly, will give the same results?

12. An account paying 7.25% annual interest, compounded semi-annually, has a future value of $1429 in 8 years.

  a) What is the present value of the account?

  b) How much more interest will have been earned than if simple interest was paid?

13. To have $5000 at the end of 8 years, how much do you need to invest today, at 6% per annum, compounded semi-annually?

14. Jerry deposited $300 into an account that earns 6.7% annual interest, compounded daily. When he closed the account, the amount had grown to $348.56. How long was the money invested?

15. Heather deposits $200 per week for 20 years into an account that earns 2.6% annual interest, compounded weekly.

  a) Draw a time line to represent this annuity.

  b) Determine the amount of the annuity.

  c) How much interest will be earned?

16. After 20 years of investing, Heather decides to retire and use the amount of her annuity to finance her retirement for the next 20 years. Use the amount from question 15b) and the same interest conditions.

  a) Draw a time line to represent Heather's retirement annuity.

  b) Determine the maximum monthly withdrawal that she can make.

  c) Determine the total amount of interest earned over the 40 years spanning the two annuities.

17. Niki needs $5200 for university tuition when she graduates from high school in 2 years. She plans to make deposits into an account that earns 6.5% per year, compounded bi-weekly.

  a) Draw a time line to represent this annuity.

  b) How much should she deposit every 2 weeks?

18. Shira has invested $18 000 in an annuity from which she plans to withdraw $650 per month for the next 4.5 years. If at the end of this time period the balance of the annuity is zero, what annual rate of interest, compounded monthly, did the account earn?

19. Instead of investing $3000 at the end of 5 years and $4000 at the end of 10 years, Steve wishes to make regular monthly payments that will amount to the same total after 10 years. Determine the monthly payment if interest is compounded monthly at an annual rate of 4%.

Chapter 6 Discrete Functions

1. Write the first three terms of each sequence. Describe the pattern in words.

   a) $t_n = 3n - 2$

   b) $f(n) = 4^n + 1$

   c) $t_n = 5n^2 - 16$

   d) $f(n) = \dfrac{n^3}{2} + 2$

   e) $t_1 = 1, t_n = 2t_{n-1} + 5$

   f) $t_1 = -2, t_n = (t_{n-1})^2 - 8$

2. Graph the first eight terms of each sequence in question 1.

3. The value of a new car bought for $45 000 depreciates at a rate of 15% in the first year and 5% every year after that.

   a) Determine the value of the car at the end of the first year, the second year, and the third year. Write these values as a sequence.

   b) Determine an explicit formula for the value of the car at the end of year n.

   c) What is the value of the car at the end of year 20? Is this realistic? Explain your thinking.

4. Given the graph, write the sequence of terms and determine a recursion formula using function notation.

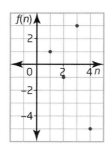

5. Write a recursion formula and an explicit formula for each sequence.

   a) 5, 7, 9, 11, …

   b) 2, 4, 16, 256, …

6. Investigate the prime-numbered rows of Pascal's triangle. Describe the property that is common to these rows but not common to the rows that are not prime-numbered.

7. Expand and simplify each binomial.

   a) $(2x + 5)^7$

   b) $(a^2 - 3b)^5$

   c) $\left(\dfrac{2}{x} + x^2\right)^6$

   d) $\left(5 - \dfrac{3}{\sqrt{n}}\right)^4$

8. State whether each sequence is arithmetic, geometric, or neither. Determine a defining equation for those that are arithmetic or geometric, and find the 12th term.

   a) 6, 11, 17, 29, …

   b) −3, 1, 5, 9, …

   c) 3, 12, 48, 192, …

   d) 2 657 205, −885 735, 295 245, −98 415, …

9. The fourth term of an arithmetic sequence is 6 and the seventh term is 27. Determine the first and second terms.

10. How many terms are in the geometric sequence 7, 21, 63, …, 3 720 087?

11. A new golf course has 480 lifetime members 3 weeks after it opens and 1005 lifetime members 6 weeks after it opens. Assume the membership increase is arithmetic.

   a) Determine the general term that represents the sequence for this situation.

   b) How many members were there at the end of the fifth week?

   c) When will there be over 2000 members?

12. Determine the sum of the first 10 terms of each series.

   a) $2 + 9 + 16 + 23 + \cdots$

   b) $5 - 25 + 125 - 625 + \cdots$

   c) $256 + 128 + 64 + 32 + \cdots$

   d) $-\dfrac{1}{3} - \dfrac{5}{6} - \dfrac{4}{3} - \dfrac{11}{6} - \cdots$

13. A ball is dropped from a height of 160 cm. Each time it drops, it rebounds to 80% of its previous height.

a) What is the height of the rebound after the 8th bounce?

b) What is the total distance travelled at the time of the 15th bounce?

Chapter 7 Financial Applications

14. Define each term.

a) principal

b) amount

c) simple interest

d) compound interest

e) annuity

f) present value

g) compounding period

15. Determine the interest earned for each investment.

a) $1000 is invested for 8 months at 5% per year simple interest.

b) $800 is placed into an account that pays 2.5% annual simple interest for 40 weeks.

c) A 90-day $10 000 treasury bill earns simple interest at a rate of 4.8% per year.

16. Alex deposited $500 into an account at 3% simple interest.

a) Write an equation to relate the amount in the account to time.

b) Sketch a graph of this relation for 1 year.

c) How long does it take to earn $10 in interest?

17. Sarah invests $750 in a term deposit, at 4.5% per annum, compounded semi-annually, for 5 years. How much interest will Sarah earn?

18. Abdul decides to invest some money so that he can have $10 000 for a down payment on a new car in 5 years. He is considering two investment options: Account A pays 3.5% per annum, compounded semi-annually. Account B pays 3.2% per annum, compounded monthly.

a) Compare the present values of the two options.

b) Which account is the better choice for Abdul? Explain your reasoning.

19. To save for her university education, Shaquilla will deposit $50 into an account at the end of each month for the next 3 years. She expects the interest rate to be 1.5% per year, compounded monthly, over that time. How much will she have saved after 3 years?

20. Wayne is 16 years old. To become a millionaire by the time he is 50 years old, how much does Wayne need to invest, at the end of every 6 months, at 4% per year, compounded semi-annually?

21. What annual interest rate, compounded monthly, is needed for Eva to accumulate $20 000 by depositing $300 at the end of each month for 5 years?

22. A rental contract calls for a down payment of $1000, and $500 to be paid at the end of each month for 3 years. If interest is at 4.5% per year, compounded monthly, what is the present value of this rental contract?

23. A retirement account contains $100 000. Barb would like to withdraw equal amounts of money at the end of every 3 months for 15 years. If interest is 5% per year, compounded quarterly, what will the size of Barb's withdrawals be?

Task

Loans and Annuities Due

a) **i)** Ali is paying off a loan by making $50 payments at the end of every month for 2 years, at 6%, compounded monthly. What is the value of the loan today?

ii) Ken is paying off a loan by making a $50 down payment and then $50 payments at the end of every month for 2 years, at 6%, compounded monthly. What is the value of the loan today?

iii) Maria is paying off a loan by making $50 payments at the beginning of every month for 2 years, at 6%, compounded monthly. What is the value of the loan today?

iv) Explain the factors in each situation that account for the differences in the results.

b) An ordinary annuity consists of payments at the end of each payment period, as you have seen in this chapter. An *ordinary annuity due* consists of the same number of payments at the beginning, rather than the end, of each payment period.

i) Which part of part a) is an annuity due? Explain.

ii) Use the results of your calculations to develop a formula for the present value of an ordinary annuity due.

iii) Use your formula to determine the present value of a loan, with $200 payments at the beginning of every 3 months for 2 years, with interest at 7%, compounded quarterly.

iv) Use your formula to determine the monthly payments at the beginning of each month on a $15 000 car loan, at 3%, compounded monthly, for 3 years.

Course Review

Chapter 1 Functions

1. Determine the domain and the range for each relation. Sketch a graph of each.

a) $y = \dfrac{3}{x - 9}$ **b)** $y = \sqrt{2 - x} - 4$

2. Which of the following is NOT true?

A All functions are also relations.

B The vertical line test is used to determine if the graph of a relation is a function.

C All relations are also functions.

D Some relations are also functions.

3. The approximate time for an investment to double can be found using the function $n(r) = \dfrac{72}{r}$, where n represents the number of years and r represents the annual interest rate, as a percent.

a) How long will it take an investment to double at each rate?

i) 3% **ii)** 6% **iii)** 9%

b) Graph the data to illustrate the function.

c) Determine the domain and range in this context.

4. Determine the vertex of each quadratic function by completing the square. Verify your answer by using partial factoring. State if the vertex is a minimum or a maximum.

a) $f(x) = 3x^2 + 9x + 1$

b) $f(x) = -\dfrac{1}{2}x^2 + 3x - \dfrac{5}{2}$

5. A small company manufactures a total of x items per week. The production cost is modelled by the function $C(x) = 50 + 3x$. The revenue is given by the function $R(x) = 6x - \dfrac{x^2}{100}$. How many items per week should be manufactured to maximize the profit for the company?

Hint: Profit = Revenue − Cost

6. Simplify.

a) $2\sqrt{243} - 5\sqrt{48} + \sqrt{108} - \sqrt{192}$

b) $\dfrac{2}{3}\sqrt{125} - \dfrac{1}{3}\sqrt{27} + 2\sqrt{48} - 3\sqrt{80}$

7. Expand. Simplify where possible.

a) $\left(\sqrt{5} + 2\sqrt{3}\right)\left(3\sqrt{5} + 4\sqrt{3}\right)$

b) $\left(4 - \sqrt{6}\right)\left(1 + \sqrt{6}\right)$

8. Find a simplified expression for the area of the circle.

9. Solve $3x^2 + 9x - 30 = 0$ by

a) completing the square

b) using a graphing calculator

c) factoring

d) using the quadratic formula

10. The length of a rectangle is 5 m more than its width. If the area of the rectangle is 15 m², what are the dimensions of the rectangle, to the nearest tenth of a metre?

11. Find an equation for the quadratic function with the given zeros and containing the given point. Express each function in standard form. Graph each function to check.

a) $2 \pm \sqrt{3}$, point $(4, -6)$

b) 4 and -1, point $(1, -4)$

12. An arch of a highway overpass is in the shape of a parabola. The arch spans a distance of 16 m from one side of the road to the other. At a horizontal distance of 1 m from each side of the arch, its height above the road is 6 m.

a) Sketch the quadratic function if the vertex of the parabola is on the y-axis and the road is along the x-axis.

b) Use this information to determine the equation of the function that models the arch.

c) Find the maximum height of the arch.

13. At a fireworks display, the path of the biggest firework can be modelled using the function $f(x) = -0.015x^2 + 2.24x + 1.75$, where x is the horizontal distance from the launching platform. The profile of a hill, some distance away from the platform, can be modelled with the equation $h(x) = 0.7x - 83$, with all distances in metres. Will the firework reach the hill? Justify your answer.

Chapter 2 Transformations of Functions

14. Test whether the functions in each pair are equivalent by

 i) testing three different values of x

 ii) simplifying the expressions on the right sides

 iii) graphing using graphing technology

 a) $f(x) = -2(x + 3)^2 + (5x + 1)$,
   $g(x) = -2x^2 - 7x - 17$

 b) $f(x) = \dfrac{x^2 - 2x - 15}{x^2 - 9x + 20}$,
   $g(x) = \dfrac{x + 3}{x - 4}$

15. Simplify and state the restrictions.

 a) $\dfrac{-x + 1}{8x} \div \dfrac{2x - 2}{14x^2}$

 b) $\dfrac{x^2 + 5x - 36}{x^2 - 2x} \div \dfrac{x^2 + 11x + 18}{8x^2 - 4x^3}$

 c) $\dfrac{x^2 - 25}{x - 4} \times \dfrac{x^2 - 6x + 8}{3x + 15}$

16. For each function $g(x)$, state the corresponding base function $f(x)$. Describe the transformations that must be applied to the base function using function notation and words. Then, transform the graph of $f(x)$ to sketch the graph of $g(x)$ and state the domain and range of each function.

 a) $g(x) = \dfrac{1}{x + 5} - 1$

 b) $g(x) = \sqrt{x + 7} - 9$

17. For each graph, describe the reflection that transforms $f(x)$ into $g(x)$.

 a)

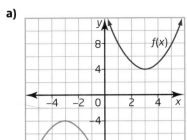

 b)

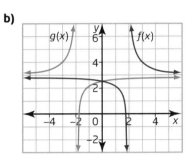

18. For each of the functions $f(x) = x^2$, $f(x) = \sqrt{x}$, and $f(x) = \dfrac{1}{x}$, write an equation to represent $g(x)$ and $h(x)$ and describe the transformations. Then, transform the graph of $f(x)$ to sketch graphs of $g(x)$ and $h(x)$ and state the domain and range of the functions.

 a) $g(x) = 4f(-x)$ and $h(x) = \dfrac{1}{4}f(x)$

 b) $g(x) = f(4x)$ and $h(x) = -f\left(\dfrac{1}{4}x\right)$

19. A ball is dropped from a height of 32 m. Acceleration due to gravity is -9.8 m/s². The height of the ball is given by $h(t) = -4.9t^2 + 32$.

 a) State the domain and range of the function.

 b) Write the equation for the height of the object if it is dropped on a planet with acceleration due to gravity of -11.2 m/s².

 c) Compare the domain and range of the function in part b) to those of the given function.

20. Describe the combination of transformations that must be applied to the base function $f(x)$ to obtain the transformed function $g(x)$. Then, write the corresponding equation and sketch its graph.

a) $f(x) = x$, $g(x) = -2f[3(x - 4)] - 1$

b) $f(x) = \frac{1}{x}$, $g(x) = \frac{1}{3}f\left[\frac{1}{4}(x - 2)\right] + 3$

21. For each function $f(x)$,

i) determine $f^{-1}(x)$

ii) graph $f(x)$ and its inverse

iii) determine whether the inverse of $f(x)$ is a function

a) $f(x) = 4x - 5$

b) $f(x) = 3x^2 - 12x + 3$

22. The relationship between the area of a circle and its radius can be modelled by the function $A(r) = \pi r^2$, where A is the area and r is the radius. The graphs of this function and its inverse are shown.

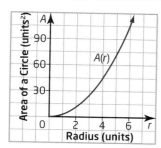

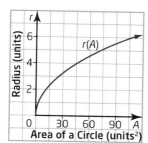

a) State the domain and range of the function $A(r)$.

b) Determine the equation of the inverse of the function. State its domain and range.

Chapter 3 Exponential Functions

23. A petri dish contains an initial sample of 20 bacteria. After 1 day, the number of bacteria has tripled.

a) Determine the population after each day for 1 week.

b) Write an equation to model this growth.

c) Graph the relation. Is it a function? Explain why or why not.

d) Assuming this trend continues, predict the population after

i) 2 weeks

ii) 3 weeks

e) Describe the pattern of finite differences for this relationship.

24. Tritium is a substance that is present in radioactive waste. It has a half-life of approximately 12 years. How long will it take for a 50-mg sample of tritium to decay to 10% of its original mass?

25. Apply the exponent rules first, if possible, and then evaluate.

a) $(-8)^{-2} + 2^{-6}$

b) $(3^{-3})^{-2} \div 3^{-5}$

c) $\left(\frac{2^3}{3^2}\right)^{-2}$

d) $\frac{(6^6)(6^{-3})}{6^2}$

26. Simplify.

a) $(4n^{-2})(-3n^5)$

b) $\frac{12c^{-3}}{15c^{-5}}$

c) $(3a^2b^{-2})^{-3}$

d) $\left(\frac{-2p^3}{3q^4}\right)^{-5}$

27. Evaluate.

a) $16^{-\frac{3}{4}}$

b) $\left(\frac{4}{9}\right)^{-\frac{1}{2}}$

c) $\left(-\frac{8}{125}\right)^{-\frac{2}{3}}$

28. Simplify. Express your answers using only positive exponents.

a) $\frac{a^{-2}b^3}{a^{\frac{1}{4}}b^{\frac{2}{3}}}$

b) $(u^{-\frac{2}{3}}v^{\frac{1}{4}})^{\frac{3}{5}}$

c) $w^{\frac{7}{8}} \div w^{-\frac{3}{4}}$

29. Graph each exponential function. Identify the

- domain
- range
- x- and y-intercepts, if they exist
- intervals of increase/decrease
- asymptote

a) $y = 5\left(\frac{1}{3}\right)^x$ **b)** $y = -4^{-x}$

30. A radioactive sample has a half-life of 1 month. The initial sample has a mass of 300 mg.

a) Write a function to relate the amount remaining, in milligrams, to the time, in months.

b) Restrict the domain of the function so the mathematical model fits the situation it is describing.

31. Sketch the graph of each function, using the graph of $y = 8^x$ as the base. Describe the effects, if any, on the

- asymptote
- domain
- range

a) $y = 8^{x-4}$ **b)** $y = 8^{x+2} + 1$

32. Write the equation for the function that results from each transformation applied to the base function $y = 11^x$.

a) reflect in the x-axis and stretch vertically by a factor of 4

b) reflect in the y-axis and stretch horizontally by a factor of $\frac{4}{3}$

33. At midnight, one hospital patient contracts an unknown virus. By 1 a.m., three other hospital patients are diagnosed with the same virus. One hour later, nine more patients are found to have the virus, and by 3 a.m., 27 more patients have the virus. The virus continues to spread this way through the hospital.

a) Make a table of values to relate the number of new patients who are diagnosed with the virus to time, in 1-h intervals.

b) Make a scatter plot. Describe the trend.

c) What type of function represents the spread of this virus? Justify your answer.

d) Determine an equation to model this relation. Explain the method you chose to determine the equation.

Chapter 4 Trigonometry

34. a) To find trigonometric ratios for 240° using a unit circle, a reference angle of 60° is used. What reference angle should you use to find the trigonometric ratios for 210°?

b) Use the unit circle to find exact values of the three primary trigonometric ratios for 210° and 240°.

35. A fishing boat is 15 km south of a lighthouse. A yacht is 15 km west of the same lighthouse.

a) Use trigonometry to find an exact expression for the distance between the two boats.

b) Check your answer using another method.

36. Without using a calculator, determine two angles between 0° and 360° that have a sine of $\dfrac{\sqrt{3}}{2}$.

37. The point P(-2, 7) is on the terminal arm of ∠A.

a) Determine the primary trigonometric ratios for ∠A and ∠B, such that ∠B has the same sine as ∠A.

b) Use a calculator and a diagram to determine the measures of ∠A and ∠B, to the nearest degree.

38. Consider right $\triangle PQR$ with side lengths $PQ = 5$ cm and $QR = 12$ cm, and $\angle Q = 90°$.

a) Determine the length of side PR.

b) Determine the six trigonometric ratios for $\angle P$.

c) Determine the six trigonometric ratios for $\angle R$.

39. Determine two possible measures between $0°$ and $360°$ for each angle, to the nearest degree.

a) $\csc A = \dfrac{7}{3}$

b) $\sec B = -6$

c) $\cot C = -\dfrac{9}{4}$

40. An oak tree, a chestnut tree, and a maple tree form the corners of a triangular play area in a neighbourhood park. The oak tree is 35 m from the chestnut tree. The angle between the maple tree and the chestnut tree from the oak tree is 58°. The angle between the oak tree and the chestnut tree from the maple tree is 49°.

a) Sketch a diagram of this situation. Why is the triangle formed by the trees an oblique triangle?

b) Is it necessary to consider the ambiguous case? Justify your answer.

c) Determine the unknown distances, to the nearest tenth of a metre. If there is more than one possible answer, determine both.

41. At noon, two cars travel away from the intersection of two country roads that meet at a 34° angle. Car A travels along one of the roads at 80 km/h and car B travels along the other road at 100 km/h. Two hours later, both cars spot a jet in the air between them. The angle of depression from the jet to car A is 20° and the distance between the jet and the car is 100 km. Determine the distance between the jet and car B.

42. Isra parks her motorcycle in a lot on the corner of Canal and Main streets. She walks 60 m west to Maple Avenue, turns 40° to the left, and follows Maple Avenue for 90 m to the office building where she works. From her office window on the 18th floor, she can see her motorcycle in the lot. Each floor in the building is 5 m in height.

a) Sketch a diagram to represent this problem, labelling all given measurements.

b) How far is Isra from her motorcycle, in a direct line?

43. Prove each identity.

a) $\dfrac{1}{\sin^2 \theta} + \dfrac{1}{\cos^2 \theta} = \left(\tan \theta + \dfrac{1}{\tan \theta}\right)^2$

b) $\csc \theta \left(\dfrac{1}{\cot \theta} + \dfrac{1}{\sec \theta}\right) = \sec \theta + \cot \theta$

Chapter 5 Trigonometric Functions

44. a) Sketch a periodic function, $f(x)$, with a maximum value of 5, a minimum value of -3, and a period of 4.

b) Select a value a for x, and determine $f(a)$.

c) Determine two other values, b and c, such that $f(a) = f(b) = f(c)$.

45. While visiting a town along the ocean, Bashira notices that the water level at the town dock changes during the day as the tides come in and go out. Markings on one of the piles supporting the dock show a high tide of 4.8 m at 6:30 a.m., a low tide of 0.9 m at 12:40 p.m., and a high tide again at 6:50 p.m.

a) Estimate the period of the fluctuation of the water level at the town dock.

b) Estimate the amplitude of the pattern.

c) Predict when the next low tide will occur.

46. Consider the following functions.

i) $y = 4 \sin \left[\frac{1}{3}(x + 30°) \right] - 1$

ii) $y = -\frac{1}{2} \cos [4(x + 135°)] + 2$

a) What is the amplitude of each function?

b) What is the period of each function?

c) Describe the phase shift of each function.

d) Describe the vertical shift of each function.

e) **Use Technology** Graph each function. Compare the graph to the characteristics expected.

47. A sinusoidal function has an amplitude of 6 units, a period of 150°, and a maximum at (0, 4).

a) Represent the function with an equation using a sine function.

b) Represent the function with an equation using a cosine function.

48. The height, h, in metres, above the ground of a rider on a Ferris wheel after t seconds can be modelled by the sine function $h(t) = 9 \sin [2(t - 30)] + 10$.

a) **Use Technology** Graph the function.

b) Determine

i) the maximum and minimum heights of the rider above the ground

ii) the height of the rider above the ground after 30 s

iii) the time required for the Ferris wheel to complete one revolution

49. Marcia constructs a model alternating current (AC) generator in physics class and cranks it by hand at 4 revolutions per second. She is able to light up a flashlight bulb that is rated for 6 V. The voltage can be modelled by a sine function of the form $y = a \sin [k(x - d)] + c$.

a) What is the period of the AC produced by the generator?

b) Determine the value of k.

c) What is the amplitude of the voltage function?

d) Model the voltage with a suitably transformed sine function.

e) **Use Technology** Graph the voltage function over two cycles. Explain what the scales on the axes represent.

Chapter 6 Discrete Functions

50. Write the ninth term, given the explicit formula for the nth term of the sequence.

a) $t_n = \frac{n^2 - 1}{2n}$

b) $f(n) = (-3)^{n-2}$

51. Write the first five terms of each sequence.

a) $t_1 = 3, t_n = \frac{t_{n-1}}{0.2}$

b) $f(1) = \frac{2}{5}, f(n) = f(n-1) - 1$

52. A hospital patient, recovering from surgery, receives 400 mg of pain medication every 5 h for 3 days. The half-life of the pain medication is approximately 5 h. This means that after 5 h, about half of the medicine is still in the patient's body.

a) Create a table of values showing the amount of medication remaining in the body after each 5-h period.

b) Write the amount of medication remaining after each 5-h period as a sequence. Write a recursion formula for the sequence.

c) Graph the sequence.

d) Describe what happens to the medicine in the patient's body over time.

Use Pascal's triangle for questions 53 and 54.

53. Expand each power of a binomial.

a) $(x - y)^6$

b) $\left(\frac{x}{3} - 2x \right)^4$

54. Write each as the sum of two terms, each in the form $t_{n, r}$.

a) $t_{5, 2}$

b) $t_{10, 7}$

55. a) State whether or not each sequence is arithmetic. Justify your answer.

    i) 9, 5, 1, −3, ...

    ii) $\frac{1}{5}$, $\frac{3}{5}$, 1, $\frac{7}{5}$, $\frac{9}{5}$, ...

    iii) −4.2, −3.8, −3.5, −3.3, −3.2, ...

  b) For those sequences that are arithmetic, write the formula for the general term.

56. For each geometric sequence, determine the formula for the general term and then write t_{10}.

  a) 90, 30, 10, ...

  b) $\frac{1}{4}$, $\frac{1}{6}$, $\frac{1}{9}$, ...

  c) −0.0035, 0.035, −0.35, ...

57. Determine the sum of the first 10 terms of each arithmetic series.

  a) $a = 2$, $d = -3$, $t_{10} = 56$

  b) $a = -5$, $d = 1.5$

58. Determine the sum of each geometric series.

  a) $45 + 15 + 5 + \cdots + \frac{5}{729}$

  b) $1 - x + x^2 - x^3 + \cdots - x^{15}$

59. A bouncy ball bounces to $\frac{3}{5}$ of its height when dropped on a hard surface. Suppose the ball is dropped from 45 m.

  a) What height will the ball bounce back up to after the seventh bounce?

  b) What is the total distance travelled by the ball after 12 bounces?

Chapter 7 Financial Applications

60. Richard deposits $1000 into a guaranteed investment certificate (GIC) that earns 4.5% per year, simple interest.

  a) Develop a linear model to relate the amount in the GIC to time. Identify the fixed part and the variable part. Graph the function.

  b) How long will it take, to the nearest month, for the investment to double?

  c) What annual rate of interest must be earned so that the investment doubles in 6 years?

61. Suppose you have $2500 to invest for 6 years. Two options are available:

  • Top Bank: earns 6% per year, compounded quarterly

  • Best Credit Union: earns 5.8% per year, compounded weekly

  Which investment would you choose and why?

62. Five years ago, money was invested at 6.75% per year, compounded annually. Today the investment is worth $925.

  a) How much money was originally invested?

  b) How much interest was earned?

63. At the end of every month, Cassie deposits $120 into an account that pays 5.25% per year, compounded monthly. She does this for 5 years.

  a) Draw a time line to represent this annuity.

  b) Determine the amount in the account after 5 years.

  c) How much interest will have been earned?

64. Murray plans to withdraw $700 at the end of every 3 months, for 5 years, from an account that earns 7% interest, compounded quarterly.

  a) Draw a time line to represent this annuity.

  b) Determine the present value of the annuity.

  c) How much interest will have been earned?

Prerequisite Skills Appendix

Angle Sum of a Triangle

Use the fact that the sum of the interior angles of a triangle is 180° to find the measure of x.

$x + 58° + 71° = 180°$

$\qquad x = 180° - 129°$

$\qquad x = 51°$

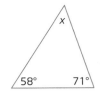

1. Find the measure of each angle x.

a)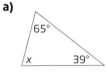

b)

c)

Apply the Sine Law and the Cosine Law

Use the sine law to solve any acute triangle given
- the measures of two angles and any side
- the measures of two sides and the angle opposite one of the given sides

To find the length of side p, first determine the measure of $\angle$P.

Apply the angle sum of a triangle.

$\angle P = 180° - 44° - 75°$

$\quad = 61°$

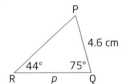

Then, use the sine law.

$$\frac{p}{\sin 61°} = \frac{4.6}{\sin 44°}$$

$$p = \frac{4.6 \sin 61°}{\sin 44°}$$

$$\doteq 5.8$$

The length of side p is approximately 5.8 cm.

Use cosine law to solve any triangle given
- the measures of two sides and the contained angle
- the measures of three sides

Use the cosine law to find b.

$b^2 = a^2 + c^2 - 2ac \cos B$

$b^2 = 8.7^2 + 6.3^2 - 2(8.7)(6.3) \cos 68°$

$b^2 \doteq 74.316$

$\ b \doteq 8.6$

The length of side b is approximately 8.6 cm.

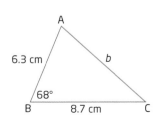

1. Determine the measure of the angle or side indicated.

a) length of s

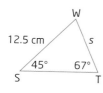

b) measure of $\angle$B

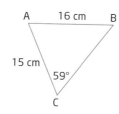

c) measure of $\angle$M

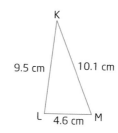

Apply Trigonometric Ratios to Problems

Various problems involving right triangles can be solved using trigonometric ratios.

An airplane that is 450 m above the ground is coming down for a landing at an angle of depression of 18°. How far, horizontally, is the plane from its landing point?

Draw and label a diagram to represent the given information.
Use the tangent ratio and solve for x.

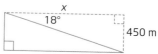

$$\tan 18° = \frac{450}{x}$$

$$x = \frac{450}{\tan 18°}$$

$$\doteq 1385$$

The plane is about 1385 m horizontally from its landing point.

1. A guy wire attached to the ground and the top of a flagpole is 6.2 m long. The wire makes an angle of 75° with the ground. How tall is the flagpole?

2. The ramp from the back of a truck is 4.0 m long. If the back of the truck is 0.6 m above the ground, at what angle is the ramp inclined?

Classify Triangles

Triangles can be classified according to their side lengths or the measures of their angles.

Classification by Side Length
- Equilateral: all three sides equal
- Isosceles: two sides equal
- Scalene: no sides equal

Classification by Angle Measure
- Right triangle: contains a 90° angle
- Acute triangle: has all angles less than 90°
- Obtuse triangle: contains an angle greater than 90°

This is a scalene
right triangle.

This is an isosceles
acute triangle.

This is a scalene
obtuse triangle.

1. Classify each triangle by its sides and angles.

a)

b)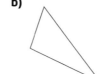

c)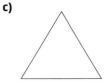

Common Factors

To factor an expression, determine the greatest common factor (GCF) of each term.

To factor $6m^2 - 15m$, write each term in expanded form.
$$6m^2 = 2 \times 3 \times m \times m$$
$$15m = 3 \times 5 \times m$$

$3m$ is the GCF.
Find the second factor by dividing the GCF into each term in the original expression.
$$\frac{6m^2}{3m} - \frac{15m}{3m} = 2m - 5$$

Therefore, $6m^2 - 15m = 3m(2m - 5)$.
A common factor can have more than one term. For example,
$3(x - 2) + x^2(x - 2) = (x - 2)(3 + x^2)$.

1. Find the GCF of each set of terms.

a) $8x$, $12y$

b) $-12a^3$, $6a^2b$, $9ab$

c) $10xy^3$, $35x^3y^2$

d) $24m^3n^2$, $-72m^2n^4$, $96m^2n^3$

e) $6(a^2 + 3)$, $-5(a^2 + 3)$

f) $3x^2y + 12xy$, $15xy^3 - 6x^2y$

2. Factor fully.

a) $16x^2 + 20x$

b) $5x^2y^2 + 10xy^3$

c) $3a^3 - 9a^2$

d) $4r^5s^2 + 16r^2s$

e) $8a^3b - 10ab + 4a^2b^2$

f) $-6x^3y - 18x^4y^3 - 36x^2y^4$

g) $12p(p + 3q) - q(p + 3q)$

h) $8x(y - 2x^2) + 20xy(y - 2x^2)$

Determine an Angle Given a Trigonometric Ratio

To determine the measure of an acute angle, use the corresponding inverse function on a scientific or graphing calculator.

If sin A = 0.3897, then
$\angle A = \sin^{-1} 0.3897$
$\angle A \doteq 22.9°$

1. Determine the measure of each acute angle, to the nearest degree.

a) cos A = 0.2598

b) sin Q = 0.8339

c) tan T = 2.4591

d) cos P = 0.7662

e) sin X = 0.3478

f) tan C = 0.6264

Direct Variation and Partial Variation

In a direct variation, one variable is a constant multiple of another variable. For example, $y = 4x$ is a direct variation. It is a linear relation that passes through the origin.

A partial variation is a linear relation between two variables that involves a fixed amount plus a variable amount.

A plumber charges $60, plus $40/h for labour.
The equation of the relationship is $C = 40t + 60$, where C represents the total cost, in dollars, and t represents the time, in hours.
The fixed part is 60 and the variable part is 40.
Use a table of values to graph the relationship.

Time (h)	Cost ($)
0	60
1	100
2	140
3	180

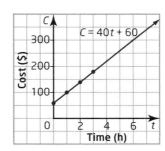

The slope of the line is $\dfrac{100 - 60}{1 - 0} = 40$.

The vertical intercept is 60.

The slope is the coefficient of the variable part and represents the hourly cost of labour. The vertical intercept is the fixed part and represents the fixed or initial cost of labour.

1. For an advertisement in the classified section, a newspaper charges $25 plus $12 per day.

   a) Write an equation to relate the total cost, C, in dollars, of the advertisement to the number, d, of days.

   b) Identify the fixed part and the variable part of this relation.

   c) Graph the relation.

   d) Determine the slope and the vertical intercept of the graph.

   e) Explain how your answers in parts b) and d) are related.

2. Irene works part-time at a clothing store. She earns $200 per week, plus a commission of 5% of her sales.

   a) Write an equation to relate her weekly salary to her sales.

   b) Identify the fixed part and the variable part of this relation.

   c) Graph the relation.

   d) Determine the slope and the vertical intercept of the graph.

   e) Explain how your answers in parts b) and d) are related.

Distributive Property

According to the distributive property, $a(x + y) = ax + ay$.
An algebraic expression in factored form can be expanded by multiplying each term in the brackets by the term outside.

For example, $3(x + 7) = 3x + 21$.

1. Expand.

   a) $2(a + b)$ b) $6(x - 4)$ c) $4(k^2 + 5)$ d) $-3(x - 2)$

   e) $5(x^2 - 2x + 1)$ f) $2x(3x - 4)$ g) $8a(3 + a)$ h) $-2x(x + y - 3)$

Evaluate Expressions

To find the percent of a number, change the percent to a decimal number. Then, multiply by the number.

$$16\% \text{ of } 50 = 0.16 \times 50$$
$$= 8$$

1. Evaluate.

   a) 45% of 120   b) 3% of 64   c) 20% of 95

   d) 5.5% of 2036   e) 4.25% of 600   f) 140% of 230

To add or subtract rational numbers in fraction form, find the least common denominator (LCD), multiply accordingly to get equivalent fractions, and add or subtract the numerators.

To evaluate $\dfrac{3}{8} - \dfrac{7}{12}$, use the LCD of 24.

$$\frac{3}{8} - \frac{7}{12} = \frac{9}{24} - \frac{14}{24}$$

Refer to **Work With Fractions** on page 494.

$$= -\frac{5}{24}$$

To multiply rational numbers in fraction form, multiply numerators and denominators. To divide, multiply by the reciprocal of the second fraction. For all operations, convert any mixed numbers to improper fractions first.

$$-\frac{5}{6} \div 2\frac{1}{2} = -\frac{5}{6} \div \frac{5}{2}$$
$$= -\frac{5}{6} \times \frac{2}{5}$$
$$= -\frac{10}{30}$$
$$= -\frac{1}{3}$$

2. Evaluate.

a) $\frac{3}{4} + \left(-\frac{1}{2}\right)$

b) $1\frac{2}{3} - \frac{5}{12}$

c) $-\frac{5}{8} + \left(-1\frac{1}{6}\right)$

d) $\frac{7}{9} \times \left(-\frac{3}{4}\right)$

e) $3\frac{1}{8} \div \left(-1\frac{1}{4}\right)$

f) $-1\frac{1}{5} \div 6$

Exponent Rules

To multiply powers with the same base, add the exponents.
$$x^3 \times x^2 = x^{3+2}$$
$$= x^5$$

To divide powers with the same base, subtract the exponents.
$$x^6 \div x^2 = x^{6-2}$$
$$= x^4$$

To raise a power to a power, multiply the exponents.
$$(x^2)^3 = x^{2 \times 3}$$
$$= x^6$$

1. Simplify, using the exponent rules. Leave answers in exponential form.

a) $2^3 \times 2^4$

b) $5^2 \times 5^4$

c) $3^5 \div 3^2$

d) $4^8 \div 4^3$

e) $(6^4)^2$

f) $(9^3)^7$

g) $a^5 \times a^5$

h) $z^4 \times z^4$

i) $3x^2 \times 2x^3$

j) $y^8 \div y^5$

k) $(p^3)^6$

l) $n^6 \div n$

m) $(12x^7) \div (-3x^4)$

n) $(2t^4)^3$

o) $(-4x^2)^4$

2. Evaluate.

a) $8^6 \div 8^4$

b) $2^2 \times 2^3 \div 2^4$

c) $3^9 \div 3^3$

d) $(2^4)^2$

e) $(4^2)^3$

f) $\left(\frac{1}{4}\right)^3$

Factor Quadratic Expressions

To factor a quadratic expression:
- check for common factors
- for expressions in the form $x^2 + bx + c$, find two integers, m and n, that have a sum of b and a product of c, and factor as $(x + m)(x + n)$
- for expressions in the form $ax^2 + bx + c$, find two integers, m and n, that have a sum of b and a product of ac, and then rewrite as $ax^2 + mx + nx + c$ and factor by grouping
- look for special products such as differences of squares or perfect squares

To factor $x^2 + 2x - 15$, note that $5 + (-3) = +2$ and $(5)(-3) = -15$.
Therefore, $x^2 + 2x - 15 = (x + 5)(x - 3)$.

In the expression $12x^2 - 60x + 75$, the number 3 is a common factor.
So, $12x^2 - 60x + 75 = 3(4x^2 - 20x + 25)$.
The coefficients of the first term and the last term are perfect squares, so that the trinomial inside the brackets may be a perfect square.
Since the coefficient of the middle term, -20, is twice the product of the square roots of 4 and 25, it is a perfect square trinomial.
Therefore, $12x^2 - 60x + 75 = 3(2x - 5)^2$.

1. Factor fully.

a) $x^2 + 6x + 8$ **b)** $x^2 - 7x + 12$ **c)** $2x^2 + 6x - 36$

d) $3x^2 - 48$ **e)** $3x^2 - 11x + 10$ **f)** $x^2 - 6x + 9$

g) $4x^2 - 100$ **h)** $2x^2 + 3x - 20$ **i)** $4x^2 - 15x + 14$

Find Primary Trigonometric Ratios

To determine the primary trigonometric ratios for $\angle A$, determine the length of the third side using the Pythagorean theorem.

$$c^2 = 5^2 - 3^2$$
$$c = \sqrt{16}$$
$$= 4$$

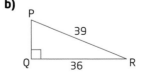

$$\sin A = \frac{\text{opposite}}{\text{hypotenuse}} \qquad \cos A = \frac{\text{adjacent}}{\text{hypotenuse}} \qquad \tan A = \frac{\text{opposite}}{\text{adjacent}}$$

$$= \frac{3}{5} \qquad\qquad\qquad = \frac{4}{5} \qquad\qquad\qquad = \frac{3}{4}$$

1. Find the primary trigonometric ratios for $\angle P$ in each triangle.

a)

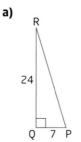

b)

Use a calculator to find the primary trigonometric ratios for any angle. For the angle 25°, sin 25° = 0.4226, cos 25° = 0.0963, and tan 25° = 0.4663, rounded to four decimal places.

2. Use a calculator to find the primary trigonometric ratios for each angle. Round each answer to four decimal places. Be sure your calculator is in degree mode.

a) 58° **b)** 79° **c)** 15°

Finite Differences

Given a table of values where the x-values change in constant steps, it is possible to determine the type of relationship that exists between the variables by calculating finite differences. The first differences are found by subtracting successive y-values. If the first differences are constant, the relationship is linear. If not, calculate the second differences by subtracting successive first differences. If the second differences are constant, the relationship is quadratic. If not, then the relationship is neither linear nor quadratic.

x	y	First Differences
1	−3	
		3 − (−3) = 6
2	3	
		13 − 3 = 10
3	13	
		27 − 13 = 14
4	27	
		45 − 27 = 18
5	45	

The first differences are not constant. So, the relationship is not linear.

x	y	First Differences	Second Differences
1	−3		
		3 − (−3) = 6	
2	3		10 − 6 = 4
		13 − 3 = 10	
3	13		14 − 10 = 4
		27 − 13 = 14	
4	27		18 − 14 = 4
		45 − 27 = 18	
5	45		

The second differences are constant. So, the relationship is quadratic.

1. Use finite differences to determine whether each relationship is linear, quadratic, or neither.

a)

x	y
1	5
2	1
3	−3
4	−7
5	−11

b)

x	y
1	−2
2	2
3	18
4	52
5	110

c)

x	y
1	15
2	28
3	39
4	48
5	55

Graphs and Lines

Graph a linear relation by using
• a table of values
• the slope and the y-intercept
• the intercepts

To graph $y = 2x - 3$, make a table of values by choosing simple values for x and substituting to calculate y.

x	y
0	−3
1	−1
2	1
3	3

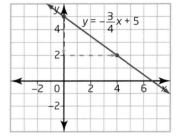

Plot the four points and draw a line through them.

To graph the line $y = -\dfrac{3}{4}x + 5$, use the y-intercept, 5, and the slope, or $\dfrac{\text{rise}}{\text{run}}$, $\dfrac{-3}{4}$.

Start on the y-axis at (0, 5). Then, use the slope to get to another point on the line. Here, counting down 3 and right 4 leads to (4, 2). Then, draw a line through the two points.

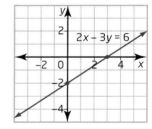

To graph $2x - 3y = 6$, use intercepts.
At the x-intercept, $y = 0$.

$2x - 3(0) = 6$
$2x = 6$
$x = 3$

The x-intercept is 3. A point on the line is (3, 0).

At the y-intercept, $x = 0$.

$2(0) - 3y = 6$
$-3y = 6$
$y = -2$

The y-intercept is −2. A point on the line is (0, −2). Draw a line through the two points.

1. Graph each line using a convenient method.

a) $y = \dfrac{2}{3}x - 4$ **b)** $y = -3x + 6$ **c)** $x + 2y = 8$

d) $5x - 3y = 15$ **e)** $y = -\dfrac{1}{2}x + 5$ **f)** $y = 4x - 7$

To determine the equation of a line when given a graph, identify the
y-intercept and the slope. Then, write the equation in slope y-intercept
form, $y = mx + b$.

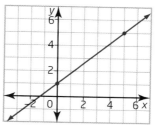

The y-intercept of this line is 1.
The line passes through the point (5, 5).
Starting from the y-intercept, the rise is 4 and
the run is 5.

The slope is $\frac{4}{5}$.

The equation of the line is $y = \frac{4}{5}x + 1$.

If you are given two points that are on the line, determine an equation for
the line by finding the slope and the y-intercept.
Find the slope of the line passing through (3, −6) and (15, 2).

$$m = \frac{2 - (-6)}{15 - 3}$$

$$= \frac{8}{12} \text{ or } \frac{2}{3}$$

Therefore, $y = \frac{2}{3}x + b$.

Substitute the point (3, −6) to solve for b.

$$-6 = \frac{2}{3}(3) + b$$

$$-6 = 2 + b$$

$$b = -8$$

The equation of the line is $y = \frac{2}{3}x - 8$.

2. Determine the equation in the form $y = mx + b$ for each line.

a)

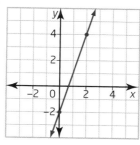

b)

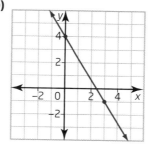

3. Determine the equation in the form $y = mx + b$ for the line that passes
through each pair of points.

a) (1, 9) and (3, 13)   **b)** (3, 1) and (−12, 8)   **c)** (−5, −14) and (10, −5)

Identify Patterns

1. Identify the next three terms in each pattern.

a) Z, ZY, ZYX, ...   **b)** −3, 2, 7, 12, ...   **c)** 3, 9, 27, ...

d) 19, 11, 3, −5, ...   **e)** $\frac{1}{2}, -\frac{2}{3}, \frac{3}{4}, -\frac{4}{5}, ...$ **f)** $54x, 18x^2, 6x^3, ...$

Linear and Exponential Growth

A graph of $y = 25x + 300$ is shown.
The relation is linear.
The y-intercept is 300 and the slope is 25.

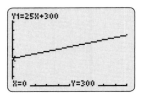

A table of values with first differences shows that the first differences are constant.

x	y	First Differences
0	300	
1	325	325 – 300 = 25
2	350	350 – 325 = 25
3	375	375 – 350 = 25

A graph of $y = 50(1.04)^x$ is shown.
The relationship is exponential.
The y-intercept is 50.

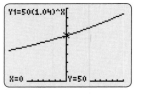

A table of values with first differences, second differences, and common ratios is shown.

x	y	First Differences	Second Differences	Common Ratios
0	50			
1	52	52 – 50 = 2		$\frac{52}{50} = 1.04$
2	54.08	54.08 – 52 = 2.08	2.08 – 2 = 0.08	$\frac{54.08}{52} = 1.04$
3	56.243	56.243 – 54.08 = 2.163	2.163 – 2.08 = 0.083	$\frac{56.243}{54.08} = 1.04$

Successive first and second differences can be obtained by multiplying by 1.04. The common ratios are all equal to 1.04.

1. Graph the relation $y = 30x + 200$.

   a) What kind of relation is this?

   b) Identify the slope and the y-intercept.

   c) Construct a table of values for $x = 0, 1, 2, 3$.

   d) Calculate the first differences and describe their pattern.

2. Graph the relation $y = 25(1.1)^x$.

   a) What type of relation is this?

   b) Identify the y-intercept.

   c) Construct a table of values for $x = 0, 1, 2, 3$.

   d) Calculate the first and second differences and describe any patterns.

   e) Calculate the common ratios of consecutive terms and describe their pattern.

Quadratic Relations

An equation in vertex form $y = a(x - h)^2 + k$ or standard form $y = ax^2 + bx + c$, $a \neq 0$, represents a quadratic relation. The graph of such a relation has a characteristic shape called a parabola.

Given an equation in vertex form, (h, k) represents the coordinates of the parabola's vertex, $x = h$ is the equation of the axis of symmetry, and a represents the vertical stretch factor. If a is positive, the parabola opens upward; if a is negative, the parabola opens downward.

For the quadratic relation $y = -3(x + 2)^2 + 5$, the coordinates of the vertex are $(-2, 5)$ and the axis of symmetry is $x = -2$. The vertical stretch factor is 3 and the parabola opens downward because a is negative.

To determine the y-intercept, substitute $x = 0$.
$$y = -3(0 + 2)^2 + 5$$
$$= -3(4) + 5$$
$$= -7$$
The y-intercept is -7.

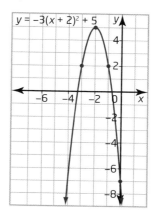

To sketch the graph, plot the vertex $(-2, 5)$. Substitute to find that when $x = -1$, $y = 2$. By symmetry, another point is $(-3, 2)$. Plot the y-intercept. Then, draw a smooth U-shaped curve passing through all four points.

1. For each quadratic relation, state
   i) the coordinates of the vertex
   ii) the equation of the axis of symmetry
   iii) the direction of opening
   iv) the y-intercept

   Then, sketch the graph of the relation.
   a) $y = 2(x - 3)^2 - 8$ **b)** $y = -4(x + 1)^2 + 3$ **c)** $y = 3(x - 5)^2 + 1$

2. Compare the graph of each quadratic function to the graph of $y = x^2$. Identify the direction of opening and state whether the parabola has been vertically stretched or compressed. Justify your answer.
   a) $y = 5x^2$ **b)** $y = -\dfrac{1}{4}(x - 1)^2$ **c)** $y = -3(x + 5)^2 + 2$

To identify the coordinates of the vertex of a quadratic relation using an equation in standard form, change to vertex form by completing the square.

If $a = 1$, then complete the square as described in the second step below.

If a is any number other than 1, then the first step is to factor this from the x-terms.

Write $y = 2x^2 - 12x + 19$ in vertex form as follows.

$y = 2(x^2 - 6x) + 19$ Factor a (i.e., 2) from the first two terms.

$\quad = 2(x^2 - 6x + 9 - 9) + 19$ Divide the coefficient of the x-term by 2 and square the result. This yields 9. Add this number to and subtract it from the expression in brackets.

$\quad = 2(x - 3)^2 + 2(-9) + 19$ Express the perfect square, $x^2 - 6x + 9$, in factored form. Multiply the subtracted value (i.e., 9) by a.

$\quad = 2(x - 3)^2 + 1$ Simplify.

The vertex is $(3, 1)$.

3. Complete the square to express each quadratic relation in the form $y = a(x - h)^2 + k$. Then, state the coordinates of the vertex.

a) $y = x^2 + 4x + 7$ **b)** $y = x^2 - 12x + 3$

c) $y = 3x^2 + 18x - 2$ **d)** $y = -2x^2 + 16x + 9$

Rearrange Formulas

To rearrange a formula to isolate a variable, apply the same steps as for solving an equation.

Solve for a in the formula $I = \dfrac{50d}{a + b}$.

$I = \dfrac{50d}{a + b}$

$I(a + b) = 50d$ Multiply both sides by $a + b$.

$a + b = \dfrac{50d}{I}$ Divide both sides by I.

$a = \dfrac{50d}{I} - b$ Subtract b from both sides.

1. Solve each formula for the variable indicated.

a) $y = -4x + 5$ for x **b)** $P = 2\ell + 2w$ for w **c)** $x^2 + y^2 = r^2$ for y

d) $V = \dfrac{1}{3}\pi r^2 h$ for h **e)** $s = \dfrac{2 - 10e}{t}$ for e **f)** $A = P(1 + rt)$ for r

Solve Equations

To solve $4(x + 2) = x + 5$, expand to remove brackets and then isolate the variable.

$4(x + 2) = x + 5$

$4x + 8 = x + 5$ Expand.

$3x + 8 = 5$ Subtract x from both sides.

$3x = -3$ Subtract 8 from both sides.

$x = -1$ Divide both sides by 3.

To check, substitute -1 for x in the original equation.

L.S. $= 4(x + 2)$ R.S. $= x + 5$

$\quad = 4(-1 + 2)$ $\quad = -1 + 5$

$\quad = 4(1)$ $\quad = 4$

$\quad = 4$

Since L.S. $=$ R.S., the solution is $x = -1$.

To solve $\dfrac{x+5}{2} - \dfrac{x}{3} = 1$, multiply both sides by the least common denominator, 6, to eliminate fractions.

$$\frac{x+5}{2} - \frac{x}{3} = 1$$

$$6 \times \left(\frac{x+5}{2} - \frac{x}{3}\right) = 6$$

$$3(x+5) - 2x = 6$$

$$3x + 15 - 2x = 6$$

$$x + 15 = 6$$

$$x = -9$$

To solve $600(1+i)^5 = 747.72$, first isolate the variable expression in brackets.

$$600(1+i)^5 = 747.72$$

$(1+i)^5 = \dfrac{747.72}{600}$ Divide both sides by 600.

$(1+i)^5 = 1.2462$

$\sqrt[5]{(1+i)^5} = \sqrt[5]{1.2462}$ Take the fifth root of both sides.

$1 + i \doteq 1.0450$ Simplify.

$i \doteq 0.0450$

1. Solve and check.

a) $7x - 5 = 3x - 17$

b) $3x - 7 = 5(x - 3)$

c) $\dfrac{x+1}{3} + \dfrac{x+5}{5} = 4$

d) $\dfrac{x+1}{2} - \dfrac{x-7}{6} = 3$

2. Solve. Round your answers to four decimal places, if necessary.

a) $\dfrac{850}{w-5} = 200$

b) $-6(p-3)^2 = -31.74$

c) $275.38 = 200(1+i)^{10}$

d) $\dfrac{2026.12}{(k+4)^3} = 5$

Solve Equations Involving Rational Expressions

To solve $\dfrac{200}{x} = 10$, isolate x.

$$\frac{200}{x} = 10$$

$200 = 10x$ Multiply both sides by x.

$20 = x$ Divide both sides by 10.

1. Solve.

a) $\dfrac{16}{x} = 8$

b) $\dfrac{a}{5} = 7$

c) $45 = \dfrac{135}{c}$

d) $\dfrac{12}{r} = \dfrac{4}{9}$

e) $\dfrac{k}{20} = \dfrac{3}{8}$

f) $\dfrac{36}{t} = \dfrac{2}{15}$

Solve Linear Systems of Equations

To determine the point of intersection of a linear system, graph the linear relations or solve the system algebraically.

To solve the linear system $y = \frac{4}{5}x$ and $6x - 5y = 10$ by graphing, find the point of intersection of the two lines. First, express the second equation in the form $y = mx + b$.

$$6x - 5y = 10$$
$$-5y = -6x + 10$$
$$y = \frac{6}{5}x - 2$$

Graph each line using the y-intercept and the slope. Then, identify the point of intersection. The point of intersection is $(5, 4)$.

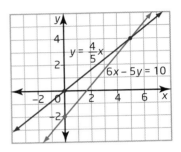

To solve a linear system algebraically, use either the substitution or the elimination method.

Substitution is suitable when one of the variables is easily isolated. The following system is best solved using the elimination method.

$$5x + 2y = 5$$
$$2x + 3y = 13$$

To make the coefficients of the y-terms the same, multiply the first equation by 3 and the second equation by 2. Then, subtract to eliminate y.

$$5x + 2y = 5 \quad ① \times 3 \rightarrow \quad 15x + 6y = 15 \; ③$$
$$2x + 3y = 13 \quad ② \times 2 \rightarrow \quad \underline{4x + 6y = 26 \; ④}$$
$$11x = -11 \; ③ - ④$$
$$x = -1$$

Substitute $x = -1$ in ①.
$$5(-1) + 2y = 5$$
$$2y = 10$$
$$y = 5$$

The point of intersection is $(-1, 5)$.

1. Graph to find the point of intersection of each pair of lines.

a) $y = 3x - 5$
$ y = 2x - 4$

b) $x + y = 1$
$ y = \frac{2}{5}x - 6$

c) $x - 3y - 2 = 0$
$ 2x + y = 4$

2. Solve algebraically to find the point of intersection.

a) $x - 2y = 7$
$ 2x - 3y = 13$

b) $y = 2x - 7$
$ 3x + y = -17$

c) $4x - 7y = 20$
$ x - 3y = 10$

d) $4x - 3y = 8$
$ 6x - 3y = 18$

e) $4x + 3y = -2$
$ 4x + y = -6$

f) $5x - 2y = 20$
$ 2x + 5y = 8$

Use Similar Triangles

In similar triangles, the corresponding angles are equal and the lengths of corresponding sides are proportional.

The triangles shown are similar because all corresponding pairs of angles are equal. Write a proportion involving corresponding sides to solve for the length of side d.

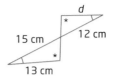

$$\frac{d}{13} = \frac{12}{15}$$

$$d = 13 \times \frac{12}{15}$$

$$d = 10.4$$

The length of side d is 10.4 cm.

1. Use similar triangles to determine the unknown length in each. If necessary, round answers to the nearest tenth.

a)

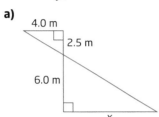

b)

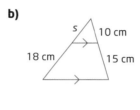

Use the Pythagorean Theorem

The Pythagorean theorem states that, in a right triangle, the square of the length of the hypotenuse is equal to the sum of the squares of the lengths of the other two sides.

To find the length, b, to the nearest tenth, write an equation using the Pythagorean theorem.

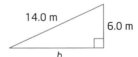

$$b^2 + 6^2 = 14^2$$

$$b^2 + 36 = 196$$

$$b^2 = 160$$

$$b = \sqrt{160}$$

$$b \doteq 12.6$$

The length of side b is 12.6 m, to the nearest tenth of a metre.

1. Determine the measure of the unknown side in each triangle. Round to the nearest tenth, if necessary.

a)

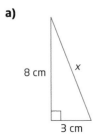

b)

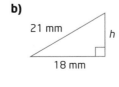

c)

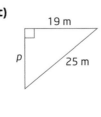

Work With Fractions

To evaluate or simplify expressions involving adding or subtracting fractions, it is best to determine the least common denominator (LCD), which is the same as determining the least common multiple (LCM) of the denominators.

To find the LCM of 24 and 30, write each number in factored form and determine the greatest common factor (GCF).
$$24 = 2 \times 2 \times 2 \times 3$$
$$30 = 2 \times 3 \times 5$$

The GCF is 2×3, or 6. Find the LCM by multiplying the GCF by the other factors of the original numbers.
$$2 \times 3 \times 2 \times 2 \times 5 = 120$$
The LCM is 120.

To find the LCM of $x^2 + x - 12$ and $x^2 - 8x + 15$, factor each expression and determine the GCF.
$$x^2 + x - 12 = (x + 4)(x - 3)$$
$$x^2 - 8x + 15 = (x - 3)(x - 5)$$
The GCF is $(x - 3)$.
The LCM is $(x - 3)(x + 4)(x - 5)$.

To add or subtract rational numbers in fraction form, find the LCM of the denominators, multiply the numerators accordingly to get equivalent fractions, and add or subtract the numerators.

To simplify $\dfrac{3x}{4} + \dfrac{2y}{10}$, first find the LCM of 4 and 10.

$$\dfrac{3x}{4} + \dfrac{2y}{10} = \dfrac{3x \times 5}{4 \times 5} + \dfrac{2y \times 2}{10 \times 2}$$ The LCM is $2 \times 2 \times 5 = 20$. Multiply to write equivalent fractions with denominator 20.

$$= \dfrac{15x}{20} + \dfrac{4y}{20}$$ Simplify.

$$= \dfrac{15x + 4y}{20}$$

1. Determine the LCM of each set.

   a) 24, 40   **b)** $-10x^2,\ 35x,\ -55x^3$ **c)** $x^2 + 7x + 12,\ x^2 - 9$

2. Add or subtract.

   a) $\dfrac{5}{9} + \dfrac{5}{6}$ **b)** $\dfrac{5}{24} - \dfrac{7}{60}$ **c)** $\dfrac{3a}{16} + \dfrac{5b}{36}$ **d)** $\dfrac{4x}{45} - \dfrac{k}{18}$

To simplify $\left(-\dfrac{14}{9}\right)\left(\dfrac{6}{7}\right)$, look for common factors to reduce the fractions.

Then, multiply numerators and multiply denominators.

$$\left(-\dfrac{14}{9}\right)\left(\dfrac{6}{7}\right) = \left(-\dfrac{\overset{2}{\cancel{14}}}{9}\right)\left(\dfrac{\overset{2}{\cancel{6}}}{\cancel{7}_{1}}\right)_{3}$$ Divide by common factors.

$$= -\dfrac{4}{3}$$ Simplify.

To divide, multiply by the reciprocal of the second fraction.

3. Simplify.

a) $\left(\dfrac{8}{15}\right)\left(\dfrac{3}{4}\right)$ 　　**b)** $\left(\dfrac{5}{6}\right)\left(-\dfrac{3}{10}\right)$ 　　**c)** $\dfrac{3}{8} \div \left(-\dfrac{9}{20}\right)$ 　　**d)** $-\dfrac{11}{30} \div \dfrac{33}{9}$

Work With Polynomials

To expand $2(x - 5)(x + 4)$, expand the brackets. Then, multiply by the outside term.

$$
\begin{aligned}
2(x - 5)(x + 4) &= 2(x^2 + 4x - 5x - 20) \\
&= 2(x^2 - x - 20) \qquad \text{Collect like terms.} \\
&= 2x^2 - 2x - 40 \qquad \text{Multiply.}
\end{aligned}
$$

A perfect square trinomial has the general form $a^2 + 2ab + b^2$ and can be expressed in factored form as $(a + b)^2$.

To factor $4x^2 + 20x + 25$, check for the general form.
$4x^2 = (2x)^2$ 　　　　$20x = 2(2x)(5)$ 　　　　$25 = 5^2$
Therefore, $4x^2 + 20x + 25 = (2x + 5)^2$.

1. Expand and simplify.

a) $3(x + 2)(x + 5)$ 　　**b)** $-2(x - 4)(x + 7)$ 　　**c)** $(x - 6)^2$

2. Factor fully.

a) $x^2 + 3x - 10$ 　　**b)** $x^2 + 14x + 49$ 　　**c)** $9y^2 - 25$

d) $3a^2 + 48a + 192$ 　　**e)** $25x^2 - 60x + 36$ 　　**f)** $-p^2 - 20p - 100$

3. What value of k makes each quadratic expression a perfect square trinomial?

a) $x^2 + 16x + k$ 　　**b)** $x^2 - 30x + k$ 　　**c)** $x^2 + 40x + k$

d) $4x^2 + 12x + k$ 　　**e)** $x^2 - 7x + k$ 　　**f)** $9x^2 - 4x + k$

Zero and Negative Exponents

Any base, other than zero, raised to the exponent zero is equal to one.
$3^0 = 1$

A base raised to a negative exponent is equal to the reciprocal of the base raised to the positive value of the exponent.

1. Evaluate.

a) $10^3 \times 10^0$ 　　**b)** 4^{-3} 　　**c)** -7^0

d) 5^{-2} 　　**e)** $(3^{-3})^2$ 　　**f)** $6^4 \times 6^{-3} \times 6^2$

g) $2^3 \div 2^{-2}$ 　　**h)** $2(3^4)^{-1}$ 　　**i)** $\left(\dfrac{2}{3}\right)^{-2}$

2. Simplify. Write your answers using only positive exponents.

a) $3x^{-4}$ 　　**b)** $(5y^{-2})^2$ 　　**c)** $2(3x)^{-3}$

d) $\dfrac{4x^5 y^6}{8x^2 y^8}$ 　　**e)** $\dfrac{(3a^{-4})2b^3}{6ab^{-3}}$ 　　**f)** $\left(\dfrac{4m^3 n^{-2}}{3m^{-4}n}\right)^{-3}$

Technology Appendix

CONTENTS

The Geometer's Sketchpad®, Geometry Software Package

	PAGE
Menu Bar	497
Creating a Sketch	497
Setting Preferences	497
Selecting Points and Objects	498
Hiding Points and Objects	498
Using a Coordinate System and Axes	499
Graphing Relations	499
Plotting Points	500
Finding a Point of Intersection	500
Using the Measure Menu	500
Labelling a Vertex	501
Changing Labels of Measures	502
Using the On-Screen Calculator	502
Using Tabulate to Construct a Data Table	502
Constructing a Slider for a Function	503
Changing the Value of a Parameter	505
Rotating a Terminal Arm About the Origin	505

TI-83 Plus and TI-84 Plus Graphing Calculators

	PAGE
Keys	506
Graphing Relations and Equations	506
Setting Window Variables	507
Setting Up a Table of Values	507
Tracing a Graph	507
Using Zoom	508
Setting the Format	508
Entering Data Into Lists	509
Using List Operations	509
Clearing Lists	509
Calculating First and Second Differences	510
Turning Off All Plots	510
Changing the Appearance of a Line	510
Turning Off an Equation	511
Finding a y-Intercept	511
Finding an Intersection Point	511
Creating a Scatter Plot	512
Turning On the Diagnostic Mode	512
Turning Off the Diagnostic Mode	512
Finding a Curve or a Line of Best Fit	513
Finding a Zero or a Maximum/Minimum Value	513
Finding the Sum of an Arithmetic or Geometric Series	514
Repeating Calculations for Other Scenarios	515
About the Finance Applications: The TVM Solver	515
What the TVM Solver Variables Represent	515
Investments and Loans (No Regular Payments)	516
Ordinary Annuities (Regular Payments)	516

The Geometer's Sketchpad®, Geometry Software Package

Menu Bar

1. **File** menu—open/save/print sketches
2. **Edit** menu—undo/redo actions/ set preferences
3. **Display** menu—control appearance of objects in sketch
4. **Construct** menu—construct new geometric objects based on objects in sketch
5. **Transform** menu—apply geometric transformations to selected objects
6. **Measure** menu—make various measurements on objects in sketch
7. **Graph** menu—create axes and plot measurements and points
8. **Window** menu—manipulate windows
9. **Help** menu—access the help system, an excellent reference guide
10. **Toolbox**—access tools for creating, marking, and transforming points, circles, and straight objects (segments, lines, and rays); also includes text and information tools

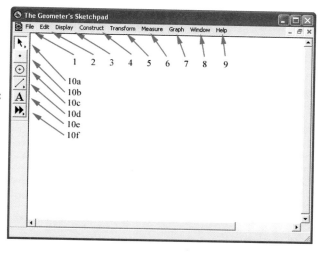

10a **Selection Arrow Tool** (Arrow)—select and transform objects
10b **Point Tool** (Dot)—draw points
10c **Compass Tool** (Circle)—draw circles
10d **Straightedge Tool**—draw line segments, rays, and lines
10e **Text Tool** (Letter A)—label points and write text
10f **Custom Tool** (Double Arrow)—create or use special "custom" tools

Creating a Sketch

- From the **File** menu, choose **New Sketch** to start with a new work area.

Setting Preferences

- From the **Edit** menu, choose **Preferences...**
- Click the **Units** tab.
- Set the units and precision for angles, distances, and calculated values such as slopes and ratios.
- Click the **Text** tab.
- If you check the auto-label box **For All New Points**, then *The Geometer's Sketchpad®* will label points as you create them.
- If you check the auto-label box **As Objects Are Measured**, then *The Geometer's Sketchpad®* will label any measurements that you define.

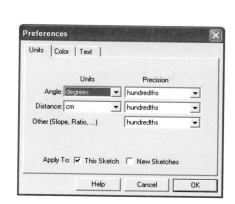

You can also choose whether the auto-labelling functions will apply only to the current sketch, or also to any new sketches that you create.

Be sure to click **OK** to apply your preferences.

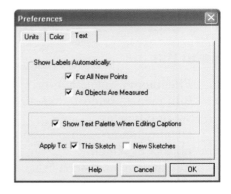

Selecting Points and Objects

- Choose the **Selection Arrow Tool**. The mouse cursor appears as an arrow.

To select a single point:
- Select the point by moving the cursor to the point and clicking it.

The selected point will now appear as a darker point, similar to a bull's-eye ⊙.

To select an object such as a line segment or a circle:
- Move the cursor to a point on the object until it becomes a horizontal arrow.
- Click the object. The object will change appearance to show it is selected.

To select a number of points or objects:
- Select each object in turn by moving the cursor to the object and clicking it.

To deselect a point or an object:
- Move the cursor over it, and then click the left mouse button.
- To deselect all selected objects, click in an open area of the workspace.

Hiding Points and Objects

Open a new sketch. Draw several objects, such as points and line segments.

To hide a point:
- Select the point.
- From the **Display** menu, choose **Hide Point**.

To hide an object:
- Select another point and a line segment.
- From the **Display** menu, choose **Hide Objects**.

Shortcut: You can hide any selected objects by holding down the (CTRL) key and typing H.

You can make hidden objects reappear by choosing **Show All Hidden** from the **Display** menu.

Using a Coordinate System and Axes

- From the **Graph** menu, choose **Show Grid**.

The default coordinate system has an origin point in the centre of your screen and a unit point at (1, 0). Drag the origin to relocate the coordinate system and drag the unit point to change the scale.

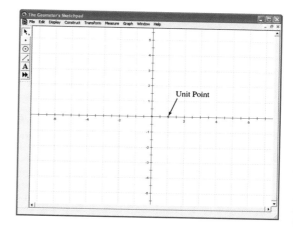

Graphing Relations

Consider the equations $y = 2x^2 - 3$ and $y = 2^{-x}$ as examples.
- From the **Graph** menu, select **Show Grid**.
- From the **Graph** menu, select **Plot New Function…**.

The calculator interface will appear.

Enter the first equation: $2 * x \wedge 2 - 3$.
- Press **OK**. The graph of the first equation appears, along with the equation in function notation. You can move the equation next to the line.

Use the same procedure to graph the second equation.

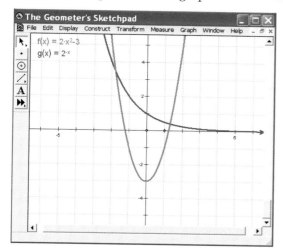

Plotting Points

- From the **Graph** menu, choose **Show Grid**.
- If you want points plotted exactly at grid intersections, also choose **Snap Points**.
- Choose the **Point Tool**.

If you have enabled **Snap Points**, a point will "snap" to the nearest grid intersection as you move the cursor over the grid.

- Click the left mouse button to plot the point.

Alternatively, you can plot points by typing in the desired coordinates.

- From the **Graph** menu, choose **Plot Points...**. A dialogue box will appear. Type the desired x- and y-coordinates in the boxes. Then, press **Plot**.
- When you are finished plotting points, click **Done**.

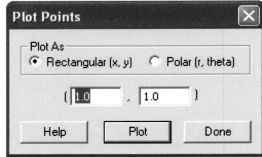

Finding a Point of Intersection

Consider the equations $y = 1400(1 + 0.12x)$ and $y = 2000(1 + 0.06x)$ as examples.

- Turn on the grid, and then plot the graphs of the two equations.
- Use the **Point Tool** to plot two points on each line, such that the intersection lies between the points.
- Select one pair of points on a line. From the **Construct** menu, choose **Segment**. Use the same procedure to construct a segment on the other line.
- Select the two segments. From the **Construct** menu, choose **Intersection**. The point of intersection will appear.
- Select the point of intersection. From the **Measure** menu, choose **Coordinates**. The coordinates of the point of intersection will appear.

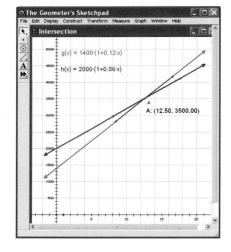

Using the Measure Menu

To measure the distance between two points:
- Ensure that nothing is selected.
- Select the two points.
- From the **Measure** menu, choose **Distance**.

The Geometer's Sketchpad® will display the distance between the points using the units and accuracy selected in **Preferences...** under the **Edit** menu.

To measure the length of a line segment:
- Ensure that nothing is selected.
- Select the line segment (but not the endpoints).
- From the **Measure** menu, choose **Length**.

To measure an angle:
- Ensure that nothing is selected.
- Select the three points that define the angle so that the second point selected is the vertex of the angle.
- From the **Measure** menu, choose **Angle**.

To calculate the ratio of two lengths:
- Select the two lengths to be compared.
- From the **Measure** menu, choose **Ratio**.

To measure the area of a triangle or other closed figure:
- Use the **Straightedge Tool** to draw a triangle.
- Select the points on the vertices of the triangle.
- From the **Construct** menu, choose **Triangle Interior**.
- Select the triangle interior.
- From the **Measure** menu, choose **Area**.

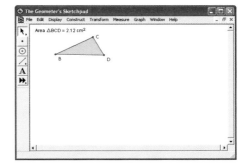

You can construct and measure the area of other closed figures in a similar manner.

To measure the slope of a line, ray, or line segment:
- Select the line, ray, or line segment.
- From the **Measure** menu, choose **Slope**.

Labelling a Vertex

To label a point on a line segment:
- Use the cursor to select the **Text Tool**.
- Move the cursor over the point on the line segment and click once.
- A letter label will appear.
- Move the cursor to the other point on the segment and click once.
- The next letter label in the alphabet will appear.
- If you double-click the point you can input the letter desired.
- Click **OK**.

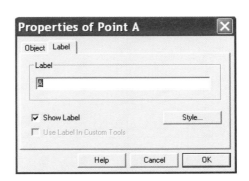

Changing Labels of Measures

- Right-click the measure and choose **Label Measurement** (or **Label Distance Measurement** depending on the type of measure) from the drop-down menu.
- Type in the new label.
- Click **OK**.

Using the On-Screen Calculator

You can use the on-screen calculator to do calculations involving measurements, constants, functions, or other mathematical operations.

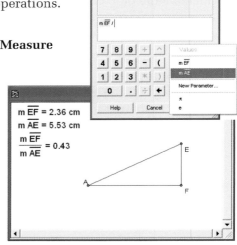

To calculate the sine ratio of two lengths:
- Select the two measures. Then, choose **Calculate** from the **Measure** menu.
- Click the **Values** button and select the first measure.
- Press the (÷) key.
- Click the **Values** button and select the second measure.
- Click **OK** and the ratio will be calculated.

Using Tabulate to Construct a Data Table

- Click the measures in the order that they are to appear in the table. This will highlight them.
- Choose **Graph** and then **Tabulate**.
- The first row of the data table will be completed.
- Select a vertex and manipulate the object.
- Double-click the table to add a row of data.
  Note: The bottom row is always the active row. It changes as you manipulate the object. If you highlight only the table, you can choose the **Graph** menu and select **Add Table Data** to add a row to the table.

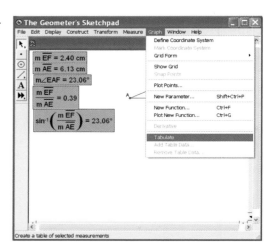

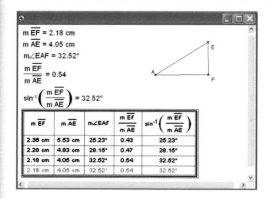

Constructing a Slider for a Function

To construct a slider for a function of the form
$y = a(x + h)^2 + k$:

- Construct a line through two points.
- Use the **Text Tool** to label the points A and B.
- Use the **Point Tool** to create another point on the line between A and B.
- Label the point C.
- Click A, B, and then C, in that order.
- From the **Measure** menu, choose **Ratio**.
- Click the white background to turn off the highlight on the ratio. Click the line and the point B to highlight them.
- Hide the line and point B by holding down the ⌃Ctrl key and pressing H. The points A and C and the ratio measure will remain.
- Construct a line segment from point A to point C.
- Select the **Text Tool** and double-click the ratio measure.
- Change its label to the letter a.

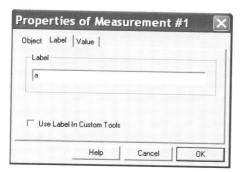

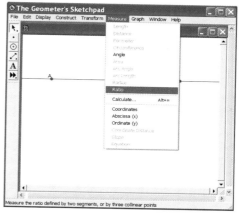

- Click the endpoints of the line segment to hide the letters A and C.
- Click the **Selection Arrow Tool** and click on the white background to turn off the highlighted ratio measure.
- Move the measure of a to the line segment.
- Select the right point and move it. **Note:** The value of a is positive when this point is on the right but negative when it is to the left of the other point.
- Manipulate the slider for the parameter a so that its value is 0.5.
- Select the measure and the slider for parameter a by holding the left mouse button until a rectangle is drawn around the objects as shown on the right.

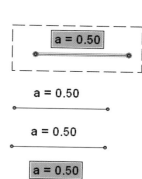

- From the **Edit** menu, choose **Copy**.
- From the **Edit** menu, choose **Paste** to insert a copy of the slider in the document.
- Move the copy below the original.
- From the **Edit** menu, choose **Paste** to insert another copy of the slider in the document.
- Move this copy below the last copy.

- Click the white background to turn off the highlight.
- Select the **Text Tool** and double-click the middle measure of a.
- Change its label to h.
- Click **OK**.
- Double-click the last measure.
- Change its label to k.
- Click **OK**.

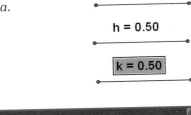

- Click the **Selection Arrow Tool**.
- Move the sliders and their values to the left side of the window.
- From the **Graph** menu, choose **Show Grid**.
- Click each of the measures a, h, and k (not the line segments).
- From the **Graph** menu, choose **Plot New Function**.

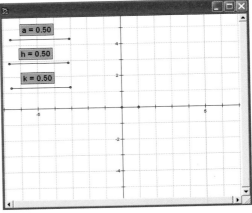

- Click (x) ^ 2 to begin the quadratic equation.
- Use the left arrow key and cursor to the beginning of the expression.
- Click the **Values** button and select the parameter a.
- Insert a multiplication symbol (*) between a and the opening parenthesis.
- Use the right arrow and cursor to the right of x.
- Insert a negative sign (−).
- Click the **Values** button and select the parameter h.
- Use the right arrow key and cursor to the far right of the expression.
- Insert an addition symbol (+).
- Click the **Values** button and select the parameter k.
- Click **OK**. The function will appear highlighted on your sketch.
- From the **Graph** menu, choose **Plot Function**. The graph of the quadratic function will appear.
- Move the right endpoints of the sliders and the values and the graph will change.

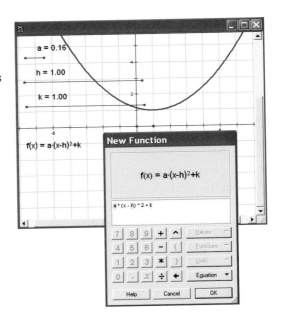

Changing the Value of a Parameter

- From the **Graph** menu, choose **New Parameter**. Set the name as b and its initial value to 3. Click **OK**.
- From the **Graph** menu, choose **Plot New Function**. Click on the parameter b, and then click on ^x and **OK**.
- Click on parameter b and press the (+) and (–) keys on the keyboard to increase or decrease the value of b in unitary increments.
- Right-click on parameter b and choose **Edit Parameter** to enter a specific value.
- Right-click on parameter b and choose **Animate Parameter**. Use the various buttons on the **Motion Controller** to see the effects of changing b continuously.

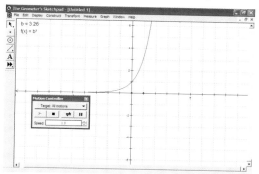

Rotating a Terminal Arm About the Origin

- From the **Graph** menu, choose **Show Grid**.
- Move the cursor to one of the increment numbers on either axis. Then, you can change the scale of both axes by dragging, so that you can create a large unit circle.

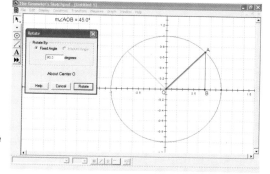

- Use the **Compass Tool** to draw a unit circle with centre (0, 0).
- Draw a line segment from the origin to the unit circle to create a terminal arm and then another one from the origin on the x-axis to create an initial arm that will form a right triangle when joined.
- To create the initial arm, select the x-axis and the point on the unit circle from the terminal arm. From the **Construct** menu, choose **Perpendicular Line**.
- Select the perpendicular line and the x-axis. From the **Construct** menu, choose **Intersection**. Select the origin and the point of intersection. From the **Construct** menu, choose **Segment**. You should now have an initial arm.
- Select the three points, making sure that the origin is your second choice. From the **Measure** menu, choose **Angle**. (Ensure that this is $45°$ by moving the point on the unit circle).
- Select the terminal arm. From the **Transform** menu, choose **Rotate**. Rotating the terminal arm by $90°$ is shown.

TI-83 Plus and TI-84 Plus Graphing Calculators

Keys

The keys on the TI-83 Plus and TI-84 Plus are colour-coded to help you find the various functions.

- The white keys include the number keys, decimal point, and negative sign. When entering negative values, use the white ((-)) key and not the grey (−) key.
- The grey keys on the right side are math operations.
- The grey keys across the top are used when graphing.
- The primary function of each key is printed on the key, in white.
- The secondary function of each key is printed in blue and is activated by pressing the (2nd) key. For example, to find the square root of a number, press (2nd) (x^2) for [√].
- The alpha function of each key is printed in green and is activated by pressing the green (ALPHA) key.

Graphing Relations and Equations

Press (Y=). Enter the equation.
To display the graph, press (GRAPH).

For example, enter $y = 2x^2 - 3x + 1$ by pressing
(Y=) 2 (X, T, θ, n) (x^2) (−) 3 (X, T, θ, n) (+) 1.
Press (GRAPH).

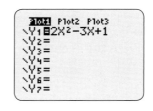

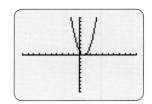

Setting Window Variables

The (WINDOW) key defines the appearance of the graph.
The standard (default) window settings are shown.

To change the window settings:
- Press (WINDOW). Enter the desired window settings.

In the example shown,
- the minimum x-value is -47
- the maximum x-value is 47
- the scale of the x-axis is 10
- the minimum y-value is -31
- the maximum y-value is 31
- the scale of the y-axis is 10
- the resolution is 1, so equations are graphed at each horizontal pixel

Note: The greater the resolution, the faster the graph plots because the horizontal pixels are omitted.

Setting Up a Table of Values

The standard (default) table settings are shown.
This feature allows you to specify the x-values of the table.

To change the **Table Set up** settings:
- Press (2nd) (WINDOW). Enter the desired values.

In the example shown,
- The starting x-value of the table is -5.
- The change in x-values is 0.5.

- Press (2nd) (GRAPH).

The table of values will appear as shown.

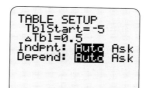
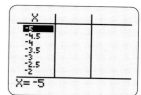

Tracing a Graph

- Enter a function using (Y=).
- Press (TRACE).
- Press (◄) and (►) to move along the graph.

The x- and y-values are displayed at the bottom of the screen.

If you have more than one graph plotted, use the (▲) and (▼) keys to move the cursor to the graph you wish to trace.

You may want to turn off all Stat Plots before you trace a function:
- Press (2nd) (Y=) for [STAT PLOT]. Select **4:PlotsOff**.
- Press (ENTER).

Using Zoom

Use the (ZOOM) key to change the area of the graph that is displayed in the graphing window.

To set the size of the area you want to zoom in on:
- Press (ZOOM). Select **1:ZBox**. The graph screen will be displayed, and the cursor will be flashing.
- If you cannot see the cursor, use the (►), (◄), (▲), and (▼) keys to move the cursor until you see it.
- Move the cursor to an area on the edge of where you would like a closer view.
- Press (ENTER) to mark that point as a starting point.
- Press the (►), (◄), (▲), and (▼) keys, as needed, to move the sides of the box to enclose the area you want to look at.
- Press (ENTER) when you are finished. The area will now appear larger.

To zoom in on an area without identifying a boxed-in-area:
- Press (ZOOM). Select **2:Zoom In**.

To zoom out of an area:
- Press (ZOOM). Select **3:Zoom Out**.

To display the viewing area where the origin appears in the centre and the *x*- and *y*-axes intervals are equally spaced:
- Press (ZOOM). Select **4:ZDecimal**.

To display an equation with the minimum and maximum *y*-values constructed to match the scale of the *x*-axis and without changing the current minimum and maximum *x*-values, so that a square grid results:
- Press (ZOOM). Select **5:ZSquare**.

To reset the axes range on your calculator:
- Press (ZOOM). Select **6:ZStandard**.

To display all data points in a Stat Plot:
- Press (ZOOM). Select **9:ZoomStat**.

To display an equation with the minimum and maximum *y*-values constructed to best show the equation without changing the current minimum and maximum *x*-values:
- Press (ZOOM). Select **0:ZFit**.

Setting the Format

To define a graph's appearance:
- Press (2nd) (ZOOM) for [FORMAT] to view the choices available.

The default settings, shown here, have some of the features on the left turned on.

To use **GridOn**:
- Pressing (2nd) (ZOOM) for [FORMAT].
Cursor down and right to **GridOn**.
- Press (ENTER).
- Press (GRAPH) to see the grid turned on.
- Press (2nd) (MODE) for [QUIT].

Entering Data Into Lists

To enter data:
- Press (STAT). The cursor will highlight the **Edit** menu.
- Press 1 or (ENTER) to select **1:Edit…**.

This allows you to enter new data, or edit existing data, in lists **L1** to **L6**.

For example, press (STAT), select **1:Edit…**, and then enter values in **L1**.
- Use the cursor keys to move around the editor screen.
- Complete each data entry by pressing (ENTER).
- Press (2nd) (MODE) for [QUIT] to exit the list editor when the data are entered.

Using List Operations

You can use a list in the list editor and apply the order of operations to produce another list. This is useful when tabulating data in a list affected by the same order of operations.

For example, for the area of a fenced-in yard:
Width = (120 − 2 × length) ÷ 3
Area = length × width

Use the list operations to compute the width values.
- Press (STAT) 1 to enter the list editor.
- Enter the given lengths into **L1**. For the example given, use 0, 10, 20, 30, 40, 50, 60.
- Press (▶) for **L2**. Cursor up to the title for **L2**.
- Press (( ) 120 (−) 2 (2nd) 1 ( )) (÷) 3 (ENTER).

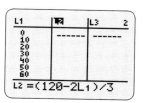

The width data are pasted into **L2**.

Use the list operations to compute the area values.
- Press (▶) for **L3**. Cursor up to the title for **L3**.
- Press (2nd) 1 (×) (2nd) 2 (ENTER).

The area data are pasted into **L3**.

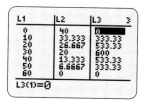

This process is useful when constructing the data for simple and compound interest problems.

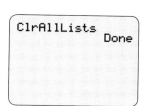

Clearing Lists

To clear all lists from the calculator without resetting the RAM:
- Press (2nd) (+) for [MEM]. Select **4:ClrAllLists**.

This will paste the **ClrAllLists** command to the home screen of the calculator.

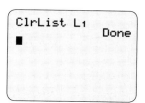

To clear all the lists:
- Press (ENTER).

You may need to clear only a specific list before you enter data into it. For example, to clear list **L1**:
- Press (STAT) and select **4:ClrList**.
- Press (2nd) 1 for [L1] and press (ENTER).

Calculating First and Second Differences

The calculator can compute the first and second differences of a list.
- Press (STAT) then select **1:Edit…**.
- Enter data into **L1**.
- Enter data into **L2**.

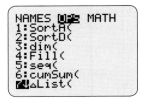

To find the first differences:
- Press (▶) and cursor over to **L3**.
- Press (▲) and cursor up to the title for **L3**.
- Press (2nd) (STAT) for [LIST]. Cursor over to the **OPS** menu. Select **7:Δ List(** to paste the command in the title for **L3**.

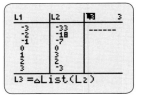

- Press (2nd) 2 ( ) (ENTER) to compute the first differences of **L2**.

To find the second differences:
- Press (▶) and cursor over to **L4**.
- Press (▲) and cursor up to the title for **L4**.
- Press (2nd) (STAT) for [LIST]. Cursor over to the **OPS** menu. Select **7:Δ List(** to paste the command in the title for **L4**.

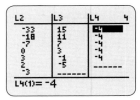

- Press (2nd) 3 ( ) (ENTER) to compute the second differences of **L2** (first differences of **L3**).

Turning Off All Plots

To turn off all the plots without resetting the RAM:
- Press (2nd) (Y=) and select **4:PlotsOff**.
- Press (ENTER).

Changing the Appearance of a Line

The default style is a thin solid line. The line style is displayed to the left of the equation.
There are seven options for the appearance of a line.

Thin line
Thick line
Dotted line
Shade upper
Shade lower
Animate with trace
Animate without trace

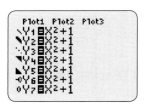

- Press (Y=) and clear any previously entered equations.
  Enter the relation $2x^2 + 2x + 1$ for **Y1**.
  Enter the relation $-3x^2 + 4x - 1$ for **Y2**.
- Press (◀) until the cursor is to the left of **Y2 =**.
- Press (ENTER) repeatedly until the thick solid line shows.
- Press (GRAPH).

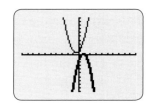

Turning Off an Equation

In the equation editor, move the cursor over the equal sign of the equation of the graph you do not want to display.

- Press (ENTER) to turn off the graph for that equation.

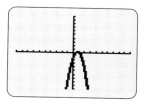

- Press (GRAPH).

Note: Any equation without a highlighted equal sign is turned off and will not be plotted.

Finding a *y*-Intercept

To find the *y*-intercept of a function:
Enter $(2x - 3)(x + 2)$ for **Y1**.
- Press (GRAPH).
- Press (TRACE) 0 (ENTER).

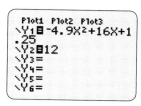

Finding an Intersection Point

There must be at least two equations in the calculator's Equation Editor.
- Press (Y=) and enter the relations for **Y1** and **Y2**.
Be sure to use the appropriate window settings.

- Press (GRAPH).

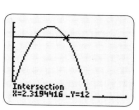

Note: An intersection point *must* be visible in order to find its coordinates. If an intersection point is not visible, adjust the window settings accordingly.

To find an intersection point:
- Press (2nd) (TRACE) and select **5:Intersect**.
- Press (ENTER) (ENTER) (ENTER).

The coordinates of the intersection point will appear at the bottom of the screen.

To find the other intersection point:
- Press (2nd) (TRACE) and select **5:Intersect**.
- Press and hold the (◄) or (►) key to move closer to the other intersection point.
- Press (ENTER) (ENTER) (ENTER).

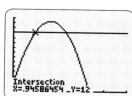

Creating a Scatter Plot

To create a scatter plot:
- Enter the two sets of data in lists **L1** and **L2**.
- Press (2nd)(Y=) for [STATPLOT].
- Press 1 or (ENTER) to select **1:Plot1...**.
- Press (ENTER) to select **On**.
- Cursor down then press (ENTER) to select the top left graphing option, a scatter plot.
- Cursor down to **Xlist** and press (2nd) 1 for [L1].
- Cursor down to **Ylist** and press (2nd) 2 for [L2].
- Cursor down to **Mark** and select a mark style by pressing (ENTER).
- Press (2nd)(MODE) for [QUIT] to exit the Stat Plots editor after you have entered the data.

To display the scatter plot:
- Press (Y=) and use the (CLEAR) key to remove any graphed equations.
- Press (2nd)(MODE) for [QUIT].
- Press (ZOOM) and select **9:ZoomStat** to display the scatter plot for the data in the lists.
- Press (WINDOW) to change **Xscl** and **Yscl** appropriately to place tick marks on both axes if they are not visible.

Turning On the Diagnostic Mode

To turn on the Diagnostic mode:
- Press (2nd) 0 for [CATALOG].
- Press (x^{-1}) for the Ds in the alphabetic list of commands.
- Scroll down to **DiagnosticOn**.
- Press (ENTER) to paste the command to the home screen of the calculator.
- Press (ENTER) to turn on the Diagnostic mode.

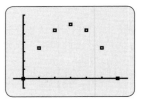

Note: If the diagnostic mode is turned on, you will see the values for r and r^2 for a linear regression and the value of R^2 for a quadratic regression.

Turning Off the Diagnostic Mode

To turn off the Diagnostic mode:
- Press (2nd) 0 for [CATALOG].
- Press (x^{-1}) for the Ds in the alphabetic list of commands.
- Scroll down to **DiagnosticOff**.
- Press (ENTER) to paste the command to the home screen of the calculator.
- Press (ENTER) to turn off the Diagnostic mode.

Finding a Curve or a Line of Best Fit

You can add a curve of best fit to data in the lists by using an appropriate model.

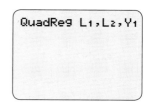

- With the scatter plot displayed, press (STAT) (▶) for the **CALC** menu.
- Select the model that would best represent the data displayed in the scatter plot:
  4:LinReg(ax+b) for a linear regression
  5:QuadReg for a quadratic regression
  0:ExpReg for an exponential regression
  C:SinReg for a sinusoidal regression
- Press (2nd) 1 for **L1** and press (,).
- Press (2nd) 2 for **L2** and press (,).
- Press (VARS) (▶) for the **Y-VARS** menu. Select **1:Function...**, and then select **1:Y1**.
- Press (ENTER) to perform the regression analysis.
- Press (GRAPH) to view the model.

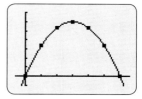

Finding a Zero or a Maximum/Minimum Value

There must be at least one equation in the Equation Editor.
- Press (Y=).
The example shows a parabola.

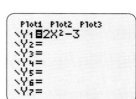

To calculate a zero (*x*-intercept), maximum, or minimum there *must* be one visible.
- Press (GRAPH).

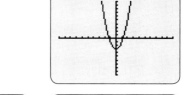

Note: If a zero (*x*-intercept), maximum, or minimum is not visible, adjust the window settings accordingly.

To find a zero:
- Press (2nd) (TRACE) 2.
- Move to the left side of a zero (*x*-intercept) by pressing and holding the left cursor key.
- Press (ENTER).

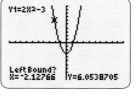

- Move to the right side of a zero (*x*-intercept) by pressing and holding the right cursor key.
- Press (ENTER).

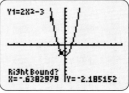

To find the value of a zero (*x*-intercept) using the calculator's guess feature:
- Press (ENTER).
A zero (*x*-intercept) is shown at the bottom of the screen.

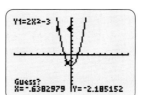

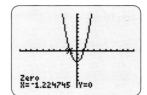

To find a minimum:
- Press (2nd) (TRACE) 3.
- Move to the left side of a minimum by pressing and holding the left cursor key.
- Press (ENTER).

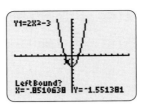
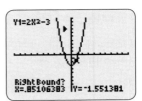

- Move to the right side of a minimum by pressing and holding the right cursor key.
- Press (ENTER).

To find the value of a minimum using the calculator's guess feature:
- Press (ENTER).
A minimum value is shown at the bottom of the screen.

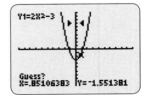

Sometimes the values of x and/or y are not exact because of the method used by the calculator to determine the values. The value for x, shown, is $-1.938E-6$. This means the number is -1.938×10^{-6} in scientific notation. Moving the decimal six places to the left will give the number in standard form ($-0.000\ 001\ 938$). In this case, assume that the x-value of the minimum is 0 rather than $-0.000\ 001\ 938$.

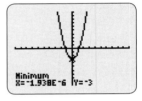

To find a maximum:
- Press (2nd) (TRACE) 4. Follow a similar procedure as above.

Finding the Sum of an Arithmetic or Geometric Series

Start by listing the first ten terms and storing them **L1**.
- Press (2nd) (STAT) for [LIST] and cursor over to the **OPS** menu.
For an arithmetic series, such as one with $a = 2$, $d = 4$, to find S_{10}:
- Select **5:seq(** and enter $2 + (x - 1) \times 4$, x, 1, 10, 1).
For a geometric series, such as one with $a = 2$, $r = -3$, to find S_{10}:
- Select **5:seq(** and enter $20 \times (-3)^{x-1}$, x, 1, 10, 1).
- Press (STO►), (2nd) 1 for [L1], (ENTER).

Now determine the sum.
- Press (2nd) (STAT) [LIST] and cursor over to the **MATH** menu.
- Select **5:sum(** and enter **L1**).
- Press (ENTER).

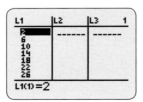

Repeating Calculations for Other Scenarios

- Press $\boxed{\text{2nd}}$ $\boxed{\text{ENTER}}$ for [ENTRY] to recall the previous calculation.
  Use the cursor keys, the $\boxed{\text{DEL}}$ key, and the [INS] command to modify the equation to fit each scenario.
- Press $\boxed{\text{ENTER}}$ to perform the new calculation.
  In the example shown, press $\boxed{\text{2nd}}$ $\boxed{\text{ENTER}}$ for [ENTRY] twice to see the first calculation again, and then alter the amount, 2600.

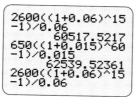

About the Finance Applications: The TVM Solver

The **TVM Solver** is used to work with annuities (for example, loans and investments with regular payments, and mortgages) and can also be used for non-annuities (for example, loans or investments with no regular payments). **TVM** stands for **T**ime **V**alue of **M**oney.

To open the TVM Solver:

- On the TI-83 Plus/TI-84 Plus, press $\boxed{\text{APPS}}$ 1 and 1.

What the TVM Solver Variables Represent

When There Are Regular Payments (Ordinary Annuities and Mortgages)

N	Number of Payments
I%	Annual Interest Rate
PV	Present Value
PMT	Payment
FV	Future Value
P/Y	Number of Payments/Year
C/Y	Number of Compounding Periods/Year
PMT: END BEGIN	Payments at End of Payment Interval

```
N=12.00
I%=7.00
PV=0.00
PMT=-200.00
•FV=2645.02
P/Y=4.00
C/Y=4.00
PMT:END BEGIN
```

A savings annuity invested at 7%, compounded quarterly, with quarterly deposits of $200, for 3 years has a future value of $2645.02.

When There Are No Regular Payments

N	Number of Years
I%	Annual Interest Rate
PV	Present Value, or Principal
PMT	Always set **PMT=0.00**.
FV	Future Value, or Final Amount
P/Y	Always set **P/Y=1.00**.
C/Y	Number of Compounding Periods/Year
PMT: END BEGIN	END or BEGIN

```
N=7.00
I%=5.00
PV=-1000.00
PMT=0.00
•FV=1418.04
P/Y=1.00
C/Y=12.00
PMT:END BEGIN
```

$1000 invested at 5%, compounded monthly, for 7 years has a future value of $1418.04.

Investments and Loans (No Regular Payments)

Final Amount If you know the principal, or present value, interest rate, compounding frequency, and term of an investment or loan, you can determine its final amount.

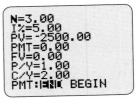

For example, to determine the final amount of a **$2500** investment earning 5% interest, **compounded semi-annually**, for **3 years**, follow these steps:

Open the **TVM Solver** and enter the values as shown:

To solve for **FV**, cursor to **FV=0.00** and press (ALPHA) (ENTER).

Term is 3 years.
Annual interest rate is 5%.
Principal is $2500.
Final amount is unknown.
2 compounding periods/year

Present Value, or Principal If you know the final amount, interest rate, compounding frequency, and term of an investment or loan, you can determine its present value, or principal.

Open the **TVM Solver** and enter the known values.
To solve for **PV**, cursor to **PV=0.00** and press (ALPHA) (ENTER).

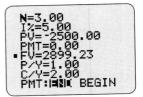

The final amount is $2899.23.

Interest Rate To find the annual interest rate, enter the known values for **N**, **PV**, **FV**, and **C/Y**. Set **I%=0.00**, **PMT=0.00**, and **P/Y=1.00**. Then, cursor to **I%=0.00** and press (ALPHA) (ENTER).

Term To find the term, in years, enter the known values for **I%**, **PV**, **FV**, and **C/Y**. Set **N=0.00**, **PMT=0.00**, and **P/Y=1.00**. Then, cursor to **N=0.00** and press (ALPHA) (ENTER).

Important Points About the TVM Solver
- Set the number of decimal places to 2.
- A value must be entered for each variable.
- Money paid out (cash outflow), such as a loan payment, is negative.
- Money received (cash inflow), such as the final amount of an investment, is positive.
- To quit the **TVM Solver** and return to the Home Screen, press (2nd) (MODE).

Ordinary Annuities (Regular Payments)

Future Value Enter the known values for **N**, **I%**, **PMT**, **P/Y**, and **C/Y** and set **PV = 0.00**, **FV = 0.00**, and **PMT:END**. Then, cursor to **FV = 0.00** and press (ALPHA) (ENTER).

Present Value Enter the know values for **N**, **I%**, **PMT**, **P/Y**, and **C/Y** and set **PV = 0.00**, **FV = 0.00**, and **PMT:END**. Then, cursor to **PV = 0.00** and press (ALPHA) (ENTER).

Payment To find the payment given the present value or the future value, enter the known values for **N**, **I%**, **PV** or **FV**, **P/Y**, and **C/Y** and set **PV = 0.00** or **FV = 0.00**, and **PMT:END**. Then, cursor to **PMT = 0.00** and press (ALPHA) (ENTER).

Answers

Chapter 1

Prerequisite Skills, pages 2–3

1. a)

b)

c)

d)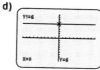

2. a) $y = 2x - 3$ **b)** $y = -\frac{1}{3}x + 2$

3. a) $y = -\frac{5}{4}x + 8$ **b)** $y = -3x + 4$

c) $y = \frac{5}{4}x - 6$

4. a) $(-1, 2)$ **b)** $(4, -3)$ **c)** $(2, 2)$

5. a) $(1, 8)$ **b)** $(5, 9)$ **c)** $(5, -1)$

6. a) $x^2 + 4x + 4$ **b)** $n^2 - 9$

c) $\frac{1}{2}t^2 - 4t + 8$ **d)** $3x^2 + 3x - 18$

e) $4k^2 - 4$ **f)** $4x^2 + \frac{14}{3}x - 2$

7. a) $(x + 5)(x - 3)$ **b)** $(x + 3)^2$

c) $(3n + 5)(3n - 5)$ **d)** $-(x + 4)(x - 3)$

e) $3(t + 1)^2$ **f)** $-5(x - 4)^2$

8. a) no   **b)** yes; $(x - 6)^2$

c) no   **d)** no

e) yes; $(x + 2)^2$ **f)** yes; $(2n + 3)^2$

9. a) 16   **b)** 25   **c)** 1   **d)** 49

e) $\frac{25}{4}$ **f)** $\frac{121}{4}$ **g)** $\frac{1}{4}$ **h)** $\frac{9}{4}$

10. a) $\frac{1}{2}(x^2 - 3x)$ **b)** $\frac{2}{3}\left(x^2 + \frac{15}{2}x\right)$

c) $-\frac{1}{5}(x^2 + 10x)$ **d)** $-\frac{3}{4}(x^2 - 12x)$

11. a) i) $(-1, -3)$ **ii)** $x = -1$

   iii) upward   **iv)** -1

b) i) $(3, 1)$ **ii)** $x = 3$

   iii) downward   **iv)** -14

12. a) $y = -(x - 2)^2 + 3$ **b)** $y = (x + 5)^2 - 1$

13. a) $y = (x + 2)^2 - 3; (-2, -3)$

b) $y = (x - 5)^2 - 30; (5, -30)$

14. a) The graph of $y = (x + 5)^2 + 2$ is the graph of $y = (x + 5)^2$ translated vertically up 2 units.

b) The graph of $y = x^2 - 4x$ is the graph of $y = x^2 - 4x + 3$ translated vertically down 3 units.

15. a)

b)

1.1 Functions, Domain, and Range, pages 12–15

1. a) This relation is a function. No vertical line can be drawn that will pass through more than one point on the line.

b) This relation is a function. No vertical line can be drawn that will pass through more than one point on the line.

c) This relation is a function. No vertical line can be drawn that will pass through more than one point on the line.

d) This relation is not a function. An infinite number of vertical lines can be drawn that will pass through more than one point on the curve.

2. a) This relation is a function. No vertical line can be drawn that will pass through more than one point on the line.

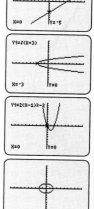

b) This relation is not a function. An infinite number of vertical lines can be drawn that will pass through more than one point on the curve.

c) This relation is a function. No vertical line can be drawn that will pass through more than one point on the line.

d) This relation is not a function. An infinite number of vertical lines can be drawn that will pass through more than one point on the circle.

3. a) domain {5, 6, 7, 8, 9}, range {5, 6, 7, 8, 9}; this relation is a function because for each value in the domain there is exactly one value in the range.

b) domain {3, 4, 5, 6}, range {−1}; this relation is a function because for each value in the domain there is exactly one value in the range.

c) domain {1}, range {−14, −8, 0, 6, 11}; this relation is not a function. The x-value 1 has five corresponding y-values.

d) domain {1, 3, 4, 5, 11}, range {1, 4, 5, 9,11}; this relation is a function because for each value in the domain there is exactly one value in the range.

e) domain {1, 2, 3}, range {−2, −1, 0, 1, 2}; this relation is not a function. The x-values 2 and 3 have two corresponding y-values.

4. a) This relation is a function because for each value in the domain there is exactly one value in the range.

b) This relation is a function because for each value in the domain there is exactly one value in the range.

c) This relation is not a function. The domain has three elements but the range has five elements. So one or more values in the domain must be associated with two values in the range.

d) This relation is not a function. The domain has one element but the range has five elements. So one value in the domain must be associated with every value in the range.

5. a) domain $\{x \in \mathbb{R}\}$, range $\{y \in \mathbb{R}\}$
  b) domain $\{x \in \mathbb{R}\}$, range $\{y \in \mathbb{R}, y \geq 0\}$
  c) domain $\{x \in \mathbb{R}, x \geq 0\}$, range $\{y \in \mathbb{R}\}$
  d) domain $\{x \in \mathbb{R}\}$, range $\{y \in \mathbb{R}, y \leq -1\}$
  e) domain $\{x \in \mathbb{R}, x \neq 3\}$, range $\{y \in \mathbb{R}, y \neq 0\}$

6. a) domain $\{x \in \mathbb{R}\}$, range $\{y \in \mathbb{R}\}$
  b) domain $\{x \in \mathbb{R}\}$, range $\{y \in \mathbb{R}, y \geq -4\}$
  c) domain $\{x \in \mathbb{R}\}$, range $\{y \in \mathbb{R}, y \leq 1\}$
  d) domain $\{x \in \mathbb{R}, -3 \leq x \leq 3\}$; range $\{y \in \mathbb{R}, -3 \leq y \leq 3\}$
  e) domain $\{x \in \mathbb{R}, x \neq -3\}$, range $\{y \in \mathbb{R}, y \neq 0\}$
  f) domain $\{x \in \mathbb{R}, x \geq -0.5\}$, range $\{y \in \mathbb{R}, y \geq 0\}$

7. Answers may vary.

8. a) $A = -2x^2 + 45x$
  b) domain $\{0 < x < 22.5\}$, range $\{0 < A < 253.125\}$

9. a) This relation is a function because for each value in the domain there is exactly one value in the range.
  Independent variable: the number of raffle tickets that a hockey team sells; dependent variable: the amount of money taken in.
  b) This relation is not a function. For any grade level, there may be students of different age levels.
  c) This relation is a function because for each value in the domain there is exactly one value in the range.
  Independent variable: the speed at which Jung Yoo walks; dependent variable: the time it takes Jung Yoo to walk to school

10. Answers may vary. Sample answers:
  a) The fourteen 3-m sections of preassembled fencing can be assembled so that the length is 12 m and the width is 9 m. This will give an area of 108 m² for the parking lot.
  b) Since the sections are 3 m in length, the sections can be assembled to give an area of 12 m by 9 m. The greatest area that can be enclosed with 42 m of fencing will occur when the width of the area is 10.5 m and the length of the area of is 10.5 m. The greatest area is 110.25 m².

11. a) range $\{0, 6, 12, 18, 24\}$ **b)** range $\{-3, 0, 5, 12, 21\}$
  c) range $\{3\}$ **d)** range $\{-1, 1, 7, 17, 31\}$
  e) range $\left\{\frac{1}{7}, \frac{1}{6}, \frac{1}{5}, \frac{1}{4}, \frac{1}{3}\right\}$
  f) range $\left\{-2\sqrt{6}, -\sqrt{21}, -4, -3, 0, 3, 4, \sqrt{21}, 2\sqrt{6}\right\}$

12. a)

b)

c) Answers may vary. Sample answers: The relation $x = y^2 - 3$ can be defined using the relations $y = \sqrt{x + 3}$ and $y = -\sqrt{x + 3}$.
  d) The x-values 6, 1, and -2 each have two corresponding y-values.

13. Answers may vary.

14. Answers may vary. Sample answers:
  a) A single point on a graph has one entry in the domain and one entry in the range.
  b) A vertical line on a graph has one entry in the domain and many entries in the range.
  c) A horizontal line on a graph has many entries in the domain and one entry in the range.

15. Answers may vary. Sample answers:
  a) $y = -x^2 + 5$ **b)** $x^2 + y^2 = 9$

16. a) $P = 0.002s + 400$:
  domain $\{x \in \mathbb{R}, 0 \leq x \leq 100\,000\}$,
  range $\{y \in \mathbb{R}, 400 \leq y < 600\}$.
  $P = 0.0025s + 400$;
  domain $\{x \in \mathbb{R}, x \geq 100\,000\}$,
  range $\{y \in \mathbb{R}, y \geq 650\}$
  b) Both relations are functions because for each value in the domain there is exactly one value in the range.

c)

 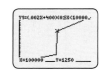

d) Answers may vary. Sample answer: At $s = 100\,000$, there is a jump discontinuity on the graph. At this number of sales, the weekly earnings for the salesperson increase from less than $600 per week to $1250 per week, and for sales greater than $100\,000, the salesperson's earnings will increase more rapidly than for sales less than $100\,000.

17. Answers may vary. Sample answer: Yes. The function $y = (x + 2)^2 + 5$ has domain $\{x \in \mathbb{R}\}$ and range $\{y \in \mathbb{R}, y \geq 5\}$. The function $y = (x - 2)^2 + 5$ has domain $\{x \in \mathbb{R}\}$ and range $\{y \in \mathbb{R}, y \geq 5\}$. The domain and range of both functions are the same.

18. a) domain $\{\theta \in \mathbb{R}\}$, range $\{y \in \mathbb{R}, 1 \leq y \leq 5\}$; the relation is a function.
  b) domain $\{x \in \mathbb{R}, -5 \leq x \leq 5\}$, range $\{y \in \mathbb{R}, -4 \leq y \leq 4\}$; the relation is not a function.

19. $\{x \in \mathbb{R}, 3 \le x < 5\}$

20. \$160

21. 48 factors

22. $-2 < x < 2$

1.2 Functions and Function Notation, pages 21–24

1. a) $\frac{63}{5}$, 9, $\frac{161}{15}$ **b)** 57, 66, 1   **c)** 128, 2, $\frac{200}{9}$

d) $-6, -6, -6$ **e)** $\frac{1}{4}, -\frac{1}{5}, -\frac{3}{2}$ **f)** $3, 0, \sqrt{\dfrac{13}{3}}$

2. a) 4   **b)** 0

 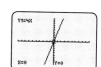

c) -4 **d)** -1

 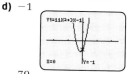

e) -6 **f)** $\frac{70}{3}$

 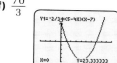

3. a) $-4; y = -4x$ **b)** $3; y = 3x$

c) $\frac{2}{3}; y = \frac{2}{3}x$ **d)** $-1; y = -x$

4. Answers will vary. For example: An example of a linear function is $y = 2x + 3$ and an example of a constant function is $y = 2$. The functions have the same domains $\{x \in \mathbb{R}\}$, but different ranges. For the function $y = 2x + 3$ the range is $\{y \in \mathbb{R}\}$ and for the function $y = 2$ the range is $\{y \in \mathbb{R}, y = 2\}$.

5. a)   **b)**

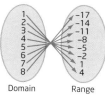 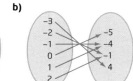

c)   **d)**

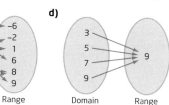

6. a) This relation is a function because for each value in the domain there is exactly one value in the range.

b) This relation is a function because for each value in the domain there is exactly one value in the range.

c) This relation is not a function. The x-value -5 has two corresponding y-values.

d) This relation is a function because for each value in the domain there is exactly one value in the range.

7. a) $\{(1, 1), (2, 4), (3, 9), (4, 16)\}$

b) $\{(-5, 11), (-4, 6), (-2, -4), (0, -14), (2, -24)\}$

c) $\{(-4, 6), (3, 6), (1, 6), (5, 6)\}$

8. a) This relation is a function because for each value in the domain there is exactly one value in the range.

b) This relation is a function because for each value in the domain there is exactly one value in the range.

c) This relation is a function because for each value in the domain there is exactly one value in the range.

9. Answers may vary. Sample answer: Mapping diagrams are visual representations of relations that are sets of ordered pairs. For visual learners, it may be easier to determine if a relation that is represented by a mapping diagram is a function by determining if there is exactly one arrow leading from each value in the domain.

10. a) $f : x \to -x + 4$ **b)** $g : x \to x^2 + 5x - 3$

c) $s : x \to \sqrt{4x - 4}$ **d)** $r : k \to -\dfrac{1}{2k - 1}$

11. Answers may vary. Sample answer: A relation is a function if for each value in the domain there is exactly one value in the range. In a mapping diagram a relation is a function if there is exactly one arrow leading from each value in the domain.

12. a)   **b)**

 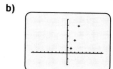

c) $y = 3x^2 - 2x + 3$

d)

13. a)

b) Answers may vary. Sample answer: This relation is a function because for each value in the domain there is exactly one value in the range.

c) Answers may vary. Sample answer: Yes. For each value in the domain there is exactly one value in the range.

14. a) domain $\{d \in \mathbb{R}, d \geq 0\}$, range $\{v \in \mathbb{R}, v \geq 0\}$

b)

15. a) $24 000   **b) i)** $3090.90   **ii)** $2769.12

c) 22 years

d) Answers may vary. Sample answer: The relation is a function because for each value in the domain there is exactly one value in the range.

16. a) domain $\{i \in \mathbb{R}, i \neq -1\}$, range $\{A \in \mathbb{R}, 0 \leq A \leq 100\}$

b)   **c)** $95.24   **d)** 11.1%

17.–18. Answers may vary.

19.

Rating, r Age, n	1	2	3	4	5
40	570	560	550	540	530
41	572	562	552	542	532
42	574	564	554	544	534
43	576	566	556	546	536
44	578	568	558	548	538
45	580	570	560	550	540

21. a) domain $\{d \in \mathbb{R}, d \geq 0\}$, range $\{v \in \mathbb{R}, v \geq 8\}$

b)

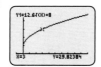

c) Answers may vary. Sample answer: This relation is a function because for each value in the domain there is exactly one value in the range.

22. D   **23.** 65   **24.** C

1.3 Maximum or Minimum of a Quadratic Function, pages 31–32

1. a) $y = (x + 2)^2 - 4$ **b)** $f(x) = \left(x + \dfrac{7}{2}\right)^2 - \dfrac{5}{4}$

c) $g(x) = \left(x - \dfrac{3}{2}\right)^2 - \dfrac{5}{4}$ **d)** $y = \left(x - \dfrac{11}{2}\right)^2 - \dfrac{137}{4}$

e) $f(x) = \left(x + \dfrac{13}{2}\right)^2 - \dfrac{161}{4}$ **f)** $y = \left(x - \dfrac{9}{2}\right)^2 - \dfrac{117}{4}$

2. a) $(-5, -19)$; minimum   **b)** $(-3, -2)$; minimum

c) $(1, 4)$; maximum   **d)** $(6, 31)$; maximum

e) $(-1, 2)$; maximum   **f)** $\left(-4, -\dfrac{7}{3}\right)$; minimum

3. a) $(1, 8)$; minimum   **b)** $(2, 5)$; maximum

c) $\left(3, \dfrac{7}{2}\right)$; minimum   **d)** $\left(\dfrac{3}{2}, -\dfrac{25}{4}\right)$; maximum

e) $\left(5, -\dfrac{3}{2}\right)$; minimum   **f)** $\left(-7, \dfrac{22}{5}\right)$; maximum

4. Answers may vary.

5. $1000

6. 130

7. 2.4 m

8. 83 km/h

9. 12 m by 6 m

10. short side 5 m, longer side 10 m

11. 25

12. a) domain $\{n \in \mathbb{R}, 0 \leq n \leq 60\}$; range $\{e \in \mathbb{R}, 0 \leq e \leq 10\}$

b) vertex: $(30, 10)$; maximum; Answers may vary. For example: The graph is a parabola opening downward, so the vertex is a maximum.

c) Answers may vary. For example: the maximum effectiveness of a TV commercial will occur after 30 viewings.

d)

13. Answers may vary. Sample answers:

a) $y = 2x^2 + 4x$ $y = 2x^2 + 2x$

$y = 2x^2$ $y = 2x^2 - 2x$

$y = 2x^2 - 4x$

b) The five parabolas are congruent and they all open upward.

c) $(-1, -2)$; $(-0.5, -0.5)$; $(0, 0)$; $(0.5, -0.5)$; $(1, -2)$

d) The x-coordinate of each vertex is the value of b multiplied by $-\dfrac{1}{4}$.

14. 7.5 cm

15. Answers may vary.

16. C   **17.** C   **18.** B

1.4 Skills You Need: Working With Radicals, pages 39–40

1. a) $12\sqrt{5}$ b) $5\sqrt{6}$ c) $-2\sqrt{35}$
   d) $-20\sqrt{15}$ e) $6\sqrt{6}$ f) $6\sqrt{22}$

2. a) $2\sqrt{3}$ b) $11\sqrt{2}$ c) $7\sqrt{3}$
   d) $2\sqrt{5}$ e) $6\sqrt{7}$ f) $14\sqrt{2}$

3. a) $\sqrt{3}$ b) $-4\sqrt{5}$ c) 0
   d) $5\sqrt{2} - 4\sqrt{5}$ e) $4\sqrt{6} - 5\sqrt{2}$ f) $-3\sqrt{10} + \sqrt{5}$

4. a) $4\sqrt{2}$ b) $37\sqrt{2}$ c) $-3\sqrt{5} - 6\sqrt{3}$
   d) $9\sqrt{7} + 8\sqrt{6}$ e) $14\sqrt{3} - 4\sqrt{2}$ f) $5\sqrt{11} + 5\sqrt{22}$

5. a) $30\sqrt{2}$ b) $-16\sqrt{7}$ c) $40\sqrt{2}$
   d) $-18\sqrt{5}$ e) $55\sqrt{6}$ f) -24

6. a) $24 - 3\sqrt{5}$ b) $5\sqrt{6} + 12$ c) $3\sqrt{2} - 3$
   d) $-8\sqrt{5} - 20$ e) $64 + 48\sqrt{6}$ f) $6\sqrt{21} - 15\sqrt{6}$

7. a) $27 + 10\sqrt{2}$ b) $-12 - 4\sqrt{2}$
   c) $5\sqrt{3} + 5\sqrt{6} + 10\sqrt{2} + 20$
   d) $-5 - 7\sqrt{5}$ e) -4 f) $-17 + \sqrt{7}$

8. a) $-\dfrac{1}{2}\sqrt{6}$ b) $2\sqrt{5}$ c) $2\sqrt{2}$
   d) $\sqrt{5} - 4\sqrt{3}$

9. a) $3\sqrt{2}$ b) $60\sqrt{2}$ c) 45   d) 2π

10. Answers may vary. Sample answer:
    $\sqrt{2880} = \sqrt{576 \times 5} = \sqrt{576} \times \sqrt{5} = 24\sqrt{5}$.

11. $15\sqrt{3}$ cm

12. 100

13. area: $12\sqrt{7}$ cm²; perimeter: $12 + 4\sqrt{7}$ cm

14. Answers may vary.

15. a) Answers may vary. Sample answer: Yes.
    $1 + \sqrt{3}$ is a solution to the equation
    $x^2 - 2x - 2 = 0$. Substitute $1 + \sqrt{3}$ for x in the
    left side of the equation. Then,
    $$\left(1 + \sqrt{3}\right)^2 - 2\left(1 + \sqrt{3}\right) - 2$$
    $$= 1 + 2\sqrt{3} + 3 - 2 - 2\sqrt{3} - 2$$
    $$= 0$$

16. a) $2 + 3\sqrt{5}$ b) $3 - \sqrt{6}$ c) $\sqrt{7}$
    d) $3 - \sqrt{3}$ e) $-2 + \sqrt{2}$

17. a) $3\sqrt[3]{2}$ b) $10\sqrt[3]{3}$ c) $5\sqrt[3]{9}$

18. Explanations may vary.
    a) $\sqrt{a} < a$ for $\{a \in \mathbb{R}, a > 1\}$.
    b) $\sqrt{a} > a$ for $\{a \in \mathbb{R}, 0 < a < 1\}$.

19. D   20. C   21. C   22. 1

1.5 Solve Quadratic Equations, pages 49–51

1. a) $-3, 1$ b) $-5, 2$ c) $-3, 3$
   d) $\dfrac{4}{3}, 1$ e) $\dfrac{1}{5}, \dfrac{1}{3}$ f) $-\dfrac{5}{2}, -\dfrac{2}{3}$

2. Answers may vary.

3. a) $\dfrac{17 \pm \sqrt{73}}{4}$ b) $\dfrac{3 \pm \sqrt{137}}{8}$
   c) $\dfrac{-1 \pm \sqrt{29}}{2}$ d) $-3 \pm \sqrt{13}$

e) $\dfrac{-1 \pm \sqrt{133}}{6}$ f) $4 \pm \sqrt{14}$

4. a) no real roots   b) one root
   c) two roots   d) two roots

5. a) $\dfrac{-3 - \sqrt{57}}{12}, \dfrac{-3 + \sqrt{57}}{12}$
   b) $6 - 2\sqrt{3}, 6 + 2\sqrt{3}$
   c) $-2, \dfrac{14}{3}$ d) 4

6. a) two distinct real roots
   b) two equal real roots
   c) no real roots
   d) two distinct real roots

7. Answers may vary. Sample answers:
   a) factor; $-\dfrac{3}{2}, 4$ b) factor; ± 5
   c) quadratic formula, complete the square,
      graphing calculator; $\dfrac{-3 \pm \sqrt{17}}{4}$
   d) factor; $-8, 0$
   e) quadratic formula, complete the square,
      graphing calculator; no solution
   f) factor; 2
   g) quadratic formula, graphing calculator;
      $\dfrac{3.7 \pm \sqrt{19.39}}{1.14}$
   h) factor; $\dfrac{4}{3}$

8. a) $k = -6, k = 6$ b) $k < -6, k > 6$

9. a)   b)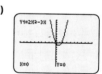

   c)

   d) $-1.1, 2.6$ e) $\dfrac{3 - \sqrt{57}}{4}, \dfrac{3 + \sqrt{57}}{4}$

10. Answers may vary.

11. a) $-8, 8, -7, 7, -13, 13$ b) $-7, 7, -2, 2$
    c) Answers may vary. Sample answer: if k can be
       factored as $k = ab$, where $a + b = -3$, then the
       equation can be solved
       $k = -2, 0, 4, 10, 18, 24, 28, 40, 54, 70, 88, 108, \ldots$

12. 4.1 s

13. a) 64.0 km/h   b) 95.2 km/h   c) 115.5 km/h

14. a) 10 m   b) 8.7 m

15. width: 3.6 m; length: 5.6 m

16. 23.0 m

17. 6 m

18. 1413 km

19. a) Yes. The stock will reach this volume at
    16.3 weeks and 33.7 weeks.

b) No. The stock will not reach a volume of 400 000 shares.

20. a) $x = -26$, $x = -24$; two distinct real roots

b) $x = -25$, $x = -25$; one double real root

c) no real roots

22. Answers may vary.

23. edge length: 10.1 cm; volume: 1030.3 cm³

24. a) 3.7 m   **b)** 20.6 m²

25. B

26. A

27. $\text{Area}_{\text{KROQ}} = \frac{1}{4} \text{Area}_{\text{MNOP}}$

1.6 Determine a Quadratic Equation Given Its Roots, pages 57–59

1. a) $f(x) = a(x + 6)(x - 3)$

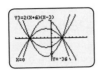

b) $f(x) = a(x + 1)(x + 1)$

c) $f(x) = a(x + 4)(x + 3)$

2. a) $f(x) = a(x^2 + 3x - 18)$

b) $f(x) = a(x^2 + 2x + 1)$

c) $f(x) = a(x^2 + 7x + 12)$

3. a) $f(x) = \frac{3}{7}(x + 3)(x - 5)$

b) $f(x) = 1.2(x + 4)(x - 7)$

c) $f(x) = 5x(3x + 2)$

4. a) $f(x) = \frac{3}{7}x^2 - \frac{6}{7}x - \frac{45}{7}$

b) $f(x) = \frac{6}{5}x^2 - \frac{18}{5}x - \frac{168}{5}$

c) $f(x) = 15x^2 + 10x$

5. a) $f(x) = 3x^2 - 6x - 30$ **b)** $f(x) = x^2 + 4x - 3$

c) $f(x) = -2x^2 - 20x - 46$

6. a) $f(x) = \frac{1}{2}(x - 1)^2 - 2$ **b)** $f(x) = -2\left(x + \frac{1}{2}\right)^2 + \frac{9}{2}$

c) $f(x) = \frac{1}{3}(x - 1)^2 - \frac{16}{3}$

7. a) $f(x) = -\frac{3}{140}x^2 + \frac{4107}{560}$

b) 7.3 m   **c)** 18.5 m

d) $f(x) = -\frac{3}{140}x^2 + \frac{111}{140}x$

e) The graphs in parts a) and d) are congruent. The graph of $f(x) = -\frac{3}{140}x^2 + \frac{111}{140}x$ is the graph of $f(x) = -\frac{3}{140}x^2 + \frac{4107}{560}$ translated 18.5 units to the right.

f)

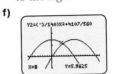

8. a) $f(x) = -\frac{1}{2}x^2 + \frac{1}{2}x + 3$

b) $f(x) = 3x^2 + 15x - 18$

c) $f(x) = -4x^2 - 8x + 60$

9. Graphs may vary.

10. Answers may vary.

11. a) $f(x) = -\frac{2}{25}x^2$ **b)** $f(x) = 3(x - 5)^2$

c) $f(x) = \frac{2}{3}(x + 1)^2$

12. a)   **b)**

 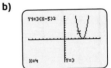

c)

13. $c = \frac{25}{4a}$

14. a) $f(x) = -2x^2 + 28x - 90$

b) $f(x) = -2x^2 + 28x - 68$

c) for $x = 6$, $y = 28$; for $x = 7$, $y = 30$

15. a)   **b)** $f(x) = -\frac{2}{5x^2} + \frac{72}{5}$

c) 14.4 m

16. a) $f(x) = -\frac{2}{5}x^2 + \frac{24}{5}x$

b) 14.4 m; the maximum heights are the same.

17. Answers may vary. Sample answer: The graph of equation developed for the arch in question 16 is congruent to the one for the arch in question 15. The graph of the arch in question 16 is the graph of the arch in question 15 translated horizontally 6 units to the right.

19. a) Yes. Answers may vary. Sample answer: The equation of a quadratic function with an x-intercept of 5 and vertex $(3, 2)$ can be found by substituting $x = 5$, $y = 0$, $p = 3$, and $q = 2$ in $y = a(x - p)^2 + q$ and solving the resulting equation to find the value of $a = -\frac{1}{2}$. The defining equation is $f(x) = -\frac{1}{2}(x - 3)^2 + 2$.

b) Yes. Answers may vary. Sample answer: The equation of a quadratic function with a vertex $(2, 4)$ that passes through the point $(5, 7)$ can be found by substituting $x = 5$, $y = 7$, $p = 2$, and $q = 4$ in $y = a(x - p)^2 + q$ and solving the resulting equation to find the value of $a = \frac{1}{3}$. The defining equation is $f(x) = \frac{1}{3}(x - 2)^2 + 4$.

c) Yes. Substitute and solve three equations of the form $y = ax^2 + bx + c$ for a, b, and c.

20. Answers may vary. Sample answer: $f(x) = x^2 + \frac{2}{3}x - \frac{2}{3}$.

22. Answers may vary.

1.7 Solve Linear-Quadratic Systems, pages 67–69

1. a) $(4, 3)$, $(5, 5)$ **b)** $(2, 17)$, $(6, 49)$
  c) $(-4, 13)$, $(2, -5)$ **d)** $(-4, 6)$, $(1, 1)$

2. Answers may vary.

3. a) The functions do not intersect.
  b) The functions intersect once.
  c) The functions intersect twice.
  d) The functions intersect twice.

4. a)   **b)**

  c)   **d)**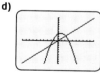

5. a) 6   **b)** -4 **c)** $-\frac{3}{2}$ **d)** $\frac{2}{3}$

6. Answers may vary.

7. $(-11, 265)$, $(3, 55)$

8. Yes, at the points $(117, -24\,524)$ and $(-262, -214\,024)$.

9. Answers may vary.

10. a) $k > -6$ **b)** $k = -6$ **c)** $k < -6$

11. a) $k > -\frac{1}{2}$ **b)** $k = -\frac{1}{2}$ **c)** $k < -\frac{1}{2}$

12. 49

13. Answers may vary. Sample answer: The vertical line $x = 2$ intersects the graph of $y = x^2 - 9$ so that part of the line is above the graph of $y = x^2 - 9$ and part of the line is below it.

14. a)   **b)** $(12, 36)$
  c) The fence should be located 37.1 m up the hill.

15. 7.5 s

16. $11{:}00 < t < 15{:}00$, or between 11 a.m. and 3 p.m.

18. a) $(2, 1)$, $(5, 0)$ **b)**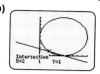

19. $(5, -7)$, $(6, 0)$

20. B

Chapter 1 Review, pages 70–71

1. a) domain $\{x \in \mathbb{R}, -2 \le x \le 2\}$, range $\{y \in \mathbb{R}, -3 \le y \le 3\}$
  b) domain $\{-2, 3, 5, 11\}$, range $\{1, 2, 3, 7\}$
  c) domain $\{1, 2, 3, 4, 5\}$, range $\{4, 6, 10, 18, 29\}$
  d) domain $\{x \in \mathbb{R}\}$, range $\{y \in \mathbb{R}, y \ge 11\}$

2. a) not a function   **b)** not a function
  c) Answers may vary. Sample anwer: This relation is a function because for each value in the domain there is exactly one value in the range.
  d) Answers may vary. Sample anwer: This relation is a function because for each value in the domain there is exactly one value in the range.

3. a) $y = 4x - 3$
  b) Answers may vary. Sample anwer: It is possible for a second function to exist that will generate these values, but the function will not be linear.

4. a)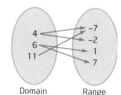

Domain   Range

  b) Answers may vary. Sample anwer: This relation is not a function. The x-values 4 and 6 have two corresponding y-values.

5. 160

6. a) 10 A   **b)** 500 W

7. a) $-70 + 8\sqrt{3}$ **b)** $-9 - 15\sqrt{6}$
  c) 22   **d)** $-12 + 43\sqrt{2}$

8. a) $5\sqrt{6} - 2$ square units   **b)** $\frac{27\pi}{2}$ square units

9. a) $\frac{1 - \sqrt{7}}{3}$, $\frac{1 + \sqrt{7}}{3}$ **b)** $\frac{4}{3}$, $\frac{5}{2}$

10. a) two distinct real roots
  b) two distinct real roots
  c) one real root

11. Answers may vary. Sample answer: Jessica is not correct. Since $\sqrt{2} + \sqrt{2} = 2\sqrt{2} \doteq 2.8$ and $\sqrt{2} \times \sqrt{2} = 2$, then $\sqrt{2} + \sqrt{2} \ne \sqrt{2} \times \sqrt{2}$.

12. a) $f(x) = -\frac{1}{2}x^2 + \frac{3}{2}x + 5$
  b) $f(x) = -5x^2 - 20x + 5$

13. a) $f(x) = -\frac{1}{40}x^2 + \frac{53}{40}x$ **b)** 17.6 m

c) Answers may vary. Sample answer: Yes. The second quadratic function is $f(x) = -\frac{1}{40}x^2 + \frac{2809}{40}$.

14. Answers may vary.

15. a) $(2, 6), (3, 11)$ **b)** $(-1, -2), (7, -26)$

16. $b = -4$

17. Answers may vary. Sample answer: No. The line $y = 2x + 1$ and the parabola $y = x^2 - 3$ do not intersect.

Chapter 1 Practice Test, pages 72–73

1. a) false **b)** true **c)** true
   d) false **e)** false

2. A **3.** B **4.** C **5.** B **6.** B

7. a) $y = -x^2 + 3$

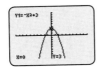

b) $x^2 + y^2 = 25$

8. a) domain $\{x \in \mathbb{R}\}$, range $\{y \in \mathbb{R}, y \geq 0\}$
   b) domain $\{0, 1, 2, 3\}$, range $\{-21, -12, -8, -5\}$

9. a) domain $\{\ell \in \mathbb{R}, \ell \geq 0\}$, range $\{T \in \mathbb{R}, T \geq 0\}$;
   b)

   c) Answers may vary. Sample answer: Yes. For each value of ℓ there is exactly one value for T.

10. $\{(1, 3), (3, 2), (4, 2), (4, 3), (7, 2), (7, 3)\}$. Answers may vary. Sample answer: No. This relation is not a function. The x-value and 7 have two corresponding y-values.

11. a) $(4, 11)$
   b) maximum; the parabola opens downward
   c) two x-intercepts

12. a) 3.75 m by 5 m **b)** 18.75 m²

13. a) $R(x) = -10(x - 10)^2 + 16\ 000$
   b) $40 **c)** $16\ 000

14. a) $-18 + 6\sqrt{6}$ **b)** $2 - x^2$

15. $\sqrt{x} + \sqrt{x} = \sqrt{x} \times \sqrt{x}$ is true for $x = 4$.
   $\sqrt{4} + \sqrt{4} = 2 + 2 = 4$ and
   $\sqrt{4} \times \sqrt{4} = 2 \times 2 = 4$.

16. a) $-2, 10$
   b) Answers may vary. Sample answer: $(4, 18)$
   c)

17. 5 m by 13 m

18. $f(x) = 8x^2 + 80x + 176$

19. a) $f(x) = -\frac{2}{5}x^2 + \frac{8}{5}x + \frac{24}{5}$ **b)** 6.4

20. $(-3, -16), (6, 2)$

21. a) Answers may vary.
   b) Answers may vary. Sample answer: The equation needs to be changed from $f(x) = 3x^2 - 4$ to $f(x) = 3x^2 - 12$.
   c) $f(x) = a\left(x^2 - \frac{7}{5}\right)$

22. Answers may vary. Sample answer: No. The quadratic function that models the path of the baseball does not intersect the linear function that models the profile of the bleachers in the first quadrant. The ball lands on the ground before it reaches the bleachers.

Chapter 2

Prerequisite Skills, pages 76–77

1. a) up; vertically stretched by a factor of 3 because $a = 3$
   b) down; vertically compressed by a factor of 0.5 because $a = -0.5$
   c) up; vertically compressed by a factor of 0.1 because $a = 0.1$
   d) up; vertically compressed by a factor of $\frac{3}{5}$ because $a = \frac{3}{5}$

2. a) $(5, 10)$ **b)** $(-6, 20)$
   c) $(1, -5)$ **d)** $(-3, -4)$

3. a)

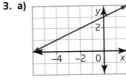

   b)

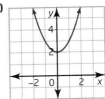

   c)

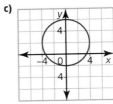

   d)

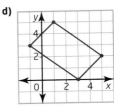

4. a)

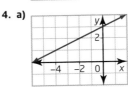

   b)

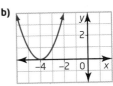

   c)

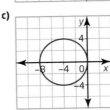

   d)

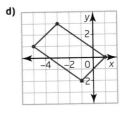

5. a)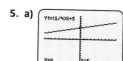
b)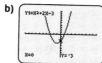

c)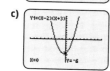
d)

6. a) $15x^2 - 24x$ **b)** $60x^3y - 120x^2y^2$
c) $-12x^3 - 39x^2 + 21x$ **d)** $6x^2 - 7x - 20$
e) $16x^2 - 25$ **f)** $52x^2 - 39x$

7. a) 8 **b)** 3 **c)** 12
d) $4xy^2$ **e)** $x^2 + 2x$ **f)** $x + 4$

8. a) $5x(3x + 2)$ **b)** $-5x^2(7x + 9)$
c) $6y^3(3x^2 - 6x + 1)$ **d)** $-5x^2(x^3 + 20x^2 + 6)$
e) $2(2x + 5)(2x - 5)$ **f)** $(6 - 11x)(x - 1)$

9. a) $(x + 2)(x + 3)$ **b)** $(x + 2)(x - 6)$
c) $(x + 9)(x - 3)$ **d)** $(x - 7)(x - 7)$
e) $(x + 8)(x - 8)$ **f)** $3(x + 5)(x - 8)$
g) $2(x + 5)(x + 5)$ **h)** $4(x + 8)(x - 8)$

10. a) $(2x + 3)(x - 5)$ **b)** $(3x + 4)(3x + 4)$
c) $2(3x + 1)(2x - 1)$ **d)** $2(3x + 1)(3x - 10)$
e) $2(2x - 3)(x + 4)$ **f)** $(5x + 8)(4x + 3)$

11. a) 630 **b)** $12x^2y^2$
c) $(x + 8)(x - 5)(x - 6)$

12. a) $\dfrac{17}{15}$ **b)** $\dfrac{23}{36}$

c) $\dfrac{2x + 3y}{12}$ **d)** $\dfrac{16x - 9y}{24}$

13. a) $-\dfrac{1}{8}$ **b)** $\dfrac{16}{5}$ **c)** $\dfrac{128}{27}$ **d)** 10

14. a) $r = \pm\sqrt{\dfrac{A}{\pi}}$ **b)** $w = \dfrac{P - 2\ell}{2}$

c) $y = \pm\sqrt{16 - x^2}$ **d)** $y = \pm\sqrt{y + 20}$

e) $x = \pm\sqrt{y^2 + 5}$ **f)** $h = \dfrac{A - 2\pi r^2}{2\pi r}$

2.1 Transformations of Functions, pages 83–85

1. a)

Yes. The functions appear to be equivalent.

b)

No. The functions do not appear to be equivalent.

c)

No. The functions do not appear to be equivalent.

d)

Yes. The functions appear to be equivalent.

e)

No. The functions do not appear to be equivalent.

2. a) Answers may vary.
b) $f(0) = 14$; $g(0) = -14$ **c)** $f(0) = 0$; $g(0) = 3$
d) Answers may vary. **e)** $f(3) = -26$; $g(3) = -17$

3. a) $x \neq 3$ **b)** $x \neq -2$
4. a) $x \geq 1$, $x \neq 5$ **b)** $x \neq -3$, $x \neq -2$
5. a) Yes; $x \neq -6$ **b)** No; $f(x) = \dfrac{x + 4}{x - 4}$, $x \neq 4$
c) No; $f(x) = x + 1$, $x \neq -5$
d) Yes; $x \neq -8$, $x \neq 6$ **e)** Yes; $x \neq 0$, $x \neq \dfrac{2}{3}$
f) No; $f(x) = x - 5$, $x \neq -\dfrac{2}{5}$

6. a) $\dfrac{1}{x - 5}$, $x \neq 5$, $x \neq 8$ **b)** $3(x - 7)$, $x \neq 7$, $x \neq 10$
c) $\dfrac{x + 3}{x + 7}$, $x \neq -7$, $x \neq 6$ **d)** $\dfrac{x + 9}{x + 5}$, $x \neq -5$, $x \neq 2$

e) $\dfrac{x + 8}{(x - 8)(x + 2)}$, $x \neq 8$, $x \neq -2$

f) $\dfrac{5x + 4}{2(x + 3)}$, $x \neq -3$, $x \neq \dfrac{2}{5}$

7. a) 32, 33, 34, 37, 44
b) -4, undefined, 0, 6, 20; the expression cannot be evaluated for $x = -1$ since it simplifies to $2x$, $x \neq -5$, $x \neq -1$.

8. a) $A = \pi r^2 - 9\pi$
b) domain $\{r \in \mathbb{R}, r > 3\}$, range $\{A \in \mathbb{R}, A > 0\}$

9. a) $V(x) = (2x + 0.5)(x - 0.5)(x + 0.5)$
b) $SA(x) = 2(2x + 0.5)(x - 0.5) + 2(2x + 0.5)(x + 0.5) + 2(x - 0.5)(x + 0.5)$
c) 0.625 m³, 6.625 m²; 1.875 m³, 11.5 m²; 7 m³, 25 m²
d) $V(x)$: domain $\{x \in \mathbb{R}, x > 0.5\}$, range $\{V \in \mathbb{R}, V > 0\}$; $SA(x)$: domain $\{x \in \mathbb{R}, x > 0.5\}$, range $\{SA \in \mathbb{R}, SA > 3\}$

10. a) $f(x) = (18 + x)(12 - x)$
b) $(18 + x)(12 - x) = 216 - 6x - x^2$
c) 15 green lights per hour

11. a)

x	$x^2 + 1$	$x^2 - 1$	$2x$	$(x^2 + 1)^2 = (x^2 - 1)^2 + (2x)^2$
2	5	3	4	$5^2 = 3^2 + 4^2$
3	10	8	6	$10^2 = 8^2 + 6^2$
4	17	15	8	$17^2 = 15^2 + 8^2$

b) hypotenuse is $x^2 + 1$; in all three cases, this side is the longest side

c) Answers may vary.

12. a)

b) The value of the expression in the denominator will never equal zero.

c) Answers may vary.

13. The simplified form of the function is $f(x) = 2x + 3$, $x \neq -6$, $x \neq 2$. The graph is the line $y = 2x + 3$ with holes at $(-6, -9)$ and $(2, 7)$.

14. $A(x) = 100 - x^2$; domain $\{x \in \mathbb{R}, \sqrt{50} < x < 10\}$, range $\{A \in \mathbb{R}, 0 < A < 50\}$

15. division by zero in the last line of the proof: $a^2 - ab = a(a - b)$ which is zero because $a = b$

16. $(2, 0)$

2.2 Skills You Need: Operations With Rational Expressions, pages 94–96

1. a) $\dfrac{22y^2}{x^2}$, $x \neq 0$ **b)** $25x^6$, $x \neq 0$

c) $\dfrac{5b}{2}$, $b \neq 0$ **d)** $\dfrac{1}{b}$, $a \neq 0$, $b \neq 0$

2. a) $2y$, $x \neq 0$, $y \neq 0$ **b)** $330x^3$, $x \neq 0$, $y \neq 0$

c) $\dfrac{2b^2}{a^4}$, $a \neq 0$, $b \neq 0$ **d)** $8ac^2$, $a \neq 0$, $b \neq 0$, $c \neq 0$

3. a) 5, $x \neq -10$ **b)** 2, $x \neq 0$, $x \neq 1$

c) $\dfrac{x + 5}{x + 7}$, $x \neq -7$, $x \neq 3$ **d)** 1, $x \neq -8$, $x \neq -\dfrac{3}{2}$

4. a) $\dfrac{x}{3(x + 10)}$, $x \neq -10$, $x \neq -\dfrac{3}{2}$, $x \neq 0$

b) $\dfrac{16x}{x + 8}$, $x \neq -8$, $x \neq -6$, $x \neq 0$

c) 1, $x \neq -7$, $x \neq -3$, $x \neq -2$

d) 1, $x \neq -5$, $x \neq 3$, $x \neq 6$

5. a) 2, $x \neq -1$, $x \neq 0$ **b)** x, $x \neq 3$

c) $\dfrac{x - 5}{x + 10}$, $x \neq -12$, $x \neq -10$, $x \neq 5$

d) 1, $x \neq -3$, $x \neq 7$

6. a) $\dfrac{x + 15}{4}$, $x \neq -6$, $x \neq 0$ **b)** $\dfrac{1}{6}$, $x \neq 0$, $x \neq 9$

c) $\dfrac{5x(x + 13)}{x - 5}$, $x \neq -2$, $x \neq 0$, $x \neq 5$

d) $\dfrac{x + 8}{x - 8}$, $x \neq -3$, $x \neq 1$, $x \neq 8$

7. a) $\dfrac{7x + 3}{90}$, no restrictions

b) $\dfrac{-x + 18}{20}$, no restrictions

c) $\dfrac{5}{12x}$, $x \neq 0$ **d)** $\dfrac{37}{24x}$, $x \neq 0$

e) $\dfrac{12 + 5a}{4ab}$, $a \neq 0$, $b \neq 0$

f) $\dfrac{26b + 55a^2}{20a^2b^2}$, $a \neq 0$, $b \neq 0$

g) $\dfrac{6b + 3ab + 4a - a^2}{3a^2b^2}$, $a \neq 0$, $b \neq 0$

h) $\dfrac{7 - ab}{9ab}$, $a \neq 0$, $b \neq 0$

8. a) $\dfrac{12}{(x - 6)(x + 6)}$, $x \neq -6$, $x \neq 6$

b) $\dfrac{15x - 84}{(x + 8)(x - 9)}$, $x \neq -8$, $x \neq 9$

c) $\dfrac{23x + 22}{(x - 6)(x + 4)}$, $x \neq -4$, $x \neq 6$

d) $\dfrac{2(x + 4)(x - 1)}{(x + 1)(x - 2)}$, $x \neq -1$, $x \neq 2$

9. a) $\dfrac{3x - 2}{(x - 1)(x - 8)}$, $x \neq 1$, $x \neq 8$

b) $\dfrac{x^2 + 2x - 4}{(x + 5)(x - 2)}$, $x \neq -5$, $x \neq 2$

c) $\dfrac{-2x^2 + 3x + 4}{(x + 1)(x + 2)(x + 7)}$, $x \neq -7$, $x \neq -2$, $x \neq -1$

d) $\dfrac{-(x - 23)(x - 1)}{(x + 11)(x - 11)(x - 3)}$, $x \neq -11$, $x \neq 3$, $x \neq 11$

10. a) Total time $= \dfrac{20x - 20}{x(x - 2)}$, $x > 2$

b) 2.25 h

11. a) $\dfrac{2}{x - 2}$, $x \neq 2$ **b)** $\dfrac{x + 2}{x - 3}$, $x \neq 3$

c) $\dfrac{-2a + 3}{2a - 5}$, $a \neq \dfrac{5}{2}$ **d)** $\dfrac{b - 3}{4b - 1}$, $b \neq \dfrac{1}{4}$

12. a) $V(x) = x(80 - 2x)(100 - 2x)$

b) $SA(x) = 2x(80 - 2x) + (80 - 2x)(100 - 2x) + 2x(100 - 2x)$

c) $\dfrac{V(x)}{SA(x)} = \dfrac{x(40 - x)(50 - x)}{2000 - x^2}$

d) $x \neq 20\sqrt{5}$, but in context $x < 40$

13. a) $R_T = \dfrac{R_1 R_2 R_3}{R_1 R_2 + R_1 R_3 + R_2 R_3}$

b) Answers may vary. Sample answer: $R_T = \dfrac{R_1}{3}$

c) Answers may vary. Sample answer: $R_T = \dfrac{R_1}{9}$

14. a) $\dfrac{V(r)}{SA(r)} = \dfrac{rh}{2(r + h)}$ **b)** $r > 0$, $h > 0$

15. a) $\dfrac{800}{V}$ **b)** $\dfrac{400}{v - 0.5} + \dfrac{400}{v + 0.5}$

c) No. Simplifying the expression in part b) gives $\dfrac{800v}{(v - 0.5)(v + 0.5)}$, which is not equivalent to the expression in part a).

16. a) 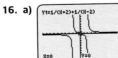   **b)** $f(x) = \dfrac{2x}{(x + 2)(x - 2)}$

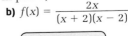

c) Answers may vary. Sample answer: The two

graphs are the same. The restrictions for both graphs are $x \neq -2$ and $x \neq 2$. Both graphs are discontinuous at $x = -2$ and $x = 2$.

18. a) $\dfrac{V_{\text{sphere}}(r)}{V_{\text{cylinder}}(r)} = \dfrac{2}{3}$ **b)** $\dfrac{SA_{\text{sphere}}(r)}{SA_{\text{cylinder}}(r)} = \dfrac{2}{3}$

c) Answers may vary. Sample answer: The ratios are the same for part a) and part b).

19. $\dfrac{-x^2 - 7x - 7}{(2x + 5)(x + 2)}$, $x \neq -8$, $x \neq -3$, $x \neq -\dfrac{5}{2}$, $x \neq -2$, $x \neq 3$

20. a) 2.718 279 57

b) 2.718 281 828… The answer for part a) is equal to e^1 up to four decimal places.

c) The result gets closer and closer to the value of e.

$\therefore$

$1 + \dfrac{1}{6 + \dfrac{1}{1 + \dfrac{1}{1 + \dfrac{1}{8}}}}$

21. B   **22.** A   **23.** −34   **24.** A

2.3 Horizontal and Vertical Translations of Functions, pages 102–104

1. a)

x	$f(x) = \sqrt{x}$	$r(x) = f(x) + 7$	$s(x) = f(x - 1)$
0	0	7	no value
1	1	8	0
4	2	9	$\sqrt{3}$
9	3	10	$\sqrt{8}$

b)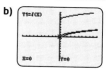

c) Answers may vary. Sample answer: Since $r(x)$ is a vertical translation of 7 units up of $f(x)$, the y-coordinate of each point of $r(x)$ is 7 more than the corresponding y-coordinate of $f(x)$. Since $s(x)$ is a horizontal translation of 1 unit to the right of $f(x)$, the x-coordinate of each point of $s(x)$ is 1 more than the corresponding x-coordinate of $f(x)$.

2. a) A'(−4, 7), B'(−2, 7), C'(−1, 3), D'(1, 3), E'(2, 4), F'(4, 4)

b) A'(−4, −5), B'(−2, −5), C'(−1, −9), D'(1, −9), E'(2, −8), F'(4, −8)

c) A'(4, 2), B'(6, 2), C'(7, −2), D'(9, −2), E'(10, −1), F'(12, −1)

d) A'(−10, 2), B'(−8, 2), C'(−7, −2), D'(−5, −2), E'(−4, −1), F'(−2, −1)

3. a) A'(−1, 8), B'(1, 8), C'(2, 4), D'(4, 4), E'(5, 5), F'(7, 5)

b) A'(−2, −8), B'(0, −8), C'(1, −12), D'(3, −12),

E'(4, −11), F'(6, −11)

c) A'(−9, 6), B'(−7, 6), C'(−6, 2), D'(−4, 2), E'(−3, 3), F'(−1, 3)

d) A'(−16, −1), B'(−14, −1), C'(−13, −5), D'(−11, −5), E'(−10, −4), F'(−8, −4)

4. a) A'(−4, 1), B'(−3, 3), C'(−1, 1), D'(0, 3)

b) A'(−4, −8), B'(−3, −6), C'(−1, −8), D'(0, −6)

c) A'(0, −2), B'(1, 0), C'(3, −2), D'(4, 0)

d) A'(−11, −2), B'(−10, 0), C'(−8, −2), D'(−7, 0)

5. a) A'(−2, 8), B'(−1, 10), C'(1, 8), D'(2, 10)

b) A'(1, −11), B'(2, −9), C'(4, −11), D'(5, −9)

c) A'(−12, 7), B'(−11, 9), C'(−9, 7), D'(−8, 9)

d) A'(−5, −13), B'(−4, −11), C'(−2, −13), D'(−1, −11)

6. a) $f(x) = x$; $y = f(x) - 9$; translate 9 units down:

domain $\{x \in \mathbb{R}\}$, range $\{y \in \mathbb{R}\}$

b) $f(x) = x$; $y = f(x) + 12$; translate 12 units up:

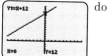

domain $\{x \in \mathbb{R}\}$, range $\{y \in \mathbb{R}\}$

c) $f(x) = x^2$; $y = f(x) + 8$; translate 8 units up;

domain $\{x \in \mathbb{R}\}$,

range $\{y \in \mathbb{R}, y \geq 8\}$

d) $f(x) = \sqrt{x}$; $y = f(x) - 12$; translate 12 units down;

domain $\{x \in \mathbb{R}, x \geq 0\}$,

range $\{y \in \mathbb{R}, y \geq -12\}$

e) $f(x) = x^2$; $y = f(x - 6)$; translate 6 units right;

domain $\{x \in \mathbb{R}\}$,

range $\{y \in \mathbb{R}, y \geq 0\}$

f) $f(x) = \dfrac{1}{x}$; $y = f(x) + 5$; translate 5 units up;

domain $\{x \in \mathbb{R}, x \neq 0\}$,

range $\{y \in \mathbb{R}, y \neq 5\}$

g) $f(x) = \sqrt{x}$; $y = f(x + 10)$; translate 10 units left;

domain $\{x \in \mathbb{R}, x \geq -10\}$,

range $\{y \in \mathbb{R}, y \geq 0\}$

h) $f(x) = \frac{1}{x}$; $y = f(x - 2)$; translate 2 units right;

domain $\{x \in \mathbb{R}, x \neq 2\}$,
range $\{y \in \mathbb{R}, y \neq 0\}$

i) $f(x) = \sqrt{x}$; $y = f(x - 9) - 5$; translate 9 units right and 5 units down; domain $\{x \in \mathbb{R}, x \geq 9\}$,

range $\{y \in \mathbb{R}, y \geq -5\}$

j) $f(x) = \frac{1}{x}$; $y = f(x + 3) - 8$; translate 3 units left and 8 units down; domain $\{x \in \mathbb{R}, x \neq -3\}$,

range $\{y \in \mathbb{R}, y \neq -8\}$

7. Answers may vary. Sample answer: The translation for question 6a) could be 9 units down or 9 units right. The translation for question 6b) could be 12 units up or 12 units left.

8. a) translate 9 units left and 3 units down;
$g(x) = f(x + 9) - 3$;
$f(x)$: domain $\{x \in \mathbb{R}, 0 \leq x \leq 8\}$,
range $\{y \in \mathbb{R}, 0 \leq y \leq 4\}$;
$g(x)$: domain $\{x \in \mathbb{R}, -9 \leq x \leq -1\}$,
range $\{y \in \mathbb{R}, -3 \leq y \leq 1\}$

b) translate 4 units right and 3 units down;
$g(x) = f(x - 4) - 3$; $f(x)$: domain $\{x \in \mathbb{R}\}$,
range $\{y \in \mathbb{R}, y \geq 0\}$; $g(x)$: domain $\{x \in \mathbb{R}\}$,
range $\{y \in \mathbb{R}, y \geq -3\}$

c) translate 4 units left and 2 units up;
$g(x) = f(x + 4) + 2$; $f(x)$: domain $\{x \in \mathbb{R}, x \geq 0\}$,
range $\{y \in \mathbb{R}, y \geq 0\}$;
$g(x)$: domain $\{x \in \mathbb{R}, x \geq -4\}$,
range $\{y \in \mathbb{R}, y \geq 2\}$

d) translate 6 units right and 3 units down;
$g(x) = f(x - 6) - 3$;
$f(x)$: domain $\{x \in \mathbb{R}, 0 \leq x \leq 12\}$,
range $\{y \in \mathbb{R}, -3 \leq y \leq 3\}$;
$g(x)$: domain $\{x \in \mathbb{R}, 6 \leq x \leq 18\}$,
range $\{y \in \mathbb{R}, -6 \leq y \leq 0\}$

9. a) translate 8 units left and 12 units up
Answers may vary in parts b) and c). Sample answers:

b) A$(-1, 1)$, B$(0, 0)$, C$(1, 1)$; A'$(-9, 1)$, B'$(-8, 0)$,
C'$(-7, 1)$; A"$(-9, 13)$, B"$(-8, 12)$,
C"$(-7, 13)$

c) A$(-1, 1)$, B$(0, 0)$, C$(1, 1)$; A'$(-1, 13)$, B'$(0, 12)$,
C'$(1, 13)$; A"$(-9, 13)$, B"$(-8, 12)$, C"$(-7, 13)$.
The final image points are the same regardless of the order of the translations. So, the order of translations is not important.

d)

e) Answers may vary.

10. Horizontal translations have the same effect as vertical translations when $c = -d$. Answers may vary.

11. a) $n(x) = x - 10$ **b)** $r(x) = x + 11$
c) $s(x) = x - 1$ **d)** $t(x) = x - 7$

12. a) $n(x) = (x - 4)^2 - 6$ **b)** $r(x) = (x + 2)^2 + 9$
c) $s(x) = (x + 6)^2 - 7$ **d)** $t(x) = (x - 11)^2 + 4$

13. a) $g(x) = \sqrt{x - 4} - 6$ **b)** $g(x) = \sqrt{x + 2} + 9$
c) $g(x) = \sqrt{x + 6} - 7$ **d)** $g(x) = \sqrt{x - 11} + 4$

14. a) $n(x) = \dfrac{1}{x - 4} - 6$, $x \neq 4$

b) $r(x) = \dfrac{1}{x + 2} + 9$, $x \neq -2$

c) $s(x) = \dfrac{1}{x + 6} - 7$, $x \neq -6$

d) $t(x) = \dfrac{1}{x - 11} + 4$, $x \neq 11$

15. a) The hybrid electric car would have to be given a head start of 33.6 m.

b)

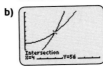

16. a) domain $\{x \in \mathbb{N}, x \geq 0\}$; the number of units of the product produced and sold is greater than or equal to 0 units; range $\{c \in \mathbb{R}, c \geq 500\}$; the cost to produce the units of the product is greater than or equal to \$500.

b) $c(x) = \sqrt{x + 10} + 500$

c) translate 10 units to the left

d) domain $\{x \in \mathbb{N}, x \geq 0\}$, range $\{c \in \mathbb{R}, c \geq 503.16\}$

17. Answers may vary.

18. D   **19.** D   **20.** B

2.4 Reflections of Functions, pages 110–112

1. a)

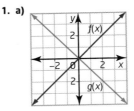

$f(x)$: domain $\{x \in \mathbb{R}\}$,
range $\{y \in \mathbb{R}\}$;
$g(x)$: domain $\{x \in \mathbb{R}\}$,
range $\{y \in \mathbb{R}\}$

b)

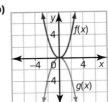

$f(x)$: domain $\{x \in \mathbb{R}\}$,
range $\{y \in \mathbb{R}, y \geq 0\}$;
$g(x)$: domain $\{x \in \mathbb{R}\}$,
range $\{y \in \mathbb{R}, y \leq 0\}$

c)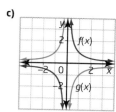

$f(x)$: domain $\{x \in \mathbb{R}, x \neq 0\}$, range $\{y \in \mathbb{R}, y \neq 0\}$; $g(x)$: domain $\{x \in \mathbb{R}, x \neq 0\}$, range $\{y \in \mathbb{R}, y \neq 0\}$

d)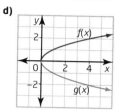

$f(x)$: domain $\{x \in \mathbb{R}, x \geq 0\}$, range $\{y \in \mathbb{R}, y \geq 0\}$; $g(x)$: domain $\{x \in \mathbb{R}, x \geq 0\}$, range $\{y \in \mathbb{R}, y \leq 0\}$

e)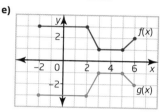

$f(x)$: domain $\{x \in \mathbb{R}, -2 \leq x \leq 6\}$, range $\{y \in \mathbb{R}, 1 \leq y \leq 3\}$; $g(x)$: domain $\{x \in \mathbb{R}, -2 \leq x \leq 6\}$, range $\{y \in \mathbb{R}, -3 \leq y \leq -1\}$

f)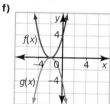

$f(x)$: domain $\{x \in \mathbb{R}\}$, range $\{y \in \mathbb{R}, y \geq 0\}$; $g(x)$: domain $\{x \in \mathbb{R}\}$, range $\{y \in \mathbb{R}, y \leq 0\}$

2. a)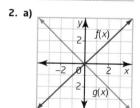

$f(x)$: domain $\{x \in \mathbb{R}\}$, range $\{y \in \mathbb{R}\}$; $g(x)$: domain $\{x \in \mathbb{R}\}$, range $\{y \in \mathbb{R}\}$

b)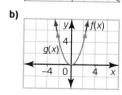

$f(x)$: domain $\{x \in \mathbb{R}\}$, range $\{y \in \mathbb{R}, y \geq 0\}$; $g(x)$: domain $\{x \in \mathbb{R}\}$, range $\{y \in \mathbb{R}, y \geq 0\}$

c)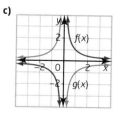

$f(x)$: domain $\{x \in \mathbb{R}, x \neq 0\}$, range $\{y \in \mathbb{R}, y \neq 0\}$; $g(x)$: domain $\{x \in \mathbb{R}, x \neq 0\}$, range $\{y \in \mathbb{R}, y \neq 0\}$

d)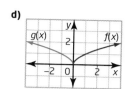

$f(x)$: domain $\{x \in \mathbb{R}, x \geq 0\}$, range $\{y \in \mathbb{R}, y \geq 0\}$; $g(x)$: domain $\{x \in \mathbb{R}, x \leq 0\}$, range $\{y \in \mathbb{R}, y \geq 0\}$

e)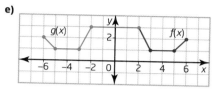

$f(x)$: domain $\{x \in \mathbb{R}, -2 \leq x \leq 6\}$, range $\{y \in \mathbb{R}, 1 \leq y \leq 3\}$; $g(x)$: domain $\{x \in \mathbb{R}, -6 \leq x \leq 2\}$, range $\{y \in \mathbb{R}, 1 \leq y \leq 3\}$

f)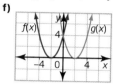

$f(x)$: domain $\{x \in \mathbb{R}\}$, range $\{y \in \mathbb{R}, y \geq 0\}$; $g(x)$: domain $\{x \in \mathbb{R}\}$, range $\{y \in \mathbb{R}, y \geq 0\}$

3. a)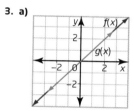

$f(x)$: domain $\{x \in \mathbb{R}\}$, range $\{y \in \mathbb{R}\}$; $g(x)$: domain $\{x \in \mathbb{R}\}$, range $\{y \in \mathbb{R}\}$

b)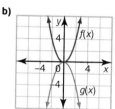

$f(x)$: domain $\{x \in \mathbb{R}\}$, range $\{y \in \mathbb{R}, y \geq 0\}$; $g(x)$: domain $\{x \in \mathbb{R}\}$, range $\{y \in \mathbb{R}, y \leq 0\}$

c)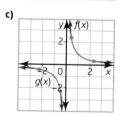

$f(x)$: domain $\{x \in \mathbb{R}, x \neq 0\}$, range $\{y \in \mathbb{R}, y \neq 0\}$; $g(x)$: domain $\{x \in \mathbb{R}, x \neq 0\}$, range $\{y \in \mathbb{R}, y \neq 0\}$

d)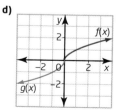

$f(x)$: domain $\{x \in \mathbb{R}, x \geq 0\}$, range $\{y \in \mathbb{R}, y \geq 0\}$; $g(x)$: domain $\{x \in \mathbb{R}, x \leq 0\}$, range $\{y \in \mathbb{R}, y \leq 0\}$

e)

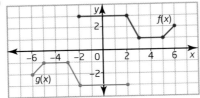

$f(x)$: domain $\{x \in \mathbb{R}, -2 \le x \le 6\}$,
range $\{y \in \mathbb{R}, 1 \le y \le 3\}$;
$g(x)$: domain $\{x \in \mathbb{R}, -6 \le x \le 2\}$,
range $\{y \in \mathbb{R}, -3 \le y \le -1\}$

f)

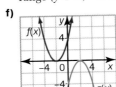

$f(x)$: domain $\{x \in \mathbb{R}\}$,
range $\{y \in \mathbb{R}, y \ge 0\}$;
$g(x)$: domain $\{x \in \mathbb{R}\}$,
range $\{y \in \mathbb{R}, y \le 0\}$

4. a) $g(x) = -\sqrt{x + 4} + 4$ **b)** $g(x) = (-x + 1)^2 - 4$

  c) $g(x) = -(-x - 5)^2 - 9$ **d)** $g(x) = -\dfrac{1}{(-x - 3)} + 6$

  e) $g(x) = -\sqrt{-x - 2} + 5$ **f)** $g(x) = -\sqrt{-x + 9} + 1$

5. a) $g(x) = f(-x)$; reflection in the y-axis

  b) $g(x) = -f(x)$; reflection in the x-axis

  c) $g(x) = -f(-x)$; reflection in the x-axis followed
    by a reflection in the y-axis

6. If a set of axes is superimposed with the origin at
the horizontal and vertical centre of the logo, "az"
is a reflection in the x-axis followed by a reflection
in the y-axis of "Te."

7. Answers may vary. Sample answer: A reflection in
the x-axis leaves the domain unchanged, but the
range may change. A reflection in the y-axis leaves
the range unchanged, but the domain may change.

8. a) i) $(-1, 0)$ and $(5, 0)$ **ii)** $(0, -5)$

  b) Answers may vary. Sample answer: $f(x) = x^3$

9. a) Since $g(x) = f(-x)$, $g(x)$ is a reflection of $f(x)$ in
    the y-axis.

  b) Since $g(x) = f(-x)$, $g(x)$ is a reflection of $f(x)$ in
    the y-axis.

  c) Since $g(x) = -f(x)$, $g(x)$ is a reflection of $f(x)$ in
    the x-axis.

  d) Since $g(x) = -f(x)$, $g(x)$ is a reflection of $f(x)$ in
    the x-axis.

  e) Since $g(x) = -f(x)$, $g(x)$ is a reflection of $f(x)$
    in the x-axis. Since $g(x) \ne f(-x)$, $g(x)$ is not
    a reflection of $f(x)$ in the y-axis. Since $g(x) \ne$
    $-f(-x)$, $g(x)$ is not a reflection of $f(x)$ in both axes.

  f) Since $g(x) = f(-x)$, $g(x)$ is a reflection of $f(x)$ in
    the y-axis.

10. Answers may vary.

11. a) Answers may vary. Sample answer: The
    x-value and the y-value in each ordered pair
    of the function is multiplied by -1 to give the
    coordinates of each ordered pair of the function
    that is reflected in the origin.

b)

 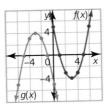

12. a)

b) $g(x) = (-x - 4)^2$

  c) Translate $f(x)$ to the left 8 units.

  d) The result of a translation of 8 units to the left of
    $f(x) = (x - 4)^2$ is $h(x) = (x + 4)^2$.

   $g(x) = (-x - 4)^2$
     $= [-1(x + 4)]^2$
     $= (-1)^2(x + 4)^2$
     $= (x + 4)^2$

  e) Answers may vary. Sample answer: No, it
    changes the orientation.

  f) Answers may vary. Sample answer: Yes, it
    works for any function that is symmetrical about
    a vertical line.

14. a)

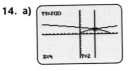

b)

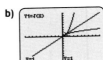

15. 0

16. D

17. Answers may vary.

18. domain $\{x \in \mathbb{R}, x \ne -2, x \ne 3\}$, range $\{y \in \mathbb{R}\}$

19. C

2.5 Stretches of Functions, pages 119–122

1. a)

x	$f(x) = x^2$	$g(x) = 5f(x)$	$h(x) = f\left(\frac{1}{4}x\right)$
0	0	0	0
2	4	20	$\frac{1}{4}$
4	16	80	1
6	36	180	$\frac{9}{4}$

b)

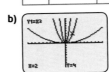

c) Answers may vary. Sample answer: The graph of $g(x)$ is the graph of $f(x)$ stretched vertically by a factor of 5. Each y-value of $g(x)$ is five times as far from the x-axis as the corresponding y-value of $f(x)$. The graph of $h(x)$ is the graph of $f(x)$ stretched horizontally by a factor of 4. Each x-value of $h(x)$ is four times as far from the y-axis as the corresponding x-value of $f(x)$.

2. a)

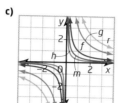

b)

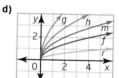

c)

d)

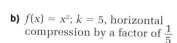

3. a) $a = 10$; the graph of $g(x)$ is a vertical stretch by a factor of 10 of the graph of $f(x)$.

b) $k = 9$; the graph of $g(x)$ is a horizontal compression by a factor of $\frac{1}{9}$ of the graph of $f(x)$.

c) $a = \frac{1}{5}$; the graph of $g(x)$ is a vertical compression by a factor of $\frac{1}{5}$ of the graph of $f(x)$.

d) $k = \frac{1}{20}$; the graph of $g(x)$ is a horizontal stretch by a factor of 20 of the graph of $f(x)$.

4. a) $f(x) = x$; $a = 10$, vertical stretch by a factor of 10

b) $f(x) = x^2$; $k = 5$, horizontal compression by a factor of $\frac{1}{5}$

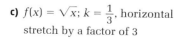

c) $f(x) = \sqrt{x}$; $k = \frac{1}{3}$, horizontal stretch by a factor of 3

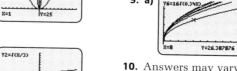

d) $f(x) = \frac{1}{x}$; $a = 4$, vertical stretch by a factor of 4

e) $f(x) = \sqrt{x}$; $k = 16$, horizontal compression by a factor of $\frac{1}{16}$

f) $f(x) = x$; $a = \frac{1}{4}$, vertical compression by a factor of $\frac{1}{4}$

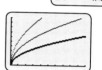

5. a)

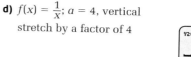

b)

6. a) vertical stretch by a factor of 3
b) vertical stretch by a factor of 5

7. Answers may vary. Sample answers:
a) A$(-2, 4)$, B$(0, 0)$, C$(2, 4)$
b) A'$(-2, 16)$, B'$(0, 0)$, C'$(2, 16)$; A"$(-1, 16)$, B"$(0, 0)$, C"$(1, 16)$
c) A'$(-1, 4)$, B'$(0, 0)$, C'$(1, 4)$; A"$(-1, 16)$, B"$(0, 0)$, C"$(1, 16)$
d) The graphs from parts b) and c) are the same.

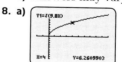

e) vertical stretch by a factor of 16
f) Answers may vary.

8. a)

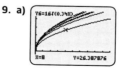

b) approximately 4.4 m/s
c) approximately 198.0 m/s

9. a)

b) 13.8 km/h

10. Answers may vary. Sample answer: Each x-value of $g(x)$ is $\frac{1}{k}$ times as far from the y-axis as the corresponding x-value of $f(x)$.

11. a) domain $\{t \in \mathbb{R}, 0 \le t \le 2.02\}$,
range $\{h \in \mathbb{R}, 0 \le h \le 20\}$

b) $h(t) = -6.2t^2 + 20$

c) The domain of the function in part b) is $\{t \in \mathbb{R}, 0 \le t \le 2.02\}$, its range is the same as the given function.

12. Answers may vary.

13. a)

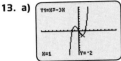

b) $g(x) = 3x^3 - 9x$; $h(x) = 27x^3 - 9x$

c)

d) No.

14. B **15.** A **16.** A **17.** (2, 1) **18.** $y = \dfrac{7}{5}x + 6$

2.6 Combinations of Transformations, pages 129–131

1. a) $a = 4, k = 1, d = 3, c = 0$; vertical stretch by a factor of 4 then translation of 3 units right

b) $a = \dfrac{1}{3}, k = 1, d = 0, c = 1$; vertical compression by a factor of $\dfrac{1}{3}$ then translation of 1 unit up

c) $a = 1, k = 1, d = -5, c = 9$; translation 5 units left and 9 units up

d) $a = 1, k = \dfrac{1}{4}, d = 0, c = 2$; horizontal stretch by a factor of 4 then translation of 2 units up

e) $a = 1, k = 5, d = 0, c = -2$; horizontal compression by a factor of $\dfrac{1}{5}$ then translation of 2 units down

f) $a = 2, k = 1, d = 0, c = -7$; vertical stretch by a factor of 2 then translation of 7 units down

2. a) $a = 3, k = 2, d = 0, c = -1$; vertical stretch by a factor of 3, horizontal compression by a factor of $\dfrac{1}{2}$, and then translation of 1 unit down

b) $a = -2, k = 1, d = 0, c = 1$; reflection in the x-axis, vertical stretch by a factor of 2, and then translation of 1 unit up

c) $a = \dfrac{1}{2}, k = 1, d = 4, c = 5$; vertical compression by a factor of $\dfrac{1}{2}$, then translation of 4 units right and 5 units up

d) $a = 1, k = -3, d = 0, c = 4$; reflection in the y-axis, horizontal compression by a factor of $\dfrac{1}{3}$, and then translation of 4 units up

e) $a = -1, k = \dfrac{1}{2}, d = 0, c = -3$; reflection in the x-axis, horizontal stretch by a factor of 2, and then translation of 3 units down

f) $a = \dfrac{1}{4}, k = 3, d = 0, c = -6$; vertical compression by a factor of $\dfrac{1}{4}$, horizontal compression by a factor of $\dfrac{1}{3}$, and then translation of 6 units down

3. a) vertical stretch by a factor of 4 and horizontal compression by a factor of $\dfrac{1}{3}$; $g(x) = 4\sqrt{3x}$

b) translation 1 unit right and 2 units up;
$$g(x) = \dfrac{1}{x - 1} + 2$$

c) horizontal stretch by a factor of 4 then translation of 2 units left;
$$g(x) = \dfrac{1}{16}(x + 2)^2$$

d) reflection in the x-axis, vertical stretch by a factor of 5, and then translation of 3 units down;
$$g(x) = -5x - 3$$

4. a) reflection in the x-axis, vertical compression by a factor of $\dfrac{1}{2}$, horizontal compression by a factor of $\dfrac{1}{2}$, and then translation of 1 unit left and 3 units down;
$$g(x) = -x - 4$$

b) reflection in the x-axis, vertical stretch by a factor of 2, horizontal compression by a factor of $\dfrac{1}{3}$, and then translation of 4 units right and 1 unit down;
$$g(x) = -18(x - 4)^2 - 1$$

c) vertical compression by a factor of $\dfrac{1}{2}$, horizontal stretch by a factor of 2, and then translation of 3 units left and 5 units up;
$$g(x) = \dfrac{1}{2}\sqrt{\dfrac{1}{2}(x + 3)} + 5$$

d) vertical stretch by a factor of 2, reflection in the
y-axis, and then translation 3 units right and
4 units up;

$$g(x) = -\frac{2}{x-3} + 4$$

5. a) $f(x) = x$

$f(x)$: domain $\{x \in \mathbb{R}\}$,
range $\{y \in \mathbb{R}\}$;
$b(x)$: domain $\{x \in \mathbb{R}\}$,
range $\{y \in \mathbb{R}\}$

b) $f(x) = x^2$;

$f(x)$: domain $\{x \in \mathbb{R}\}$,
range $\{y \in \mathbb{R}, y \geq 0\}$;
$e(x)$: domain $\{x \in \mathbb{R}\}$,
range $\{y \in \mathbb{R}, y \geq -5\}$

c) $f(x) = x^2$;

$f(x)$: domain $\{x \in \mathbb{R}\}$,
range $\{y \in \mathbb{R}, y \geq 0\}$;
$h(x)$: domain $\{x \in \mathbb{R}\}$,
range $\{y \in \mathbb{R}, y \geq 0\}$

d) $f(x) = \sqrt{x}$;

$f(x)$: domain $\{x \in \mathbb{R}, x \geq 0\}$,
range $\{y \in \mathbb{R}, y \geq 0\}$;
$j(x)$: domain $\{x \in \mathbb{R}, x \geq 7\}$,
range $\{y \in \mathbb{R}, y \geq 0\}$

e) $f(x) = \frac{1}{x}$;

$f(x)$: domain $\{x \in \mathbb{R}, x \neq 0\}$,
range $\{y \in \mathbb{R}, y \neq 0\}$;
$m(x)$:
domain $\{x \in \mathbb{R}, x \neq -8\}$,
range $\{y \in \mathbb{R}, y \neq 0\}$

f) $f(x) = \frac{1}{x}$

$f(x)$: domain $\{x \in \mathbb{R}, x \neq 0\}$,
range $\{y \in \mathbb{R}, y \neq 0\}$;
$r(x)$: domain $\{x \in \mathbb{R}, x \neq 3\}$,
range $\{y \in \mathbb{R}, y \neq 1\}$

6. a)

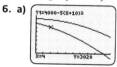

b) No. The second skydiver will not catch up to
the first skydiver before they have to open their
parachutes at 800 m.

c) $g(t)$: domain $\{t \in \mathbb{R}, t \geq -10\}$,
range $\{g \in \mathbb{R}, 0 \leq g \leq 4000\}$;
$h(t)$: domain $\{t \in \mathbb{R}, t \geq 0\}$,
range $\{h \in \mathbb{R}, 0 \leq h \leq 4000\}$

7.

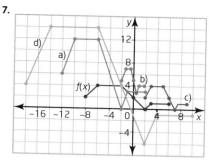

8. a) approximately 121 Hz

b) domain $\{v \in \mathbb{R}, 0 \leq v \leq 40\}$,

range $\left[f \in \mathbb{R}, \dfrac{83\ 000}{93} \leq f \leq \dfrac{83\ 000}{73}\right]$

9. Answers may vary.

10. a)

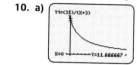
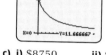

b) $11\ 666.67

c) i) $8750　　　**ii)** $7000　　　**iii)** $2692.31

12. a)

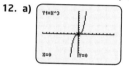

b) i) $g(x) = 3(x + 2)^3$　　　**ii)** $h(x) = -64(x - 3)^3 + 5$

13. a) Apply a horizontal translation of 2 units right
and a vertical translation of 1 unit up to the
circle $x^2 + y^2 = 25$.

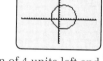

b) Apply a horizontal translation of 4 units left and
a vertical translation of 5 units up to the circle
$x^2 + y^2 = 9$.

14. Answers may vary.

15. C

2.7 Inverse of a Function, pages 138–141

1. a) $\{(5, 1), (2, 4), (-3, 5), (0, 7)\}$;
function: domain $\{1, 4, 5, 7\}$, range $\{-3, 0, 2\ 5\}$
inverse: domain $\{-3, 0, 2\ 5\}$, range $\{1, 4, 5, 7\}$

b) $\{(5, 3), (0, 4), (-5, 5), (-10, 6)\}$;
function: domain $\{3, 4, 5, 6\}$,
range $\{-10, -5, 0, 5\}$
inverse: domain $\{-10, -5, 0, 5\}$, range $\{3, 4, 5, 6\}$

c)

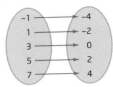

function: domain $\{-4, -2, 0, 2, 4\}$,
range $\{-1, 1, 3, 5, 7\}$
inverse: domain $\{-1, 1, 3, 5, 7\}$,
range $\{-4, -2, 0, 2, 4\}$

d)

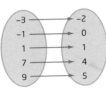

function: domain $\{-2, 0, 1, 4, 5\}$,
range $\{-3, -1, 1, 7, 9\}$
inverse: domain $\{-3, -1, 1, 7, 9\}$,
range $\{-2, 0, 1, 4, 5\}$

2. a)

function: domain $\{-5, -2, 1, 4, 7\}$,
range $\{-2, 0, 2, 4, 6\}$
inverse: domain $\{-2, 0, 2, 4, 6\}$,
range $\{-5, -2, 1, 4, 7\}$

b)

function: domain $\{-6, -4, -1, 2, 5\}$,
range $\{2, 3, 4, 5\}$
inverse: domain $\{2, 3, 4, 5\}$,
range $\{-6, -4, -1, 2, 5\}$

3. a)

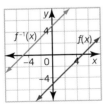

The inverse of $f(x)$ is a
function because it passes
the vertical line test.

b)

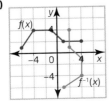

The inverse of $f(x)$ is not a
function. It does not pass
the vertical line test.

c)

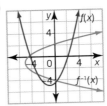

The inverse of $f(x)$ is not a
function. It does not pass
the vertical line test.

4. a) $f^{-1}(x) = \dfrac{x}{2}$ **b)** $f^{-1}(x) = \dfrac{x + 5}{6}$

c) $f^{-1}(x) = -x + 10$ **d)** $f^{-1}(x) = \dfrac{5x - 4}{2}$

5. a) $f^{-1}(x) = \pm\sqrt{x - 6}$ **b)** $f^{-1}(x) = \pm\sqrt{\dfrac{x}{4}}$

c) $f^{-1}(x) = \pm\sqrt{x - 8}$ **d)** $f^{-1}(x) = \pm\sqrt{2x - 20}$

6. a) $f^{-1}(x) = \pm\sqrt{x - 6} - 3$

b) $f^{-1}(x) = \pm\sqrt{-x + 1} + 10$

c) $f^{-1}(x) = \pm\sqrt{\dfrac{x + 75}{2}} - 6$

d) $f^{-1}(x) = \pm\sqrt{\dfrac{x - 8}{-3}} - 6$

7. a) i) $f^{-1}(x) = \dfrac{-x + 6}{5}$ **ii)**

iii) The inverse of $f(x)$ is a function because it
passes the vertical line test.

b) i) $f^{-1}(x) = 3x + 24$ **ii)**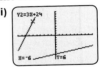

iii) The inverse of $f(x)$ is a function because it
passes the vertical line test.

c) i) $f^{-1}(x) = \pm\sqrt{x - 16} + 8$

ii)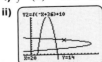

iii) The inverse of $f(x)$ is not a function because
it does not pass the vertical line test.
The x-value $x = 20$ has two corresponding
y-values.

d) i) $f^{-1}(x) = \pm\sqrt{-x + 36} + 10$

ii)

iii) The inverse of $f(x)$ is not a function because
it does not pass the vertical line test.

8. a) domain $\{v \in \mathbb{R}, v \geq 0\}$, range $\{d \in \mathbb{R}, d \geq 0\}$

b) $v = \sqrt{10d}$ domain $\{d \in \mathbb{R}, d \geq 0\}$, range $\{v \in \mathbb{R}, v \geq 0\}$; The inverse function represents the muzzle speed, in metres per second, for distances, in metres, travelled by the projectile.

c) Answers may vary.

9. a) approximate domain $\{t \in \mathbb{R}, t \geq 1\}$, range $\{d \in \mathbb{R}, d \geq 0\}$

b) Answers may vary. Sample answer: The first second is pure acceleration.

c) $t = \dfrac{d + 12.5}{11.8}$; domain = $\{d \in \mathbb{R}, d \geq 0\}$; approximate range = $\{t \in \mathbb{R}, t \geq 1\}$

d) Yes. Bolt's coach was close to being correct. The inverse function can be used to determine that Bolt could have run the 100-m race in 9.53 s.

10. Answers may vary.

11. a) $g(x)$ is not the inverse of $f(x)$ since $g(x)$ is not a reflection of $f(x)$ in the line $y = x$.

b) $g(x)$ is the inverse of $f(x)$ since $g(x)$ is a reflection of $f(x)$ in the line $y = x$.

c) $g(x)$ is not the inverse of $f(x)$ since $g(x)$ is not a reflection of $f(x)$ in the line $y = x$.

d) $g(x)$ is the inverse of $f(x)$ since $g(x)$ is a reflection of $f(x)$ in the line $y = x$.

12. a) $y = \dfrac{5}{9}(x - 32)$; x represents the temperature, in degrees Fahrenheit; y represents the temperature, in degrees Celsius

b)

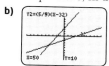

c) $-40°$; Answers may vary. Sample answer: The original and the inverse function intersect at the point $(-40, -40)$.

13. a) $t = 5 - \sqrt{\dfrac{-d + 70}{2.8}}$; the inverse represents the time, t, in seconds, before the brakes are applied, for a given stopping distance.

b) function: domain $\{t \in \mathbb{R}, 5 \leq t \leq 10\}$, range $\{d \in \mathbb{R}, 0 \leq d \leq 70\}$ inverse: domain $\{d \in \mathbb{R}, 0 \leq d \leq 70\}$, range $\{t \in \mathbb{R}, 5 \leq t \leq 10\}$

c) Answers may vary. Sample answer: The distance travelled will be less in successive time intervals.

14. Eve's car: $\sqrt{40}$ s;

Byron's car with 1-s head start: $\sqrt{80} - 1$ s;

Byron's car with 2-s head start: $\sqrt{80} - 2$ s;

Byron's car with 3-s head start: $\sqrt{80} - 3$ s;

Byron's car with 4-s head start: $\sqrt{80} - 4$ s

15. a) i) $f^{-1}(x) = \pm\sqrt{\dfrac{x}{2}}$ **ii)**

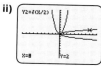

iii) $\{x \in \mathbb{R}, x \geq 0\}$ **iv)**

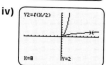

b) i) $f^{-1}(x) = \pm\sqrt{x - 2}$

ii)

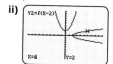

iii) $\{x \in \mathbb{R}, x \geq 0\}$ **iv)**

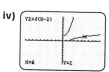

c) i) $f^{-1}(x) = \pm\sqrt{x} + 3$

ii)

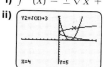

iii) $\{x \in \mathbb{R}, x \geq 3\}$ **iv)**

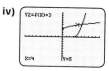

16. a) $f^{-1}(x) = \dfrac{x - 7}{3}$

b) $f(f^{-1}) = x$ and $f^{-1}(f) = x$

c) $f^{-1}(x) = \pm\sqrt{x + 6}$; $f(f^{-1}) = x$ and $f^{-1}(f) = x$

d) Answers may vary. Sample answer: For a linear function, f, and its inverse, f^{-1}, $f(f^{-1}) = x$ and $f^{-1}(f) = x$.

18. a) $f^{-1}(x) = x^2 - 3, x \geq 0$

b) function: domain $\{x \in \mathbb{R}, x \geq -3\}$, range $\{y \in \mathbb{R}, y \geq 0\}$ inverse: domain $\{x \in \mathbb{R}, x \geq 0\}$, range $\{y \in \mathbb{R}, y \geq -3\}$

c)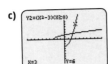

19. a) $r = \sqrt[3]{\dfrac{3V}{4\pi}}$ the inverse of the equation represents the radius, r, of a sphere in terms of the volume, V, of the sphere.

b) $V = \dfrac{4}{3}\pi r^3$: domain $\{r \in \mathbb{R}, r \ge 0\}$,

range $\{V \in \mathbb{R}, V \ge 0\}$

$r = \sqrt[3]{\dfrac{3V}{4\pi}}$; domain $\{V \in \mathbb{R}, V \ge 0\}$,

range $\{r \in \mathbb{R}, r \ge 0\}$

20. a) $f^{-1}(x) = \dfrac{1}{x}$

b) Answers may vary. Sample answer: The graph of $f(x)$ is a reflection of itself in the line $y = x$. Therefore, the inverse of $f(x) = \dfrac{1}{x}$ is the same function: $f^{-1}(x) = \dfrac{1}{x}$.

21. a) $f^{-1}(x) = \dfrac{1}{x} + \dfrac{16}{5}$

b) $f(x)$: domain $\left\{x \in \mathbb{R}, x \ne \dfrac{16}{5}\right\}$,

range $\{y \in \mathbb{R}, y \ne 0\}$; $f^{-1}(x)$:

domain $\{x \in \mathbb{R}, x \ne 0\}$, range $\left\{y \in \mathbb{R}, y \ne \dfrac{16}{5}\right\}$

22. a) i) $g(x)$ and $f(x)$ are not inverses of each other

ii) $g(x)$ and $f(x)$ are inverses of each other

iii) $g(x)$ and $f(x)$ are inverses of each other

iv) $g(x)$ and $f(x)$ are not inverses of each other

b) i)

ii) f and g are inverses if the domain of f is restricted to $x \ge 5$.

iii)

iv) f and g are inverses if the domain of g is restricted to $x \ge 0$.

23. A   **24.** A   **25.** C

26. (3, 4) and (4, 3)

1. a) equivalent   **b)** not equivalent

2. a) $\dfrac{1}{x + 3}, x \ne -7, x \ne -3$

b) $x + 8, x \ne 8$

3. a) $1600 - 4x^2$ **b)** $0 < x < 20$

4. a) $xy, x \ne 0, y \ne 0$ **b)** $10a^2b^4, a \ne 0, b \ne 0$

c) $\dfrac{2x + 15}{6x^2}, x \ne 0$

d) $\dfrac{x + 2}{(x - 4)(x - 6)}, x \ne 4, x \ne 6$

5. a) $\dfrac{x(x + 1)}{3}, x \ne -7, x \ne -2$

b) $2, x \ne -10, x \ne 2, x \ne 6$

c) $\dfrac{-5x^2 - 22x - 6}{(x + 5)(x + 2)(x - 2)}, x \ne -5, x \ne -2, x \ne 2$

d) $\dfrac{2x(x + 62)}{(x + 16)(x + 2)(x - 10)}, x \ne -16, x \ne -2, x \ne 10$

6. $\dfrac{V}{SA} = \dfrac{x(40 - 2x)}{(40 + 2x)}, 0 < x < 20$

7. a) A'(0, 6), B'(1, 7), C'(4, 8), D'(9, 9)

b) A'(3, 0), B'(4, 1), C'(7, 2), D'(12, 3)

8. a) $f(x) = x^2; y = f(x + 7) - 8$; translate 7 units left and 8 units down;

$f(x)$: domain $\{x \in \mathbb{R}\}$, range $\{y \in \mathbb{R}, y \ge 0\}$; $g(x)$: domain $\{x \in \mathbb{R}\}$, range $\{y \in \mathbb{R}, y \ge -8\}$

b) $f(x) = \sqrt{x}; y = f(x - 6) + 3$; translate 6 units right and 3 units up;

$f(x)$: domain $\{x \in \mathbb{R}, x \ge 0\}$, range $\{y \in \mathbb{R}, y \ge 0\}$; $g(x)$: domain $\{x \in \mathbb{R}, x \ge 6\}$, range $\{y \in \mathbb{R}, y \ge 3\}$

c) $f(x) = \dfrac{1}{x}; y = f(x + 3) + 1$; translate 3 units left and 1 unit up;

$f(x)$: domain $\{x \in \mathbb{R}, x \ne 0\}$, range $\{y \in \mathbb{R}, y \ne 0\}$; $g(x)$: domain $\{x \in \mathbb{R}, x \ne -3\}$, range $\{y \in \mathbb{R}, y \ne 1\}$

9.

$f(x)$: domain $\{x \in \mathbb{R}\}$, range $\{y \in \mathbb{R}, y \ge -4\}$

a) domain $\{x \in \mathbb{R}\}$, range $\{y \in \mathbb{R}, y \ge -4\}$

b) domain $\{x \in \mathbb{R}\}$, range $\{y \in \mathbb{R}, y \le 4\}$

c) domain $\{x \in \mathbb{R}\}$, range $\{y \in \mathbb{R}, y \le 4\}$

10. a) i) $g(x) = -\sqrt{x} - 5$ **ii)** $g(x) = -\dfrac{1}{x} + 7$

b) $h(x) = \sqrt{-x} + 5$ **ii)** $h(x) = -\dfrac{1}{x} - 7$

11. a) $a = 4$; $g(x) = 4x^2$;

f(x): domain $\{x \in \mathbb{R}\}$,
range $\{y \in \mathbb{R}, y \geq 0\}$;
g(x): domain $\{x \in \mathbb{R}\}$,
range $\{y \in \mathbb{R}, y \geq 0\}$

b) $k = 5$; $g(x) = (5x)^2$;

f(x): domain $\{x \in \mathbb{R}\}$,
range $\{y \in \mathbb{R}, y \geq 0\}$;
g(x): domain $\{x \in \mathbb{R}\}$,
range $= \{y \in \mathbb{R}, y \geq 0\}$

c) $k = \dfrac{1}{3}$; $g(x) = \left(\dfrac{1}{3}x\right)^2$;

f(x): domain $\{x \in \mathbb{R}\}$,
range $\{y \in \mathbb{R}, y \geq 0\}$;
g(x): domain $\{x \in \mathbb{R}\}$,
range $\{y \in \mathbb{R}, y \geq 0\}$

d) $a = \dfrac{1}{4}$; $g(x) = \dfrac{1}{4}x^2$;

f(x): domain $\{x \in \mathbb{R}\}$,
range $\{y \in \mathbb{R}, y \geq 0\}$;
g(x): domain $\{x \in \mathbb{R}\}$,
range $\{y \in \mathbb{R}, y \geq 0\}$

12. a) $f(x) = x$; vertical stretch by a factor of 5

b) $f(x) = \dfrac{1}{x}$; horizontal compression by a factor of $\dfrac{1}{4}$

c) $f(x) = x^2$; horizontal compression by a factor of $\dfrac{1}{3}$

d) $f(x) = \sqrt{x}$; horizontal compression by a factor of $\dfrac{1}{9}$

13. a) vertical stretch by a factor of 3, then translation of 6 units left; $g(x) = 3\sqrt{x + 6}$

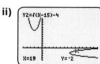

b) reflection in the x-axis, horizontal compression by a factor of $\dfrac{1}{6}$, and then translation of 5 units down; $g(x) = -6x - 5$

c) vertical compression by a factor of $\dfrac{1}{5}$, then translation of 4 units up;
$g(x) = \dfrac{1}{5}\left(\dfrac{1}{x}\right) + 4$ or
$g(x) = \dfrac{1}{5x} + 4$

d) reflection in the x-axis, vertical stretch by a factor of 2, horizontal compression by a factor of $\dfrac{1}{3}$, and then translation of 4 units left and 6 units down;
$g(x) = -2[3(x + 4)]^2 - 6$

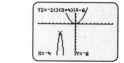

14. a) $f(x) = x$;

f(x): domain $\{x \in \mathbb{R}\}$,
range $\{y \in \mathbb{R}\}$;
g(x): domain $\{x \in \mathbb{R}\}$,
range $\{y \in \mathbb{R}\}$

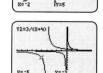

b) $f(x) = \dfrac{1}{x}$;

f(x): domain $\{x \in \mathbb{R}, x \neq 0\}$,
range $\{y \in \mathbb{R}, y \neq 0\}$;
g(x): domain $\{x \in \mathbb{R}, x \neq -4\}$,
range $\{y \in \mathbb{R}, y \neq 0\}$

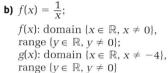

c) $f(x) = \sqrt{x}$;

f(x): domain $\{x \in \mathbb{R}, x \geq 0\}$,
range $\{y \in \mathbb{R}, y \geq 0\}$;
g(x): domain $\{x \in \mathbb{R}, x \geq 0\}$,
range $\{y \in \mathbb{R}, y \leq 1\}$

d) $f(x) = x^2$;

f(x): domain $\{x \in \mathbb{R}\}$,
range $\{y \in \mathbb{R}, y \geq 0\}$;
g(x): domain $\{x \in \mathbb{R}\}$,
range $\{y \in \mathbb{R}, y \geq 0\}$

15. a) i) $f^{-1}(x) = \dfrac{x + 5}{7}$ **ii)**

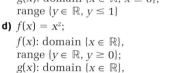

iii) Yes. $f^{-1}(x)$ is a function.

b) i) $f^{-1}(x) = \pm\sqrt{\dfrac{x - 9}{2}}$ **ii)**

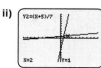

iii) No. $f^{-1}(x)$ is not a function.

c) i) $f^{-1}(x) = \pm\sqrt{x - 15} - 4$

ii)

iii) No. $f^{-1}(x)$ is not a function.

d) i) $f^{-1}(x) = \pm\sqrt{\dfrac{x + 30}{5}} - 2$

ii)

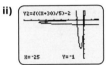

iii) No. $f^{-1}(x)$ is not a function.

16. a) $E = 600 + 0.05s$, where E represents Jai's weekly earnings, in dollars, and s represents Jai's weekly sales, in dollars.

b) $s = \dfrac{E - 600}{0.05}$

c) The inverse function represents Jai's weekly sales, s, in dollars, as a function of her weekly earnings, E, in dollars.

d) $3500

Chapter 2 Practice Test, pages 144–145

1. B **2.** C **3.** D **4.** C **5.** B

6. Answers may vary. Sample answer: No. The two expressions are not equivalent. The first expression is not defined for $x = 7$. The second expression is defined for $x = 7$. The first expression can be simplified to $6x + 15$. The second expression can be simplified to $5x + 15$. Since the expressions are not equivalent when simplified, the given expressions are not equivalent.

7. The inverse of $f(x)$ is not a function.

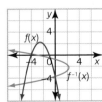

8. a) $\dfrac{x - 8}{(x + 7)(x - 3)}, x \neq -15, x \neq -7, x \neq 3$

b) $\dfrac{(x + 10)(x + 2)}{(x + 5)(x - 3)}, x \neq -10, x \neq -5, x \neq 3$

c) $\dfrac{-x + 57}{(x - 7)(x - 2)}, x \neq 2, x \neq 7$

d) $\dfrac{x^2 + 15x + 42}{(x + 6)(x + 3)}, x \neq -6, x \neq -3$

9. a) $f(x) = x^2$

b) vertical stretch by a factor of 4, horizontal compression by a factor of $\dfrac{1}{3}$, and then translation of 2 units left and 9 units up

c)

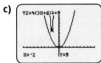

$f(x)$: domain $\{x \in \mathbb{R}\}$, range $\{y \in \mathbb{R}, y \geq 0\}$; $g(x)$: domain $\{x \in \mathbb{R}\}$, range $\{y \in \mathbb{R}, y \geq 9\}$

10. a) $f(x) = \sqrt{x}$

b) vertical compression by a factor of $\dfrac{1}{5}$, horizontal compression by a factor of $\dfrac{1}{2}$, and then translation of 8 units right and 3 units down

c)

$f(x)$: domain $\{x \in \mathbb{R}, x \geq 0\}$, range $\{y \in \mathbb{R}, y \geq 0\}$; $g(x)$: domain $\{x \in \mathbb{R}, x \geq 8\}$, range $\{y \in \mathbb{R}, y \geq -3\}$

11. a) $f(x) = \dfrac{1}{x}$

b) vertical stretch by a factor of 2, horizontal stretch by a factor of 2, and then translation of 5 units up

c)

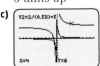

$f(x)$: domain $\{x \in \mathbb{R}, x \neq 0\}$, range $\{y \in \mathbb{R}, y \neq 0\}$; $g(x)$: domain $\{x \in \mathbb{R}, x \neq 0\}$, range $\{y \in \mathbb{R}, y \neq 5\}$

12. a) i) $f^{-1}(x) = \dfrac{x - 8}{3}$ **ii)**

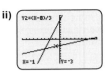

iii) Yes. $f^{-1}(x)$ is a function.

b) i) $f^{-1}(x) = \pm\sqrt{\dfrac{x - 8}{6}} + 9$

ii)

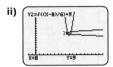

iii) No. $f^{-1}(x)$ is not a function.

c) i) $f^{-1}(x) = \pm\sqrt{\dfrac{x + 100}{3}} - 6$

ii)

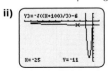

iii) No. $f^{-1}(x)$ is not a function.

13. a) $R = (80 + 5x)(120 - 15x)$

b) R: domain $\{x \in \mathbb{Z}, 0 \leq x \leq 8\}$, range $\{R \in \mathbb{R}, 0 \leq R \leq 10\,800\}$

c) $x = \pm\sqrt{\dfrac{R - 10\,800}{-75}} - 4$; the number of $5 increases as a function of the revenue, R, in dollars; domain $\{R \in \mathbb{R}, 0 \leq R \leq 10\,800\}$, range $\{x \in \mathbb{Z}, 0 \leq x \leq 8\}$

d) 2 $5 increases

14. a) $T = \dfrac{19\,200}{(160 + w)(160 - w)}$; domain $\{w \in \mathbb{R}, -160 < x < 160\}$, range $\{T \in \mathbb{R}, T \geq 0.75\}$

b)

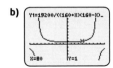

c) Answers may vary. Sample answer: No. The minimum time to complete the round trip occurs when there is no prevailing wind. While some time will be made up, it will always take longer to complete the trip when wind is involved.

15. a)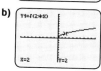

b) For lesser values of ℓ, in litres, the graph has greater values of m, in litres per 100 km.

c) $m_{\text{Imperial}} = \dfrac{235}{1.2\,\ell}$

d) Answers may vary. Sample answer: horizontal compression by a factor of $\dfrac{1}{1.2}$

Chapter 3

Prerequisite Skills, pages 148–149

1. a) C **b)** A **c)** B

2. Answers may vary.

3. a) x^5 **b)** y^9 **c)** m^2 **d)** h

e) a^7b^6 **f)** x^2y^2 **g)** $a^4b^8c^{12}$ **h)** $9u^2v^6$

i) $\dfrac{a^2b^4}{16}$ **j)** $-\dfrac{27w^6}{64r^9}$

4. a) 128 **b)** 729 **c)** 32 000 **d)** 1

e) 64 **f)** 5 **g)** 6561 **h)** 64

5. a) missing values in the y-column: 4, 2, 1

b) Answers may vary. Sample answer: Divide each previous term by 2.

c) missing values in the y-column:

$4, 2, 1, \dfrac{1}{2^2}, \dfrac{1}{2^3}, \dfrac{1}{2^n}$

6. a) 1 **b)** $\dfrac{1}{16}$ **c)** $-\dfrac{1}{216}$ **d)** $\dfrac{1}{9}$

e) 1 **f)** -1 **g)** $\dfrac{25}{16}$ **h)** $\dfrac{1}{9}$

7. a) $\dfrac{1}{x}$ **b)** $\dfrac{1}{y^6}$ **c)** $\dfrac{u}{v}$ **d)** $\dfrac{1}{16a^4b^2}$

8. a) i) $\{x \in \mathbb{R}\}$ **ii)** $\{y \in \mathbb{R}\}$

iii) x-intercept 8; y-intercept 4

b) i) $\{x \in \mathbb{R}\}$ **ii)** $\{y \in \mathbb{R}, y \geq -5\}$

iii) x-intercepts -8, 2; y-intercept -2

9. a)
i) $\{x \in \mathbb{R}\}$
ii) $\{y \in \mathbb{R}, y \geq -9\}$
iii) x-intercepts -3, 3; y-intercept -9

b)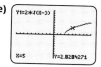
i) $\{x \in \mathbb{R}, x \geq -4\}$
ii) $\{y \in \mathbb{R}, y \geq 0\}$
iii) x-intercept -4; y-intercept 2

10. Translate 2 units right and 1 unit down.

11. a)   **b)**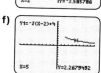

11. a)

b)

c)

d)

e)

f)

3.1 The Nature of Exponential Growth, pages 155–157

1. a)

Day	Population	First Differences	Second Differences
0	20		
1	80	60	
2	320	240	180
3	1 280	960	720
4	5 120	3 840	2 880
5	20 480	15 360	11 520

Answers for parts b) to e) may vary. Sample answers:

b) Yes; the values in each difference column increase by a factor of 4.

c) Differences in each column are 4 times the previous difference in that column.

d) Yes.

e)

Third Differences	Fourth Differences
540	
2160	1620
8640	6480

Yes.

2. Answers may vary. Sample answer: Since $10^3 = 1000$, $10^2 = 100$, and $10^1 = 10$, following the pattern of dividing by 10 suggests $10^0 = 1$.

3. a) $\dfrac{a \times a \times a}{a \times a \times a}$ **b)** 1 **c)** a^0

d) Answers may vary. Sample answer: $a^0 = 1$

4. a) 1 **b)** 1 **c)** 1 **d)** 1

5. a)–b) Answers may vary.

c) i) 81 **ii)** 19 683 **d)** 6 **e)** 6

6. a) i) $\{x \in \mathbb{R}, x > 0\}$ **ii)** $\{y \in \mathbb{R}, y = 0\}$

iii) linear and horizontal along the x-axis

b)

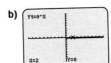

c) Answers may vary. Sample answer: The **Trace** operation does not give a value for $x = 0$.

7. a) i) 10 people   **ii)** 20 people

b) Answers may vary.

c) Answers may vary. Sample answer: Yes; the ratio of successive first differences is 2.

8. Answers may vary. Sample answer: Take the Double Deal; it is worth the most after 2 weeks.

9. a) $p = 200 \times 3^t$ **b)**

Answers for parts c) and d) may vary. Sample answers:

c) 961; the graph is easier to use.

d) 106 288 200; the equation is easier to use.

10. a) 0.05; $A = P(1.05)^t$

b)–c)

Number of Compounding Periods (years)	Amount ($)	First Differences	Second Differences
0	100		
		5	
1	105		0.25
		5.25	
2	110.25		0.26
		5.51	
3	115.76		0.28
		5.79	
4	121.55		

d)

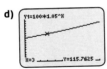

Answers for parts e) and f) may vary. Sample answers:

e) The points between values have no meaning because the payment of interest is not continuous.

f) The function is exponential because each value in the chart is greater than the previous by a factor of 1.05.

11. a) $2249.73   **b)** $2737.14

12. a) approximately 10.24 years

b) approximately 4 more years

13. Answers may vary.

14. a) approximately 5.7 days, approximate population 25 600 bacteria cells

b) approximately 2.6 days faster

15. Answers may vary. Sample answers:

a) The Double Deal is still the best choice, because it still pays more.

b) $0.03

16. C   **17.** D   **18.** B

19. $\frac{1}{9}$

20. $\frac{1}{2} + \frac{1}{3} + \frac{1}{6}; \frac{1}{4} + \frac{1}{4} + \frac{1}{2}$

3.2 Exponential Decay: Connecting to Negative Exponents, pages 166–169

1. a) $\frac{1}{3}$ **b)** $\frac{1}{x}$ **c)** $\frac{1}{y^2}$

d) $\frac{1}{ab}$ **e)** $-\frac{1}{x^2}$ **f)** $\frac{1}{x^2}$

2. a) 5^{-2} **b)** k^{-3}

3. a) $\frac{1}{36}$ **b)** $\frac{1}{32}$ **c)** $\frac{1}{10\ 000}$

d) $\frac{1}{729}$ **e)** $\frac{1}{2}$ **f)** $\frac{5}{8}$

4. a) 16   **b)** $\frac{1}{256}$ **c)** 100 000

d) $\frac{1}{5}$ **e)** 49   **f)** $\frac{1}{16}$

g) 9   **h)** 4

5. a) m **b)** $-\frac{6}{v^9}$ **c)** p^7

d) $\frac{3}{w^2}$ **e)** k^{12} **f)** $\frac{b^6}{4a^2}$

6. a) 64   **b)** $\frac{1\ 000\ 000}{729}$ **c)** $\frac{16}{81}$

d) $-\frac{8}{125}$ **e)** 8   **f)** 1600

7. a) a^2b^2 **b)** $512u^3$ **c)** $\frac{w^4}{g^8}$

d) $\frac{27b^6}{64a^9}$ **e)** $\frac{b^9}{27a^6}$ **f)** $\frac{x^4}{y^2}$

8. a)

Time (days)	Amount of W-187 remaining (mg)
0	100
1	50
2	25
3	12.5
4	6.25

b) $f(x) = 100\left(\frac{1}{2}\right)^x$, where f is the amount of W-187 remaining, in milligrams, on day x.

c)

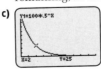

d) 0.781 25 mg   **e)** 4.3 days

f) The function $f(x) = 100(2^{-x})$ can also be used, as $\left(\frac{1}{2}\right)^x = (2^{-1})^x$, which is equal to 2^{-x}.

9. a) i) $\frac{1}{9}$ **ii)** $\frac{1}{27}$ **b)** $\frac{1}{243}$ **c)** $\frac{1}{243}$

d) Answers may vary. Sample answer: The two answers are the same. This illustrates that the product rule applies to negative exponents.

e) Answers may vary.

10.–11. Answers may vary.

12. a) 20 000 is the initial value of the car; 0.7 represents the remaining value of the car (as a percent) after each year; and t represents the time since purchase, in years.

b) i) $14 000   **ii)** $9800

c)

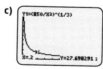

d) approximately 6.5 years

13. a) Answers may vary. Sample answer: Substituting negative values for n will give amounts of Pu-239 before the beginning of the study.

b) i) 100 mg   **ii)** 400 mg

14.–15. Answers may vary.

17. $767.90

18. 2.1×10^{20} N

19. a) $F = \dfrac{GMm}{r^2}$

b) Answers may vary. Sample answer: This is an inverse square relationship because the force between two objects is proportional to the inverse of the square of the distance, r, separating those objects.

c) Answers may vary.

20. Answers may vary.

21. A   **22.** D   **23.** B

3.3 Rational Exponents, pages 175–177

1. a) 4   **b)** -10 **c)** $\dfrac{1}{2}$ **d)** $\dfrac{2}{3}$

2. a) 3   **b)** $\dfrac{2}{5}$ **c)** 2   **d)** -10

3. a) 4   **b)** 16   **c)** -1024 **d)** $\dfrac{1}{1000}$

4. a) $\dfrac{1}{2}$ **b)** $\dfrac{1}{125}$ **c)** 128

d) 4   **e)** $\dfrac{27}{1000}$ **f)** $\dfrac{9}{4}$

5. a) $x^{\frac{1}{2}}$ **b)** $m^{\frac{13}{12}}$ **c)** $w^{\frac{1}{6}}$

d) $a^{\frac{1}{2}}b^{\frac{5}{3}}$ **e)** $y^{\frac{1}{3}}$ **f)** $u^{\frac{1}{6}}v^{\frac{1}{9}}$

6. a) k **b)** $\dfrac{1}{p^{\frac{3}{2}}}$ **c)** $\dfrac{1}{y^2}$

d) $w^{\frac{2}{3}}$ **e)** $\dfrac{4}{3}x^{\frac{1}{3}}$ **f)** $\dfrac{5}{49}y^{\frac{4}{3}}$

7. 4000 cm²

8. a) $A = \ell^2$ **b)** $\ell = A^{\frac{1}{2}}$

c) i) 6 m   **ii)** 13 cm   **iii)** $4\sqrt{5}$ m

d) $S = 6\ell^2$, $\ell = \left(\dfrac{S}{6}\right)^{\frac{1}{2}}$

e) i) 5 m   **ii)** 10 cm   **iii)** $5\left(\dfrac{5}{3}\right)^{\frac{1}{2}}$ m

9. a) $V = \ell^3$ **b)** $\ell = V^{\frac{1}{3}}$

c) i) 4 m   **ii)** 7 cm   **iii)** approximately 2.49 m

10. a) B and C are correct

Answers for parts b) and c) may vary. Sample answers:

b) Since B and C are equivalent, both are correct.

c) It is called the square-cube law because the square of the volume is related to the cube of the surface area.

11. a) i) 600 cm²   **ii)** approximately 205.2 m²

Answers for parts b) to d) may vary. Sample answers:

b) I used $S = 6V^{\frac{2}{3}}$, since it gives the surface area in terms of the volume.

c) i) 343 m³   **ii)** approximately 15.2 cm³

d) I used $V = \left(\dfrac{S}{6}\right)^{\frac{3}{2}}$, since it gives the volume in terms of the surface area.

12. a) 1.72×10^{-17} **b)** 1.9 times as long

c) 1.1×10^{11} m

13. a) $r = \left(\dfrac{T}{k}\right)^{\frac{2}{3}}$ **b)** 7.87×10^{11} m

15. a) $V = \pi r^2 h$ **b)** $r = \sqrt{\dfrac{V}{\pi h}}$

16. a) $SA = 2\pi r^2 + 2\pi rh$

b) $SA = \dfrac{2V}{h} + 2\sqrt{\pi h V}$

c) $SA = \dfrac{1}{5}V + 2\sqrt{10\pi V}$

d) 554.5 m²

17. a) $V = \sqrt[3]{\dfrac{850}{P^2}}$ **b)** 2.04 m³

c)

d) Answers may vary. Sample answer: This relation is a function since there is exactly one volume for each given pressure value.

18. A   **19.** 5

3.4 Properties of Exponential Functions, pages 185–187

1. a) B   **b)** D   **c)** C   **d)** A

2. a) Answers may vary.

b) Answers may vary. Sample answer: No; there are many exponential functions with these properties.

3. a) Answers may vary.

b) Answers may vary. Sample answer: No; there are many exponential functions with these properties.

4. $y = 4(2^x)$

5. $y = 24\left(\dfrac{1}{2}\right)^x$

6. a) C   **b)** approximately 2.2 mg

7. a)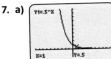

i) $\{x \in \mathbb{R}\}$
ii) $\{y \in \mathbb{R}, y > 0\}$

iii) no x-intercept; y-intercept 1
iv) always decreasing **v)** $y = 0$

b)

i) $\{x \in \mathbb{R}\}$
ii) $\{y \in \mathbb{R}, y > 0\}$

iii) no x-intercept; y-intercept 2
iv) always increasing **v)** $y = 0$

c)

i) $\{x \in \mathbb{R}\}$
ii) $\{y \in \mathbb{R}, y < 0\}$

iii) no x-intercept; y-intercept -1
iv) always increasing **v)** $y = 0$

8. a) i) **ii)**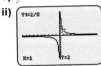

Answers for parts b) and c) may vary. Sample answers:

b) They are alike in that they both have a horizontal asymptote at $y = 0$. They differ in that $f(x)$ is increasing for all $x \in \mathbb{R}$ and $r(x)$ is decreasing on the intervals $x < 0$ and $x > 0$ ($r(x)$ is not defined at $x = 0$). $r(x)$ also has a vertical asymptote at $x = 0$.

c) They have the same horizontal asymptotes.

9. a) i) 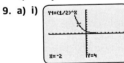 **ii)**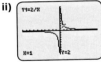

Answers for parts b) and c) may vary. Sample answers:

b) They both have a horizontal asymptote at $y = 0$. They differ in that $g(x)$ is decreasing for all $x \in \mathbb{R}$ and $r(x)$ is decreasing on the intervals $x < 0$ and $x > 0$ (it is not defined at $x = 0$). $r(x)$ also has a vertical asymptote at $x = 0$.

c) They have the same horizontal asymptotes.

10. Answers may vary. Sample answers:

a) The two graphs are identical.

b)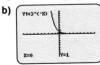

c) Since $\frac{1}{3} = 3^{-1}$, $\left(\frac{1}{3}\right)^x = (3^{-1})^x$, which can be simplified to 3^{-x}.

11. a) $\{x \in \mathbb{R}, x \geq 0\}$ **b)** $\{y \in \mathbb{R}, 0 < y \leq 2\}$
c) 2 V **d)** 0 V
e) approximately 1 ms

12. Answers may vary. Sample answers:

a) The value of 0.75 is the base of the exponential function and the 2 represents a horizontal compression by a factor of $\frac{1}{2}$.

b)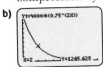

c) The base of the exponential function is between 0 and 1, indicating that the number of revolutions per minute is decreasing.

d) i) 2250 **ii)** 712

13. a) $\frac{1}{4}$

b) Answers may vary. Sample answer: Substitute $t = 0$ and $V = 2$ to find V_0. Then, substitute $t = 0.001$ and $V = 1$ from the graph, as well as the given values for R and C to find b.

c)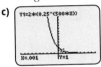

d) domain $\{x \in \mathbb{R}\}$, range $\{y \in \mathbb{R}, y > 0\}$
e) domain $\{x \in \mathbb{R}, x \geq 0\}$, range $\{y \in \mathbb{R}, 0 < y \leq 2\}$. Answers may vary. Sample answer: The restriction is made because the circuit only begins to discharge at $t = 0$.

14. a) $S = \frac{(3V)^{\frac{1}{2}}}{5}$

b) Answers may vary. Sample answer: domain $\{V \in \mathbb{R}, V > 0\}$

c) The side length of the base will increase by a factor of $\sqrt{2}$.

15. a) $SA = 2V + 2(V\pi)^{\frac{1}{2}}$
b) $SA \doteq 4.77$ m²; $d \doteq 1.00$ m
c) $\{V \in \mathbb{R}, V > 0\}$ **d)**

16. 1, 3 **17.** A **18.** A

3.5 Transformations of Exponential Functions, pages 196–198

1. a) translate 2 units up
b) translate 3 units right
c) translate 4 units left
d) translate 1 unit right and 5 units down

2. a) 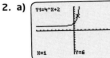 **b)**

c)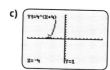

d)

3. a) $y = 5^x - 3$

b) $y = 5^{x-2}$

c) $y = 5^{x + \frac{1}{2}}$

d) $y = 5^{x + 2.5} + 1$

4. a) vertical compression by a factor of $\frac{1}{2}$

b) horizontal compression by a factor of $\frac{1}{4}$

c) reflection in the x-axis

d) reflection in the y-axis and horizontal compression by a factor of $\frac{1}{2}$

5. a)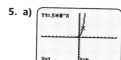

b)

c)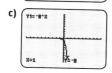

d)

6. a) $y = -7^x$

b) $y = 3(7^x)$

c) $y = 7^{\frac{x}{2.4}}$

d) $y = 7(7^{-x})$

7.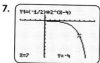

8.

9. a)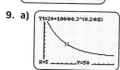

b) $T = 20$; room temperature

c) approximately 28.7 min

10. a)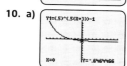

b) i) $\{x \in \mathbb{R}\}$

ii) $\{x \in \mathbb{R}, y > -1\}$

iii) $y = -1$

11. a)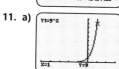

b) $y = 3^{2x}$; horizontal compression of the graph of $y = 3^x$ by a factor of $\frac{1}{2}$

c) $y = 81^{\frac{1}{2}x}$; horizontal stretch of the graph of $y = 81^x$ by a factor of 2

d) Answers may vary. Sample answer: Since 3^{2x} and $81^{\frac{1}{2}x}$ both equal 9^x, all three functions are equivalent.

12. Answers may vary. Sample answers:

a) $y = 2^{3x}$, $y = 64^{\frac{1}{2}x}$

b) Since 2^{3x} and $64^{\frac{1}{2}x}$ both equal 8^x, all three functions are equivalent.

13. Answers may vary. Sample answers:

a) $y = 2^{x+1} + 4$

b) There are many possible functions. Many transformations of different functions can produce the function in part a).

14. Answers may vary. Sample answers:

a) $y = 2(2^x)$ **b)** $y = 2^x + 1$, $y = 2^{x+1}$

c) All functions have base 2, and when $x = 0$ is substituted into each equation, the result is $y = 2$.

15. Answers may vary.

16. a)

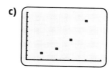

b) Answers may vary. Sample answer: The number of squares is growing exponentially as a power of 2.

c) $s = 2^n$ **d) i)** 32   **ii)** 1024

17. a)–b)

Term Number (n)	Number of Toothpicks (t)	First Differences	Second Differences
1	7		
2	12	5	
3	22	10	5
4	42	20	10

c)

Answers for parts d) to f) may vary. Sample answers:

d) The function that expresses t in terms of n is exponential, since the ratio of successive finite differences is always 2.

e) $t = 5(2^{n-1}) + 2$

f) This function results from a vertical stretch by a factor of 5 and a translation of 1 unit right and 2 units up.

18.–19. Answers may vary.

21. Answers may vary. Sample answers:

a) 2 white squares, 3 short horizontal rectangles, 2 short vertical rectangles, 2 slightly longer vertical rectangles

b) The growing patterns of the different types of pieces all seem to be exponential.

c) $t = 7(2^{n-1}) + 2$

d) They are all translations of the function $y = 2^n$. The function in part c) results from a vertical stretch of the function in question 16 by a factor of 5 and a shift of 1 unit right and 2 units up. The function in part c) results from a vertical stretch of the function in question 17 by a factor of $\frac{7}{5}$ and a shift of $\frac{4}{5}$ units down.

22. a)

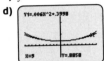

Answers for parts b) to f) may vary. Sample answers:

b) This graph resembles a quadratic function.

c) $y = 0.006x^2 + 0.3998$

d)

Y1=.006X^2+.3998

X=5   Y=.0858

e) The graphs are similar, but the quadratic equation is slightly lower than the catenary function for the graphed domain.

f) This difference is magnified as the values of x get larger in the positive and negative directions.

23. 117   **24.** B   **25.** $\{y \in \mathbb{R}, y > -3\}$ **26.** A

3.6 Making Connections: Tools and Strategies for Applying Exponential Models, pages 207–209

1. a) D   **b)** C   **c)** A

2. Answers may vary.

3. Answers may vary. Sample answers:

a) Yes; the data appear to be exponential.

b) I estimate that $a = 100$ and $b = 1.1$. I arrived at these values by calculating the ratio of successive first differences.

d) $259.37

e) approximately 7 years

4. a)

Time (half-hour intervals)	Number of People Who Just Heard the News
0	1
1	2
2	4
3	8
4	16
5	32

Answers for parts b) to d) may vary. Sample answers:

b)

The trend is increasing.

c) The data seem to follow an exponential function, since the ratio of successive first differences is constant.

d) $P = 2^n$, where P represents the number of people that know and n represents the number of half-hour increments.

5. Answers may vary. Sample answers:

a) No, as eventually everyone in the company will know the news.

b)

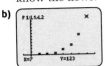

At the beginning of the 24-h period, only Gina knows the news. After each half-hour interval, twice as many people hear the news, which gives the points (0, 1), (1, 2), (2, 4), (3, 8), (4, 16), (5, 32), and (6, 64). Since $1 + 2 + 4 + 8 + 16 + 32 + 64 = 127$, after six half-hour intervals have elapsed there are only $250 - 127 = 123$ people are left who know the news. All of these people hear the news in the next interval, at (7, 123). After this time, no one will learn of the news, and so all remaining coordinates have a y-value of 0.

6.–7. Answers may vary.

8. Answers may vary. Sample answers:

a)

The data appear to be linear.

b) The data seem to follow a linear relation, as the increase in y-values is consistently around 30 to 40 pandas per year. A linear model is $P = 35x + 800$ and an exponential model is $P = 800(1.04^x)$, where x is the number of years and P is the number of pandas.

c) linear model: 1220 pandas; exponential model: 1281 pandas

d) Answers may vary. Sample answer: linear model: 34.3 years, exponential model: 23.4 years

9. Answers may vary. Sample answers:

a) $y = 100(1.023)^x$, where y represents the CPI and x represents the time, in years (2002 is $x = 0$).

b) The average Canadian's earnings are growing at a rate that is slightly greater than the CPI, as the value of the base of the exponent is slightly greater.

10. Answers may vary.

11. Answers may vary. Sample answers:

a) Earnings for Ontarians are greater than earnings for all Canadians.

b) The only province that has a greater average weekly salary than Ontario is Alberta. The three territories have consistently had greater average weekly earnings than Ontario.

12.–15. Answers may vary.

Chapter 3 Review, pages 210–211

1. D

2. Answers may vary.

3. a) 1   **b)** Answers may vary.

4. a) $A = 250\left(\frac{1}{2}\right)^n$, where n is the number of years and A is the amount radioactive material remaining, in milligrams.

   b) 0.244 mg   **c)** approximately 2.3 years

5. Answers may vary. Sample answers:

   a) $A = 250(2^{-n})$

   b) Since $b^{-x} = \frac{1}{b^x}$, which can be written as $\left(\frac{1}{b}\right)^x$, then $\left(\frac{1}{2}\right)^n = 2^{-n}$, so the equations are equivalent.

6. a) $\frac{1}{10}$ **b)** $\frac{1}{16}$ **c)** $\frac{2}{9}$

   d) $\frac{126}{125}$ **e)** 5   **f)** $\frac{64}{27}$

7. a) $\frac{1}{x^3}$ **b)** $\frac{6}{k}$ **c)** $\frac{1}{w}$

   d) uv^5 **e)** z^6 **f)** $\frac{b^2}{4a^2}$

8. a) 4   **b)** 5   **c)** -5

   d) $\frac{1}{2}$ **e)** 9   **f)** 10 000

   g) $-\frac{1}{64}$ **h)** $\frac{16}{9}$ **i)** $\frac{25}{9}$

9. a) $x = 2^{\frac{1}{2}} U^{\frac{1}{2}} k^{-\frac{1}{2}}$

   b) $x = \sqrt{\dfrac{2U}{k}}$ **c)** 8 cm

10. a)

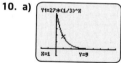

   b) i) $\{x \in \mathbb{R}\}$ **ii)** $\{y \in \mathbb{R}, y > 0\}$
   iii) no x-intercepts; y-intercept 27
   iv) The function is decreasing over its domain.
   v) $y = 0$

11. $y = 10(2)^{2x}$ or $y = 10(4^x)$

12. a) 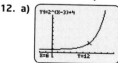   **b) i)** $\{x \in \mathbb{R}\}$
                         ii) $\{y \in \mathbb{R}, y > 4\}$
                         iii) $y = 4$

13. a) vertical stretch by a factor of 2
   b) horizontal compression by a factor of $\frac{1}{2}$
   c) reflection in the x-axis and the y-axis
   d) reflection in the y-axis, horizontal compression by a factor of $\frac{1}{5}$, translation of 2 units left

14. a)

Number of Bounces, n	Height, h (cm)	First Differences	Second Differences
0	100		
1	76	−24	
2	57	−19	5
3	43	−14	5
4	32	−11	3
5	24	−8	3

Answers for parts b) to f) may vary. Sample answers:

b)

The data seem to follow an exponential curve.

c) $y = 100(0.75)^x$

d) i) According to the mathematical model, the ball should never stop bouncing, as it will always bounce to a height that is 75% of the previous bounce, which will never equal 0.
   ii) In the real situation, the ball will eventually stop bouncing.

e) There is also a slight loss of energy due to air resistance and friction. Eventually, these factors will cause the ball to stop bouncing.

Chapter 3 Practice Test, pages 212–213

1. B   **2.** C   **3.** A   **4.** A

5. a) 7   **b)** $\frac{1}{125}$ **c)** 1   **d)** 2

   e) -32 **f)** $\frac{256}{81}$ **g)** $\frac{4}{3}$ **h)** $\frac{625}{16}$

6. a) $\frac{1}{x^3}$ **b)** $\frac{1}{p^5}$ **c)** $\frac{1}{2k^4}$

   d) $a^{\frac{7}{6}}$ **e)** $\frac{1}{y^4}$ **f)** $\frac{v^6}{u}$

7. Answers may vary, but should be of the form $y = a(2^x)$ for some value of a.

8. a) C   **b)** A   **c)** D   **d)** B

9. a)   **b) i)** $\{x \in \mathbb{R}\}$
                         ii) $\{y \in \mathbb{R}, y > 3\}$
                         iii) $y = 3$

10. a) vertical compression by a factor of $\frac{1}{3}$
   b) horizontal compression by a factor of $\frac{1}{4}$
   c) reflection in the x-axis, reflection in the y-axis
   d) reflection in the y-axis, horizontal compression by a factor of $\frac{1}{3}$, translation of 2 units left

11. Answers may vary. Sample answers:
   a) $M = 80\left(\frac{1}{2}\right)^{\frac{t}{2.5}}$, M is the mass remaining, in milligrams, after t days.

b)

The function is a decreasing exponential function: as the values of t increase, the values of M decrease.

c) $\{t \in \mathbb{R}, t \geq 0\}$ **d) i)** approximately 5 mg

ii) approximately 1.25 mg

e) approximately 10.8 days

12. a) 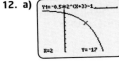   **b) i)** $\{x \in \mathbb{R}\}$

                               ii) $\{y \in \mathbb{R}, y < -1\}$

                               iii) $y = -1$

13. 30 m

14. Answers may vary. Sample answers:

a)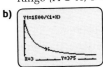

Yes; the data appear to be exponential in nature as are not increasing the y-values linearly.

b) $y = 1987.6(1.0805)^x$ **c)** $\{x \in \mathbb{R}, x \geq 0\}$

d) approximately 3417

e) approximately 9 years, assuming the rate of population growth increases at the same rate

Chapters 1 to 3 Review, pages 214–217

1. a) domain $\{x \in \mathbb{R}, -4 \leq x \leq 4\}$, range $\{y \in \mathbb{R}, -3 \leq y \leq 3\}$; this is not a function because a vertical line can be drawn that will pass through more than one point on the relation.

b) domain $\{-2, -1, 0, 1, 2\}$, range $\{1, 4, 9, 25\}$; this is a function because for each value in the domain there is exactly one value in the range.

c) domain $\{x \in \mathbb{R}\}$, range $\{y \in \mathbb{R}, y \geq -4\}$; this is a function because every vertical line intersects the relation at exactly one point.

2. a) $f: x \rightarrow \sqrt{1 - 3x}$; $f(-1) = 2$

b) $f: x \rightarrow \dfrac{2x + 1}{x^2 - 4}$; $f(-1) = \dfrac{1}{3}$

3. a) domain $\{i \in \mathbb{R}, i \geq 0\}$, range $\{A \in \mathbb{R}, 0 \leq A \leq 1500\}$

b)

c) approximately \$1456.31

d) 50%

4. a)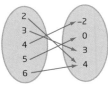

b) Since every value in the domain maps to exactly one value in the range, this is a function.

5. 333.3 m by 500 m

6. a) \$17.50   **b)** \$9187.50

7. a) $x = \dfrac{2 \pm \sqrt{10}}{2}$ **b)** $x = \dfrac{6 \pm 2\sqrt{6}}{3}$

8. a) 2   **b)** 2   **c)** 2

9. The length is approximately 8.81 m and the width is approximately 2.27 m.

10. a) $f(x) = \dfrac{1}{3}x^2 - \dfrac{1}{3}x - 4$ **b)** $f(x) = 2x^2 - 8x + 2$

11. a) 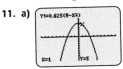   **b)** $f(x) = 9 - x^2$

                                   c) 9 m

12. a) $\left(\dfrac{5 + \sqrt{33}}{4}, \dfrac{15 + \sqrt{33}}{2} \right), \left(\dfrac{5 - \sqrt{33}}{4}, \dfrac{15 - \sqrt{33}}{2} \right)$

b) $\left(\dfrac{17 + \sqrt{321}}{4}, \dfrac{-9 - \sqrt{321}}{8} \right),$

      $\left(\dfrac{17 - \sqrt{321}}{4}, \dfrac{-9 + \sqrt{321}}{8} \right)$

13. $b = 5$

14. a) yes   **b)** no

15. a)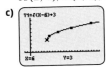

$A'(0, 4)$, $B'(1, 5)$, $C'(4, 6)$, $D'(9, 7)$, $E'(16, 8)$

b)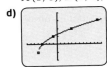

$A'(2, 0)$, $B'(3, 1)$, $C'(6, 2)$, $D'(11, 3)$, $E'(18, 4)$

c)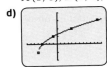

$A'(6, 3)$, $B'(7, 4)$, $C'(10, 5)$, $D'(15, 6)$, $E'(22, 7)$

d)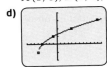

$A'(-5, -1)$, $B'(-4, 0)$, $C'(-1, 1)$, $D'(4, 2)$, $E'(11, 3)$

16. a) domain $\{x \in \mathbb{R}\}$,
range $\{y \in \mathbb{R}, y \geq -4\}$

b) domain $\{x \in \mathbb{R}\}$,
range $\{y \in \mathbb{R}, y \leq 4\}$

c) 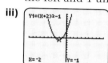 domain $\{x \in \mathbb{R}\}$,
range $\{y \in \mathbb{R}, y \leq 4\}$

17. a) i) $f(x) = x^2$

ii) $g(x) = f(x + 2) - 1$; translation of 2 units to
the left and 1 unit down

iii)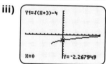

iv) $f(x)$: domain $\{x \in \mathbb{R}\}$, range $\{y \in \mathbb{R}, y \geq 0\}$;
$g(x)$: domain $\{x \in \mathbb{R}\}$, range $\{y \in \mathbb{R}, y \geq -1\}$

b) i) $f(x) = \sqrt{x}$

ii) $g(x) = f(x + 3) - 4$; translation of 3 units to
the left and 4 units down

iii)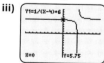

iv) $f(x)$: domain $\{x \in \mathbb{R}, x \geq 0\}$,
range $\{y \in \mathbb{R}, y \geq 0\}$;
$g(x)$: domain $\{x \in \mathbb{R}, x \geq -3\}$,
range $\{y \in \mathbb{R}, y \geq -4\}$

c) i) $f(x) = \dfrac{1}{x}$

ii) $g(x) = f(x - 4) + 6$; a translation of 4 units
to the right and 6 units up

iii)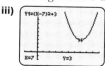

iv) $f(x)$: domain $\{x \in \mathbb{R}, x \neq 0\}$,
range $\{y \in \mathbb{R}, y \neq 0\}$;
$g(x)$: domain $\{x \in \mathbb{R}, x \neq 4\}$,
range $\{y \in \mathbb{R}, y \neq 6\}$

d) i) $f(x) = x^2$

ii) $g(x) = f(x - 7) + 3$; translation of 7 units to
the right and 3 units up

iii)

iv) $f(x)$: domain $\{x \in \mathbb{R}\}$, range $\{y \in \mathbb{R}, y \geq 0\}$;
$g(x)$: domain $\{x \in \mathbb{R}\}$, range $\{y \in \mathbb{R}, y \geq 3\}$

18. a) $t = \dfrac{20}{v + 1.5}$ **b)** $t = \dfrac{20}{v}$

c)

d) Shane's time would be approximately 48 min.

19. a) i) $g(x) = -2x^2 + 7x - 3$ **ii)** $h(x) = 2x^2 + 7x + 3$

b) i) $g(x) = -\sqrt{x} + 3$ **ii)** $h(x) = \sqrt{-x} - 3$

c) i) $g(x) = -\dfrac{1}{x + 2}$ **ii)** $h(x) = -\dfrac{1}{x - 2}$

20. a) $a = 2$; $g(x) = 2x^2$;
domain $\{x \in \mathbb{R}\}$,
range $\{y \in \mathbb{R}, y \geq 0\}$

b) $a = 9$; $g(x) = 9x^2$
or $g(x) = (3x)^2$;
domain $\{x \in \mathbb{R}\}$,
range $\{y \in \mathbb{R}, y \geq 0\}$

c) $a = \dfrac{1}{16}$; $g(x) = \dfrac{1}{16}x^2$
or $g(x) = \left(\dfrac{x}{4}\right)^2$;
domain $\{x \in \mathbb{R}\}$,
range $\{y \in \mathbb{R}, y \geq 0\}$

d) $a = \dfrac{1}{3}$; $g(x) = \dfrac{1}{3}x^2$;
domain $\{x \in \mathbb{R}\}$,
range $\{y \in \mathbb{R}, y \geq 0\}$

21. a) base function $f(x) = x$;
vertical stretch by a factor of 7

b) base function $f(x) = \dfrac{1}{x}$;
horizontal compression by a
factor of $\dfrac{1}{5}$

c) base function $f(x) = x^2$;
horizontal compression
by a factor of $\dfrac{1}{3}$

d) base function $f(x) = \sqrt{x}$;
horizontal compression
by a factor of $\dfrac{1}{6}$

22. Answers may vary. Sample answers:

a) vertical stretch by a factor of 4, horizontal translation of 3 units to the left

b) reflection in the x-axis, horizontal compression by a factor of $\frac{1}{5}$, vertical translation of 2 units down

c) reflection in the x-axis, vertical stretch by a factor of 3, horizontal compression by a factor of $\frac{1}{2}$, translation of $\frac{9}{2}$ units to the left and 4 units down

23. a) i) $f^{-1}(x) = \dfrac{x + 3}{11}$

ii)   **iii)** function

b) i) $f^{-1}(x) = \pm\sqrt{\dfrac{x - 4}{3}}$

ii) 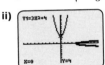   **iii)** not a function

c) i) $f^{-1}(x) = \pm\sqrt{x - 19} - 8$

ii) 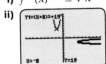   **iii)** not a function

d) i) $f^{-1}(x) = \pm\sqrt{\dfrac{1}{2}\left(x - \dfrac{103}{8}\right)} + \dfrac{3}{4}$

ii) 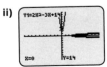   **iii)** not a function

24. a) $f(x) = 450 + 0.06x$ **b)** $f^{-1}(x) = \dfrac{x - 450}{0.06}$

c) The inverse represents Issa's total sales as a function of her total weekly earnings.

d) \$9500

25. a) $y = 3^x$ **b)** $y = x^2$

c) $y = \left(\dfrac{1}{3}\right)^x$ **d)** $y = 3x$

26. C

27. a) $M(t) = 200\left(\dfrac{1}{2}\right)^{\frac{t}{3}}$ **b)** approximately 19.8 g

c) approximately 10 years

d) $M(t) = 200(2^{-\frac{t}{3}})$

e) Since $b^{-x} = \dfrac{1}{b^x}$, which can be rewritten as $\left(\dfrac{1}{b}\right)^x$, then $\left(\dfrac{1}{2}\right)^{\frac{t}{3}} = 2^{-\frac{t}{3}}$.

28. a) $\dfrac{1}{9}$ **b)** $\dfrac{1}{25}$ **c)** $\dfrac{1}{8}$

d) $\dfrac{28}{27}$ **e)** 25   **f)** $\dfrac{243}{32}$

29. a) $\dfrac{1}{x^5}$ **b)** $\dfrac{1}{2n^5m^8}$ **c)** a

d) $\dfrac{b}{mn^4}$ **e)** s^{20} **f)** $\dfrac{b^6}{9a^2}$

30. a) 3   **b)** -10 **c)** -2

d) 7   **e)** $\dfrac{5}{6}$ **f)** 27

g) 16   **h)** $-\dfrac{1}{625}$ **i)** $\dfrac{243}{32}$

31. a)

b) i) $\{x \in \mathbb{R}\}$ **ii)** $\{y \in \mathbb{R}, y > 0\}$

iii) no x-intercept; y-intercept 64

iv) The function is decreasing for all values of x.

v) $y = 0$

c) $y = 64(4^{-x})$; since $b^{-x} = \dfrac{1}{b^x}$, which can be rewritten as $\left(\dfrac{1}{b}\right)^x$, then $\left(\dfrac{1}{4}\right)^x = 4^{-x}$.

32. a)

Yes; an exponential curve best describes the data.

b) $y = 1500(1.05^x)$

c) $\{x \in \mathbb{R}, x \geq 0\}$

d) approximately 2327, assuming the population increases at the same rate

e) approximately 14.2 years, assuming the population increases at the same rate

33. a) $M(t) = 100\left(\dfrac{1}{2}\right)^{\frac{t}{1.5}}$

b) The graph follows an exponential decay curve.

c) $\{t \in \mathbb{R}, t \geq 0\}$

d) i) approximately 2.48 mg

ii) approximately 0.16 mg

e) approximately 7.6 days

Chapter 4

Prerequisite Skills, pages 220–221

1. a) scalene, right

b) isosceles

c) equilateral

d) isosceles, right

2. a) 60°

b) 70°, 70°

c) 60°, 60°, 60°

d) 45°, 45°

3. a) 17 m

b) 8.5 cm

4. a) 8 cm ✓

b) 3.6 m

5. a) $\sin A = \dfrac{3}{5}$, $\cos A = \dfrac{4}{5}$, $\tan A = \dfrac{3}{4}$, $\sin C = \dfrac{4}{5}$, $\cos C = \dfrac{3}{5}$, $\tan C = \dfrac{4}{3}$

b) $\sin A = \dfrac{12}{13}$, $\cos A = \dfrac{5}{13}$, $\tan A = \dfrac{12}{5}$, $\sin C = \dfrac{5}{13}$, $\cos C = \dfrac{12}{13}$, $\tan C = \dfrac{5}{12}$

6. a) $\sin 30° = 0.5$, $\cos 30° = 0.8660$, $\tan 30° = 0.5774$

b) $\sin 45° = 0.7071$, $\cos 45° = 0.7071$, $\tan 45° = 1$

c) $\sin 60° = 0.8660$, $\cos 60° = 0.5$, $\tan 60° = 1.7321$

7. a) 32°   **b)** 41°   **c)** 30°

8. a)

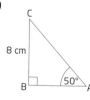

Answers may vary. Sample answer: Use the tangent ratio because the opposite side is given and the adjacent side is asked for.

b) 6.7 cm   **c)** 40°

9. Answers may vary. Sample answers:

a)

b) Yes.

c) Using the sine ratio, the angle is 75°, which is within the safe angle range.

10. 16.4 m   **11.** 10.4 cm

12. a) Answers may vary. Sample answer: Use the cosine law because two sides and their contained angle are given.

b) 14 m   **c)** 82°

13. Answers may vary. Sample answer: The two given angles add to 90°, so the third angle is 90°, and the primary trigonometric ratios can be applied to find the measure of c, which is approximately 21.4 cm.

4.1 Special Angles, pages 228–231

1. Answers may vary. Sample answer: All exact values for the trigonometric ratios are either identical to the value displayed on the calculator or are found to be the same when the exact value is calculated with a CAS.

2. In all cases, exact values are identical to those found by a calculator.

3. a)

 $\sin 30° = \dfrac{1}{2}$, $\cos 30° = \dfrac{\sqrt{3}}{2}$, $\tan 30° = \dfrac{1}{\sqrt{3}}$

b)

$\sin 60° = \dfrac{\sqrt{3}}{2}$, $\cos 60° = \dfrac{1}{2}$, $\tan 60° = \sqrt{3}$

4.

θ	$\sin\theta$ Exact	$\sin\theta$ Calculator	$\cos\theta$ Exact	$\cos\theta$ Calculator	$\tan\theta$ Exact	$\tan\theta$ Calculator
0°	0	0	1	1	0	0
30°	$\dfrac{1}{2}$	0.5	$\dfrac{\sqrt{3}}{2}$	0.8660	$\dfrac{1}{\sqrt{3}}$	0.5774
45°	$\dfrac{1}{\sqrt{2}}$	0.7071	$\dfrac{1}{\sqrt{2}}$	0.7071	1	1
60°	$\dfrac{\sqrt{3}}{2}$	0.8660	$\dfrac{1}{2}$	0.5	$\sqrt{3}$	1.7321
90°	1	1	0	0	undefined	error

5. a) 60°

b) $\sin 120° = \dfrac{\sqrt{3}}{2}$, $\cos 120° = -\dfrac{1}{2}$, $\tan 120° = -\sqrt{3}$

6.

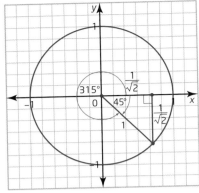

$$\sin 315° = -\frac{1}{\sqrt{2}}, \cos 315° = \frac{1}{\sqrt{2}},$$
$$\tan 315° = -1$$

7.

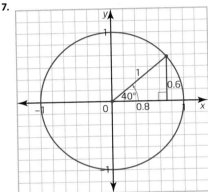

sin 40°		cos 40°		tan 40°	
Diagram	Calculator	Diagram	Calculator	Diagram	Calculator
0.6	0.6428	0.8	0.7660	0.8	0.8391

8.

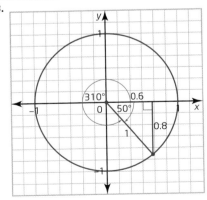

sin 310°		cos 310°		tan 310°	
Diagram	Calculator	Diagram	Calculator	Diagram	Calculator
−0.8	−0.7660	0.6	0.6428	−1.3	−1.1918

9.

θ	$\sin \theta$	$\cos \theta$	$\tan \theta$
0°	0	1	0
90°	1	0	undefined
180°	0	−1	0
270°	−1	0	undefined
360°	0	1	0

10. a) First quadrant: sin θ, cos θ, tan θ;
second quadrant: sin θ; third quadrant: tan θ;
fourth quadrant: cos θ

b) C: only cosine is positive; A: all are positive;
S: only sine is positive; T: only tangent is positive

11. a)   **b)** 5 m

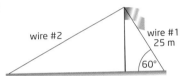

12. a) $12\sqrt{2}$ km

b) Answers may vary. Sample answer: Using the
Pythagorean theorem, the answer is $12\sqrt{2}$ km.

13. a)

b) 43.3 m

c) Answers may vary. Sample answer: The angle
that the second wire makes with the ground
is not needed because you can use similar
triangles to find the wire's length or you can
calculate the length using the Pythagorean
theorem.

d) 30°

14. a)

θ	$\sin \theta$	Quadrant	Sign
30°	0.5	first	+
150°	0.5	second	+
210°	−0.5	third	−
330°	−0.5	fourth	−

b) Yes, because the signs all follow the CAST rule.

c) i) 30° **ii)** −30°

d)

θ	$\cos \theta$	Quadrant	Sign
60°	0.5	first	+
120°	−0.5	second	−
240°	−0.5	third	−
300°	0.5	fourth	+

e) Answers may vary. Sample answer:

θ	tan θ	Quadrant	Sign
45°	1	first	+
135°	−1	second	−
225°	1	third	+
315°	−1	fourth	−

15. Answers may vary.

16. 30°, 30 m

17. 40 m

19.–21. Answers may vary.

22. B   **23.** A   **24.** C

4.2 Co-Terminal and Related Angles, pages 237–240

1. a) $\sin \theta = \frac{12}{13}$, $\cos \theta = \frac{5}{13}$ $\tan \theta = \frac{12}{5}$

b) $\sin \theta = \frac{4}{5}$, $\cos \theta = -\frac{3}{5}$, $\tan \theta = -\frac{4}{3}$

c) $\sin \theta = -\frac{4}{5}$, $\cos \theta = -\frac{3}{5}$, $\tan \theta = \frac{4}{3}$

d) $\sin \theta = \frac{5}{\sqrt{29}}$, $\cos \theta = \frac{2}{\sqrt{29}}$, $\tan \theta = \frac{5}{2}$

e) $\sin \theta = -\frac{3}{\sqrt{10}}$, $\cos \theta = -\frac{1}{\sqrt{10}}$, $\tan \theta = 3$

2. a) $\sin \theta = \frac{3}{5}$, $\cos \theta = -\frac{4}{5}$, $\tan \theta = -\frac{3}{4}$

b) $\sin \theta = -\frac{4}{5}$, $\cos \theta = \frac{3}{5}$, $\tan \theta = -\frac{4}{3}$

c) $\sin \theta = -\frac{8}{17}$, $\cos \theta = -\frac{15}{17}$, $\tan \theta = \frac{8}{15}$

d) $\sin \theta = -\frac{5}{\sqrt{34}}$, $\cos \theta = \frac{3}{\sqrt{34}}$, $\tan \theta = -\frac{5}{3}$

e) $\sin \theta = \frac{2}{\sqrt{5}}$, $\cos \theta = \frac{1}{\sqrt{5}}$, $\tan \theta = 2$

f) $\sin \theta = -\frac{1}{\sqrt{10}}$, $\cos \theta = \frac{3}{\sqrt{10}}$, $\tan \theta = -\frac{1}{3}$

3. a) $\cos A = \frac{15}{17}$, $\tan A = \frac{8}{15}$

b) $\sin B = -\frac{4}{5}$, $\tan B = -\frac{4}{3}$

c) $\sin C = \frac{5}{13}$, $\cos C = -\frac{12}{13}$

d) $\cos D = -\frac{\sqrt{5}}{3}$, $\tan D = \frac{2}{\sqrt{5}}$

e) $\sin E = \frac{\sqrt{11}}{6}$, $\tan E = -\frac{\sqrt{11}}{5}$

f) $\sin F = \frac{12}{\sqrt{193}}$, $\cos F = \frac{7}{\sqrt{193}}$

4. Answers may vary. Sample answers:
a) 315° **b)** 30° **c)** 660° **d)** 80° **e)** 590° **f)** 170°

5. Answers may vary. Sample answers:
a) 480°, 840°, 1200°   **b)** −30°, −390°, −750°

6. a) $\sin A = -\frac{1}{\sqrt{2}}$, $\cos A = \frac{1}{\sqrt{2}}$, $\tan A = -1$

b) $\sin B = -\frac{\sqrt{3}}{2}$, $\cos B = -\frac{1}{2}$, $\tan B = \sqrt{3}$

c) $\sin C = 0$, $\cos C = -1$, $\tan C = 0$

d) $\sin D = \frac{1}{\sqrt{2}}$, $\cos D = \frac{1}{\sqrt{2}}$, $\tan D = 1$

e) $\sin E = \frac{\sqrt{3}}{2}$, $\cos E = \frac{1}{2}$, $\tan E = \sqrt{3}$

f) $\sin F = 1$, $\cos F = 0$, $\tan F$ is undefined

7. 150°, 210°

8. 135°, 315°

9. 45°, 315°

10. 90°, 270°

11. a) $\sin A = \frac{9}{\sqrt{97}}$, $\cos A = -\frac{4}{\sqrt{97}}$, $\tan A = -\frac{9}{4}$;

$\sin B = \frac{9}{\sqrt{97}}$, $\cos B = \frac{4}{\sqrt{97}}$, $\tan B = \frac{9}{4}$

b)

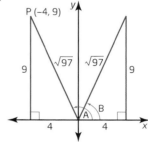

$\angle A = 114°$, $\angle B = 66°$

12. a) $\sin E = -\frac{5}{\sqrt{34}}$, $\cos E = -\frac{3}{\sqrt{34}}$, $\tan E = \frac{5}{3}$;

$\sin F = \frac{5}{\sqrt{34}}$, $\cos F = \frac{3}{\sqrt{34}}$, $\tan F = \frac{5}{3}$

b)

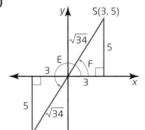

$\angle E = 239°$, $\angle F = 59°$

13. Answers may vary.

14. a) $\sqrt{p^2 + q^2}$

b) $\sin \theta = \frac{q}{\sqrt{p^2 + q^2}}$, $\cos \theta = \frac{p}{\sqrt{p^2 + q^2}}$, $\tan \theta = \frac{q}{p}$

c)

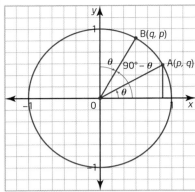

d) $\sin(90° - \theta) = \dfrac{p}{\sqrt{p^2 + q^2}}$,

$\cos(90° - \theta) = \dfrac{q}{\sqrt{p^2 + q^2}}$,

$\tan(90° - \theta) = \dfrac{p}{q}$

e) The sine and cosine ratios are reversed, while the two tangent ratios are reciprocals of each other.

15. 90°, 40 m

17. $\sqrt{3}\,s$

18. $\sqrt{2 + \sqrt{2}}\,\ell$

19. Answers may vary.

20. A   **21.** C   **22.** C

4.3 Reciprocal Trigonometric Ratios, pages 246–248

1. a) $\sin 20° = 0.342$, $\cos 20° = 0.940$,
$\tan 20° = 0.364$, $\csc 20° = 2.924$,
$\sec 20° = 1.064$, $\cot 20° = 2.747$

b) $\sin 42° = 0.669$, $\cos 42° = 0.743$,
$\tan 42° = 0.900$, $\csc 42° = 1.494$,
$\sec 42° = 1.346$, $\cot 42° = 1.111$

c) $\sin 75° = 0.966$, $\cos 75° = 0.259$,
$\tan 75° = 3.732$, $\csc 75° = 1.035$,
$\sec 75° = 3.864$, $\cot 75° = 0.268$

d) $\sin 88° = 0.999$, $\cos 88° = 0.035$,
$\tan 88° = 28.636$, $\csc 88° = 1.001$,
$\sec 88° = 28.654$, $\cot 88° = 0.035$

e) $\sin 153° = 0.454$, $\cos 153° = -0.891$,
$\tan 153° = -0.510$, $\csc 153° = 2.203$,
$\sec 153° = -1.122$, $\cot 153° = -1.963$

f) $\sin 289° = -0.946$, $\cos 289° = 0.326$,
$\tan 289° = -2.904$, $\csc 289° = -1.058$,
$\sec 289° = 3.072$, $\cot 289° = -0.344$

2. $\sin 315° = -\dfrac{1}{\sqrt{2}}$, $\cos 315° = \dfrac{1}{\sqrt{2}}$, $\tan 315° = -1$,

$\csc 315° = -\sqrt{2}$, $\sec 315° = \sqrt{2}$, $\cot 315° = -1$

3. $\sin 120° = \dfrac{\sqrt{3}}{2}$, $\cos 120° = -\dfrac{1}{2}$, $\tan 120° = -\sqrt{3}$,

$\csc 120° = \dfrac{2}{\sqrt{3}}$, $\sec 120° = -2$, $\cot 120° = -\dfrac{1}{\sqrt{3}}$

4. $\sin 270° = -1$, $\cos 270° = 0$, $\tan 270°$ is undefined, $\csc 270° = -1$, $\sec 270°$ is undefined, $\cot 270° = 0$

5. a) 42°   **b)** 53°   **c)** 67°

d) 63°   **e)** 41°   **f)** 53°

g) no such angle, because the cosecant ratio is positive in the first quadrant

h) no such angle, because the reciprocal of a secant ratio with value $\dfrac{2}{5}$ is a cosine ratio with value $\dfrac{5}{2}$, which exceeds 1, the cosine ratio's maximum value

6. 135°, 225°

7. 135°, 315°

8. a) $\sin \theta = \dfrac{12}{13}$, $\cos \theta = -\dfrac{5}{13}$, $\tan \theta = -\dfrac{12}{5}$,

$\csc \theta = \dfrac{13}{12}$, $\sec \theta = -\dfrac{13}{5}$, $\cot \theta = -\dfrac{5}{12}$

b) $\sin \theta = -\dfrac{3}{5}$, $\cos \theta = -\dfrac{4}{5}$, $\tan \theta = \dfrac{3}{4}$,

$\csc \theta = -\dfrac{5}{3}$, $\sec \theta = -\dfrac{5}{4}$, $\cot \theta = \dfrac{4}{3}$

c) $\sin \theta = \dfrac{15}{17}$, $\cos \theta = -\dfrac{8}{17}$, $\tan \theta = -\dfrac{15}{8}$,

$\csc \theta = \dfrac{17}{15}$, $\sec \theta = -\dfrac{17}{8}$, $\cot \theta = -\dfrac{8}{15}$

d) $\sin \theta = -\dfrac{7}{25}$, $\cos \theta = \dfrac{24}{25}$, $\tan \theta = -\dfrac{7}{24}$,

$\csc \theta = -\dfrac{25}{7}$, $\sec \theta = \dfrac{25}{24}$, $\cot \theta = -\dfrac{24}{7}$

e) $\sin \theta = \dfrac{40}{41}$, $\cos \theta = \dfrac{9}{41}$, $\tan \theta = \dfrac{40}{9}$,

$\csc \theta = \dfrac{41}{40}$, $\sec \theta = \dfrac{41}{9}$, $\cot \theta = \dfrac{9}{40}$

f) $\sin \theta = -\dfrac{3}{\sqrt{13}}$, $\cos \theta = -\dfrac{2}{\sqrt{13}}$, $\tan \theta = \dfrac{3}{2}$,

$\csc \theta = -\dfrac{\sqrt{13}}{3}$, $\sec \theta = -\dfrac{\sqrt{13}}{2}$, $\cot \theta = \dfrac{2}{3}$

g) $\sin \theta = -\dfrac{3}{\sqrt{34}}$, $\cos \theta = \dfrac{5}{\sqrt{34}}$, $\tan \theta = -\dfrac{3}{5}$,

$\csc \theta = -\dfrac{\sqrt{34}}{3}$, $\sec \theta = \dfrac{\sqrt{34}}{5}$, $\cot \theta = -\dfrac{5}{3}$

h) $\sin \theta = \dfrac{7}{\sqrt{53}}$, $\cos \theta = -\dfrac{2}{\sqrt{53}}$, $\tan \theta = -\dfrac{7}{2}$,

$\csc \theta = \dfrac{\sqrt{53}}{7}$, $\sec \theta = -\dfrac{\sqrt{53}}{2}$, $\cot \theta = -\dfrac{2}{7}$

9. $\sin P = \dfrac{15}{17}$, $\cos P = \dfrac{8}{17}$, $\tan P = \dfrac{15}{8}$;

$\csc P = \dfrac{17}{15}$, $\sec P = \dfrac{17}{8}$, $\cot P = \dfrac{8}{15}$

10. 12°, 168°

11. 102°, 258°

12. 162°, 342°

13. 124°

14. Answers may vary.

15. 90°, 60 m

17. Answers may vary.

18. $\sin B = \dfrac{d}{\sqrt{c^2 + d^2}}$, $\cos B = -\dfrac{c}{\sqrt{c^2 + d^2}}$,

$\tan B = -\dfrac{d}{c}$, $c \neq 0$, $\csc B = \dfrac{\sqrt{c^2 + d^2}}{d}$, $d \neq 0$,

$\sec B = -\dfrac{\sqrt{c^2 + d^2}}{c}$, $c \neq 0$

19. $\sin A = -\dfrac{2\sqrt{t}}{t + 1}$, $t \geq 0$, $t \neq 1$

20. a) 14   **b)** 23   **c)** 300 m²

   d) Answers may vary. Sample answer: Because angle parking spaces extend into the street more than 3 m, more of the street would be taken up for parking.

   e) 707 m², which is consistent with the prediction in part d) for the reason stated

21. a)

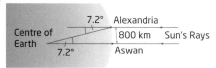

   Answers may vary. Sample answer: Assume that the sun's rays are parallel when they reach Earth. This is valid, as the distance from Earth to the sun is so large. Also assume that the 800-km separation between the two cities is a linear measure, instead of an arc measure, even though the surface of Earth curves. This is also valid, because the measure of 800 km is small relative to Earth's dimensions.

   b) 6370 km   **c)** 6371.0 km   **d)** 24° north

22. $\sqrt{22}$ **23.** 58   **24.** 65 km

4.4 Problems in Two Dimensions, pages 254–258

1. a) Since the triangle is a right triangle, primary trigonometric ratios are the most appropriate tool.

   b) Since two angles and a side are given, the most appropriate tool is the sine law.

   c) Since two angles and a side are given, the most appropriate tool is the sine law.

   d) Since two sides and their contained angle are given, the most appropriate tool is the cosine law.

2. a) 6.3 cm   **b)** 5.2 m   **c)** 10.6 cm   **d)** 16.8 km

3. 53°

4. Answers may vary. Sample answer: The golfer needs to hit the ball at least 67 m to clear the water. Since he can only hit the ball 60 m, he should go around the hazard.

5. a)

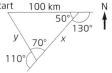

   b) 274 km

6. a)

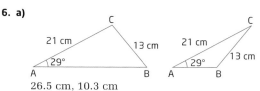

26.5 cm, 10.3 cm

   b)

18.3 m. Explanations may vary. Sample explanation: The second diagram cannot be solved because the sum of the given angle and the calculated value of the second angle (an obtuse angle) is greater than 180°.

7. $20\sqrt{181 + 90\sqrt{2}}$ m

8. $50(\sqrt{3} - 1)$ m

9. 32.2°

10. 38 m

11. a) 42 km   **b)** 22.7° east of south

12. $25(\sqrt{2} - 1)$ m

13. Answers may vary.

14. a) Answers may vary. Sample answer: Since the given angle is not contained within the two given sides, two triangles are possible.

   b)

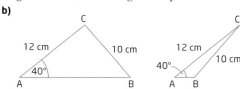

   c) 15.6 cm, 2.8 cm; both are valid solutions

   d) Answers may vary. Sample answer: There is only one valid solution; it is not possible to draw the second triangle.

   e) 18.4 cm

15. a) Answers may vary. Sample answer: There is no solution; the 7-cm-long side is not long enough to enclose a triangle.

   b) 7.7135 cm

16. Answers may vary.

17. 55°, 50 m

18. 74 min

19. a) 23.5° is the tilt angle of Earth as it spins on its axis.

   b)

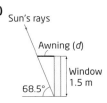

   c) 0.59 m   **d)** 1.27 m

20. a)

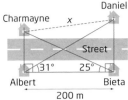

b) Answers may vary. Sample answer: You can use primary trigonometric ratios to determine the distance from Albert's house to Charmayne's house, and do the same for the distance from Bieta's house to Daniel's house. The difference between these two measures represents the length of one of the legs of a right triangle, with the other leg being 200 m in length. Use the Pythagorean theorem to find the hypotenuse, which represents the required distance.

c) 202 m

22. Answers may vary.

23. 3.8°

24. a)

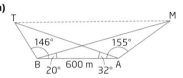

b) Answers may vary. Sample answer: Use the known angles to determine the measures of the missing angles in the triangle. Use the sine law in each triangle to find the missing side lengths, and then use the cosine law to find the distance from T to M.

c) 11 073 m

25. a) 10:14 a.m., 1:46 p.m.

b) Answers may vary. Sample answer: The shadow can be on either side of the flagpole, which means that an equal number of hours and minutes on each side of noon will create the required shadow.

26. Answers may vary.

27. B

28. 7 min 45 s

29. B

4.5 Problems in Three Dimensions, pages 265–269

1. 38°

2. a) $\sqrt{3} + 1$ m

b) $2 + 2\sqrt{3}$ m

c) $4\sqrt{2 + \sqrt{3}}$ m

3. 47.8°

4. a)

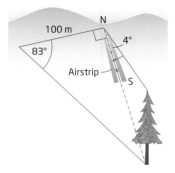

b) Answers may vary. Sample answer: Use the tangent ratio to calculate the distance from the departure point of the runway to the base of the tree: 814.4 m.　　**c)** 57 m

d) The height is sufficient to clear the trees but not by enough to be safe.

5. 35.3°

6. a) 3.3 km　　**b)** 3.3 km　　**c)** 173 m

d) Answers may vary. Sample answer: Assume that the minimum height above point C where the circle exists does not affect the radius of the circle. This is a reasonable assumption based on the calculated values.

7. Jodi, in approximately 3 min 10 s (versus approximately 3 min 33 s for Leanna)

8. a)

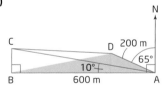

b) 9 min 29 s

9. a)–b) Answers may vary.

c) 109.5°

d) Answers may vary.

10. a)

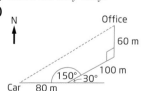

b) 184 m

11. $\theta = 45°$, 50 m

12. 56.8 m

13.–14. Answers may vary.

15. $\sqrt{3}R - 2r$

16. $\sqrt{\dfrac{2}{3}}s$

17. 49.1°

18. a) Answers may vary. Sample answer: The vertices of the triangle are not on a flat surface, so the sum of the angles does not equal 180°. In other words, the shape is not really a triangle.

b) The sum of the angles will be greater than 180°, as Earth's surface is convex.

19. Answers may vary. Sample answers:

a) The intersection of the two spheres is a circle, as the two surfaces contact each other around a common radius.

b) The third satellite creates two points of intersection with the circle created by the intersection of the first two spheres.

c) The final satellite eliminates one of the two points of intersection of the three spheres, narrowing the location to a single point.

20. 20 min 47 s, by the cutter

21. B   **22.** C

4.6 Trigonometric Identities, pages 273–275

1. Answers may vary.

2. The graph is a horizontal line through $y = 1$.

3.–10. Answers may vary.

11. Answers may vary. Sample answer: No, as the graph only shows that the expression is true for the range of values chosen on the display of the calculator. You would need to show that it is true for all values in the domain.

12.–13 Answers may vary.

14. 30°, 20 m

15.–16. Answers may vary.

16. Answers may vary.

18. Answers may vary. Sample answers:

a) Since the second equation traces over the first when graphed, it appears that the equation is an identity.

b) $\sin 60° = 2 \sin 30° \cos 30°$,
$\sin 90° = 2 \sin 45° \cos 45°$,
$\sin 180° = 2 \sin 90° \cos 90°$. Therefore, the equation is true for the given values of the angle.

19. Answers may vary. Sample answers:

a) Since the second equation traces over the first when graphed, it appears that the equation is an identity.

b) $\cos 30° = \sin 60°$, $\cos 45° = \sin 45°$, $\cos 60° = \sin 30°$. Therefore, the equation is true for the given values of the angle.

c) From the unit circle, it can be seen that the side opposite θ is the adjacent side for $90° - \theta$.

d) $\sin \theta = \cos (90° - \theta)$, $\tan \theta = \dfrac{1}{\tan(90° - \theta)}$

20. Answers may vary. Sample answers:

a) Since the second equation traces over the first when graphed, it appears that the equation is an identity.

b) $\sin 30° = \sin 150°$, $\sin 45° = \sin 135°$, $\sin 90° = \sin 90°$. Therefore, the equation is true for the given values of the angle.

c) From the unit circle and using the CAST rule, it can be seen that the relation is true.

d) $\cos \theta = -\cos (180° - \theta)$

21. C   **22.** C   **23.** D

Chapter 4 Review, pages 276–277

1. $\sin 210° = -\dfrac{1}{2}$, $\cos 210° = -\dfrac{\sqrt{3}}{2}$, $\tan 210° = \dfrac{1}{\sqrt{3}}$

2. $5(\sqrt{3} - \sqrt{2})$ m, 1.6 m

3. a) $\sin \theta = \dfrac{12}{13}$, $\cos \theta = -\dfrac{5}{13}$, $\tan \theta = -\dfrac{12}{5}$

b) $\sin \theta = -\dfrac{4}{5}$, $\cos \theta = \dfrac{3}{5}$, $\tan \theta = -\dfrac{4}{3}$

c) $\sin \theta = -\dfrac{4}{5}$, $\cos \theta = \dfrac{3}{5}$, $\tan \theta = -\dfrac{4}{3}$

d) $\sin \theta = -\dfrac{3}{\sqrt{13}}$, $\cos \theta = -\dfrac{2}{\sqrt{13}}$, $\tan \theta = \dfrac{3}{2}$

e) $\sin \theta = -\dfrac{5}{\sqrt{26}}$, $\cos \theta = \dfrac{1}{\sqrt{26}}$, $\tan \theta = -5$

f) $\sin \theta = \dfrac{4}{\sqrt{65}}$, $\cos \theta = -\dfrac{7}{\sqrt{65}}$, $\tan \theta = -\dfrac{4}{7}$

4. a) $\cos A = \dfrac{3}{5}$, $\tan A = \dfrac{4}{3}$

b) $\sin B = -\dfrac{15}{17}$, $\tan B = -\dfrac{15}{8}$

c) $\sin C = \dfrac{12}{13}$, $\cos C = -\dfrac{5}{13}$

d) $\cos D = -\dfrac{\sqrt{33}}{7}$, $\tan D = \dfrac{4}{\sqrt{33}}$

5. a) 194°, 346°   **b)** 37°, 323°   **c)** 212°, 32°

6. a) $\sin \theta = -0.9231$, $\cos \theta = -0.3846$, $\tan \theta = 2.4$, $\csc \theta = -1.0833$, $\sec \theta = -2.6$, $\cot \theta = 0.4167$

b) $\sin \theta = 0.6$, $\cos \theta = -0.8$, $\tan \theta = -0.75$, $\csc \theta = 1.6667$, $\sec \theta = -1.25$, $\cot \theta = -1.3333$

c) $\sin \theta = 0.8824$, $\cos \theta = 0.4706$, $\tan \theta = 1.875$, $\csc \theta = 1.1333$, $\sec \theta = 2.125$, $\cot \theta = 0.5333$

d) $\sin \theta = -0.96$, $\cos \theta = 0.28$, $\tan \theta = -3.4286$, $\csc \theta = -1.0417$, $\sec \theta = 3.5714$, $\cot \theta = -0.2917$

7. 104°, 256°

8. a) Yes; as there is a unique value for the angle.

b) 270°

9. a)

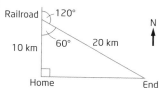

b) cosine law, since two sides and their contained angle are given

c) $10\sqrt{3}$ km, 17.3 km

Answers • MHR **555**

10. a) Answers may vary.

b)

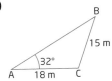

c) 27 m, 4 m

11. 321 m

12. a) 11.7 km   **b)** 8.2°

13.–15. Answers may vary.

Chapter 4 Practice Test, pages 278–279

1. B   **2.** D   **3.** D   **4.** D   **5.** C

6. a)

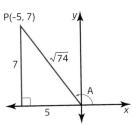

b) $\sin A = \dfrac{7}{\sqrt{74}}$, $\cos A = -\dfrac{5}{\sqrt{74}}$, $\tan A = -\dfrac{7}{5}$,

$\csc A = \dfrac{\sqrt{74}}{7}$, $\sec A = -\dfrac{\sqrt{74}}{5}$

7. a)

b) $50(3 - 2\sqrt{2})$ m

c) The horizontal distance at the initial point (300 m of cable at an angle of 60°) is 150 m. At the second point (200 m of cable at an angle of 45°), the horizontal distance is 141.4 m. Therefore, the balloon moves horizontally toward the tether point.

8. a)

b) Answers may vary. Sample answer: Once the diagram is split into its component triangles, use the primary trigonometric ratios and the cosine law to determine the distance from home.

c) 12.0 km   **d)** 45.2° west of south

9. 3.6 km

10. 2.3 km

11.–13 Answers may vary.

Chapter 5
Prerequisite Skills, pages 282–283

1. a) 2.6 cm   **b)** 5 cm   **c)** 10 cm

2. a) $\sin 30° = \dfrac{1}{2}$, $\cos 30° = \dfrac{\sqrt{3}}{2}$,

$\sin 60° = \dfrac{\sqrt{3}}{2}$, $\cos 60° = \dfrac{1}{2}$

b) $\sin 120° = \dfrac{\sqrt{3}}{2}$, $\cos 120° = -\dfrac{1}{2}$, $\sin 150° = \dfrac{1}{2}$,

$\cos 150° = -\dfrac{\sqrt{3}}{2}$, $\sin 210° = -\dfrac{1}{2}$,

$\cos 210° = -\dfrac{\sqrt{3}}{2}$, $\sin 240° = -\dfrac{\sqrt{3}}{2}$,

$\cos 240° = -\dfrac{1}{2}$, $\sin 300° = -\dfrac{\sqrt{3}}{2}$, $\cos 300° = \dfrac{1}{2}$,

$\sin 330° = -\dfrac{1}{2}$, $\cos 330° = \dfrac{\sqrt{3}}{2}$

c) $\sin 45° = \dfrac{1}{\sqrt{2}}$, $\cos 45° = \dfrac{1}{\sqrt{2}}$, $\sin 135° = \dfrac{1}{\sqrt{2}}$,

$\cos 135° = -\dfrac{1}{\sqrt{2}}$, $\sin 225° = -\dfrac{1}{\sqrt{2}}$,

$\cos 225° = -\dfrac{1}{\sqrt{2}}$, $\sin 315° = -\dfrac{1}{\sqrt{2}}$,

$\cos 315° = \dfrac{1}{\sqrt{2}}$

d) $\sin 0° = 0$, $\cos 0° = 1$, $\sin 90° = 1$, $\cos 90° = 0$, $\sin 180° = 0$, $\cos 180° = -1$, $\sin 270° = -1$, $\cos 270° = 0$

3. domain $\{x \in \mathbb{R}\}$, range $\{y \in \mathbb{R}, y \geq 0\}$

4. Answers may vary. Sample answer: $y = \sqrt{25 - x^2}$

5. a)

b) The second function is translated 3 units up from the first function and the third function is translated 2 units down from the first function.

6. a)

b) The second function is translated 3 units to the right of the first function and the third function is translated 2 units to the left of the first function.

7. a) $y = (x + 5)^2 - 3$ **b)** $y = (x - 4)^2 + 7$

8. The parabola is translated 2 units to the right and 2 units up. The equation of the transformed function is $y = (x - 2)^2 + 2$. The vertex of the transformed parabola is (2, 2).

9. a)

b) The second function is stretched vertically by a factor of 2 compared to the first function and the third function is compressed vertically by a factor of $\frac{1}{2}$ compared to the first function.

10. a)

b) The second function is stretched vertically by a factor of 2 compared to the first function and the third function is compressed vertically by a factor of $\frac{1}{2}$ compared to the first function.

11. $y = 4x^2$

12. $y = 9(x - 4)^2$

13. a)

b) Answers may vary. Sample answer: The second function is a reflection in the x-axis of the first function.

14. a) i) $y = (x + 2)^2$ **ii)** $y = (x - 2)^2$

b) Answers may vary. Sample answer: The two functions are reflections of each other in the y-axis.

15. a) $y = \frac{1}{2}(x + 4)^2 + 1$ **b)**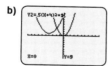

16. The function has been stretched vertically by a factor of 3, reflected in the x-axis, and translated 4 units to the right and 8 units up.

17. $k = 12$

18. $k = 10\ 800$

5.1 Modelling Periodic Behaviour, pages 290–293

1. a) periodic; the pattern of y-values repeats on a regular basis

b) not periodic; the pattern of y-values does not repeat on a regular basis

c) periodic; the pattern of y-values repeats on a regular basis

d) periodic; the pattern of y-values repeats on a regular basis

2. a) amplitude 1.5, period 5

c) amplitude 1, period 6

d) amplitude 0.75, period 3.5

3.–4. Answers may vary.

5. Answers may vary. Sample answer: My graphs

have common characteristics with those of my classmates, but the actual graphs are different, because an infinite number of periodic functions can be drawn with each set of characteristics.

6. a) -3 **b)** 2   **c)** 8

d) Answers may vary. Sample answer: It is not possible to determine because the x-value of 40 is not a multiple of the period added to or subtracted from one of the given x-values of the given points on the function.

7. Answers may vary.

8. Answers may vary. Sample answer: No, because the two points may not be in the same relative position on the periodic function. In the graph shown, $f(-2) = f(1)$. However, the period is 6, not $1 - (-2) = 3$.

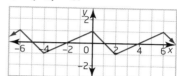

9. a)

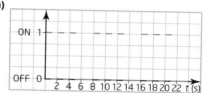

b) It is periodic because the pattern of y-values repeats on a regular basis.

c) 8 s   **d)** 0.5

10. a)

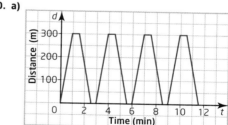

b) 3 min   **c)** 150 m

11. Answers may vary. Sample answers:

a) This could possibly be periodic because the seasons will influence the prices of produce. However, factors such as drought could cause the prices to not follow a periodic function.

b) Interest rates tend to be governed by varying economic conditions that are not periodically predictable.

c) The phases of the moon are such that the illuminated portion of the moon is periodic.

d) As long as the breathing is normal, the function that describes the volume of air in the lungs as a function of time is periodic.

12. Answers may vary. Sample answer: Solar activity is periodic. This rise and fall in sunspot counts varies in a cyclical way. The length of the cycle is about 11 years on average.

13. Answers may vary. Sample answer: No, based on the strict definition of a periodic function. However, science describes some motions, such as damped harmonic motion, as "periodic" even if amplitude is either continuously increasing or decreasing. See the example in question 23 on page 293.

14. a) approximately 12 h 20 min

   b) 1.3 m   **c)** 1:00 a.m.

15. Answers may vary. Sample answers:

   a) The distance will start at zero, increase to a maximum value of 12 800 km, and then decrease to zero as Quito returns to its starting position. As the rotation continues, the same values of *d* will exist as existed during the first rotation, thus forming a repeating pattern.

   b) 24 h   **c)** 6400 km

   d) The cosine law is an appropriate tool, since *y*, representing the lengths of the two sides of the triangle, is constant, and it is the angle that is changing. Select a suitable step, such as 1 h, and determine the angle between the two sides of the triangle. Use the cosine law to calculate the value of *d*. Continue for 24 h.

16. Answers may vary. Sample answers:

   a) In Ottawa, Ontario, the average maximum monthly temperature is about 21 °C (in July) and the average minimum monthly temperature is about −11 °C (in January). The amplitude of this pattern is 16 °C, being half the difference between the maximum value and the minimum value.

   b) The period of the function will be 12 months, because the weather patterns in an area usually change in the same pattern on a yearly basis.

17. Answers may vary.

18. a) The wave form of the note played has a regular repeating pattern.

   b) 0.002 s

   c) As the frequency of the note increases, the period decreases. The frequency is the reciprocal of the period.

19. Answers may vary.

20. Answers may vary. Sample answers:

   a) Because of the tilt of Earth on its axis, hours and minutes of daylight anywhere on any given day depend on the position of Earth as it orbits the sun. Since a complete orbit takes 1 year (about 365 days), the data will show a periodic pattern over several years through successive Earth orbits.

   b) just over 14 h

   c) approximately 12 h 30 min

22. a) 1 s, 200 m

b)

Angle of Beam (degrees)	Time (seconds)	Distance of Beam (metres)
30	1	200
60	2	115.5
90	3	100
120	4	115.5
150	5	200

   c) As the beam approaches 180°, the distance that it travels becomes very large. When it reaches 180°, it no longer reaches the cliff.

   d) After 6 s, the beam will reach the 0° position. After this, it will again hit the cliff.

   e) The graph shows the function from 0° to 180°. From 180° to 360°, the light does not hit the cliff.

   f) Answers may vary. Sample answer: It is periodic, since the pattern will repeat every 12 s (which is the period of the function).

   g) Answers may vary. Sample answer: The pattern has no amplitude because there is no maximum value in the function.

23. Answers may vary. Sample answers:

   a)

x	y
17	2
70	1.25
135	1
195	0.9
250	0.6
315	0.4
365	0.25

   b)

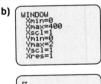

   c) The data seem to follow an exponential model.

   d) $y = 2.146(0.99)^x + 0.25$

   e)

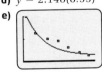

The fit is not perfect, but it seems to generally show the behaviour of the data.

24. C   **25.** B   **26.** C   **27.** A

5.2 The Sine Function and the Cosine Function, pages 299–301

1. Answers may vary. Sample answers:

   a)

A cosine function models the horizontal displacement, because the horizontal displacement starts at 8 m and decreases to 0 at 90°, a characteristic of the cosine function.

b)

A sine function models the vertical displacement, because the vertical displacement starts at 0 and moves through to a maximum at 90°, a characteristic of the sine function.

2. a)

b) Answers may vary. Sample answer: The more complex function has more detail in its wave form, creating a more complex sound. They both have a period of 360° and all x-intercepts of $y = \sin x$ are also x-intercepts of the more complex function (the more complex function has more x-intercepts, however).

c)

Answers may vary. Sample answer: Again, the second harmonic is far more complex than the $y = \sin x$ function, with more x-intercepts and a more complex wave form, even more complex than the $y = \sin x + \sin 2x$ wave form. The second harmonic and $y = \sin x$ have the same period and all x-intercepts for $y = \sin x$ are shared with the second harmonic.

3. a)

b)

c) 6 cycles   **d)** 72 cycles

4. a)

x	$\tan x$
0	0
10	0.176
20	0.364
30	0.577
40	0.839
50	1.192
60	1.732
70	2.747

x	$\tan x$
75	3.732
80	5.671
85	11.430
86	14.301
87	19.081
88	28.636
89	57.290

b) Answers may vary. Sample answer: As the angle gets closer to 90°, the tangent function value gets larger and larger. This means that as x approaches 90°, the tangent function value approaches infinity. At a value of 90°, the tangent function is undefined.

c) Answers may vary, as students will extend their tables of values differently, but should all lead to the graph in question 4d).

d)

e)

f)

The asymptotes will be located at 450° and 630°.

g)

The asymptotes will be located at −90°, −270°, −450°, and −630°.

h) Answers may vary. Sample answer: Yes, the tangent function is periodic, as the y-values repeat in a periodic pattern. The period of the tangent function is 180°.

5. Answers may vary. Sample answers:

a) All vertical lines that can be drawn intersect $y = \tan x$ at exactly one point. Therefore, it is a function.

b) Since there is no maximum or minimum of a tangent function, the amplitude is not defined.

c) The tangent function is increasing on the intervals (0°, 90°), (90°, 270°), and (270°, 360°). The tangent function does not exist at 90° and 270°.

d)

e)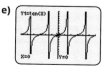

f) domain $\{x \in \mathbb{R}, x \neq 90 + 180n, n \in \mathbb{Z}\}$, range $\{y \in \mathbb{R}\}$

6. a)

b) Answers may vary. Sample answer: The graph of $y = \csc x$ has asymptotes where the sine function is zero, has minimum values of 1 and maximum values of -1 in the appropriate areas between the asymptotes, and moves either upward toward positive infinity for the areas above the x-axis or downward toward negative infinity for the areas below the x-axis as the function approaches the asymptotes.

c)

d) Answers may vary. Sample answer: $y = \csc x$ is a function. No vertical line can be drawn that will pass through more than one point on the line.

e) domain $\{x \in \mathbb{R}, x \neq 180n, n \in \mathbb{Z}\}$, range $\{y \in \mathbb{R}, |y| \geq 1\}$

7. a)

b) Answers may vary. Sample answer: The graph of $y = \sec x$ has asymptotes where the cosine function is zero, has minimum values of 1 and maximum values of -1 in the appropriate areas between the asymptotes, and moves either upward toward positive infinity for the areas above the x-axis or downward toward negative infinity for the areas below the x-axis as the function approaches the asymptotes.

c)

e) domain $\{x \in \mathbb{R}, x \neq 90 + 180n, n \in \mathbb{Z}\}$, range $\{y \in \mathbb{R}, |y| \geq 1\}$

8. a)

b) Answers may vary. Sample answer: The graph of $y = \cot x$ has asymptotes where the tangent function is zero. Where the tangent function has asymptotes, the cotangent function is zero. Anywhere the tangent function is either 1 or -1, the cotangent function is also 1 or -1.

c)

e) domain $\{x \in \mathbb{R}, x \neq (90°)n, n \in \mathbb{Z}\}$, range $\{y \in \mathbb{R}\}$

9. a) 1 **b)** $(135 + 180n)°, n \in \mathbb{Z}$

c)

10. $0 \leq x < 45°$ or $225° < x \leq 360°$

11. $-45°, 45°$

12. C

5.3 Transformations of Sine and Cosine Functions, pages 309–312

1. a)

vertical stretch by a factor of 4, amplitude 4

b)

vertical stretch by a factor of $\frac{3}{2}$, amplitude $\frac{3}{2}$

c)

vertical stretch by a factor of 5, amplitude 5

d)

vertical stretch by a factor of $\frac{5}{4}$, amplitude $\frac{5}{4}$

2. a)

vertical stretch by a factor of 3, amplitude 3

b)

vertical compression by a factor of $\frac{1}{2}$, amplitude $\frac{1}{2}$

c)

vertical stretch by a factor of 2, amplitude 2

d)

vertical compression by a factor of $\frac{2}{3}$, amplitude $\frac{2}{3}$

3. a) horizontal compression by a factor of $\frac{1}{5}$, period 72°

b) horizontal stretch by a factor of $\frac{3}{2}$, period 540°

c) horizontal stretch by a factor of 6, period 2160°

d) horizontal stretch by a factor of 2, period 720°

e) no horizontal stretch, period 360°

f) horizontal compression by a factor of $\frac{1}{8}$, period 45°

g) horizontal compression by a factor of $\frac{1}{12}$, period 30°

h) horizontal stretch by a factor of $\frac{4}{3}$, period 480°

4. Answers may vary. Sample answers:
a) $y = 5 \sin 3x$; $y = 5 \cos [3(x + 90°)]$
b) $y = -3 \sin 4x$; $y = 3 \cos [4(x + 67.5°)]$

5. Answers may vary. Sample answers:
a) $y = 4 \cos 2x$; $y = 4 \sin [2(x + 45°)]$
b) $y = -2 \cos 3x$; $y = 2 \sin [3(x - 30°)]$

6. a) phase shift right 50°, vertical shift up 3
b) phase shift left 45°, vertical shift down 1
c) phase shift right 25°, vertical shift up 4
d) phase shift left 60°, vertical shift down 2

7. a) phase shift left 30°, no vertical shift
b) phase shift right 32°, vertical shift up 6
c) phase shift left 120°, vertical shift down 5
d) phase shift right 150°, vertical shift up 7

8. a) i) phase shift left 100°, vertical shift up 1
ii) no phase shift, vertical shift up 3
iii) phase shift left 45°, vertical shift down 2
iv) phase shift right 120°, vertical shift up 2

b) i)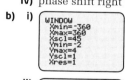

ii)

iii)

iv)

9. a) i) no vertical shift, amplitude 1
ii) vertical shift down 1, amplitude 3
iii) vertical shift up 2, amplitude 1
iv) vertical shift down 3, amplitude 4

b) i)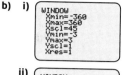

ii)

iii)

iv)

10. a) 10 cm   **b)** 90 cm   **c)** 0.5 s
d) The value of k will change from 720 to 240, so the equation becomes $y = 40 \sin 240t + 50$.

11. a) i) amplitude 5, period 90°, phase shift left 60°, vertical shift down 2
ii) amplitude 2, period 180°, phase shift left 150°, vertical shift down 5
iii) amplitude 0.5, period 720°, phase shift right 60°, vertical shift up 1
iv) amplitude 0.8, period 100°, phase shift right 40°, vertical shift down 0.4

b) i)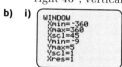

ii)

iii)

iv)

12. a) physical: $y = \sin\left(\frac{360°}{23}\right)t$; emotional: $y = \sin\left(\frac{360°}{28}\right)t$; intellectual: $y = \sin\left(\frac{360°}{33}\right)t$

b)

c) Answers may vary. Sample answer: days 6, 75, 120, 141

d) Answers may vary. Sample answer: days 20, 61, 89, 108, 132

13. a) $y = 4 \sin kt$ **b)** $y = \sin kt$
  c) 16 m from the source

14. a) $y = 4 \sin x + 4$ **b)** $30°$ to the right

c) Answers may vary. Sample answer: No, because no matter what the period of the function is, the y-intercept of $\sin kx = 0$ is always 0 for any value of k.

15.–16. Answers may vary.

18. a) Answers may vary. Sample answer: There are five points of intersection, as there are three common zeros, and in the two intervals between the zeros, there is one more point of intersection each, for a total of five.

b)

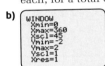

Yes. My prediction was correct.

c) $\left(60°, \dfrac{\sqrt{3}}{2}\right)$

d) Answers may vary. Sample answer: There are nine points of intersection, as there are five common zeros, and in the four intervals between the zeros, there is one more point of intersection each, for a total of nine.

e)

Yes. My prediction was correct.

f) Answers may vary. Sample answer: There are seven points of intersection. There are three common zeros. There are two points of intersection between each adjacent pair of zeros.

19. Answers may vary.

20. C

21. Answers may vary.

5.4 Graphing and Modelling With $y = a \sin[k(x - d)] + c$ and $y = a \cos[k(x - d)] + c$, pages 318–321

1. a) amplitude 5, period $90°$, phase shift $25°$ to the right, vertical shift 3 units up

b) amplitude 2, period $20°$, phase shift $40°$ to the left, vertical shift 5 units down

c) amplitude 3, period $3°$, phase shift $30°$ to the right, vertical shift 2 units up

d) amplitude $\dfrac{3}{4}$, period $540°$, phase shift $60°$ to the right, vertical shift $\dfrac{1}{2}$ unit up

2. a) amplitude 3, period $72°$, phase shift $45°$ to the right, vertical shift 4 units up

b) amplitude 2, period $15°$, phase shift $80°$ to the left, vertical shift 1 unit down

c) amplitude 3, period $5°$, phase shift $10°$ to the right, vertical shift 3 units up

d) amplitude $\dfrac{5}{2}$, period $480°$, phase shift $40°$ to the right, vertical shift $\dfrac{1}{2}$ unit up

3. a) Answers may vary. Sample answer: Apply the amplitude of 3, apply the vertical shift of 1 unit down, and apply the horizontal compression by a factor of $\dfrac{1}{2}$.

b) $f(x)$: domain $\{x \in \mathbb{R}\}$, range $\{y \in \mathbb{R}, -1 \leq y \leq 1\}$
  $g(x)$: domain $= \{x \in \mathbb{R}\}$, range $\{y \in \mathbb{R}, -4 \leq y \leq 2\}$

c) $h(x) = 3 \sin [2(x + 60°)] - 1$

4. a) Apply the amplitude 4, the vertical shift of 2 units down, and the horizontal compression by a factor of $\dfrac{1}{3}$.

b) $f(x)$: domain $\{x \in \mathbb{R}\}$, range $\{y \in \mathbb{R}, -1 \leq y \leq 1\}$
  $g(x)$: domain $\{x \in \mathbb{R}\}$, range $\{y \in \mathbb{R}, -6 \leq y \leq 2\}$

c) $h(x) = 4 \cos [3(x - 60°)] - 2$

5. a) $y = 5 \sin [3(x + 30°)] - 2$ **b)** $y = 5 \cos 3x - 2$

6. a) $y = \dfrac{1}{2} \sin \left[\dfrac{1}{2}(x + 180°)\right] + 1$

b) $y = \dfrac{1}{2} \cos \dfrac{1}{2}x + 1$

7. a) $y = 4 \cos [3(x + 30°)] - 1$

b)

8. a) amplitude 10, period 360°, phase shift right 45°, vertical shift 10 units up

b) maximum 20, minimum 0

c) 315°, 675°, 1035°   **d)** 2.93

9. a) amplitude 5, period 180°, phase shift 30° to the right, no vertical shift

b) maximum 5, minimum −5

c) 75°, 165°, 255°   **d)** 2.5

10. Answers may vary.

11. a) Apply the amplitude of 5, $y = 5 \sin x$; apply the vertical shift of 4 units down, $y = 5 \sin x - 4$; apply the horizontal compression by a factor of $\frac{1}{6}$, $y = 5 \sin 6x - 4$; and translate the function 120° to the right, $y = 5 \sin [6(x - 120°)] - 4$.

b) $f(x)$: domain $\{x \in \mathbb{R}\}$, range $\{y \in \mathbb{R}, -1 \le x \le 1\}$

$g(x)$: domain $\{x \in \mathbb{R}\}$, range $\{y \in \mathbb{R}, -9 \le x \le 1\}$

c)

12. a) Apply the amplitude of 6, $y = 6 \cos x$; apply the vertical shift of 2 units up, $y = 5 \cos x + 2$; apply the horizontal compression by a factor of $\frac{1}{5}$, $y = 6 \cos 5x + 2$; and translate the function 60° to the left, $y = 6 \cos [5(x + 60°)] + 2$.

b) $f(x)$: domain $\{x \in \mathbb{R}\}$, range $\{y \in \mathbb{R}, -1 \le y \le 1\}$

$g(x)$: domain $\{x \in \mathbb{R}\}$, range $\{y \in \mathbb{R}, -4 \le y \le 8\}$

c)

13. a) Answers may vary. Sample answer:
$y = -2 \cos 3x$

b)

14. a) $y = 2 \sin [4(x - 30°)] + 3$

b) Answers may vary. Sample answer:
$y = 2 \cos [4(x - 52.5°)] + 3$

15. Answers may vary. Sample answers:

a) The graphs of $y = \sin x$ and $y = 2 \sin x$ have the same period, but different amplitudes, with $y = 2 \sin x$ having an amplitude that is twice the amplitude of $y = \sin x$.

b) The amplitude of the second curve is less than the amplitude of the first. The two curves look slightly phase-shifted from each other.

c) Answers may vary.

16. Answers may vary. Sample answers:

a) $y = 4 \cos 30x + 10$

b) $y = 4 \sin [30(x + 3)] + 10$

c) $y = 4 \sin [30(x - 3)] + 10$

d) $y = 4 \cos [30(x - 6)] + 10$

e) Answers may vary.

18. Answers may vary. Sample answer: No. This does not work if p is a zero of the function (that is, $q = 0$). It does work for all other points.

If $q \ne 0$, then $a = \dfrac{q}{\sin p}$.

19. Answers may vary. Sample answers:

a)

b) The graph will have missing sections where the graph of $y = \sin x$ has negative y-values.

c)

X	Y1
180	0
181	ERROR
182	ERROR
183	ERROR
184	ERROR
185	ERROR
186	ERROR

X=180

d) Since the entire function will now be above the x-axis, there will be no missing section of the curve.

e)

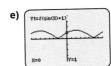

20. Answers may vary. Sample answers:

a) Three transformations are needed: a horizontal compression by a factor of $\frac{1}{2}$, a phase shift of $45°$ to the right, and a vertical shift of 1 unit down, giving the equation $y = \sin [2(x - 45°)] - 1$.

b) Three transformations are needed: a horizontal compression by a factor of $\frac{1}{2}$, a phase shift of $45°$ to the left, and a vertical shift of 1 unit down, giving the equation $y = \sin [2(x + 45°)] - 1$.

21. $75°$ **22.** C   **23.** B

5.5 Data Collecting and Modelling, pages 328–332

In these answers, the data are modelled using sine functions. Answers using cosine functions are possible.

1. Answers may vary. Sample answers:

a) maximum 3 m, minimum 1.5 m, amplitude 0.75

b) 2.25 m up

c) d is about 0.4 s to the right.

d) period 2 s, $k = 180$

e) $y = 0.75 \sin [180(x - 0.4)] + 2.25$

f)

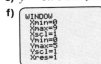

2. Answers may vary. Sample answers:

a) maximum 3 m, minimum 0.5 m, amplitude 1.25

b) 1.75 m up

c) d is about 0.2 s to the right.

d) period 2.5 s, $k = 144$

e) $y = 1.25 \sin [144(x - 0.2)] + 1.75$

f)

3. a) maximum 12 m, minimum 2 m

b) high tide at 8:00 a.m.; low tide at 2:00 p.m.

c) 11.3 m

d) 12:46 a.m., 3:14 a.m., 12:46 p.m., 3:14 p.m.

4. a) maximum 13 000, minimum 3000

b) maximum in October, at $t = 10$; minimum in April, at $t = 4$

c) 12 330 people

d) January 6, $t = 6$ days, and July 24, $t = 7$ months 24 days

5. Answers may vary. Sample answers:

a) $y = 180.7 \sin [30(x - 2.6)] + 199.3$

b) domain $\{x \in \mathbb{R}, 1 \le x \le 12\}$, range $\{y \in \mathbb{R}, 18 \le y \le 380\}$

6. a) $y = 10 \sin (x + 240°) + 14$

b) $y = 10 \cos (x + 150°) + 14$

c) The phase shift of the curves will be altered by an additional $30°$. $y = 10 \sin (x + 210°) + 14$; $y = 10 \cos (x + 120°) + 14$

7. The new equations are as follows:

a) $y = 10 \sin (x + 240°) + 16$

b) $y = 10 \cos (x + 150°) + 16$

8. a) $\frac{1}{30}$ s

b) maximum 70 mm, minimum -30 mm, amplitude 50 mm

c) maximum at $\frac{1}{120}$ s, minimum at $\frac{1}{40}$ s

d) 70 mm

9. a) by a factor of $\sqrt{2}$

b) You must decrease the length by a factor of 4.

c) Answers may vary.

d) The period would increase by a factor of $\sqrt{6}$.

10.–11. Answers may vary.

12. a) period 24 h. Answers may vary. Sample answer: Smog is often created from human activity that generally repeats from day to day, so a period of 24 h is appropriate.

b) maximum 55, minimum -5, amplitude 30

c) maximum at 10 a.m., minimum at 10 p.m.

d) Answers may vary. Sample answer: The interval from 7:45 a.m. to 12:15 a.m.

13.–16. Answers may vary.

18. a) Answers may vary. Sample answer: $y = 10 \cot [15(12 - x)], 6 < x \le 12$

b)

19. B   **20.** D   **21.** D

5.6 Use Sinusoidal Functions to Model Periodic Phenomena Not Involving Angles, pages 337–342

1. a) $y = 8 \sin [30(t - 2.5)]$

b) high tide at 5:30 p.m., low tides at 11:30 a.m. and 11:30 p.m.

2. a) $y = 5 \cos 30t$

b) Answers may vary. Sample answer: The graphs of $y = 5 \sin [30(t + 3)]$ and $y = 5 \cos 30t$ are the same.

3. Answers may vary. Sample answer: During a brownout, the voltage drops. This means that the amplitude of the function decreases. All other properties of the function remain the same. An example is $V = 100 \sin 21\ 600t$, where the peak voltage drops from 170 V to 100 V.

4. a) maximum 850, minimum 250, amplitude 300

b) vertical shift up 550   **c)** phase shift 0

d) 6 years, $k = 60$ **e)** $y = 300 \sin 60x + 550$

f) Answers may vary, but all graphs should match the shape of the graph given.

5. a) maximum 26 m, minimum 2 m   **b)** 12 h

c)

d) from 1:13 a.m. to 2:47 a.m., and from 1:13 p.m. to 2:47 p.m.

e) Answers may vary. Sample answer: Factors such as wind conditions and boat traffic in the harbour need to be considered.

6. a) $y = 8 \sin [30(x - 2)] + 14$

b)

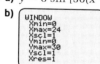

c) Answers may vary. Sample answer: Since the water level has a minimum value of 6 m, and only 3 m of water are needed for a safe landing, it is never considered unsafe to land at this time of year.

7. a) $\dfrac{1}{50}$ s   **b)** $k = 18\ 000$ **c)** 240 V

d) $V = 240 \sin 18\ 000t$

e)

Answers may vary. Sample answer: The domain is set from 0 s to $\dfrac{1}{25}$ s with each tick representing $\dfrac{1}{100}$ s. Each tick on the y-axis represents 100 V.

8. a) period $\dfrac{1}{3}$ s   **b)** $k = 1080$

c) 6   **d)** $V = 6 \sin 1080t$

e)

Answers may vary. Sample answer: The domain is set from 0 to $\dfrac{2}{3}$ s with each tick representing $\dfrac{1}{6}$ s. Each tick on the y-axis represents 5 V.

9. Answers may vary. Sample answers:

a) $y = 75 \sin [36(x - 18)] + 85$

b)

c) Answers may vary.

10. Answers may vary. Sample answers:

a) 2010, 2020, and 2030

b) 2015, 2025, and 2035

c) The variation in the maximum values is from approximately 123 to 163 and the variation in the minimum values is from approximately 8 to 12.

11. a) $N(t) = 25 \sin [90(t - 1)] + 75$

b)

c) Answers may vary. Sample answer: The phase shift to the right is because, as the prey population (the food supply) increases, the number of predators grows. This increase continues, until the predators begin to deplete the prey population (the food supply), which results in a decrease in the number of predators a short time later.

12. Answers may vary.

13. Answers may vary. Sample answers:

a) $y = 700\ 000 \cos [30(t - 2)] + 900\ 000$

b)

c) 1 593 187 000 m³

14. a)

b) Answers may vary. Sample answer:
$y = 4.19 \sin [30(x + 8.98)] + 12.35$

c)

d) Answers may vary. Sample answer: 9 h 21 min

15. Answers may vary.

16. Answers may vary. Sample answers:

a) $y = \sin 432\,000t + 1.4$

b)

c) 0.000 47 min, 0.000 78 min, or 0.028 s, 0.047 s

17. a)

b) Answers may vary. Sample answer: $\sin x$
controls the amplitude of $\sin 10x$ such that the
pattern is a grouped series of maximum and
minimum values where, within the grouping,
the amplitudes increase to a maximum before
decreasing to a minimum. This pattern repeats
twice in 360° as $y = \sin 10x$ has more wave
forms within 0 to 360°, but they are controlled
by the one wave form of $y = \sin x$ within this
same domain.

c) Answers may vary.

18. Answers may vary.

19. a) $y = 24 \sin 9720t + 94$

b)

c) 0.0015 s and 0.0170 s

20. a)

b) Answers may vary. Sample answer: The two
functions are completely out of phase with each
other, meaning that the addition of two parts of
the function will always result in a total y-value
of 0. This is why the coating is non-reflective.

c) $y = \cos (x + 90°)$

21. Answers may vary.

22. D   **23.** 121

Chapter 5 Review, pages 344–345

1. a) The function is periodic because the y-values
repeat in a regular pattern.

b) 3   **c)** maximum 5, minimum 1

d) 2   **e)** 360°

2. a)
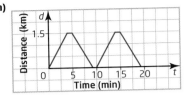

b) 0.75 km

c) Answers may vary. Sample answer: It would
take less time to get to and from the airport and
parking lot, so more cycles would exist in a
20-min period. This would not affect the
portions of the graph associated with the stops
at the terminal and parking lot.

3.

4.

5. a) 1   **b)** 360°

c) 60° to the left   **d)** 3 units up

e)

f) The new equation is $y = \cos (x - 60°) - 3$. The
graph shifts to the right 120° and down 6 units
compared to the graph of $y = \cos (x + 60) + 3$.

6. a) amplitude 30, period 1 s, phase shift 0.25 cm to
the right, vertical shift 45 cm up

b) 15 cm

c) domain $\{t \in \mathbb{R}\}$, range $\{y \in \mathbb{R}, 15 \le y \le 75\}$

d) The vertical shift must change from 45 cm to 50
cm. The new equation is
$y = 30 \sin [360(t - 0.25)] + 50$.

7. a)

Month (21st day)	Time (decimal format)
1	7.67
2	7.07
3	6.28
4	5.42
5	4.78
6	4.62
7	4.92
8	5.47

Month (21st day)	Time (decimal format)
9	6.02
10	6.60
11	7.25
12	7.72

b) $y = 1.55 \sin [0.5(x + 3.3)] + 6.24$;
amplitude 1.55, period 12 months,
phase shift 3.3 left, vertical shift 6.24 up

c)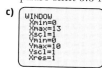

8. January 7 at 7:39 a.m.; July 7 at 4:49 a.m.

9. a) $y = 40 \sin 360t + 90$

b)

c) 4.8 L

d) $y = 40 \cos [360(t - 0.25)] + 90$

e) $y = 40 \sin (720t) + 90$

f) Answers may vary. Sample answer: The amplitude does not change because the maximum and minimum volume of blood in the left ventricle does not change regardless of any increase in the heart rate.

Chapter 5 Practice Test, pages 346–347

1. D **2.** B **3.** C **4.** A **5.** C **6.** B **7.** C **8.** A

9. a) 3 **b)** 90°

c) 60° to the left **d)** 2 units down

e)

f) domain $\{x \in \mathbb{R}\}$, range $\{y \in \mathbb{R}, -5 \le y \le 1\}$

10. Answers may vary. Sample answers:

a) $y = 4 \cos 4x - 2$

b) $y = 4 \sin (4x + 22.5°) - 2$

11. a) $y = \dfrac{1}{4} \sin \left[\dfrac{1}{2}(x + 180°)\right] + \dfrac{1}{2}$

b)

12. a) amplitude 2, period 120°, phase shift 120° to the right, no vertical shift

b) maximum 2, minimum −2

c) 30°, 90°, 150° **d)** 2

13. a) $y = 2 \sin [6(x - 15°)] + 1$

b) Answers may vary. Sample answer: The period of the function changes from 60° to 30°; so the equation is $y = 2 \sin [12(x - 15°)] + 1$.

14. Answers may vary. Sample answers:

a) $y = 17 \sin [30(x - 4)] + 79$

amplitude 17, period 12, phase shift 4, vertical shift 79

b)

The fit of the curve is good with respect to the data.

c) Approximately 95% will be employed on June 15.

d) This will result in a damped periodic function, with the amplitude decreasing to 90% of the value in the previous month, due to the 10% decrease.

15. a) $y = 9 \sin (x + 270°) + 11$

b) $y = 9 \sin (x + 225°) + 11$

c)

Answers may vary. Sample answer: Similarities: same amplitude, period, and vertical shift, because the wheel turns with these characteristics no matter where it is loaded. Differences: phase shift, because the loading dock of the ride changes position.

Chapters 4 and 5 Review, pages 348–349

1. a) $\sin 315° = -\dfrac{1}{\sqrt{2}}$, $\cos 315° = \dfrac{1}{\sqrt{2}}$, $\tan 315° = -1$

b) $\sin 315° = -0.7071$, $\cos 315° = 0.7071$, $\tan 315° = -1$

2. a) $\sin 255° = -1.0$, $\cos 255° = -0.3$, $\tan 255° = 3.7$

b) $\sin 255° = -0.9659$, $\cos 255° = -0.2588$,
$\tan 255° = 3.7321$

3. $\sin \theta = -\dfrac{1}{\sqrt{10}}$, $\cos \theta = \dfrac{3}{\sqrt{10}}$, $\tan \theta = -\dfrac{1}{3}$,

$\csc \theta = -\sqrt{10}$, $\sec \theta = \dfrac{\sqrt{10}}{3}$, $\cot \theta = -3$

4. $\cos Q = -\dfrac{8}{17}$, $\tan Q = -\dfrac{15}{8}$

5. $\theta = 159°, 339°$

6. $187°, 353°$

7. a)

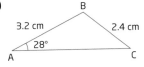

b) 280 km

8. a)

b) First triangle: $\angle C = 39°$, $\angle B = 113°$, $b = 4.7$ cm; second triangle: $\angle C = 141°$, $\angle B = 11°$, $b = 1.0$ cm

9. 3.0 km

10. 32.3 m, 11.4 m

11.–12. Answers may vary.

13. a) The y-values repeat in a regular pattern.
b) 7   **c)** maximum 3, minimum -4
d) amplitude 3.5   **e)** period 2

14. a) $45°$ and $-135°$

b)

15. a) 3   **b)** $180°$
c) $45°$ to the right   **d)** 1 unit down
e)

f) The equation becomes
$y = 3 \sin [4(x - 45°)] - 1$.

16. a) $y = \dfrac{1}{2} \sin [\dfrac{1}{3}(x + 270°)] + \dfrac{1}{4}$

b)

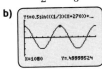

17. a) amplitude 2, period $120°$, phase shift $120°$, no vertical shift

b) maximum $\dfrac{1}{4}$, minimum $-\dfrac{1}{4}$
c) $45°, 135°, 325°$ **d)** $-\dfrac{1}{4}$

18. Answers may vary. Sample answers:
a) $d = 1.5 \sin 24t + 0.2$
b) amplitude 1.5, period 15 s, no phase shift, vertical shift up 0.2
c) 1.5 m

19. Answers may vary. Sample answers:
a) $A = 2000 \sin 30x + 3000$
b)

c) All the properties of the sine function remain the same, except for a phase shift to translate the sine function to a cosine function. Sample function: $A = 2000 \cos [30(x - 3)] + 3000$

Chapter 6

Prerequisite Skills, pages 352–353

1. a)   **b)**

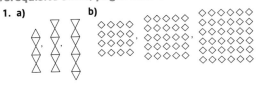

c) EEEEE, FFFFFF, GGGGGGG
d) PQRST, PQRSTU, PQRSTUV
e) 15, 18, 21   **f)** $-25, 30, -35$
g) $-9, -13, -17$ **h)** $\dfrac{1}{6}, \dfrac{1}{7}, \dfrac{1}{8}$
i) $5x, 6x, 7x$

2. a) 2   **b)** -10 **c)** $\dfrac{1}{2}$ **d)** $\dfrac{-m + 7}{m + 2}$

3. a) 2   **b)** $\dfrac{1}{4}$ **c)** $2^{\frac{1}{3}}$ **d)** $2^{\frac{t-1}{3}}$

4. a) 1   **b)** 5
c) $t^2 - 7t + 11$ **d)** $4t^2 - 6t + 1$

5. a)

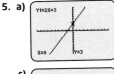

b)

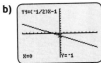

c)

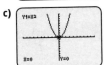

d)

e)

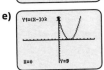

f)

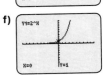

g)

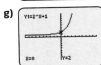

h)

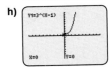

6. a) $y = -\dfrac{3}{7}$ **b)** $t = 0$ **c)** $a = \dfrac{3}{2}$ **d)** $x = 44$ **e)** $x = 6$

7. a) 4.8 **b)** 105 **c)** 0.48
d) 20 **e)** 0.051 **f)** 980

8. a) $\dfrac{4}{5}$ **b)** $-\dfrac{3}{14}$ **c)** $\dfrac{24}{5}$
d) $-\dfrac{39}{2}$ **e)** $\dfrac{1}{6}$ **f)** $\dfrac{11}{5}$

9. a) quadratic **b)** linear **c)** neither

10. Answers may vary. Sample answer: For a linear function, the first differences are the same. The value of the first differences for the linear function $y = 3x - 1$ is 3. The slope of the linear function $y = 3x - 1$ is also 3. The value of the first differences for a linear function is equal to the value of m in a linear function of the form $y = mx + b$.

11. Answers may vary. Sample answer: For a quadratic function, the second differences are the same. The value the second differences for the quadratic function $y = 2x^2 - 5x - 3$ is 4. The value of the second differences of a quadratic function is equal to the value of $2a$ in a quadratic function of the form $y = ax^2 + bx + c$.

12. a) $(3, 1)$ **b)** $\left(-\dfrac{8}{3}, \dfrac{49}{3}\right)$
c) $\left(\dfrac{228}{13}, -\dfrac{112}{3}\right)$ **d)** $(5, 4)$

6.1 Sequences as Discrete Functions, pages 360–363

1. a) 2, 5, 8 **b)** $-3, -8, -13$ **c)** 1, 3, 9
d) $\dfrac{1}{2}, \dfrac{1}{4}, \dfrac{1}{8}$ **e)** $1, \dfrac{1}{2}, \dfrac{1}{3}$ **f)** 24, 48, 96

2. a) -35 **b)** 29 **c)** 142
d) $\dfrac{13}{12}$ **e)** 168 **f)** -2048

3. Answers may vary. Sample answers:
a) The first term is 4. Multiply each term by 4 to get the next term.
next three terms: 1024, 4096, 16 384
b) The first term is 7. Subtract 1 from each term to get the next term.
next three terms: 3, 2, 1
c) The first term is -3. Subtract three from each term to get the next term.
next three terms: $-15, -18, -21$
d) The first term is 100. Divide each term by 10 to get the next term.
next three terms: 0.01, 0.001, 0.0001
e) The first term is 5. To get each subsequent term in the sequence, increase the absolute value of the previous term by 5 and then multiply the result by $(-1)^{n+1}$.
next three terms: 25, -30, 35
f) The first term is $\dfrac{1}{3}$. Multiply each term by $\dfrac{1}{3}$ to get the next term.
next three terms: $\dfrac{1}{243}, \dfrac{1}{729} \dfrac{1}{2187}$

g) The first term is x. Add $2x$ to each term to get the next term.
next three terms: $9x, 11x, 13x$
h) The first term is 4. Add 4 to each term to get the next term.
next three terms: 20, 24, 28
i) The first term is a. Multiply each term by r to get the next term.
next three terms: ar^4, ar^5, ar^6
j) The first term is 0.2 To get each subsequent term in the sequence, increase the absolute value of the previous term by 0.2 and then multiply the result by $(-1)^{n+1}$.
next three terms: 1, -1.2, 1.4

4. a)

Term Number, n	Term, t_n	First Differences
1	2	
2	4	2
3	6	2
4	8	2

$f(n) = 2n$; domain $\{n \in \mathbb{N}\}$

b)

Term Number, n	Term, t_n	First Differences
1	2	
2	1	-1
3	0	-1
4	-1	-1

$f(n) = -n + 3$; domain $\{n \in \mathbb{N}\}$

c)

Term Number, n	Term, t_n	First Differences
1	3	
2	6	3
3	9	3
4	12	3

$f(n) = 3n$; domain $\{n \in \mathbb{N}\}$

d)

Term Number, n	Term, t_n	First Differences	Second Differences
1	0		
2	3	3	
3	8	5	2
4	15	7	2

$f(n) = n^2 - 1$; domain $\{n \in \mathbb{N}\}$

e)

Term Number, n	Term, t_n	First Differences	Second Differences
1	3		
2	6	3	
3	11	5	2
4	18	7	2

$f(n) = n^2 + 2$; domain $\{n \in \mathbb{N}\}$

f)

Term Number, n	Term, t_n	First Differences	Second Differences
1	−10		
2	−9	1	
3	0	9	8
4	17	17	8

$f(n) = 4n^2 - 11n - 3$; domain $\{n \in \mathbb{N}\}$

5. a) $f(n) = n^2$, domain $\{1, 2, 3, 4\}$

b) $f(n) = 2n$, domain $\{1, 2, 3, 4\}$

c) $f(n) = \frac{1}{2}n - \frac{3}{2}$, domain $\{1, 2, 3, 4\}$

d) $f(n) = 4n - 11$, domain $\{1, 2, 3, 4\}$

6. a) discrete; Answers may vary. Sample answer: The function is a distinct set of points.

b) continuous; Answers may vary. Sample answer: The function is a continuous line.

c) discrete; Answers may vary. Sample answer: The function is a distinct set of points.

7. Answers may vary. Sample answers:

a) The first term and each alternate term after this term in the sequence is 1. The second term and each alternate term after this term in the sequence is the set of natural numbers.
Next three terms: 5, 1, 6

b) The first term and each alternate term after this term in the sequence is the set of natural numbers. The second term in the sequence is 5 and each alternate term after this term is 5 more than the preceding alternate term.
Next three terms: 4, 20, 5

c) The first term in the sequence is 3. Multiply each term by $\sqrt{5}$ to get the next term.
Next three terms: $75\sqrt{5}$, 375, $375\sqrt{5}$

d) The first term in the sequence is $\frac{1}{2}$. Multiply each term by $\frac{1}{2}$ to get the next term.
Next three terms: $\frac{1}{32}, \frac{1}{64}, \frac{1}{128}$

8. Answers may vary. Sample answers: Each term in the sequence is a multiple of 7.

a) 98 is a part of this sequence. 98 is a multiple of 7.

b) 110 is not a part of this sequence. 110 is not a multiple of 7.

c) 378 is a part of this sequence. 378 is a multiple of 7.

d) 575 is not a part of this sequence. 575 is not a multiple of 7.

9. a)

b) Answers may vary. Sample answer: The curve is an exponential curve. If the growth rate were greater the curve would be steeper.

c) 6.5772, 6.6561, 6.736, 6.8168, 6.8986, 6.9814, 7.0652, 7.15, 7.2358, where each number is in billions.

10. a)–b)

Year	Value
0	35 000.00
1	28 000.00
2	22 400.00
3	17 920.00
4	14 336.00
5	11 468.80
6	9 175.04
7	7 340.03
8	5 872.03
9	4 697.62
10	3 758.10
11	3 006.48
12	2 405.18
13	1 924.15
14	1 539.32
15	1 231.45

c)

d) $f(n) = 35\,000(0.80)^n$

e) This is a discrete function. The depreciated value of the car is calculated on a yearly basis.

11. $\frac{1}{2}, \frac{1}{3}, \frac{1}{4}, \frac{1}{5}, \frac{1}{6}$

12. a) Answers may vary.

b)

Stage Number	Line Segment Length	Number of Line Segments	Perimeter of the Snowflake
1	1	3	3
2	$\frac{1}{3}$	12	4
3	$\frac{1}{9}$	48	$\frac{16}{3}$
4	$\frac{1}{27}$	192	$\frac{64}{9}$
5	$\frac{1}{81}$	768	$\frac{256}{27}$
6	$\frac{1}{243}$	3072	$\frac{1024}{81}$

c) Line Segment Length: $f(n) = \left(\frac{1}{3}\right)^{n-1}$;
Number of Line Segments: $f(n) = 3(4)^{n-1}$;
Perimeter of the Snowflake: $f(n) = 3\left(\frac{4}{3}\right)^{n-1}$

d) Line Segment Length: 1.0622×10^{-11};
Number of Line Segments: 2.1111×10^{14};
Perimeter of the Snowflake: 2242.3954

13. Answers may vary. Sample answers:

a) $f(n) = (-4)(-2)^{n-1}$; −65 536

b) $f(n) = \dfrac{n}{2n - 1}; \dfrac{15}{29}$

c) $f(n) = \sqrt{n}; \sqrt{15}$

d) $f(n) = 2^{n-1}; 16\ 384$

e) $f(n) = \dfrac{1}{n}; \dfrac{1}{15}$

f) $f(n) = (-1)^{n-1}; 1$

14. Answers may vary.

15. a) 50, 100, 200, 400, 800, 1600

b) $f(n) = 50(2)^{n-1}$

c) \$409 600.00; Answers may vary. Sample answer: No. This amount seems to be too great for the sales on the 14th day of a new small business.

16. $f(n) = 2100 - 110n$; 12 years

17. a) 1.7321, 1.3161, 1.1472

b) Answers may vary. Sample answer: The numbers are getting smaller and approaching 1.

c) 1

18. $f(n) = \dfrac{n(n + 1)(2n + 1)}{6}$

19. B   **20.** B   **21.** B

6.2 Recursive Procedures, pages 370–372

1. a) 4, 7, 10, 13

b) 7, 13, 25, 49

c) $-3, -1.8, -1.56, -1.512$

d) 50, 25, 12.5, 6.25

e) 8, -20, 66, -190

f) 100, 5000, 250 000, 12 500 000

2. a) 9, 7, 5, 3

b) $-1, 3, -9, 27$

c) $3, \dfrac{3}{2}, \dfrac{1}{2}, \dfrac{1}{8}$

d) 18, 20, 22, 24

e) 0.5, -0.5, 0.5, -0.5

f) 25, -12.5, 6.25, -3.125

3. a) $t_1 = 5, t_n = t_{n-1} + 6$ **b)** $t_1 = 4, t_n = t_{n-1} - 3$

c) $t_1 = 4, t_n = 2t_{n-1}$ **d)** $t_1 = -4, t_n = \dfrac{1}{2}t_{n-1}$

e) $t_1 = -5, t_n = -3t_{n-1}$

4. a) 40, 70, 100, 130, ...; $t_1 = 40, t_n = t_{n-1} + 30$

b) $1, -2, 4, -8; t_1 = 1, t_n = t_{n-1}(-2)$

5. Answers may vary. Sample answer:
$t_1 = 206, t_n = t_{n-1}$

6. a) 50, 54, 62, 74

b) Answers may vary. Sample answer: There are 50 seats in the first row. The number of seats in the second row is the number of seats in the first row increased by 4. The number of seats in the third row is equal to the number of seats in the second row increased by 8. The number of seats in the fourth row is equal to the number of seats in the third row increased by 12. The number of seats in subsequent rows is equal to the number of seats in the previous row increased by 4 multiplied by the result that you get if you subtract one from the number that the row is designated as.

c) $t_1 = 50, t_n = t_{n-1} + 4(n - 1)$

7. a)

Year	House Value (\$)
0	250 000
1	250 000 + 0.03 × 250 000 = 257 500
2	257 500 + 0.03 × 257 500 = 265 225
3	265 225 + 0.03 × 265 225 = 273 181.75
4	273 181.75 + 0.03 × 273 181.75 = 281 377.20
5	281 377.20 + 0.03 × 281 377.20 = 289 818.52
6	289 818.52 + 0.03 × 289 818.52 = 298 513.08
7	298 513.08 + 0.03 × 298 513.08 = 307 468.47
8	307 468.47 + 0.03 × 307 468.47 = 316 692.52
9	316 692.52 + 0.03 × 316 692.52 = 326 193.30
10	326 193.30 + 0.03 × 326 193.30 = 335 979.10

b) 257 500, 265 225, 273 181.75, 281 377.20, 289 818.52, 298 513.08, 307 468.47, 316 692.52, 326 193.30, 335 979.10

c) $t_n = 1.03t_{n-1}$; \$389 491.86

8. a) 1, 7, 58, 3376   **b)** 8, 4, 2, 1

c) 3, 6, 12, 24   **d)** $-5, 14, -24, 52$

e) $\dfrac{1}{2}$, 4, 18, 74

f) $a + 3b, a + 7b, a + 11b, a + 15b$

9. a) 2, 2, 6, 10   **b)** 1, 2, 2, 4

c) 5, 7, -2, 9   **d)** $-2, 3, -3, 6$

e) $1, -4, -4, 16$ **f)** $3, 1, 7, -3$

10. 0, 2, 5, 9, 14, 20; $t_1 = 0, t_n = t_{n-1} + n$

11. $t_1 = 1, t_n = t_{n-1} + 2n - 1$

12. a) $-8, -12, -20, -36$

b) $t_1 = -8, t_n = 2t_{n-1} + 4$

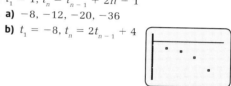

13. Answers may vary. Sample answers:

a) 1, 9, 25, 49; $t_1 = 1, t_n = t_{n-1} + 8(n - 1)$

b) $2, \dfrac{5}{2}, \dfrac{10}{3}, \dfrac{17}{4}; t_1 = 2, t_n = t_{n-1} + \dfrac{n(n-1) - 1}{n(n-1)}$

c) $\dfrac{1}{3}, \dfrac{1}{9}, \dfrac{1}{27}, \dfrac{1}{81}; f(1) = \dfrac{1}{3}, f(n) = \dfrac{f(n-1)}{3}$

d) 4, 7, 10, 13; $t_1 = 4, t_n = t_{n-1} + 3$

e) $-3, 0, 5, 12; f(1) = -3, f(n) = f(n-1)$

f) 2, 8, 32, 128; $f(1) = 2, f(n) = 4f(n-1)$

14. a) 3, 7, 15, 31; $t_n = 4(2^{n-1}) - 1$

b) $1, \dfrac{1}{2}, \dfrac{1}{4}, \dfrac{1}{8}; t_n = \dfrac{1}{2^{n-1}}$

c) 10, 0, -10, -20; $t_n = 20 - 10n$

d) $-2, -\dfrac{5}{2}, -\dfrac{8}{3}, -\dfrac{11}{4}; t_n = \dfrac{1 - 3n}{n}$

15. a) Answers will vary.

b) area $= \dfrac{3}{4}$ square units

c) Answers will vary.

d) $1, \dfrac{3}{4}, \dfrac{9}{16}, \dfrac{27}{64}, \dfrac{81}{256}$, ...; recursive: $t_1 = 1$,
$t_n = \dfrac{3}{4}t_{n-1}$: explicit $f(n) = \left(\dfrac{3}{4}\right)^{n-1}$

16. Answers may vary. Sample answers:

a) $t_1 = 2, t_n = t_{n-1} + 2n$

b) $t_1 = 3, t_n = t_{n-1} + n^2$

c) $t_1 = 2, t_n = (t_{n-1})^2 + 1$

d) $t_1 = -1, t_n = t_{n-1} + 3^{n-2}$

18. a) $1.5, -3, 6, -12, 24$ **b)** $-4, 0, 9, 25$

19. Answers may vary.

20. a) sequence as exact numbers:

$1, 1, 2, \dfrac{3}{2}, \dfrac{5}{3}, \dfrac{8}{5}, \dfrac{13}{8}, \dfrac{21}{13}, \ldots;$

sequence as approximate numbers: 1, 1, 2, 1.5, 1.667, 1.6, 1.625, 1,615, ...;

Answers may vary. Sample answer: The sequence is converging and approaching 1.618.

b) Answers will vary.

21. a) Answers may vary.

b) $\dfrac{\pi}{4}, \dfrac{\pi}{4}, \pi, \dfrac{9\pi}{4}, \dfrac{25\pi}{4}, 16\pi; 26\pi$ square units

22. Answers may vary.

6.3 Pascal's Triangle and Expanding Binomial Powers, pages 378–379

1. 6; Answers may vary. Sample answer: The number not on the diagonal is equal to the sum of the three numbers that are on the diagonal. Examples may vary.

2. a) 256   **b)** 4096

c) 1 048 576   **d)** 2^n

3. a) $t_{5,4}$ **b)** $t_{9,6}$

c) $t_{26,18}$ **d)** $t_{a+1, b+1}$

4. a) $t_{3,1} + t_{3,2}$ **b)** $t_{11,8} + t_{11,9}$

c) $t_{27,13} + t_{27,14}$ **d)** $t_{16, x-1} + t_{16, x}$

5. a) $x^5 + 10x^4 + 40x^3 + 80x^2 + 80x + 32$

b) $y^4 - 12y^3 + 54y^2 - 108y + 81$

c) $4096 + 6144t + 3840t^2 + 1280t^3 + 240t^4 + 24t^5 + t^6$

d) $1 - 5m + 10m^2 - 10m^3 + 5m^4 - m^5$

e) $16x^4 - 96x^3y + 216x^2y^2 - 216xy^3 + 81y^4$

f) $a^{10} + 20a^8 + 160a^6 + 640a^4 + 1280a^2 + 1024$

6. a) 1   **b)** 26   **c)** 16   **d)** $n + 1$

7. a) 1   **b)** 7   **c)** 4   **d)** 495

8. a) 8   **b)** 11   **c)** 14   **d)** 16

9. Answers may vary. Sample answers:

a) $t_{5,2} - t_{4,1}$ **b)** $t_{7,3} - t_{6,2}$

c) $t_{13,9} - t_{12,8}$ **d)** $t_{29,14} - t_{28,15}$

10. a) top row: 8, 1; bottom row: 45, 10

b) middle left: 35; bottom right: 28 ; middle cell 21

c) middle left: 11; middle right: 165; bottom row: 66, 220

d) top left: 21; middle right: 70; bottom row: 84, 126

11. Answers may vary.

12. Answers may vary. Sample answer: If you write Pascal's triangle as a right triangle, then the sum of the diagonals form the Fibonacci sequence, 1, 1, 2, 3, 5, 8, 13, ...

13. Row 0: 1; Row 1; 2: Row 2: 6; Row 3: 20; Row 4: 70; 1, 2, 6, 20, 70; Answers may vary. Sample answer: The numbers are located at the centre of every other row in Pascal's Triangle. Answers may vary. Sample answer: $t_n = t_{2(n-1), n-1}$

14. $x = -2; n = 9$

15. Answers may vary. Sample answer: The top term is 1. The first and last terms of each row n are generated by increasing the denominator of first and last terms of row $n - 1$ by 1. Every other term in a row is obtained by subtracting the term to its immediate right from the term immediately above andto the right. Using this pattern the next three rows in the triangular array are as follows:

$$\dfrac{1}{6} \quad \dfrac{1}{30} \quad \dfrac{1}{60} \quad \dfrac{1}{60} \quad \dfrac{1}{30} \quad \dfrac{1}{6}$$

$$\dfrac{1}{7} \quad \dfrac{1}{42} \quad \dfrac{1}{105} \quad \dfrac{1}{140} \quad \dfrac{1}{105} \quad \dfrac{1}{42} \quad \dfrac{1}{7}$$

$$\dfrac{1}{8} \quad \dfrac{1}{56} \quad \dfrac{1}{168} \quad \dfrac{1}{280} \quad \dfrac{1}{280} \quad \dfrac{1}{168} \quad \dfrac{1}{56} \quad \dfrac{1}{8}$$

16. Answers may vary. Sample answer: The numbers in the rows where the first term after the 1 is a prime number are multiples of the prime number.

17. 89 ways

18. C   **19.** B   **20.** A

6.4 Arithmetic Sequences, pages 385–387

1. a) $a = 12, d = 3; 21, 24, 27, 30$

b) $a = 6, d = -2; 0, -2, -4, -6$

c) $a = 0.2, d = 0.15; 0.65, 0.8, 0.95, 1.1$

d) $a = -30, d = 6; -12, -6, 0, 6$

e) $a = 5, d = -6; -13, -19, -25, -31$

f) $a = \dfrac{1}{2}, d = \dfrac{1}{2}; 2, \dfrac{5}{2}, 3, \dfrac{7}{2}$

2. a) arithmetic; the first term is $a = 3$ and the common difference between the consecutive terms is $d = 2$

b) not arithmetic; the first term is $a = 2$, the difference between consecutive terms is not equal

c) not arithmetic; the first term is $a = 4$, the difference between consecutive terms is not equal

d) arithmetic; the first term is $a = 13$ and the common difference between the consecutive terms is $d = -6$

e) arithmetic; the first term is $a = -12$ and the common difference between the consecutive terms is $d = 7$

f) arithmetic; the first term is $a = 0$ and the common difference between the consecutive terms is $d = 1.5$

3. a) $5, 7, 9; t_n = 2n + 3$

b) $-2, -6, -10; t_n = -4n + 2$

c) $9, 5.5, 2; t_n = -3.5n + 12.5$

d) $0, -\dfrac{1}{2}, -1; t_n = -\dfrac{1}{2}n + \dfrac{1}{2}$

e) $100, 110, 120; t_n = 10n + 90$

f) $\dfrac{3}{4}, \dfrac{5}{4}, \dfrac{7}{4}; t_n = \dfrac{1}{2}n + \dfrac{1}{4}$

g) $10, 10 + t, 10 + 2t$; $t_n = tn + 10 - t$

h) $x, 3x, 5x$; $t_n = 2nx - x$

4. a) 40 **b)** -47 **c)** $\dfrac{15}{2}$ **d)** 2

5. a) $-1, 1, 3$ **b)** $-2, -3, -4$

 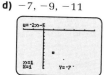

c) $2, 0, -2$ **d)** $-7, -9, -11$

e) $0.75, 1.25, 1.75$ **f)** $0.3, 0.5, 0.7$

6. t_{32}

7. a) 40 **b)** 30 **c)** 89 **d)** 35

8. Answers may vary.

9. a) $a = \dfrac{5}{2}, d = \dfrac{1}{2}; 1, \dfrac{1}{2}, 0$

b) $a = -6, d = \dfrac{5}{2}; \dfrac{3}{2}, 4, \dfrac{13}{2}$

c) $a = 2a, d = -b; 2a - 3b, 2a - 4b, 2a - 5b$

10. a) $a = 5, d = 4; t_n = 4n + 1$

b) $a = -4, d = 6; t_n = 6n - 10$

c) $a = -8, d = -3; t_n = -3n - 5$

d) $a = 3 - 22x, d = 4.5x; t_n = 4.5xn + 3 - 26.5x$

11. a) $t_1 = 5, t_n = t_{n-1} + 4$

b) $t_1 = -4, t_n = t_{n-1} + 6$

c) $t_1 = -8, t_n = t_{n-1} - 3$

d) $t_1 = 3 - 22x, t_n = t_{n-1} + 4.5x$

12. a) $t_n = 2n$ **b)** $t_n = 10n$

c) $t_n = -10n + 5$ **d)** $t_n = -3n + 2$

13. a) \$5500

b) 20 winners; Answers may vary. Sample answer: The 20th winner will receive \$500. The amount left after this prize is paid out will be \$0.

14. \$130 500, if $n = 0$ represents his current salary and $n = 1$ represents his salary at the end of the first year.

15. 822 members

16. $-9, -27$

17. 83

18 Answers may vary. Sample answers:

a) arithmetic; Each term after the first term is found by adding a common difference of 3 to the previous term.

b) not arithmetic; Each term after the first term and the second term is found by multiplying the previous term by 4 and then adding the term

that is 2 before the current term. The terms in the sequence do not have a common difference.

c) not arithmetic; Each consecutive term is found by squaring the previous term. The terms in the sequence do not have a common difference.

d) not arithmetic; Each term after the first term is found by multiplying the previous term by -2 and then subtracting 5. The terms in the sequence do not have a common difference. Answers may vary.

19. $\dfrac{7x + 10y}{4}, \dfrac{5x + 6y}{2}, \dfrac{13x + 14y}{4}$

20. $x = 5$; the first three terms are 5, 9.5, 14

21. 4, 11, 18, 25, ...

22. a) $(-1, 2)$ **b)** $(-1, 2)$

c) Answers may vary.

23. C

24. Answers may vary.

25. B **26.** C **27.** D

6.5 Geometric Sequences, pages 392–394

1. a) arithmetic; The first term is $a = 5$ and the common difference is $d = -2$.

b) geometric; The first term is $a = 5$ and the common ratio is $r = -2$.

c) geometric: The first term is $a = 4$ and the common ratio is $r = \dfrac{1}{10}$.

d) geometric: The first term is $a = \dfrac{1}{2}$ and the common ratio is $r = \dfrac{1}{3}$.

e) neither: The first term is $a = 1$, but there is no common difference or common ratio between the consecutive terms.

f) neither: The first term is $a = 1$, but there is no common difference or common ratio between the consecutive terms.

2. a) 2; 16, 32, 64

b) $-3; -243, 729, -2187$

c) $-1; \dfrac{2}{3}, -\dfrac{2}{3}, \dfrac{2}{3}$

d) $-0.5; 37.5, -18.75, 9.375$

e) $1; -15, -15, -15$

f) $10; 3000, 30\ 000, 300\ 000$

g) $0.5, 4.5, 2.25, 1.125$

h) $x^2; x^9, x^{11}, x^{13}$

3. a) $t_n = 54\left(\dfrac{1}{3}\right)^{n-1}; \dfrac{2}{243}$

b) $t_n = 4(5)^{n-1}; 1\ 562\ 500$

c) $t_n = \left(\dfrac{1}{6}\right)\left(\dfrac{6}{5}\right)^{n-1}; 0.716\ 636\ 16$

d) $t_n = 0.0025(10)^{n-1}; 250\ 000$

4. a) 5, 10, 20, 40

b) 500, -2500, 12 500, $-62\ 500$

c) 0.25, -0.75, 2.25, -6.75

d) $2, 2\sqrt{2}, 4, 4\sqrt{2}$

e) $-1, -0.2, -0.04, -0.008$

f) $-100, 20, -4, 0.8$

5. a) 7   **b)** 6   **c)** 12

     d) 21   **e)** 8   **f)** 7

6. a) arithmetic; $a = x, d = 2x$

     b) geometric $a = 1, r = \frac{x}{2}$

     c) neither

     d) geometric; $a = \frac{5x}{10}, r = \frac{1}{100}$

7. 10

8. 7

9. after 14 7-h periods, the bacteria count will be 1.64×10^6

10. a) $\frac{100}{9}$ Ci/km²

     b) $1 = \frac{100}{9}\left(\frac{1}{2}\right)^{\frac{t}{30}}$; 104.2 years

     c) Answers may vary.

11. 46 656

12. a) Answers may vary.

     b) $A = 1\left(\frac{8}{9}\right)^{n-1}$

     c) 0.106 684 square units

     d) Answers may vary.

13. a) Number of Voters, V: $V = (1\,000\,000)(1.026)^n$, where n is the number of 4-year periods since 1850

     b) Answers may vary. Sample answer: discrete; the elections are held once every 4 years

     c) 2 791 865

14. a) 25   **b)** 12, 36, and 108

16. $y = \frac{1}{5}, y = 6$

17. a) $x = 6, y = 24; x = -6, y = -24$

     b) $x = 16, y = -128$

18. $x^2 + x, x^3 + x^2, x^4 + x^3$

19. 22.47% per year

20. Case 1: $x = 2, y = 12$; Case 2: $x = 8, y = 24$

21. C   **22.** B   **23.** $50\sqrt[3]{2}$

6.6 Arithmetic Series, pages 400–401

1. a) 39   **b)** -12 **c)** -90

     d) 130   **e)** $-\frac{49}{6}$ **f)** $180x$

2. a) $a = 5, d = 4, S_{20} = 860$

     b) $a = 20, d = 5, S_{20} = 1350$

     c) $a = 45, d = -6, S_{20} = -240$

     d) $a = 2, d = 0.2, S_{20} = 78$

     e) $a = \frac{1}{2}, d = \frac{1}{4}, S_{20} = 57.5$

     f) $a = -5, d = -1, S_{20} = -290$

3. a) 18   **b)** 1020   **c)** 270   **d)** 1120

4. a) 375   **b)** 2170   **c)** -1480 **d)** 0

5. a) 4564   **b)** -3630 **c)** $-35\,409.3$ **d)** 87

6. $-27, -22, -17$

7. 3925

8. a) $1190\sqrt{7}$ **b)** $-550x$ **c)** $22b$ **d)** $\frac{90}{x}$

9. Answers may vary. Sample answers:

     a) not arithmetic; the first term is -2, the differences between the four terms in the series are not equal

     b) arithmetic; the first term is $2x^2$, the common differences between the three terms in the series is equal to x^2

     c) arithmetic; the first term is a, the common differences between the three terms in the series is equal to $2b$

     d) not arithmetic; the first term is $\frac{17}{20}$, the differences between the three terms in the series are not equal

10. 68 cans

11. 1860 cm

12. a) 15   **b)** Answers may vary.

13. $S_n = \frac{n}{2}(3n - 1)$

14. a) $x = 0, x = 4$

     b) if $x = 0$, sum $= 45$; if $x = 4$, sum $= 305$

16. $S_n = \frac{7}{2}n^2 - \frac{13}{2}n$

17. 124; 15

18. $2 + 6 + 10 + 14 + \dots$

19. A

20. C

21. 14 706

22. $x = 7$

23. Answers may vary.

24. $\frac{20}{21}$

6.7 Geometric Series, pages 408–409

1. a) geometric; The first term is $a = 4$ and the common ratio is $r = 5$.

     b) geometric; The first term is $a = -150$ and the common ratio is $r = -\frac{1}{10}$.

     c) not geometric: The first term is $a = 3$, but there is no common ratio between the consecutive terms.

     d) geometric: The first term is $a = 256$ and the common ratio is $r = -\frac{1}{4}$.

2. a) $a = 2, r = 3, S_8 = 6560$

     b) $a = 24, r = -\frac{1}{2}, S_{10} = \frac{1023}{64}$

     c) $a = 0.3, r = 0.01, S_{15} \doteq \frac{10}{33}$

     d) $a = 1, r = -\frac{1}{3}, S_{12} = \frac{132\,860}{177\,147}$

     e) $a = 2.1, r = -2, S_9 = 359.1$

     f) $a = 8, r = -1, S_{40} = 0$

3. a) 3066   **b)** -2730

c) 2 615 088 483   **d)** $2.999\ 999\ 97 \times 10^{10}$

e) 10 922.5   **f)** $\dfrac{29\ 524}{81}$

4. a) $\dfrac{9841}{243}$ **b)** $\dfrac{889}{64}$ **c)** ≈ 1333.3 **d)** $\dfrac{6305}{6561}$

5. a) 2735   **b)** -510 **c)** 64 125   **d)** $\dfrac{463}{729}$

6. a) $\dfrac{-242\sqrt{3}}{\sqrt{3}+1}$ **b)** $\dfrac{63\sqrt{2}x}{\sqrt{2}-1}$ **c)** $\dfrac{3(x^{15}-1)}{x-1}$

7. a) $\dfrac{1275}{64}$ **b)** $\dfrac{31\ 248\sqrt{5}}{\sqrt{5}-1}$ **c)** $\dfrac{1(x^{k}-1)}{x-1}$

8. 7 terms

9. $\dfrac{58\ 025}{48}$

10. $r = 2$; $S_k = 3(2^k - 1)$ or $r = -3$, $S_k = \dfrac{-3}{4}[(-3)^k - 1]$

11. a) $S = 25(2^x - 1)$, where S is the total amount of prize money and x is the total number of tickets drawn.

b)

16 prizes can be given out if the total amount of prize money is \$2 million

12. a) $\dfrac{1280}{729}$ m   **b)** approximately 98.6 m

13. a)

Stage	Line Segment Length	Total Length
1	1	1
2	$\dfrac{1}{3}$	3
3	$\dfrac{1}{9}$	9
4	$\dfrac{1}{27}$	27
5	$\dfrac{1}{81}$	81
6	$\dfrac{1}{243}$	243

b) $LSL = \left(\dfrac{1}{3}\right)^{n-1}$; $\dfrac{1}{243}$ units

c) $TL = (3)^{n-1}$; 243 units

d) Answers may vary.

15. $a = 5$, $b = 10$, $c = 20$ or $a = 20$, $b = 10$, $c = 5$

16. $3 + 6 + 12$ or $3 - 6 + 12$

17. $a = 6$, $r = 2$, $t_{10} = 3072$, $S_{10} = 6138$

18. $n = 8$

19. Sequence 1: $b = -\dfrac{1}{3}$, $S_5 = -\dfrac{11}{6}$;

Sequence 2: $b = 3$, $S_5 = 124$

Chapter 6 Review, pages 410–411

1. a) 6, 12, 22, 36   **b)** $1, \dfrac{3}{2}, \dfrac{5}{3}, \dfrac{7}{4}$

2. a)

Term Number, n	Term, t_n	First Differences
1	-8	
2	-11	-3
3	-14	-3
4	-17	-3

$f(n) = -3n - 5$;
domain $= \{n \in \mathbb{N}\}$

b)

Term Number, n	Term, t_n	First Differences	Second Differences
1	3		
2	2	-1	
3	-3	-5	-4
4	-12	-9	-4

$f(n) = -2n^2 + 5n$;
domain $= \{n \in \mathbb{N}\}$

3. a) 5, 1, -3, -7 **b)** 3, 4, 5, 6

4. a) $t_1 = -2$, $t_n = t_{n-1} + 9$

b) $t_1 = 1$, $t_n = -3t_{n-1}$

5. a) $x^5 + 20x^4 + 160x^3 + 640x^2 + 1280x + 1024$

b) $y^4 - 24y^3 + 216y^2 - 864y + 1296$

c) $m^4 + 8m^3n + 24m^2n^2 + 32mn^3 + 16n^4$

d) $729p^6 - 1458p^5q + 1215p^4q^2 - 540p^3q^3 + 135p^2q^4 - 18pq^5 + q^6$

6. a) 35, 56

b)

```
              1
            1   1
          1   2   1
        1   3   3   1
      1   4   6   4   1
    1   5  10  10   5   1
  1   6  15  20  15   6   1
1   7  21  35  35  21   7   1
1   8  28  56  70  56  28   8   1
```

The tetrahedral numbers are found in the fourth diagonals of Pascal's triangle starting with the 1's on the ends of row 3. The tetrahedral numbers are 1, 4, 10, 20, 35, 56, 84, ... The two diagonals have the value 20 in common.

7. a) $a = 3$, $d = -2$; $t_n = 5 - 2n$, -5, -7, -9, -11

b) $a = \dfrac{2}{3}$, $d = \dfrac{1}{4}$; $t_n = \dfrac{n}{4} + \dfrac{5}{12}$, $\dfrac{5}{3}$, $\dfrac{23}{12}$, $\dfrac{13}{6}$, $\dfrac{29}{12}$

8. a) 1, 5, 9   **b)** 1, −3, −7

9. a) 145 seats   **b)** 245 seats

10. a) arithmetic; The first term is $a = -1$ and the common difference is $d = 10$.

    b) neither: The first term is $a = 1$, but there is no common difference or common ratio between the consecutive terms.

    c) geometric; The first term is $a = -2$ and the common ratio is $r = -3$.

11. a) −2, 2, −2   **b)** −12, −24, −48

12. 1177.3 m

13. a) $a = 50, d = -5; 50$ **b)** $a = -27, d = 6; 600$

14. $48 985

15. a) −1450   **b)** 120

16. a) 94 158 416   **b)** −2728

17. a) 272.221 95   **b)** 9841.499 924

18. 1023 cm²

Chapter 6 Practice Test, pages 412–413

1. D   **2.** B   **3.** B   **4.** C   **5.** B

6. a) 4, −1, −6, −11, −16   **b)** 1, 10, 23, 40, 61

    c) $\dfrac{1}{8}, \dfrac{1}{2}, 2, 8, 32$ **d)** 1, 1.2, 1.4, 1.6, 1.8

    e) 2.5, 3, 3.5, 4, 4.5

    f) −6, −12, −24, −48, −96

7. a) $f(n) = 64\left(\dfrac{1}{2}\right)^{n-1}; t_1 = 64, t_n = t_{n-1} \times \dfrac{1}{2}$

    b) $f(n) = -23 + 3n; t_1 = -20, t_n = t_{n-1} + 3$

    c) $f(n) = 84 - 4n; t_1 = 80, t_n = t_{n-1} - 4$

    d) $f(n) = -4000\left(-\dfrac{1}{4}\right)^{n-1}; t_1 = -4000,$

    $t_n = t_{n-1} \times \left(-\dfrac{1}{4}\right)$

    e) $f(n) = -3(2)^{n-1}; t_1 = -3, t_n = t_{n-1} \times 2$

    f) $f(n) = -14\sqrt{2} + 2\sqrt{2}n; t_1 = -12\sqrt{2},$

    $t_n = t_{n-1} + 2\sqrt{2}$

8. a) 46   **b)** −3072   **c)** 5120   **d)** −55

9. a) 86 093 442   **b)** 425

    c) 1.0×10^{-29} **d)** −11.25

10. a) 20   **b)** 15

11. a) 1.6, 1.68, 1.764

    b) $t_1 = 1.6, t_n = 1.05t_{n-1}; 1.944\ 81$ t

12. a) $\dfrac{25\ 575}{64}$ **b)** −855

13. a) −2470   **b)** 2592

14. a) $\dfrac{671\ 846}{81}$ **b)** 5115

15. a) $b^5 - 15b^4 + 90b^3 - 270b^2 + 405b - 243$

    b) $64x^6 - 960x^5y + 6000x^4y^2 - 20\ 000x^3y^3$
    $+ 37\ 500x^2y^4 - 37\ 500xy^5 + 15\ 625y^6$

16. a) 8   **b)** −7

17. 1380

18. Answers may vary. Sample answer: A is equal to B. Each pair of numbers in A could be factored as a difference of squares as follows:

$A = (50 + 49)(50 - 49) + (48 + 47)(48 - 47) + \ldots$
   $+ (4 + 3)(4 - 3) + (2 + 1)(2 - 1)$
  $= (99)(1) + (95)(1) + \ldots + (7)(1) + (3)(1)$
  $= 99 + 95 + \ldots + 7 + 3$.

The sum of this series is 1275. The sum of series B is $50 + 49 + 48 + 47 + \ldots + 2 + 1$, or 1275.

19. 32 paths

20. 66.8%

21. 3930

22. $54 908.48

23. Answers may vary.

Chapter 7

Prerequisite Skills, pages 416–417

1. a) linear

b) $m = 40, b = 400$

c) and **d)**

x	$y = 40x + 400$	First Differences
0	400	
1	440	40
2	480	40
3	520	40
4	560	40

The first differences are constant.

2. a) exponential

b) (0, 100)

c) and **d)**

x	$y = 100(1.05)^x$	First Differences	Second Differences
0	100		
1	105	5.00	
2	110.25	5.25	0.25
3	115.76	5.51	0.26
4	121.55	5.79	0.28

Neither the first differences nor the second differences are constant.

e) $\dfrac{105}{100} = 1.05, \dfrac{110.25}{105} = 1.05, \dfrac{115.75}{110.25} = 1.05,$

$\dfrac{121.55}{115.76} = 1.05$. All common ratios are the same value, 1.05.

3. a) linear function; first differences are constant

b) exponential function; the ratio of successive y-values is the same, 0.9

4. a) direct   **b)** partial

    c) partial   **d)** direct

5. a) $C = d + 3$

    b) Fixed: $3, Variable: $1 per kilometre

    c)

    d) slope = 1, vertical intercept = 3

    e) Answers may vary. Sample answer: slope is the coefficient of the variable part and vertical intercept is the fixed part of the relation

6. a) All terms differ by a constant difference.

    b) $a = 7, d = 3$ **c)** $t_n = 3n + 4$

7. a) $-2, 3, 8, 13$ **b)** $a = -2, d = 5$

8. 25 050

9. a) It is geometric because consecutive terms have a common ratio.

    b) $a = 3, r = 2$ **c)** $t_n = 3(2)^{n-1}$

10. a) $-2, -6, -18, -54$ **b)** $a = -2, r = 3$

11. 21.578 563 59

12. $a = 2$

13. a) 80   **b)** 780   **c)** $\dfrac{250}{1.32}$ **d)** 0.065

14. a) 153.5791   **b)** -0.92

    c) 0.0328 or -2.0328 **d)** ± 1.0309

15. a) 36 months   **b)** $\dfrac{15}{52}$ years

    c) $\dfrac{26}{73}$ years   **d)** 39 weeks

    e) $\dfrac{240}{73}$ months   **f)** $\dfrac{75}{13}$ months

16. a) 104   **b)** 4   **c)** 42

    d) 12   **e)** 4   **f)** 7

7.1 Simple Interest, pages 424–425

1. a) $117   **b)** $21.88   **c)** $15.99   **d)** $14.10

2. a) $212, $224, $236, $248, $260

    b) $a = 212, d = 12$

    c) $t_n = 200 + 12n$; this is a linear model that represents the amount of the $200 investment at the end of the nth year.

3. a) All first differences are $39, representing the amount of simple interest earned each year.

    b) $650; $t = 0$ is the start of the investment

    c) 6%

4. a) $A = 650 + 39t$

    b) Answers may vary. Sample answer: This is a partial variation since the initial amount is not $0. The linear model contains a fixed part, and a 650, variable part $39t$.

    c) 16 years 8 months

5. a) $1500   **b)** 8%

    c) $A = 120t + 1500$ **d)** 12 years 6 months

6. a) $I = 120t$

b) 12 years 6 months; the same as 5d)

7. a) $A = 11.25t + 250$

    b)

    c) approximately 4 years 5 months

    d) approximately 8.2%

8. a) $561.88   **b)** $61.88

    c) repay in approximately 14 months

9. approximately 10.7%

10. a) $280   **b)** $2280

11. 17.8 months

12. a) Bank: $A = 5500 + 682t$, Dealership: $A = 5700 + 605t$

    b)

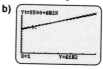

    c) Answers may vary. Sample answer: The bank loan is a better deal if the loan is repaid in less than 2.6 years. The dealership loan is a better deal if the loan is repaid in more than 2.6 years.

13. a) $r = \dfrac{A - P}{Pt}$ **b)** approximately 5.4%

    c) Answers may vary.

14. a) $t = \dfrac{A - P}{Pr}$ **b)** Answer may vary.

7.2 Compound Interest, pages 433–435

1. a) $632.66   **b)** $132.66

2. a) $1222.01   **b)** $372.01

3. a) 0.0075   **b)** 0.02   **c)** 0.03   **d)** 0.005

4. a) 12   **b)** 8   **c)** 9

    d) 14   **e)** 6

5. a) $n = 6, i = 0.0875$ **b)** $n = 12. i = 0.015$

    c) $n = 24, i = 0.002$ **d)** $n = 15, i = 0.0225$

6. a) $1661.54   **b)** $261.54   **c)** $241.50

7. $2.06

8. a) **i)** $360   **ii)** $457.41

    iii) $483.67   **iv)** $490.02

    The order from best to worst for Karin is the order given in the problem i) , ii) , iii), iv).

    b) Answers may vary. Sample answer: The greater the number of times interest is paid, the more interest accumulates.

9. approximately 11%

10. approximately 8%

11. Answers may vary. Sample answer: First Provincial Bank; it pays more interest.

12. a) $2149.19   **b)** $149.19

    c) Answers may vary. Sample answer: She earns $130.81 less, but Chloe can access the money in the chequing account with no penalty.

13. a) i) 9 years   **ii)** 8 years   **iii)** 6 years

   b) Answers may vary. Sample answer: The Rule of 72 is close but not exact. The results using the compound interest formula are: **i)** 9 years, **ii)** 8.04 years, and **iii)** 6.12 years.

14. approximately 4.36 years

16.–17. Answers may vary.

18. A   **19.** C

20. a) $1610.51   **b)** $1645.31
   c) $1648.61   **d)** $1648.72

7.3 Present Value, pages 441–443

1. a) $548.47   **b)** $885.57

2. $400.00

3. a) $516.85   **b)** $290.36

4. a) $2499.98   **b)** $921.42

5. annually

6. approximately 5 years 4 months

7. a) Investment A: $7712.54, Investment B: $7808.59

   b) Answers may vary. Sample answer: Investment A; more interest is earned.

8. Bank A is better; he will pay slightly less in interest charges. Bank A will lend him $1533.65, bank B will lend $1531.10.

9. a) $314.63   **b)** $126.65

10. $712.02

11. approximately 13.3%

12. a) Answers may vary. Sample answer: As the number of compounding periods increases, the present value decreases.

   b) Answers may vary. Sample answer: The more frequent the interest payments, the smaller the amount you need to deposit to have a fixed amount in 5 years.

13. a) $2.00   **b)** $0.14

14. $27 683.79

15. a) $4429.19

   b) $7570.81; represents the future value of the last investment in her portfolio

   c) 6%

16. a) $PV = \dfrac{800}{(1.06)^t}$

   b)

   The graph is exponentially decaying.

   c) Answers may vary. Sample answer: The horizontal scale of the graph is time in years.

   d) Answers may vary. Sample answer: The graph provides information on the present value of the investment.

   e) Answers may vary. Sample answer: No, in the context any negative value of t corresponds to a date after the time that the account's future value is $800.

18. Answers may vary. Sample answer: The new graph is a mirror image of the original. It is exponentially growing and represents the future value of an $800 investment as a function of time. The interest is 6% per year, compounded annually.

19. $PV = \dfrac{FV}{1 + rt}$

20. $3402.67

21. D

7.4 Annuities, pages 453–455

1. $2653.19

2. a) A time line for the future value of an annuity with $R = 250$, $n = 6$, and $i = 0.045$.

   b) $1679.22   **c)** $179.22

3. a) A time line for the future value of an annuity with $R = 35$, $n = 104$, and $i = 0.001$.

   b) $3834.00   **c)** $194.00

4. $2277.45

5. $449.44

6. a) $3289.83   **b)** 6%

7. 1.6 percentage points

8. a) $42 059.39   **b)** $13 259.39

9. Answers may vary. Sample answer: I agree with his advisor that increasing the frequency of the deposit and the frequency of the compounding period will increase the amount of the annuity. He also invests more per year by depositing $40 per week as
$40 × 52 = $2080 and $160 × 12 = $1920.

10. Answers may vary. Sample answer: He should switch to the weekly deposits since it is worth more than the other two possibilities at the end of the 7 years.

11. Option A pays $533 704.47 more.

12. a) $87.33   **b)** Answers may vary.

13. a)

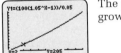

   The graph shows exponential growth.

   b) Answers may vary.

   c) regular payment = $100 and interest rate = 5% per year

   d) Answers may vary.

14. a) $P = 100n$ **b)**

   c) Answers will vary. Sample answer: The interest earned will be the difference between the two functions. $I(n) = \dfrac{100(1.05^n - 1)}{0.05} - 100n$

15. B

16. A

17. (0, 10), (6, 2), (10, 0)

18. B

7.5 Present Value of an Annuity, pages 461–463

1. $106 593.02

2. a) A time line for the present value of an annuity with $R = 1000$, $n = 4$, and $i = 0.08$.
b) $3312.13

3. a) A time line for present value of an annuity with $R = 650$, $n = 20$, and $i = 0.016$.
b) $11 050.38   **c)** $1949.62

4. $1614.14

5. $2830.60

6. $152 917.37

7. a) Answers may vary. Sample answer: No, she will not have enough to retire and live off her lottery winnings.
b) $1 242 519.27

8. approximately 8%

9. approximately 20.1%

10. a) Option A: $567.36   Option B: $187.33
b) Option A: $808.32   Option B: $743.88
c) Answers may vary. Sample answer: Option A earns more interest, but option B allows Jordan to withdraw more.

11. $8217.75

12. $1585.60

13. a) Answers may vary.   **b)** Answers may vary.
c) $632 490.38   **d)** $54 274.33
e) Answers may vary.

15. Answers may vary.

16. a) 0.412 392% per month
b) $1163.21

17. a) $1022.99   **b)** $235.58
c) $156 254

Chapter 7 Review, pages 464–465

1. a) $102.60   **b)** $822.60

2. approximately 2 years 10 months

3. a)

b) Answers may vary. Sample answer: The relation is linear, as the graph is a straight sloping line.
c) The vertical intercept of $750 represents the amount borrowed.
d) The slope of $48.75 represents the interest per year.

4. a) $1241.15   **b)** $406.15

5. a) The graph grows exponentially over time.

b) The vertical intercept of $1000 represents the initial amount in the account.
c) The slope will be increasing for increasing values of time.

6. a) 10 years 9 months
b) Answers may vary. Sample answer: No. The interest rate and period is not changing and the ratio of the amount to the principal is still 2:1.

7. $816.30

8. a) $33 758.66   **b)** $11 241.34

9. approximately 6.15%

10. quarterly

11. a) A time line for the future value of an annuity with $R = 2400$, $n = 4$, and $i = 0.043$.
b) Answers may vary. Sample answer: The series is geometric as consecutive terms have a common ratio.
c) $10 237.14   **d)** $637.14

12. a) $48 100.11   **b)** $9 700.11

13. $341.94

14. a) 6 years
b) 6%; 4 compounding periods per year
c) $5007.60   **d)** $992.40

15. $109 449.87

16. $1798.97

Chapter 7 Practice Test, pages 466–467

1. D   **2.** B   **3.** B   **4.** C   **5.** A

6. a) $33.60   **b)** $223.20
c) 15.05%

7. $516.61

8. a) 3 years, as the annuity lasts for 36 months
b) 6%, with 12 payments per year
c) $15 734.44   **d)** $1 334.44

9. Answers will vary. Sample answer: Option A is better because it pays more in interest.

10. approximately 6.9%

11. approximately 5.97%

12. a) $808.35   **b)** $151.81

13. $3115.83

14. 817 days

15. a) A time line for the future value of an annuity with $R = 200$, $n = 1040$, and $i = 0.0005$.
b) $272 723.63   **c)** $64 723.63

16. a) A time line for the present value of an annuity with $R = 336$, $n = 1040$, and $i = 0.0005$.
b) $336.36
c) $141 814.40

17. a) A time line for the future value of an annuity with R, $n = 52$, and $i = 0.0025$.
b) $93.77

18. 33.6%

19. $52.04

Chapters 6 and 7 Review, pages 468–469

1. a) 1, 4, 7; Answers may vary.
 b) 5, 17, 65; Answers may vary.
 c) −11, 4, 29; Answers may vary.
 d) $\frac{5}{2}$, 6, $\frac{31}{2}$; Answers may vary.
 e) 1, 7, 19; Answers may vary.
 f) −2, −4, 8; Answers may vary.

2. a) 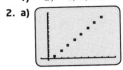 **b)**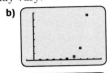

 c) 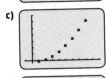 **d)**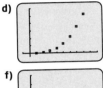

 e)  **f)**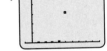

3. a) $38\ 250$, $\$36\ 377.50$, $\$34\ 520.63$
 b) $V(n) = 38\ 250(0.95)^{n-1}$
 c) $\$14\ 433.78$. Answers may vary.

4. 1, −1, 3, −5; $f(1) = 1$, $f(n) = f(n-1) + (-2)^{n-1}$

5. a) $t_n = 2n + 3$; $t_1 = 5$, $t_n = t_{n-1} + 2$
 b) $t_n = 2^{2^{n-1}}$; $t_1 = 2$, $t_n = (t_{n-1})^2$

6. Answers may vary.

7. a) $128x^7 + 2240x^6 + 16\ 800x^5 + 70\ 000x^4$
 $+ 175\ 000x^3 + 262\ 500x^2 + 218\ 750x + 78\ 125$
 b) $a^{10} - 15a^8b + 90a^6b^2 - 270a^4b^3 + 405a^2b^4$
 $- 243b^5$
 c) $\frac{64}{x^6} + \frac{192}{x^3} + 240 + 160x^3 + 60x^6 + 12x^9 + x^{12}$
 d) $625 - \frac{1500}{\sqrt{n}} + \frac{1350}{n} - \frac{540}{n\sqrt{n}} + \frac{81}{n^2}$

8. a) neither
 b) arithmetic, $t_n = 4n - 7$, $t_{12} = 41$
 c) geometric, $t_n = 3(4)^{n-1}$, $t_{12} = 12\ 582\ 912$
 d) geometric, $t_n = 2\ 657\ 205\left(-\frac{1}{3}\right)^{n-1}$, $t_{12} = -15$

9. $t_1 = -15$, $t_2 = -8$

10. 13 terms

11. a) $t_n = 175n - 45$ **b)** 830 members
 c) after 12 weeks

12. a) 335 **b)** −8 138 020
 c) 511.5 **d)** $-\frac{155}{6}$

13. a) 26.84 cm **b)** 1383.71 cm

14. a) The principal is the amount of money initially invested or borrowed.
 b) The amount is the value of an investment or loan at the end of a time period.

c) Simple interest is the interest calculated only on the original principal using the formula $I = Prt$, where I is the interest, in dollars; P is the principal, in dollars; r is the annual rate of interest, as a decimal; and t is the time, in years.

d) Compound interest is the interest that is calculated at regular compounding periods.

e) An annuity is a sum of money paid as a series of regular payments.

f) The present value is the principal invested or borrowed today to result in a given future amount, given specified interest and time conditions.

g) The compounding period is the time interval after which compound interest is calculated.

15. a) $\$33.33$ **b)** $\$15.38$ **c)** $\$118.36$

16. a) $A = 500 + 15t$
 b)  **c)** 8 months

17. $\$186.90$

18. a) Account A: $\$8407.29$ Account B: $\$8523.25$
 b) Answers may vary. Sample answer: Account A is the better choice because it requires a smaller initial amount.

19. $\$1839.94$

20. $\$7031.73$

21. 4.2%

22. $\$17\ 808.46$

23. $\$2378.99$

Course Review, pages 471–477

1. a) domain $\{x \in \mathbb{R}, x \neq 9\}$,
 range $\{y \in \mathbb{R}, y \neq 0\}$

 b) domain $\{x \in \mathbb{R}, x \leq 2\}$,
 range $\{y \in \mathbb{R}, y \geq -4\}$

2. C

3. a) i) 24 years **ii)** 12 years **iii)** 8 years
 b)

 c) domain $\{r \in \mathbb{R}, r > 0\}$, range $\{n \in \mathbb{R}, n > 0\}$

4. a) minimum $\left(-\frac{3}{2}, -\frac{23}{4}\right)$ **b)** maximum $(3, 2)$

5. 150 items

6. a) $-4\sqrt{3}$ **b)** $7\sqrt{3} - \frac{26}{3}\sqrt{5}$

7. a) $39 + 10\sqrt{15}$ **b)** $3\sqrt{6} - 2$

8. 6π

9. a)–d) all solutions are $x = 2$, $x = 25$

10. 2.1 m by 7.1 m

11. a) $y = -6x^2 + 24x - 6$ **b)** $y = \frac{2}{3}x^2 - 2x - \frac{8}{3}$

12. a)

   b) $y = -\frac{2}{5}(x - 8)(x + 8)$

   c) 25.6 m

13. Answers may vary. Sample answer: Yes, they intersect at a horizontal distance of approximately 142 m.

14. a)   **i)** The functions appear to be equivalent.

    ii) Algebraically the functions are equivalent.

    iii) The functions seem to yield the same graph.

   b)   **i)** The functions appear to be equivalent.

    ii) Algebraically the functions are not equivalent.

    iii) The functions yield the same graph except at $x = 5$.

15. a) $-\dfrac{7x}{8}$, $x \neq 0$, $x \neq 1$

   b) $\dfrac{-4x(x - 4)}{x + 2}$, $x \neq -9$, $x \neq -2$, $x \neq 0$, $x \neq 2$

   c) $\dfrac{(x - 5)(x - 2)}{3}$, $x \neq -5$, $x \neq 4$

16. a) $f(x) = \frac{1}{x}$; $y = f(x + 5) - 1$; translate left 5 units and down 1 unit;

domain $\{x \in \mathbb{R}, x \neq -5\}$,
range $\{y \in \mathbb{R}, y \neq -1\}$

   b) $f(x) = \sqrt{x}$, $y = f(x + 7) - 9$; translate left 7 units and down 9 units;

domain $\{x \in \mathbb{R}, x \geq -7\}$,
range $\{y \in \mathbb{R}, y \geq -9\}$

17. a) reflection in the x-axis and then the y-axis

   b) reflection in the y-axis

18. a)   **i)** $g(x) = 4x^2$; reflection in the y-axis and a vertical stretch by a factor of 4;

domain $\{x \in \mathbb{R}\}$,
range $\{y \in \mathbb{R}, y \geq 0\}$

    ii) $h(x) = \frac{1}{4}x^2$; vertical compression by a factor of $\frac{1}{4}$; domain $\{x \in \mathbb{R}\}$,

range $\{y \in \mathbb{R}, y \geq 0\}$

    iii) $g(x) = 4\sqrt{-x}$; reflection in the y-axis and a vertical stretch by a factor of 4; domain $\{x \in \mathbb{R}, x \leq 0\}$, range $\{y \in \mathbb{R}, y \geq 0\}$

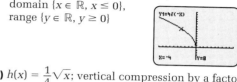

    iv) $h(x) = \frac{1}{4}\sqrt{x}$; vertical compression by a factor of $\frac{1}{4}$;

domain $\{x \in \mathbb{R}, x \geq 0\}$,
range $\{y \in \mathbb{R}, y \geq 0\}$

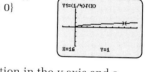

    v) $g(x) = -\frac{4}{x}$; reflection in the y-axis and a vertical stretch by a factor of 4; domain $\{x \in \mathbb{R}, x \neq 0\}$, range $\{y \in \mathbb{R}, y \neq 0\}$

    vi) $h(x) = \frac{1}{4x}$; vertical compression by a factor of $\frac{1}{4}$; domain $\{x \in \mathbb{R}, x \neq 0\}$, range $\{y \in \mathbb{R}, y \neq 0\}$

   b)   **i)** $g(x) = 16x^2$; horizontal compression by a factor of $\frac{1}{4}$; domain $\{x \in \mathbb{R}\}$, range $\{y \in \mathbb{R}, y \geq 0\}$

    ii) $h(x) = -\frac{1}{16}x^2$; reflection in the x-axis and a horizontal stretch by a factor of 4; domain $\{x \in \mathbb{R}\}$, range $\{y \in \mathbb{R}, y \leq 0\}$

iii) $g(x) = \sqrt{4x}$; horizontal compression by a
factor of $\frac{1}{4}$;

domain $\{x \in \mathbb{R}, x \geq 0\}$,
range $\{y \in \mathbb{R}, y \geq 0\}$

iv) $h(x) = -\sqrt{\frac{1}{4}x}$; reflection in the x-axis and a

horizontal stretch by a factor of 4;
domain $\{x \in \mathbb{R}, x \geq 0\}$,
range $\{y \in \mathbb{R}, y \leq 0\}$

v) $g(x) = \frac{1}{4x}$; horizontal compression by a factor

of $\frac{1}{4}$;

domain $\{x \in \mathbb{R}, x \neq 0\}$,
range $\{y \in \mathbb{R}, y \neq 0\}$

vi) $h(x) = -\frac{4}{x}$; reflection in the x-axis and a
horizontal stretch by a factor of 4;
domain $\{x \in \mathbb{R}, x \neq 0\}$,
range $\{y \in \mathbb{R}, y \neq 0\}$

19. a) domain $\{t \in \mathbb{R}, 0 \leq t \leq 2.56\}$,
range $\{h \in \mathbb{R}, 0 \leq h \leq 32\}$
b) $h(t) = -5.6t^2 + 32$
c) Answers may vary. Sample answer: only the
domain changes, domain $\{t \in \mathbb{R}, 0 \leq t \leq 2.39\}$

20. a) reflection in the x-axis, vertical stretch by a
factor of 2, horizontal compression by a factor
of $\frac{1}{3}$, and then translation
of 4 units right and

1 unit down;
$g(x) = -6x + 23$

b) vertical compression by a factor of $\frac{1}{3}$, horizontal
stretch by a factor of 4, and then translation of
2 units right and 3 units up; $g(x) = \frac{4}{3(x-2)} + 3$

21. a) i) $f^{-1}(x) = \frac{x + 5}{4}$ **ii)**

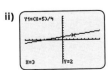

iii) The inverse is a function.

b) i) $f^{-1}(x) = \pm\sqrt{\frac{x + 9}{3}} + 2$

ii)

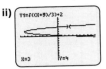

iii) The inverse is not a function.

22. a) domain $\{r \in \mathbb{R}, r \geq 0\}$, range $\{A \in \mathbb{R}, A \geq 0\}$

b) $r = \sqrt{\frac{A}{\pi}}$; domain $\{A \in \mathbb{R}, A \geq 0\}$,

range $\{r \in \mathbb{R}, r \geq 0\}$

23. a)

Day	Number of Bacteria
0	20
1	60
2	180
3	540
4	1 620
5	4 860
6	14 580
7	43 740

b) $y = 20(3)^t$

c)

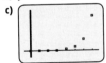

This is a function because each element in the
domain corresponds to exactly one element in
the range.

d) i) 95 659 380 **ii)** 209 207 064 100

e) Answers may vary. Sample answer: The
consecutive values in each difference column
increases by a factor of 3.

24. approx 40 years

25. a) $\frac{1}{2^5} = \frac{1}{32}$ **b)** $3^{11} = 177\ 147$

c) $\frac{3^4}{2^6} = \frac{81}{64}$ **d)** 6

26. a) $-12n^3$ **b)** $\frac{4c^2}{5}$ **c)** $\frac{b^6}{27a^6}$ **d)** $-\frac{243q^{20}}{32p^{15}}$

27. a) $\frac{1}{8}$ **b)** $\frac{3}{2}$ **c)** $\frac{25}{4}$

28. a) $\frac{b^{\frac{7}{3}}}{a^{\frac{9}{4}}}$ **b)** $\frac{\sqrt[20]{v^3}}{u^{\frac{2}{5}}}$ **c)** $w^{\frac{13}{8}}$

29. a)

domain $\{x \in \mathbb{R}\}$,
range $\{y \in \mathbb{R}, y > 0\}$, no
x-intercept, y-intercept is 5,
always decreasing, and
asymptote $y = 0$

b)

domain $\{x \in \mathbb{R}\}$,
range $\{y \in \mathbb{R}, y < 0\}$, no
x-intercept, y-intercept is -1,
always increasing, and
asymptote $y = 0$

30. a) $A = 300\left(\dfrac{1}{2}\right)^t$ **b)** domain $\{t \in \mathbb{R}, t \geq 0\}$

31. a)

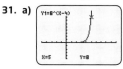

No effect on domain, range, or asymptote.

b)

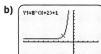

No effect on the domain, but the asymptote changes to $y = 1$ and the range changes to $\{y \in \mathbb{R}, y > 1\}$.

32. a) $y = -4(11)^x$ **b)** $y = 11^{-\frac{3}{4}x}$

33. a)

Time (1-h intervals)	Number of New Patients Diagnosed
0	1
1	3
2	9
3	27
4	81
5	243
6	729
7	2187

b)

c) exponential

d) $y = 3^t$

34. a) $30°$

b) $\sin 240° = -\dfrac{\sqrt{3}}{2}$, $\cos 240° = -\dfrac{1}{2}$,

$\tan 240° = \sqrt{3}$; $\sin 210° = -\dfrac{1}{2}$,

$\cos 210° = -\dfrac{\sqrt{3}}{2}$, $\tan 210° = \dfrac{1}{\sqrt{3}}$

35. a) $15\sqrt{2}$ km   **b)** Answers may vary.

36. $60°$, $120°$

37. a) $\sin A = \dfrac{7}{\sqrt{53}}$, $\cos A = -\dfrac{2}{\sqrt{53}}$, $\tan A = -\dfrac{7}{2}$

$\sin B = \dfrac{7}{\sqrt{53}}$, $\cos B = \dfrac{2}{\sqrt{53}}$, $\tan B = \dfrac{7}{2}$

b) $\angle A = 106°$, $\angle B = 74°$

38. a) 13 cm

b) $\sin P = \dfrac{12}{13}$, $\cos P = \dfrac{5}{13}$, $\tan P = \dfrac{12}{5}$

$\csc P = \dfrac{13}{12}$, $\sec P = \dfrac{13}{5}$, $\cot P = \dfrac{5}{12}$

c) $\sin R = \dfrac{5}{13}$, $\cos R = \dfrac{12}{13}$, $\tan R = \dfrac{5}{12}$

$\csc R = \dfrac{13}{5}$, $\sec R = \dfrac{13}{12}$, $\cot R = \dfrac{12}{5}$

39. a) $25°$, $155°$ **b)** $100°$, $260°$ **c)** $156°$, $336°$

40. a)

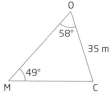

Since the triangle has no right angle, it is an oblique triangle.

b) It is not necessary to consider the ambiguous case because two angles and a side are given.

c) 39.3 m, 44.3 m

41. 38.7 km

42. a)

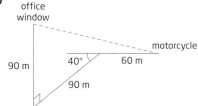

b) 167.6 m

43.–44. Answers may vary.

45. a) 12 h and 20 min

b) 1.95 m   **c)** 1:00 a.m.

46. a) i) amplitude 4   **ii)** amplitude $\dfrac{1}{2}$

b) i) $1080°$ **ii)** $90°$

c) i) $30°$ to the left   **ii)** $135°$ to the left

d) i) 1 unit down   **ii)** 2 units up

e)

47. a) $y = 6 \sin\left[\dfrac{12}{5}(x + 37.5°)\right] - 2$

b) $y = 6 \cos\left(\dfrac{12}{5}x\right) - 2$

48. a)

b) i) maximum 19 m, minimum 1 m

ii) 10 m   **iii)** 3 min

49. a) 0.25 s   **b)** 1440

c) 6 V   **d)** $V = 6 \sin 1440t$

e)

Each tick mark on the x-axis represents 0.125 s. Each tick mark on the y-axis represents 1V.

50. a) $\dfrac{40}{9}$ **b)** -2187

51. a) 3, 15, 75, 375, 1875

b) $\frac{2}{5}, -\frac{3}{5}, -\frac{8}{5}, -\frac{13}{5}, -\frac{18}{5}$

52. a)

5-h Interval	Amount of Medication (mg)
0	400
1	600
2	700
3	750
4	775
5	787.5
6	793.75
7	796.875
8	798.437 5
9	799.218 75
10	799.609 375
11	799.804 687 5
12	799.902 343 8
13	799.951 171 9
14	799.975 585 9

b) 400, 600, 700, 750, 775, ..., 799.975 585 9;
$t_n = 400 + 0.5t_{n-1}$

c)

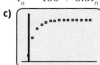

d) Answers may vary. Sample answer: Over time the amount of drug remaining in the body will vary between 800 mg right after a dose and 400 mg just before the next dose is taken.

53. a) $x^6 - 6x^5y + 15x^4y^2 - 20x^3y^3 + 15x^2y^4 - 6xy^5 + y^6$

b) $\frac{x^4}{81} - \frac{8x^4}{27} + \frac{24x^4}{9} - \frac{32x^4}{3} + 16x^4 = \frac{625}{81}x^4$

54. a) $t_{4,1} + t_{4,2}$ **b)** $t_{9,6} + t_{9,7}$

55. a) i) arithmetic; the first term is 9 and the common difference between the consecutive terms is −4

ii) arithmetic; the first term is $\frac{1}{5}$ and the common difference between the consecutive terms is $\frac{2}{5}$

iii) not arithmetic; the first term is −4.2 and the difference between consecutive terms is not equal

b) i) $t_n = -4n + 13$ **ii)** $t_n = \frac{2}{5}n - \frac{1}{5}$

56. a) $t_n = 90\left(\frac{1}{3}\right)^{n-1}, t_{10} = \frac{10}{2187}$

b) $t_n = \frac{1}{4}\left(\frac{2}{3}\right)^{n-1}, t_{10} = \frac{128}{19\,683}$

c) $t_n = -0.0035(-10)^{n-1}, t_{10} = 3\,500\,000$

57. a) −115   **b)** 17.5

58. a) $67\frac{362}{729}$ **b)** $\frac{x^{16} - 1}{-(x + 1)}$

59. a) approximately 1.26 m

b) approximately 179.7 m

60. a) $A = 1000 + 45t$, with 1000 representing the fixed part and $45t$ representing the variable part

b) 22 years 3 months   **c)** 16.7%

61. Answers will vary. Sample answer: Top Bank; it pays more in interest.

62. a) $667.27   **b)** $257.73

63. a) A time line for the future value of an annuity with $R = 120$, $n = 60$, and $i = 0.004\,375$.

b) $8213.00   **c)** $1013.00

64. a) A time line for the present value of an annuity with $R = 700$, $n = 20$, and $i = 0.0175$.

b) $11 727.02   **c)** $2272.98

Prerequisite Skills Appendix, pages 478–495

Angle Sum of a Triangle, page 478

1. a) $x = 76°$ **b)** $x = 76°$ **c)** $x = 36°$

Apply the Sine Law and the Cosine Law, page 478

1. a) 9.6 cm   **b)** 53.5°   **c)** 69.3°

Apply Trigonometric Ratios to Problems, page 479

1. 6.0 m   **2.** 8.6°

Classify Triangles, page 480

1. a) isosceles acute triangle

b) scalene obtuse triangle

c) equilateral triangle

Common Factors, page 480

1. a) 4   **b)** 3a   **c)** $5xy^2$

d) $24m^2n^2$ **e)** $a^2 + 3$ **f)** $3xy$

2. a) $4x(4x + 5)$ **b)** $5xy^2(x + 2y)$

c) $3a^2(a - 3)$ **d)** $4r^2s(r^3s + 4)$

e) $2ab(4a^2 - 5 + 2ab)$ **f)** $-6x^2y(x + 3x^2y^2 + 6y^3)$

g) $(p + 3q)(12p - q)$ **h)** $4x(2 + 5y)(y - 2x^2)$

Determine an Angle Given a Trigonometric Ratio, page 481

1. a) 75°   **b)** 57°   **c)** 70°

d) 40°   **e)** 20°   **f)** 32°

Direct Variation and Partial Variation, page 481

1. a) $C(d) = 25 + 12d$

b) fixed part = 25 ($25); variable part = 12 ($12 per day)

c)

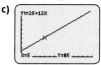

d) slope = 12, vertical intercept 25

e) Answers may vary. Sample Answer: The slope of the graph is equal to the variable part of the equation. The vertical intercept of the graph is equal to the fixed part of the equation.

2. a) $E = 200 + 0.05s$, where E represents Irene's total earnings and s represents her total sales.

b) fixed part = 200 ($200); variable part = 0.05 (5% commission of her sales)

c)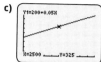

d) slope = 0.05, vertical intercept 200

e) Answers may vary. Sample Answer: The slope of the graph is equal to the variable part of the equation. The vertical intercept of the graph is equal to the fixed part of the equation.

Distributive Property, page 482

1. a) $2a + 2b$ **b)** $6x - 24$ **c)** $4k^2 + 20$
d) $-3x + 6$ **e)** $5x^2 - 10x + 5$ **f)** $6x^2 - 8x$
g) $24a + 8a^2$ **h)** $-2x^2 - 2xy + 6x$

Evaluate Expressions, page 482

1. a) 54   **b)** 1.92   **c)** 19
d) 111.98   **e)** 25.5   **f)** 322
2. a) $\dfrac{1}{4}$ **b)** $\dfrac{5}{4}$ **c)** $-\dfrac{43}{24}$
d) $-\dfrac{7}{12}$ **e)** $-\dfrac{5}{2}$ **f)** $-\dfrac{1}{5}$

Exponent Rules, page 483

1. a) 2^7 **b)** 5^6 **c)** 3^3
d) 4^5 **e)** 6^8 **f)** 9^{21}
g) a^{10} **h)** z^8 **i)** $6x^5$
j) y^3 **k)** p^{18} **l)** n^5
m) $-4x^3$ **n)** $8t^{12}$ **o)** $256x^8$
2. a) 64   **b)** 2   **c)** 729
d) 256   **e)** 4096   **f)** $\dfrac{1}{64}$

Factor Quadratic Expressions, page 484

1. a) $(x + 4)(x + 2)$ **b)** $(x - 3)(x - 4)$
c) $2(x + 6)(x - 3)$ **d)** $3(x + 4)(x - 4)$
e) $(3x - 5)(x - 2)$ **f)** $(x - 3)(x - 3)$
g) $4(x + 5)(x - 5)$ **h)** $92x - 5)(x + 4)$
i) $(x - 2)(4x - 7)$

Find Primary Trigonometric Ratios, page 484

1. a) $\sin P = \dfrac{24}{25}$; $\cos P = \dfrac{7}{25}$; $\tan P = \dfrac{24}{7}$
b) $\sin P = \dfrac{12}{13}$; $\cos P = \dfrac{5}{13}$; $\tan P = \dfrac{12}{5}$
2. a) $\sin 58° = 0.8480$; $\cos 58° = 0.5299$; $\tan 58° = 1.6003$
b) $\sin 79° = 0.9816$; $\cos 79° = 0.1908$; $\tan 79° = 5.1446$

c) $\sin 15° = 0.2588$; $\cos 15° = 0.9659$; $\tan 15° = 0.2679$

Finite Differences, page 485

1. a) The first differences are constant, 4. So, the relationship is linear.

b) The first differences are not constant. So, the relationship is not linear. The second differences are not constant. So, the relationship is not quadratic.

c) The first differences are not constant. So, the relationship is not linear. The second differences are constant, -2. So, the relationship is quadratic.

Graphs and Lines, page 486

1. a) 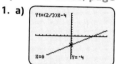   **b)**

c) 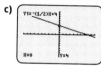   **d)**

e) 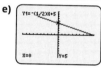   **f)**

2. a) $y = 3x - 2$ **b)** $y = -\dfrac{5}{3}x + 4$

3. a) $y = 2x + 7$ **b)** $y = -\dfrac{7}{15}x + \dfrac{12}{5}$
c) $y = \dfrac{3}{5}x - 11$

Identify Patterns, page 487

1. a) ZYXW, ZYXWV, ZYXWVU
b) 17, 22, 27   **c)** 81, 243, 729
d) $-13, -21, -29$ **e)** $\dfrac{5}{6}, -\dfrac{6}{7}, \dfrac{7}{8}$
f) $2x^4, \dfrac{2}{3}x^5, \dfrac{2}{9}x^6$

Linear and Exponential Growth, page 488

1.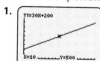
a) linear
b) slope = 30; y-intercept 200

c)

x	y	First Differences
0	200	
1	230	30
2	260	30
3	290	30

d) The first differences are all 30.

2.

a) exponential

b) y-intercept 25

c)

x	y	First Differences	Second Differences	Common Ratios
0	25			
1	27.5	2.5		1.1
2	30.25	2.75	0.25	1.1
3	33.275	3.025	0.275	1.1

d) The common ratios are all 1.1.

Quadratic Relations, page 489

1. a) **i)** $(3, -8)$ **ii)** $x = 3$
iii) upward **iv)** 10

b) **i)** $(-1, 3)$ **ii)** $x = -1$
iii) downward **iv)** -1

c) **i)** $(5, 1)$ **ii)** $x = 5$
iii) upward **iv)** 76

2. a) upward, stretched vertically by a factor of 5; Since $a > 0$ $(a = 5)$, the parabola opens upward. Since $a > 1$, the parabola is stretched vertically by a factor of 5.

b) downward, compressed vertically by a factor of $\frac{1}{4}$; Since $a < 0$ $\left(a = -\frac{1}{4}\right)$ the parabola opens downward. Since $0 < a < 1$, the parabola is compressed vertically by a factor of $\frac{1}{4}$.

c) downward, stretched vertically by a factor of 3; Since $a < 0$ $(a = -3)$ the parabola opens downward. Since $a < -1$, the parabola is stretched vertically by a factor of 3.

3. a) $y = (x + 2)^2 + 3; (-2, 3)$
b) $y = (x - 6)^2 - 33; (6, -33)$
c) $y = 3(x + 3)^2 - 29; (-3, -29)$
d) $y = -2(x - 4)^2 + 41; (4, 41)$

Rearrange Formulas, page 490

1. a) $x = \dfrac{-y + 5}{4}$
b) $w = \dfrac{P - 2\ell}{2}$
c) $y = \pm\sqrt{r^2 - x^2}$
d) $h = \dfrac{3v}{\pi r^2}$
e) $e = \dfrac{2 - st}{10}$
f) $r = \dfrac{A - P}{Pt}$

Solve Equations, page 490

1. a) $x = -3$ **b)** $x = 4$ **c)** $x = 5$ **d)** $x = 4$
2. a) $w = 9.25$ **b)** $p = 0.7$ or $p = 5.3$
  c) $i = -2.0325$ or $i = 0.0325$ **d)** $k = 3.4$

Solve Equations Involving Rational Expressions, page 491

1. a) $x = 2$ **b)** $a = 35$ **c)** $c = 3$
d) $r = 27$ **e)** $k = \dfrac{15}{2}$ **f)** $t = 270$

Solve Linear Systems Equations, page 492

1. a) $(1, -2)$ **b)** $(5, -4)$ **c)** $(2, 0)$
2. a) $(5, -1)$ **b)** $(-2, -11)$ **c)** $(-2, -4)$
d) $(5, 4)$ **e)** $(-2, 2)$ **f)** $(4, 0)$

Use Similar Triangles, page 493

1. a) $x = 9.6$ m **b)** $s = 12$ cm

Use the Pythagorean Theorem, page 493

1. a) 8.5 cm **b)** 10.8 mm **c)** 16.2 m

Work With Fractions, page 494

1. a) 120 **b)** 1008 **c)** $770x^4$
d) $(x + 3)(x + 4)(x - 3)$
2. a) $\dfrac{25}{18}$ **b)** $\dfrac{11}{120}$
  c) $\dfrac{27a + 20b}{144}$ **d)** $\dfrac{8x - 5y}{90}$
3. a) $\dfrac{2}{5}$ **b)** $-\dfrac{1}{4}$ **c)** $-\dfrac{5}{6}$ **d)** $-\dfrac{1}{10}$

Work With Polynomials, page 495

1. a) $3x^2 + 21x + 30$ **b)** $-2x^2 - 6x + 56$
  c) $x^2 - 12x + 36$
2. a) $(x + 5)(x - 2)$ **b)** $(x + 7)(x + 7)$
  c) $(3y + 5)(3y - 5)$ **d)** $3(a + 8)(a + 8)$
  e) $(5x - 6)(5x - 6)$ **f)** $-(p + 10)(p + 10)$
3. a) 64 **b)** 225 **c)** 400
d) 9 **e)** $\dfrac{49}{4}$ **f)** $\dfrac{4}{9}$

Zero and Negative Exponents, page 495

1. a) 1000 **b)** $\dfrac{1}{64}$ **c)** -1
d) $\dfrac{1}{25}$ **e)** $\dfrac{1}{729}$ **f)** 216
g) 32 **h)** $\dfrac{2}{81}$ **i)** $\dfrac{9}{4}$
2. a) $\dfrac{3}{x^4}$ **b)** $\dfrac{25}{y^4}$ **c)** $\dfrac{2}{27x^3}$
d) $\dfrac{x^3}{2y^2}$ **e)** $\dfrac{b^6}{a^5}$ **f)** $\dfrac{27n^9}{64m^{21}}$

Glossary

absolute value
The distance of a number from zero on a real number line.

$|3| = 3$ and $|-3| = 3$

acute angle
An angle whose measure is less than $90°$.

acute triangle
A triangle in which each of the three interior angles is acute.

algebraic modelling
The process of representing a relationship by an equation or a formula, or representing a pattern of numbers by an algebraic expression.

amount
The value of an investment or loan at the end of a time period, calculated by adding the principal and interest.

amplitude
Half the distance between the maximum and minimum values of a periodic function.

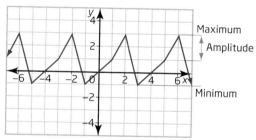

angle bisector
A line that divides an angle into two equal parts.

angle in standard position
An angle with vertex at the origin and initial arm on the positive x-axis.

angle of depression
The angle, measured downward, between the horizontal and the line of sight from an observer to an object.

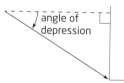

angle of elevation
The angle, measured upward, between the horizontal and the line of sight from an observer to an object.

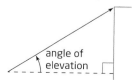

annual rate of interest
The rate at which interest is charged, as a percent, per year.

annuity
A sum of money paid as a series of equal payments at regular intervals of time.

arithmetic sequence
A sequence where the difference between consecutive terms is a constant.

arithmetic series
The indicated sum of the terms of an arithmetic sequence. $S_n = \frac{n}{2}[2a + (n - 1)d]$ gives the sum of the first n terms of an arithmetic series with first term a and common difference d.

associative property
$a + (b + c) = (a + b) + c$ for addition and $a \times (b \times c) = (a \times b) \times c$ for multiplication.

asymptote
A line that a curve approaches more and more closely, but never touches.

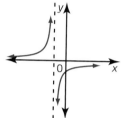

B

base function
The simplest form of various functions: linear $f(x) = x$, quadratic $f(x) = x^2$, radical $f(x) = \sqrt{x}$, rational $f(x) = \frac{1}{x}$.

base (of a power)
The number used as a factor for repeated multiplication.

In 6^3, the base is 6.

binomial
A polynomial with two terms.

$3x + 4$ is a binomial.

C

CAST rule
An acronym that tells which primary trigonometric ratios are positive in which quadrant.

Sin	All
Tan	Cos

circle
The set of all points in the plane that are equidistant from a fixed point called the centre.

coefficient The factor by which a variable is multiplied.

In the term $8y$, the coefficient is 8; in the term ax, the coefficient is a.

common difference The difference between any two consecutive terms in an arithmetic sequence.

For the sequence 1, 4, 7, 10, …, the common difference is 3.

common ratio The ratio of any two consecutive terms in a geometric sequence.

For the sequence 1, 2, 4, 8, 16, …, the common ratio is 2.

commutative property $a + b = b + a$ for addition and $ab = ba$ for multiplication.

completing the square Part of a process by which a quadratic function in standard form can be written in vertex form.

compound interest Interest that is calculated at regular compounding periods and is added to the principal to earn interest for the next compounding period.

compounding period The time interval after which compound interest is calculated.

compression A transformation that is a stretch by a factor less than 1.

conjecture A generalization, or educated guess, made using inductive reasoning.

constant term A term that does not include a variable.

continuous function A function that maps real numbers to real numbers and has a graph that is a curve with no holes or jumps.

continuous graph A graph that consists of an unbroken line or curve.

cosecant ratio The reciprocal of the sine ratio.

$$\csc A = \frac{1}{\sin A}$$

cosine law The relationship between the lengths of the three sides and the cosine of an angle in any triangle.

$$a^2 = b^2 + c^2 - 2bc \cos A$$

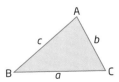

cosine ratio In a right triangle, the ratio of the length of the adjacent side to the length of the hypotenuse.

$$\text{cosine} = \frac{\text{adjacent}}{\text{hypotenuse}}$$

cotangent ratio In trigonometry, the reciprocal of the tangent ratio.

$$\cot A = \frac{1}{\tan A}$$

coterminal angles Angles in standard position that have the same terminal arm.

counterexample An example that demonstrates that a conjecture is false.

cube root Given a number z, the number a such that $a^3 = z$.

$\sqrt[3]{8} = 2$, because $2 \times 2 \times 2 = 8$, or $2^3 = 8$.

cycle One complete pattern of a periodic function.

dependent variable In a relation, the variable whose value depends on the value of the independent variable. On a coordinate grid, the values of the dependent variable are on the vertical axis.

In $d = 4.9t^2$, d is the dependent variable.

depreciation The amount by which an item decreases in value.

discontinuity A point at which a function is not defined. The graph has a break at this point.

$f(x) = \frac{1}{x}$ has a discontinuity at $x = 0$.

discrete function A function that is made up of separate points that are not connected.

discriminant In the quadratic formula, the quantity under the radical sign, $b^2 - 4ac$.

distance between two points The length of the line segment joining the points.

For points (x_1, y_1) and (x_2, y_2),

$$d = \sqrt{(x_2 - x_1)^2 + (y_2 - y_1)^2}.$$

distributive property $a(b + c) = ab + ac$.

domain The set of all values of the first coordinates of the ordered pairs, or the independent variable, in a relation.

double root The solution of an equation where two roots are the same.

The equation $(x - a)^2 = 0$ has a double root at $x = a$.

elements The individual members of a set.

entire radical A radical in the form $\sqrt{n}$, where $n > 0$.

$\sqrt{29}$ and $\sqrt{\frac{5}{3}}$ are entire roots.

equilateral triangle A triangle with all three sides equal.

equivalent expressions Expressions that have the same value for all values of the variable(s).

explicit formula A formula for the nth term of a sequence, from which the terms of the sequence may be obtained by substituting 1, 2, 3, and so on, for n.

$t_n = 2n + 1$ is an explicit formula for the arithmetic sequence 3, 5, 7, 9, ….

exponent The raised number that denotes repeated multiplication of a base.

In $3x^4$, the exponent is 4.

exponential decay A pattern of decay in which each term is multiplied by a constant amount, between 0 and 1, to produce the next term.

exponential equation An equation that has a variable in an exponent.

$3^x = 81$ is an exponential equation.

exponential function A function in which a variable is an exponent. It can be defined by an equation of the form $y = ab^x$, where $a \neq 0$, $b > 0$, and $b \neq 1$.

exponential growth A pattern of growth in which each term is multiplied by a constant amount, greater than 1, to produce the next term.

extrapolate To estimate values lying outside the range of given data. To extrapolate from a graph means to estimate coordinates of points beyond those that are plotted.

 F

factor To express a number as the product of two or more numbers, or an algebraic expression as the product of two or more other algebraic expressions. Also, the individual numbers or algebraic expressions in such a product.

Fibonacci sequence The sequence of numbers 1, 1, 2, 3, 5, 8, …. Each term, after the first two terms, is the sum of the preceding two terms.

finite differences Differences found from the y-values in a table of values with evenly spaced x-values. See first differences and second differences.

first differences Differences between consecutive y-values in a table of values with evenly spaced x-values.

x	y	First Differences
1	3	
		$5 - 3 = 2$
2	5	
		$7 - 5 = 2$
3	7	
		$9 - 7 = 2$
4	9	
		$11 - 9 = 2$
5	11	

fractal A curve that generates itself by replacing each side of its original shape with a generator and iterating the process.

function A relation in which each value of the independent variable (the first coordinate) corresponds to exactly one value of the dependent variable (the second coordinate).

future value The amount that a principal invested or borrowed will grow to, given specified interest and time conditions.

 G

generalize To determine a general rule or conclusion from examples. Specifically, to determine a general rule to represent a pattern or relationship between variables.

geometric mean If a, x, and b are consecutive terms of a geometric sequence, then x is the geometric mean of a and b.

geometric sequence A sequence where the ratio of consecutive terms is a constant.

1, 3, 9, 27, … is a geometric sequence with common ratio 3.

geometric series The indicated sum of the terms of a geometric sequence. $S^n = \dfrac{a(r^n - 1)}{r - 1}$ gives the sum of the first n terms of a geometric series with first term a and common ratio r.

graphing calculator A hand-held device capable of a wide range of mathematical operations, including graphing from an equation, constructing a scatter plot, determining the equation of a line of best fit for a scatter plot, making statistical calculations, and performing elementary symbolic manipulation. Many graphing calculators will attach to scientific probes that can be used to gather data involving physical measurements, such as position, temperature, and force.

graphing software Computer software that provides features similar to those of a graphing calculator.

greatest common factor (GCF) The expression with the greatest numerical coefficient and greatest degree that is a factor of two or more terms.

The GCF of $12ab$ and $8bc$ is $4b$.

 H

half-life The length of time for an unstable element to spontaneously decay to one half of its original amount.

hypotenuse The longest side of a right triangle.

I

identity An equation that is true for all values of the variable for which the expressions on each side of the equation are defined.

image point Any point that has been transformed from a point on the original figure or graph.

independent variable In a relation, the variable whose value determines that of the dependent variable. On a coordinate grid, the values of the independent variable are on the horizontal axis.
  In $d = 4.9t^2$, t is the independent variable.

inequality A mathematical statement that contains one of the symbols $<$, $\leq$, $>$, $\geq$, or $\neq$.

initial arm The arm, or ray, of an angle in standard position that is on the positive x-axis.

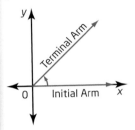

integer The set of whole numbers and their opposites, represented by $\mathbb{Z}$.

intercept The distance from the origin of the xy-plane to the point at which a line or curve crosses a given axis.

interest rate The percent of the principal that is earned, or paid, as interest.

interpolate To estimate values lying between elements of given data. To interpolate from a graph means to estimate coordinates of points between those that are plotted.

interval An unbroken part of the real number line, such as $-3 < x < 5$.

invariant points Points that are unaltered by a transformation.

inverse of a function A function and its inverse undo each other. A function f and its inverse f^{-1} have the property that if $f(a) = b$, then $f^{-1}(b) = a$.

irrational number A number that cannot be written in the form $\frac{a}{b}$, where a and $b \in \mathbb{Z}$ and $b \neq 0$.

  $\sqrt{2}$, $\sqrt{3}$, and π are irrational numbers.

isosceles triangle A triangle with exactly two equal sides.

L

least common denominator (LCD) The least common multiple of the denominators of two or more rational expressions.

least common multiple (LCM) The least multiple that two or more expressions share.
  The LCM of $2x$ and $3x^2$ is $6x^2$.

like radicals Numbers that have the same radicand.
  $2\sqrt{3}$ and $8\sqrt{3}$ are like radicals.

like terms Terms that have exactly the same variable(s) raised to exactly the same exponent(s).
  $3x^2$, $-x^2$, and $2.5x^2$ are like terms.

line of symmetry A line such that a figure coincides with its reflection image over the line.

line segment The part of a line that joins two points.

linear relation A relation between two variables that appears as a straight line when graphed on a coordinate system. May also be referred to as a linear function.

M

mapping diagram A graphical representation that relates the values in one set, the domain, to a second set, the range, using directed arrows from domain to range.

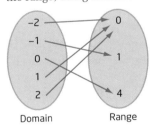

mapping notation A style of writing a function using an arrow.
  $f(x) \rightarrow ax^2 + bx + c$.

mathematical model A mathematical description of a real situation. The description may include a diagram, a graph, a table of values, an equation, a formula, a physical model, or a computer model.

mathematical modelling The process of describing a real situation in mathematical form.

mean The sum of a set of values divided by the number of values.
  The mean of 2, 4, 6, and 8 is 5.

midpoint The point that divides a line segment into two equal points. For the line segment joining points (x_1, y_1) and (x_2, y_2), the midpoint is $\left(\dfrac{x_1 + x_2}{2}, \dfrac{y_1 + y_2}{2} \right)$.

mixed radical A radical in the form $a\sqrt{b}$, where $a \neq \pm 1$ and $b > 0$.
$3\sqrt{10}$ and $\frac{1}{2}\sqrt{7}$ are mixed radicals.

monomial An algebraic expression with one term.
$7x$ is a monomial.

natural number A number in the sequence 1, 2, 3, 4, …, represented by $\mathbb{N}$.

non-linear relation A relationship between two variables that does not fit a straight line when graphed.

oblique triangle A triangle that is not right-angled.

obtuse angle An angle that measures more than 90° but less than 180°.

obtuse triangle A triangle containing one obtuse angle.

ordinary annuity A series of equal payments made at the end of each payment period.

origin The point of intersection of the x-axis and the y-axis on a coordinate grid.

parabola A symmetrical U-shaped curve that is the graph of a quadratic function. The domain is any real number.

Pascal's triangle A triangular arrangement of numbers with 1 in the first row, 1 and 1 in the second row, and where each number in the succeeding rows is the sum of the two numbers above it in the preceding row.

payment interval The time between successive payments of an annuity.

payment period Another name for the payment interval.

perfect square A number that is the square of a whole number.

perfect square trinomial The trinomial that results from squaring a binomial.

perimeter The distance around a polygon.

period The horizontal length of one cycle of a periodic function.

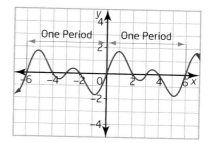

period (of a pendulum) The time it takes to complete one back-and-forth swing.

periodic function A function that has a pattern of y-values that repeats at regular intervals.

phase shift The horizontal translation of a trigonometric function.

point of intersection The point that is common to two non-parallel lines.

polynomial An algebraic expression formed by adding or subtracting monomials.

power A product obtained by using a base as a factor one or more times.
5^3, x^6, and a^m are powers.

present value The principal invested or borrowed today to result in a given final amount, given specified interest and time conditions.

present value of an annuity The principal that must be invested today to finance a series of regular withdrawals.

primary trigonometric ratios The three ratios, sine cosine, and tangent, defined in right triangles.

$\sin A = \dfrac{\text{opposite}}{\text{adjacent}}$

$\cos A = \dfrac{\text{adjacent}}{\text{hypotenuse}}$

$\tan A = \dfrac{\text{opposite}}{\text{adjacent}}$

prime number A number with exactly two factors—itself and 1.
2, 5, and 13 are prime numbers.

principal An amount of money invested or borrowed.

principal square root The positive square root of a number.

prism A three-dimensional figure with two parallel, congruent polygonal bases. A prism is named by the shape of its bases, for example, rectangular prism, triangular prism.

probability The ratio of the number of favourable outcomes to the number of possible outcomes.

product rule To multiply powers of the same base, add the exponents.
$$x^a \times x^b = x^{a+b}$$

proportion An equation that states that two ratios are equal.

Pythagorean identity In trigonometry, $\sin^2 \theta + \cos^2 \theta = 1$ for all values of θ.

Pythagorean theorem In a right triangle, the square of the length of the longest side is equal to the sum of the squares of the lengths of the other two sides.

quadrant One of the four regions formed by the intersection of the x-axis and the y-axis.

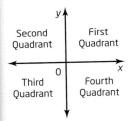

quadratic equation An equation of the form $ax^2 + bx + c = 0$, where a, b, and $c \in \mathbb{R}$ and $a \neq 0$.

quadratic expression An expression of the form $ax^2 + bx + c$, where a, b, and $c \in \mathbb{R}$ and $a \neq 0$.

quadratic formula The formula $x = \dfrac{-b \pm \sqrt{b^2 - 4ac}}{2a}$ that gives the roots of a quadratic function of the form $y = ax^2 + bx + c$, where $a \neq 0$.

quadratic function A function defined by a quadratic equation.
In standard form: $y = ax^2 + bx + c$, where a, b, and $c \in \mathbb{R}$ and $a \neq 0$.
In factored form: $y = a(x - r)(x - s)$, where $a \neq 0$ and r and $s \in \mathbb{R}$ and are the x-intercepts.
In standard form: $y = a(x - h)^2 + k$, where $a \neq 0$ and the vertex is at (h, k).

quotient identity In trigonometry, $\dfrac{\sin \theta}{\cos \theta} = \tan \theta$ for all values of θ.

quotient rule To divide powers of the same base, subtract exponents.
$$x^a \div x^b = x^{a-b}$$

radical expression An expression involving the square root of an unknown.

radical sign The symbol $\sqrt{\ }$.

radicand A number or expression under a radical sign. In $\sqrt{ab}$, the radicand is ab.

range of a relation The set of the second coordinates of the ordered pairs in a relation.

ratio A comparison of two quantities with the same units.

rational expression The quotient of two polynomials. $\dfrac{3}{k-1}$ and $\dfrac{a^2 + b^2}{a+b}$ are rational expressions.

rational number A number that can be expressed as the ratio of two integers, where the divisor is not zero. 0.75, $\dfrac{3}{8}$, and -2 are rational numbers.

real number A member of the set of all rational and irrational numbers, represented by $\mathbb{R}$.

reciprocal identities In trigonometry, the reciprocals of the primary trigonometric ratios.
$$\csc \theta = \frac{1}{\sin \theta}, \sec \theta = \frac{1}{\cos \theta}, \cot \theta = \frac{1}{\tan \theta}$$

reciprocals Two numbers that have a product of 1. x and $\dfrac{1}{x}$ are reciprocals.

recursion formula A formula by which each term in the sequence is generated from the preceding term or terms. $t_1 = 1$, $t_n = t_{n-1} + 3$ is a recursion formula for the arithmetic sequence 1, 4, 7, 10, ...

reflection A transformation in which a figure is reflected over a reflection line.

reflex angle An angle that measures more than $180°$ but less than $360°$.

regular payments Payments of equal value made at equal time periods.

regular withdrawals Withdrawals of equal value made at equal time periods.

relation An identified pattern between two variables that may be expressed as ordered pairs, a table of values, a graph, or an equation.

restriction Any value that must be excluded for a variable.

$\frac{8y}{y + 1}$ has restriction $y \neq -1$.

rhombus A parallelogram in which the lengths of all four sides are equal.

right angle An angle that measures 90°.

right bisector of a line segment A line that is perpendicular to a line segment and divides the line segment into two equal parts.

right prism A three-dimensional figure with two parallel, congruent polygonal bases and lateral faces that are perpendicular to the bases.

right triangle A triangle containing a 90° angle.

roots The solutions of an equation.

scalene triangle A triangle with no sides equal.

secant A line that intersects a curve at two distinct points.

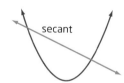

secant ratio In trigonometry, the reciprocal of the cosine ratio.

$\sec A = \frac{1}{\cos A}$

second differences Differences between consecutive first differences in a table of values with evenly spaced x-values.

x	y	First Differences	Second Differences
1	2		
		5 − 2 = 3	
2	5		5 − 3 = 2
		10 − 5 = 5	
3	10		7 − 5 = 2
		17 − 10 = 7	
4	17		9 − 7 = 2
		26 − 17 = 9	
5	26		

sequence A set of numbers, terms, or items, usually separated by commas, arranged in an order that can be identified by a pattern or rule.

series The sum of the terms of a sequence.

similar triangles Triangles that have the same shape but different size. Corresponding sides are in proportion and corresponding angles are equal.

simple interest Interest calculated only on the original principal using the formula $I = Prt$, where I is the interest, in dollars; P is the principal, in dollars; r is the annual rate of interest, as a decimal; and t is the time, in years.

sine law The relationship between the lengths of the sides and their opposite angles in any triangle.

$\frac{a}{\sin A} = \frac{b}{\sin B} = \frac{c}{\sin C}$

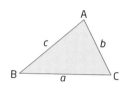

sine ratio In a right triangle, the ratio of the length of the opposite side to the length of the hypotenuse.

$\sin e = \frac{\text{opposite}}{\text{hypotenuse}}$

sinusoidal function A function with the curved form of a sine wave that is used to model periodic data.

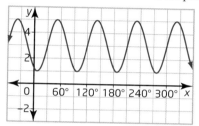

slope A measure of the steepness of a line. The slope of a line, m, containing the points $P(x_1, y_1)$ and $Q(x_2, y_2)$ is

$m = \frac{\text{vertical change}}{\text{horizontal change}}$ or $\frac{\text{rise}}{\text{run}}$

$= \frac{\triangle y}{\triangle x}$

$= \frac{y_2 - y_1}{x_2 - x_1}, x_2 \neq x_1$

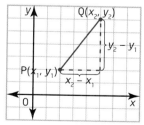

slope y-intercept form of a linear equation The equation of the line with slope m and y-intercept b is given by $y = mx + b$.

square root A number that is multiplied by itself to give another number.

straight angle An angle that measures 180°.

stretch A transformation that results in the distance from the x-axis of every point growing by a scale factor greater than 1 (vertical stretch) or the distance from the y-axis of every point growing by a scale factor greater than 1 (horizontal stretch).

symmetry A quality of a plane figure so that it can be folded along a fold line so that the halves of the figure match exactly.

system of equations Two or more equations that are considered together.

 T

tangent line A line that touches a curve at one point and equals the slope of the curve at that point.

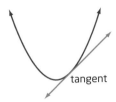

tangent

tangent ratio In a right triangle, the ratio of the length of the opposite side to the length of the adjacent side.

$$\text{tangent} = \frac{\text{opposite}}{\text{adjacent}}$$

term A number or a variable, or the product or quotient of numbers and variables.
   The expression $x^2 + 5x$ has two terms: x^2 and $5x$.

term (of a sequence) A single value or object in a sequence.

terminal arm The arm, or ray, of an angle in standard position that is not on the positive x-axis.

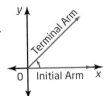

time line A diagram used to illustrate the cash flow of an annuity.

transformation A change made to a figure or a relation such that the figure or the graph of the relation is shifted or changed in shape.

translation A slide transformation that results in a shift of the original figure without changing its shape.

translation image The image of a plane figure after a translation.

trigonometric equation An equation that contains one or more trigonometric functions.

trinomial A polynomial with three terms.
   $x^2 + 3x - 1$ is a trinomial.

TVM (Time-Value-Money) Solver A feature of graphing calculators that is used for financial calculations.

 U

unit circle A circle of radius 1 unit that is centred at the origin.

 V

variable A letter or symbol, such as x, used to represent an unspecified number.
   x and y are variables in the expression $2x + 3y$.

vertex A point at which two sides of a polygon meet.

vertex of a parabola The point of the parabola at which the graph intersects the axis of symmetry. It is the minimum point on a parabola that opens upward, or the maximum point on a parabola that opens downward.

vertical line test A method of determining whether a relation is a function. If every vertical line passes through exactly one point on the graph of a relation, then the relation is a function.

 W

whole number A number in the sequence $0, 1, 2, 3, 4, 5, \ldots$.

 X

x-intercept The x-coordinate of the point where a line or curve crosses the x-axis.

 Y

y-intercept The y-coordinate of the point where a line or curve crosses the y-axis.

 Z

zero of a function Any value of x for which the value of the function is 0.

zero product property The property that, if the product of two real numbers is zero, then one or both of the numbers must be zero.

Index

A

ambiguous case, 249–254
amount (in financial calculations), 418, 419, 420, 421, 422, 423
amplitude, 285, 289
angle in standard position, 223
angles
  co-terminal, 236, 237
  determining with reciprocal trigonometric ratios, 245
  of elevation, 280
  initial arm, 223, 227
  reference, 223
  in standard position, 223
  sum in a triangle, 263
  terminal arm, 223, 227
  in unit circles, 245
annual rate of interest, 418, 419, 420, 421–422, 423, 426–431, 449–450
annuities, 444–452, 456–460, 470
area
  formula, 11
  function, 10–11, 13
arithmetic sequences, 380–387, 389, 395–401
arithmetic series, 395–401
associative property, 37
asymptotes, 9, 13, 100, 180, 181, 184, 189–190

B

becquerels (Bq), 388
binomial powers, 373–377

C

career connections
  bioinformatician, 387
  building inspector, 231
  forensics, 122
  investment trader, 455
  medical radiation technologist, 169
  mining engineer, 15
  perfusionist, 301

circle
  equation of, 10
  proving identities with, 270–271
  reference angles, 223
  unit, 222–224, 227, 233–235, 245, 302–303
classifying functions, 286–287
co-terminal angles, 236, 237
common difference, 382, 384, 385
common ratio, 389, 390, 391, 427
commutative property, 37
completing the square, 26, 30
compound interest, 426–432
compounding period, 429–431, 445–452, 459–460
compressions, 115–117, 119, 124, 126, 190–193, 195, 325
conjugates, 37
continuous functions, 358
cosecant ratio, 243, 244, 245
cosine
  curve, 298
  law, 221, 222, 241, 249, 250, 253–254, 264
  ratio, 234, 237, 244
  transformations, 308
cotangent ratio, 243, 244
cube roots, 171, 172
curve of best fit, 201–202, 204–205
cycles, 285, 289

D

data
  modelling sinusoidal functions with, 322–324, 327
  patterns in, 4–5
decay, 160–165, 183, 203–205
dependent variables, 4
depreciation, 203–205, 359–360
discrete functions, 354–360, 364–369, 373–377, 380–385, 388–391, 395–399, 402–407, 414
discriminant, 47–48, 61, 65, 67
distance, 92–93, 136–137

distance-speed-time formula, 92–93
distributive property, 37, 38
domain, 8–15, 100
  determining, 8–9, 11
  of inverse of a function, 134
  mapping diagrams, 18–19
  restrictions on, 9, 11
  in stretches and compressions, 115–116, 128

E

entire radical, 35–36, 38
explicit formulas, 355–357, 359–360
exponential decay/depreciation, 160–169, 178, 183, 203–205, 206
exponential functions, 178–198
  analysing a graph, 180–181
  graph characteristics, 178–180
  graphing, 178–182, 184, 189–195
  growth, 150–154, 199–203, 206
  models, 199–206
  properties of, 178–187
  transformations of, 188–198
  writing an equation, 182–183, 184
exponential growth, 150–154, 199–203, 206
exponential models, 199–206
exponents
  of binomials, 373–377
  effects on graphs, 178–179
  in fraction form, 171–174
  with fractional bases, 165, 166
  half-lives, 160–164, 183
  indicating decay, 160–169, 178, 183
  indicating growth, 150–154
  negative, 164–165, 166, 171, 172, 173–174
  rational, 170–177
  zero, 153, 154

F

factored form, 25, 27–28
factoring (partial), 27–28
families of quadratic functions,
    53–54, 57
Fathom™, 201–203
Fibonacci sequence, 366
financial mathematics, 415–477
    amount, 418, 419, 420, 421,
    422, 423
    annual rate of interest, 418,
    419, 420, 421–422, 423,
    426–431, 449–450
    annuities, 444–452, 456–460,
    470
    compound interest, 426–432,
    436–441, 445–446, 447–452,
    458–460
    compounding periods,
    429–431, 445–452, 459–460
    determining the interest rate,
    431–432
    future value, 437–441, 445,
    447, 457–458
    investing, 437–440, 446–452
    loans, 436, 440, 470
    present value, 436–441,
    456–460
    present value of an annuity,
    456–460
    principal, 418, 419, 420–423,
    426–431
    regular payments, 444–452
    regular withdrawals,
    456–460
    retirement savings, 456–460
    simple interest, 418–423
    time lines, 445, 446, 448,
    457, 458
fourth roots, 171, 172
function notation, 17–24, 132,
    356–357
functions
    classifying, 286–287
    continuous, 358
    defined, 4, 11
    discrete, 354–360, 364–369,
    373–377, 380–385, 388–391,
    395–399, 402–407, 414
    inverse of, 133–134,
    134–136, 137

types of, 358–359
future value, 437–441, 445, 447,
    457–458

G

geometric sequences, 388–391,
    402–407
geometric series, 402–407
graphing
    connecting equations, graphs,
    and functions, 6
    equivalent expressions,
    79–81
    exact trigonometric ratios and
    angles, 241–242
    exponential decay/
    depreciation, 162, 163–164,
    166, 203–205
    exponential functions,
    178–182, 181, 184, 189–195,
    190, 191, 193–194
    exponential growth, 153, 154,
    199–201
    inverse of a function,
    133–134, 134–136, 137
    parabolic path, 29–30
    points of intersection in
    linear-quadratic systems, 63
    quadratic equations, 44,
    45–46, 52–59
    scatter plots, 343
    simple interest calculation,
    420–421
    sine functions, 302–303,
    304–306
    sinusoidal functions,
    302–303, 304–306, 313–314,
    316–317
    sinusoidal models, 325–327
    translations, 97–98
growth, 150–154, 199–203, 206

H

half-lives, 160–164, 183, 218,
    368, 388

I

identities, 270–275
independent variables, 4

index of a root, 171
initial arms, 223, 227
interest
    compound, 426–432,
    436–441, 445–446, 447–452,
    458–460
    determining the rate,
    431–432
    simple, 418–423
intervals, 178
inverse of a function, 132–137
irrational numbers, 34
irrational roots, 45

L

least common denominator
    (LCD), 90–92
least common multiple (LCM),
    90–91, 92
line of symmetry, 27
linear function machine, 16–17
linear-quadratic systems, 60–69
loans, 436, 440, 470

M

mapping diagram, 18–19
mapping notation, 19–20
maximum or minimum value,
    25–33
mixed radicals, 35–36, 38

N

notation
    function, 16–20, 356–357
    inverse of a function, 132,
    137
    mapping, 19–20
    set, 9, 11

P

parabolas
    determining direction of
    opening, 25, 26
    determining equations for,
    52–59
    families of, 53–54
    and maximum or minimum
    value, 25–33

and projectile path, 29–30, 33
partial factoring, 27–28
Pascal's triangle, 373–377
patterns
in common ratios, 427
in exponential growth, 150–151, 153, 154, 162, 166
in fractals, 351, 353
Pascal's triangle, 373–377
periodic, 284–289, 294–298, 333–337
in sequences, 354–360, 364, 365–369, 373–377, 380–385, 388–391, 395–399, 402–407, 414
perfect square trinomials, 26
perfect squares
forming mixed radicals from, 35, 38
and irrational numbers, 34, 35
and simplifying entire radicals, 35, 38
periodic functions, 284–350
amplitude, 285, 289
classifying, 286–287, 289
cosine, 298, 308
cycles, 285, 289
graphing, 286–289
modelling, 284–289
not involving angles, 333–343
patterns, 284–289, 294–298, 333–337
periods, 285, 289
sine, 294–298, 302–303, 304–308
sinusoidal, 295, 304–308, 313–318, 322–327, 333–337, 343
periodic phenomena not involving angles, 333–343
period, 285, 289
polynomial expressions, 78–81, 83
polynomials in rational expressions, 89–90, 91–92, 93
population data, 158–159, 324, 336
powers *see* exponents

present value, 436–441, 456–460
present value of an annuity, 456–460
principal, 418, 419, 420–423, 426–431
pyramids, 38, 280, 380–382
Pythagorean identity, 219, 271–272, 273
Pythagorean theorem, 225, 233, 265

Q

quadratic equations
determining exact, 55–56
determining for quadratic functions, 52–59
solving, 43–51
quadratic formula, 44, 46–47
quadratic functions, 25–33
determining equations for, 52–59
factored form, 25, 27–28
families of, 53–54, 57
forms of, 25
maximum or minimum value, 25–33
partial factoring, 27–28
standard form, 25
vertex form, 25, 26
quotient identity, 271, 272, 273

R

radical signs, expressions under, 10, 11
radicals, 34–42, 171–174
adding, 36, 38
entire, 35–36, 38
mixed, 35–36, 38
multiplying, 37, 38
subtracting, 36, 38
radicands, 35, 171
range, 8–15, 100
of inverse of a function, 134
mapping diagrams, 18–19
in stretches and compressions, 115–116, 128
rational exponents, 170–174
rational expressions, 81, 83
adding and subtracting,

90–92, 93
multiplying and dividing, 88–90, 93
with polynomials, 89–90, 91–92, 93
reciprocal identities, 271, 273
reciprocal trigonometric ratios, 243–248
recursion formula, 366–367, 369, 383
recursive procedures, 365–372, 427–428
reference angles, 223
reflections, 98, 105–112, 124, 127, 129, 190–192
regression, 200, 204–205, 206
regular payments, 444–452
regular withdrawals, 456–460
relations
properties of, 5
quadratic, 9
and tables of values, 5
vertical line test, 6–7, 11
restrictions on a variable, 81, 83
retirement savings, 456–460
roots, 171
cube, 171, 172
determining quadratic equations using, 52–59
fourth, 171, 172
irrational, 45
negative, 135
square, 38, 41–42, 45, 46–47, 172, 173, 174

S

scatter plots, 205
secant ratio, 65, 67, 243, 244
sequences, 354–414
arithmetic, 380–387, 389, 395–401
arithmetic series, 395–401
common difference, 382, 384, 385
common ratio, 389, 390, 391, 427
determining type of, 389
explicit formulas, 355–357, 359–360, 369
Fibonacci, 366
geometric, 388–391, 402–407

geometric series, 402–407
Pascal's triangle, 373–379
recursion formulas, 366–367, 369, 383
recursive procedures, 365–372
terms of, 355, 356, 364, 384, 390–391, 396–399, 405–406, 407
set notation, 9, 11
side-side-angle, 249
simple interest, 418–423
sine
  graphing, 302–303, 304–306
  law, 221, 249, 250, 251–253, 254, 262–263
  ratio, 233–234, 237, 244, 245, 294, 296–298
  transformations, 304–312
  wave, 295, 323
sinusoidal functions, 295, 304–343
  graphing, 302–303, 304–306, 313–315, 316–317, 322–323
  modelling, 333–343
  sine forms, 306–308
  transformations, 304–312
sinusoidal models, 322–350
  determining values with, 325–327
  graphing, 325–327
  of periodic phenomena not involving angles, 333–343, 333–350
  to make predictions, 325, 327
  using data to construct, 322–324, 327
slope y-intercept form, 61
speed, 92–93, 136–137
spreadsheets, 41, 162, 381, 440, 452
square roots, 38, 47
  with denominators, 45, 46–47, 172, 173, 174
square-cube law, 176
squares
  completing to find vertex, 26, 30
  difference of, 37
  perfect, 26, 34, 35, 38
standard form for quadratic functions, 25

stretches, 98, 113–122, 124, 125, 128, 129, 190–192, 195
systematic trial, 163

T

table of values, 5, 180
tangent
  line, 65
  ratio, 234–235, 237, 244
terminal arms, 223, 227, 236, 237
terms of a sequence, 355, 356, 364, 384, 390–391, 396–399, 405–406, 407
The Geometer's Sketchpad®, 123–124, 194, 222, 223, 227, 259–260, 355
time
  in distance-speed-time formula, 92–93, 136–137
  in interest calculations formula, 418–423
time lines (financial), 445, 446, 448, 457, 458
transformations, 75–146
  combinations of, 126–128, 129
  compound, 189, 191–192
  compressions, 115–117, 119, 124, 126, 190–193, 195, 325
  cosine, 308, 316, 318
  of exponential functions, 188–198
  order of, 125–129
  reflections, 98, 105–112, 124, 127, 129, 190–192
  sine, 304–316
  stretches, 98, 113–122, 124, 125, 126, 128, 129, 190–192, 195
  translations, 97, 98–99, 100–101, 123, 125, 126, 129, 190, 307–308
translations, 98–99, 100–101, 123, 126
  horizontal, 98, 100–101, 126, 190
  order of, 125, 126
  sine, 307–308
  vertical, 97, 98, 99, 126, 189
triangles

determining reciprocal trigonometric ratios, 244
  oblique, 251
  Pascal's, 373–379
  right, 225, 263
  side-side-angle, 249
  solving, 261–265
  special, 225, 227
  sum of angles in, 263
trigonometric functions, 281–350
trigonometric ratios, 219–280
  ambiguous case, 249–260
  cosecant, 243, 244, 245
  cosine, 234, 237, 244, 298
  cotangent, 243, 244
  exact, 222–223, 227, 241–242
  identities, 270–275
  primary, 233–234, 237, 250, 254, 262–264
  reciprocal, 243–248
  secant, 243, 244
  sine, 233–234, 237, 244, 245, 262, 263, 294, 296–298
  tangent, 234–235, 237, 244, 250, 262
  three-dimensional problems, 261–269
  two-dimensional problems, 249–260
  in unit circles, 222, 222–224, 227, 233–235, 245, 302–303
trigonometric tools, 221
trinomials, perfect square, 26
TVM Solver, 438, 439, 447, 450, 460

U

unit circle, 222–224, 226–227, 245, 294–295, 302–303

V

variables
  dependent, 4, 5
  independent, 4, 5
  restrictions on, 81, 83
vertex form
  completing the square, 26
  for quadratic functions, 25, 26

vertex of a parabola, 9, 11
   completing the square, 26,
   28–29
   finding, 11, 25–26, 30
   finding algebraically, 11
   maximum or minimum
   value, 26–29
   partial factoring to find,
   27–28
vertical line test, 6–7, 11

y-intercept, 2, 24, 25, 65, 68,
   104, 112, 153
   for tangent line to quadratic
   function, 65

zero principle, 27
zeros
   of a function, 29
   of a quadratic function, 33,
   54–55, 57

Photo Credits

t = top, b = bottom, l = left, r = right

1 Daniel Stein/iStock, 3 © Steve Prezant/Corbis, 4 Gordon M. Grant / Alamy, 10 Gordon M. Grant / Alamy, 15 JUPITERIMAGES/ Comstock Images / Alamy, 16 Science Museum of Brussels/Wikipedia Commons, 25 Dieter K. Henke/iStock, 43 THE CANADIAN PRESS / COC ANDRE FORGET, 52 © Michel Van Loon | Dreamstime.com, 60 gkphotography / Alamy, 66 © CORBIS SYGMA, 69 Reimar / Alamy, 74 Visions of America, LLC / Alamy, 75 © Giorgio Fochesato/iStock, 77 © Stefan Witas/iStock, 78 DETLEV VAN RAVENSWAAY / SCIENCE PHOTO LIBRARY, 92 © Ankevanwyk | Dreamstime.com, 97 © Alvaro García Gamero/Maxx Images, 122 © Kay Ransom/iStock, 125 © Francis G. Mayer/CORBIS, 128 © Jacom Stephens/iStock, 132 Mike Greenslade, 139 Bill Frakes /Sports Illustrated/ Getty Images, 146 Robert Fried / Alamy, 147 NASA / SCIENCE PHOTO LIBRARY, 149 © Stocktrek Images/Corbis, 150 Michael Cogliantry/Photonica/ Getty Images, 154 Tischenko Irina/Shutterstock, 157 © Visuals Unlimited/Corbis, 160 Pickering Nuclear, photo courtesy of Ontario Power Generation, 169 Noel Hendrickson/Digital Vision/Getty Images, 170 © NASA/ESA/Kalas and Graham/epa/Corbis, 176 WARNER BROS / THE KOBAL COLLECTION, 178 © Caro / Alamy, 188 Roland W. Meisel, 199 © Ana Abejon/iStock, 218 © CORBIS/Maxx Images, 219 David Maisel Photography/UpperCut Images/Getty Images, 222 © Blaine Harrington III/CORBIS, 231 © Atsuko Tanaka/Corbis, 232 © G. Bowater/Corbis, 243 Kim Steele/Getty Images, 249 Wilbur E. Garrett/ National Geographic/Getty Images, 256 © Zheng Dong | Dreamstime.com, 257 Nick Gregory / Alamy, 261 Michael Dunning/Photographer's Choice/Getty Images, 265 © Marco Manzini/iStock, 267 Brian Bailey/Taxi/Getty Images, 268 © Tammy Peluso/ iStock, 269 © Firefly Productions/CORBIS, 270 Pascal Rondeau/Getty Images, 277 Dick Hemingway, 278 © Sherri Camp/iStock, 279 Arco Images GmbH / Alamy, 280 © Oleg Albinsky/iStock, 281 Altrendo Nature/Getty Images, 283 Leslie Garland Picture Library / Alamy, 284 CP PHOTO/Belleville Intelligencer - Jeremy Ashley, 292 RIA NOVOSTI / SCIENCE PHOTO LIBRARY, 294 © Fancy/Veer/ Corbis, 301 Jonathan Kirn/Getty Images, 304 © 2009 Gary Schultz/AlaskaStock.com, 311 Srdjan Draskovic / Alamy, 313 Michael Taylor, 322 AP Photo/Rene Macura, 329 Stephen Dorey ABIPP / Alamy, 332 Karl Weatherly/Getty Images, 333 SALLY BENSUSEN (1987) / SCIENCE PHOTO LIBRARY, 334 John Elk III/Lonely Planet Images/Getty Images, 336 © Tom Brakefield/zefa/Corbis, 338 © Wendy Holden/ iStock, l 341 Peter Dazeley/Stone/Getty Images, r 341 CP PHOTO - Steve White, r 342 Leslie Garland Picture Library / Alamy, l 342 ECKHARD SLAWIK / SCIENCE PHOTO LIBRARY, 345 Richard Levine / Alamy, 347 © Eric Hood/iStock, 348 Lawrence Berkeley National Laboratory, 349 CP PICTURE ARCHIVE/Lethbridge Herald - Rob Olson, 350 Roland W. Meisel, 351 Dr. Wolfgang Beyer/Wikipedia Commons, 354 Liz Van Steenburgh/Shutterstock, 359 © Drive Images / Alamy, 365 Photolibrary/Getty Images, 368 Pete Saloutos/Uppercut Images/Getty Images, 373 Wikipedia Commons, 380 © Laura Young/iStock, 387 Andreas Kindler/Johner Images/ Getty Images, 388 CENTRE JEAN PERRIN / SCIENCE PHOTO LIBRARY, 395 Olga Skalkina/Shutterstock, 402 Kevin C. Cox/Getty Images, 414 © Thevinman | Dreamstime.com, 415 © Paul Thompson; Eye Ubiquitous/CORBIS, 417 Copyright © David Young-Wolff / PhotoEdit, 418 © Sean Locke/iStock, 426 © Suprijono Suharjoto/iStock, 436 © Spencer Grant / PhotoEdit, 444 Scott Maxwell / LuMaxArt/ Shutterstock, 455 © John Foxx/Maxx Images, 456 Bernd Fuchs/Firstlight, 467 © Eric Hood/iStock, 470 © FogStock / Alamy